Chocolate Lovers

SWEET STORIES ABOUT LOVE, FRIENDSHIP, AND INAPPROPRIATE BEHAVIOR

Cheryl-
Thanks for
supporting
my vagina ;

TARA SIVEC

xo
Tara S

DISCLAIMER

This is a work of adult fiction. The author does not endorse or condone any of the behavior enclosed within. The subject matter is not appropriate for minors. Please note this novel contains profanity, explicit sexual situations, alcohol and drug consumption.

Table of Contents

Futures and Frosting

Troubles and Treats

Table of Contents

Seduction and Snacks

A CHOCOLATE COVERED LOVE STORY

1.

Arby's Anyone?

Hello, my name is Claire Morgan and I never want to have children.

For those of you out there who feel the same way, is it just me or does it seem like you're in the middle of a horrible Alcoholics Anonymous meeting whenever someone finds out you never want children? Should I stand up, greet the room as a whole, and confess what brings me to the seventh circle of Hell I constantly find myself in? It's a house of horrors where pregnant women asking me to touch their protruding bellies and have in-depth discussions about their vaginas surround me. They don't understand why the words placenta and afterbirth should never be used in a sentence. Ever; especially over coffee in the middle of the day.

You know what brought me to this decision? The video we saw in health class in sixth grade. The one set back in the seventies that had some woman screaming bloody murder with sweat dripping off of her face while her husband lovingly patted her forehead with a towel and told her she was doing great. Then the camera panned down to the crime scene between her legs: the blood, the goo, the gore, and the humungous porn bush that now had a tiny little head squeezing its way out. While most of the girls around me were saying, "Awwwwwww!" when the baby started to cry, I looked around at them in revulsion muttering, "What the hell is wrong with you people? That is NOT normal." From that moment on, my motto was: I'm never having children.

"So, Claire, what do you want to be when you grow up?"

"I'm never having children."

"Claire, did you choose a major yet?"

"I'm never having children."

"Would you like fries with that?"

"I'm never having children."

Of course there are always those in your life who think they can change your mind. They get married, have a baby, and then invite you over expecting you to be overcome with emotion when you take a look at their new little miracle. In truth, all you can do is look around at the house they haven't had time to clean in six weeks, smell their body they haven't had time to bathe in two weeks, and watch their eyes get a little squirrelly when you ask them the last time they got a good night's sleep. You see them laugh at every burp and smile at every fart. They manage to bring poop into every single conversation, and you have to wonder whom the crazy one really is here.

Then you have the people who believe your flippancy is due to some deep, dark, secret issue with your uterus that you're overcompensating for, and they look at you and your vagina with pity. They whisper behind your back and then suddenly it turns into a horrible game of "Telephone," and the whole world thinks you have life-threatening fertility issues where pregnancy will cause your vagina to spontaneously combust and your left tit to fall off. Stop the insanity! All my bits are in working order and as far as I know, I don't have exploding vagina syndrome.

The simple truth is, I just never thought pushing a tiny human out of me which turns my vagina into something resembling roast beef that no man would ever want look at, let alone bang, was a stellar idea. End of story.

And let's face it people, no one is ever honest with you about childbirth. Not even your mother.

"It's a pain you forget all about once you have that sweet little baby in your arms."

Bullshit. I CALL BULLSHIT. Any friend, cousin, or nosey-ass stranger in the grocery store that tells you it's not that bad is a lying sack of shit. Your vagina is roughly the size of the girth of a penis. It has to stretch and open and turn into a giant bat cave so the life-sucking human you've been growing for nine months can angrily claw its way out. Who in their right mind would do that willingly? You're just walking along one day and think to yourself, "You know, I think it's time I turn my vagina into an Arby's Beef and Cheddar (minus the cheddar) and saddle myself down for a minimum of eighteen years to someone who will suck the soul and the will to live right out of my body so I'm a shell of the person I used to be and can't get laid even if I pay for it."

It just stands to reason that after all the years of preaching I did to everyone around me about how I was never having children, I was the first of my friends to have one much to their horror, which I was highly offended by. I mean really, any idiot can raise a child. Case in point: my mother. She was absent the day they handed out parenting handbooks and instead turned to the age old, brilliant wisdom of Doctor Phil and fortune cookies to educate me, and I turned out just fine. Okay, maybe that wasn't the best example. I'm not a serial killer, so at least I have that going for me. More on my mother later.

I suppose saying I hate children is a little harsh, considering I'm a mother now, right? And it's not like I hate *my* kid. I just strongly dislike *other people's* dirty faced, snotty nosed, sticky handed, screaming, puking, shitting, no-sleeping, whining, arguing, crying little humans. Give me a cat over a kid any day. You can open up a bag of Meow Mix, plop it down on the floor next to a bucket of water, go on vacation for a week, and come home to an animal that is so busy licking it's own ass that it has no idea you were even gone. You can't do that with a kid. Well, I guess you could, but I'm sure it's frowned upon in most circles. And if my kid could lick his own ass, I'd have saved a shit load of money on diapers, I can tell you that.

To say I was a little worried about becoming a mother given my aversion to childbirth and children in general is an understatement. They say that when you have your own child, the first time you look into his or her eyes you will fall instantly in love and the rest of the world disappears. They say you'll believe your child can do no wrong, and you will love them unconditionally right from the very first moment. Well, whoever "they" are should seriously limit the amount of crack they smoke and stop talking out of their ass while their Arby's vaginas are flopping around in their grandma panties.

The day I had my son I looked down at him and said, "Who the hell are you? You look nothing like me."

Sometimes it isn't love at first sight. *What to Expect When You Weren't Expecting to Get Knocked Up That One Time at a Frat Party* and the rest of the all-knowing baby books like to leave that part out. Sometimes you have to learn to love the little monsters for something other than the tax deductions they provide you. Not all babies are cute when they're born no matter how many new parents try to convince you otherwise. This is yet another lie the half-baked "theys" lead you to believe. Some babies are born looking like old men with wrinkled faces, age spots, and a receding hairline.

When I was born, my father George took my hospital picture over to his friend Tim's house while my mom was still recuperating in the hospital. Tim took one look at my picture and said, "Oh sweet Jesus, George. You better hope she's smart." It was no different with my son, Gavin. He was funny looking. I was his mother, so I could say that. He had a huge head, no hair, and his ears stuck out so far I often wondered if they worked like the Whisper 2000, and he was able to pick up conversations from a block away. During my four day hospital stay, all I kept doing whenever I looked at his huge head was speak in a Scottish accent and quote Mike Meyers from *So I Married an Ax Murderer.*

"He cries himself to sleep at night on his huge pilluh."

"That thing's like Spootnik. It's got its own weather system."

"It's like an orange on a toothpick."

I think he heard me talking about him to the nurses and formulated a plan to get back at me. I firmly believe at night in the nursery he and all the other newborns struck up a conversation and decided it was time for a revolution. Viva la newborns!

I knew I should have kept him in my room the whole time I was there. But come on people, I needed some rest. Those were the last days I would ever get to sleep again, and I took full advantage of it. I should have kept a better eye on which kid they put his bassinet next to at night though. I knew that little brat Zeno would be a bad influence on my kid. He had "anarchy" written all over his face. And who names their kid Zeno anyway? That was just asking for an ass kicking on the playground.

Gavin was quiet, never fussed, and he slept all the time in the hospital. I laughed in the face of my friends who came to visit and told me he wouldn't be like this once we left. In reality, Gavin did the laughing, waving his tiny little fist of fury in the air for his brothers in the Newborn Nation. I swore I heard, "Infant Pride! Baby Power!" every time he made noises in his sleep.

The moment I got him in the car to go home, the jig was up. He screamed his head off like a wild banshee and didn't stop for four days. I had no idea what a wild banshee was or if they even existed, but if they did, I was sure they were loud as fuck. The only good thing about this whole ordeal was the fact that my kid refused to leave my body via my lady bits. No roast beefy beaver for this woman. All the baby books written by women who had the most perfect birth experience in the world said you should talk to your child in the womb. That was about the only piece of advice I took from those things. Every day I told him if he ruined my vagina I would video tape his birth and show all his future girlfriends what happened to your who-ha when you had sex, ensuring that he will never, ever get laid. Fuck playing Mozart and reading Shakespeare. I went with the scared straight method.

All my threats to him in the womb paid off. He sat there with his arms crossed for twelve hours and refused to move down the shoot. This was perfectly fine by me. C-section, here I come. I would go through having my gut sliced open again in a minute if I could skip the whole baby part and just get the four days at an all-inclusive location that served you breakfast, lunch, and dinner in bed, gave you a twenty-four hour morphine drip, and sent you packing with a thirty-day supply of Vicodin.

Before I get too excited thinking about legal narcotics without the ear-bleeding scream of a newborn, maybe I should go back to the night that got me into this mess. My horoscope that day should have been a warning of things to come: "You'll score a bunch of great computer gadgets and jewelry from your neighbors, who happen to die when you go into their house, shoot them, and take all their things."

I don't know what it should have been a warning of, but come on! Does that not have "bad omen" written all over it? The one and only time in my life I decide to have a one-night stand so I can finally give up the V-card, I get pregnant. I'm telling you, the universe hates me.

I was twenty years old and in my second year of college, well on my way to a degree in Business Administration. Aside from the constant ribbing from my best friend Liz, on the state of my virginity, life was good. Well, college student good. I didn't have VD, none of my friends had been roofied, and at the end of the semester, I had avoided needing to sell my organs to science to pay for food and pot.

Let me just say I do not condone illegal drug use in any way. Unless it's an all natural herb that doesn't make me feel guilty for eating an entire box of Peanut Butter Captain Crunch while watching hours of *The Joy of Painting* with Bob Ross. "Oh green water, oh that's pretty, and a happy little tree right over there." It also chills Liz out during finals so she isn't screaming and climbing the walls like a rabid howler monkey. Remember that whole "Hugs not Drugs" shit they tried to cram down our throats in high school? We fooled them. You don't have to choose. You can totally have both and not die. But seriously, kids, don't do drugs.

I remember that night fondly. And by fondly, I mean with bitter resentment toward all things alcoholic and with a penis.

8

2.

Beer Pong May Cause Pregnancy

It was a Friday night and we were spending it the usual way - at a frat party with a bunch of drunken frat boys and sorority freaks of nature. I really don't understand how Liz managed to drag me to these things week after week. These were not our people. Our people were back at the dorms listening to Pink Floyd, "The Darkside of the Moon" and watching *The Wizard of Oz* while arguing over whether or not the last season of *Dawson's Creek* jumped the shark. (Pacey and Joey forever!) We did not belong with the crowd of trust fund babies that thought student loans had something to do with a foreign exchange student. As we made our way over to a portable bar on one side of the room, I could hear two completely wasted tools argue back and forth about who paid more for their Coach purse and who slept with the most guys last week. One of them claimed she was ashamed she brought the other to the party since she was wearing a pair of Louboutins that was "so last year." These were the future leaders of our country, ladies and gentlemen. Christ, I felt like I was watching a live scene from *Heathers* ("I brought you to a Remington party and what's my thanks? It's on a hallway carpet. I got paid in puke."). Thankfully, Liz interrupted me before I handed one of them a cup of liquid drainer.

"Oooh what about that one? He's cute. And he has good teeth," she announced excitedly as she tipped her head towards a guy in a sweater vest manning the keg.

"Jesus Liz, he's not a horse," I moaned, rolling my eyes and taking a sip of lukewarm beer.

"But you could ride him all night long if you play your cards right," she said with a creepy used car salesman wink and a nudge of her shoulder.

"I'm concerned about you Liz. I really think you spend entirely too much time thinking about my hymen. You're secretly in love with me aren't you?"

"Don't flatter yourself," she replied distractedly as she scoped out more guys. "Come to think of it, I did bat for the other team in high school after one of Tom Corry's Friday night parties. We never got past second base though. Someone knocked on the bathroom we were in and it suddenly occurred to me that I liked penis," she mused.

I stared at her profile like she had two heads…or her hand in a vagina. Why is it that I'm just now finding out my best friend went through a lesbian phase? Every time I look at her now I'm going to picture vagina-hand. A little hand that looks like a who-ha chasing me around the house and watching me while I sleep. Vagina-hand is always watching. Vagina-hand sees you.

Liz looked beyond my shoulder and then leaned in closer. "Two tangos staring at us at your six."

I rolled my eyes again and sighed at the attempt Liz was making to be covert.

"Five bucks says free drinks will be ours if we play our cards right," she said conspiratorially.

"Liz, we're surrounded by kegs of beer and we were handed a plastic cup when we walked in. I'm pretty sure that equals free booze," I told her, holding up my red Solo cup in front of her as a reminder.

"Oh shut it. You're ruining the moment. If we were at a bar right now, they'd totally be buying us drinks."

"If we were legal."

"Details," she scoffed with a wave of her ominous vagina-hand.

She fluffed up her hair, and then pulled the front of her shirt down lower so she showed enough cleavage to blind a man.

"Liz, if you sneeze there's going to be a nip slip. Put those things away before you poke an eye out."

"They're coming over!" she squealed, batting my hands away as I tried to pull her shirt back up to cover the twins.

"Jesus, is there a homing beacon on those things?" I muttered. I shook my head in amazement at the power that was her boobs. "Your tits are like Bounty. The quicker dick picker upper," I muttered as I finally turned around to get a look at who was coming over. I'm pretty sure to an outsider I looked like Elmer Fudd when he saw Bugs Bunny dressed up like a girl and his eyes popped out of his head and his heart stretched out the front of his shirt. If the music weren't so loud you would be able to hear "ARRROOOOOOGA!"

"Hello there ladies."

Liz not so subtly elbowed me when the one that looked like a linebacker spoke. I briefly raised my eyebrows at the shirt he wore that strained against the muscles of his chest and read, "I'm not a gynecologist but I'll take a look." My attention immediately focused on the guy standing next to him with his hands in his pockets. The long-sleeved t-shirt he wore with the sleeves pushed up to his elbows hugged his body nicely and I could see the subtle outline of muscles in his chest and arms. They were nothing compared to Hooked on Steroids standing next to him, but they were perfect to me. I wanted him to turn around so I could see how great his ass looked in the well-worn jeans he had on. Unlike a lot of the college guys around here who were going through some sort of weird Justin Bieber-hair phase, this guy kept his light brown hair cut short, with just enough length on top for some messy spikes. He wasn't too tall, wasn't too short, he was just right. And just...beautiful. I wanted to punch my own face for calling a guy beautiful but it was true. He was so pretty I wanted to frame him and put him on my nightstand in a totally non-creepy, non-Hannibal Lector skin-suit-wearing kind of way. He looked bored and like he'd rather be anywhere but at this party. Before I could introduce myself and tell him he was my soul mate, someone bumped into me roughly from behind and I stumbled forward, smacking gracefully into his chest and spilling my beer all over the floor at our feet.

Holy hell he smelled good. Like boy and cinnamon and a tiny hint of cologne that made me want to rub my nose in his shirt and take a deep breath. Okay, so that might have thrown me back into creepy territory. I didn't want him to start calling me the shirt sniffer. That's a nickname that just doesn't go away. Like vagina-hand.

His hands flew out of his pockets and grabbed onto my arms to steady me while I was busy trying not to motorboat his tee shirt and flee the scene in mortification. I heard the sound of cackling laughter behind me and turned to see that one of the Heathers was responsible for my graceful entrance into this guy's life. It turns out slamming into someone is hilarious and her equally offensive twin joined in on the finger pointing and laughing.

What is this, a bad teen movie from the nineties? Did they expect me to cry and go running out of the room while dramatic music played over my exit?

"Jesus, what's your damage Heather?" a masculine voice said irritably.

Their laughter immediately stopped and they looked behind me in confusion. I whipped my head around and stared at the guy in awe, noticing that I still had my hands pressed against his chest and that I could feel the heat from his skin through his thin t-shirt.

"Did you just quote 'Heathers'?" I whispered. "That is my favorite movie ever."

He looked down at me and smiled, the piercing blue of his eyes boring a hole right through me.

"I had a huge crush on Winona Ryder before the whole shoplifting thing," he said with a shrug, his hands still wrapped around my upper arms.

"My name isn't Heather," a whiny voice protested behind me.

"Wow, Winona Ryder," I stated with a nod of my head.

Jesus, I had absolutely no game. Being in close proximity to a guy this hot turned my brain to mush. I just wanted to hear him speak again. His voice made me want to take my pants off.

"I kind of have a thing for quirky, intelligent, dark-haired chicks," he said with a smile.

"Why did he call me Heather? He knows my name is Niki," came the shrill voice from behind me again.

I'm a quirky, intelligent, dark haired chick! Me, me, me, pick me! And who the hell keeps whining and ruining my perfect moment? I will cut a bitch.

"Um, hellloooo!"

The man of my dreams broke eye contact with me to look over my shoulder. "Niki, your voice is making my ears bleed and killing my buzz."

I heard her huff and storm off. At least I think that's what she did. I was still staring at this guy and wondering how soon was too soon to drag him into a spare bedroom. He looked back at me and removed one of his hands from my arms to brush my bangs out of my eyes with his fingers. The simplicity of the action and the ease in which he performed it made it feel as though he'd done it a thousand times before. I wanted to slyly give Liz a big cheesy grin and a thumbs up but she was busy talking to this guy's friend a few feet away.

"You want to go refill your drink, maybe play a game of beer pong or something?"

I want to reach in my pants, pull out my virginity, wrap it up and put a bow on it. Or maybe stick it in a gift bag from Target and give it to him like a present with a nice card that says "Thank you for being you! Just a little virginity to show you my gratitude!"

"Sure," I replied with a shrug, totally playing it cool. It's probably best to play a little hard to get. You don't want to look too eager.

☉ ☉ ☉

"Oh God, don't stop," I panted as he kissed a trail down my neck and fumbled clumsily with the button of my jeans. After five rounds of beer pong and hours of talking, laughing and standing so close to him that it soon became impossible to refrain from touching him, I forgot the meaning of "hard to get". With a boldness I could only achieve through copious amounts of alcohol, I wrapped a hand behind his neck after losing the last round, pulled him to me, and kissed him with everything I had in me in front of all the people still left at the party that hadn't yet passed out in a pile of their own vomit. I grabbed his hand and dragged him down the hallway and shoved him into the first room we came to. I hoped Liz would have been close by to give me some sort of encouragement or last minute pointers about what I was about to do, but she disappeared after I announced to the room that she would be giving free PAP tests at the end of the night with her lesbian approved hand.

As soon as we got into the dark room we attacked each other: sloppy, drunken kisses, hands groping all over the place, slamming into random furniture as we stumbled and laughed our way to the bed. I tripped over something on the floor that may or may not have been a person and fell backwards, luckily onto the bed, dragging the guy right along with me. He landed roughly on top of me and it felt like the wind was knocked out of me.

"Shit, sssorry. You'kay?" he slurred as he pushed himself up on his arms, taking some of his weight off of me.

"Yep, good," I wheezed. "Now take your clothes off."

I was so buzzed I almost laughed when he dragged himself off me and took his pants and boxer briefs off. The moonlight shining through the bedroom window provided just enough illumination for me to see what he was doing even though the alcohol coursing through my veins made him look like he was on a tilt-a-whirl. He pushed everything down to his ankles without bending his knees, then stood up and shuffled back to the bed. Thankfully, the miniscule part of my brain that hadn't yet been taken over by beer and tequila shots reminded me it was never a good idea to laugh at a man when he took his pants off. It was just so funny though! I've seen plenty of penises before, just not in living color and two feet from my body. That thing stuck straight out and was pointing right at me. I swear, in my head I could hear the penis talking.

"Aaarrrggg, ahoy me matey, thar's a great grand vagina over yonder."

Penises talk like pirates when I'm drunk - probably because Liz calls them one-eyed snakes. And pirates wear patches and only have one eye and...holy shit, Captain Hookpenis was coming closer.

I should probably focus.

He crawled on top of me and kissed me, his scallywag bumping into my leg. This time I did laugh, pulling my mouth away from his and giggling until I snorted. I was drunk as shit, thinking about walking the plank and there was a penis smacking against my thigh in a strange bedroom that may or may not have a dead person on the floor. How can you not chortle like a schoolgirl at that shit? He was oblivious to my convulsions of laughter as he moved his head to the side and kissed my neck. And Jeeeeeeesus if that didn't sober me up long enough to realize how good it felt.

"Ohhhhh yesssssssss," I moaned out loud, surprising myself that I'd actually vocalized the words that were sloshing around in my fuzzy, beer-addled brain.

His lips moved up to the spot right behind my ear and when his tongue slid lightly against the skin there, it shot a tingle right between my legs that surprised me. My hands moved up to clutch onto his hair and hold his head in place. I didn't really think anything about this night was going to feel good. It was all about getting this crap out of the way; enjoying myself was a small perk I didn't expect. After a few minutes of fumbling with my jeans, he finally got them unbuttoned and yanked them down my legs, taking my underwear with them. His hands slid up the sides of my body, taking my shirt with them until it was pulled over my head and tossed in the general direction of my jeans. The liquid courage reignited long enough for me to take off my bra and fling it to the side, the sound of the material smacking into the wall making me realize I was now lying on a bed completely naked with a guy kneeling between my legs, staring down at all I had to offer.

Oh my God. This is really happening. I'm naked in front of a guy. Am I really going to do this?

"Jesus, you're so fucking beautiful."

Yes, the answer is yes! If he keeps talking to me like that he can stick it in my ear.

He let his eyes roam over my body and then quickly yanked his shirt off and threw it across the room. My hands automatically reached up to his chest so I could touch him as he sunk back down on top of me. His chest was hard and his skin was smooth. I touched every inch of him I could reach. I wrapped my hands around the back of his neck and pulled him down to me and kissed him. He tasted like tequila and sunshine. Despite our inebriated states, I was enjoying his kisses. Now that we were naked and in bed, they weren't so frantic. They were actually soft and sweet and made me sigh a little into his mouth. He pulled one of my legs up and wrapped it around his hip and I could feel the head of his penis right at my opening.

Oh shit, this is it. This is really happening. And why am I talking to myself when I have my tongue in someone's mouth and he's getting ready to stick his penis in me?

Oh my God …

Even though I was drunk as a skunk at the time, I still remembered what happened after that. Less than two seconds later he was inside me and I was waving good-bye to my virginity. I wanted it to last forever. I saw stars, came three times that night and it was the most beautiful experience of my life.

Yeah right. Are you kidding me? Have you lost your virginity lately? It hurts like a mother effer and it's awkward and messy. Anyone that tells you she had anything even close to resembling an orgasm during the actual event itself is a lying sack of shit. The only stars I saw were the ones behind my eyelids as I squeezed them shut and waited for it to be over.

But let's be honest here, this is exactly how I expected it to be. It's not his fault it wasn't anything to write home about. He was as sweet and gentle as he could possibly be with me considering the amount of alcohol we consumed during the night. We were both drunk as hell and I lost my virginity to a guy whose name I didn't know because I didn't want any distractions and I didn't have time for a relationship. With the state of my virginity out of the way, I could focus more on school and my career and Liz would stop treating every party we went to like a meat market. It went exactly according to my plan. That is, until my period was a week late and I realized I ate an entire loaf of bread and seven sticks of string cheese while I sat at the kitchen table looking at the calendar and wishing I'd paid more attention to math in kindergarten because there was no fucking way I counted right.

3.

Have You Seen This Sperm Donor?

Sometimes I blame my lack of desire to have children on my mother. She wasn't a bad mother; she just didn't really know what she was doing. She realized early on that living in a small town out in the country wasn't for her and that sitting around day after day watching television with my dad and dealing with a sassy pre-teen wasn't all that she wanted out of life. She wanted to travel, go to art shows, concerts and movies, she wanted to be free to come and go as she pleased and not have to answer to anyone. My mom told me once that she never stopped loving my dad. She just wanted more than he could give her. They divorced and she moved out when I was twelve to get a condo in the city about thirty miles away. I never felt like she abandoned me. I still saw her all the time and talked to her on the phone every day. And it's not like she didn't ask me to go with her when she moved out. She did, but I think it was only because she felt like it was expected. Everyone knew I'd choose to stay with my father. I was and always would be a daddy's girl. As much as I loved my mother, I felt like I had more in common with my dad and it just seemed natural that I should stay with him.

Even though she didn't live with us, my mother still tried to nurture me as best she could. Her parental skills weren't all that great to begin with though, and after she moved out, they pretty much turned into one big train wreck. Regardless of what people might think, she really did love me; she just acted more like a friend most of the time than a mother. Three days after she moved out, she called and told me that according to something she saw on *Oprah*, we needed to do something life altering so that we could forge a stronger bond between us. She suggested getting matching tattoos. I reminded her that I was twelve and it was illegal. I have enough *Chicken Soup for the Mother/Daughter Blah, Blah, Blah* reference books she's given me over the years to open my own bookstore and have been tagged in one too many photos of her and I on her Facebook page with the caption "Me and my BFF!".

People thought it was strange the way the three of us lived, but it worked for us. My dad didn't have to listen to my mother nagging in his ear all day long about how he never took her anywhere, and my mother was free to do as she pleased while still having a close relationship with us. Some people just aren't meant to live together. My parents got along much better when there was a twenty-five minute car ride separating them.

Aside from the advice she received from bad talk shows, my mother used the *Parenting with Idioms* book to raise me. Every piece of advice ever given to me was in the form of a one-liner she read in a book or heard Paula Deen use on the Food Network. Unfortunately, they never made sense and were never used in the correct context. When you're six years old and you tell your mother someone at school made you cry and she replies with, "Don't pee down my back and tell me it's raining," you sort of learn to handle things on your own and stop asking for her advice.

When I found out I was pregnant, I didn't immediately have dreams of being some independent, womens' lib, equal rights, "I don't shave my legs because the man won't keep me down" type of person, perfectly content to do things on her own without the help of anyone. I'm not a martyr. As stubborn and self-sufficient as I was, I knew I would need help.

As soon as I took eleventy-billion home pregnancy tests, after drinking a gallon of milk so I would have enough pee for all of them, I realized I needed to hunt this guy down. Of course, this was after I

Googled "milk and pregnancy tests" to make sure I didn't just spend thirty-seven minutes of my life staring in horror at positive pregnancy tests littered all over my bathroom that may or may not be correct because pasteurization messed with the hormones in your body and created a false positive.

It doesn't, just in case you were wondering.

I was a twenty-year-old full-time college student, and according to my mother, "You don't have two nickels to pull out of a duck's ass with a penny in its name." My dad, George, worked the same job he had since he was eighteen and made just enough to pay his bills and help me with my room and board. Thank God my dad's best friend Tim was right all those years ago. I was smarter than I looked and received a full ride to the University of Ohio, so I didn't have the burden of student loans or grants. Unfortunately though, that meant I went to school full time and worked my ass off, taking twice the course load as other students, leaving no time for a job and no money saved.

In some ways I took after my mother. I wanted more out of my life than waiting tables at Fosters Bar and Grill where I worked all through high school. I wanted to travel, work hard and one day own my own business. Unfortunately, life doesn't throw curveballs; it throws an eight pound, one ounce infant at your face when you're looking the other way. Life is a vindictive little bitch. I was smart enough to know I couldn't do this by myself and wanted more than anything to keep the inconvenience of my mistake away from my dad for as long as possible. Any other woman would probably call her mother to cry and plead for help as soon as the stick turned pink, but at the time, I wasn't in the mood for my mother to tell me that "Rome was not built with two birds in your bush". That left me with the person who helped put me into this situation. Unfortunately, I had no idea who the guy was I slept with. I was too mortified by my actions that night to ever repeat the performance so I knew without a doubt Mr. Beer Pong was the father. I just had to find him. Who the hell gave a guy her virginity and never even bothered to ask him what his name was?

Oh yeah, that would be me.

The first day I decided to try and find him was spent talking to every single dumb jock that lived at the frat house where the party occurred. No one there had any clue who I was talking about when I tried to describe this guy and the friend he had with him that night. It could have been due to the fact that everyone I talked to smelled like a brewery and stared at my boobs the entire time I was there. Or maybe it was because I wasn't fluent in stupid. Really, either option was viable. On the way back to the apartment I shared with Liz, after my hunting expedition, all I wanted to do was kick my own ass. The morning after when I woke up, I felt silly admitting that the feel of his arm wrapped around my waist made me sigh a little. I should have stayed. I should have waited until he woke up, thanked him for a good time and put his number in my phone. But as much as I itched to run my fingers through his hair or slide my hand down his cheek, I knew I couldn't. At that point, I couldn't afford any distractions in my life and that's exactly what he would have been. If we were together, stone-cold sober, I knew I could have easily lost myself in him and forgot everything I had been working towards all my life. I found it was much easier to brush something off and say you did it because you were drunk than admit you made a mistake. I didn't think sleeping with him was a mistake really, just the way I went about it and my actions the next morning. Instead of sticking around, I slithered out from under his arm and the warmth of his body and thought about how bad it would have been if I woke up next to some ugly troll. At least he was hot as hell in the light of day, and I didn't have to perform a coyote ugly and chew my own arm off to get out from under him. I threw on my clothes as fast as I could and left him naked and sound asleep in bed. No one moved as I stepped over the lifeless bodies spread throughout the house and performed the morning-after walk of shame, out the door and into the bright morning light.

I turned around a total of six times to go back to that house and wait for him to wake up. And each time, I talked myself out of it with the same argument. I used him to finally get rid of my stupid virginity. Did I really want to know why he did it? I was definitely not the best looking girl in that place. People tell me I'm cute and I guess I probably am, but what exactly did he see when he looked at me? Maybe he could just tell I would be a sure thing that night. I'd rather remember him as the sweet, buzzed, hot guy who rid me of my virginity and made me laugh. I didn't want to know if he was some skeezy womanizer that was sleeping his way through the student directory, and I was just lucky enough he finally made it to the M's.

When I got home that day, Liz made me retell the story over and over so she could squeal and tell me how happy she was for me and that it was no big deal she struck out with his buff friend because she found some guy named Jim who was all alone at the party and it was love at first sight.

Her squealing and patting on the back continued until five weeks later when she came home from class and found me sitting on the bathroom floor surrounded by little white plastic sticks that all said "Pregnant" on them, crying hysterically with snot running down my lip as I rambled incoherently about milk and cows taking pregnancy tests.

For two months Liz helped with my crusade to find this guy. She never got his friend's name either because as soon as she made eye contact with Jim "the rest of the world disappeared" or some disgusting shit like that. We contacted the admissions office and we poured through a dozen yearbooks in the hopes that we might recognize him in one of the pictures. We even tried locating that skanky chick Niki that slammed into me, with no luck.

Did these people just appear out of thin air or something? How is there no fucking record of their existence at this school?

Liz even tried talking to the guys at the frat house herself, taking Jim along with her, but she didn't have any better luck than I did. She did however come home completely trashed because every guy she talked to made her and Jim do a shot every time they said the words "goat testicles". Honestly, I have no idea how that word came up in their conversation so many damn times. Do you have any clue how annoying drunk people are when you are forced to be sober? Especially drunk people who are in love, touchy-feely and quoting Walt Whitman to each other while you've got red, puffy eyes from crying, haven't showered in four days and just got done throwing up the contents of your stomach because you saw a commercial about goldfish - the crackers, not the real fish. But those damn things looked so much like real fish all I could think about was swallowing a live, slimy goldfish that stared at me with its beady little eyes before I put him on my tongue.

I knew the chances of me finding this guy were slim to none. I couldn't very well move into the frat house and be the boys' token pregnant roommate in the hopes he would one day come back there before the child I was carrying was in college and possibly living there himself.

I also couldn't hold off on telling my dad any longer. I saw the campus nurse that morning and she confirmed with a blood test that I was pregnant, and going by my calculations of the one and only time I had sex, I was thirteen weeks along.

Now, I'm all for a woman's right to choose. I believe it is your body and do with it as you may and blah, blah, blah. With that being said, as much as I dislike tiny little humans, I could never get rid of my own flesh and blood, by abortion or adoption. It just wasn't something I was personally comfortable with. So, with Liz holding my hand, I took the chicken shit way out and told my dad over the phone.

Let me explain something about my dad. He's six-foot-four, two hundred and fifty pounds, has tattoos up and down his forearms of snakes and skulls and other scary shit, and he always looks pissed off at the world. He scared the shit out of several boys in high school when they knocked on the door and my dad would answer. When I came to the door, they'd tell me they thought my dad was going to kill them and I'd reassure them that no, that's just the way his face always looks.

In all honesty, my dad was a nice guy. He got his tattoos when he was young and in the army and he always had a scowl on his face because he was exhausted. He worked twelve-hour days, seven days a week for months at a time before he got a day or two off. He wasn't big on talking about his feelings or being affectionate, but I knew he loved me and would do anything for me. He was a great guy, but he was still a force to be reckoned with and God help the person who ever hurt his little girl. Liz started spewing Chuck Norris quotes in high school and replacing Chuck's name with my dad's. She did it so much that I find myself doing it from time to time. He reacted to the pregnancy news pretty much like I expected him to.

"Well, I'll get your room ready so you can come back home when the semester is done. And if you find this guy in the meantime, let me know so I can rip off his balls and shove them down his throat," he said in his usual deep, monotone voice.

If you spelled George Morgan wrong on Google it didn't say, "Did you mean George Morgan?" It simply replied, "Run while you still have the chance."

After the semester ended, I applied for a leave of absence with the school so they would hold my scholarship. They would only keep it active for one year before I would have to reapply. I never intended to be away from school that long, but I also never intended on a baby completely fucking up my life. Er, I mean, bringing me years of great joy.

For the next six and a half months, I worked as much as my growing stomach and cankles would allow so I could save plenty of money for after he was born. Unfortunately, in the small town of Butler, there's not much to choose from employment-wise that would pay well. Unless of course I wanted to be a stripper at the town's one and only strip club, The Silver Pole. The owner approached me at the grocery store when I was seven months. In the middle of the cereal aisle he told me there were plenty of patrons in his club that thought the pregnant body was beautiful. If there weren't children around at the time, I would have told him off. Oh, who was I kidding? If Jesus himself was standing next to me, I would have still told that douche bag that if he ever came anywhere near me again I would rip his dick off and choke him with it. I would have apologized to Jesus before leaving though, of course.

On the bright side, the president of the Butler Elementary PTA was standing there with her six year old and heard every word. I guess I shouldn't hold my breath waiting for the invitation to join, huh? Shoot. Now where am I going to find the will to live?

With my pregnant stripping career over before it started and my proverbial tail stuck between my legs, I groveled for my old job as a waitress at Fosters Bar and Grill. Luckily, the Fosters still owned it from when I worked there in high school, and they were more than happy to help me out considering my *situation*.

When people in a small town talked about you to your face, they whispered the words that they believed might offend someone if they were to overhear your conversation. In my opinion, they should be whispering words like "fuck," "anal sex" or "Did you hear Billy Chuck got caught with his pants around his ankles down at the Piggly Wiggly with his dog Buffy?" Whispering the word "situation" kind of defeated the purpose. I whispered random words all the time just to mess with them.

"Mrs. Foster, the *bathroom* is out of toilet paper."

"Mr. Foster, I need to leave *early* to go to the doctor."

I talked to Liz every single day after I moved back home, and she kept up her search of the missing sperm donor when she had time. Her family was from Butler as well so she came home to visit me as often as she could but towards the end of my pregnancy, she just didn't have time to make the three and a half hour drive as often. Her professors convinced her to double up on her course load so she could graduate a year early with her degree in Small Business, majoring in Entrepreneurship with minors in Marketing and Accounting. With her full-time studies, part-time internship with an at-home consulting firm and her blossoming relationship with Jim, I knew she had a lot on her plate and didn't begrudge her any of her successes or happiness. I was a big enough person to admit that I was only a tiny bit jealous. Liz and I always talked about owning businesses together. About how we'd rent out buildings right next to one another with a door that led into both and how we'd live in a loft upstairs and throw awesome parties every weekend. We also dreamed about both of us marrying one of the members of N'Sync and living a life of polygamy with our new band N'Love.

Fingers still crossed on that one.

In all of our talk about the future, Liz never really cared what kind of business she ran, she just wanted it to be hers and be in charge. I always knew I wanted to own a candy and cookie shop.

As far back as I can remember I was always in the kitchen covering something in chocolate or baking cookies. My dad always joked that I could never sneak up on him because he could smell the chocolate on me from a mile away. I was pretty sure it leaked out of my pores at this point. I was so happy that my best friend's dream was coming true. I tried not to dwell too much on the fact that my dream was going on the back burner until God knew when.

I missed seeing Liz every day once I moved back home, and I was sad that my future needed to be put on hold, but nothing was as depressing as going into labor on my twenty-first birthday. While all of my friends celebrated their twenty-first birthdays by drinking every alcoholic beverage on the menu, sitting on the floor of a public restroom while singing along to the music piped through the speakers and then hanging out of the passenger-side window of a car on the way home screaming, "I'M DRUNK FUCKERS!" I was stuck in a hospital trying not to punch every twat nurse in the face that kept telling me it wasn't time for my epidural.

I decided then and there that someday, I was going to be a labor and delivery consultant. I was going to stand next to every single woman in labor and every time a nurse or a doctor or hell, even the woman's husband said something stupid like, "Just breathe through the pain," it would be my job to squeeze the living fuck out of their reproductive organs until they were curled up in the fetal position asking for their mommies and I'd say, "Just breathe through the pain, asshole!" And anyone that gave the new mother a dirty look after an eight pound, one ounce bloody, gooey, screaming pile of tiny human was cut out of her stomach when she asked her father to grab the bottle of vodka out of her overnight bag because, "morphine and vodka sounds like a stellar way to celebrate the birth of my spawn," would get their McJudgy glare smacked right off their face.

And I guess that brings us up to speed.

The next four years were spent working my ass off trying to make enough money to set aside for my future business, while raising my son and trying not to sell him to gypsies on a daily basis.

After a while, the search for Mr. Cherry Popper fell by the wayside as life got in the way. It didn't mean I never thought about him. Every time I looked at my son, I couldn't help but think about him. Everyone told me that Gavin looks exactly like me. And I guess he does to an extent. He has my nose, my lips, my dimples and my attitude. But his eyes were a whole other story. Every single day when I looked into the crystal blue pools of my son's eyes, I saw his father. I saw the way the corners of his eyes crinkled when he laughed at something I said, I saw the way they sparkled when he animatedly told me a funny story and I saw the sincerity in them each time he brushed the hair out of my eyes that night. I wondered where he was, what he was doing and if *Heathers* was still one of his favorite movies. Every so often I would be struck with a sharp stab of guilt at the fact that this man would never get to meet his son, but it's not like I didn't try. There's only so much I could do. I wasn't about to put out an ad in the paper that says, "Hey, world! So this one time, at a frat party, I was a total slut and let a stranger go where no man has gone before and now I have a son. Won't you please help me find my baby daddy?"

Jim became more of a permanent fixture in my life as well as Liz's. I probably talked to him on the phone as much as I did her. It was a no-brainer that the two of them would be Gavin's godparents. They spoiled him rotten and I liked to put all the blame on Liz for the mouth on that kid. I didn't think anyone screamed louder than I did when I found out Jim asked Liz to marry him and that they were going to move to Butler to be closer to her family and me. As soon as they moved back, Liz began tirelessly working and researching for the next few years to get a solid business plan in place. She told me a few months ago that she finally figured out what she wanted to sell, but she didn't want to tell me until she was certain she could do it. After that phone call, the most I saw of Liz was a blur as she ran from one appointment to the next. She was constantly on the phone with realtors and banks, running back and forth to her lawyer's office to sign paperwork and making daily trips up to the county courthouse to get all of the small business forms completed. I reluctantly agreed during a night of girl-time, after five too many dirty martinis, that I would help her out on a part-time basis as a consultant. I think my exact words were "I love you Liz. And I love vodka. I shall hug you and squeeze you and call you Lizdka." Liz considered that a yes.

All Liz told me about the job was that it could be considered sales and I would have a blast doing it. Being a bartender, I considered myself pretty damn good at sales.

"What? You say your wife dumped you for a woman in her book club? Here, try a bottle of Patrón."

"Oh no, your best friend's neighbor's ex-wife's dog was hit by a car? Here, Johnnie Walker should do the trick."

Liz liked to make even the most mundane things suspenseful and wanted to keep me in the dark and surprise me about what I would be selling. And since I was drunk at the time, I would have agreed to sell do-it-yourself enema kits and she knew it. I worked a few hours almost every night at the bar after Gavin went to bed and made some money putting together candy and cookie trays for parties around town but I could always use the extra cash, so I was okay with it as long as helping Liz out didn't cut into my time with Gavin too much.

Tonight was my "orientation" so to speak. I was going to tag along with Liz to one of her engagements so I could get a feel for the business. Jim was watching Gavin for the night so I offered to drive, dropping him off when I picked Liz up.

They met us out in the driveway as I pulled in. Liz was lugging the biggest suitcase I had ever seen behind her and shooed Jim's hand away when he tried to help her heft it into my trunk. I should have taken Jim's knowing smirk when we pulled away as a huge red flag. In my defense, I don't get out much. I assumed we would be selling something like candles, tupperware or beauty products; all things that Liz loved. I should have known better. Or paid closer attention to the words "Bedroom Fun" stitched into the side of the suitcase in pink, elegant script.

4.

Sex and Chocolate

"He was my favorite uncle. Good old Uncle Willie. I sure am gonna miss him."

I rolled my eyes and drained the last of my beer, listening to my best friend Drew on the barstool next to me try to pick up one of the waitresses.

"Oooooh, you poor baby. You must be so sad," she told him, eating up all of his bullshit and running her hands through his hair.

"I'm devastated. Practically horny with grief."

"What did you say? I couldn't hear you over the music," she shouted.

I snorted and looked over her head to make eye contact with Drew, giving him a look that clearly said, "I cannot believe the words that are coming out of your mouth."

With a kiss on his cheek and a smack to her ass, they parted ways and he swiveled around on his bar stool to take a swig of his drink.

"Your Uncle Willie died two years ago. And you hated him," I reminded Drew.

He slammed his beer down on the bar and turned to face me.

"Have you forgotten the awesomeness that was *Wedding Crashers*, Carter? Grief is nature's most powerful aphrodisiac, my friend."

Drew had been my best friend since kindergarten, and yet sometimes, the things he said still amazed me. The fact that he was a good friend and was here for me in my time of need helped me overlook his obnoxious and man-whorish behavior most of the time.

Drew flagged the bartender over and ordered up two shots of tequila. At this rate I would be going home on a stretcher. My organs were going to start shutting down from liquor running through my veins instead of blood and I'm pretty sure there was a little person in my brain whispering the words to "Ice, Ice Baby" and messing with my vision.

Drew and I both worked for the same automotive plant and were recently transferred from the plant in Toledo to the one a few hours away in Butler. We shared an apartment together in Toledo, but after two years of listening to him bang his way through the white pages, the yellow pages, and eight business directories within a ten mile radius, I decided not sharing a small space with him anymore was a necessity. I still had a ton of unpacking to do in the small ranch-style home I was renting and was starting to regret letting Drew convince me to drown my sorrows in the bottom of a bottle. He knew me too well though and knew that if I was at home, I wouldn't be unpacking. I'd be sitting there alone, staring at a picture of my ex wondering why the hell I wasted so many years with her.

The bartender poured the shots, letting them overflow and Drew grabbed them both, handing one over to me and raising his in the air. I reluctantly did the same with mine and tried to focus on holding my hand steady while the room tipped sideways.

Drew's empty hand flew out and grabbed onto my elbow, yanking me upright and spilling some of the shot on my hand.

Oops, guess that was me tipping, not the room.

"Before you face plant off your stool, fucker, I'd like to make a toast. To my best friend, Carter: may he never fall victim to another two-timing, gold-digging whore."

We downed the shots and slapped the glasses on the bar.

"Thanks for not fucking her buddy," I mumbled, trying not to slur.

"Dude, first of all, I'd never fuck any girl you were even remotely interested in, let alone dating for a long period of time. And second,

I could never accept a proposition from that skank. I wouldn't do that to my penis. He's done nothing wrong and doesn't deserve the punishment of her vagina."

I sighed, smacked my elbows on top of the bar and rested my head in my hands.

"My poor penis. I should buy him a gift," I muttered to myself.

Finding out my girlfriend of two years was cheating on me two days before we were supposed to move here together and start a new life was a huge pain in my ass. And my penis.

Drew's grief counselor, the waitress, walked back over to console him and interrupted my penis pity party. At the same time, a rush of air surrounded me as someone quickly walked by, his or her shoes clicking on the hardwood floor. I breathed in right at that moment and the smell of chocolate overwhelmed me and instantly transported me back in time to five years ago.

"Mmmmm you smell so good. Like chocolate chip cookies," I muttered with a raspy, hung-over voice as I pulled her incredibly soft body against my own.

Wow, she doesn't have any bones. Like, at all. Where the fuck are her bones? Am I still drunk? Did I sleep with a blow-up doll? Again? I peeled my eyes open one at a time so the rays of sun shining in the room wouldn't make me go blind. Once my eyes adjusted to the light, I looked down and groaned. Nope, not drunk, just hugging a pillow. I let go of the pillow, rolling over onto my back and flinging my arm out to the side of me to stare up at the ceiling.

She was gone. And I didn't even get her name. What kind of a dick was I? She wasn't too interested in knowing my name either though, so I guess we were even. As drunk as I was last night, I could remember every single second. I closed my eyes and pulled to mind how great her ass looked in those jeans, the smell of her skin, the sound of her laugh and the way her body felt like it was made to fit against mine. I scanned through every memory I had, but for some reason, her face just wouldn't come into focus no matter how hard I tried. God dammit, how was I going to find her if I couldn't remember her face and didn't know her name? I was the king of jackasses. I knew she was beautiful, even if I couldn't remember everything. Her skin was soft and her hair felt like silk and her lips on me could make me whimper like a girl. And best of all, she made me laugh. Not many girls made me laugh. They never got my jokes or were too uptight for my sense of humor. But she got me.

Last night obviously wasn't my best performance. I hope to God I didn't have whiskey dick and was able to at least get it up and keep it up. Shit. She probably ran out of here as fast as she could this morning because I sucked so badly. I never had a one-night stand before; I didn't know what the protocol was for something like this. Would it be wrong for me to hunt her down? Even if she wanted nothing to do with me ever again, I needed to at least apologize for my God-awful skills last night.

And truth be told, I just wanted to see her again. I wanted to know if she was real or if I just imagined how perfect she was. I grabbed the pillow and brought it up to my face, breathing the smell of chocolate in deep and smiling. I might not have remembered everything, but I remembered her smell. It was like hot chocolate on a cold winter's day, chocolate cake baking in an oven on a rainy afternoon...

Oh my God, I sound like a chick. I need to watch some ESPN and get in a bar fight, pronto.

The sound of the toilet flushing in the connecting bathroom had me bolting upright in bed. Holy shit! Was that her?

I swung my legs around off the bed and started to get up right when the door opened.

"*Fucking hell dude, don't ever sleep in a bathtub. That shit is for the birds. My ass is killing me,*" *Drew complained as he shuffled over to the bed, turned around and let his body fall back onto the end, settling after a few bounces. He threw his arm over his eyes and groaned.*

"*Why the fuck does morning have to come so early?*" *he whimpered.*

I sighed in disappointment, holding the sheet in place so I could lean over and grab my jeans that were crumpled on the floor with my boxer-briefs still shoved inside them.

"*I'm never drinking again,*" *he promised.*

33

"You said that last week," I reminded him as I flung the sheet off of me so I could put my pants on.

What. The. Fuck?

"Oh shit. Fucking shit. Mother fucking shit balls."

This can't be good. This really, really cannot be good.

"What are you whining about over there, Nancy?" Drew asked as he removed his arm from across his eyes and sat up.

"My dick is bleeding. Drew – MY DICK IS BLEEDING!"

I was screeching like a girl. I knew it, he knew it, and pretty soon the whole house would know it. But my dick was bleeding. Did you hear me? My fucking dick was fucking bleeding. FUCK! It's not supposed to bleed. Ever.

I thought I was having a heart attack. I couldn't breathe. I didn't know much, but I did know the rules about owning a dick. Rule number one: It should never bleed. Rule number two: There was no rule number two. IT SHOULD NEVER FUCKING BLEED.

Did I sleep with a nutcase that decided to carve my dick like a jack-o-lantern while I slept? Or maybe her vagina had teeth. My dad used to always tell me when I was a teenager to stay away from them, because they bite. I thought he was kidding. Oh God, I can't look. What if some of it is missing?

"Calm down. Let's assess the situation," Drew said, crossing one leg over the other and folding his hands on his knee. "Have you noticed any of the following: unidentified discharge, burning sensation when you urinate, lower abdominal pain, testicular pain, pain during sex, fever, headache, sore throat, weight loss, chronic diarrhea or night sweats?"

He sounded like a fucking commercial for syphilis.

"Eeew dude, no. I just have blood on my dick," I answered irritably, pointing to the problem but refusing to look.

He leaned over and looked down at my lap.

"Looks okay to me," he said with a shrug as he stood up. "You probably just bagged a virgin."

I sat there with my bloody, non-chlamydia infested dick flapping in the breeze and my jaw hanging open.

A virgin? That can't be right.

I glanced back down in my lap and took a closer look. Okay so it wasn't the bloody slaughter I originally thought I saw. My dick hadn't been Texas Chainsaw Massacred. There were just a few pink streaks. I wore a condom though. How in the hell does something like this happen? You use those God dammed things as water balloons in middle school and couldn't get them to pop even if you threw them at a bed of nails. The one time you need them to stay in one piece they decide to say, "fuck this shit". It was like condom anarchy.

But more importantly - Holy hell! Why would she let me take her virginity? Why in the fuck would she give something like that to me when I was completely shit-faced and couldn't even make it sort of enjoyable for her? What an epic fail. I probably ruined sex for her forever. She's probably thinking right now "Seriously? That's what I waited for? What a joke."

"I have to find out who she is. I need to apologize," I mumbled to myself, standing up and pulling my boxers and jeans on.

"Whoa, dude. You didn't even get her name? Wow, you're kind of a dick," Drew said with a laugh, walking over to the bedroom door and opening it.

I threw my shirt over my head and then followed behind him, hopping on one foot to slide my shoes on.

"Thanks for making me feel a whole lot better Drew. Really. You're a stellar friend," I said sarcastically as we maneuvered our way through a house full of passed out drunks.

"Hey, it's not my fault you banged and bailed bro," he stated as he took a giant step over a naked chick wearing just a sombrero and opened the front door.

"I didn't bang and bail. In case you failed to notice, I woke up alone in bed this morning."

"With a bloody johnson," he added, walking down the steps of the porch.

"With a fucking bloody johnson," I repeated with a groan. "Shit. I have to find this girl. Do you think it's wrong for me to ask your dad to use his private detective resources to find out who she is?"

Drew's dad opened his own PI agency a few years ago when he decided following the rules of the police department didn't fit in with his busy schedule.

"Are you asking me if it's ethically wrong or if I think it's wrong? Because those are two very different questions my friend," he replied as we crossed the street and got into his car parked by the curb. *If only Drew took after his father in some way...*

"I have to find her Drew," I said as he started up the car.

"Then find her we shall my little virginity thief!"

"We never found her, did we big guy?" I muttered to Drew, who I assumed was still sitting next to me.

"Are you speaking to anyone in particular or do your shot glasses usually respond?" replied a very un-Drew-sounding voice.

☉ ☉ ☉

"Now, if you'll direct your attention to the one Claire is holding, that is called the Purple Pussy Eater. It has four speeds: Yes, More, Faster and Holy Shit Balls. It's also got a g-spot stimulator that is sure to tickle your fancy. Could you hold it up a little higher so everyone can see, Claire?"

I shot Liz a look that clearly said "bend over so I can shove this thing up your ass sideways" before I raised the rubber penis above my head with absolutely no enthusiasm.

The living room full of completely trashed women screamed in excitement and bounced up and down in their seats when I raised my arm, like the thing I was holding above my head was the actual penis of Brad Pitt. It's plastic, people. And it's filled with double A's, not sperm.

"Go ahead and pass it around for me, Claire," Liz said sweetly as she reached into her suitcase for yet another rubber rod.

I held my arm out lifelessly in front of me for the drunk-ass sitting closest to grab, but she was too busy complaining about how her husband's spunk always tastes like garlic.

Please God don't let me ever come face-to-face with this man, I beg of you. I will look at his crotch and see cloves of garlic popping out of his dick.

"Yo, Lara," I called, trying to get her attention so she could take this dildo out of my hand.

"Claire, remember to use her Bedroom Fun Party name!" Liz reminded me in a sickeningly sweet voice that was starting to make my ears bleed.

I gritted my teeth and imagined raising my arm back up and chucking the fake phallus right at her forehead so she would have a permanent dick head mark right in the middle of her face that people would point and laugh at. Is that a birthmark? No, it's a dick mark.

"Excuse me, *Luscious Lips Lara*?" I enunciated politely while trying not to vomit in my mouth.

Really, was it necessary for everyone to come up with a stupid ass nickname? That was the first thing Liz made everyone do when they got here. Come up with a sexual nickname for yourself using the first letter of your first name. And you were only allowed to call each other by those names all night.

Luscious Lips Lara, Juicy Jenny, Raunchy Rachel, Tantalizing Tasha…

Who thought up this shit? Oh, that's right, Liz - my former best friend. The one who decided to start a sex toy business without telling me so she could con me into working for her.

She should have let me come up with the names. Twat Face Tasha, Jizzbucket Jenny, Loose Labia Lara…those didn't make me want to jam a pencil in my eye.

Liz finished up the rest of her stupid party while I imagined I was doing anything else but this, like getting a Brazilian wax, water boarded by Navy Seals or my big toe shot off at close range for a gang initiation. Any of those would be preferable to talking with complete strangers about lubrication, nipple clamps and anal beads.

I gave her the silent treatment as we drove to the bar an hour later. I was offered an extra shift tonight that I couldn't pass up and Liz was going to keep me company in between customers. I should just open the car door and throw her out of the moving vehicle for what she did to me tonight, but I didn't want to ruin someone else's car if they ran her over.

"You can't ignore me forever, Claire. Quit being a dick," she complained.

"Speaking of dick...really, Liz? Sex toy parties? At what point in our friendship did you think I would EVER want to sell Pocket Pussies for a living? And another thing, Pocket Pussies? What kind of man needs something called a Pocket Pussy? Do men really need to release their seed out into the wild so much that they need to stick a fake vagina in their pocket that they can whip out at a moment's notice?"

Liz rolled her eyes at me and I resisted the urge to reach over the console and punch her in the vagina.

Pussy Punch: when a Twat Tap just isn't enough.

"Claire, quit being such a drama queen. I don't expect you to sell my sex toys forever; just until I can hire a few more consultants. Think about it Claire, this is the perfect opportunity for us. What was the one thing you noticed that was missing from this party tonight?" she asked, turning sideways in her seat to look at me as I got off at the exit for the bar.

"Dignity," I replied flatly.

"Funny. Snacks, Claire. Well, good snacks at least. They had bowls of chips and store bought cookies and enough liquor to choke a horse. These are women with money, Claire. Money they don't mind throwing away on Pocket Pussies for the husbands they don't want to screw anymore or clitoral stimulators for the "friend" they know whose husband has never given them an orgasm. What goes better with sex than chocolate?"

Sex and chocolate. My chocolate. My chocolate-covered yummy goodness that I couldn't sell as often as I liked because as a single mother working in a bar, it was hard to market yourself. The majority of people I was surrounded by cared more about who was buying the next round than what kind of desserts to have at their next party.

"The building I rented has the potential to be turned into two separate spaces. One of them with a kitchen," Liz continued. "A very large kitchen where you can perform your magic and when women book their parties they can order dessert trays at the same time."

I took my eyes off the road long enough to look over and Liz, expecting to see a sarcastic smile on her face and waiting for her to say "Just kidding! Wouldn't that be great though?" When none of that happened and she just sat there in her seat staring at me expectantly, I blinked back tears that I hadn't even realized were forming in my eyes.

"What are you talking about?" I whispered shakily in the dark car.

"Okay so I did something big. Something that's probably going to piss you off because you're going to think it's charity or pity, but really, all I did was get the ball rolling. The rest is up to you," she explained. "I've looked everywhere for a building for my business and everyplace I see is too big or too small and way overpriced. My realtor called me a few weeks ago and told me the owners of Andrea's Bakery right on Main Street came into some money and wanted to sell their space as quickly as possible, retire and move to Florida. It was like a sign, Claire. The price is right, the location is perfect and it's exactly what we always dreamed about, minus the whole Justin Timberlake penis time-share. With one sheet of drywall, we've got enough room for two connecting businesses: my sex toys and your desserts."

I bit my lip to stop myself from crying. I never cried.

"But I really wanted to share JT's penis with you," I told her with a sad look, trying to take the seriousness out of this situation before I started to ugly cry. No one likes an ugly crier. It's uncomfortable for all parties involved.

After a few minutes of neither one of us saying a word in the dark car, Liz couldn't take it anymore.

"Will you say something already?"

I let out a huge breath and tried to calm my racing heart.

"Liz I don't…I can't believe you…the money…" She put her hand on my arm as we pulled into the parking lot of Fosters.

"Don't turn into a pansy-ass on me just yet. Take some time and think about it. You know the trust fund my grandfather left me has been eating its way through my pocket so we're not even going to discuss money right now. Talk it over with your dad, come and check out the kitchen at the store and then we'll talk. In the meantime, you're going to get your hot little ass in that bar and serve me up some cocktails. I've got some new products to test out on Jim after your dad picks Gavin up later," she said with a wink before getting out of the car.

I sat there for a few minutes after she got out wondering what the hell just happened. My best friend was always a force of nature, but this just defied logic. Did she really just tell me she bought me a business? With every step of my life I felt like I'd made wrong turns. Nothing was going the way I planned. I wanted this more than anything, but part of me was afraid to really get my hopes up. Who knows though? Maybe good things were finally going to start happening in my life.

I glanced at the clock on the dashboard and realized I spent entirely too long sitting in my car and now I was late for my shift. I ran through the parking lot and threw open the side door, tying my little black apron around my waist as I went. Mr. and Mrs. Foster have seen one too many episodes of *True Blood* and recently decided we should adopt the same uniform as Merlotte's. Tiny black shorts and tiny white t-shirts with the word "Fosters" stamped across our tits in green. It could be worse. At least I don't have to make sure I'm wearing enough "flare" or sing some demented version of "Happy Birthday" with the rest of the staff. "Happy birthday to you, with beer goggles on you don't look like you should moo, happy birthday dear random stranger who's dressed like a hooker, happy birthday to you!"

I ran behind Liz already seated on a stool at the bar sipping her usual drink of vanilla vodka and Diet Coke and waved to T.J., the bartender I was taking over for tonight. Thankfully the men didn't have to wear the same uniform. I didn't think I could handle seeing a couple of these guys in tiny shorts with their hairy balls popping out of the leg holes.

On a slow night, I would have just hopped my ass up onto the bar and swung my legs around to get behind it, but the place was packed tonight. I had to do it the right way and go under the hinged, lift-top part of the bar at the opposite end. I jogged past some poor drunk schmuck that held his head in his hands, moaning, and made a mental note to call him a cab if he was here by himself.

Once I was behind the bar and got the skinny from T.J. on the customers here tonight and what they were drinking, he left to go home and I got to work getting refills for the regulars. One of the waitresses brought in an order for ten shots of the cheapest whiskey we had. I rolled my eyes and went to the end of the bar where we kept all of the whiskey. What is wrong with these people? Cheap whiskey equals a bad hangover and having the craps all the next day. I started lining up the shot glasses on my tray when I heard the drunken moaner speak.

"We never found her, did we big guy?"

Oh Jesus. I hate the really tanked ones. I hope this guy isn't a crier. He sounds pitiful. And if he pukes on my bar I'm going to rub his nose in it like a dog that shit on the carpet.

"Are you speaking to anyone in particular or do your shot glasses usually respond?" I asked without looking up as I added a few more shot glasses to the tray and reached under the bar for the bottle of Wild Turkey, trying not to make gagging noises as I unscrewed the top and the disgusting smell wafted up to my nose.

I saw Return of the Living Drunk whip his head up out of the corner of my eye while I filled the glasses.

"You know, the first sign of insanity is when inanimate objects talk to you. Or maybe it's the first sign of alcohol poisoning," I mused to myself.

"Who the hell is ordering that rot gut? They're going to have the shits all day tomorrow."

I laughed that even drunk, he was able to come to the same conclusion as me. Picking up the tray of shots and a bowl of lemon slices, I turned around to tell him so - and stopped dead in my tracks at the sight before me.

What. The. Fuck?

I felt the tray full of glass and booze tipping out of my raised hand but there was nothing I could do to stop its descent to the floor. I stood there like a statue, staring straight ahead as the glasses shattered around my feet and liquid splashed up onto my legs.

5.

Snickers Finger Arm Teeth

It happened in slow motion. Well, for me it happened in slow motion. Probably because the amount of alcohol I've consumed tonight has digested half of my brain cells, and I feel like I'm in the Matrix.

I wonder if I could lean back on my bar stool and do that cool move from the movie where I dodge bullets in slow motion while suspended in mid-air? I need a cool black leather jacket and my hair slicked back. I wonder if they used wires or if that Keanu guy could really bend like that? I bet he does that yoga shit. He looks like the kind of guy that does Downward Facing Dog.

Heh, heh, downward dog. That's funny. I should get a dog.

Wait, what was I doing? Oh, yeah. The bartender turned around and stared at me and before I could even get a good non-drunken haze look at her. I watched the entire tray of shots tip right out of her hand. They crashed to the floor before I had a chance to react, the sound of glass breaking rising above the drone of music and loud voices.

I should have jumped into action and vaulted across the bar to help her. Because you know, right now I had cat-like reflexes—if the cat drank three times its weight in tequila because it just found out its girlfriend of two years never wanted to have kids and decided to turn her vagina into a wiener-warmer for half the population of Toledo.

I should get a cat or two. They're pretty low maintenance. Maybe I can even teach it to piss in the toilet like Jinxy from *Meet the Fockers*.

Can a guy turn into a crazy cat lady? I suddenly pictured myself as an old man shuffling along the sidewalk covered in cat hair and meowing at everyone who walked by.

On second thought, no cats. I shouldn't be allowed to think when I'm drinking.

The bartender ducked down behind the bar, and I forgot about cats pissing for a minute so I could stand up and lean over as far as I could without the bar stool flying out from under me to see if she needed help.

And by "help" I meant checking to make sure she wasn't bleeding and then sitting back down before the room tilted too far to the left and I made an ass of myself.

My good deed ended before it began when a tiny little thing with long blonde hair, who looked strangely familiar, got behind the bar and walked over to the spot I was trying to see and looked down.

"Jesus, butterfingers, are you…"

A hand flying up from behind the bar, latching onto her forearm and yanking her down roughly cut her off. She disappeared with a yelp and I shook my head at why women were so weird. And such whores.

Fuck you, Tasha. And fuck cats that don't piss in toilets. And fuck you, Keanu Reeves, and your dog.

Drew sat back down next to me and yelled out, "Yo, bartender!"

The girl with the blonde hair popped up suddenly from behind the bar with her mouth wide open, staring right at me.

"Can we get a couple shots of tequila?" Drew asked her. She didn't even look in his direction, just stared at me without even blinking, like we were in some sort of fucking staring contest.

I'll show her. I'm the mother-fucking king of staring contests.

Drew leaned over and snapped his fingers in front of her face a few times.

"Hellloooo?"

Dammit! I blinked.

But she never moved from her spot kneeling behind the bar with just her little head peeking over the top of it. What the fuck was wrong with this woman? She was starting to freak me out.

"Um, tequila please?" I asked questioningly, enunciating each word as best as my drunken mouth would allow. So really, it came out as "Ufff, shakira pea?"

A huge psychotic smile broke out on her face and she quickly stood up.

"So what can I get you?" she asked me brightly, resting her hands on top of the bar and leaning into them.

Drew and I slowly turned to face one another. We both shrugged and I turned back to look at her, but not before noticing that Drew was busy tucking his shirt back into his jeans.

"T-e-q-u-i-l-a," I said very slowly, wondering if this bartender was drunker than me.

Her smile got bigger if that's even possible.

"Whiskey, coming right up!"

She quickly spun around and immediately tripped over what I assumed was the other bartender, still down there picking up broken glass. Blondie caught herself from falling, huffed and reached down to pull the other girl up. There was some swearing, loud whispering and tugging back and forth before she was finally able to pull the other one up roughly. Her long, wavy brown hair hung in a curtain, obscuring her face as she stood there with her head down. More whispering and erratic hand gesturing continued between the them, then they each turned and stomped off in the same direction, both taking turns smacking the other in the arm as they walked away. My eyes went immediately to the brunette's ass in the tiny black shorts as she walked away.

"I hate to see you go, but I love watching you leave," I said with a snort.

Drew punched me in the arm and I reluctantly looked away from her great ass and long legs before I started drooling.

"So, did you strike out with the waitress?" I asked him as we waited for whatever it was the chick decided to bring us to drink.

"No, I just fucked her in the bathroom. She tasted like beef jerky and Captain Morgan. Strange, yet oddly satisfying. She threw up when she came though. She's got issues."

"How in the fuck has your dick not fallen off yet?" I asked with disgust.

"Don't be a hater just because you dipped your wick in the same crotch-rot for two years. I like to test the waters, sample the merchandise. Plus, I've got a stamp card for the Quickie Mart by my house. One more box of condoms and I get a free twenty ounce of Pepsi."

The ladies were back with our drinks before I could come up with a clever retort. The short blonde with the staring problem slammed a bottle of Johnnie Walker Blue Label down on the bar, while the other one stood a few feet behind her with her hair still shading her face.

"So boys, what are we drinking to tonight?"

Since she wasn't staring at me like that creepy clown Pennywise from the movie *It* anymore, I figured she wasn't dangerous.

"If you share a drink with us, I might be inclined to tell you," I said with a wink.

At least I thought it was a wink. She was looking at me funny; maybe I just squinted really hard. I tried again.

Fuck, why was it so hard to fucking wink?

"Is something wrong with your face?" she asked.

I had been out of the game for too long. I couldn't even get drunk and flirt anymore. I could, however, get drunk and look like a stroke victim. I just shook my head and pointed at the shot glasses, signaling her to pour them.

"You'll have to excuse my friend here," Drew said with a pat to my back. "He's still mourning the loss of a shitty girlfriend and he's not happy I made him go out instead of sitting at home watching "Beaches" and diddling his vagina."

"Shut up, dick-fuck," I muttered as I grabbed one of the shots the blonde poured.

Turning her head, she called to the girl behind her. "Get your sweet ass up here and do a shot with these lovely gentlemen."

"I'm working, Liz. I can't drink," she said, gritting her teeth.

My ears perked up at the sound of her voice like I was a dog and someone just said, "cookie." The shot was halfway to my lips and I held it in place as she took a step forward and shook the hair out of her eyes.

Holy shit, she was beautiful. And not beer goggles beautiful. I was pretty sure that if I were sober she'd still look good. Long, wavy brown hair, smooth skin and the most gorgeous brown eyes I'd ever seen.

"Oh shut your yap. You know the Fosters could care less if you drink while you're on the job. You're like the daughter they never had."

Those eyes. There was something about them that made it impossible for me to look away.

"Liz, the Fosters have a daughter."

"Patty plays softball and can bench press two hundred and fifty pounds. Her dick is probably bigger than this guy's," she said, hooking her thumb towards Drew.

"Heeeeey," Drew said defensively.

I couldn't stop staring. I just wanted her to look at me. Why wouldn't she look at me? Her friend wouldn't shut up and she wouldn't look at me.

"Sorry, big guy. I'm sure you have a very nice dick."

"Well, thank you. How about you and I..."

"Don't even finish that sentence," she said with a roll of her eyes and a shake of her head. "I saw you sneak into the women's bathroom to fuck Jerky Jade not more than twenty minutes ago. Are you seriously flirting with me right now?"

"Jerky Jade? I thought her name was Alison."

"You're such a man whore. Her name is Jade. She always smells like beef jerky so we call her Jerky Jade. And you stuck it to her. You stuck your penis in her meaty vagina."

While Drew and Blondie continued their verbal sparring, I continued to stare at the quiet one. I wanted to touch her hair and see if it was as soft as it looked. I bet I could use her hair as a pillow, a silky, furry hair pillow that I could finger all night to help me get to sleep.

No, that doesn't sound creepy at all. I should really stop drinking. Who keeps putting alcohol in my alcohol?

"Jesus, Liz, keep it down. She's right over there."

My ears perked up like a dog's again when she spoke and pointed in the general direction of the chick that smelled of Slim Jims.

I hope I don't start barking.

"Oh, please, like she doesn't know about the smell of meat products wafting from her lady parts. I think she rubs bologna down there to attract men. Lunch meat is her sex pheromone."

The brunette shook her head in irritation. "If I do a shot, will you please stop talking about Jade's disgusting vagina and never, ever use the word meat product in a sentence?"

"Woof!"

Three sets of eyes all turned to look at me.

"Did I just bark out loud?"

Three heads bobbed up and down in unison.

"I dated a guy once that had wet dreams almost every night. I'd wake up to him humping his pillow and howling in his sleep," Liz said wistfully, taking the heat off of me for a minute.

The beautiful one came right up to the bar then and grabbed the shot glass closest to me but still wouldn't look up. She kept her eyes down in the glass like it held the meaning of life.

"So, what are we drinking to?" she asked the shot glass.

"Do your shot glasses usually respond?" I asked with a laugh, throwing her words from earlier back at her.

Her eyes shot up to mine and I felt like I had been punched in the gut. Her eyes were so bright and shiny they looked like melted chocolate.

Fuck. Why the hell was I obsessing about chocolate again? It had been years since I thought about that night and now all of a sudden I couldn't get away from it. I thought I smelled it earlier and that stupid flashback floated through my mind, and now I was comparing this chick's eyes to it. It was chocolate for fuck's sake. It was everywhere. There was nothing special about chocolate.

Except *she* had smelled like chocolate.

After that night, I'm ashamed to say I went through a phase for a few months of smelling lotion and soap at every single store I was in but they never smelled exactly right. The only thing that came even remotely close was real chocolate. I used to wonder if she rubbed Hershey's behind her ears instead of perfume. And then I'd wonder if she tasted like chocolate, and I'd have to rub one out after kicking myself in the ass for not tasting her that night.

Who was I kidding? It hadn't been years since I thought about her. Every fucking time I was within a mile radius of someone eating chocolate I thought about her. Shit. It was all Tasha's fault that I was here right now obsessing about chocolate. My job relocation was going to give us a brand new start in a new place. The fighting between us those last couple of months was brutal, and we both agreed a change of scenery would do our relationship a world of good. Knowing she was going to make the move to this small town with me made it not seem so shitty. Fucking cocksucker. Literally. Too bad it was never my cock she sucked. She did it once and said she had TMJ or some shit and never did it again.

TMJ my ass.

Women were the devil. They led you along for years, making you think you would have a future together and then one day you came home and found her on her knees with the neighbor's dick in her mouth and porn playing on the television. It was all fun and games until someone else's dick was in your girlfriend's TMJ mouth. And it wasn't even good porn that was playing. It was Looney Toons porn. I shit you not folks. She sucked our neighbor off while Daffy Duck took it up the ass from Bugs Bunny shouting, "P-p-p-p-p-weathe Bugs, harder." That is some serious shit that could never be unseen.

Does it matter that I'm pretty sure I never loved Tasha? That every day with her felt like I was just biding my time until I found *her* again? I knew it was shitty of me and I probably deserved to walk in on her gargling with the neighbor's spunk, but it still sucked.

Clearing my head of duck-fucking rabbits and depressing thoughts, I raised my glass in the air with an angry growl and waited for the other three to do the same.

"We're drinking to all of the lying bitches in this world that wouldn't know how to tell the truth if it smacked them in the fucking face. Cheers!"

I threw back the shot and slammed my glass down, wondering why the beautiful girl in front of me hadn't drank hers and instead stood staring at me with a look of horror on her face. I watched her friend elbow her and she quickly sucked that shot down like a champ. And then proceeded to pour herself another. And another. And then, like ten more after that - in a row. She'd obviously overcome her decision that it wasn't a good idea to drink on the job. Drew and I just kind of sat there watching her in awe. I mean, I drank like ten times that much tonight, but not all at once.

Half the bottle was gone by the time Liz reached over and took it out of her hands.

"Okay there, home slice, I think that's enough for now."

I was seriously losing my ability to focus at this point. I wanted to ask her if I could suck on one of her fingers and see if it tasted like a Snickers bar. I wanted to ask her what her name was and tell her I didn't always do stuff like this, but she was already walking away and I couldn't figure out how to lift up my arm to signal her back. I stared down at my arm resting on the bar and it just sat there like a little piece of shit slacker. I stared really hard at it and thought about it moving, but it didn't work.

Fucking arm. It must be in a union and on a break. I can't feel my teeth.

"Drew, I can't feel my teeth." I tapped my finger against them. I had dreams all the time that my teeth were falling out. Fuck, what if this was one of those dreams? But it can't be a dream because I don't remember falling asleep. In my dreams my teeth were always falling in my lap and there was blood everywhere and no one cared that I was spitting them all out. Every tooth I touch just falls right out and no one looked at me funny even though that was some crazy shit, right? I ran my fingers around the hard edges of all my teeth.

Never mind. It's fine. Teeth are still there.

"Yeah, I think it's time to say nighty-night and get you home, little buddy," Drew said as he got up from his stool and threw a wad of bills down on the bar before pulling my dead arm up and swinging it over his shoulders. I looked up at Drew as he helped me walk out of the bar. "I wanna eat her Snickers finger but my arm teeth won't feel."

I didn't remember much after that.

6.

I Got a Big Weiner

I was having the best dream ever. It was one of those hot dreams where you're having sex and you start having an orgasm and you slowly wake up in the middle of it and you don't know if you really did just have an orgasm or if it was part of the dream, but you know you want it to keep going. I was warm and cozy under the covers, and I slid my hand down between my legs to either do it again or finish it. Right when my fingers started to slip inside my underwear, I opened my eyes and screamed.

"HOLY SHIT!"

My son stood there next to the bed just staring at me. Seriously, two inches from my face just staring at me like those creepy twins in *The Shining*. I waited for him to start saying, "Come play with us" in their freaky twin voices while I tried not to have a heart attack.

"Gavin, seriously. You can't just stand here and stare at Mommy. It's weird," I grumbled as I put my hand to my aching head and tried to calm my pounding heart.

Sweet Jesus, who kicked me in the head and shit in my mouth last night?

"You said a bad word, Mommy," he informed me as he clambered onto my bed and straddled my waist. My other hand joined the first one on my head and I held on tight, fearing the entire thing was going to explode all over the room.

"Yes, Mommy said bad words. Sometimes mommies say bad words. Just don't ever repeat them, got it?"

He started bouncing up and down on my stomach like he was riding one of those stupid hopping balls with handles.

"Gavin, come on. Mommy doesn't feel good," I complained.

He stopped bouncing and leaned forward to sprawl his body out on top of me, putting his face right up to mine.

"Do you want me ta' beat up your friends, Mommy?" he whispered conspiratorially.

I removed my hands from my head and opened my eyes to look at him.

"What are you talking about, Gav?"

He brought his hands up and put them on my chest, resting his chin on top.

"Your friends, Mommy. The ones who maded you sick," he said in a voice that clearly screamed, "Duh."

I wrapped my arms around his little body and shook my head at him. "I have no idea what you're talking about, buddy."

He let out an exasperated sigh. Poor kid. He got stuck with a dumb mother.

"Papa says your friends Johnny, Jack and Jose maded you sick. Friends shouldn't do stuff like that, Mommy. If Luke maded me sick, I'd punch him in the nuts!"

"Gavin! Come on, we don't say things like that," I scolded him.

"Fine," he huffed. "I'd tickle him in the nuts."

Jesus Christ on a waffle cone. There's a reason why some animals in the wild eat their young.

"Just don't talk about nuts," I said with a sigh, rolling over so he slipped down onto the bed next to me with a giggle as he went.

"My best friend Luke talks about nuts. He showed me his wiener once. Do girls have wieners? Papa took me to breakfast and I ate fwee pancakes wif syrup and sausages, and Papa let me have Dr. Pepper last night wif dinner, and I told him I'm not allowed to have pop wif dinner but he told me not to tell you, and I said okay but I forgot. Can we go to the park?"

Make it stop. Please God just make it stop.

"SO HOW YOU FEELING THERE CLAIRE?" my dad screamed at the top of his lungs as he lounged against the doorframe to my room with a cup of coffee in his hand.

I squinted one eye open and peered at him through it, trying to muster up a dirty look but my face hurt too much to do that.

"Really funny there, old man. Don't make me come over there and punch you. When I don't feel like puking. And my legs start to work again," I muttered as Gavin fidgeted and kicked and scrambled his way over top of me to get off the bed.

He ran across the room to my dad and threw himself at his legs, his head smacking into the family jewels.

"Shit! Gavin, you gotta be careful there, buddy," my dad wheezed as he picked him up.

"Papa, can we go to the shit-park?"

I have to give it to my dad, he never laughed at that shit. Er, stuff. I don't know how the hell he always kept his composure. As long as Gavin didn't do that sh..stuff in public and embarrass the hell out of me, it was hard not to laugh.

"Gavin, remember the talk we had last night about big-people words? Well, *shit* is one of those big-people words. You don't say it," my dad said sternly as he looked into Gavin's eyes.

"Can I says it when I'm a big boy?"

"Yes, you can SAY it when you're a big boy," he replied.

Gavin seemed satisfied with that answer and forgot all about the shit-park. My dad put him down and he ran out the door and down the hall to his room.

"Thanks for watching him last night after Liz got home to Jim," I said as I pushed myself up in bed and leaned against the headboard.

"Yep."

He stood there staring at me silently while he sipped his hot coffee. He knew something was up. I liked to have some drinks every now and then, but getting tanked like I did last night, especially at work, meant something bad happened. Thank God Liz stayed with me at the bar all night and made sure I didn't drop any more glasses or puke in someone's lap.

I don't even know how I'm supposed to process what happened last night. Or more to the point, *who* happened last night. As soon as I saw his face, I knew. Those eyes were a dead giveaway. Aside from the fact that I used to dream about those blue eyes and would remember his face no matter how much time had passed, I've had to look into those same eyes every single day for the past four years.

Fuck!

I'm pretty sure the wet dream I was having this morning was about him too.

Double fuck!

His voice was a dead giveaway as well. That deep raspy voice that murmured the words "Jesus, you're so fucking beautiful" in that dark bedroom five years ago floated through my mind all the time. After I tipped the tray full of glasses and dropped down behind the bar, I sent a panicked look to the other end where Liz sat. Without hesitating, she got to my side to see what was wrong. My frantic words of "OH MY GOD, OH MY GOD, OH MY GOD, IT'S HIM, HOLY SHIT LIZ IT'S HIM AND HE'S HERE AND HE SAW ME AND OH MY GOD I CAN'T DO THIS RIGHT NOW!" spurned her into action and she popped her head up to get a better look at him. After just a few seconds she dropped back down to my hiding place and with a squeal and a clap of her hands she confirmed it was him.

My dad stood there in the doorway tapping his foot, waiting for me to proceed. I needed more time to think about what I was going to do, but I never kept anything from my dad. With a huge dramatic sigh, I let it out. "He came into the bar last night."

Dad stared at me questioningly for a few seconds before it clicked and his eyes grew wide and his mouth fell open. He knew exactly whom I was referring to. There were only a small handful of men in my life, and we both knew I would call them by name if I were talking about them. The only person we ever referred to as "he" over the last few years was….

Fuck! I still don't know his God damn fucking name!

"Did you get his name this time?" my dad asked sarcastically, practically reading my mind.

I shook my head and let it drop into my hands.

My dad let out a sigh. "Well, if he comes back into the bar and you need me to kill him, let me know. I can make it look like an accident."

If you're George Morgan's enemy and you can see him, it's too late; he already killed you and you just don't realize it yet.

⊙ ⊙ ⊙

After a shower and two cups of coffee, I almost felt human. I checked my voicemail while Gavin got dressed and there was a message from Liz. She told me to meet her at the old location of Andrea's Bakery as soon as I woke up. She wanted me to look at the place before I had a chance to freak out about the bomb she dropped on me in the car the previous night. Liz knew me entirely too well. She knew as soon as I came to my senses I would tell her there was absolutely no way I would let her buy me a freaking business. She was out of her mind. Forcing me to meet her at the shop was cheating as far as I was concerned. Liz was smart though; I'll give her that. She knew this would take my mind off of my other *situation*.

Butler was a small college town that had a town square right in the heart of it where all of the mom-and-pop-type stores were located. Andrea's Bakery was situated on the busiest corner. I had to clamp down my excitement as I buckled Gavin into his car seat and headed towards downtown. I would not get my hopes up about this yet. There were entirely too many things to work out and consider. How much rent would I have to pay Liz? What would Gavin and I do about healthcare? Would Liz and I be partners with this whole thing or two separate entities just sharing a space? Could our friendship survive something like this? Would Gavin have to skip college and spend his life as a male prostitute just to make end's meet because I stuck every penny into a business that tanked?

Fuck, this was going to throw me into a panic attack.

"Are we going to Auntie Wiz's house?" Gavin asked from the backseat, looking out his window at the cars and houses we passed.

I looked at him in the rearview mirror and reminded myself that whatever I did was all for him. He deserved the best life, and I was determined to give that to him.

"No, bud, we're not going to her house. But we are going to see her," I told him as I pulled up in front of the building a few minutes later.

I sat in the car for a minute staring at our building. It was right on the corner and windows took up the entire front of the store, wrapping around to take up the whole other side as well. It was the perfect corner store where we could each have our own window displays. Andrea's Bakery had recently been repainted bright white and had brand new flower boxes installed beneath the windows overflowing with Gerbera daisies in every color. It looked beautiful.

Our building, *our* window displays. Jesus, I'm already thinking of it as mine. Liz is an evil genius and I haven't even walked inside yet.

Speaking of the she-devil, Liz stepped out of one of the doors, holding it open with her hip.

"Stop gawking and get your ass in here," she yelled out to me, before turning around and walking back inside.

Gavin unfastened his seat belt and tried to open his door but the childproof lock prevented him from doing so.

"Come on, Mommy," he complained. "Auntie Wiz said to get our ass in dare."

"Gavin, language," I said, rolling my eyes at his refusal to listen as I got out and walked around to open his door. I grabbed his hand and helped him jump down out of the car.

"Be good, you got it?" I asked as we walked up onto the sidewalk. "Don't run, don't yell, don't touch anything and stop saying bad words or you're going home to take a nap."

"Naps can suck it."

I will not sell him to gypsies. I will not sell him to gypsies.

A bell dinged above the door as I opened it, and Gavin yanked his hand out of mine to go running into Liz's arms.

"Ooooooh, my handsome man is here!" Liz squealed as she scooped him up and swung him around. "What's new, little man?" she asked as she set him down on top of the counter next to her.

"Mommy don't feel good today and I got a big wiener!"

Liz barked out a laugh.

"Gavin, please. Enough with the wiener talk," I complained

"But, Mommy, look," he said as he attempted to unbutton his jeans. "My wiener is really big and tall right now and it feels funny."

"Ooookay," I said as I quickly walked over and stopped him from whipping it out. "No one needs to see it and remember what I told you the other night?"

Gavin nodded in understanding and I slid him down off of the counter and told him to go look out the front window to count the cars that go by. When his face and hands were plastered against the window, I turned to face Liz who was silently laughing with her hand over her mouth.

"It's not funny," I hissed at her in a loud whisper. "Why the fuck didn't anyone tell me four-year-olds get woodies? I am not equipped to deal with this shit, Liz."

She wiped tears out of her eyes and looked at me apologetically. "I'm sorry, Claire, but seriously. That is some funny shit right there. Sorry, I know nothing about four-year-old boys. When the hell did it first happen?"

"ONE!" Gavin yelled from in front of the window as a car went by.

"The other night after his bath. He was lying on the floor on his towel and I gave him a book to read while I ran down the hall to get his pajamas out of the dryer," I started.

"TWO!" came another yell from Gavin.

"I walked in the room and he rolled over onto his back and that thing stuck straight up into the air like a lightening rod. It was horrific. He kept smacking at it and saying it felt funny. Jesus Christ, will you stop laughing!"

"FWEE!"

"I'm sorry. I'm sorry!" Liz gasped in between laughs.

"And of all the books he could have been reading when it happened, it had to be Barney. My son gets a hard-on for fucking BARNEY," I screeched and quickly turned around to make sure Gavin didn't hear me.

Liz was hysterical at this point. Her mouth was closed and her shoulders were shaking. Every time she tried to breathe and not laugh she snorted and then choked.

"Did you ask your dad about it?" she asked between giggles and coughs.

I rolled my eyes before responding as I thought back to the conversation I'd attempted to have with my dad the other morning.

"You know my dad. As soon as I said the word *penis* he turned and walked out of the room and told me to call my mother. And she was just as much help as you are right now. When I asked her if it was normal she replied, "Does a one-legged duck swim in circles?" I hung up on her after ten straight minutes of her doing that hyperventilating laugh thing after I told her about the Barney Boner."

Liz finally calmed down and we both turned to check and make sure Gavin was still occupied.

"Now every time it happens he wants to show me and say 'Mom! Look at my big wiener!' So I just told him it was normal and it happens to all little boys and it just wasn't something he should go walking around telling people."

Liz patted me on the back and gave me a look of pity. "Well, that's just proof you need a man in your life, Claire. And speaking of men in your life…."

"Don't. Don't even go there," I threatened, pointing my finger in her face so she knew I was serious. "I am so not ready to have this discussion with you right now. I'm still wondering if last night was a dream and that wasn't really him. Maybe I was just imagining things in the haze of alcohol. I mean, in all the bars, in all the towns, in all the world…"

"Easy there, Humphrey Bogart, it was him. I immediately recognized him and the friend he had with him. That was the guy who tried to make out with me that night right after telling me he usually liked girls with bigger tits but since I was pretty he would make an exception."

I knew I was full of shit trying to convince myself that maybe it wasn't him. But having Liz confirm it made me feel like a dumb ass.

"Fuck. Fuck, fuck, fuck. Did you see his eyes? God, those were Gavin's eyes. They were that same weird blue-grey color with a black outline. What the fuck am I going to do?" I asked in a panic.

"TEN!"

"Gavin, four comes after three," Liz yelled to him while I tried not to throw up on the floor.

"That's boring," he announced.

"Come on, let me give you the tour before he starts showing his penis to all the people walking by and gets an indecent exposure ticket before the ink is dry on this place," Liz said as she grabbed my hand. "You're going to stop worrying about this right now and just enjoy taking a look at your dreams coming true. We'll worry about blue-eyes later."

☉ ☉ ☉

I was still in shock and awe mode as I drove us home two hours later. Gavin fell asleep as soon as the car started, so I didn't have any nonsense chatter about wieners and nuts coming from the backseat to break up my thoughts. The kitchen at the store was much nicer than I remembered from the years I spent stopping in there for a cup of coffee and a muffin, and it was stocked with supplies I only dreamed of using, let alone owning. There was an industrial-sized, two-door reach-in freezer with a matching three-door reach-in fridge, a heavy-duty electric range with six burners, two Cyclone convection ovens, a holding cabinet that could keep sixteen trays of chocolates cool, a refrigerated bakery case that was right below the front counter and two copper kettles to melt chocolate, caramel or pretty much anything I needed. Right in the middle of the room was a four-foot by six-foot island with a cooling marble countertop - perfect for making candy. In all the time I'd patronized Andrea's Bakery, I always loved the open floorplan. I loved how when you were at the counter paying you could see into the kitchen and watch someone making cakes or pies.

It was too much and I told Liz that as I walked around the kitchen, letting my hand trail over all of the equipment. She tried to tell me that the previous owners recently upgraded everything so all of the stuff in the kitchen came with the space, but I knew she was lying. I'd been in Andrea's Bakery not that long ago and spoke with the manager. I knew for a fact they didn't upgrade. Plus, Liz could never look me in the eyes when she lied and she swore twice as much.

"Liz, this is too much. I can't let you do this."

"Oh for fuck's sake, Claire. This fucking shit came with the fucking place and the previous fucking owners just want to fucking get rid of it."

Liar liar, fucking pants on fucking fire.

Liz's side of the store was just as nice, only without the amazeballs kitchen that my side had. She showed me where she wanted the wall to go that would separate the two spaces right down the middle, but not extend all the way to the front. She wanted enough room up by the windows for customers to walk back and forth between the two stores. It would provide just enough privacy in case my customers weren't too keen on looking at the dildos, lingerie and lube on Liz's side and she said we could put a door back by my kitchen where the two of us could easily go back and forth without going to the main parts of the stores. The front of both of our sides had a counter where a cash register would go. Liz's side had display tables littered throughout the front so she could display the items she would have for sale. Mine was left empty right now, so I could possibly add some tables for people to sit down in the future. I realized she made changes to the place long before she clued me in, knowing full well I wouldn't be able to turn it down once I saw the hard work she put in to it. Where my side was wide open so when you were standing in front, you could see the entire kitchen in the back, Liz's side had a wall right behind the front counter since the only thing in the back of her store would be inventory. She'd thought of everything and I was completely amazed at all she'd done in such a short amount of time.

While Gavin ran amok, we sat down on the floor with all of the paperwork strewn around us. We were knee deep in zoning permits, sales tax licenses, business plans, insurance policies and a hundred other different forms that made my head spin. This dream was so close I could touch it, but the fear of not being able to afford it had me biting my fingernails down to stubs. I could take up extra shifts at Fosters to save some more money and of course there was the additional income I would get from suffering through a bunch of Liz's sex toy parties, but it still wouldn't be enough to swing the rent and I refused to let Liz invest any more of her money for me. Liz called my father before I could protest and he met us up at the shop to take a look around.

"So, what do you think?" I asked him as he opened up the fuse box and took a look inside.

"Wiring is good. The kitchen is on a separate circuit from the security system," he replied.

"That's not what I mean."

I wanted him to knock some sense in to me like he was famous for. Tell me I was insane for thinking I could do something like this; call me an asshole for having my head in the clouds.

My dad closed the fuse box and turned around to stare up at the ceiling.

"You know how when you were in college I was paying your room and board every month?" he asked as he checked out all of the light fixtures. "Well, for the past five years, I've been putting that money into a savings account every month just in case you needed it one day. With the interest it's earned, it's a little over fifty thousand right now."

My mouth dropped open in shock and Liz, who was standing close by and not even trying to pretend that she wasn't eavesdropping, started squealing loud enough to break the sound barrier. She jumped up and down and flung her arms around my dad while I stood there trying to process what he'd just told me.

"Mr. Morgan, if you weren't my best friend's father I would totally hump your leg right now," Liz told him excitedly.

"There's a…I have…my dog's at the vet," my dad stuttered awkwardly as he pulled himself away from Liz and walked out of the store.

"You're dad doesn't have a dog," Liz stated as the bell over the door jingled with his departure.

"Nope. Your dry humping threats have finally made him go insane."

It took another hour for Liz to convince me that it wasn't selfish to take the money my dad offered. It was money he put away for me to do with as I wished, so why shouldn't I use it to start up the business I've always dreamed of? With money worries out of the way for the time being, Liz asked me to make up a tray of items to take to the party she booked me to do tomorrow afternoon. Jenny, a friend of her cousin, was having it and she was a computer designer. She offered to help Liz with brochures and flyers and things like that. Liz let her know I would be doing her party and that I needed help creating something to advertise my store as well. She agreed to help us out as long as she got to test out some free samples. I'd let her sample my vagina if she did this for me.

After the party, I was going to head over to Liz and Jim's house for dinner and some wine so we could talk more and come up with names for our business.

Our business. I repeated those words over and over to myself as I drove home from the store, trying to make it sink in. It was all happening so fast. Just two days ago the idea of owning my own business was a pipe dream that I figured was years and years away from ever happening.

I pulled into my driveway and quietly unbuckled a sleeping Gavin so I could take him in the house and lay him down. As I lifted him out of his car seat and held his head to my shoulder, he wrapped his arms around my neck and squeezed.

"You hafta mow the lawn wiffa snake marshmallow," he mumbled sleepily. "I slipped on a penny."

I let out a chuckle at my son's sleep-talking habits as I walked into the house and got him situated in his bed.

I wonder if *he* talks in his sleep too.

Liz sufficiently took my mind off of Gavin's father all morning, but now that I was alone with my thoughts, his reappearance in my life screamed through my head and it was all I could think about. For all I knew, he could have been passing through town and I'll never see or hear from him again. He was too drunk to remember me the first time we met, and obviously history was repeating itself. He had no clue who I was last night.

I refused to admit it stung a little that I hadn't made any kind of impact on him almost five years ago, when I had to live with a reminder of him every single day.

7.

Open Mouth, Insert Vodka

She rested her elbows against the bar and leaned closer to me. Her eyes mesmerized me. They looked like pools of Hershey's chocolate syrup. It was her. All these years and I could finally see her face. She was just as stunning as I remembered.

"I've been looking everywhere for you," I said.

She laughed and goose bumps rose on my arms. I remember that laugh; it was like music to my ears. She reached across the top of the bar and ran her hand down my arm and rested it on top of my own.

"Do your shot glasses usually talk to you?" she asked with a smile.

"Wait, you're the girl from the bar," I said in confusion.

"Am I?" she asked with a smirk.

She leaned completely across the top of the bar and pressed her cheek to mine, her lips close to my ear.

"Ask me what my favorite movie is," she whispered.

I turned my head and slid my nose against her cheek. She still smelled like chocolate. But that didn't make sense. Someone started knocking on the door to the bar and she pulled away and whipped her head around in that direction. She started backing up as the banging continued.

"Wait! Don't go. Just tell me your name," I pleaded.

She kept backing away and I stared at her face, memorizing every single detail: brown eyes, thick chestnut hair, full-heart-shaped lips, and a dimple on each cheek.

That's what the girl from the bar looked like. But this one had the same eyes and the same voice as MY girl. What the hell is going on?

"Please, tell me your name!" I yelled after her.

I jerked awake to the sound of banging and my heart pounding like I just ran a marathon. I slid my hand through my hair and flopped back down, trying to remember what I had just been dreaming about. It was right there at the edge of my consciousness but I just couldn't grasp onto it. There was something I needed to remember about that dream. I closed my eyes and tried to bring it back. The silence lasted for two seconds before the pounding against my front door started again and interrupted my thoughts.

"SHUT THE FUCK UP!" I screamed at the incessant banging, irritated that I couldn't make myself remember.

Oh, sweet Jesus, I am never drinking again.

I have the weirdest dreams every fucking time I drink. Why the hell can't I remember this one? I picked up a pillow from next to me and hugged it against my ears, trying to muffle the sound of my door being kicked in.

"Open the door, goat-fucker!" Drew's muffled yell shouted as he continued to pound his fist against my front door. I know if I don't get up, he'll keep making noise and then I'd have to kill him.

The banging continued as I sat up, threw the covers off angrily and stumbled through the rental house with my eyes closed. I still had boxes of shit all over the place that I had yet to unpack and I kicked them angrily out of the way as I went. I made it to the front door without breaking any limbs and flung it open with an angry growl.

"Holy shit, dude, you don't look so hot," Drew said as he shouldered his way past me and into my house, wearing one of his signature t-shirts. I swear this guy owned at least two hundred fifty of these things. Today's shirt said, "I pooped today".

"Sure, come on in Drew," I muttered to myself as I slammed the door shut and followed him to the living room. "You totally interrupted a good dream I was having. At least I think it was a good dream, I can't remember."

"Were you dreaming about the hot bartender you couldn't stop drooling over last night?" he asked with a laugh.

"Funny," I deadpanned as I leaned against the doorway and crossed my arms in front of me.

"If only I were kidding, dude. Her friend with the blonde hair asked me if you rode the short bus to the bar after you picked up your beer and poured it down the front of your shirt instead of your mouth—which was wide open staring at the bartender's ass.

Wow, definitely not one of my better nights.

"Maybe I should go up there and apologize to…."

Shit, I was drawing a blank.

"Yet another girl whose name you didn't get." Drew finished. "At least this time we know where she works. This place is a fucking mess," he said as he shoved boxes away with his foot so he could make his way over to the couch.

"Did you just come over here to insult me, or is there a reason for this early morning visit?"

"Early? It's twelve-thirty, dumb ass. We've got orientation at one," he said as he slid a box of books over and flopped down on the couch.

"SHIT! Are you kidding me?" I yelled as I ran into the kitchen, tripping over boxes along the way. Sure enough, the clock on the microwave read twelve thirty-four. Fucking hell. I do not need to be late for orientation at the new plant. I pulled the front of my t-shirt up over my nose, took a whiff and cringed. I smelled like a distillery.

I ran to the bathroom and took the fastest shower known to man and threw on a clean long-sleeved t-shirt and pair of jeans. Drew broke every speed limit, and we managed to get to the Butler Automotive Plant with five minutes to spare.

The plant was closed for production on Sundays, so our small group of transfers was the only people that would be here today. There were about twenty of us that transferred from different plants around the United States and would start working tomorrow. All of the plants basically ran the same way, so we wouldn't need to learn how to do our jobs or anything. We would just get all of our paperwork to fill out for Human Resources and watch a few videos about the history of the company and about how you shouldn't sexually harass your co-workers. The latter was always our favorite. It was the same video they've been showing for over thirty years that they recorded back in the seventies and it was set to porno music. Getting a group of rowdy, blue-collar workers together in one room and putting in a tape that shows a guy in a leisure suit putting his hand on his secretary's ass and you've got complete and total anarchy, ladies and gentlemen.

We walked through the employee entrance to the plant and went into a conference room right by the door. Drew and I signed our names in to the attendance log hanging on the door and took a seat at one of the tables towards the back of the room. We looked around at all of the other people that would be starting with us, seeing if we recognized anyone.

"So, what kind of a douche bag do you think our foreman will be?" Drew said in a low voice. A guy sitting on the other side of Drew leaned forward and spoke before I could answer.

"He's actually an okay guy. He's been here for about twenty years and as long as you don't fuck up, he leaves you alone to do your work. I'm Jim Gilmore," the guy said, holding his hand out for us to shake while Drew provided the introductions.

"Hey, man, I'm Drew Parritt and this is Carter Ellis."

We each shook his hand while Drew kept talking.

"So how long have you worked here?"

"Only a few months. My fiancé and I just moved here from Toledo," he said.

"Seriously? That's where we just moved from. We worked at the Toledo Automotive Plant and got relocated here," I explained.

Jim laughed. "Small world I guess. My fiancé is originally from Butler and we met in college at The University of Ohio. She wanted to move back here as soon as we graduated, so here we are."

"Hey, we went to a party one weekend there. Gee, Carter, you probably don't remember that party, do you?" Drew asked sarcastically, knowing full well just how much I remembered about that party.

"Shut up, asshole," I grumbled. "So Jim, how come you had to come to orientation today?"

"They suckered me into coming to give you guys a tour of the plant when it's over and introduce you to your foreman."

"As long as he leaves me alone and doesn't ride my ass, we'll get along just fine," Drew said.

"I thought you liked it when big, burly men rode your ass," I joked.

"You must have me confused with you and that new vagina you grew. Remind me again when the last time it was you got laid? Because I'm pretty sure I got my dick wet last night while you barked like a dog and passed out in the parking lot."

"I don't think I'd be bragging about tapping some girl's ass that has a meat-product nickname for her vagina," I reminded him.

"Yeah, that wasn't really my finest hour. I'm so disappointed in myself I can practically taste it."

"Does it taste like semen?" I asked.

"Fuck you. She wasn't a dude," Drew replied, leaning back in his chair and crossing his arms in front of him.

"Jim, please tell me you know some hot girls," Drew begged.

He let out a chuckle. "You might be in luck boys; my fiancé has a few single friends."

"Don't worry about the pussy here to the right of me," Drew said while Jim took a drink of his bottled water. "He's been hung up on a one-night-stand he had five years ago with a girl that smelled like Cocoa Puffs."

Jim spit out some of his water and started choking on the rest. Drew had to reach over and pat him on the back. After he recovered, he sat there staring at me funny.

What the fuck is up with people staring at me lately? Last night at the bar and now today. There was something wrong with the people in this town.

Just then, one of the supervisors walked in and shoved the sexual harassment video into the machine. Everyone started clapping and cheering as soon as the music started.

"Why don't you guys come over tonight for dinner and some drinks," Jim said over the rowdy employees as he started to turn back around to face the front of the room. "My fiancé can see if you guys are worthy enough for her friends," he said with smirk.

☉ ☉ ☉

"Hey, Claire, does this lube really taste like strawberry cheesecake?"

"Um, sure," I replied.

"Does the Jack Rabbit hit your g-spot or do I need to get something else for that?"

"Are you sure this massage oil candle burns cool? The last time my boyfriend and I tried hot oil, his penis got second degree burns."

Kill me. Just kill me right now.

"Where exactly do you put the cock ring on a guy? We must not have put it in the right spot because after a few minutes it got lost in my vagina. That was an awkward emergency room trip, let me tell you."

I'm going to lose my shit if someone asks me one more fucking question that I can't answer. That's all anyone has been doing for the last half hour. FUCK! These people need to just buy something already and quit talking to me.

"Do you let a guy use a vibrator on you? I've heard that's really hot."

"Okay look," I shouted, holding my hands up so they'd shut their yaps. "I have zero experience with any of this shit. I'm only doing this as a favor to my friend so I can make some extra money for my new business. I have had exactly one and a half sexual partners in my life and they were both pretty shitty experiences. The first one was in college and we were both completely trashed, I never got his name and he knocked me up. The next one was a friend of mine, and I decided to try it again and see if got any better. His dad had a key to his house and walked in on us two thrusts in, which completely killed any mood that might have been started. I've decided that my vagina is cursed. My orgasms have all been self-induced and have never been with anything that required batteries, a special cleaner, instructions or a weapon of mass destruction warning. If you want to place an order, I'll be in the kitchen. Try the chocolate-covered potato chips."

I turned and stalked out of the room and straight into the kitchen. Where was a giant, gaping hole in the floor to swallow you up when you needed one? Every woman in there was probably talking about what a loser I was and how they were going to tell everyone they knew to never do business with us. Shit, Liz was going to fire me. I was going to have to tell people I got fired from selling dildos. I can't even sell fake cocks to a room full of horny women. How do you come back from that shit? And on top of it all, I just spilled my deepest, darkest secrets to a room full of strangers.

"Oh, honey, you poor thing," Jenny said as she hurriedly walked into the kitchen and threw her arms around me. One thing new people learned about me real quick - don't invade my personal space or you will get punched in the neck.

I stood there stiff as a board with my arms out to the side. I don't understand huggers. I really don't. A nice, solid pat on the back worked just fine.

"I'm buying you a Jack Rabbit," Jenny proclaimed.

"Whoa, no, really that's okay," I tried to argue as I pulled out of the hug. That thing scared the shit out of me - four speeds, ears and beads that spun around. You should have to get a permit from the city to even power that thing up.

After several minutes of cajoling, Jenny managed to pull me back into the living room, and after she announced that she was going to buy me a toy, the whole room erupted in agreement. Much to my mortification, all of them began commenting to one another about what they were going to buy me. I had to draw the line when they started talking about throwing me a Vibrator Virgin party. I heard the words penis-shaped ice cubes and penis pasta salad, and I started getting a headache from hell. Any moment now they were all going to join hands and sing Kumbaya to my vagina—my poor, unloved vagina that never knew the pulsating touch of a rubber penis. I'm sorry vagina, I should have taken better care of you, I guess.

At the end of the show, I sold twice as much as normal because everyone bought two of everything, one for themselves and one for me. If my vagina wasn't covered in cotton and jeans, it might have taken offense to their looks of pity. I swore as they all placed their orders they looked down between my legs. Now, I know how chicks with huge boobs feel when a guy won't look you in the eyes.

When the last girl left with a hug for Jenny and me and a goodie bag of fun in her hand, we both collapsed on the couch in the living room.

"Thanks for doing the party tonight, Claire," she said with a smile. "And thanks for the awesome tray of desserts. Seriously, you have a gift. Those chocolate-covered pretzels drizzled with caramel almost gave me an orgasm. And that's saying a lot considering I was surrounded by fibrillators all night."

My eyes popped open and I raised my head from it's spot resting on the back of the couch to stare next to me at Jenny's profile while she absentmindedly check out her manicured nails. She was a nice person and we got along really well, but some of the things that came out of her mouth tonight boggled the mind.

"Um, Jenny do you mean *de*fibrillators?"

Why she was even using that word in a sentence about a sex toy party was beyond my scope of imagination, unless she assumed something in my bag of tricks would stop someone's heart. Come to think of it, I almost had a heart attack when I saw the size of the

Grape Gargantuan. Where exactly is a woman supposed to stick that thing - in the Hoover Damn to plug it up?

"Wait, what did I say? I meant vibrator. Oh my gosh that's so weird!"

I just shook my head and got up off of the couch to pack up all of the stuff into the extra suitcase Liz gave me for the supplies. Just my luck, I get to keep all of this shit in my house. If anything ever happened to me and the police or some other authority figure had to go through my house, I was going to be completely humiliated from beyond the grave if they find this suitcase.

Oh, Jesus, what if my dad found this thing? He was going to think I was a freak. What woman needed a suitcase with thirty-seven vibrators and nineteen bottles of lube? Shit, I needed to store this stuff at Liz's house. I didn't tell my dad yet about Liz's part of the business. No girl should ever be forced to have a conversation about dildos with her father. That was just wrong on so many levels. He could find out the first time he walked into the store just like everyone else.

"So, I'll get started on your flyer this week as soon as you send me photos of the items you want featured on it. I'm going to do one for you, one for Liz and then one that combines both of your stores. You said you guys were going to get together tonight and decide on a name?" Jenny asked.

"Yeah, I'm headed over to her and Jim's house tonight," I explained as I zipped the suitcase closed. "Hey, why don't you come with me? You can help us brainstorm."

"Oh, I don't know. I don't want to impose."

I pulled the plastic handle out of the top of the case and glanced over at her.

"You will definitely not be imposing. You already know Liz and she always makes enough food to feed an army. Really, she won't mind at all."

"Well, if you think it will be okay, I guess I'll stop by. I really need to get out and have some fun. Maybe she can find me a single man. I'm so desperate that I might settle for ugly and unemployed as long as he has decent hygiene and knows how to go down on me."

I stared blankly at her, wishing I could erase that that entire sentence from my memory.

"I'm going to finish cleaning up here, and I might try to fit an orgasm in too. I'll just meet you there."

I'm pretty sure my head just exploded.

"Um, Jenny? Did you just say you were going to try and fit an orgasm in?"

Please God, let me have heard her wrong.

"Well, duh! I have to make sure what I bought works properly don't I? If it doesn't get me off fast enough, I'm returning it. I have a two point five minute rule."

Oh Jesus. Please don't let her give me a used vibrator with her vagina funk all over it. What the fuck am I supposed to do with that? Do I need a HAZMAT suit to handle a returned vibrator? This was not a topic included in my new employee packet.

"Okay, well, I'll just see you at Liz's house then," I said as I ran from her house, pulling my suitcase on wheels behind me as fast as the wobbly legs on that thing would allow.

☉ ☉ ☉

Fifteen minutes later I was walking up to Liz and Jim's house and letting myself in. Liz flew around the corner into the foyer with a panicked look on her face.

"Elizabeth Marie Gates, you owe me big time. That was the single most horrific experience of my life," I yelled at her while I unbuttoned my coat.

"Claire, I have to tell you..."

"When I invited Jenny over for dinner, she decided to tell me she was going to pencil in some alone time with her vibrator before coming here," I said in horror, interrupting her. "I'm not going to be able to look her in the eye at all tonight."

"Claire, there's something…"

"You could have warned me that these women would be asking me a thousand questions about lube and g-spots that I wouldn't have a fucking clue how to answer. 'Oh, all you need to do is stand there and take everyone's orders,'" I complained in my best Liz voice as I yanked my jacket off.

"You need to…"

"I lost my shit after the question on cock rings getting stuck in vaginas and told them all about my stellar sexual history. Jesus H. Christ, Liz, a woman who has had one point five lays and didn't even come close to getting off during them should NOT be selling sex toys!" I screeched, throwing my coat on the hook next to the door and turning back to face her.

"Claire, you might want to keep it…"

"I told them about Max, Liz. MAX! The thing we swore to never speak of again. I told them all about him getting two thrusts in before his dad walked in on us," I said as I started walking backwards out of the foyer. "I can tell by that horrified look on your face that you realize how awesome this evening was for me."

"Don't say any…"

"Why in the hell did you ever think I would be good at this?" I asked as I came to a stop in the living room. "By the end of the night, every woman in that room was giving my vagina sad looks. My vagina is going to get a complex Liz. It's already judging me because it's only gotten off with my hand. And I don't count dry humping your leg that one time we were really drunk after finals freshman year," I argued as Jim came up next to me with a bottle of Grape Three Olive vodka in his hand.

I glanced at him and then back to Liz.

"Why the hell are you staring at me like that?" I asked her. Her mouth was open and she kept looking behind me over my shoulder.

Oh fuck.

I looked at Jim and he gave me a reassuring smile and held the bottle of vodka out to me.

Oh fucking fuck.

"There's someone behind me, isn't there?" I whispered.

Liz just nodded her head. I swallowed thickly and blindly reached to my side to grab the bottle out of Jim's hand. He already took the cap off for me so I brought it up to my lips and took and huge swig of it, my eyes watering as the burn of the alcohol slid down my throat and warmed my stomach. I slowly turned to face the music and die of humiliation. When I finally made it all the way around, the bottle of vodka slipped out of my grasp. Thank God for Jim's quick reflexes. His hand shot out and grabbed the bottle before it crashed to the floor.

"So, who wants another drink?" Liz asked cheerily from behind me.

8.

Cuckoo for Cocoa Puffs

Orientation took a few hours. When we were done, Jim, Drew and I decided to stop for a drink before heading over to Jim's house. We were sitting by the window at a tall table in a sports bar in the next town over. I really liked Jim. He was down-to-earth and friendly. He gave us a bunch of tips on places to go and things to do in this area. The conversation flowed easily and it felt like we had known this guy for years.

"I think I need to hear some more about Miss Cocoa Puffs," Jim said after he took a drink of his beer. I closed my eyes, wishing he forgot all about that comment Drew made back at the plant.

"I thought you'd never ask," Drew said with a smile as he leaned back in his chair and put his hands behind his head.

"Oh, you are so not telling this story, asshole," I said.

"Carter, I am the best possible person TO tell this story. I have an outside perspective on the situation and can give a better recollection of the events that took place that night. Plus, I've had to deal with your whiny ass for the past five years and your constant need to stop in chick stores and smell girly lotions. Maybe Jim can talk some sense into that brain of yours."

I could feel my face turning red and it wasn't because it was stuffy in here. I could not believe Drew was saying this shit. I would really need to evaluate his best friend status when this night was over. His membership card to the Carter Ellis Friendship Club was getting revoked. And yes, I realized I sounded like a complete douche just by thinking that.

"So, it goes like this," Drew began, completely ignoring the pissed-off looks I was throwing in his direction. "Five years ago, we crashed a frat party at your alma matter."

"Wait, so neither one of you went to school there?" Jim interrupted excitedly.

Try to contain your excitement at my humiliation, dick.

"Nope," Drew said, popping the 'p'. "Heard about it from a friend of a friend…you know how it goes. Anywho, we get to this party and little Carter here sees this girl across the room right when we get there. I swear to fuck you could almost hear "Dream Weaver" start playing and see stars circling his head. He stares at her for like a half hour before I finally tell him to quit being a pussy and to go talk with her. She's got a hot friend so I'm all over that shit."

I rolled my eyes at his retelling of the story. As I recall, Drew made me take him to see a voodoo priestess he found in the yellow pages that week because he said the friend put a hex on his penis. For two weeks he slept with a two-pound package of boneless, skinless chicken breasts on his junk since he refused to sacrifice a live chicken.

"So, he starts talking to her. They're doing some stupid movie-quoting shit that bored the fuck out of me, and I turned my charms onto her friend to pass the time. We totally hit it off and left those two losers to their geekiness. This girl was smokin' hot and had an ass that wouldn't quit. We found the closest empty bedroom and fucked like rabbits all night."

Drew had a faraway look in his eyes like he was remembering every detail.

"That's funny, because you couldn't remember shit about her the next day except for the fact that she put a curse on your twigs and berries so they would shrivel up and fall off. All of a sudden you have perfect clarity? You woke up in the bathtub alone, dip shit," I said with a laugh.

"Hey, we're talking about you, not me. And I thought we agreed to never ever speak of *the curse* again. Her highness, Zelda Crimson-Grass stressed how important that was," he stated seriously.

"So, anyway, where was I?" Drew asked, after looking over each of his shoulders in case the great and powerful Zelda, who charged thirty-five dollars a minute and accepted Visa, Mastercard and traveler's checks, was standing behind him holding a voodoo doll with pins stuck between its legs. "Carter wakes up the next morning freaking the fuck out because he thinks his dick is falling off."

Jim laughed and clunked his bottle of beer down on the table to wipe off the drops that dribbled down his chin. "Okay, why the hell would you think your dick was falling off?"

I huffed. "Because…"

"Because Carter here banged a virgin whose name he never got and had a bloody one-eyed snake," he said, interrupting me with a laugh.

I thought I heard Jim growl a little under his breath and I looked his way to see what his deal was, but he brought his beer back up to his mouth right then and wasn't looking at me. I must have just imagined it. I turned to face Drew to find him still laughing.

"Okay, seriously, you are making this whole thing sound really awful. You need to work on your storytelling skills, idiot," I complained.

"There is nothing about what I've said that isn't true. You're just pissed off after all these years of searching you have never been able to smell her again."

No, that didn't sound weird at all.

After getting a strange, almost angry vibe from Jim the last several minutes, he finally seemed to relax.

"Wow, so you actually looked for this girl and never found out who she was?" Jim asked.

Drew started to answer him, but I punched him in the arm.

"You shut your mouth. It's my turn," I said to him.

I sighed. I hated thinking about this part. For some reason it made my chest hurt.

"Yes, I looked for her. I would have given anything just to talk to her again and I don't care how much of a pussy that makes me sound. I asked everyone on that fucking campus and no one could tell me anything. I even went to admissions and tried to bribe the secretary into letting me look through yearbooks," I explained.

"Ha ha. She called the cops on you, remember?" Drew laughed.

"Um, yeah I remember. She called the cops because *you* told her we needed to look at pictures of all the female student body, pun intended, to see which one gave me a hard-on. She thought I was a pervert."

"So, why did you want to find her so badly? I mean, everyone has one-night-stands at some point. Most guys would consider themselves lucky they didn't have to deal with the whole morning-after bullshit," Jim stated.

I should feel embarrassed about this shit, but in all honesty, I didn't. Even though we just met him, I felt like Jim was the type of guy I could confide in and he wouldn't judge me, as opposed to my ex-best friend who was miming the act of playing a violin to go along with my sad tune.

"There was something about her," I said with a shrug. "Something that drew me in and made me want to just be near her. We talked for hours while we played beer pong. She got my sense of humor and we had the same taste in music and movies. Everything I can remember about her just makes me want to find her and see if she really existed. And it had nothing to do with the sex. Although, I would like to apologize to her for ruining her first time since I was completely trashed. It's more than that though. No woman has ever been on my mind as much as her. And it drives me fucking crazy that I can't remember her face," I said irritably as I flicked my beer bottle cap across the table.

Understanding seemed to wash over Jim's face and he nodded his head. The anger I swore I saw flash in and out of his features during this entire exchange suddenly vanished.

"Okay, now that you got all the touchy-feely shit out of the way, tell him about the creepy stalker shit you do," Drew said pointedly.

"Fuck you. It's not stalker shit."

"Right, because dragging my ass into every single fucking girly store and making me stand there while you smell everything that's made with chocolate, made near chocolate or made by something that shits chocolate isn't weird at all. And don't think I haven't forgotten about that last time a few months ago when the clerk asked us how long we'd been dating and you put your arm around me and said, "Well, sugar plum, this big, strong, sexy beast and I have been together for ages now," he said, mimicking the high-pitched voice I used at the time.

Jim threw his head back and laughed and even I had to snicker at the memory. When Drew turned to run out of the store I smacked him on the ass. It really was priceless.

"Alright, so after five years I can't get the smell of her out of my head. Big fucking deal. And it's not like I Google every store that sells lotion and just go down the list every weekend. If I happen to be in a store that sells lotions or soap, I go and smell a few to see if by some off chance I'll find the one that smells like she did. I just can't pass up the chance to find that smell again. It drives me God damn crazy."

Both men sat there staring at me. Fuck, I really was growing a vagina.

"You, my friend need to bang this chick out of your system once and for all. We really need to find you a nice girl that won't fuck you over and will make you forget about the Count Chocula Cooter," Drew said with a sad shake of his head.

"I may have just the girl for you," Jim said with a smirk.

"Perfect!" Drew proclaimed with a hard smack to my back. "You see, little buddy? There just might be hope for you yet. Hey, maybe we can even convince her to slather some Three Musketeers on her vagina. We'll just tell her you have a Willy Wonka fetish," Drew said with a laugh, finishing off his beer.

I kicked the leg of his chair while he leaned back on two of them. While I watched him windmill his arms to get his balance and not fall backwards onto the hardwood floor, I thought I heard Jim whisper something that sounded like, "That won't be necessary."

⊙ ⊙ ⊙

When we got to Jim' house, his fiancé came out of the kitchen to greet us and Drew and I both stopped dead in our tracks.

"Hey, aren't you the girl from the bar last night?" I asked. It was the woman with blonde hair that hadn't been afraid to call Drew out on his lame attempt at trying to get in her pants. "Liz, right?"

As soon as she saw us her eyes got wide and her mouth flew open. But she gained her composure quickly and smiled.

"Wow, I'm surprised you remembered. When you left the bar you were crying and singing at the top of your lungs 'I got ninety-nine problems and the bitch is all of them'."

I grimaced at the memory that frankly, I didn't remember at all.

"Really, don't worry about it," she laughed when she saw my discomfort. "It was quite fun pointing and laughing at you all night," she teased.

"Remind me never to get drunk around you again. I might wake up with my head shaved," I said with a laugh. Liz motioned for us to follow her the rest of the way into the living room.

"Don't worry, I'd never do something like that," she promised with a smile as we all found a place to sit and she relaxed next to Jim on the couch.

"Don't lie, sweetie," Jim laughed as he swung his arm around Liz and rested it on the back of the couch. "The night I met you, I had to pry a black Sharpie marker out of your hand because you were going to write, "insert penis here" on some guy's cheek with an arrow pointing to his mouth. Wasn't he passed out in some room in a ba-"

Liz jumped up from the couch suddenly and grabbed Jim's hand.

"Hon, can I talk to you for a second in the kitchen?" she asked, pulling him up before he could answer.

"Sorry, we'll be right back," Jim said over his shoulder as he was quickly ushered out of the room.

Drew leaned forward, placed his elbows on his knees and whispered across the coffee table to me.

"Fuck, that chick still looks so damn familiar. I hope I didn't sleep with her. That would be kind of awkward, right? I mean, we just met this guy. He's nice. I don't want to have to tell him I've seen his girlfriend's vagina. He might not let us eat dinner and I'm fucking starving."

"Drew, I'm pretty sure she would have said something by now if that happened," I assured him.

"I don't know man. She looked surprised to see us just now. I bet you they're in there right now arguing about my penis. What do you think she's saying? Do you think she's telling him it was the best sex she's ever had? I haven't gotten in a fight in a while. Maybe I should stretch."

"Jesus, how do you fit your ego through doorways?" I asked as the sound of the front door opening and closing stopped Drew's musings.

Faster than I've ever seen anyone move, Liz flew out of the kitchen and bolted to the front door. They had a foyer around the corner from the living room so we couldn't see who had just gotten here, but we could definitely hear her.

"Elizabeth Marie Gates, you owe me big time. That was the single most horrific experience of my life."

Holy fuck, I know that voice. And why am I suddenly thinking about barking dogs?

Muted voices filled the room as Jim sauntered in from the kitchen with a giant bottle of grape vodka in one hand and two bottles of beer in the other. He cocked his head and stared at Drew with a funny look on his face and for a minute, I wondered if maybe Drew was right about sleeping with Liz. After a few seconds though, he smirked like he just remembered the punch line to an inside joke, placed the beers on the coffee table in front of Drew and me and turned to face the direction of the foyer but didn't move from where he was standing.

The voice from the foyer suddenly got really loud.

"I lost my shit after the question on cock rings getting stuck in vaginas and told them all about my stellar sexual history. Jesus H. Christ, Liz, a woman who has had one point five lays and didn't even come close to getting off during them should not be selling sex toys!"

Ouch. We should probably not be listening to this. She's going to be pissed.

Jim unscrewed the lid to the vodka and tossed it down on the coffee table where it clattered a few times before coming to a stop. I thought he was going to take a drink straight from the bottle or something, but he just stood there holding on to it, as if waiting for something. At least Liz was trying to get her to talk a little quieter. We heard a few of her attempts but they went completely unnoticed.

Shit, one of us should say something. Alert her to our presence by walking around the corner or coughing or something. But like the assholes we are, we just sat there waiting to hear more.

The name Max was yelled and something about him getting two thrusts in before his dad walked in on them. Okay, now I wanted to hear more. Drew must have had the same idea because both of us leaned our bodies closer to the door so we could hear better. Fortunately, there was no need for that. Suddenly, everything was loud and clear as she walked with her back to us into the living room while Liz followed her, shaking her head frantically.

"Why in the hell did you ever think I would be good at this?" she said as she came to a stop and put her hands on her hips.

It was the girl from the bar last night. Hallelujah! And don't judge me just because I knew it was her as soon as I saw her ass. That was a really, really nice ass right there. I wanted to get down on my knees and praise God and the makers of the jeans she was wearing. I wanted to fuck that ass.

Wait, that didn't come out right. I mean, yeah what guy wouldn't? But she might not be into that sort of thing. That's something you have to discuss with a woman. You don't just go poking around or you'll get punch in the face and the words, "EXIT ONLY!" screamed at you.

The word 'vagina' being yelled right at that moment was the only thing that pulled my mind and my dream dick out of this chick's ass.

"By the end of the night, every woman in that room was giving my vagina sad looks. My vagina is going to get a complex, Liz."

Jim was the only one of us with any brains at this point. He walked over to the two women and stood quietly next to the one with the great ass, vodka bottle still in hand.

"It's already judging me because it's only gotten off with my hand. And I don't count dry humping your leg that one time we were really drunk after finals freshman year."

I have now lost all motor function. Someone check and see if I just came.

"Oh my God, I think I just wet myself," Drew whispered excitedly.

"Why the hell are you staring at me like that?" the woman asked irritably as she looked back and forth between Liz and Jim. She whispered something and Liz just nodded her head and looked in our direction. By the speed with which her hand flew out and grabbed the vodka bottle and chugged it, I'm guessing she just realized there were other people in the room listening to her talk about blah, blah, blah, masturbation, blah, blah, girl-on-girl-action. She slowly turned her body around and her eyes flew right to mine. I felt like the wind had been knocked out of me and watched the bottle of vodka slip from her hands. Jim calmly stuck his arm out and caught the bottle before it hit the floor, while I just sat there staring at the most beautiful woman I had ever seen.

Okay, I knew I saw her last night, but I was drunk and objects in drunken eyes may appear hotter than they actually are. My recollection of her face in my mind might not have been as accurate as I thought it was. Thankfully, she was just as beautiful as I remembered.

And now I felt really bad that she looked so horrified by everything she blurted out to Liz when she thought no one else was here.

"So, who wants another drink?" Liz asked cheerfully as she moved around the brown-haired beauty.

Drew and I wordlessly lifted our beer bottles to show Liz we were all set. She grabbed onto the poor girl's arm and dragged her into the living room. I watched her bring the vodka bottle back up to her lips and take another swig as she walked. Liz snatched the bottle away from her and slammed it down on the coffee table.

"Carter, this is *Claire*. Claire, this is *Carter*," Liz said, emphasizing our names for some reason. I feared for Liz's life a little right now. I was afraid Claire might claw her eyes out.

"We sort of met last night," I said with a smile, trying to move the attention to me and save Liz from disfigurement.

Claire let out a hysterical laugh.

Liz sat down on the couch, pulling Claire down next to her.

"Well, we have a few minutes before dinner will be ready. Jim tells me you guys just moved here from Toledo, is that right?" Liz asked as Jim walked in front of the women to take a seat on the other side of Claire.

I nodded my head. "Yeah, we were transferred here from the Toledo Automotive plant."

I turned my gaze back to Claire. Her knee was bouncing up and down at a frantic pace. Liz reached over and put her hand on it to stop the movement.

"So, Claire, how long have you been a bartender?" I asked. I wanted to know everything there was about her. And I wasn't going to lie, I was dying to hear her voice again and learn more about her vagina and how often she found herself humping girlfriends. Shit, please don't let me get a hard-on right now.

"Almost five years," she said as another awkward laugh bubbled out of her and Jim reached up to pat her on the back a few times.

How much of the vodka did she chug from that bottle?

"Liz, I can't take it anymore," Drew interrupted. "You look so fucking familiar."

Claire jumped to her feet, her knee slamming into the coffee table and knocking over the two beer bottles. Thankfully they were already empty.

"I think I heard the timer go off on the oven. Liz, did you hear the timer go off?" she asked.

Liz shook her head casually. "Nope. Definitely didn't hear the timer," she said with a smile.

I watched as Claire turned her back to us and faced Liz.

"The timer definitely went off. You just didn't hear it because you weren't paying attention. We need to go check on the food. Because the timer. It went off."

"Hey, Liz," Drew said. "I think she's trying to tell you the timer went off!"

He laughed at his own joke and I reached over and smacked his arm.

Watching her go from horrified, to embarrassed, to nervous was fascinating. She was like a beautiful train wreck and I couldn't stop watching.

Liz sighed and finally stood up, smiling at Drew and me while she excused herself and followed Claire into the kitchen.

Drew leaned over and whispered in my ear, "Did you see the way Liz looked at me? I think I definitely banged her."

9.

Claire's Coochie Kills

Oh, Jesus Christ. Oh, fuck. Can a person die from humiliation? Shitfuckdamn.

"I think I'm having a heart attack. Or maybe a stroke. Which is the one that makes your left arm numb?"

I've lost all brain function. This is it. I'm dying. Tell my folks I love them.

"A stroke," Liz said in a deadpan voice as she followed me into the kitchen.

"Shit. I'm having a stroke. Feel my pulse. Does it feel weird to you?" I asked, thrusting my arm out to her.

Liz smacked my hand away. "For fuck's sake, Claire, get a grip."

"Carter. His name is Carter. And he has no idea who I am," I whined.

Fuck, I hate whiny girls. I'm turning into an insecure, whiny girl. I'm going to have to kick my own ass. Liz bent down in front of the oven and took a peek at the lasagna cooking inside. She stood back up and crossed her arms in front of her chest, leaning her hip against the front of the oven.

"You think you have it bad? That fucktard Drew thinks he slept with me. I can see it in his eyes. He's trying to remember if he knows what I look like naked. Like I would ever let my lady bits near someone who wears an "I pooped today" shirt. He doesn't even remember hitting on me that night or how close he was to having cock and balls permanently drawn on his face. I wonder if he remembers the hex I put on his dumb stick? He really believed I was a witch that night. What an idiot."

"Really Liz? You're comparing the fact that a guy doesn't remember telling you he'd make out with you because you had nice tits to my sperm-donoring one-night-stand sitting twenty feet away and not know who the fuck I am? Really? Is that what you're doing right now because I just want to make sure I understand this correctly and didn't accidentally hit a bong full of bad crack on the way over that I don't know about," I ranted.

Liz rolled her eyes at me. "Jesus, Cranky VonHyperAss, simmer down."

I put my hands on my hips and gave her my best "I'm gonna fuck you up look".

"Okay, so this isn't the most ideal situation for meeting back up with your baby daddy, I'll give you that. But it's done. He's here and there's nothing we can do about it now. After all these years of wondering, you finally know who he is so you can tell him about Gavin. So pull up your big-girl thongs and get your ass out there."

We stared at each other blankly for a moment.

"I know what you were going for with that but it didn't work so well," I told her.

"Yeah, I realized that as soon as I said it. Next time I'll just stick with big-girl panties."

I started pacing back and forth across the kitchen.

"What are the fucking odds, Liz? First, he shows up in the bar out of the clear blue and now he's here. In your house. And he's talking to me like I'm some new chick he just met that he wants to get to know."

"Well, technically, you *are* some new chick he just met," she said with a shrug, like it was no big deal. "I know we wondered last night if he just didn't recognize you because he was drunker than Mel Gibson when he called his wife a pig in heat, but I think it's safe to say, he really doesn't remember who you are. It's time to face facts, Claire. Your vagina just isn't that memorable."

"Fuck you," I mumbled.

"Not tonight dear, I've got a headache."

It wasn't her fault she could be so nonchalant about this whole thing. I never really told her just how much I actually thought about him over the years. She had no idea how much that man sitting out in her living room had occupied my thoughts and dreams. In all the scenarios I made up in my head about someday finding him, they always began the same way. He remembered me, and everything about that night immediately and apologized for never trying to find me. We would kiss in the rain, jump hand-in-hand together into a pool and ride horses together along the beach.

Or maybe I've seen one too many tampon commercials.

Seeing him again, knowing that he had no clue about the night we spent together, sucked big time. Especially since I was raising a reminder of that night and had to think about it every time I looked at my son.

"How am I supposed to even begin telling him about Gavin when he has no idea who I am? He is never going to believe me. He's going to think I'm some nut job who's looking for child support." I stopped my pacing and moved to stand next to Liz by the oven.

"Not necessarily. Jim didn't realize who Drew was until just before you got here when I dragged him into the kitchen, but he knew immediately who Carter was. Said he talked all about you this afternoon when they were at the bar. He knew right away when the poor guy mentioned something about you smelling like chocolate."

I stopped my manic pacing and stared at her. My heart started beating furiously again.

"What?!"

"I guess he told Jim about a girl, and I quote," she paused and brought her hands up to make air quotes, "'that he met at a frat party and how he's thought about her for five years.' Jim didn't get a chance to elaborate on what all was said because you chose that moment to walk into the house telling everyone about your neglected vagina and two-pump-chump Max."

"Fucking hell," I whispered.

"That's why Jim invited them over. I didn't have a chance to tell him that we saw Carter last night at the bar so he had no idea until our kitchen pow-wow."

He DID remember me! Well, not me-me, but the 'me' from that night. The 'me' he met at the party. The 'me' whose virginity he took.

I need to stop saying 'me'.

"A little advanced notice would have been nice. You know there's this nifty little gadget called a cell phone right?" I complained.

"Oh, shut the fuck up. I was just as surprised as you were. They got here right before you did and Jim had all of thirty seconds to blurt out what was going on while we hung up their coats," she argued as she pulled plates down out of the cupboard.

"There is no way you were even remotely as surprised as me. If I woke up tomorrow with my tits sewn to the curtains, I wouldn't be this much in shock," I replied petulantly.

"Hey, I tried to shut you up. Several times. It's not my fault everyone now knows you have an irritable vagina. Heh, irritable vagina!" she laughed at her own joke. "Maybe it's like irritable bowel and you can get some medication for it."

Jim chose that moment to stick his head in the kitchen.

"If you two yentas are finished discussing Claire's rabid who-ha, me and the boys would like to eat sometime this century."

"You and 'the boys?' You just met them today. Does the Ya-Ya Brotherhood already have a secret handshake and a password?" Liz joked.

Jim made a production of grabbing his crotch. "Secret hand-shake - check. And the password is 'Claire's Coochie Kills'."

I threw an oven-mitt at him, hitting him square in the face. Just then the buzzer to the oven went off and the doorbell rang.

"That's probably Jenny," Liz said as she opened the oven door and pulled out the pan of lasagna. Being the good friend that I am,

I had the foresight to send her a text with the news about Jenny joining us for dinner.

"Perfect timing. We'll all sit down and eat, she will inevitably say a bunch of stupid shit and everyone will forget about your pikachu. That should give you enough time to figure out a way to tell Carter his boys can swim."

☉ ☉ ☉

Fifteen minutes later we were all seated around the dining room table, filling up our plates. Thankfully, my earlier embarrassment was pushed to the side while I watched Drew fall all over Jenny. Unfortunately, I couldn't ignore the Carter situation since he was sitting right across from me and I couldn't stop staring at him.

Fuck he's hot. I mean, really, really hot. He filled out a lot in five years. I bet he works out. He's probably a runner. He's got that lean look to him. I wonder who cuts his hair? It looks like he pays a small fortune to make it look like he doesn't care what it looks like. Totally works for him.

Shit! Focus. Who cares what kind of hair products he uses? How are you going to tell this man he's a father?

Hey Carter, how about this crazy weather we've been having? Speaking of crazy, your spunk has a crazy backstroke.

The hum of conversation around the table shook me from my thoughts.

"So, I was in the left-hand lane and some idiot tried to come over to where I was. I had to slam on my brakes so I didn't hit the medium."

Everyone stopped what they were doing and waited for Jenny to correct her mistake. Unless she really meant that she almost ran her car into someone who could communicate with the dead.

"Um, Jenny, do you mean *median?*" Jim asked when the silence around the table lasted for far too long.

She paused with her fork halfway to her mouth and looked at him funny. "Isn't that cement thingy in the middle of the highway called a medium?"

Carter tried to cover up a laugh by coughing, and I saw Drew punch him in the side.

"It's alright, Jenny. You can call it whatever you want to," Drew said, patting her hand in reassurance.

"Oh, Claire, I forgot to tell you. The purchase I made tonight worked awesome!"

I should never have taken a drink of my water at that moment. As soon as the words left Jenny's mouth, I took a deep breath in shock and the water went down the wrong pipe. I started hacking and coughing, tears running down my face as Liz put her fork down and started smacking me on the back.

"What did you buy?" Drew asked as over a mouthful of noodles and sauce, completely ignoring the fact that I was dying across the table from him.

Carter at least gave me a concerned look and did that half-sitting, half-standing thing like he was getting ready to vault over the table to make sure I was okay. His concern for me was hot.

Hey Carter, speaking of hot - your hot beef injection had a play date with my eggs.

"The best vibrator I've ever owned," Jenny announced proudly, answering Drew's question.

It was his turn to choke. Some of the lasagna flew out of his mouth as he pounded his fist against his chest and Carter reached over to slap his palm against his back.

It was starting to look like a Heimlich convention in here.

"Seriously, Liz, you have some great products for sale. I can't wait to try out the rest of the stuff I bought. What about you, Claire? Did you get some alone time yet with all the toys everyone bought you tonight?" she said with a wink and a wag of her eyebrows.

"Wait, the girls at the party bought *you* vibrators?" Liz questioned, suddenly forgetting about the fact that everyone was supposed to be thinking of something other than my down-there-place.

"Nope, this isn't at all uncomfortable. Thanks for asking," I said under my breath, with a roll of my eyes.

"Can we go back to what Jenny was saying? I'd like some more details about her alone time: location, mood lighting, standing up or sitting down and if she's in need of a spotter next time. I have excellent upper body strength," Drew said with a wink as he recovered from having noodles lodged in his windpipe.

"Eeew," I muttered.

"So you really sell sex toys?" Carter said to me with a dreamy look in his eyes as he leaned in my direction with his elbows resting on the table.

I could feel my face heating up. This was not a conversation I wanted to have with him of all people. I was trying to figure out a way to tell him his love mayonnaise had mad skills and no one at this table could stop talking about vibrators.

"Technically, she doesn't sell them. She's just doing it as a favor to me," Liz chimed in, saving me from trying to explain. "We're starting up a business together. I'm selling sex toys and she'll sell cookies and candies."

"I like sex and....caaaaandy yeeaaahhh," Drew sang, completely fucking up the words to the song.

"Oh, so in answer to your question Liz—yes!" Jenny said over top of Drew's poor rendition of the sex and candy song. "Everyone tonight bought Claire a vibrator! How many did you end up with? Eleven?" Jenny asked. "I still can't believe you have never used one on yourself. That's just insanity right there. No orgasm comes close to the ones you can have with one of those puppies."

This was not happening right now. This was a dream wasn't it? Like one of those where you're in front of your entire high school naked and everyone is pointing at you and laughing. Except this time, I'm lying on the dining room table naked and everyone is pointing dildos at me.

"Oh my gosh, I know right?" Liz agreed, leaning forward so she could see around me. "I can have multiple orgasms in seconds with the Jack Rabbit."

Liz was a traitor. Benedict Liz. That's what I was calling her from now on. Fucking Benedict Liz.

"No offense baby," she said sheepishly to Jim.

"None taken, love. As long as you get off, I'm happy," he said with a smile as he leaned over and kissed her shoulder.

"Claire, you absolutely have to go home tonight and use the Jack Rabbit. And then call me immediately after and give me a report," Jenny said excitedly.

"No, she shouldn't go with JR her first time out of the gate, that will scar her for life. She needs to ease herself into using toys. Did anyone buy you a bullet?" Liz asked casually with a glance in my direction. "A bullet is the best bet for your first time. It's small, doesn't make a lot of noise but it's powerful as shit," Liz explained. "It will take you thirty seconds, *tops.*"

Are these people seriously discussing how I should give myself an orgasm at the dinner table like they were discussing the directions for putting together a bookshelf? Insert slot A into your vagina and twist. What the fuck is happening right now?!

"Sorry," I said to Carter. "My vagina isn't usually dinner topic conversation."

He was the only one that heard me since everyone else at the table was...fuck! Still talking about my God damned vagina.

"Maybe she should use the blue dolphin. It's so cute with its bottlenose and adorable little eyes and fin! She could make up a whole story about it swimming up her channel!" Jenny proclaimed.

Carter laughed and gave me a reassuring smile and for some strange reason I wanted to climb over the table and lick his mouth.

"Alright, now I'm curious. Bullets, rabbits, dolphins…are we still talking about vibrators or are you freaky people into bestiality? I want to see these things and what they can do. Claire, go out to your car and bring them in," Drew said as he pulled his cell phone out of his pocket. "This thing has a video camera on it somewhere…" he trailed off, pushing a bunch of buttons.

"Um, no. I am not bringing in vibrators that I have neither confirmed nor denied to receiving. So shut up and eat your dinner, all of you."

"Too bad that Max guy didn't have a bullet on him. You could have at least gotten off before his dad came home," Jenny laughed.

"Ooooh, is this the guy you were talking about when you walked in the door? What happened?" Drew asked, momentarily forgetting about filming amateur porn on his cell phone.

"No. Absolutely not," I protested.

"Come on, Claire, it's no big deal, just answer it," Jenny begged with a laugh.

"Come on, Claire," Drew argued while I sat there with my arms folded glaring at him.

"Answer the question, Claire!" Drew and Jenny said sternly at the same time while trying to reign in their laughter.

"Yeah, because I've never heard the *Breakfast Club* reference before," I muttered.

"Awww, don't feel bad, Claire. Everyone's got an embarrassing sex experience. Hell, Carter here had sex with a virgin when he was drunk one time in college and never found out her name."

Somewhere in heaven, baby Jesus is weeping. Or maybe that's just the sound of my dignity dying. I'm sure Jim, Liz and I looked like we just witnessed a horrific car accident. And technically, we kind of did. I felt like blocking off the table with crime scene tape. "Keep it movin' folks, there's nothing to see here - just my self-respect being flushed down the crapper."

I'm pretty sure I stopped breathing and Liz smacked Jim in the chest so he'd close his mouth which was currently stuck in the "holy shit, did that just happen?!" wide open position. I wondered for a minute if this whole thing was one big elaborate plan to trip me up and get me to confess and that everyone at the table was in on it. My eyes glanced over to Carter to see his reaction and he looked embarrassed, not like he wanted to wring my neck for keeping a secret from him that he knew and he knew that I knew that he knew.

Aaaaack!

I started tapping my foot nervously, my leg bouncing up and down. Liz reached over under the table and put her hand on my knee.

"Drew, Jesus, man," Carter muttered, shaking his head.

"Claire..."

I interrupted Liz. She was giving me a look that clearly said now was a perfect opportunity to come clean, but I wasn't ready for that yet. This was not something you blurted across the table in front of people. Instead, I let the word vomit flow.

"So, I used to work with this guy Max at the bar. We were pretty good friends and seemed to have a lot in common."

I conveniently skipped over the part that our primary mutual interest was that we were both single parents at the time.

"We tried to tack on a friend with benefits thing a few years ago. His recently widowed father had just retired and moved in to the apartment above his garage. It was the middle of summer and we were all in the house watching a movie. His dad decides to get up and go fishing for a few hours. So, he leaves and we start going at it on the couch."

Everyone at the table stopped eating and stared at me as the story flew from my mouth in one long, continuous run-on sentence.

I can't believe I'm doing this. I'm covering up one humiliation with another.

"So, we're naked from the waist down and he dives right in. Exactly two seconds later, the front door opens and in walks his dad. He's too busy trying to get through the door with a fishing rod and a tackle box that he doesn't notice us scrambling around on the couch trying to throw a blanket over the bottom half of us."

Drew's shoulders were shaking in silent laughter, Carter looked sorry for me and everyone else just nodded their heads up and down since they had heard this story before.

"So, his dad walks right into the living room, sits down in the middle of the floor with his back to us and starts organizing his tackle box and rambling to us about how the lake was closed for fishing. Meanwhile, we're under a heavy, wool blanket on the couch behind him in the middle of July."

"Totally not suspicious at all," Carter joked.

I finally looked at him and when I realized he wasn't outright laughing *at* me, I took a deep breath to go on.

"Yeah, not at all considering Max didn't have air conditioning and it was about ninety-eight degrees out that day."

Drew shook his head in amusement. "So what the hell did you do?"

"Well, I sat there horrified and Max started digging in the couch cushions for his boxers. The more he dug, the more the blanket was threatening to get pulled right off of my naked lap. I was holding on to that thing for dear life while his dad continued to mumble about lures and bait three feet in front of us. Max finally finds his boxers and shorts and starts shimmying into them under the blanket. Meanwhile, I'm still trying to hang onto the blanket and dig for my underwear at the same time, but can't find them anywhere. I found my shorts though so I yank those on and almost scream in victory when Max flings the blanket off of our lap because I was sweating my ass off under that thing."

Everyone was thoroughly amused by my story, and I didn't mind too much at this point since they weren't talking about me getting myself off or Carter's cherry popping blunder.

"You're forgetting the best part, Claire," Jim reminded me.

"Oh yeah. So when Max yanked the blanket off of us, my underwear must have been stuck somewhere in there. It went flying through the air and hit his dad in the back of the head."

"So what did you do?" Carter asked.

"I did what any self-respecting, grown woman would do when faced with a situation like that. I stood up, ran like hell out of that house and pretended like it never happened."

⊙ ⊙ ⊙

The rest of the night went pretty well; aside from the wide-eyed looks and head nods in Carter's direction Liz kept shooting me every couple of minutes when there was a lull in the conversation. She seriously expected me to just blurt this shit out in between courses in front of everyone. "Why yes, this apple pie is delicious. Did you know apple comes from the Latin word *alum*, which means *you knocked me up?*"

We finished dinner and Liz made the men do the dishes so she, Jenny and I could start brainstorming some names for the business. We had it narrowed down to three that we loved and couldn't decide between. And then the guys joined us and the suggestions immediately went in the gutter. It's amazing, really, how quickly they can go from zero to filthy.

Plastic Penises and Pastries.

Cocks and Cookies.

Sex and Candy (I'll give you one guess who suggested that one).

Lubes and Lady Fingers.

Cock Rings and Confectioneries.

I sat on the couch the entire time pretending to pay attention but all I could do was stare at Carter. Every time he smiled I felt like someone punched me in the stomach, which was just stupid. I didn't even know him. He was a one-night-stand.

A one-night-stand I felt comfortable enough with to give him one of the most important gifts a girl has to give and the little time I spent with him was enough to create a lasting memory of how alike the two of us were. It was also enough time to create another lasting memory that I've had to love, nurture and mold all by myself into something that I hope resembles a well-behaved child and will not need years of therapy due to my parenting skills.

None of the similarities in our personalities or how attracted I was to him then and now has any bearing on this moment, though. As soon as I tell him he's a father and has a four-and-a-half year old son, he was probably going to hate me. At least I had nine months to get used to the idea. What single, gorgeous man in his twenties wanted to be told he was now saddled with the giant responsibility of a kid for the rest of his life?

He was going to head for the hills when I told him. He was going to scream, turn and run - like one of those cartoon characters that go charging through a door and all you see is a giant hole in the wood shaped like them running. I needed to just prepare myself for that. And it wasn't like I could blame him. It was a completely insane situation that no one in his or her right mind would ever believe. Gavin and I did quite well on our own so far anyways. You couldn't miss something you never had. If he chose to never speak to us again, so be it.

So why did the thought of that suddenly make me sad?

I glanced at my watch and realized it was almost ten o'clock. I needed to get home and relieve my dad of babysitting duty.

"Hey, where are you off to? It's not even ten yet," Drew said as I stood up from the couch and started moving to the foyer to grab my coat.

"Sorry, I need to get home to Ga...et some laundry finished," I said, stumbling over my words.

Dammit, I almost said Gavin. I am a chicken-shit. I should have just said it and gotten it over with. Liz winced at my almost-slip and Jim coughed.

"I'll call you tomorrow and we can *go over a few more things*," Liz said with a raise of her eyebrows.

I know by "go over a few more things" she meant that she was going to beat the shit out of me for not saying something to Carter tonight.

Super, looking forward to it.

I waved good-bye to everyone and quickly walked out into the foyer. I had just gotten my coat on when Carter came rushing around the corner.

"Hey, I'll walk you out to your car," he said as he opened the front door for me with a smile.

I stood there like an idiot, just staring at him. I should tell him. Right now, while we're out here alone.

Hey, you don't remember me, but I'm the one whose virginity you took five years ago and well, guess what? It's a boy!

I couldn't do it. I broke my stare and walked out the door, rushing down the steps to my car and putting as much distance between us as I could. Didn't Liz say that Carter mentioned to Jim something about his "mystery girl" smelling like chocolate? I didn't need him putting the connection together. Not now. I needed more time. I needed to figure out what to say and find out what kind of guy he really was. Did he even want children? Did he plan on staying in town for long or was he going to put in for another transfer? Maybe he already had six other children spread around the world that he didn't support. Oh God, what if he decides he wants to be a father to Gavin and sticks around, then something happens to all the mothers of his illegitimate children and suddenly he gets custody of them and we have not one but seven children? And they all hate us because we were never there for them and Gavin turns to life on the streets and turning tricks for crack because a homeless guy named Fromunda Cheese told him crack ISN'T whack. I needed more time. I needed to formulate a plan that kept Gavin out of the hood. I also needed to calm down. It's not like Carter was begging for my attention or asking to see me again. He was being nice and walking me to my car. End of story.

Carter followed right behind me and stopped by the hood as I opened the door and turned to face him.

"I'd like to see you again, Claire," he said softly.

"Well fuck me gently with a chainsaw," I muttered, as I stood there with the car door open.

His mouth dropped open and for a second I thought I saw recognition flash across his face.

Shit, I just quoted *Heathers*. I didn't even realize what I was saying. The non-bat-shit crazy part of me willed him to remember, to put two and two together and realize that *I* was the girl from the frat party. Jesus, we'd practically acted out the entire movie while we played beer pong. We traded quotes back and forth until our sides ached from laughing. But his silence proved that whatever memories he may have had about me were still locked up tight in the far recesses of his mind.

"Call me. Liz can give you my number," I blurted before I could change my mind. I scrambled into the car, started it up and pulled quickly out of the driveway, glancing into the rearview mirror to see Carter, still standing in the driveway, get smaller and smaller as I drove away.

10.

Seduction and Snacks...and Snafus

I couldn't stop staring at Claire all through dinner. I felt bad that everyone seemed to be picking on her, but she was so adorable when she got embarrassed. Her cheeks flushed pink and she looked down at her lap and tugged on her left ear lobe.

Jesus, I just used the word adorable like I was talking about a fucking puppy. Wait, that didn't sound right, although if she *was* a puppy, she'd probably be fucking something because she's so hot. So in reality, she *would* be a fucking puppy. I mean come on, what dog wouldn't want to tap that ass? I need to stop watching Animal Planet. Claire is not a puppy - one that fucks or one that doesn't. Period.

I had a hard time finishing my dinner. The lasagna was amazing, but all I could think about was Claire pleasuring herself with a vibrator.

Or her hand.

Or a vibrator and her hand.

Or a vibrator and her hand and my hand.

Well, hello there, Mr. Hard-on.

I clearly had issues when it came to this woman I just met. Part of me wanted to rip that guy Max's head off just because he got to touch her, kiss her and be inside her. But when she was finished with the story, I just wanted to find him so I could point and laugh at him. What kind of a douche tried to have sex with a woman on his couch with his daddy living there, coming and going as he pleases? Real smooth there, buddy. I stopped being jealous of the guy at that point.

Now, all I wanted to do was show her how a real man should act. I had an irrational need to show her everything she'd been missing.

Right, because I am the king of all things sexual. My penis can make grown women weep in the streets.

Things got silly as the men drank more beer and the women tried thinking up business names for Liz and Claire's place. I didn't know why they shot down "Candy-Coated Cunnilingus." That was brilliant. And it made me think of sucking on a Jolly Rancher, brushing the wet piece of candy between Claire's legs and then sliding my tongue along candy trail.

Then I remembered the one time in middle school when I put a half-eaten Jolly Rancher on my dresser and somehow it fell into one of the drawers. Three socks, a pencil and a G.I. Joe guy were stuck to it when I found it a month later.

Probably wasn't a good idea to put something like that anywhere near a vagina, especially Claire's vagina. No harm should ever come to Claire's vagina.

I was probably imagining things, but I swear every time I glanced over at her she looked away quickly. It made me smile to myself thinking that she might be staring at me too. I knew Drew was right. I needed to stop fantasizing about a girl I was never going to see again. It was five years ago for God's sake. I was acting like a pussy, holding on to the tiny bit of information I had on her. For all I know she looks like Sloth from *The Goonies* now and smells like Drew's sweaty balls. I tried to forget about her by getting into a relationship with Tasha a couple of months after that frat party. Almost five years later and I was still stuck in the same rut of fantasizing about someone I'd never see again. To be fair though, I should have known from the start that Tasha and I weren't the best idea. We spent the majority of our time together in some sort of argument or another. She had a jealous streak that bordered on psycho and hated that I didn't behave the same way if another man glanced in her direction. What I should have done was hold out for someone like Claire: someone

sweet, and funny and smart; someone who didn't have a whole other side to her like Tasha. Right in front of me was a beautiful woman that made me think dirty thoughts just by watching her breathe. I needed to cut this shit out and take a chance.

Aside from the jealousy and fighting, I knew one of the main reasons Tasha and I didn't last was because I just wasn't able to give the relationship one-hundred percent because I couldn't stop wondering if *she* might still be out there somewhere.

That and the fact that Tasha's vagina had the same slogan as McDonalds: Over ten billion served.

I digress.

I needed to put a stop to this stupid fixation on some faceless mystery girl who could very well be a figment of my imagination. I needed take a chance on someone who was sitting right here in front of me or I was going to be alone forever. I was too busy contemplating my pathetic life to notice that Claire was no longer across from me and had gotten up to leave. She was already rounding the corner into the foyer when I snapped out of it.

I sat there staring at her back (fine, her ass) long enough for Drew to punch me in the arm. He not so subtly nodded his head in the direction she went and suddenly I realized all eyes were on me. They were looking at me like, "what the fuck are you waiting for?" Liz narrowed her eyes at me and I'm not gonna lie, I was a little scared of her. I jumped up from the couch and ran out of the room, catching her right as she finished putting her coat on. Circling behind her back, I opened the door and stood next to it.

She was surprised by my presence and jumped a little at the sound of my voice and the door opening. I couldn't tear my eyes away from her. I need to kiss her. I need to kiss her like I need to breathe. What the fuck is this woman doing to me? Before I made a complete ass of myself by drooling or pushing her up against the wall so I could attack her lips, she turned and walked through the door without saying a word to me after I told her I'd walk her to her

car. I had an irrational need to spend more time with her. I wanted
to learn what made her blush (aside from talk about her vagina),
what song was on repeat on her iPod and what her favorite book was.
I wanted to hear her say my name.

Fuck, I wanted to hear her sigh, shout and scream my name.

So, I told her just that. Well, not all of it. I didn't want her to get a
restraining order. I watched the corners of her mouth twitch when I
said her name, almost like it made her happy to hear it. For a second,
I thought she would just get in the car and peel out of the driveway
without answering me. Then she muttered something that I almost
didn't hear over the sound of a car starting next door. The words she
spoke forced my mouth to drop open and pushed the memory of a
dream I had recently to the forefront of my mind.

"Ask me what my favorite movie is."

She interrupted my thoughts by telling me to call her. By the time
I remembered where I knew that quote from, her car had pulled out
of the driveway and was speeding down the street.

◉ ◉ ◉

For the next two weeks Claire and I talked every night on the phone.
Unfortunately, the plant put me on night shift and overtime for the
first few weeks so our schedules never meshed so we could see each
other. The only spare time we both had to talk was during my first
fifteen-minute break around midnight every night. I always apologized to her for calling at such a shitty time but she swore it was
absolutely perfect. For the first time in as long as I can remember, I
actually looked forward to going to work because I knew I'd get to
hear Claire's voice. Drew, who worked directly across from me on
the assembly line, got entirely too much pleasure out of watching
me rush to a quiet corner of the plant to make the call. The first
time, he asked me where I was going and when I didn't answer, he
followed me the entire way, shouting to every single person that I

was calling my parents to tell them I was coming out of the closet. A well-placed punch to the nuts curbed his desire to do that ever again, but people were still coming up to me and patting me on the back in congratulations.

For fifteen minutes every single night, Claire and I talked about nothing and everything all at the same time. I told her about growing up with two older brothers who confirmed my belief in the boogey man and had their friends call me and tell me they were Santa Clause and that I would never get another toy again if I didn't clean their rooms while wearing a pair of their underwear on my head.

Claire told me about her parents' divorce and her decision to live with her father, who I hadn't even met and already feared. He went to a birthday party the previous weekend and when trying to break up a fight, some guy said to him "What are you going to do about it Grandpa?" Claire's dad knocked him out with one punch and said "THAT'S what I'm going to do about it, asshole." Claire tried to convince me that her dad was a giant teddy bear, but where I come from, you're not afraid to meet a teddy bear in a dark alley at night for fear that he'll scalp you and tattoo his name on your ass.

I regrettably told her about Tasha and the reason for the breakup. I even spilled my guts to her about how I didn't know if I ever even really loved Tasha and was just biding my time until the right person came along. I didn't tell her more about the one-night-stand from college that Drew brought up at dinner that night and she never asked about it, thankfully. Even though it was easy to talk to Claire about Tasha, it seemed wrong to talk to her about the woman I'd dreamed about for five years. Claire was sweet and smart and funny and I didn't want to taint any of that with a stupid dream. The more I talked to Claire and got to know her, the more it became clear that she could be the one I was waiting for. I felt like the majority of the time we talked more about me than we did her and when I pointed that out, she just laughed and said there wasn't much to tell because her life was so boring. Still, with each phone call I learned something new about her and I was willing to spend as long as it took to know everything there was to know about her.

Finally, after fifteen days of hovering in corners at work away from the loud machines to listen to Claire's soft, husky voice as she lay curled up in bed under the covers talking to me, I was going to see her again. The plant finally gave me a Saturday off of work and I was more than happy to spend it checking out Claire and Liz's shop (fine, Claire's ass). Claire had sent me a few pictures on my cell phone in the last week and from what I could tell, they were making enormous progress on the place. In reality, I didn't care if I was meeting Claire in a garbage dump; as long as I could be close to her I would be happy.

At ten that Saturday morning, I pulled up in front of the address Claire gave me for the shop. I sat in the car for a minute, tapping my fingers against the steering wheel. I probably got around three hours of sleep last night. All I did was toss and turn, thinking about seeing Claire again and being close enough to touch her. I'm not gonna lie though, the thing that gave me the sleepless night was the quote she used absentmindedly on the phone the previous night. It was the second time she'd used it around me and no matter how much I tried to push it from my mind, that stupid nagging thought about *her* popped back up. A lot of people have seen the movie *Heathers*. And really, "fuck me gently with a chainsaw" could be a very popular way to say "holy shit" nowadays.

Uh-huh, yeah right.

Her use of that saying could be the biggest fucking coincidence in the history of the world, or I just boarded the crazy train headed straight for cuckoo city. I pulled my cell phone out of the cup holder and checked the time, smiling when I saw the picture of Claire that I was using as my screen background. I caught a lot of shit from Drew when he saw it, but I didn't care. I covertly asked Liz to send a picture of Claire to me and she was more than happy to oblige. The picture she sent was a black and white close up of Claire, laughing unabashedly at something, with one hand held up to her face and her fingers spread in such a way that you could still see her beautiful smile, the mirth in her eyes and the dimples in her cheeks. It was stunning, and I only hoped I would be able to put that look on Claire's face myself one of these days and be there to witness it.

Looking at the picture of Claire on my phone erased the confusion and questions from my mind and made me just want to concentrate on her, not ghosts from the past. I shut the engine off and got out, finally taking a good look at the building I parked in front of. I was impressed. It was bigger than I thought it would be and it looked great from the outside. I could see Liz through the front window on what must have been her side of the store, so I rounded the front of the car and stepped up on the sidewalk. I started walking towards the front door and had to stop short when a little boy went flying in front of me, arms and legs flailing all over the place.

"Gavin, get your ass back here!"

On instinct, my arm flew out and I grabbed onto the back of the kid's shirt, halting his progress of running away. A guy, probably close to fifty, jogged over to where I was.

"Hey, thanks for stopping him," he said, looking down at the boy with a stern face that would have made me cringe if I was on the receiving end of it. I let go of his shirt, confident that the little runaway wasn't going anywhere now that he'd been caught.

"Gavin, how many times have I told you that you can't just take off when you get out of the car? You have to hold my hand."

The kid shrugged. "I don't know. I was just hurryin' my ass to the ice cream store 'fore it all meltses."

I covered my mouth with my hand to hide my laugh. This kid had balls! The poor guy just rolled his eyes at the boy and let out a sigh.

"If you enjoy your sanity at all, don't have kids," the guy said to me before grabbing the kid's hand and walking away.

"Thanks for the advice!" I yelled to him as the two of them walked into the ice cream shop next door.

Liz noticed me on the sidewalk through the window just then and opened the door for me.

"Good morning!" she said brightly as I walked inside.

Everywhere I looked I saw bras, underwear and all sorts of frilly shit on hangers and displayed on tables. I could almost feel my dick shriveling up and retreating back inside my body. I didn't mind taking this stuff off of a woman, but standing in the middle of a room surrounded by this crap made me feel entirely too in touch with my feminine side.

Jesus fuck, what is THAT?

"That's a ball gag mask, Carter. I take it you aren't into bondage?" Liz asked seriously, noticing the direction of my gaze.

"Uh, I...umm..."

Is it hot in here all of a sudden?

"Have you ever tied up a partner? Used whips? Experimented in anal play? Had a threesome? Would you say you're more of a dominant or a submissive? When was the last time you were checked for STD's?"

"What? I mean, I..."

"How many sexual partners have you had in the last five years? Have you ever been convicted of a sex crime against another human, animal or plant?"

"ELIZABETH!"

Oh thank God. I don't think I've ever been happier to hear the sound of Claire's voice.

"I've got my eye on you," Liz whispered, looking me up and down and doing the whole two-finger point from her eyes to mine.

"Duly noted," I muttered as I walked past her and over to the doorway behind the counter where Claire was currently standing with her hands on her hips. Since she was busy staring over my shoulder shooting dirty looks at Liz, I had the opportunity to take her in unnoticed. It was unbelievable how she seemed to have gotten even more beautiful than the last time I saw her. Maybe it was because I knew her so much better than before. Her hair was up in a messy ponytail with stray pieces falling down around her face. I noticed a smudge of flour or maybe powdered sugar on her cheek and I wanted to lick it off. My dick got hard just thinking about tasting her skin.

"I'll deal with you later, Liz," Claire threatened.

"Shut your mouth and get your scraggly ass back in the kitchen where you belong, whore!"

Claire rolled her eyes and jerked her head behind her.

"Come on, I'll show you my part of the store."

She reached for my hand like it was the most natural thing in the world. When our skin touched I had a hard time forcing my feet to move. I just wanted to stand there and stare at her. Claire smiled at me and turned, pulling me gently along behind her. We walked through the storage room of Liz's store and it took everything in me not to reach out and grab her ass. Fuck, she was wearing jeans again. This woman in a pair of jeans should be illegal. My brain didn't work when she wore jeans.

"And here is my half of Seduction and Snacks," Claire stated proudly as we left Liz's storage room and entered her kitchen. With her hand still in mine, she led me through the kitchen to the front of the store, pointing things out to me. Where Liz's store was all dark colors and rich fabrics, Claire's side was light and airy and full of bright colors. In the front of the store, she had three light yellow walls and one light pink wall. Behind the counter there was just enough wall hanging down from the ceiling to hold three large chalkboards, filled with all the store had to offer along with prices. Below the chalkboards, the wall ended and you could see straight into the kitchen. All around the room were framed pictures of cupcakes, candies and different sayings that had to do with her business. A pink and brown wooden sign on one wall stated "Money can't buy happiness but it can buy chocolate, which is kind of the same thing." and a yellow and brown one by the door read "A balanced diet is a cookie in each hand." Aside from the warm, inviting atmosphere, the smell alone would put you in a good mood. For once, the smell of chocolate didn't bother me like it usually did. Maybe, because Claire was standing right next to me, and all I could think about was tasting her instead of the memories that scent usually brought me. I moved a step towards her and took the fact that she didn't move away or let go of my hand as a good sign.

"Seduction and Snacks is a great name. It's probably more appropriate than Blow Jobs and Baked Goods."

She laughed nervously, but still didn't move away from my close proximity. This near to her, I could see that her eyes weren't just liquid brown. They also had tiny specs of gold in them that made it look like someone had sprinkled a handful of glitter in them.

"The place looks great," I told her, taking another step in her direction, wanting to be as close to her as possible. I reached down by her side and slid my free hand into hers, the fingers of both of our hands intertwining. She swallowed and licked her lips nervously but didn't move.

"Thanks," she mumbled, her eyes staring straight at my lips.

Fuck, did she want me to kiss her? Should I do it? Just lean in and press my lips to hers? Why do I feel like a twelve year old that has no experience? Why can't I stop asking myself these annoying questions?

I took one last step, closing the distance between us. I let go of her hands so I could slide mine behind her and rest them on her lower back, pulling her flush against me in the process. Her hands flew up to my chest but she didn't push me away. She rested them there and finally looked up into my eyes.

"It smells good in here. What did you make?" I asked quietly, leaning my head down closer to her lips, thankful that she was finally in my arms and amazed at how right she felt there.

"N-nothing," she stammered. "I was just making a list of all the supplies I need to order and stocking the flour on the shelves."

I stopped with my lips hovering directly over hers. I could feel her breath on me, and I had to count to ten to stop myself from pushing her back against the door and pushing myself between her legs.

"It smells like chocolate in here," I whispered, ghosting my lips back and forth across hers.

I had absolutely no self-control being this close to her. Two weeks of only hearing her voice was like the most torturous foreplay in the world. I kissed the corner of her mouth, her cheek and right below her ear, taking in a deep breath of her skin. All of the blood rushed to my head and my arms tightened around her small waist.

Whoa, what the fuck?

I could feel her heart thumping in her chest which was pressed against my own, but that wasn't what made the room suddenly seem tipsy.

This can't be right. Why in the hell is my subconscious playing tricks on me right now? I kissed the spot below her ear again just to make sure I wasn't losing my mind and felt her shudder in my arms. I took another deep breath of her skin, nuzzling my nose into the soft pieces of hair that rested against the side of her neck.

Jesus Christ, I have officially gone off the deep end. How is it possible that she smells like this? I stood there and just breathed her in. Five years of searching for this and it was right here in my arms. And now I was going to look like a total assy pervert because it was killing me. I need to know what that smell is. It had to be some kind of lotion or some shit and in some crazy, twisted act of fate, Claire used the same product. Once that mystery is solved, I can finally, once and for all, let go of this nonsense.

"It's probably just me. I always smell like chocolate," she whispered, her arms sliding up to my shoulders and around my neck, her fingers gently sliding through the hair at the nape. Something about the feel of her fingers sliding against the back of my head felt so familiar that it was my turn to shiver.

Did you just quote Heathers? That is my favorite movie ever.

I kind of have a thing for quirky, crazy, intelligent, dark-haired chicks.

I forgot how to breathe for a minute as bits and pieces of the past tried to make their way to the forefront of my mind. She felt so good in my arms; like she belonged there or maybe she'd been there before…

No, don't be a dick. Claire is sweet and beautiful and a nice girl. Don't confuse her with a memory, especially not now.

"Well, fuck me gently with a chainsaw."

"Ask me what my favorite movie is."

The past, present and stupid dreams were all flying around in my brain trying to fight for first place. Suddenly I had a memory of falling down on top of her on a strange bed. Her body was soft in all the right places and her skin was smooth and I couldn't get enough of touching her. She made the most amazing noises when I licked the skin of her neck right below her ear. I remembered pushing into her and squeezing my eyes shut because she was so fucking tight and hot, and I didn't want it to end before we even got started. I remembered moving slowly in and out of her and hoping to God it felt good for her because I wanted to do this forever with only her. I remembered waking up the next morning, breathing in the smell of chocolate that still lingered on the pillow and the sheets and praying that I'd be able to find out who she was.

I pulled away from Claire enough so I could see her face. I stared into her eyes, willing every single one of my memories to come back to me so I wouldn't feel so confused. Her fingers continued to play with my hair on the back of my head, bringing everything into focus.

"What's your favorite movie?" I whispered.

I held my breath, desperate for the answer. I watched her face go from content to puzzled to nervous. Why was she nervous? It was a simple question. Unless…

She looked back and forth between my eyes and I watched her blink back tears. Seeing her eyes like this, so bright and nervous jarred a memory loose and I choked on a breath. With perfect clarity I saw myself above her, pulling her leg up and wrapping it around my hip while I stared down into her eyes. I remembered looking into her eyes as I pushed inside of her and forcing myself to stop when I saw her quickly blink back tears.

I remembered hearing her gasp like she was in pain and I asked her if she was okay. She never answered me; she just stared up at me with those beautiful, bright brown eyes, pulled my face down to hers and kissed me. Claire's face, Claire's eyes, Claire's body...

Heathers, she whispered.

My mind flew back to the present at the sound of her whispered admission. All I could do was stare at her in disbelief. The feel of her in my arms, her breath on my face, the sound of her laughter and the way she blushed when she was embarrassed, I remembered it all. Bumping our shoulders together conspiratorially as we played beer pong, the way her lips felt the first time I kissed her...it was her. *It was Claire.*

"My favorite movie. It's *Heathers,*" she repeated, mistaking my stunned silence for a hearing impairment. She stared at me like she was willing me to remember. Hoping that I would finally get a clue as to why she and Liz acted so weird when they met me. Why she was so nervous around me that night we showed up at Jim and Liz's and tried to avoid looking me in the eyes at all cost. Why everyone at the table looked like they'd seen a ghost when Drew brought up the virgin comment. Why she was reticent to share too much with me during our many conversations over the last few weeks - I already knew everything about her. She'd shared it all with me that night so many years ago.

"It's you," I whispered, bringing my hand up to cup her cheek. "Holy shit."

She let out a watery laugh and closed her eyes, leaning her forehead against my chin.

"Oh thank God," she muttered to herself, but loud enough for me to hear.

I reached under her chin and pushed her face back up so I could see her.

"Why didn't you say anything? You probably thought I was a complete asshole."

She smirked at me. "I did. At first. Liz wanted to kick your ass."

"I think she still does," I deadpanned.

She smiled and it made my knees weak.

"Honestly, I didn't know what to think when I first saw you and you didn't say anything. I figured you were just a typical asshole that had countless one-night-stands in college. But after some of the stuff Jim told us you said, Liz figured out pretty quickly that you must have just been too drunk that night to remember everything about me. I'm still going with the idea that I just wasn't very memorable to begin with."

She laughed at her own words but I could tell that idea bothered her.

"Don't even joke about that. Do you have any idea how long I've looked for you? How bat shit crazy Drew thinks I am because I keep trying to find lotion that smells like chocolate and nothing ever comes close to the way I remembered you? I was beginning to think I imagined you."

I pulled her body back against mine and rested my forehead against hers; afraid to let go of her for fear she would disappear again. How could this be real? Drew is never going to believe this. Fuck, I still didn't believe it. Now that she was this close, I could smell her skin without even trying and it made me smile.

"You either didn't have as much to drink that night as I did or you just have a damn good memory. How in the hell did *you* recognize *me*?" I asked.

Claire opened her mouth to speak, but right then, the door to the store burst open and she pulled back out of my arms suddenly as we both turned in that direction. The little boy with the mouth flew through the door and I let out a laugh, figuring he had gotten away from his dad again.

"Mommy! I gots ice cream!" he yelled as he ran towards us.

I stood there with my mouth open as Claire bent down and caught the little guy as he threw himself into her arms. She looked up at me in complete and utter horror.

Holy shit. She has a kid. I've been looking for her for five years and she went off and had a kid. Well doesn't this suck donkey dick.

"Sweetie, that kid is about two steps away from getting one of those kid leash things they sell at the store. Or a shock collar. I wonder if you need a concealed carry permit to get a taser."

In walked the dad I saw earlier, and I tried not to cringe as he walked over to where Claire was crouched down still hugging the boy and looking a little bit like she might puke.

Claire has an old man fetish. This guy has to be pushing fifty. I'd puke too if I was her. That's kind of gross. She's touched those old, wrinkly balls. When he cums I bet it's just a puff of smoke poofing out of his elderly penis. The guy finally glanced over at me, looking me up and down.

"Who are you?" he asked, obviously forgetting our encounter just moments ago due to the Alzheimer's.

"You have old balls," I mumbled angrily.

"George! I thought I saw your car pull up a little bit ago!" Liz exclaimed as she walked over from her side of the store and right up to Claire, helping her off the floor. I stared at the back of the guy's head as Liz walked over and he turned to give her a hug. He's got thinning hair for fuck's sake. Can his balls even grow hair anymore? I want to punch his hairless, old balls.

Claire looked nervously back and forth between Old Man Winter and me. I wonder what he would think about the fact that Claire and I had a past - and that she almost made out with me right before he got here and interrupted us.

"I slept with your wife," I stated, crossing my arms in front of me and staring him down.

All three of them gaped at me with equal looks of confusion on their faces.

"You swept wif my Nana? Did she read you a bedtime story? Papa says she snores."

George took a step towards me and I actually gulped. Regardless of how old his balls were, I was sure he could kick my ass. Or kill me and make it look like an accident.

"Dad," Claire said in warning.

Dad? Oh, fuck. I really *am* an asshole. I have Tourette's of the mouth. Claire never once mentioned his name when she talked about him. This was the man who punched someone in the face for calling him Grandpa. And now I just told him he had old balls. He was going to straight up murder me.

"Shit. I didn't sleep with your wife. Total mistake."

He stopped walking towards me and if I had a brain I would have kept my mouth shut from that point on. Obviously I was drunk the day they were handing those things out.

"I got confused. I meant to say I slept with your daughter."

I heard Liz groan and saw Claire's mouth fall open.

"But it's not what you think," I continued quickly. "I mean, we were both really, really drunk and I didn't even know who she was until a minute ago."

Oh my God, stop. STOP!

One of his eyebrows cocked and I swear I heard him crack his knuckles.

"She smells like chocolate and I don't like to be spanked," I blurted in a panic.

"Jesus Christ..." George muttered, shaking his head.

I saw Claire smack Liz from behind George. Liz was snorting with laughter. Of course she found this funny.

"I don't like to be spanked either. How's come I don't have hair on my balls? Mommy, you aren't going to spank him are you?"

"Yes, Mommy, tell us. Are you going to spank Carter for being a bad boy?" Liz said in her best Marilyn Monroe voice. In the chaos of the shit storm that was happening, I never really got a good look at the kid Claire was holding. His back had been facing me up until a few seconds ago and I hadn't been paying much attention when I caught him from running away outside. Claire had to shift him to her other arm so she could smack Liz. He was staring right at me now. He was a really good-looking kid. But that wasn't surprising since he looked just like her. But there was something about him...

I cocked my head to the side and he did the same. I realized no one was speaking but I couldn't take my eyes off of him. The edges of my vision started to turn black and I felt like I was going to pass out. He had my eyes. He had my fucking eyes! I quickly tried to do the math but my brain was a jumbled mess and I couldn't remember what number comes after potato!

What the fuck is happening right now? This couldn't be real. My sperm betrayed me. I suddenly had a vision of my sperm swimming around and talking in Bruce Willis's voice like in *Look Who's Talking*. "Come on! Swim faster! This little shit has no idea we escaped from the condom! Yippee-ki-yay, motherfucker!"

My Bruce Willis sperm is badass and thinks he's John McClane from *Die Hard*. That is the only explanation for this fuckery.

"Who are you?" I asked the kid with my eyes when I finally found my voice.

"I'm Gavin Morgan, who the hell are you?"

11.

Good Vibrations

Oh fuck.

My dad was going to kill Carter before I even got a chance to tell him that he was a father. Although, I was pretty sure that ship has sailed. He's either mentally challenged or in shock. Or I completely missed the fact that he liked to shout about hairy balls and being spanked.

Gavin *did* like to talk about his balls all the time. Could be hereditary...

"Who are you?" Carter whispered, staring straight at Gavin like he was trying to figure out the square root of Pi in his head.

"I'm Gavin Morgan, who the hell are you?"

"GAVIN!" we all scolded, except for Carter. He still looked like he might throw up.

Shit, this was so not how I saw this happening. I knew after all of our conversations and how much I'd gotten to know Carter that I was going to have to come clean soon. And I had planned on telling him today, easing him into it.

After I supplied him with enough alcohol to choke a horse.

"This is one of Mommy's friends, buddy," I told Gavin. "Friend" seemed better than "the father you never knew you had" or "the guy who knocked Mommy up" at the moment. I could wait until he was a teenager to scar him with that information.

Gavin started to get bored with the lack of excitement in the room since everyone pretty much just stood there and waited for

Carter's brain to explode. Gavin had the attention span of a two year old with ADD on crack. He started to squirm in my arms so I put him down. I held my breath as he stalked right over and stood in front of Carter with his hands on his hips.

"You're Mommy's fwiend?" he questioned.

Carter just nodded with his mouth open and no sound coming out. I'm pretty sure he didn't even hear Gavin. Someone could have asked him if he liked to watch gay porn while painting pictures of kittens and he would have nodded his head.

Before anyone could react, Gavin pulled back one of his little fists of fury and slammed it right into Carter's manhood. He immediately bent over at the waist, clutching his hands between his legs and gasping for breath.

"Oh my God! Gavin!" I yelled, as I scrambled over to him, bent down and turned him around to face me while my dad and Liz laughed like hyenas behind me.

"What is wrong with you? We don't hit people. EVER," I scolded.

While Carter tried to breathe again, my dad managed to stop laughing long enough to apologize.

"Sorry, Claire, that's probably my fault. I let Gavin watch *Fight Club* with me last night."

I am Claire's complete mortification.

"Your fwiends got you sick the other night. You said he was your fwiend," Gavin explained, like it made all the sense in the world.

This just made my dad laugh even louder.

"Not helping, Dad," I growled through clenched teeth.

"You don't make my mommy sick, dicky-punk!" Gavin yelled at Carter, putting his two little fingers up by his eyes, and then pointing them right at Carter just like Liz had done to him earlier.

"Jesus Christ," Carter wheezed. "Did he just threaten me?"

"Jesus Cwist!" Gavin repeated back.

Liz scurried over then and scooped Gavin up into her arms.

"Okay, little man, how about me, you and Papa go for a walk and talk about big-people words?" she asked him as she walked over to my dad and grabbed him around the elbow.

I stood up and shot her a look of thanks. She just smiled and dragged my dad out the door with Gavin talking her ear off about something he saw on *Spongebob.*

When Carter and I were finally alone, I chanced a look at him. He didn't look pissed. He didn't look sad. He just looked like he had no idea where he was or what day it was. We stood there looking at each other for several minutes until the silence finally got to me.

"Would you please say something?" I begged.

Just moments ago I was blissfully happy that he finally figured out who I was. He held me close and he was going to kiss me. Now everything was ruined and it was my fault for not telling him sooner.

Carter shook his head as if trying to clear it.

"That was a kid," he stated. "I don't like kids."

I bit my tongue. He was still in shock. I couldn't just go off on him because he said something like that. Hell, I don't even like kids and I live with one. I love my kid, but that doesn't mean I like him all the time.

"I used a condom. I know I used a condom," he said in an accusatory tone, shooting me a panicked look.

Okay, that was it for the tongue biting. The pleasure I'd felt earlier when he'd had his body pressed up against mine and his lips on my neck flew right out the window.

"Really? You can actually remember that? Because I'm pretty sure up until about twenty minutes ago you had no fucking idea who I even was. You're right, though, you did use a condom. You put it on three thrusts *after* you took my virginity. But let me clear something up for you there Einstein, they aren't one-hundred percent effective, especially when they aren't used properly," I fumed.

"I dry heave whenever anyone pukes. And I don't know how to change a diaper," he said in horror.

"Carter, he's four. He doesn't wear diapers. And he's not Linda Blair from *The Exorcist*. He doesn't walk around spewing vomit all day," I said with a roll of my eyes.

"My wiener hurts. I need a drink," he muttered before turning and walking out the door.

⊙ ⊙ ⊙

By the time Liz and my dad came back to the store with Gavin, I was in no mood to talk to either one of them. I put Gavin in the car and went home without saying a word. I was probably acting like a big baby, but I didn't care. I was mad at them for thinking this whole thing was funny, I was mad at myself for not telling Carter as soon as I saw him, and I was mad that I was mad about all this.

Who cares that he freaked out and would probably never talk to us again? It wasn't like we were missing out on anything. Gavin had no idea who he was. How could you miss something you never had?

But I *did* have him. Literally. And even thought I was fucked up at the time, I know what I'm missing. For two weeks he opened up to me and I knew so much more about him than I did before. I know he loves his family and wants more than anything to have one of his own someday. I know he's a hard worker and would do anything for those he loved. For just a moment, it was nice to have him here. To be in the same room with him, to see him smile and hear him laugh, to feel his arms around me and know I wasn't alone in this crazy parenthood thing.

Shit. I was good and fucked. I *did* care. I wanted him in my life, and in Gavin's life. I wanted Gavin to know his father and I wanted Carter to know what kind of an awesome little person he helped to create. I want to spend more time with him and I want him to know me. Not the partial version I gave him on the phone for fear of slipping up about Gavin or the chocolate-scented fantasy version he held onto all these years, the *real* me. The one who put her dreams on hold to raise his son, the one who would do it all over again in a minute if it meant she got to have Gavin in her life, the not so perfect crazy me who jumps to conclusions and freaks out about the most mundane things and who would give anything to go back to that morning five years ago and stay curled up in that boy's arms who smelled like sweet cinnamon and whose kisses were hotter than an inferno.

I spent the rest of the day cleaning the house from top to bottom. This was a sure sign I was agitated. I hate cleaning.

I was on my hands and knees pulling shit out from under the couch. A pop-tart wrapper, a sucker stick and a sippy cup with something chunky in it that was probably milk at one time.

Jesus, Gavin hasn't used sippy cups in over a year.

"Mommy, are we havin' people over for a party?"

"No, we're not having a party, why?" I asked him as I picked up two pennies, a nickel and four empty fruit snack wrappers.

"Cuz you're cleanin'. You only clean when people are comin' over."

I pulled my head out from under the couch and sat back on my feet.

"I do not only clean when people are coming over," I argued.

"Do too."

"No I don't."

"Uh-huh."

"Do not."

"Do too."

Gaaaaah! I'm arguing with a four-year old.

"Gavin, enough!" I yelled. "Go clean your room."

"Freakin' hell," he mumbled.

"What did you just say?" I asked him with a stern voice.

"I love you mommy," he said with a smile before he threw his arms around me and squeezed.

God dammit. I am way too easy.

I ignored three calls from Liz throughout the day and one from my dad. Liz's voicemails weren't surprising.

"Stop being a dick. Call me."

"Did you pull the stick out of your ass yet?"

"…OH YES! Harder Jim! Oh fuck yes…"

That bitch actually butt-dialed me while she had sex with Jim.

My dad's voicemail showed just how concerned he was for my well being.

"Did I leave my Budweiser hat at your house last week?"

As the day wore on, I started to feel sorry for Carter. I mean really, he did kind of get blindsided. One minute he was leaning in to kiss me, and the next he found out he was the father of a four-year-old.

Good God, he almost kissed me.

My hand paused in the process of putting our plates from dinner into the dishwasher, and I stared off into space as I remembered what happened between us before everything went to shit. I should be trying to think of what I was going to say to Carter when we spoke again, but the memory of this morning was too fresh in my mind and it had been too long since I let a man get that close to me. My body was starved for affection. And even *I* couldn't deny that some small part of me had always dreamed about being with Carter again. Completely sober this time so I could remember every single detail. I was embarrassed to admit that he had always been the star in my spank bank reel. Except it was always made-up things since not much about our first encounter could be used as masturbation material aside from the kisses and how hot he looked. I had real life facts to use now. His lips had been soft and warm on the sensitive skin of my neck. I felt the tip of his tongue sneak out and taste me and I wanted more. His breath against my cheek made my heart speed up and warmth explode between my legs. When his firm hands and strong arms wrapped around me and pulled me up against him, I felt every inch of his body, including how much he wanted me. I had been on a small handful of dates over the years that never went much beyond kissing. None of those men ever made me feel even a tiny bit of what Carter did. I never craved more with any of them; I never daydreamed about what it would be like to feel their lips and tongues moving over every inch of my naked body. What would it be like to be with him without the haze of alcohol? Would he take his time? Would his hands be strong and demanding on my body, or soft and gentle? The beep of a new text message on my phone startled me from my fantasies, and I almost dropped the plate I was holding. I shoved it into the dishwasher and shut the door before walking over to the table and snatching up my cell.

If you're not going 2 call me, @ least do something 2 ease your tension. Take bullet U got @ Jenny's party out for a test drive. Report back 2 me 2morrow ~ Liz, The Bullet Bitch

I rolled my eyes and deleted her text without responding. Why am I not surprised that Liz just sent me a text ordering me to masturbate? I turned the light off in the kitchen and made my way down the hall to peek in on Gavin. He was sound asleep so I quietly shut his bedroom door and walked across the hall to my own room. After throwing on a tank top to wear to sleep and brushing my teeth, I was curled up in bed staring at the ceiling, thinking about Carter.

And his hands.

And fingers.

And lips.

Fuck!

Shouldn't I be thinking about how I was going to deal with this situation? My one-night-stand shows up after almost five years and he was just as gorgeous as ever and he was making me feel things I had no business feeling. I should be making plans. Driving over to his house so I could apologize for the way this huge bomb was dropped on him. I had nine months to prepare myself for this. He had no time and no one there he trusted or really knew to help him get a grip.

My heart threatened to melt as my brain quickly switched gears and I thought about the look on his face when he finally recognized me. Had he really been looking for me all this time? It just seemed so impossible and far-fetched. But Jesus, the look in his eyes when he realized it was me…it was almost too much. He looked like a dying man that had just been given the reprieve of life. His face lit up and his smile made me weak in the knees.

No, that was his tongue and the hard-on you felt poking you in the hip.

God he smelled amazing. He still smelled like cinnamon and boy. Well, that would be man now wouldn't it? And my-oh-my, what a man. I rubbed my thighs together when I felt that familiar tingle between my legs. Shit, I was never going to fall asleep at this rate. Or make any important decisions. I felt like a live wire about ready to burst into flames. I ran my fingertips over my bottom lip as I remembered the feel of his lips gently brushing back and forth over them. God I wanted him to kiss me so badly right then. I wanted to feel his tongue against mine, and I wanted to see if he still tasted the same as he did all those years ago. I was agitated and now, horny as hell. I knew I needed to take care of this or I'd never get to sleep. I *wanted* to take care of this with thoughts of Carter fresh on my mind, but suddenly, the thought of my own hand bringing me the release I needed didn't sound very thrilling. I wanted it to be his hands touching me, his fingers sliding through me and pushing me over the edge. My hand just wasn't going to do it for me at this point. I reluctantly glanced over at the black suitcase leaning against my wall and gave it a dirty look.

"God dammit, Liz," I muttered to myself as I angrily flung the covers off of me and stormed over to the suitcase. I pulled open the zipper, reached in and closed my hand around one of the clear plastic, factory-sealed bags containing what I needed. As soon as it was in hand, I paused and looked around the room to make sure no one had seen me. You know, just in case I suddenly lived with ten people who might be standing in my room watching me without my knowledge. I huffed in frustration, crawled back into bed and leaned against the headboard. I was an independent, twenty-four year old grown-ass woman. Why the hell was I so freaked out about using a vibrator? This was the twenty-first century for Christ sakes. My grandma probably owned one of these things.

Uuuughhh, *gag*. I just threw up in my mouth a little. Note to self: thinking about masturbating grandmas is not, I repeat NOT on the list of approved spank bank material.

Determined to do this thing before I had any more disgusting thoughts about relatives that may or may not own a battery operated boyfriend, I tore open the plastic with my teeth and dumped the contents of the package onto my lap. I picked up the blue, oval, plastic remote, letting the twelve inches or so of thin cord that was attached to the remote unfold until a small, silver cylinder was dangling from the end in front of my eyes like a pendulum, slowly swaying back and forth.

You're getting very horny. I'm going to count backwards and when I get to one, you will be a satisfied woman.

I rolled my eyes and scooted my body down until I was lying flat on my back. Setting the remote down by my hip, I stared at the little silver peanut of pleasure. I had a moment of panic trying to figure out if I really believed in ghosts and if I did, were they watching me right now? Was Mr. Phillips, the dirty old man who lived across the street when I was little and died of a heart attack when I was twelve, standing in the corner waiting for me to diddle myself? Was my great-grandma Rebecca standing there waiting to yell at me and tell me I was going in time out if I couldn't keep it down?

Son of a bitch!

"You better be worth all this self-doubt, my little friend," I threatened the battery operated toy.

I shook my head at my stupidity for talking out loud to a vibrator, closed my eyes and flicked the damn thing on with my free hand that was still resting on the remote before I lost my nerve.

That thing may be little, but it had a kick. It jerked alive in my hand and if there weren't any ghosts in my room before, the whirring sound of this thing was sure to wake those fuckers up from the dead and bring them right to the source of the noise to see what the ruckus was.

I flew under the covers, dragging the bullet with me and hugging it tight against my stomach in an effort to muffle the noise. When you were little and you were afraid of the boogey man, getting under the covers meant he couldn't see you or grab your foot while you were sleeping. True story. I figured the same rules applied with dead people watching you masturbate. Under the covers means it wasn't really happening. You can't see me! My sheets are magic and they make my vagina disappear!

Oddly, the vibrations of this thing against my stomach felt good. Sort of like a massage that lulled some calm into me. Calm is good. I need calm. I took a deep breath, relaxed into the mattress and closed my eyes once again, conjuring up images of Carter from this morning Carter's eyes, Carter's mouth, Carter's wet, warm tongue dipping between my breasts.

Okay, that didn't happen. But this was a diddling daydream and I could make daydream-Carter lick me if I wanted to. And I wanted to. I wanted him to lick and suck on my neck. I wanted him to lick and suck on my nipples. I wanted him to lick and suck a trail down my stomach and sink his mouth between my legs. My hand holding the bullet followed the same path Carter's mouth did in my mind, until the tiny vibrating tube rested right outside of my underwear.

Whoa. Okay, this is good.

I pushed the bullet a little harder against myself and my hips jerked forward as tiny pinpricks of pleasure shot through me.

"Jesus, God...." I mumbled, along with a few other incoherent words of shock and awe.

My hips rocked against the vibrator and I let out a small, whimpered moan at how good this felt. This was insane. I was not going to last more than a minute with this thing. I could feel the wetness in my underwear and the throbbing all through my sex and suddenly I wanted more than anything to feel the cold, smooth metallic toy directly against my bare skin. Faster than I've ever moved, I slid the bullet away and up to my stomach and pushed it and my hand beneath my underwear, quickly shoving it back where it belonged. As soon as the vibrations and the smooth metal came in direct contact with the bareness between my legs, a loud moan escaped from my lips, my head flew back and my eyes squeezed shut. With this thing pulsating between my legs, I didn't really need images of Carter, but I still wanted them. I pictured his smooth fingers pushing into me, his lips pulling my nipple into his mouth and his thumb rubbing circles around the very sensitive area the bullet currently touched. The sensations were almost too much and I cried out in surprise, arching my back as the first wave of an orgasm rocked through my core while I rubbed the bullet quickly against me.

"Holy hell," I moaned as I rode wave after wave of pleasure that made my toes curl. I was panting from my release and the energy slowly drained out of me but my hands still slid the bullet through my wetness and rubbed it quickly against my overly sensitive clit out of their own accord. Before I could even form a coherent thought, another orgasm, slightly less intense than the first, pulsed through me and put a stop to all of my movements. My mouth was open but no sound came out as I held my breath and felt the intense throb of my release pound through me. Several minutes passed before my brain started to function again. I yanked the bullet out of my underwear before I had a chance to and turn into one of those crazy nut jobs on the show *My Strange Addiction* who locked herself in her room and did nothing but masturbate and watch the Food Network all day. I quickly shut the vibrator off, the sudden lack of a buzzing sound making the room seem eerily quiet all of a sudden.

I lay there like a slug in the bed, unable to lift any of my limbs for several minutes while my eyelids drooped with fatigue. When I finally recovered the use of my arms, I reached over to the nightstand without sitting up, grabbed my cell phone and started a new text.

Bullet Bitch: Homework assignment completed. My vagina will never be the same. ~ Claire

⊙ ⊙ ⊙

A knock on the door shook me from my thoughts. Okay, maybe not thoughts, catatonic state might have been more accurate. I'd done nothing but go to work and stare at the empty walls in my house for two days since Claire dropped the bomb on me. I shuffled morosely over to the door and threw it open. Drew stood there wearing a black shirt that said "Alice in Chains" with a picture of Alice from *The Brady Bunch* wearing a ball gag, handcuffs and chains. He smiled and held up a six-pack of beer.

"Sober man enters, drunk man leaves."

I shut the door in his face and walked back over to my spot on the couch.

He reopened the door himself and walked in.

"Alright, Mary, there's no need to act like a baby," he said as he set the beer on the coffee table and flopped down on the couch next to me. My nose curled up in disgust at the smell coming from him.

"Jesus, Drew, what the fuck is that smell?" I moaned as I covered my nose with my hand.

"Don't be a hater. I picked it up today. It's Tim McGraw's cologne."

"You mean it's Tim McGraw's balls. That smells like pure cat piss dude."

"Fuck you," Drew grumbled.

"No thanks. The smell of piss does nothing for me."

Drew huffed and crossed his arms over his chest and stared me down.

"Alright, out with it. Before I run to the store and buy you Midol and tampons."

My head fell to the back of the couch. I knew I was being a little bitch but I couldn't help it. My world just blew up in my face.

"She has a kid. I'm somebody's dad," I muttered.

"Yeah, I got that already from the voicemail you left me last night. Although, I have to say, trying to decipher "Bruce Willis got her pregnant with my chocolate hairy balls at the frat party" took some time to figure out. Luckily, I was able to get a hold of Jim and Liz since you wouldn't answer my calls."

"What the hell am I going to do?" I asked him as I lifted my head up to look at him.

"First of all, you're going to talk to her and get the whole story. I know you're in shock but sitting around here all day fingering your vagina isn't going to make anything better. So, man up. Go talk to her. You spent all these years trying to find her and here she is, right in front of you. So she's got a little baggage. Who doesn't?"

"A little baggage? Drew, she has a son. That's more than a little baggage," I complained.

"Wake up and look in the mirror baby-daddy. He's your son too. And you spent the last few years trying to fuck her out of your system with some chick you could barely stand. That's not just baggage, that's luggage, bags, suitcases, carry-ons, back-packs and Clinique make-up bags."

I gave him a questioning look.

"What? I like to moisturize. Healthy skin is the sign of a healthy life. I need a make-up bag for my exfoliators, pore cleansers and firming skin lotion."

Drew stood up and turned to face me.

"In the words of the great Maury Povich, 'you ARE the father'."

I thanked him for the beers and the pep talk and watched him leave for his date with Jenny. Not a surprise there, considering the way he almost humped her leg at dinner the night they met. According to Drew, they'd spent every waking moment together since then. People were going out, falling in love, living their lives and I was stuck here with my head up my ass Googling litigations against condom companies and realizing that I CAN'T HANDLE THE TRUTH.

Could I do this? Could I really be someone's dad?

I guess there was only one way to find out.

12.

P.O.R.N.

The next week flew by pretty quickly when I wasn't thinking about Carter, which was practically every second of every day.

Okay, so I guess it didn't really fly so much as go so fucking slowly I wanted to shove a rusty fork in my eye. I wanted to talk to him and see if he was okay but every time I decided to pick up the phone and get his number, I put it right back down. Regardless of how shitty the way he found out was, now he knew. If he wanted to know the whole story, if he had questions or concerns or just wanted to bite my head off, the ball was in his court. He knew where I worked, and he knew how to find me if he wanted to talk. Maybe I was being stubborn, but oh well. I was a girl and it was my right to stomp my foot and hold my breath.

I handled two parties for Liz this week and got three orders for cookie trays from the women there so things were looking up in that regard. Aside from the parties, I was keeping fairly busy. During the day, I baked and finished getting things ready at the shop and in the evenings, I bartended and tried not to stare at the door every time someone walked in, hoping it was Carter.

By Thursday I had tested out every single product from Liz's magic suitcase and decided to Hell with men. I was going to marry the Jack Rabbit. We were going to run away together and would be very happy making little tiny Jack Rabbit babies together. That thing was going to have to grow some arms and legs though. After a few years of being married to JR, I was not going to be able to walk anymore. JR would have to carry me to Pleasure Town.

I spent all day Thursday in the kitchen at the shop making white chocolate covered potato chips and baking Snickers Surprise cookies for the party I was doing Saturday night. It would be the last party I would do since the shop was opening next week. Now that I knew what all the fuss was about with these sex toys, I was a little sad to see the parties go. Liz told me I could keep my suitcase of fun though.

I made her sign a waiver that stated that in the event of an emergency or the death of Claire Donna Morgan, she was required to remove the suitcase from the premises within fifteen minutes of said emergency and/or death. It was always a good idea to have a plan like this in place. God forbid your dad or your grandmother got to the scene first and found your stash. You just couldn't allow that to happen. It's also probably a good idea to have them delete your Internet history. No one really needs to wonder why you Googled "turtle having orgasm" or were closely watching an EBay auction of a Jesus candle with a penis.

Don't judge me. Google is my enemy after a few glasses of wine.

I was under similar contractual obligations to get to Liz and Jim's house and erase the web history on their computer within fifteen minutes and dispose of any and all pornographic movies in their nightstand, under their bed, on the top shelf of their closet, saved on their DVR, packed in the third box from the left in the garage and in the cupboard in the kitchen where the cutting boards are.

I'm not kidding. She made me a list.

As I dipped a potato chip into the big silver bowl of melted white chocolate, I looked out to the front of the store and smiled. Gavin was lying on his stomach by the windows coloring a picture. When I walked out there a little while ago, he covered it up and told me I wasn't allowed to see it. I held the chip above the bowl to let the excess chocolate drip off and then set it down on the sheet of wax paper next to me just as I heard the door open connecting mine and Liz's store.

"You can just turn right back around and go back to your side. For the last time, I am not going to tell you on a scale of one to "holy shit" how good my orgasm was last night with the butterfly vibrator."

135

"Well that sucks. Can I at least watch next time?"

My head jerked up and my mouth hung open at the sound of Carter's baritone voice.

Why the fuck am I always talking out of my ass around him? And why the hell is he standing there looking so God dammed hot that I want to mount his face.

"Um, you're dripping," he said.

"I know," I muttered, staring at his lips.

He laughed and I blinked myself back to reality as he pointed at the bowl.

"I meant the bowl is tipped. The chocolate is dripping out."

My head flew down and I muttered profanities as I righted the bowl and used my fingers to wipe the drips off of the lip of the bowl and the counter.

Carter walked over to stand next to me and just like our last few encounters, his close proximity forced my pulse into overdrive.

"I'm sorry I snuck up on you like that. Liz caught me as I was getting out of my car and dragged me into her side so she could hand me my ass," he explained as I concentrated on wiping up the chocolate and tried to ignore the heat from his body. "I hope you don't mind me dropping by like this. I feel like such a dick that it's taken me this long to talk to you."

I stood there like an idiot, trying not to touch anything since my fingers were full of chocolate. I turned my head to the side and found his face inches from my own. I saw the sincerity in his eyes, and I knew I could never be mad at him about this.

"It's okay, believe me. I've had a lot of time to get used to the idea. I'm sorry that it was sprung on you like that out of the blue. I swear that I fully intended to tell you. I don't want you to think I intentionally kept this from you. I planned on telling you from the start. I was just trying to figure out how. And then it all blew up before I could do anything about it," I explained.

I realized right then that I didn't want him to be mad at me. I wanted more than anything for him to be able to handle this and to stick around. Spending the last week going to bed without hearing his voice was sad and depressing. Having him here right now made me realize just how much I missed him.

"We have a lot of things to talk about I guess. You have no idea how many questions are swirling around in my head right now," he said.

I nodded my head and before I could say anything, he changed the subject.

"But for right now, I am in a kitchen with a beautiful woman who has melted chocolate all over her fingers," he said with a smirk.

Before I could grab a towel, he reached over and wrapped his hand around one of my wrists and pulled my hand towards him. I held my breath as he opened his mouth and slid my chocolate-coated index finger into his mouth. The pad of my finger slid along the roughness of his tongue as he sucked all of the chocolate off; then he slowly pulled my finger back out through his warm, wet lips.

Check please!

"Mommy, I finished coloring my picture!"

The excited yell and pounding footsteps of Gavin as he barreled into the kitchen doused a bucket of cold water all over my vagina. For once, I was glad I had a built-in cock-blocker in the form of a four year old. I was one more finger suck away from dropping Carter down on the floor and showing him that I was quite bendy.

Quickly wiping my hands on the apron I wore, I turned away from Carter and bent down to my son's level.

"Can I see your picture now?"

Gavin held it tight to his chest and shook his head no.

"Sorry, Mommy. I maded this picture for the little maggot," he said earnestly.

I heard Carter laugh behind me.

"Um, did you say 'little maggot'?" I asked.

"Yup," he said, popping the 'p'.

"Do I even want to know who you're talking about?"

Gavin pointed behind me to Carter.

"Him. Papa called him dat the day we met him."

I groaned in embarrassment. One of these days my father was going to have to realize that Gavin is a parrot.

"I don't like your name. It's weird. And you don't look so little to me," Gavin said to Carter. "But I still drewed you a picture."

He reached around me and handed the paper to Carter. I took a quick glance at it and realized it was a picture of a big stick figure being punched in the junk by a little stick figure.

"Well, at least now I have a photo to commemorate our first meeting," Carter deadpanned quietly.

"Gavin, how about you just call him Carter," I said, looking to Carter with my eyebrows raised in question to make sure he was okay with that.

He nodded his head at me and smiled, then squatted down so we were both eye-level with Gavin.

"Thank you very much for my picture," he said with a smile.

Gavin wasn't big on strangers, mostly because I put the fear of God into him when we had the discussion about stranger-danger. In hindsight, telling him all strangers wanted to eat him wasn't my finest hour. Having to explain to a bunch of crying children in line to see Santa why my kid was screaming "DON'T GO NEAR HIM! HE'LL EAT YOUR FINGERS!" was no picnic. Liz had to talk me out of taking him to the vet and getting a GPS chip put in his neck. Something told me though that anyone who took my kid would bring him back within the hour. They wouldn't be able to take the kicks to the nuts and the cursing.

Gavin didn't usually talk to strangers unless I prompted him to do so. The ease with which he talked to Carter surprised me.

"You're welcome, Carter. My papa is coming to get me so Mommy can give beer to people. Papa lets me watch movies that Mommy don't let me watch and I get to have pop and I wanna get a dog but my friend Luke has a jeep that he rides in the yard and

I hurted my knee and it got cut and Mommy put a band-aid on it and told me to 'shake it off' so I wouldn't cry and did you know vampires suck?"

"Gavin!" my dad bellowed before I got a chance to.

He had walked into the store during Gavin's run-on-sentence and was almost to the kitchen when he heard him drop that bomb. I quickly stood up and faced him with my hands on my hips.

"Dad, I told you he wasn't allowed to watch that movie."

"Hey, Carter, I'm team Jacob, bitch!" Gavin yelled.

"Gavin Allen! Do you want me to put soap in your mouth?" I asked him sternly.

Gavin shrugged. "Soap tastes like Fruity Pebbles."

My dad came around the counter and picked up Gavin before I could punt him like a football.

"Sorry, Claire, *Vampires Suck* was on cable the other night and there was nothing else on. You'll be happy to know that he covered his eyes during the s-e-x stuff," he explained.

"Super," I muttered.

"I saw boobs!" Gavin yelled happily.

"Okay, he may have peeked a few times," my dad admitted after Gavin's announcement.

Of all the times for Gavin to act completely like…well, Gavin, of course it had to be when Carter showed up. No wonder he hadn't said a peep in the last few minutes. He was probably stunned stupid.

I glanced behind me and saw Carter standing completely still, staring over my shoulder at my dad. I turned back around in time to catch my dad doing the whole two-finger eye-point to Carter that Gavin and Liz did the other day.

Oh for fuck's sake. It's like we suddenly have a family salute.

"Dad, quit it. Carter, you haven't been formally introduced. This is my dad, George."

Carter stuck his hand out towards him, "It's a pleasure to…"

"Cut the s-h-i-t," my dad cut him off."

Somehow he didn't sound as threatening when he had to spell everything. This could work as long as Gavin was here as a buffer.

"I've got my eye on you. I was in 'Nam and still have shrapnel in my skin from the b-o-m-b-s. You like the smell of napalm in the morning son?"

"DAD! Enough!" I scolded.

I leaned over and gave Gavin a kiss on the cheek.

"I'll see you later, baby. You be good for Papa okay?"

He slyly reached over and tried to pull the front of my shirt down.

"Lemme see your boobs."

I grabbed his hand before he could give everyone a peep show and shot a dirty look to my dad who was just standing there laughing.

"Hey, I did *not* teach him that. He must be a boob man."

Carter laughed but quickly stopped when my dad looked over at him.

"Are you a boob man Carter?" he asked menacingly.

"I…well…um…I…don't."

I rolled my eyes at my dad and rescued Carter from him.

"Say goodbye to Carter," I told Gavin.

"Bye, Carter!" Gavin said with a smile and a wave as my dad turned and headed out of the kitchen.

"Papa, what's 'Nam? Is it a park? Can we go there?" I heard Gavin ask as they walked out the front door. With a big sigh I turned to face Carter.

"Sorry about that," I said sheepishly. "I will completely understand if you turn around right now and run far, far away. Really, I won't hold it against you."

"Claire?"

I stopped fidgeting with my apron and finally looked up at him.

"Shut up," he said with a smile.

⊙ ⊙ ⊙

After my dad and Gavin left, Carter helped me clean up the kitchen and put everything away. We talked more in depth than we had on the phone now that I wasn't so worried about slipping up. I finally found out that Carter was crashing the frat party that night and didn't even go to The University of Ohio. He felt awful about all the time I spent with Liz and Jim trying to find him, and I felt guilty all over again about leaving him that morning. Especially right now, when he was being so nice and amazingly understanding about everything.

For the time being, Carter was sticking around. I wasn't going to hold my breath though. He said he wanted to spend time with us and do this the right way, but he also hasn't spent time alone with Gavin yet.

As Gavin so nicely put it, I had to give beer to people tonight, so after we finished cleaning Carter walked me down the street to the bar so we could continue talking. I remembered how easy it was to talk to him five years ago and how he seemed to get me and my humor when no one else did. He made me feel comfortable and he made me laugh. All of those things happened when we talked on the phone but sometimes it was harder to duplicate that level of comfort when you were face to face. In all honesty, it almost seemed easier to be with him like this, to be able to gauge his face for reactions to things I said and to see his expressions when I told him something about Gavin. It made me wish I'd done so many things differently. I was sad that he had missed out on the beginning of Gavin's life. He saw him now as a walking, talking, mouthy little boy, but he didn't get to experience the best parts, the parts that made his attitude and temper tantrums and bad habits all worthwhile - the first smile, the first words, the first steps, the first bear hug, and the first, "I love you."

Those were all the things that kept me from selling my child at a garage sale on a daily basis, and Carter didn't have those things. It worried me that his expectations might be too high. What if he just couldn't form a connection with Gavin? I felt connected to Carter in a way I never had with anyone else. He made me feel things I'd only dreamed about. But I didn't have just myself to consider anymore. I had to think about my son and how all of this was going to affect him.

For now, I suppose I needed to just let Carter into our lives and see where it took us.

When we got to the bar, I changed quickly into my black shorts and Fosters Bar and Grill t-shirt and was surprised to see Carter making himself comfortable at the bar when I came out of the bathroom.

I got behind the counter and walked over to stand in front of him.

"I thought you were going home," I said as I leaned onto my elbows.

He shrugged at me and smiled. "I figured, why go home to an empty house when I can sit here and stare at a hot chick all night."

I felt myself blushing and tried to suppress the giddy smile I felt coming on.

"Well, you're outta luck. It's just me here tonight."

No, I am absolutely not fishing for compliments.

"Then I guess it's a good thing that you are the hottest, sexiest woman I have ever seen."

Here, fishy, fishy, fishy.

I leaned over the bar a little to bring myself closer to him and he did the same. I didn't care that I was at work, I wanted to kiss him. And there were hardly any people here right now anyway. It was still early.

I licked my lips as I stared at his mouth and I heard him groan quietly. One more inch and I could run my tongue across his top lip.

"OUCH!"

I jerked away from Carter and yelled when something smacked against the back of my head.

Rubbing my hand against the spot, I turned around to see T.J. with both his arms in the air doing a victory dance.

"Direct hit, Morgan! That's another point for me!" he yelled as he ran over to the chalkboard behind the bar at the opposite end from me and put a tally mark under his name.

"Son of a bitch," I muttered as I turned back around to Carter.

"Um, what the hell was that about?" he asked with a laugh.

Before I could tell him it was just T.J. being a dick, the man in question ran up and stood next to me behind the bar. He slapped a ping pong ball down on the top right in front of Carter.

"That, my man, is a little something we like to call P.O.R.N."

"Wow, your idea of porn and mine are slightly different," Carter said as he picked up the ping pong ball and rolled it around in his hands.

"No, no, no. Not porn. P.O.R.N.," T.J. spelled out.

Carter looked completely lost.

"It's just this little game we play when it's slow in here," I said.

T.J. rested one hand on the bar and the other on his hip.

"Claire, don't underestimate the awesomeness that is P.O.R.N. You are completely devaluing the one thing that makes me not want to kill myself every time I come to work. A little more respect for P.O.R.N. please."

T.J. turned his attention to Carter. "Claire made up the rules," T.J. said excitedly as he pulled a piece of paper out from under the bar.

"Rules?" Carter questioned. "Don't you just throw the ball at someone?"

T.J. pushed the paper across the top of the bar and Carter picked it up to read through it.

"Au contraire my friend. There always need to be rules in P.O.R.N. Otherwise, he'll throw a ball, she'll throw a ball, they'll all throw a ball…it'll be anarchy."

"Alright there, *Breakfast Club*, walk away before I break the ten-foot distance rule and chuck one at your face," I told him.

T.J. walked away and Carter laughed as he read the rules out loud.

"Rule number one: P.O.R.N. is more fun with friends, invite them. Otherwise, you just look pitiful engaging in P.O.R.N. alone. Rule number two: Sharp objects should never be used in P.O.R.N. Poking someone's eye out will ruin the moment. Rule number three: Sneak attacks or "back door action" must come with advanced warnings or have prior approval. Rule number four: Only two balls allowed in play at all times to avoid ball-confusion, unless approved by the judges. Rule number five: P.O.R.N. is over when the other player(s) say it's over. Otherwise, someone is left holding useless balls."

Yes, sometimes I act like a twelve year old boy. Don't judge me.

"So what exactly does P.O.R.N. stand for and how do I get in on this action?" Carter asked with wag of his eyebrows.

"Well, the official title is Pong Organization Rules and Notices. But sometimes we shorten it to 'throwing shit at each other.' Frankly, I'm not sure you can handle P.O.R.N., Carter. It's an intense game of skill, determination and craftiness," I explained with a grin as I took the ball from his hand, turned quickly and whipped it across the bar to hit T.J. square in the ass as he was wiping down one of the tables.

"MOTHER FUCK!" T.J. yelled.

"It's all about being talented with your hands really," I said as I turned back around to face Carter.

I have absolutely no idea where this boldness shit was coming from. I felt like I was channeling Liz.

"Don't worry, Claire, I'm pretty good with my hands. I have a feeling I'd be *excellent* at P.O.R.N. It's all about how you angle your fingers and the stroke you use…when throwing the ball. Sometimes you have to do it slow and gentle, and other times you have to do it hard and fast."

Sweet baby innuendos, Batman.

"What time do you get off?"

In about ten seconds.

"Not until one. I have to close by myself tonight," I told him while I squeezed my thighs together and thought about his fingers stroking and pushing and hard and fast and gentle and…fuck!

"Can I just wait here while you work? I can help you close up and we can talk…or whatever," he said as he stared at my lips.

YES! Holy shitballs mother of YES! Yes, yes, fuck yes!

"Yeah, whatever," I said with a shrug as I walked away to stock the beer cooler and stick my vagina in there to cool it down.

13.

Quivering Loins

For the next couple of hours I stared at Claire's ass – er, I mean watched her work and chatted with her when she had a few seconds.

I also became a proud member of Team P.O.R.N. when I managed to throw a ping pong ball that ricocheted off of T.J.'s head and hit Claire in the tits. There was talk of making me the team captain after that one. Claire told me I really knew how to handle my balls, and I started to wonder if I was turning more than a little pervy by the fact that it turned me on whenever she said "balls."

I wonder what it would take to get her to say "cock?"

T.J. walked by just then, untying his apron and stowing it under the bar. I probably should have felt a little jealous at the fact that he was a good looking guy and he got to be in close proximity to Claire all the time, but watching them interact just made me laugh. They were like brother and sister with the way the shoved each other, threw insults back and forth and tattled to anyone who would listen. As a result, I decided I liked T.J. and I didn't have to kill him.

"Hey, T.J., do me a favor. Get Claire to say 'cock' and I'll give you twenty bucks."

"Deal," he said automatically before turning away from me.

All of the patrons were gone and Claire had just switched on the "closed" sign and was in the process of walking back from the front door.

"Hey, Claire, remember that one guy who came in here a few months ago, smacked your ass and called you Cutie Claire? What was it you called him?"

"A cocksucker," she replied distractedly as she got back behind the bar and began organizing bottles.

With a dreamy smile on my face, I slid a twenty across the bar to T.J. and he walked away. This was going to be a beautiful friendship. If he could get her to say, "Fuck me hard Carter," I might buy him a pony.

T.J. said good-bye and walked out the door while Claire finished straightening up. After a few minutes, she came around the corner of the bar and sat down next to me on a stool.

"You look exhausted," I told her as she rested her chin in her hand and let out a sigh.

"Is that a nice way of telling me I look like shit?" she teased.

"Absolutely not. If you looked like shit, I'd tell you. I would also tell you if the jeans you're wearing make your ass look big, if something you cooked tasted like it came from the bottom of my shoe or if a joke you told was not funny at all."

"Wow, that's very kind of you," she said with a laugh.

"It's what I do."

We sat there for several minutes just looking at each other. None of this seemed real yet. I couldn't believe she was sitting here in front of me. I couldn't believe she was still so remarkable and funny and beautiful and I couldn't believe she had a child, *my* child.

"You kind of amaze me, you know that?" I said, breaking the silence.

I watched the blush brighten up her cheeks and she looked away, her gaze locked on a drink napkin that she started to shred.

"I'm not that great, believe me."

I shook my head in disbelief at how she clearly didn't see herself very well.

"Are you kidding me? You hooked up with a total loser one night at a frat party, got pregnant, had to give up your dreams and quit school, worked your ass off and raised an awesome little boy and now you're opening your own business. If that's not amazing, I don't know what is."

She continued to rip up the napkin at an even faster pace while I continued.

"You're strong and confident and beautiful and you make everything look so damn easy. I am so grateful to have met you again. I will be forever in your debt for taking care of...of our son. You've done such an amazing job with him and you're so selfless that I am just in awe."

Whew, I said it. *My son.* Gavin is my son. Oddly, it didn't make me want to hurl myself on a rusty nail.

She still wasn't looking at me, though, and it was starting to make me nervous. And I felt really bad for the drink napkin that now resembled a small pile of snow. I reached over and placed my hand on top of hers to make her stop fidgeting with the mess.

"Hey, what's wrong?" I asked.

She finally turned her face towards mine and I'm not gonna lie, it really freaked me out to see tears in her eyes. I didn't do crying. At all. If she asked me to set myself on fire right now I would do it just so I wouldn't have to see her cry.

"Gavin is wonderful. He is smart and perfect, he's funny and he's the best little boy in the world. He has his moments, but he's very well behaved and just perfect. Perfect! Every single person who meets him adores him and I love every second of being his mom..." she trailed off.

I knew she was sugarcoating things. If she said the word "perfect" one more time I was going to start crying myself. I didn't want the watered-down version. I wanted to know it all, everything I missed - the good, the bad and the ugly. Her foot was tapping nervously on the rung of the bar stool, and she looked like she was about to explode. I knew with everything going on right now she had to be under a lot of stress. She was a single mom with a lot on her plate and I knew for a fact Gavin wasn't flawless. What kid was? But she definitely wanted me to think so. Was she really afraid I would change my mind if I knew the horrors of being a parent? I'd always wanted to have kids someday. It was one of the biggest issues between Tasha and me. I knew it wasn't all rainbows and kittens. I knew it could suck the life out of you and make you second-guess your sanity.

"It's okay if you want to complain. I can only imagine how tough it is for you."

"I love Gavin," she repeated with conviction.

I chuckled a little at how panicked she looked.

"No one is questioning that. But you don't have to act like you have everything under control a hundred percent of the time. I'm not going to think less of you *or* Gavin if you need to vent, believe me. I want to know everything. I wasn't lying when I said that to you earlier."

She was softening a little. The napkin was finally free from her abuse and her foot wasn't tapping maniacally anymore. She still looked at me warily, though. I knew one way I could get her to calm down and open up. I stood up and leaned over the top of the bar, reaching my arms as far as I could, and wrapped my hand around what I needed.

I sat back down, grabbed a clean shot glass that rested upside down on the bar and filled it with Three Olive Grape Vodka, which I now knew to be her favorite. I set the bottle back down on the bar and slid it out of the way.

"Be honest," I said as I pushed the shot glass in front of her.

She bit her lip, looked down at the shot glass and then back at me. She was like an open book and I could see all of the conflicting emotions as they ran across her face until she finally let go.

"IloveGavintodeathbuthedrivesmefuckingcrazy!" she said as fast as she could and snapped her mouth shut immediately.

"Take a shot," I told her, nodding at the shot glass in encouragement.

Without hesitating, she picked up the glass and tipped it back, slamming it down onto the bar when she was done.

"Keep going," I told her as I leaned closer to her and poured more vodka into the shot glass.

"The first time he said, 'Mommy,' my heart completely melted. But that kid never shuts up. Ever. He even talks in his sleep. One time when we were driving he was going on and on about sheep and french fries and his wiener and the lawn mower; I stopped the car in the middle of the street and got out. After I walked around the car and then got back in, he was still talking, asking me if lawn mowers have wieners. He never. Stops. Talking."

"Take a shot," I said again with a smile.

She downed it, slamming the glass in front of me this time so I could refill it. I did, pushing it back towards her.

"I gained fifty-six pounds when I was pregnant with him. Do you have any idea what it's like to look down and not be able to see your vagina?"

"Uh, no," I muttered.

"My ass had its own zip code."

"If it makes you feel better, it is an awesome ass," I told her honestly.

"Thank you."

I poured another and didn't even need to prompt her to drink it.

"His hugs are a magical cure for everything. But do you have any idea how much a baby shits and pukes and cries? He projectile vomited every bottle he drank. Drink, burp, spew. Lather, rinse, repeat."

Down went the shot.

"He didn't sleep through the night until he was three and a half years old. I got so fed up I told him Shasta the Sleep Monster lived under his bed and would bite his feet if he got out of it in the middle of the night for anything other than the house being on fire."

She tipped her head back and finished another shot.

"I can't believe you don't hate me right now," she said.

"Why would I ever hate you?"

"Because I basically used you for sex and then never spoke to you again," she explained.

"Honey, where I come from, that's like Christmas to a guy," I said with a laugh, trying to lighten her mood. "I should be the one apologizing to you." I reached out with my hand and turned her face towards me.

God she was so beautiful. And I was a complete dick for wanting to take advantage of her being a little tipsy. But fuck, I needed to kiss her. I waited five years to taste her again. She tilted her head so that she could rub her cheek against the palm of my hand, and I almost forgot what I had been trying to say to her.

"Granted, we were both pretty out of it that night, but if I would have ever known that you had never…that you…that I was your first, I would have done things a hell of a lot differently," I admitted.

Like stare at your naked body and memorize every inch of it, swirl my tongue around your nipples and suck them into my mouth until you moaned my name. I'd taste your skin and bury my face between your legs and make you come so hard you'd forget your name.

"Holy fuck," she whispered with a glazed look in her eyes.

"I just said all of that out loud didn't I?"

She sat there staring at me with her mouth open, and I worried that I royally fucked up. It was too soon for me to talk about her vagina and how much I wanted to become BFF's with it. Sure, I spent the past five years glorifying every single thing I could remember about her, and I worried over the past week that maybe my memories were better than reality, but that was just stupid. She was just as amazing sitting here in front of me as she was in my dreams, and I needed her to know that. I opened my mouth but before I could get the words out, she jumped down off of the stool, mumbling something about stocking beer in the cooler in the back. She brushed past me and I was left sitting on my stool with a bottle of vodka and the smell of chocolate lingering in the air.

Oh my God. Oh holy fucking shit.

I was such a fucking coward. I ran away from him as fast as I could and now I was in the storage room pretending to stock beer.

I'd taste your skin and bury my face between your legs and make you come so hard you'd forget your name.

Jesus Christ on a cracker. I had no experience with this shit. I wanted to hump his leg as soon as those words left his mouth. He clearly didn't mean to say them out loud based on the shocked expression on his face.

"Shit!" I muttered loudly, punching an empty case of beer.

Except it wasn't empty and my fist connected with full cans of beer.

"Son of a bitchfuck!" I cursed while I shook my bruised hand, kicking my foot out and connecting with a bottle of tequila that went rolling across the floor.

"I hope this alcohol abuse isn't because of something I said."

I turned around to find Carter lounging against the doorframe. Why does he always have to witness my mortifying stupidity?

"I mean really, what has that bottle of tequila ever done to you?" he asked as he started to walk towards me.

"You mean aside from impairing my judgment so that I lost my virginity to some really hot guy I met at a frat party, got knocked-up and never got the guy's name because I am a complete and total bitch and now that he's here I feel like I am so out of my league whenever he's around because I have zero experience with this shit?" I rambled.

Carter stopped right in front of me and gave me a crooked grin. "You think I'm hot?"

I rolled my eyes at his attempt to lighten the mood and completely gloss over my nervous admission.

"You know, you're absolutely right. That tequila is a real asshole. Go ahead and kick the shit out of it. You might as well finish off the beer, too. I saw him looking at you funny."

I laughed at the ridiculousness of this conversation. I wasn't drunk but I was pleasantly buzzed enough from our earlier game of Truth or Truth to be able to see the humor in this situation. When I stopped laughing, he reached out and brushed a piece of hair off of my cheek that had escaped my ponytail and it reminded me so much of the night we met that I let out a small sigh.

"Let's get something straight here. You are not a bitch. I don't blame you for anything that you did. I'm not going to lie and say that it didn't totally suck ass to wake up the next morning and not have you there with me and then spend five years wondering if I had imagined you. But I would never think you were a bitch for doing what you did," he said as he inched closer. "I wasn't lying before when I said I would have done things very different with you that night," he said softly as he moved so close to me that our chest and thighs were touching. I swallowed roughly as he brought his hand up and rested it on my hip.

"I would have kissed you more," he said, leaning in and placing a soft kiss on the corner of my mouth.

"I would have held your body up against mine longer so I could feel every inch of you," he whispered against my cheek as he wrapped his other arm around my waist and pulled me up tighter against him.

His hand that rested on my hip slid up the side of my body. It grazed up my ribs and brushed against the side of my breast until his palm was flat over my heart.

"I would have touched you everywhere and took the time to feel your heart beat against my hand."

I licked my lips and tried to control my breathing. God, I loved the way he smelled, the way he spoke and his hands on me. How had I lived so long without these things?

"Most of all, I would never have taken even one sip of alcohol that night so that every single moment with you would have been etched into my brain and the memory of how your skin felt against my hands would be clear as a bell."

I was certain he could hear the pounding of my heart echoing through the room. I knew he could feel how fast it was beating with each word he spoke.

"Fuck, Claire," he muttered. "Just being close to you drives me crazy."

He bent his knees slightly and then pushed up against me so I could feel exactly what he was talking about. Both my hands flew to his shoulders in an effort to hold on and pull him closer. My one leg automatically lifted to wrap around his waist and bring him closer to me. His lips ghosted over my neck, and I was pretty sure I moaned. When he was back by my ear he whispered, "If this is too much, too soon, just tell me to stop and I will."

Was it too soon? Was I acting like a complete slut right now rubbing myself all over him? I was a mother for fuck's sake.

A mother that had never been laid properly and was horny as fuck.

"If you stop, I will straight up murder your ass," I whispered as his lips found their way to mine and connected.

No sooner had our mouths collided than I felt his tongue gently push its way past my lips. I slid my tongue against his, and he moaned into my mouth, pushing his hips into me harder. I was tingling all over like in some cheesy romance novel. My breasts were heaving and my loins were quivering.

I HAD QUIVERING LOINS!

I felt like I was going to explode if he didn't touch me. I wanted him to touch me so much it almost hurt. I am so not good at dirty talk. Just the thought of saying "touch my *ack* pussy" made me want to cringe. I could try "let your fingers do the walking" or maybe "put your digits in my divot."

Focus Claire!

Oh my God his tongue was like magic. Where the hell did he learn to kiss? I bet his dad taught him.

Wait no. That sounded gross.

Jesus, I was turning into a puddle of goo and so was my underwear.

TOUCH MY VAGINA!

If I screamed it in my head maybe he'd figure it out. His tongue circled mine and his hand went down to my ass to slide me up and down against his hardness.

PUT YOUR HAND ON MY VAG!

My leg slid down his hip and the feel of the rough denim of his jeans against my bare thigh made me whimper. He walked us backwards and pushed me up against the wall of the storage room, deepening the kiss and slowing it down at the same time. My hands were clutching the hair at the back of his neck so hard I think I pulled some out by the roots.

His hand that was palming my ass moved away and I almost yelled in frustration until I felt him slide it around to the front of my thigh and slowly inch it up towards the hem of my shorts.

OH MY GOD HE'S GOING TO TOUCH MY VAGINA!

Did I remember to put on sexy underwear and not period panties? You know what I'm talking about. The ginormous granny panties that you only wore when the crimson tide is flowing. The ones you'd never allow man or beast to see.

He broke the kiss as his fingers snuck under the leg of my shorts and – oh thank you sweet baby Jesus and the wise guys, I just remembered I put a Victoria's Secret thong on when I got dressed earlier.

"I know this doesn't make up for the shittiness of that night, but I want to make you feel good, Claire. Can I touch you?" he asked softly against my lips while he looked into my eyes.

Could he not feel my quivering loins and the brain screams?

I need your fingers inside me!

Yep, you guessed it.

"Fuck. That was the hottest thing I have ever heard."

I didn't have time to be mortified that I'd spoken out loud. He was doing what I asked and his hand was sliding all the way under the edge of my shorts until I felt his fingers slide up the front of my underwear.

"Holy fuck," I muttered and jerked my hips into his hand.

No one had ever touched me like this. I thought touch was all the same and brought on the same feelings whether it was a guy or myself fumbling around down there.

Clearly I was mistaken.

Carter's fingers moving up and down ever so slowly against the thin scrap of satin made me want to scream my head off in pleasure.

"I can feel how wet you are," he whispered as his fingers moved to the side and toyed with the edge of my underwear.

Hearing dirty talk from other people always made me blush and feel embarrassed for them and the weird stuff that came out of their mouths. I mean really, can they hear themselves? It's corny and all "fuck me harder big boy" and "oh you're so tight baby." Who says that crap? Obviously I had been missing out on Carter's dirty talk. It was hot. And I didn't want him to stop. He could talk about how tight, wet and fan-fucking-tastic I was all night long. He placed several small kisses to my lips as he took his sweet time working his fingers under the thin scrap of material and used the heel of his hand to push the leg of my shorts open wider to give him better access. I held my breath and tried not to think about the fact that I'd never had a guy touch me like this. That was just sad, really. And even more depressing was the fact that I was feeling sorry for myself when his fingers were getting ready to go for a swim at the Y.

I broke up the pity party when I felt two of his fingers come in contact with my bare, wet skin.

"Oh my God," I mumbled, letting my head fall back against the wall with a thud.

Yep, much better than my own fingers. My own fingers were now going to feel like Sinbad's hands in the movie *Houseguest* when he gets Novocain all over them and they flop around like dead fish, knocking shit off of the table. His fingers were smooth and soft and holy fuck they were touching me, feeling just how much I wanted this and that Liz forced me get waxed regularly.

Note to self: apologize to Liz for calling her a Sadistic Vagina-Nazi Bitch every time she made a Brazilian wax appointment for me. Because of her dedication to my who-ha, Carter doesn't have to discover a wildebeest in my pants right now and stop what he's doing to go in search of a weed whacker.

He swooped in and placed an open-mouthed kiss on my neck and slowly pushed a finger inside of me, letting his thumb rest against my clit while he gave me time to adjust to what he was doing.

He held his finger perfectly still inside me, and I clutched harder onto the back of his head and pushed my hips forward, making his finger go in deeper and his thumb slide against me.

This was too much and not enough and I felt like this was going to be over long before I wanted it to because the way he moved his fingers was pure genius. And that was just shocking in and of itself. I always needed a full reel of clips from porn movies flipping through my mind in order to finish. I couldn't think about anything but what he was doing to me right now. *Naughty Neighbors, MILF Madness* - none of those were necessary.

He started pushing and pulling his finger in and out of me slowly and did some glorious maneuver where he curled his finger before he started pulling it out that made me want to pant like a dog and lick the side of his face. His lips and tongue found every inch of my neck and his thumb circled faster until I was rocking my hips into his hand almost forcefully.

I was whimpering and moaning and I didn't have time to be embarrassed that I sounded kind of like a dirty slut or that there was a real live guy who was really touching my vagina because I was really one second away from exploding.

Really.

He pulled his finger out of me and used the pad of two fingers to circle my clit until I completely fell apart against his hand.

"Ohhh, oh, God! Fuck. Carter!"

His fingers didn't stop and he swallowed my cries with his mouth while I pushed against his hand, never wanting this feeling to stop. I made all kinds of noises into his mouth while he continued to kiss me and pull every ounce of my orgasm out of me until my legs were trembling and I could barely stand. When I stopped moving my hips and the last of my release faded away, he pulled his hand out from my shorts and wrapped his arm around me, kissing me slowly, letting his tongue lazily slide against my own. I didn't know how long we stood there in the storage room wrapped in each other's arms kissing. I could have spent hours kissing him and never come up for air.

We finally pulled our mouths apart and stood there staring at each other.

"That was the hottest thing I've ever seen. I should have done that five years ago," Carter said with a smile.

"Baby, if you would have done that five years ago, I would have handcuffed my vagina to your arm and made you do that to me every single day."

Carter laughed and then his face immediately got serious.

"Claire, I need to ask you something. And it's really important."

Oh my God, he was going to ask me to have a threesome. Or tell me he was really from Canada and needed a green card and that's the only reason he was here. Oh shit, what if he didn't like my vagina? Did it feel funny? I should have felt around down there more often. My gyno never complained. In fact, he told me I had a very nice uterus. Why the hell didn't Carter like my vagina? Shit, what if he was into dendrophilia and liked to have sex with trees?

"I'd like to spend some time with Gavin."

I knew he was going to say that.

"It's okay if you don't feel comfortable with me being alone with him just yet since he really doesn't know me. But I'd like to come over and see him."

I couldn't stop the smile that took over my face. Not only did his fingers deserve a major award, like a leg lamp or a national monument erected in his name (heh, heh, erected!), he actually took the initiative and asked to spend time with Gavin - even after getting punched in the nuts and threatened with the two-finger eye-watching signal.

Gavin would finally get to hang around a man other than my father and Jim.

And I'd get to have Carter tiptoe through the twolips again soon.

14.

Captain Narcolepsy

"So what you're telling me is, our little Claire's got hardwood floors, terracotta pie, a leather sausage wallet, a who-ha with no hair-ha," Drew yelled over the noise of the assembly line.

"Wow, I am really regretting that I told you anything about last night," I yelled back.

I reached above me for the hydraulic drill attached to the rig in the ceiling and pulled it down to fasten the car door to the body of the vehicle. I had three minutes before the next car came down the line and having to deal with Drew being an ass was going to make me screw everything up and force the line to shut down.

That and the fact that I really couldn't stop thinking about what had happened between Claire and I last night in the back room of the bar. Sweet Jesus she was beautiful when she came. And the little sounds she made…fuck, just thinking about them was making Carter Junior stand up and start begging for her. I hope she didn't think things were going too fast because I really wanted a repeat performance. And I didn't even care about not getting off. Watching her and feeling her come apart in my hands was enough satisfaction for me.

"Dude, you know your secret is safe with me. I will never tell a soul that you got to third base with your baby-mama last night and that Chewbacca does not live in her underwear. At least now I don't have to worry about you."

I turned off the drill and looked across the car at Drew who was attaching the front door handle.

"Why were you worried about me?"

"Aww, bro, come on. You were one step away from lathering chocolate ganache on your dick and trying to give yourself a blow job," he said.

"Did you just say ganache?"

Drew shrugged. "Yeah. Jenny makes me watch the Food Network all the time now. Ever since she started designing the flyers for Claire, she's decided she wants to learn how to cook. She spent twenty minutes the other day looking up a recipe online for frosting made with *confederate* sugar."

Laughter bubbled out of me and I got back to work on the car.

"Did you tell her to try looking in the Deep South for that sugar? You might also want to warn her about the Rebel sugar," I laughed.

"Come on, man. Don't be a dick. I didn't have the heart to tell her it was called convection sugar."

Nope, not going to touch that one.

"So, are you and Jenny going to Claire's tonight?" I asked, changing the subject.

Claire was definitely on board with letting me see Gavin. She figured starting off in a group setting would be the best thing so she invited everyone over to her place tonight for dinner.

"Wouldn't miss it for the world. I even got a new shirt just for the occasion," Drew said with a smile.

⊙ ⊙ ⊙

At six o'clock I knocked on Claire's door. I heard footsteps pounding against the floor and suddenly the door was flung open.

I looked down at the little man that stood there staring at me and I couldn't help but smile. Jesus he looked so much like Claire. But his eyes…wow they were exactly the same as mine.

"Hi there Gavin," I said as I pulled a wrapped present out from behind my back and handed it to him. "I got this for you."

Gavin snatched it out of my hand, turned and ran away from the door screaming for Claire.

"MOOOOOOOM! That guy bought me sumfin!"

I laughed and stepped into the house, closing the door behind me.

Claire lived in a small, Cape Cod bungalow and the first thing I noticed when I walked into the living room was how homey it was. There were candles lit on the coffee table and the mantle of the fireplace and the smell of dinner coming from the kitchen was mouth watering. I walked around the room looking at all of the pictures she had on practically every surface: pictures of her when she was little, pictures of her with her dad, pictures of her friends and pictures of Gavin. My heart clenched when I saw a picture of Claire, her belly round with our son. She looked so young. I lifted the picture off of the mantle to get a better look. This was how she looked when I met her, minus the pregnant belly. Looking at this picture made me sad and angry - not with her. I could never be angry with her for anything. We were both young and stupid and neither one of us used any brains that night. I was just upset that I had missed this. I had missed watching her stomach grow, I missed being able to put my hand on her and feel him kick.

"OWWWW!" I yelped as I felt a foot connect with my shin.

I looked down to see Gavin standing there, staring at me.

So much for missing out on feeling him kick. I think my shin will remember that forever.

"Hey, I forgotted your name. Can I just call you dog poop?"

Before I could formulate any type of response to that request, I heard Claire's voice from behind me.

"Gavin!"

"I didn't do it!" he swore, with a panicked look on his face.

"Yeah, right," she deadpanned. "This nice man's name is Carter, remember? Stop trying to call everything dog poop."

I turned to find her leaning against the doorframe leading into the kitchen given Carter the evil eye.

"Don't take offense," she said, turning her gaze to me. "Last week, every time you asked him a question he replied, "stupid fat cows are stupid" no matter what the question was."

I laughed, grateful that the whole dog poop thing wasn't just because he already decided he hated me. Claire made her way across the room to where I was and glanced down at the picture still in my hand.

"Oh my God, please don't look at that picture. I look like I have a giant tumor growing out of me. A tumor that kicked the shit out of my vagina and made me pee myself when I sneezed," she said with a groan. "I just told you I peed my pants didn't I?" she asked.

"Yeah, you kind of did. It's okay, I'll only send a text to four of my contacts about it instead of my whole phone book."

I suddenly realized we were toe-to-toe and I was close enough to kiss her. I leaned forward to do just that, completely forgetting that we weren't alone in the room.

"Mo-om, can I open my pwesent now?"

We stopped inches from each other's mouths and looked down next to us.

Claire sighed and leaned back away from me.

"Yes, you can open your present now," she replied.

He plopped down on the floor right where he was and started tearing into the paper, pieces of it flying in every direction.

"You didn't have to get him anything," she said softly to me.

I shrugged. "It's no big deal, just something little."

"Mommy, look! It's crayons and markers and paint and wow I can color stuffs and make pictures!" Gavin said excitedly, holding everything up for Claire to see.

"That's awesome, baby. Can you go put them in Mommy's room on my bed and we'll play with them later?"

"But I wanna paint now," Gavin complained, dropping the box of crayons on his foot. "Shit!"

"Gavin Allen!" Claire yelled.

I knew I shouldn't laugh, so I looked away and thought of dead puppies and that scene from *Field of Dreams* where Kevin Costner's character got to play catch with his dad. God dammed scene got me every time.

"The next bad word that comes out of your mouth is going to get you a spanking, do you understand me? Tell Carter thank you for the present and go in your room until it's time for dinner."

"Thanks, Carter," Gavin mumbled as he trudged down the hall.

When he was out of earshot I started laughing, and Claire smacked me in the arm.

"Sorry, but he is funny as hell."

She rolled her eyes at me and walked back to the kitchen with me following behind her.

"Yes, he's a riot. Come back to me after you've been out in public with him. Like, say in church. And when it gets to a really quiet part and all you can hear is the fountain in the back of the church and then Gavin's voice say really loudly "Mom! I hear Jesus taking a piss!" It's not so funny then."

I glanced at the counter behind her and my jaw dropped. Covered over every available surface were chocolate, cookies and candy – every kind imaginable.

"Am I in Willy Wonka's workshop?"

She laughed and opened up the lid of a huge pot on the stove and stirred the contents.

"Well, I decided to make you guys my guinea pigs tonight. And Jenny is going to take a few pictures of some of the items for my advertisements since I don't have anything better than my cell phone camera."

I stared dreamily at everything. I may have a slight weakness to sweets.

"Holy hell, what are those things?" I asked pointing to a row of white chocolate clumps the size of my fist with caramel on top.

"Oh, those are something new I'm experimenting with. I melted a bowl of white chocolate, added crushed up pretzels and potato chips to it and then once the dropped spoonfuls solidified, I drizzled caramel on top. I may have gone a little overboard on the size of them. Right now they're called Globs."

Sweet Mary in heaven. I wanted to ask this woman to have my babies. Oh, wait…

A knock sounded on the front door and Claire asked me to answer it for her while she set the table and finished up.

Jenny and Drew were the next to arrive. I held the door open for them and shook my head at Drew while Jenny walked in and made her way into the kitchen to talk to Claire.

"Really, Drew?" I asked, looking at his shirt.

There was a picture of a little kid on it shooting a gun above his head. The shirt read, "Don't hit kids. No, seriously. They have guns now."

"What? Kids nowadays are the devil. This shirt is a PSA for you, dude. You'll thank me one day. So, where is the little guy? Does he need his diaper changed or anything? Maybe I can show him my car or give him some candy," he said as he looked around me and rubbed his hands together.

"He's four Drew. He doesn't wear diapers. And you might want to dial down the creepy kidnapper vibe just a notch."

"Whatever. Take me to your demon seed," Drew said.

We walked past the kitchen and I stuck my head in and asked Claire if it was okay to head back to Gavin's room. She told me where it was and we went down the hall and found him sitting on the floor in the middle of his room, squirting a tube of toothpaste right onto the carpet.

"Whoa there, big guy. What are you doing?" I asked as I quickly made my way over to him and took the now empty bottle out of his hand.

He just shrugged his shoulders. "I don't know."

Shit. What do I do? Should I go get Claire? I don't want the kid to think I'm a traitor though. He would get mad at me for tattling on him. Wait, I was the adult. I couldn't let him walk all over me. I needed to let him know who's the boss. And right now, it wasn't Tony Danza.

"I'm pretty sure you're not supposed to be putting toothpaste on your floor, are you?" I asked.

"That's a dumb question, Carter. Of course he's not supposed to put toothpaste on the floor," Drew said seriously.

I looked back over my shoulder and gave him a dirty look.

"I know that. I'm trying to get him to admit what he did was wrong," I said through clenched teeth.

"Okay there, Dr. Phil. I'm pretty sure he knows it's wrong otherwise he wouldn't have done it. Kids are dumb. They do things they aren't supposed to all the time because they can. Being an adult sucks. I could never get away with putting toothpaste on my floor now."

It was like dealing with two children.

"Why would you...you know what? Never mind," I said, turning back around to face Gavin.

"Your mom wouldn't be too happy about you making this mess. How about you show me where the towels are and we'll clean it up before she sees it."

There. He won't hate me for telling on him and I still let him know it was bad. I am an awesome parent.

Obviously Gavin was very excited to clean if it meant we didn't tell Claire what he did. I briefly wondered if she was going to find out and possibly cut my penis off or smother me in my sleep. And then I wondered if I told her, would Gavin punch me in the nuts again, or maybe go for the throat this time? I don't know whether to fear my kid or his mother.

Twenty minutes later, the carpet was good as new and Drew and I were sitting Indian-style in the middle of Gavin's room, praying to every higher power we knew that the girls wouldn't walk in the room right this minute.

Gavin had decided we should play dress up. We tried getting him to play something manly like cops and robbers, running with scissors or lighting shit on fire - anything but this. Unfortunately, you couldn't win an argument with a four year old no matter how much you tried. Drew and I were both currently dressed as babies, complete with pacifiers in our mouths and holding on to stuffed animals. He stuck us each in these giant sun hats of Claire's that flopped down over our faces. Drew's was pink and mine was white. I drew the line at putting on one of his old, unused diapers that he found in a drawer in his closet from before he was potty trained.

"Hey, Uncle Drew, I have a secret to tell you," Gavin said.

Drew pulled the pacifier out of his mouth.

"Give it to me."

Gavin leaned in by his ear and whispered just loud enough for me to be able to hear him.

"You smell like beef and cheese."

Gavin pulled back from Drew's ear and Drew rolled his eyes at him.

"Dude, your secret sucks," he said.

"YOU SUCK!" Gavin yelled.

"Guys, dinner is ready so you should…"

Claire's words were cut off when she rounded the corner of the room and caught us. The abrupt halt to her feet caused Jenny, who had been following close behind, to smack into the back of her. Claire put her hand over her mouth to hide her giggles. Jenny couldn't have cared less about shielding her enjoyment of the situation. She bent over at the waist laughing her ass off out loud and pointing.

"Oh my God, someone tell me they have a camera," Jenny said in between laughs.

"Do you want me to spit up? Because I'm not afraid to go there," Drew threatened.

Both of us ripped off our baby crap while the girls laughed and gave Gavin high-fives. Drew and I stood up while Jenny lifted Gavin into her arms and told him how awesome he was and cooed all over him. He ate up every word and I swear that kid smirked at us as he put his head down on Jenny's chest - which was currently on full display with her low-cut top and push-up bra.

"Oh my God, I am so jealous of that kid right now. I wish I were cradled to her tits. Cradled like a baby," Drew whispered.

"Do you hear yourself right now?" I asked as we all walked out of Gavin's room and into the dining room where we were greeted by Liz and Jim who were already seated.

◉ ◉ ◉

After an extremely delicious dinner where there was only minimal fighting between the two children, and by children I mean Drew and Gavin, Claire started bringing out tray after tray of all her sweet goodies.

Now all I could think of were Claire's sweet goodies on a tray; her delicious num-nums on a silver platter. I would love to eat her off of a tray. I want to lick her Globs.

"Carter, do you want some?"

"Fuck yes."

"Awwwww, Carter said the t-u-l word mom!" Gavin tattled.

Oops.

"Who taught you how to spell?" Drew asked with a sneer.

"Dude, I'm four," Gavin replied.

I excused myself to go to the bathroom before I did something even more embarrassing. I stood there peeing and trying not to think about Claire being naked on a tray when the bathroom door suddenly opened and Gavin walked in.

"Oh, hey there, Gavin," I said nervously as I tried to turn my body away from him without interrupting the flow. "Uh, I'm kind of going to the bathroom here buddy. Can you shut the door?"

He did as I asked, however, he didn't leave the room before he shut the door. Now he was locked in a small, enclosed space with me while I tried to take a piss. And now he was staring at my junk. Okay, this wasn't awkward at all.

"Um, Gavin can you look somewhere else? Oh hey, look at that duck in the tub. That's pretty cool."

Still staring. Was this something I should be concerned with?

"Wow, Carter. You've got a HUGE wiener."

Suddenly, Gavin being in the bathroom with me didn't seem so bad. If only he could have been in the bathroom with me in eighth grade and passed that little tidbit around for Penny Frankles to hear, I might not have gone to the eight grade graduation dance solo.

I finished pissing, zipped up my pants and flushed the toilet, all while trying not to pat myself on the back. Yeah, I had a huge wiener. You bet your sweet ass I did. I almost needed a wheelbarrow to carry it around. And because a toddler said it, it must have been true.

We got back to the table and I couldn't keep the shit-eating grin off of my face.

"What are you smiling about? Do you have gas?" Drew joked.

"Hey, Mommy, Carter has a HUGE wiener," Gavin said around a mouthful of cookie, holding his hands up in the air about three feet apart, like you do when you're telling someone how big the fish is you just caught.

Claire quickly reached over and pushed Gavin's arms down while everyone else at the table laughed. I just sat back and smiled and tried to keep my anaconda penis tucked under the table so it wouldn't scare anyone.

"Hey, Uncle Drew, you wanna hear a dirty joke?" Gavin asked excitedly.

"I don't know, will it get you punched?" Drew replied seriously. It was almost touching how concerned Drew was with getting Gavin in trouble.

"The pig fell in the mud and walked across the street to the dirt and then climbed the roof!" Gavin shouted, falling immediately into a fit of giggles at his "dirty joke".

Everyone chuckled at Gavin's attempt at humor - except Drew.

"Dude, that wasn't funny at all," Drew said with a straight face.

"You wanna piece of me?" Gavin shouted, holding his little fist up in the air at him.

"Alright, that's enough. Gavin, go put your pajamas on, and I'll be in shortly to read you a story," Claire told him.

Gavin scampered down off the chair, giving one last threatening look to Drew before running to his room. Five pairs of eyes all turned their attention to Drew.

"What?" he asked. "It wasn't funny and I totally didn't get it."

"Okay Claire," Liz said, turning her face away from Drew, probably so she wouldn't feel the need to choke him. "Time for the real show. Tell us what you've got here," she said, pointing to all the trays on the table.

Claire went around the table pointing out what each item was. Snicker Surprise cookies, homemade turtles, Pretzel Turtles, White Chocolate Buckeyes, white and milk chocolate covered potato chips, pretzels, cashews, peanuts, raisins, rice krispies, bacon and a cookie called a Cranberry Hootycreek – which Drew kept calling a Hooterpeep.

Everything was amazing and I think we were all in a sugar coma by the time we sampled everything. Jenny circled the table and snapped a few pictures of everything for the advertisements before we inhaled the stuff and Claire blushed a bright shade of red at all the compliments we threw at her.

"I definitely got some good pictures, Claire. I think for the front cover of the brochure we should pacifically focus on the chocolate-covered stuff," she explained.

"You mean specifically?" Jim asked.

"That's what I said," she replied. "Pacifically."

"Hey, Claire, can I come with you to put Gavin to bed?" I asked, hoping to divert the attention from Jenny's weird use of the English language.

Her face lit up with my question, which instantly made me grateful I had the foresight to ask.

We left everyone to clean up the dining room table and walked back to Gavin's room to find him asleep on top of his toy box. I laughed as soon as I saw him.

"Don't laugh," she whispered with a smile on her face. "That's not the funniest place I've seen him fall asleep. I've got an entire photo album dedicated to his sleeping habits. On the back of the couch like a cat, sitting up at the dinner table, face down at the dinner table, under the Christmas tree in a pile of toys, in his closet, on the toilet…you name it he's fallen asleep on it. He's like a horse. He can practically fall asleep standing up. Jim gave him the Indian name of Chief Sleepsanywhere and Liz recently changed it to Captain Narcolepsy."

She moved quietly into the room and scooped his little body up easily, placing a kiss to his head as she walked over to his bed. I leaned against the doorjamb, trying not to get too sentimental and girly at just how sweet it was to see her taking care of him. She covered him up with a blanket, smoothed back the hair off of his head and kissed him again before turning around and walking to me.

"So, Mr. Ellis, how freaked out are you right now by all of this domesticated parenting crap?" she asked.

There was a smile on her face as she stood right in front of me but I could tell it was just there for show. She really was nervous about how I was handling all of this. I glanced over her shoulder at the little boy that was fast asleep in his bed and my heart started beating faster. I had an undeniable urge to grab onto him and never let him go, to protect him from anything bad that might come his way and to shelter him from scary things like the boogey man and clowns.

Shut up, clowns are scary as fuck.

I looked back down at the incredible woman standing in front of me and knew I felt the same way about her.

"I don't want the boogey man to get you and I hate clowns," I blurted out.

She laughed and patted my cheek in sympathy. I sucked at this. I didn't do well under pressure. I cared about her and Gavin and I just wanted her to know I wasn't going anywhere. How fucking hard was that to say?

"That's not what I mean. I mean, yes, I hate clowns. They are dumb and creepy and grown men should never wear anything with polka dots or giant shoes."

God dammit, stop the word vomit!

Before I could open my mouth and stick a giant clown shoe in any further, Claire covered my mouth with her hand.

"It's okay if you're freaked out. I wouldn't blame you. Believe me, this is a lot to take in," she said softly. "All of a sudden you go from single and free to having a built-in family."

I took a deep breath and tried it again, reaching up and pulling her hand away from my mouth and resting it flat against my chest.

"Let me just start off by saying I really, really suck ass at doing the whole "touchy-feely, talk about my feelings" shit. Although if you ask Drew, he would surely disagree since he spent five years listening to me whine like a baby about how much I wanted to find you. After all that time and spending years driving everyone around me crazy just trying to find your smell again, I am not about to fuck this up and run screaming into the night."

Her thumb moved back and forth over my chest and she brought her other hand up to my cheek before leaning forward and placing a soft kiss on my lips. When she pulled her face back, I wrapped my arms around her small waist and rested my forehead against hers.

"I know after I found out I fled the scene like a hit-and-run driver, but I promise you Claire, I will never get spooked again."

She pulled back and looked me in the eye, the corners of her mouth turning up in a smile.

"Did you really just quote *Cocktail* to me right now?"

"Yes, yes I did. If you'd like me to go all crazy Tom Cruise and jump up and down on a couch for you, I'll totally do it."

"ARE YOU KIDDING ME?! I WOULD RATHER TAKE IT UP THE ASS!"

Drew's booming voice from the living room pulled our attentions away from each other. We took one last look at Gavin before closing his door, and then walked hand in hand down the hall to find everyone sitting around the living room playing a twisted game of "Would You Rather".

Claire and I sat down next to each other on the couch. I put my arm around her shoulders and she snuggled into my side. Nothing had felt this perfect in a long time.

"All right, my turn," Drew said. "Jim, would you rather have your porn name be Hugh G. Rection or Mike Unstinks?"

15.

I'm a Dirty Slut

"Chains and whips excite me...c-c-c-come on, come on...S-S-S-S-M-M-M..."

"Gavin Allen Morgan, if you don't stop singing that song I am going to put you on the curb for the garbage men to pick up," I yelled for the tenth time today as I finished cleaning up the kitchen from lunch.

"That's boring," Gavin muttered before stomping off to his room.

"Speaking of garbage, when is that Christy guy going to be here?" my dad asked from his seat at the kitchen table.

Why is everyone determined to get on my nerves today?

"It's CARTER, Dad. Stop being an ass. He'll be here when he wakes up."

My dad made a production of looking down at his wrist where there wasn't even a watch.

"It's 12:48. What kind of a slacker is this guy?"

I threw the dishtowel on the counter and turned to give my dad a dirty look.

"He works the nightshift, Dad. We've been over this already. One more comment out of you and I'm changing your Facebook status to "I love penis.""

I walked over to the fridge to add a few things to my shopping list that hung off of the freezer and tried not to glance at the clock. I was definitely anxious to see Carter.

I was up to my eyeballs in stuff for the grand opening and Carter was working a lot of overtime so we hadn't seen each other since the night of dinner a week earlier. But we talked on the phone and he

174

also called a few times just to talk to Gavin, which totally made my heart melt.

Thoughts of our time in the storage room earned me extra credit in Liz Homework by making my way through my suitcase of "who needs a man" products for a second time. Liz got all choked up on the phone when I told her. It was a beautiful moment for the two of us.

I was working at the bar tonight so Carter was going to give me a ride up there. I called Liz and told her she and Jim should come so Carter wouldn't be bored.

"I think maybe I'll hide behind the couch and jump out when he gets here. Put the fear of George into him," my dad said with a nod of his head.

"Not funny. And don't you mean 'fear of God'?"

He shrugged. "Same thing."

God said, "Let there be light" and George Morgan flipped the switch.

This was the most my dad had spoken about Carter since they met. Granted, it wasn't very flattering but hey, it was progress. At least he was acknowledging his existence and not thinking up new ways to kill him. Dad had been going down the alphabet for a week now and finally stopped at the letter S.

Death by shopping cart suffocation, in case you were wondering.

The doorbell rang and I hurried to answer it. I wiped my hands on the front of my jeans, smoothed my hair and bent forward to reach my hand down the front of my shirt and tug each of the girls up so their prime real estate was on full display. I stood back up, took a deep breath and flung the door open. My heart actually skipped a beat when I saw Carter standing there.

"You know there are windows on either side of your door right? And that your curtains are see-through?" Carter said with a smirk.

Why? WHY, for the love of God!

"I would give you my entire paycheck for a month if you bent over in front of me and fluffed your boobs again," he said as he stepped through the door, and I closed it behind him.

I closed my eyes, fully prepared to be mortified and not make eye contact, but before I could wish for a giant hole in the floor to swallow me up, Carter's lips were on mine. He slid his arm around my waist and pulled me up against him, cupping my cheek with his hand as he slid his tongue past my lips and slowly stroked it through my mouth. I could kiss this man for days and never get enough. His lips moved against mine, soft and sensually, while his hand slid from my cheek, down my neck, and stopped on the bare skin right above my heart. I wanted to reach up and push his hand down into my bra. My fists clutched onto the front of his shirt and a whimper escaped from me as his hand inched just a tiny bit lower. If my mouth wasn't fused to his right now, I might wonder if I said that last part out loud. Or maybe he could read my mind.

Touch my boobs. Do it. The power of my mind commands you.

His hand stopped its downward descent and I wanted to scream. His tongue continued to slide against mine ever so slowly and I really wished I had one of those green flags from the NASCAR races. I would've waved that thing all around. Wave it in the air like I just don't care.

Carter, start your engine! You have been given the green flag. All systems go. Hit the gas and let your hand grab the boob.

"If you touch my daughter's boobs while I'm standing right here, I'm gonna have to put taffy in your trachea until you terminate."

Carter and I broke apart so fast you would have thought we were teenagers that just got caught having sex instead of grown adults that had a child together.

"Did your dad just tell me he was going to choke me to death with taffy?" Carter whispered.

"Yeah. He's on the letter T. Behave or an umbrella up your Uranus will be in your future," I whispered back.

My father walked over to us and looked Carter up and down.

"You got any tattoos, son?"

Carter looked at me in confusion and I just shrugged my shoulders. You never knew what was going to come out of my dad's mouth.

"Uh, no. No, sir, I do not," Carter replied.

"You own a bike?"

"Well, I have a pretty nice mountain bike that's still in storage because I just haven't had time to take it out for a..."

"Motorcycle, Cathy," my father interrupted with a sigh of annoyance. "Do you own a motorcycle?"

Carter shook his head, "No, and my name is Cart-"

"You ever been arrested or get in a bar fight?" my dad interrupted.

"No, I've never been arrested or gotten into any kind of fight, Mr. Morgan," Carter said with a confident smile.

My dad leaned over towards me.

"Claire, are you sure this kid isn't gay?" he whispered to me.

"Jesus, Dad! No, he's not gay," I yelled back.

"Hey..." Carter said, insulted by my dad's question.

My dad turned to face Carter and sighed.

"Fine, you can date my daughter and get to know your son. But if you knock her up again..."

"DAD!"

My dad looked over at me with my hands on my hips and smoke practically coming out of my ears and then continued with his warning like I wasn't there.

"...I will comb the face of the earth, hunt you down like a dog, and drop her cranky ass off on your doorstep. I'm not dealing with another nine months of Miss Pissy Pants over there."

Oh for the love of God.

I looked back and forth between them as they stared each other down.

Carter nodded his head and stuck out his hand for my dad to shake.

"Deal," Carter said as they shook on it.

Wonderful. One big happy cray-cray family.

Just then, Gavin flew through the living room holding something above his head.

"Carter! Look at the new sword I gots!"

Christ almighty!

My son was running into the room with my Jack Rabbit above his head like he was a gladiator going into battle – a gladiator with a purple "sword" that had five speeds.

"Oooh, what does this button do?" Gavin asked as he stopped and pressed the button that made the beads swirl around.

I flew over to him and tried to snatch it out of his hand, but he wouldn't let go. I frantically pressed all of the buttons to get it to stop while I played tug-of-war with Gavin and suddenly I hit one that switched it to warp speed and made the whole top part start rotating and vibrating so hard Gavin's arms shook.

"M-m-m-m-m-o-o-o-o-m-m-m-m-m th-th-th-th-i-i-i-i-s-s-s-s t-t-t-i-i-ck-l-e-s-s."

Fucking hell. When did this kid get so strong?

"Gavin. Cut it out. This is not a toy," I said through gritted teeth.

I was playing tug-of-war with a rubber penis and my son. This is not okay people!

"It is too a toy. Why do you get all the good toys?" Gavin huffed as he put all of his weight into pulling the thing out of my hand and I actually stumbled forward.

"No, really guys don't worry. I've got this," I said sarcastically at my dad and Carter. They were standing shoulder-to-shoulder, a few feet away watching the show. They looked at each other and burst out laughing.

Of course. NOW they bonded - when I was trying to wrestle a sex toy out of my kid's hand.

"Gavin, let go NOW!" I yelled.

"You better do as your mom says, Gavin. She gets grumpy when she can't play with her toy," my dad laughed.

Carter laughed right along with him until I shot him a look that clearly said "If you don't shut the fuck up and help me, I will never let you in my pants again."

His mouth quickly shut and he finally moved.

"Hey, Gavin, I got something for you I left on the front porch. And it's a much better toy than your mom's. Why don't you run out and grab it," Carter suggested.

Gavin released his death grip on the vibrator without another word and ran out the front door.

"You are so lucky you helped me when you did or there would have been serious repercussions," I told Carter angrily.

Obviously he didn't get the severity of the situation since he was actually giggling right now. And my dad was wiping tears out of his eyes. Then I looked down and realized I had been enunciating my point by shaking the vibrator in Carter's face.

I quickly put my arm down, opened one of the end table drawers and shoved the damn thing inside just as Gavin ran back into the house with a toy gun, cowboy hat and sheriff's badge stuck to his shirt.

"Bad boys, bad boys, whatcha gonna do, whatcha gonna do when they cut your wiener," Gavin sang as he pointed his gun at random objects.

"Wow, cops have gotten pretty hardcore lately," Carter muttered.

☉ ☉ ☉

I forgave Carter on our ride to the bar because come on, look at him. I couldn't hold a grudge and fantasize about his penis. It was a major conflict of interest.

Business was just starting to pick up at the bar as the after-work crowd started filing in around seven. Liz and Jim ate dinner with Carter at one of the booths and the three of them moved over to the bar after they were done. On one of my many trips walking past them, Carter reached out and grabbed my arm. He swiveled his seat to the side so he could pull me between his legs. I set my empty tray on top of the bar next to him and he rested his hands on my hips.

"Remember when I told you that I would always tell you if your ass looked fat?" he asked.

Oh man, I knew I shouldn't have licked the bowl of milk chocolate clean last night after I finished making turtles. I could feel my thighs getting bigger while I stood here. Were they rubbing together tonight when I walked? I bet he was worried my rubbing thighs were going to start a spark.

Only you can prevent thigh fires. That Smokey the Bear jerk only cared about the forest. Fuck the forest. My vagina could catch on fire because Carter thought I was fat.

"Shut your brain off. I wasn't going to tell you that you looked fat," he scolded.

I knew that.

"I was just going to say, I forgot to also mention that I will always tell you when your ass looks so fucking amazing that I want to wrap my hands around it every time you walk by."

I bit my bottom lip and smiled.

"Anything else?"

Yeah, I was fishing for compliments again. I just had a meltdown about a thigh inferno. I earned this.

"Yes," Carter answered after kissing me softly. "I will also always tell you when your legs look so long and sexy that all I can think about is having them wrapped around my waist."

He kissed my lips again.

"And I will always tell you when you are so beautiful that somebody better call God, because he's missing an angel."

"Awww, did you just use a cheesy pick-up line on me?" I asked.

"I've been waiting to use that since I was fifteen," Carter said with a smile.

"Are you guys done yet? I just threw up in my mouth a little listening to this shit," Liz muttered from her seat on the other side of Carter.

"Well aren't you two just the cutest couple?"

I turned away from Carter when I heard the female voice behind me dripping with sarcasm.

"Tasha, what the fuck are you doing here?" Carter demanded as he stood up behind me.

Whoa, fucking whoa! Tasha? The ex? This was who Carter dated before he came here? Isn't this just a pickle on the crap sandwich that is my life? Of course she had to look like a porn star. Miles of long blonde hair, bright blue eyes and a perfect complexion. Not to mention the tiniest waist known to man and the nicest set of boobs I've ever seen. They had to be fake. Real boobs weren't that perfectly round. If I didn't hate her on sight, I might have asked her if I could touch them. She looked familiar. She flipped her hair behind one shoulder and it suddenly came to me how I knew her.

"Hey, you were at Jenny's sex toy party a few weeks ago."

I felt Liz walk up next to me.

"Oh yeah, I remember her. Twat Face Tasha," Liz said with a smile as she crossed her arms in front of her.

Twatty huffed in irritation. "It was Tantalizing Tasha."

"Nope, I'm pretty sure it was Twat Face," Liz said, looking to me for confirmation.

I nodded in agreement.

"Oh it definitely was. She probably doesn't remember because we talked about it behind her back," I said with a shrug.

Before I knew it, Cunty was up in my face.

"Listen slut, just because you're Carter's new flavor of the week doesn't make you anything special."

All hell broke loose then. Carter started yelling at Tasha, Tasha yelled at all of us and Liz pushed her away from me. I just stood there in the middle of the commotion in shock.

"That's enough Tasha," Carter said angrily. "Tell me what you want, or leave. You will not just show up here out of the blue and insult Claire."

She gave me another snide look before turning her gaze back on Carter.

"Wow, it sure didn't take you long to find some little whore to dip your wick into, did it?" Tasha asked Carter sarcastically.

Oh hell no! She did *not* just call me a whore.

I took a step towards her, my hands shaking with the urge to punch that smug look off of her face.

"That's pretty rich considering I heard you fucked your way through the phone book when you were with Carter. Your vagina is a giant gaping hole like the one the iceberg left on the Titanic. It's a crime scene in your pants with hundreds of people screaming in horror and trying to jump the fuck off."

I didn't even know what I was saying at this point. I was just spouting nonsense because I was pissed. And it looked like I hit the nail on the head - or the vagina. Tasha charged me like a bull. Everyone moved at once. I moved out of the way, as Carter, Liz and Jim all got in front of me and grabbed onto Tasha while she screamed about killing me. It turns out, porn star-slut-ex-girlfriends aren't so pretty when they have tomato-red faces, spit flying out of their mouths and their limbs are flailing all over the place.

Carter finally managed to grab Tasha's elbow and started pulling her with him over to the front door while she continued to yell insults and death threats at me. Carter made eye contact with me and mouthed '*I'm sorry*' before he disappeared out the front door with the nut job.

I'm not gonna lie, I was a little freaked out. It felt like everyone in the place was looking at me. It was so loud in here, no one had any clue what had just happened, but it still unnerved me. I hated being the center of attention. And I hated how insecure I felt because right now, Carter was outside, alone, with his ex-girlfriend. Granted, she was obviously one window lick away from riding the short bus, but that knowledge did nothing to ease my mind.

I let one of the other waitresses know when she walked by that I was going to take a break for a few minutes. Liz pushed me down onto her barstool and Jim stood behind me rubbing my shoulders to try and ease the tension. Neither of them said much. I think they were waiting for me to have a mental breakdown or curl up in the fetal position and suck my thumb. I had never been in any kind of a fight before. I talked a good game but the first time someone came at me I ran the other way. One time in high school, Liz and I were walking through the mall and some crazy emo chick walked by us and slammed her shoulder into mine. Without thinking, I turned and shouted, "Stop writing poetry and crying and watch where you're going!"

She stopped dead in her tracks and turned around, along with the rest of her depressed, too-much black eye make-up posse. I quickly stuck the straw of my cherry slush in my mouth and pointed my thumb at Liz.

"What did we miss, kids?" Drew asked, coming up behind us a few minutes later with his arm around Jenny as the rest of us just stood there staring at the door where Carter had disappeared.

I turned around to face him and his shirt that said, "I shaved my balls for this?"

"Somebody just tried to kill me," I told him in a horrified voice.

"What? Who?" Drew asked.

"Tasha." Liz said with disgust.

Jenny immediately looked guilty.

"Oh shit! She was here already? Claire, I'm so sorry. Tasha is all my fault."

"What the hell are you talking about? You know that crazy bitch?" Liz asked.

"We went to college together and she called me a few weeks ago and said she'd be in town and wanted to get together. That's why she was at the sex toy party. She was only supposed to stay for that weekend but she decided to stick around longer. I had no idea she knew Carter until a little bit ago. She asked me if I knew Carter and said she was an old friend and wanted to say hi. It wasn't until after I told her where you guys were going to be tonight that I remembered she used to date a guy named Carter. That's why we came up here. I really thought we'd get here before her so I could fix this."

Drew removed his arm from around Jenny and turned to face me, jumping into action.

"Okay, Claire, here's what we need to do first. Do you know how to throw a punch?" Drew asked as he grabbed my arms and stared seriously into my eyes.

"What? No. What are you talking about? I'm not going to fight her," I said with a roll of my eyes.

"You don't understand. I've known this freak for years. Did she threaten you?" Drew asked.

"Yeah, that cum dumpster said she'd kick Claire's ass," Liz told him.

"Oh it's on now! It's on like *Frogger!*" Drew shouted in excitement.

"Don't you mean *Donkey Kong*?" Jim asked as he stood behind Liz and slid his arms around her waist.

"I never really liked Donkey Kong. So it was never *on*. Frogger just works better for me."

"Drew, nothing is going to be *on*. I have never been in a fight and I'm not going to start now. Carter took her outside and is hopefully telling her to go to hell. Problem solved," I said.

Drew looked at me in horror. "Claire, I don't think you understand the seriousness of this situation. Now, as much as I hate Tasha like a fire burning rash on my dick, she's still hot. And Claire, you're a total MILF."

I looked at him in confusion. "Drew, what the hell does this have to do with anything?"

"It's like you don't even know me Claire," Drew said sadly with a shake of his head.

He let go of my arms and stepped back, wiping an imaginary tear from under his eye.

"Jim, help me out here man. I'm too upset to continue."

Jim untangled his arms from Liz and took a step forward to pat Drew on the back.

"As Drew has pointed out Claire, you're hot. And while we all agree that Cray-Cray needs to be put in her place, unfortunately, she's hot too. And you're both chicks with long hair. And we're in a restaurant that has approximately four different flavors of Jell-O in the back room," Jim explained seriously.

"Oh my God are you fucking kidding me?" Liz asked. "This is about wanting to see two chicks fight in a pool of Jell-O?"

"Liz. It's ALWAYS about wanting to see two chicks fight in a pool of Jell-O. Never, ever forget that," Drew said without any trace of humor in his voice. "Jell-O is *delicious*."

Liz looked over at me. "You know, even though these two morons are speaking with their dicks right now, you should probably learn how to hit something. You know, just in case Carter can't talk any sense into her. If she comes back in here, obviously we'll all take her out, but what if she sneaks up on you when you're unloading groceries from your car? Or jumps up from your backseat while you're driving down the highway?" she asked.

"Oh my God, what is wrong with you?! This is not helping me AT ALL!" I screeched.

"Alright, that was probably an exaggeration. Besides, her tits are too big to squeeze down in the backseat of a car. You'd totally see her first," Liz replied with a shrug. "And now, you can learn how to pop one of those implants without breaking a nail."

This was really not happening was it? I didn't want to learn how to fight. I should have kept my mouth shut with the twat face, giant vagina comments.

Drew turned to face me and put both of his hands up in the air with his palms facing out.

"Alright, strap on your brass balls and hit me," Drew said, widening his stance.

I stood there with my hands on my hips looking around at everyone. They all stood there waiting for me to punch Drew's hands.

"This is the dumbest idea ever," I complained.

"Come on Claire, let 'er rip. Then you can go outside and tear her shit up like a Cyclops," Jenny said.

"Cyclops?" Jim asked.

"You know, that other name for like, a hurricane or tornado. Cyclops."

We all cocked our heads at her in confusion.

Drew sighed. "It's cyclone, baby."

I took that moment to wind back and punch Drew's hand so I could take him by surprise. Drew looked at me in confusion while I bounced back and forth on my toes like a boxer. That felt good. That felt *really* good. I hit the shit out of his hand. Bring it on bitch!

"Claire, what the fuck was that?" Drew asked.

"Scared you, didn't I? That was my fist of fury, BITCH!" I yelled.

Drew put his hands on his hips and stared at me.

"You have the punching power of a drunken baby. I hope you throw down your vagina harder than that. Otherwise, I feel bad for Carter's penis."

"Why are we feeling bad for my penis?"

Carter came up behind me before I could tell Drew that my vagina and Carter's penis were none of his business.

"So what's up, man? What the hell did Slut Bag McFuckstick want?" Drew asked.

Carter sighed. "Oh just to tell me what a big mistake she made turning her vagina into a twenty-four hour 7-11. And how "you don't know what you got till it's gone.""

"Wow, she quoted a Cinderella song. She's not afraid to bring out the big guns is she?" Liz asked.

Everyone was laughing and making a big joke about this, but it wasn't funny. It wasn't funny at all. That bitch wanted to kill me. Or at least punch me in the face. Did everyone forget about that fact already? She wanted to punch me. In the face. With her FIST.

"I hate to break up the fun, but Crazy Train wants to beat up my face."

Liz gave me a reassuring look.

"Calm down Long Duk Dong. You may punch like a grandma after drinking a forty-ounce, but remember Claire – you know how to *take* a punch. That's what's most important here right now," Liz said with a pat to my back.

I looked at her in confusion for a few seconds before I remembered what she was talking about - drunken fight club night last year.

"I'm sorry, but why does Claire know how to take a punch? I'm not sure I like where this is going," Carter said nervously.

"Well, last year Jim made us watch *Fight Club* for like, the tenthousandth time. And while I'm all for a little shirtless Brad Pitt action, Claire and I decided to take a shot every time Edward Norton talked in third person. By about twenty minutes in, we were trashed. I don't know whose idea it was, but Claire and I started our own fight club in the living room," Liz explained.

"It was your idea, Liz. You stood up in front of me, lifted your shirt and said "Punch me in the stomach as hard as you can, fucker.""

Jim started laughing as he remembered back to that night. It wasn't my finest hour. I punched even worse when I was drunk, barely even grazing Liz's skin. She, however, could punch like a WWF wrestler on steroids.

"Oh yeah, that's right! That was one of the best ideas I've ever had while drunk. We punched each other back and forth until you started wheezing and yelled, "I am Claire's internal bleeding and you need to cut this shit out!""

Carter looked back and forth between us just shaking his head in disbelief.

"Don't worry about our girl, Carter. She went a good ten rounds before she tapped out," Jim said with a laugh. "And you'll be happy to know I got it all on video."

"Was there Jell-O? Tell me there was Jell-O?" Drew asked excitedly.

⊙ ⊙ ⊙

My shift ended a few hours after that and I desperately needed a drink after tonight's events. I threw my apron behind the bar and everyone moved back to a large table so we could all sit together. After we sat down at the table, Carter told us what happened outside. Tasha claimed that she made a huge mistake and she wanted Carter back. He laughed in her face and told her to take her crab-infested vagina back to Toledo. He also informed her that he had always wanted me, even when he was with her and now that he found me, he was never letting me go.

Cue the applause.

I lost track of how many drinks I consumed the rest of the night. Every time I set my empty glass down it was magically refilled. I think Carter knew I was stressed about the Tasha situation and wanted me to just relax and have a good evening.

Or he wanted to get me drunk and take advantage of me.

My lady bits started jumping up and down, clapping her hands and screaming, "Yes please!"

I kept looking towards the door expecting Tasha to come charging back in. After a while though, I didn't know which door she would come through since there were at least thirty of them when I looked in that direction.

I glanced down into my glass, trying to count the ice cubes and lost track after one.

Wow, what did they put in this vodka?

Carter kept looking over at me and smiling and it took everything in me not to straddle his lap. I really wanted to make some sort of move, but I didn't know the first thing about that crap. My hand was on his thigh and I slowly moved it upwards. I stopped just a few inches below the bulge I couldn't stop staring at. I want to rub my vagina all over that shit.

Yes, I was aware that I was sitting here at a table full of people, just staring down in Carter's lap like it was a desert oasis and I hadn't sipped water in months.

I thought about things I could whisper in his ear that might turn him on.

"We should have the sex."

Carter laughed and kissed my cheek.

"I thought that out loud didn't I?"

"Yes, you definitely thought that out loud," he said with a smile.

I turned away from him and grabbed Liz's arm, pulling her up with me.

"Be right back," I mumbled to the table in general.

I pulled Liz over to the bar, about ten feet away from the table.

"I don't know how to sex," I complained.

"Um, what?" Liz asked.

"I mean, sexy. I don't know how to sexy."

Liz laughed.

"You mean you don't know how to *be* sexy?"

I just nodded. Liz got me. My best friend was the best ever. She was so pretty and nice and pretty.

"Hon, you're doing just fine. In case you hadn't noticed, Carter hasn't been able to keep his hands off of you all night. And you couldn't see it, but when you put your hand on his leg, he kept swallowing and staring off into space like he was trying not to jizz in his pants."

I was starting to panic. Which was probably the booze talking but so what? I didn't know the first thing about seducing a guy. I was going to make a total fool of myself.

"You're seriously freaked out about this?" Liz asked, all traces of humor gone from her face when she saw how worried I was.

"I feel like I'm going to puke, I'm so nervous."

Liz sighed. "Claire, you're a hot bitch. You could stand there and do nothing and he'd still want to hump your leg. You just need some confidence. Repeat after me, "I am a dirty, dirty slut.""

Liz stood there with her hands on her hips waiting for me to comply. I looked back nervously at Carter but he was deep in conversation with Drew.

"This is ridiculous," I complained.

"What's ridiculous is that you don't think you can be slutty. Do you honestly think I would be friends with you if I thought there wasn't a dirty whore lurking in there somewhere? Give me a little credit please. You are the quintessential lady in the streets, freak in the sheets."

"You need to stop quoting *Urban Dictionary*," I told her.

Carter had probably been with lots of women - women who could suck a golf ball through a garden hose and dance on a pole. Liz meant well, but I just didn't know if I could pull this off.

"You're starting to piss me off. Just say it. I am a dirty, dirty slut."

I rolled my eyes. I might as well do what she says or she'll never let it go.

"I'm a dirty, dirty slut," I mumbled quietly.

Well that *did* feel a little good saying it out loud. Maybe Liz was on to something.

"Come on dirty girl, you can do better than that. Do it again, and put your vagina into it," Liz encouraged.

I took a deep breath and said it a little louder. Thank God there was music playing and people talking.

"Wow, did you see that?" Liz asked. "Carter's disco stick just shriveled up and died. You suck at this, and not in a good way. Again!"

I clenched my fists at my sides and my breathing sped up. I could be a dirty slut; I could be dirtier than a hooker at a gang-bang.

Okay, maybe not that dirty.

I took in a big gulp of air and let out all of my nerves, all of my anxiety and all of my irrational fears with one sentence.

"I AM A DIRTY, DIRTY SLUT!"

Unfortunately, the jukebox decided to move to a new song right then, so the decibel level of the bar had dropped considerably. I was too busy empowering the slut within to notice. Too bad for me no one else had been preoccupied with anything other than my screaming confirmation.

Everyone within shouting distance immediately started clapping and cheering. There were a few catcalls and wolf whistles and one over-zealous person who yelled, "Save a drum, bang a dirty slut!"

Jenny smacked Drew in the arm for that one.

Everyone felt so sorry for me that free drinks were sent to me for the next hour. And I couldn't be rude. I had to drink them. Which was why Carter was now helping me walk into my house because my feet just did not want to cooperate and - oh look, pizza!

I stumbled away from Carter and flipped open the cardboard box my dad left on the counter, shoveling an entire piece into my mouth.

"Mfmmff soooo fucking good," I mumbled around bites.

Carter stood behind me holding onto my hips to steady me while I inhaled two more pieces and guzzled two glasses of water.

"Fuck, this pizza is like...good and shit," I told him, wiping my greasy hands on a towel next to the box.

Alright, enough stalling. Time to do this shit.

I turned in Carter's arms and gave him my best sultry look, chanting my mantra over and over.

I'm a dirty slut. I'm a dirty slut.

"Are you okay Claire? Do you have something in your eye?"

Carter cupped my cheeks and tilted my head back so he could look in my eye that did NOT have anything in it but sex appeal.

I am a drunk, dirty slut. I am a drunk, dirty slut.

I pulled my face away from his hands and decided to stick with a smile. It was safer.

I could do this; I could so totally do this.

I lifted the hem of my shirt up over my stomach, my black lace bra, and my head.

Except, my shirt got caught in the bobby pins on the top of my head. I was standing here in front of Carter with my shirt stuck around my head and chin and my arms stuck out in front of my face.

I am the great Cornholio. I am the great Cornholio. I need TP for my bunghole.

I started snorting and Carter bent his knees so he could peek into the opening of my shirt.

"Baby, what are you doing?" he asked with a laugh.

"I might need some help getting nuded," I said through snorts of laughter.

"Did you say neutered?"

Carter's question just made me laugh even harder, which naturally made me cry - deep, heaving sobs with snot running down my nose.

Ladies and gentlemen, we have now entered the drunk crying portion of our evening. Please put your seatbacks in the upright position and try not to stare at the train wreck to your left.

Carter helped me get my shirt back on and put his hands back on my face, wiping away the tears with his thumbs.

"Hey, why the tears? What's wrong?" he asked softly.

That just made me cry harder. He was so nice and pretty and... nice. I sniffled loudly.

"I just wanted to be a slut so you'd like me and I don't want your penis to be disappointed and Twat Face is going to beat me up because I called her vagina a clown car."

Carter chuckled at my ramblings, bent down and scooped me up into his arms bridal-style. He walked down the hall towards my room, and I laid my head on his chest.

"First of all, I will never let Tasha beat you up, so don't even give that another thought," he reassured me as he gently set me down on my bed. He grabbed a couple of tissues from my nightstand and handed them to me as he knelt down next to my bed.

"Second," he said softly as I blew my nose and he held up the covers so I could crawl under. "You don't need to do anything to be dirty or sexy. You are already all of those things and more just by breathing. I am in a constant state of horniness whenever I'm near you or thinking about you. I don't want you to be nervous or worried about anything involving you and me and sex. You are everything I have ever wanted Claire. Never doubt that."

I really wish I wasn't drunk. I would so put his penis in my mouth right now.

Carter groaned and I was too drunk to care that I had just said that out loud. I snuggled into the covers.

"If you keep saying things like that, I am going break the rule I made to myself when I found you again," Carter said with a shake of his head as he pulled the covers up around my shoulders and smoothed my hair off of my cheek.

"What rule?" I whispered, unable to keep my eyes open any longer.

Carter leaned forward and put his lips by my ear.

"The rule that the next time I'm inside you, you will remember and enjoy every single second."

I wanted to tell him he was awfully cocky but that just made me think of cock and wonder why male roosters were called cocks.

I passed out singing Alice in Chains "They Come to Snuff the Rooster" lyrics.

16.

They're Called Nipples

Claire's body slid down the front of mine and she got to her knees, flicking the button of my jeans open as she went. The sound of my zipper sliding down filled the quiet room. I looked down at her on her knees and had to force myself not to grab onto her hair roughly and push her where I wanted her. Her soft, smooth hands reached into my pants and pulled my erection out, holding it right by her full lips. She glanced up at me through hooded eyes and smiled before she plunged her warm, wet mouth down on me. She swallowed the entire length and swirled her tongue around and around. She hallowed out her cheeks, sucking as hard as she could while she moved her mouth up and down. The tip touched the back of her throat with each suck in and caused me to moan loudly. Her hand pumped quickly up and down my length right below her mouth and I could feel my balls tighten with the force of my release. She ran her tongue from base to tip, swirling it around the head several times before pulling back and saying, "What's wrong with your wiener?"

I moaned again and tried to push her head forward so she could take me back in her mouth.

"Hey, what's wrong with your wiener?"

I jerked awake and turned my head, screaming at the top of my lungs when I saw Gavin standing a foot away from me on the couch, staring down between my legs. I followed his line of sight and groaned when I saw the huge morning wood I sported poking up under the blanket.

I sat up quickly and bunched the blanket around my lap as best I could as Claire came running into the living room, a look of panic on her face from my scream moments ago.

"What happened?" she asked in alarm as she ran over and knelt down next to Gavin.

Stop thinking about Claire on her knees. Stop thinking about Claire on her knees. Think about that old lady from Titanic naked.

Gavin pointed to me. "Carter's got a big wiener, Mom. Sumfin's wrong with him. He was making the same noises I do when my tummy hurts."

Claire smothered a laugh and finally looked me in the eyes.

"I guess I don't need to ask if you slept well!" she said brightly.

I shook my head at how chipper she was this early in the morning after last night.

"How are you even able to function this morning?" I asked, looking her over. Aside from looking a little sleepy, she still looked amazing. Her hair was wild, she had a little bit of make-up smudged underneath one eye and she wore an old tank top and shorts that had seen better days, yet she was the most beautiful woman I had ever seen.

She laughed and pointed to Gavin.

"You learn real quickly that as a parent, you don't have time for a hangover. Extra Strength-Rapid Release Tylenol and I have become very close over the years."

The phone rang and she hurried out of the living room to answer it, leaving Gavin to stand there and stare at me.

"So, how was your sleepover at Grandpa's last night?" I asked as I flung the blanket off of me now that my morning glory was under control.

He shrugged.

"Do I have a vagina?"

I stared blankly at him, not quite sure I heard him correctly.

"Uh, what?" I asked, swinging my legs around and placing my feet on the floor.

He let out a huff of irritation with me.

"I said, do I have a vagina?"

I turned towards the kitchen to see Claire on the phone, pacing back and forth. Shit, I was on my own with this one. How the hell does he even know the word vagina? Wait, maybe he doesn't. He's four for fuck's sake. He probably thinks vagina means Cleveland.

"Well, Gavin, um…do you know what that words means?"

Please say Cleveland. Please say Cleveland.

"Papa watched a movie last night and the guy said he felt like he was driving around in a vagina. Can I drive a vagina? Does a vagina have windows and a horn?"

Oh holy mother of shit.

"Shit. Son of a bitch!" Claire cursed as she walked back into the living room.

Gavin opened his mouth but Claire was quick to cut him off.

"Don't you even think about repeating what I said. Go to your room and find some clothes to wear. You have to go to work with Mommy today."

Gavin scampered off and his vagina comment was momentarily forgotten when I saw the look of worry on Claire's face.

"What's going on? What happened?"

She flopped down next to me on the couch, rested her head on the back of it and closed her eyes.

"My dad was supposed to watch Gavin today so I could finish up some things at the shop but he got called in to work," she said with a sigh.

Light bulb.

"I can watch him for you," I said immediately.

She lifted up her head and stared at me with her mouth open.

"Seriously, Claire, let me do this for you. I would be happy to take him today and get to spend some time with him."

After forty minutes of Claire listing all of the small objects he could fit into his mouth, making me repeat the number for Poison Control back to her eight times and drawing me a diagram with stick figures on a paper towel of how to do CPR, Gavin and I kissed Claire good-bye, got into my car and headed to the library for story time.

It was a public place, full of kids and parents who knew how to take care of kids in case I had a problem or questions. What could possibly go wrong?

⊙ ⊙ ⊙

"...and the sex? Oh you can just kiss that shit good-bye right now. Before we had our son my wife was a dirty little whore. She'd give me blow jobs while I drove down the freeway, she'd dress up in a naughty nurse uniform and greet me at the door when I got home from work and whenever we went out, we always pulled the car over on the way home and fucked in the front seat."

The man sitting next to me let out a great big sigh. He was another father I met when Gavin and I arrived at the library. He was there with his three year old son and eight year old daughter. His daughter was from a previous relationship and he had his son with his current wife. We started talking when I sat down next to him on one of the couches while the boys sat in a circle with a bunch of other kids a few feet away listening to the librarian read them a book. After telling him the condensed version of my relationship with Claire and Gavin, I asked him for some parenting tips since he'd been around the block a lot longer than me. Little did I know it would turn into a "how much kids fucked up my life" speech.

"But after our son was born, my penis got put on the "do not call" list. Sometimes, if I listen really closely, I can often hear the sound of "Taps" being played from my lonely balls," he whispered to me as he waved his hand and smiled at his son.

Jesus. Claire and I hadn't even got to the sex part yet. Was this really how it would be? Before I demanded that this guy tell me something good so I wouldn't have nightmares tonight, his daughter Finley ran over to him with a book in her hands.

"Daddy, can you read me this book about horses?" she asked sweetly as she climbed up onto his lap.

"Sure, baby girl," he replied, wrapping an arm around his daughter and taking the book from her hand.

See? Look at how sweet kids could be. They might be little hellions sometimes but they definitely had hearts of gold. And there was nothing sweeter than watching a father with his daughter.

"Oh Jesus, Mary and Joseph...where did you get this book?" the man asked as a few parents looked in his direction and shot him dirty looks.

I glanced over to see what the problem was and noticed the book in his hand read *The Big Book of Lesbian Horse Stories*. My mouth fell open in horror and I looked around to see if anyone had noticed that there was porn in the children's section of the library.

"Honey, go pick out another book," he told her calmly as he hid the book behind his back.

"But I want that one, it's got horses in it," she argued.

"Well, you can't read that one. That's a big person book. It's not for kids."

Finley rolled her eyes and huffed, handing him the other book she brought over with her, *Poop Eaters*.

This time, her father was the one to roll his eyes. *Poop Eaters?* Again? Really, Finley, you need to find another hobby."

"She's got this thing about poop," he told me as he took the book from her. "When she was little, she used to finger-paint her room with the poop in her diaper."

He chuckled at the memory and I covered my mouth with my hand to keep the vomit inside. I stared at the little girl's hands expecting to see it covered in shit.

"A few times when we were at the park she would run up to me and say she had a present for me. She'd hold out her hand and it would be filled with cat poop she found in the sand box. Ahhhh, good times," he said with a bob of his head.

A few times? This happened more than once? Poop finger-painting? Poop presents? Shouldn't kids be born with the knowledge that you never touch poop? Is Gavin aware that this is a rule no one should ever break?

I looked over at him rummaging through a box of books someone placed next to the reading circle and wondered if he would find poop in there and bring it to me. What if he tried to finger-paint *me* with it? I'd scream. And you can't scream in the library. What do I do? WHAT DO I DO?

"So yeah, good luck with the whole father thing, dude," the man said to me as he stood up to leave.

I sat there on the couch trying to stop the panic attack I was pretty sure I was having. I need a paper bag to breathe into. Why the fuck didn't I bring a paper bag? Oh Jesus. Poop hands. POOP HANDS!

"Carter! Hey, Carter!" Gavin shouted as he ran towards me and several other adults shushed him.

I stared at his hands, praying to God there wasn't shit on them. How would I explain to Claire that I made our son walk home from the library because I didn't want shitty handprints inside my car? I winced as he raced towards me, bracing myself for a shit pie to the face or a shit ball to the arm. He was running so fast he couldn't stop himself in time and he slammed into my legs with an "oomph."

Oh fuck, please let there not be shit on my legs right now.

As soon as he hit my legs, he scrambled up onto my lap, careful not to drop whatever was clutched in his hand. One can never be too careful with a handful of shit, obviously.

He put his knees on my thighs and I felt him crawl up onto my lap. My eyes were squeezed so tightly closed that I was giving myself a headache.

Oh sweet Jesus. Here it comes. A shit sandwich. He's going to make me pretend to eat it like kids do when they make you a Play-Doh cookie. The term "shit-eating grin" will finally have meaning in my life.

"I got you sumfin' Carter. Guess which hand?" he said excitedly.

Oh, God, please don't make me choose. It will always be the hand without shit in it.

Gavin quickly grew impatient with my silence. "Come on, Carter, open your eyes. Don't be a wuss."

I swallowed nervously, trying to think of all the ways to disinfect shit from your skin.

Does bleach burn? Probably after I took a layer of skin off with sandpaper, it would. I slowly opened one eye at a time until I could see that Gavin had his arms behind his back.

"Come on, pick one of my arms and see what I gots," he said excitedly.

"Gee, I guess I'll pick that hand," I said unenthusiastically as I tapped his right arm.

Good-bye clean, shitless skin. I'll remember you fondly.

Gavin bounced up and down on my thighs and swung his right arm around in front of him.

"You picked the right one! Here ya go!" he said excitedly.

I looked down nervously and breathed a deep sigh of relief when I saw what was in his hand.

A book – a beautiful, crisp, brand new library book. Not a book covered in shit, or a book made out of shit. Just a book. The title read, *Come on Get Happy!*

I took it from his little hand and held it up in the air to look at the picture of puppies frolicking in a field on the front cover.

"This is a pretty awesome book. How come you picked this one?" I asked him as he put the hand that used to hold the book up on my shoulder and looked me in the eye.

"Because I like you. And Mommy says it's nice to do things that make people happy. I want you to be happy."

All I could do was sit there and stare at him. I got it now. I got why Claire hadn't crumbled when she found out she was pregnant, why she dropped out of college and gave up everything for this little boy. I suddenly realized that my heart was sitting there on my lap and even though I wasn't here for the first four years of his life, I loved him unconditionally simply because he was mine. He was a part of me. I knew without a doubt, I would give my life to make sure he was safe. I wrapped my arms around his little body, hoping he didn't still think of me as a stranger and would let me hug him.

He leaned into me without hesitation and I rested my forehead against his.

"Buddy, I am already the happiest guy in the world," I told him softly.

Gavin stared at me for a few minutes and then pulled his other arm out from behind his back. "Good, then after you read that one, you can read this one."

I pulled away from him and glanced down in his hand at a book titled *The Vagina Monologues.*

⊙ ⊙ ⊙

After we left the library, I took Gavin to get ice cream and then we headed back to Claire's house. True to form, Gavin talked the whole way home and I started to wonder if he was like a record player that was skipping and maybe I needed to smack the side of him to get him to stop.

I resisted the urge. Barely.

When we got back to the house, I sat down on the couch and Gavin grabbed a photo album from one of the end table drawers and curled up on my lap with it. He flipped through all of the pages, explaining each picture to me. I saw every single birthday, Christmas, Halloween and everything in between that I missed, and with Gavin's commentary about each event, it almost felt like I had been there.

I also learned quite a few things about Claire. Like the fact she has cousin she can't stand.

"That's Heather. She's Mommy's cousin. Mommy says she's a whore," Gavin said, pointing at the group photo that looked like it was taken at some sort of family reunion.

I also learned that Gavin seemed to have a penchant for squirting things all over the house, showcased by at least five pages in the photo album. I guess I should have taken a picture of the toothpaste incident a few weeks ago.

"Gavin, how come there are so many pictures of you making messes?" I asked as I flipped to the next page that showed a picture of him sitting on the kitchen floor in a pile of coffee grounds, cereal, oatmeal and what looked like syrup. "I hope you cleaned up all this stuff for Mommy."

"Cleaning is ridiculous," he replied.

Considering the current state of my own home, I couldn't really argue that fact.

We continued to look at the rest of the pictures in that album and four others before I noticed that Gavin was unusually quiet on my lap. I glanced down and saw that he had fallen asleep sitting up. I awkwardly scooped my hands under his legs and carried him to his room exactly how he fell asleep - with his back against my chest and his legs dangling down off of my hands. I knew there was some sort of rule about "never wake a sleeping baby" and I figured that had to apply to toddlers as well since they could get into much more trouble than a baby.

After getting him tucked into bed, I came back out into the living room and relaxed on the couch. I turned on the TV, flipping through the channels until I found something to watch. An hour later, right when I started to doze off, my phone buzzed for probably the tenth time since I left the house earlier with Gavin. I smiled as I pulled my phone out of my pocket, knowing it would be Claire again.

How's it going? Is everything ok? ~ Claire

I couldn't even be offended that she was so worried. It was understandable. Surprisingly, being alone with Gavin wasn't bad at all. He was really well behaved, better than any child I had ever been around.

Perfect. Gavin just got his first lap dance. He's hopped up on Red Bull and crack right now and I found out he doesn't like whiskey. ~Carter

I laughed to myself and hit send. My phone buzzed immediately with her reply, like I knew it would.

I hope you at least sprang for the hot chick and not some butter face with VD. And your son prefers vodka, like his mother. ~Claire

My laugh at her reply was so loud I glanced down the hall to make sure it didn't wake Gavin. I quickly typed a reply back. Even though she made a joke, I knew without a doubt she was masking a tiny bit of fear.

Everything is fine, Mom. Same as it was five minutes ago when you asked ;) ~Carter

My phone buzzed not five seconds later.

Oh shut up! It's not him I'm worried about. I was afraid you were duct taped to a chair or had your head shaved by now. ~Claire

The doorbell rang and as I got up to find out who it was, I quickly sent off another text letting her know that our son was not able to overpower me.

Yet.

I opened the door to find Drew standing there with a box in his hands.

"What are you doing here?" I asked.

Drew pushed past me into the house.

"Nice to see you too, pig fucker. I've got all of Claire's flyers, brochures and whatever other shit Jenny was doing for her. She asked me to drop them off here for her. What are *you* doing here? And why are you still wearing the same clothes from last night? Did you finally bump uglies with your MILF?"

I took the box out of his hand and rolled my eyes at him.

"Will you shut up already, dick? Gavin is sleeping."

Drew looked past me towards Gavin's room.

"Good, I've got a present for the little spawn," he said with a smile as he pulled a shirt out of his back pocket. He held it up in front of me and all I could do was shake my head.

"You didn't. Oh my God, Claire is going to kill you," I told him.

I looked down at my watch, realizing that Gavin had been out for quite a while.

"Hey, how long do kids sleep?" I asked.

"You're asking me? How the fuck should I know? When was the last time you checked on him?"

I looked at him blankly.

Shit, I was supposed to check on him? He was asleep. What the hell could happen while he was asleep?

I turned and ran down the hall to Gavin's room with Drew right on my heels.

"Shit! Oh fucking shit."

Gavin's bed was empty, the covers thrown back like he woke up and flung them off.

I charged into the room, looking behind the door, under the bed and in the closet.

"Oh, Jesus. I lost him. I already fucking lost him!" I yelled in panic as I rummaged through his closet and pulled out a stuffed clown from the bottom of the pile.

Didn't that kid from *Poltergeist* get sucked into his closet by an evil clown? Shit!

"You didn't lose him. It's not like he could have gotten far. There's only one way out of this house and he would have had to walk right past you to get to it."

Drew walked out of the bedroom while I stood there trying not to cry as I choked the fuck out of the stupid clown that took my kid.

Claire was going to hate me. Our son was sucked into the pits of Hell while I was watching *General Hospital*. God damn you, Brenda and Sonny for making me lose focus.

What if he crawled into the ventilation and passed out somewhere in the walls? Oh my God, he could have gotten into the fridge and suffocated. Didn't they tell you to put rope around your fridge? Or wait, that was just when you put it out to the curb, wasn't it?

Fuck! I didn't know anything!

"Carter! I found him!" Drew yelled from down the hall.

I raced out of Gavin's room and down the hall, finding Drew standing in the doorway of the bathroom laughing his ass off.

"What the hell are you laughing about?" I asked angrily as I pushed passed him.

And then I saw it – Gavin sitting on the edge of the sink, with white shit all over his face.

"Gavin, what did you get all over your face? Is that Mommy's make-up?"

He shook his head.

"Nope, it's this," he said, handing me the empty tube.

I took it from him and looked down. Diaper rash cream. My son put diaper rash cream all over his face. And when I say all over his face, I mean it. Practically every surface was covered, including his lips.

Drew came up behind me and looked over my shoulder.

"Dude, he put ass cream on his face. You do know I'm going to have to start calling your son Ass Face now, right?" Drew laughed.

"Shut up, dicky," Gavin told him.

"You shut up. You're the one with the ass face," Drew retorted.

I got a washcloth out of the linen closet and ran it under the sink.

"Both of you shut it and quit arguing," I told them as I started to scrub the white shit off of Gavin's face. What the fuck do they make this stuff out of, cement? It's like it's been spackled on. And why does this towel smell like mint?

The white goo was starting to come off, but in its place was now blue goo. What the…?

I held up the towel and noticed it was full of whatever this blue stuff was. I brought it up to my nose and smelled it.

"There's toothpaste on this towel," I muttered.

Drew reached into the linen closet to grab me another one.

"Eeeew, what the fuck?" he said, dropping the towel on the ground.

I looked at his hands and they were covered with toothpaste. I walked back to the closet and picked up a few of the towels. Each one was smeared with toothpaste. And stuck way in the back corner of one of the shelves was the empty tube.

I turned back around to face Gavin.

"Why did you put toothpaste all over everything?"

He shrugged. "I don't know."

I managed to find a clean towel at the bottom of the pile on one of the shelves and got Gavin cleaned up. Drew took him to play in his room while I cleaned up the toothpaste and diaper rash cream mess and put all of the minty-fresh towels into the wash. I was walking past the front door after I started the washing machine when Claire walked in.

"Honey, you're home," I said with a smile.

She laughed and came up to me, snaking her arms around my waist.

"Would I sound really girly if I told you how awesome it is to walk in the door and see you here?" she asked.

I kissed the tip of her nose.

"Yeah, you'd totally sound like a needy chick. Just don't start getting clingy otherwise it's going to get really awkward."

She smacked my chest and rolled her eyes at me.

"I'm pretty sure you might like my kind of clingy," she said with a smirk as she brought her hips up against mine. I put my hands on her waist and rubbed her against the hard-on I had since she walked in the door.

"I think you might be right, Miss Morgan," I said, as I leaned forward to kiss her.

"Get your hands off my woman!"

I pulled my lips away from Claire's and we both laughed at the sound of Gavin's angry rant.

"Gavin, what are you wearing?" Claire asked as she stepped out of my arms and walked over to him.

Drew walked up behind him and smiled.

"Hey there, hot stuff! Like the shirt I got him?"

Gavin stood proudly, pulling the hem of his shirt down so Claire could read it.

"Hung like a five-year-old?" she read, giving Drew the evil eye.

"I could have gotten him one like mine. They had it in his size," Drew said.

I think we can all say the shirt Gavin was wearing was a lot better than having one on that said, "Stare at me in disgust if you want to blow me."

Claire kicked Drew out, after thanking him for dropping off her stuff from Jenny, and decided to let Gavin keep the shirt on because, let's be honest, it was just too funny to take off. I was nowhere near ready to leave Claire and Gavin yet, but I needed a shower and some clean clothes. Since Claire worked all day, I invited her and Gavin over to my place for dinner. And I told her to pack a bag for both of them.

⊙ ⊙ ⊙

I was frantically racing around my bedroom trying to find some-thing to wear that said, "I want to bang your brains out after our kid goes to sleep but I don't want to look too slutty or desperate." I washed and conditioned my hair three times, shaved my legs twice and put on enough lotion that Carter might be able to just borrow my legs the next time he wanted to jerk off. I stood by my dresser, holding up a pair of white lace thongs and tried to keep my towel wrapped around me by squeezing my arms against the sides of my boobs. I threw the white underwear back in the drawer. White was for virgins. I didn't want to be a virgin. I wanted to be a freak - a freaky hot chick that wore slutty red underwear. But not too slutty.

My cell phone rang and I struggled with the towel as I pawed through my dresser and reached for the phone. I answered it and held it against my ear with my shoulder.

"Wear the low-rise, red, lace boy shorts with the matching push-up bra."

"Liz, what the fuck? How do you...I didn't..." I stammered into the phone.

She let out a dramatic sigh.

"Well, crotch rot, since you weren't going to tell me you'd be riding the Carter Express tonight, I had to find out elsewhere."

"Liz, I just found out thirty minutes ago. I was going to call you, I swear. How the fuck do you know anyway?"

"Oh, Jim ran into Carter buying condoms at the grocery store - extra small. I didn't realize they made them in children's sizes."

"Ha ha, very funny, thunder cunt," I replied sarcastically. "Speaking of giant vaginas, I haven't gotten any butt dials from you lately. Has Jim taken a break from spelunking in your bottomless pit lately?"

Gavin walked into my room then with his *Toy Story* backpack on. He was very excited at the idea of having a sleepover at Carter's house. He argued with me that he could pack his own bag. I'd have to sneak a look into it when he was busy. The last time he went to my dad's, he packed one dirty sock, eight stuffed animals and a plastic fork.

"Liz, I have to go. Your godson just walked in and I need to finish getting ready," I explained as Gavin scrambled up onto my bed and started jumping up and down on it.

I snapped my fingers and pointed to the bed. He immediately kicked his legs out in front of his body and landed on his butt.

"Make sure you pack children's Benadryl and duct tape. You don't need anyone yelling, "Mommy," when there's a penis in you. And no matter how much Carter tries to tell you otherwise, it is never hot if he says it. Never. Trust me."

I really didn't need the mental image of Jim screaming, "Mommy," while he railed Liz. I quickly ended the call and grabbed the red bra & underwear set from my second drawer. Liz bought it for me two years prior to wear on a blind date she'd set me up on. The guy showed up an hour early asking if we could just hit it so he could go. Apparently his mom needed her car back and wanted him to clean his room before she got home. Needless to say, the tags never got removed from the red lace underwear.

I shimmied into the bra while Gavin sat there staring at me through the mirror. I learned early on that it was impossible to do anything by yourself when you had a toddler. Covering myself up and running to hide behind a door if he walked in when I was getting dressed just made him even more curious and inquisitive. And by inquisitive, I mean annoying. It was best to just go about my business and if questions arose, I could handle them in a proficient and mature manner. In theory.

"Are you puttin' your boobs on mom?" Gavin asked.

I laughed and shook my head at his question.

"Well, this bra is mostly padding so I guess I *am* putting my boobs on."

I turned around to face him as I finished pulling the straps up and reached for my jeans I left laying across the foot of the bed.

"Hey, Mom, what are those red thingys?" he asked.

"What red things?" I replied distractedly as I pulled on my jeans and stood there staring at the four different shirts I laid out.

"The red thingies on your boobs."

I closed my eyes and bowed my head.

Okay, this was my chance to be an adult. He asked a reasonable question, so I should give him a reasonable answer. Right? But he's only four. What is the appropriate age to learn the word "nipples?" Should I be honest with him or make something up? He was going to preschool in a few months. What if they were talking about baby bottles or saw a kitten drinking milk from its mother? If I made something up, my kid was going to be all, "Nuh-uh teacher. My mommy said those are called noo-noo-cows and they're just there for decoration."

My son would grow up scarred for life when everyone made fun of him for putting a noo-noo-cow on a baby bottle. I could hear Robert Dinero's voice in my head.

"I have noo-noo-cows, Greg, can you milk me?"

"They're called nipples, Gavin."

Honesty is the best policy. Let's go with that.

He sat there for a few minutes not saying anything. I was mentally patting myself on the back for being a good parent and being able to be truthful with my son.

"Nipples," he said softly.

I nodded my head, proud that he had no problem using the big-people word and not something silly. I still had nightmares about the fact that my father called a vagina a choo-choo-laney when I was growing up.

"Nipples, nipples, nipples. That's fun to say!"

Shit. I may have spoken too soon.

He jumped down off of the bed and ran out of my room, singing "Twinkle, Twinkle Little Star" but replaced each and every word with "nipple."

17.

Duct Tape for the Win

Trojan, Durex, Lifestyles, Trojan Magnum (oh yeah, my three foot cock definitely needed those), Contempo, Vivid and Rough Rider.

Seriously? There was a condom brand called Rough Rider? Why not just go with Fuck Her Hard and be done with it?

I stood in the "Family Planning" aisle of the grocery store, trying to decide which condom brand was more effective. Family Planning… give me a break. How many people came to this aisle because they were planning a family? They came to this aisle to AVOID planning a family.

I couldn't buy Trojan. Every time I opened the box I heard that goddamn jingle from the commercial, "Trojan Man!" and then I thought of a guy on a horse. Durex made me think of Playtex, which made me think of tampons, which made me think of periods, which made me want to dry heave. Lifestyles made me think of Robin Leach and caviar. Fish eggs were not sexy and neither was Robin Leach.

I wasn't going to make myself look like a major asshole and buy Trojan Magnum. If I bought those things, I'd have to talk like Dirty Hairy in the bedroom. "Do you feel lucky today, seeing my giant penis, punk?"

Claire probably wouldn't take too kindly to me calling her a punk before I had sex with her.

Contempo just sounded boring, like contemporary music, John Tesh or some shit like that. Snooze fest. If people fell asleep while you were having sex with them, you needed to get your shit together.

Rough Rider was already out so that left me with Vivid. Vivid video was a porn making company. And the things I wanted to do to Claire could definitely be in porn. I think dressing up like a FedEx guy so I could deliver my big package to the horny housewife while she bent over the kitchen sink may have to wait at least a few weeks though.

I grabbed the forty-eight-count bulk box that came with a free bottle of KY Warming Liquid and a vibrating cock ring and threw them in the cart. The cock ring scared me just a little. The idea of something vibrating by my balls made me nervous. What if it short-circuited? Great Balls of Fire didn't need to occur in the bedroom. And the smell of burning nut hair was sure to kill the mood.

"Stop worrying. I'm sure Claire isn't going to even notice that you have a tiny tally whacker."

I turned around to see Jim standing in the aisle with a smirk and a box of tampons in his hand.

"Very funny, asshole. Looks like you're on the rag this week. Make sure to get yourself some Midol and a copy of *Terms of Endearment* so you can have yourself a good cry," I quipped.

"Hey, *Terms of Endearment* is a very touching, beautiful story about the dynamics in a mother/daughter relationship. Show some respect for Shirley McClain and Debra Winger for fuck's sake. That movie won five Oscars for…"

"Jesus, calm down, Nancy. Does Liz know you're using her vagina today?" I asked in mock horror.

Jim smiled, "I'm going to pretend you didn't say that because if I told Liz, she would cut your nut sack off, dude."

He was right about that. Liz was a bulldog with rabies and mad cow disease. She would fuck me up if I crossed her.

"Since I just caught you buying condoms, and Claire is like a sister to me, I feel I must say a few words at this time," he explained, shoving aside some bottles of lube on a shelf next to him so he could put his box of tampons down and cross his arms in front of him.

I nodded. "By all means."

"I like you, Carter, but I met Claire first and I'm engaged to her best friend, so that means, by chick laws, I have to like her more. I feel it's necessary that I use the words of some of the greats in history to establish the sincerity of the situation we find ourselves in."

He paused and I waited for him to continue by resting my elbow on the handle of my cart.

"You mess with the bull, you get the horns."

"If you want to throw down fisticuffs, I've got Jack Johnson and Tom O'Leary waiting for ya, right here."

"I'll get you my pretty and your little dog too."

"I will gouge out your eyeballs and skull-fuck you."

I nodded my head, impressed. *Full Metal Jacket?* I asked.

"Yep."

"Nice touch," I replied.

Jim turned around and grabbed his tampons off of the shelf.

"Well, alrighty then. My work here is done. I've got a few more items to pick up so I'll talk to you later."

⊙ ⊙ ⊙

An hour and a half later, I managed to clean up the house, change the sheets on my bed, make up the extra bed in the spare room for Gavin and set up a couple of the things I bought for him over the past week. Maybe it was a little bit much, but oh well. I'd missed out on four years of birthdays, Christmases, Valentine's Days, Arbor Days, Sundays and every other day I could have bought him something. I had a lot of time to make up for.

My son was going to spend the night at my house.

I kind of wanted to jump up and down and clap my hands like a girl. I was excited to curl up with him on the couch in his pajamas and watch the new movie I picked up earlier. I couldn't wait to tuck him into bed and wake up with him tomorrow morning and get him breakfast. I wanted to experience all of the things that made up his day. I wanted to hear him laugh, listen to him talk and watch him interact with Claire.

Claire.

Beautiful, smart, funny, sexy Claire who was going to be spending the night at my house as well. I couldn't wait to wake up with her next to me in the morning. I missed out on that five years ago, and I wasn't about to go without this time. I wanted her face to be the first thing I saw when the sun came up and her body curled up next to mine to be the first thing I felt. But most of all, I wanted to be coherent for every single second. I didn't want the haze of alcohol to take anything away from this night for either one of us.

I hope she didn't think it was too forward of me to buy condoms. If she didn't want to do anything, there was no way I would pressure her. But if she asked my throbbing python of love to come out and play, I wasn't going to complain.

I just poured a box of noodles into a pot of boiling water when the doorbell rang. I set the timer on the stove and quickly walked through the living room and answered the door. As soon as it opened, Gavin barged past me and into the living room.

"Hi Carter! Mommy has nipples! Do you have nipples?" he asked as he took off his backpack and dumped the contents in the middle of the floor.

"Oh my God, Gavin, filter!" Claire scolded as she walked through the doorway, rolling her eyes at me. I laughed as I shut the door behind her and tried not to grab her ass or sniff her hair.

Jesus, she really did have a great ass.

"What's the deal with the nipples question?" I asked as we both stood in the entry to the living room, watching Gavin sort through the stuff he brought.

"He was in my room when I got dressed earlier and he asked me what they were. I thought I should be honest with him and now I realize it was a big mistake. He spent the whole way here singing,

"All I want for Christmas are my two front nipples." I almost opened the door and shoved him out into oncoming traffic," Claire said with a laugh.

"Mommy stopped the car and unlocked the doors and told me to get out and walk," Gavin informed me.

"Okay, *almost* isn't exactly accurate," she told me with a shrug. "In my defense, I did tell him if he said the word "nipples" one more time I was going to stop the car and make him walk. According to his pediatrician, it's important to always follow through with your threats."

I helped Claire take her coat off and scooped up Gavin's that he'd thrown on the floor and hung both of them up in the closet.

"Maybe now isn't the best time to tell you that he asked me if I he had a vagina this morning and then asked me to read him *The Vagina Monologues* at the library."

Claire groaned and shook her head.

"What the hell am I going to do when he starts preschool in a few months? He's going to be like that kid in the movie, *Kindergarten Cop*, except he's going to announce, "Boys have a penis and girls have a vagina and my mommy has nipples!" I wrapped my arm around her waist and pulled her against my side, noting again how good her body felt next to mine.

"You mean what the hell are *we* going to do?" I corrected her. I needed to make sure she understood that I wasn't going to change my mind about all of this.

"Don't forget, he's also going to tell everyone just how huge my wiener is. At least I hope he is. Maybe I should remind him about the awesomeness that is my wiener."

Claire raised her eyebrows at me and I realized that didn't come out right at all.

"That sounded a lot skeezier than I meant it too."

Claire turned her body into mine so that we were chest-to-chest and my back was to Gavin. She rested her arms on my shoulders, letting her fingers play with the hair on the back of my neck. I got goose bumps on my arms and Mr. Happy just woke up from his evening nap and started drooling.

"Can we please ban the word wiener?" she asked with a laugh.

I glanced over my shoulder at Gavin. He had his back to us and was busy talking to his Batman figurine, asking it if it had nipples. I looked back at Claire and let my hands slide down her hips and around to her ass to pull her up against me.

"Only if you use the word 'cock' from now on," I told her with a smirk.

She pushed her hips into me and I let out a groan when she came in contact with my raging erection.

"T.J. told me you paid him twenty dollars the other night to get me to say that."

Shit. T.J. was going down the next time we played P.O.R.N. He was going to get a ball right to his throat. I placed my lips to the corner of her mouth and then kissed a path across her cheek. When I got to the soft skin right behind her ear, I let my tongue snake out so I could taste her.

She let out a little moan and pushed her hips back into me. She turned her face so her lips hovered by my ear.

"Cock, cock, c-o-c-k," she whispered, drawing out the syllables in the last one.

"Holy fucking hell…" I mumbled, wrapping my arms around her waist and hugging her tightly so her hips stopped moving against me.

The timer in the kitchen went off and all thoughts of Claire's lips and "cock" were put aside. I unwound myself from her and we all made our way into the kitchen so I could finish the spaghetti.

Dinner went very well even though Claire had to remind Gavin every ten seconds to stop talking and eat. I've never heard a kid talk so much in my life about anything and everything and I enjoyed every second of it. After dinner was over, I sent Claire and Gavin to the spare bedroom while I cleaned up the dishes.

A few seconds later, I heard Gavin's yell.

⊙ ⊙ ⊙

I grabbed Gavin's hand and we took off towards the back of the house where Carter said the spare room was. I thought it was really sweet that Carter had made up a room for Gavin.

We got to the door and I pushed it open. Gavin took a step inside and let out a yell.

"WHAT THE FRIGGIN' HELL?"

He immediately ran into the room and I stood there with my mouth open, unable to muster up the ability to tell him to watch his mouth.

Carter had Toys 'R' Us in his spare room. There was a fucking tree house in the corner! A tree house! How did he even get that in here?

I slowly took in every inch of the room and then did it again just to make sure I wasn't seeing things. Nope, there was definitely a pile of at least one hundred stuffed animals in the corner, a bunk bed with race car blankets, three Hotwheels tracks that intersected all over the room, a pile of puzzles, a drawing table filled with coloring books and crayons, and a shelf filled with multicolor bins that held cars, monster trucks, army men, Legos and God knows what else. Gavin zipped all around the room, touching everything.

"Holy shit," I muttered.

Gavin stopped his climb up into the tree house and looked at me.

"Mom, you can't say shit," he scolded.

I laughed hysterically.

"Oh yes I can. I can say shit. I'm an adult for shit's sake. You're the one that can't say shit. Shit! Shitballsack!"

I could feel the burn in the back of my throat and a sting in my eyes that indicated I was going to cry. Shit! That did it. Now I was in love with the jerk. He bought my...our son a fucking toy store. He wouldn't have done this if he weren't serious. I know he told me he was - several times. I wanted so much to believe him, but I didn't just have myself to think about. I couldn't really move forward and turn this into something real until I was one hundred percent certain he would never leave Gavin. He could leave me, he could change his mind about us and I knew I'd survive. But I would never, ever let my son be hurt like that. Looking around this room, thinking about how easily he let us take over his life and change whatever plans he had for his future, I knew without a doubt I wanted him to be Gavin's dad. He wasn't just a sperm donor anymore. He was a father. And I knew he would be a damn good one.

I let the tears slip out of my eyes and run down my cheeks as I smiled at our son, happily checking out all of his new toys. I heard a throat clear behind me and I whipped around to see Carter standing there sheepishly with his hands in his pockets.

"So, um, how much trouble am I in? I didn't plan on getting this much but once I got to the store, I couldn't help myself. They make Hotwheels that change color in the water, Claire! And a garbage truck named Stinky that moves on its own and picks up toys and then burps. Did you know there was something called Moon Sand? Oh, oh and Aqua Sand that strangely looks like siding insulation when you put it in the water but when you pull it out..."

I launched myself into his arms and cut off his words with my lips. He was obviously surprised but caught me easily in his arms and returned my kiss. I poured everything I had into that kiss, all of my happiness, all of my trust and all of my love. I let him know with my lips just how thankful I was to have been blessed with a man like him in my life. I could have kissed him for days and never come up for air. The only thing that made me stop was the sound of absolute silence in the room behind us.

I broke from the kiss and Carter let out a groan of complaint, which made my girly parts tingle knowing that he didn't want to stop. Keeping my arms around him, I turned my head around.

"Where's Gavin?"

"Ooooh this is warm. And it makes my hands tingle," we heard Gavin say from another room.

I sighed. "Shit, what did he get into now?" I muttered as I reluctantly pulled out of Carter's arms.

Carter started to smile but immediately got a horrified look on his face. He turned and raced out of the room before I could ask him what was wrong. I followed after him and was right on his heels when he rounded the corner to his bedroom. It was like something out of a movie. Carter jumped up and dove through the air, arms stretched out in front of him like Superman. He sailed across the room and landed on his stomach on the bed right next to Gavin, but not before smacking something out of his hand. I just stood there with my mouth open, trying to understand what the hell was going on.

"Heeeeey," Gavin complained with a frown.

Carter was face down on the bed, his shoulders shaking so hard that Gavin's body was bouncing. Was he crying? Oh my God, was he having a nervous breakdown?

"Carter, what the hell?" I asked.

"What the hell, Carter?" Gavin repeated.

"Gavin!" I scolded while Carter continued to have a seizure or whatever the hell he was doing.

"But Mooooom, he took my lotion," Gavin pouted.

I walked up to the bed to see what Gavin was pointing at. A small tube of something was by Carter's hand on the bed. As soon as I got close enough to see it, Carter grabbed it and flipped over on his back. And now I could see that he wasn't dying from an epileptic seizure, he was laughing his ass off.

"It's not funny, Carter. You took my lotion," Gavin complained.

This only made Carter laugh harder until he was gasping for breath. I looked at him in confusion. He just lifted his arm and handed me the tube of...KY Warming Liquid?

Oh Jesus fucking hell. Lube? He put lube on his hands. It only took seconds for me to notice that condoms surrounded Gavin. A couple of them open and out of their wrappers.

"Your balloons suck, Carter," Gavin complained.

I collapsed on the bed next to Carter and laughed right along with him.

⊙ ⊙ ⊙

Twenty minutes into *Toy Story 2*, Gavin fell fast asleep with his head on Carter's lap. I got up to go to the bathroom and grabbed my cell phone off of the kitchen table so I could sneak a picture. It was just too cute not to document.

I tapped Carter on the shoulder once I stowed my phone away and pointed to Gavin and then motioned back to his room. He awkwardly tried to finagle his arms around Gavin and you could tell he was freaked out about waking him up.

"It's okay," I whispered to him. "He won't wake up."

Carter shook his head and muttered something that sounded like "Yeah right, until suddenly he disappears and you realize he's been eaten by a clown."

He moved quickly, scooping Gavin into his arms like he'd done it a thousand times before and Gavin never batted an eyelash at the disruption. I followed behind Carter down the hall and smiled at the sight of Gavin with his head nestled into the crook of Carter's neck and his arms hanging limply at his sides. We walked into the bedroom, stepping over all of the toys so we wouldn't trip, and I stood back while Carter gently put Gavin down on the bottom bunk and covered him up. It took everything in me not to sob when he brushed Gavin's hair off of his forehead like I usually did every night.

"My lunch box makes cow nipples," Gavin mumbled in his sleep before rolling over to face the wall.

Carter looked back at me.

"What the hell was that?" he whispered with a laugh.

I stepped around him, bent over and kissed Gavin's head.

"Your son talks in his sleep," I informed Carter as I took his hand and pulled him off the bed. "I was kind of hoping it was hereditary. I don't talk in my sleep and if you don't either, then maybe it has to do with what he eats before bed."

Carter held onto my hand as we walked across the room. "Sorry to say, I don't talk in my sleep. What does he eat before bed?"

"LSD, shrooms, the usual bedtime snack for toddlers."

Before we got to the door, Carter let go of my hand, walked over to the wall and plugged in a nightlight that was shaped like a race-car. He joined me at the doorway and took my hand again.

"See? This is what's wrong with the youth of America," he whispered. "Too many chocolate chip cookies and not enough acid."

I just stood there looking at him. A room full of toys *and* a night-light? This man had thought of everything.

"What?" he asked, when I didn't move.

"You just amaze me, that's all," I told him with a smile as I pulled him out into the hall, shutting the door to Gavin's room behind me.

We walked silently down the hall to Carter's bedroom, both of us knowing without a doubt that this was the next step. I wanted to sleep with him again the first moment I saw him in the bar. It felt like this was a long time coming, but here, in this moment, it finally felt right.

Carter shut the door to his room and I reached around him to lock it just in case. Gavin slept like the dead, but he was in a strange place so I didn't know how well he'd do. Maybe that was selfish of me, but after five long years and no alone time, I think I deserved this. Plus, I'd much rather get a knock on the door warning us he was awake instead of him just barging in and asking why we were wrestling naked.

The only light in the room came from a small lamp on the bed-side table that cast a soft glow around the room. We stood there by the door just staring at each other. The weird thing was it wasn't awkward at all. I wanted to take it all in. I wanted to remember every single second of this moment. I didn't want to just have bits and pieces of a drunken night flowing in and out of my mind. I wanted to remember every touch, every look and every feeling. I would never regret the first time we had sex because it brought me Gavin. But this time would mean more, because this time, I loved this man with all of my heart.

In just a few minutes I was going to be totally naked in front of him.

Oh my God, in just a few minutes I was going to be naked. In front of Carter.

Shit, I have stretch marks on my ass. Okay, just keep his eyes off of my naked ass.

He reached down and took my hand, pulling me to his chest. He didn't let go of my hand as he wrapped both of our arms behind my back, clasping our fingers together. His other hand came up to rest on my cheek while he looked into my eyes.

"Before we do this, you need to know something," he whispered.

He's going to tell me he's gay.

"I am one hundred percent, absolutely in love with you and Gavin."

My lip quivered and my heart soared. I closed my eyes and tried to keep the tears inside as I rested my forehead against his. Once I got my emotions under control, I pulled back so I could see his face.

"I love you too, Carter," I whispered back.

A smile lit up his face and I brought my hand up and let my fingers trace the shape of his lips. He kissed me fingertips and started walking me backwards towards the bed. I loved the way he looked at me, like I was his whole world. I didn't think we even made eye contact our first time together.

When the back of my knees hit the edge, he leaned me backwards, holding me tight and lowering me slowly, until I felt the softness of the bed against my back and the hard heat of Carter against my front. His arm held me tight around my waist and he lifted me just enough so he could move us both further onto the bed. I brought my legs up and wrapped them around his hips. I placed both of my hands against his cheeks and craned my neck up so I could kiss him. The kiss started out gentle and sweet but quickly changed. I could feel his hardness right in the apex of my thighs and a burst of heat surged through me and dampened my under-wear. Carter shifted his hips slightly and I whimpered into his open mouth. That sound must have gave him the "all systems go" signal because he pushed his tongue deep into my mouth and moved the hardness in his jeans right against me. I moved my hands down to hem of his shirt and slid them underneath. The heat of his smooth skin instantly warmed my chilled hands as I moved them up the front of his stomach and chest. I pushed my forearms higher to raise his shirt up the front of his body. He broke the kiss to reach back behind him and grasp a handful of his shirt, yanking it up over his head and tossing it to the side.

He raised himself above me on one arm, repeating the motions I just performed on him. He flattened his hand on the lower part of my stomach, his fingers slipping under the hem of my shirt. He watched his hand as it slowly moved up my stomach and between my breasts. I grabbed the bottom of my shirt and pulled it up, arch-ing my back so I could get it off of me and toss it in the same direc-tion that his shirt went. His flattened palm that rested on my chest slid to the side, running over the top of my breast that spilled out of the top of my red, lace push-up bra. I sighed, closing my eyes and tilting my head back as his hand engulfed my breast over the top of my bra.

"You are so beautiful," he whispered as he kneaded the soft mound, making me moan. Before I could think any coherent thoughts, his fingers slipped the edge of my bra away and his head dipped down so his warm, wet lips could capture my nipple and pull it into his mouth.

Chocolate Lovers

I was done for at that point. My hands slapped down onto his shoulders and my nails dug into his skin as he swirled his tongue around and around. How did I never know that there was a nerve that connected from my nipple right to my vagina? Holy hell! Every time he sucked I felt a tingle down there and it was driving me insane.

"You have too many clothes on," I muttered as I reached between us to unbutton and unzip his jeans. He pulled away from me and stood up next to the bed to pull his pants and boxer briefs down while I unfastened my own jeans.

Holy shit, there's his penis - his mighty, mighty penis that was going to be inside of me any second now. Does it look bigger? Maybe it's the lighting. This lighting better not be like dressing room lighting and make my ass look bigger.

"You're making me self-conscious staring at my penis so hard. It doesn't do any tricks, so I hope you're not waiting for it to juggle or anything," Carter said with a smile as he leaned down and hooked his fingers into the waistband of my jeans and underwear and slowly started to pull them down my legs.

Don't think about the c-section scar or the stretch marks around it. If you don't think about them, they aren't real.

Shit, he's going to see me naked. Maybe if he glanced away or closed his eyes, I would look better. It could be like that Old Spice commercial.

Look down, back up, now look at me. I'm a Maxim model.

"I'm just wondering if you have a permit for that thing and if it's going to fit in me," I joked, slyly resting my hands over top of the scar nestled at the top of the little triangle of pubic hair I had. Okay, I wasn't really joking. How the fuck did that thing get in there last time and why didn't I walk funny the next morning?

Carter saw through my actions and immediately pulled my hands away and held them down at my sides.

224

If I suck in my stomach any harder I'm going to pull a muscle.

"Don't cover yourself up, please. I love every inch of your body," he said sincerely as he rested one knee on the bed next to my thigh and placed a soft kiss right on top of the c-section scar. He loved every inch of my body *before* Gavin stretched it out like a rubber band on a slingshot. Granted, his memory of my body that night wasn't very clear, but I'm pretty sure he'd remember that my ass didn't have a map of stretch marks on it back then and I could very well teach a geography class with it if getting naked in front of students wasn't frowned upon.

He let go of one of my hands and used his arm to hold himself up as he leaned over me and looked at my body. The tips of his fingers followed the line of my scar back and forth several times. He had a sad look in his eyes for a moment, and I absolutely would not allow that when we were seconds away from having sexy time. I took his fingers and moved them up, placing them over top of my breast.

All right, I'm getting better at this. That wasn't awkward at all. I wanted his hand on my boob, so I put his hand on my boob. Done.

He looked up and smiled at me then knelt down on the floor next to the bed. I gave him a questioning look as he slid both of his hands down my hips, across my thighs and skimmed them back behind my knees. I started to tell him to get back up here when all of a sudden he pulled me towards him until my knees were bent at the edge of the bed and my legs hung down on either side of him. Before I could utter a protest, he leaned down and kissed the inside of my thigh.

Oh, Jesus. Oh holy fuck, he's going to put his mouth on me.

The tip of his tongue made a trail from the inside of my thigh to my hipbone where he placed his lips and sucked gently. I squeezed my eyes shut and fisted the sheets as he kissed his way from my hip to my pubic bone.

Oh fuck, he was right there. I was wet as hell and he could probably smell me now. I should have eaten strawberries or melon or a dozen roses or an entire mint plant. Did that work for women? I read an article that it worked for men. Their spunk tasted like what they ate. Did my vagina taste like spaghetti right now? God dammit! I shouldn't have eaten dinner.

His hands glided back up my legs to the tops of my thighs until his thumbs slid through the lips of my sex. He stopped kissing the area all around my triangle of curls, pulled his head up a little and watched what he was doing with his fingers. I had one eye open at this point so I could see what his next move was. Even though I was freaking out about the fact that my vagina might taste like Chef Boyardee, it was kind of hot to watch Carter stare at me as his hands rested on my thighs and he slid his thumbs up and down through my wetness.

His thumbs slid up one last time, spreading me open as he went. He groaned, and before I could apologize for not letting my lady parts gargle with mouthwash, he dipped his head and wrapped his lips and tongue around me.

A strangled cry flew from my mouth as I arched my back and smacked my hand down on the bed.

All embarrassment was forgotten when his mouth made contact with me. Every thought flew out of my mind and all I could do was feel what he was doing to me. He licked and sucked me into his mouth, letting his lips and tongue slide down to my opening and back up. He flattened his tongue and lapped over top of my clit, up and down, over and over again. The roughness of his tongue and his warm breath hitting my wet skin made me gasp and start moving my hips with the rhythm of his tongue. He moved his lips away, using just the firm tip of his tongue to flick back and forth against the most sensitive spot at a feverish pace.

I could already feel the tingles of my orgasm lurking just beyond my reach. I could hear the sounds of his lips and tongue on me and I didn't even give a shit right now how much those sounds echoed around the quiet room. Carter was going to make me have an orgasm with his mouth and just thinking that in my head made every inch of me throb and my hips thrust faster against him. His tongue slid down my slit and pushed its way inside me. My legs started to shake with the need for release and I could hear myself panting with need. He pushed his tongue in and out of me slowly, over and over, before sucking his way back up. He kissed my clit like he kissed my mouth all those times before - soft lips, swirling tongue, sucking skin. One of his hands moved away from my thigh and I felt the tip of his finger swirling against my opening. Around and around his finger teased while his mouth continued to devour me.

In the haze of pleasure I heard myself chanting, "yes, yes" over and over, encouraging him to push his finger inside. His lips and his tongue never stopped their ministrations against me while he complied with my wishes. His long finger slowly glided into me until he was so deep I could feel his knuckles pressed against my skin. With boldness I never knew I possessed, I grabbed onto the back of his head and held him against me, my hips thrusting erratically while his finger began moving in and out of me. He moved his head from side to side so that his mouth glided back and forth over me while he continued pushing and pulling his finger out of me. Before I knew it, my orgasm was rushing through me. I clutched his hair with my fists and held him in place while I bucked my hips and shouted in pleasure.

"Oh God! Ohhhhhh YES!"

Carter continued to lick every drop while I panted and whimpered through my release and slowly came down from the high. If I didn't pull him away, he would probably never stop. But I needed him now. I let go of my death grip on his hair, yanked on his arms and tugged him up my body. He crawled up the length of me, hovered over top of my body and smiled.

"You taste so fucking good. I could do that all night."

Once again, Carter's dirty talk surprisingly turned me on. I'm pretty sure I let out a growl as I slid my hand down between our bodies and wrapped it around his hardness that rested against my inner thigh. I channeled my dirty slut and pumped my hand up and down his smooth, hard length. I rubbed my thumb back and forth over the wetness that leaked out of the tip, spreading it all around.

"Fuck, shit I need to be inside you," Carter mumbled incoherently. He quickly slid his hands all around the top of the bed next to us and blindly reached for one of the condoms. When his hand finally made purchase, he stood up on his knees between my legs and I watched him take the condom out of the wrapper, place it on the tip of his penis and slide it down. I never really thought something like that would be hot, but son of a bitch! Watching him touch himself, even if it was just to put on a condom was fuck-awesome. As soon as he was sheathed, I reached back down between us and wrapped my hand around his length, needing to touch him. He leaned down over top of my body, wrapping his arm around my waist so he could pull me against him and slide us up to the middle of the bed. I slung my free arm around his shoulders and pulled him closer so I could position him right at my opening. I bent my knees so that his body was cradled in between my legs. He pushed his hips forward just enough that the swollen head slipped inside.

So different from our first time and yet, the same. His body still fit against mine like it was made to be there. His skin against mine still made my entire body tingle with anticipation. I moved my hand off of him and wrapped it around his back, clutching on to him tightly.

He looked into my eyes and I blurted out, "I love you."

He let out a shuddering breath. "So much," he whispered in reply. "I will never, ever regret our first time, but I would give anything if it would have gone a little more like this."

I pulled him even closer to me until he bent his elbows and rested his forearms on either side of my head, angling his wrists so his hands could smooth the hair off of my forehead.

"The only thing that matters to me now is that I'm here with you," I replied softly.

He looked into my eyes while he placed a soft kiss on my lips and slowly pushed himself the rest of the way inside me.

Jeeeeeeesus.

All the air left my lungs and I thanked the wet vagina Gods that there was enough lubrication down there and he didn't have to force his way in. He didn't move and I could tell he was holding his breath. I should be the one holding my breath. He pretty much just stuck a giant red whiffle ball bat into a straw. I felt full and I was completely shocked how I could stretch to fit him. And even more shocked about how good it felt to have him inside me this time. He started breathing again as he slowly pulled back out and just as gently pushed back in.

"Fuck, you feel so good," he groaned as he continued to leisurely move in and out of me. I could tell he was trying to hold back in fear of hurting me. I knew it killed him to think about how he hurt me our first time together, but I was a virgin then, the pain was inevitable. I didn't need him to control himself so rigidly. Not now. I wanted to feel his passion and the force of his need for me. I boldly slid my hands down his back, clutching onto his ass and pushed him deeper inside me.

"More," I moaned against his lips.

He immediately pulled almost all the way out and then pushed back in hard, slapping his pelvis against me. Holding himself perfectly still, he let out a shuddering breath and rested his forehead against mine.

"Shit, I'm sorry. I don't want to hurt you. I just want you so badly," he whispered.

"I'm not going to break, Carter. Please, don't hold back. I need you."

He pulled his head away from mine so he could look into my eyes and I tried to convey to him as best I could that I was okay. He must have seen the truth. His arm moved from next to my head as he let his hand skim down the side of my body until it got to my thigh. He wrapped his hand around my leg and lifted it up high so my knee rested against the side of his body. He placed another sweet kiss to my lips, pulled his hips back and slid his length out of me. I tightened my leg against his side in anticipation, and then he pushed back all the way inside of me in one swift motion. He went much deeper this time and I pushed my hips forward to meet his thrust. He moaned against my lips and I swallowed the sound with my mouth, kissing him with everything I had in me. My hands still clutched his ass and I pushed harder against him so he would continue. He didn't hesitate, beginning a rhythm with his movements in and out of me. He kept up a steady pace, slamming into me as deep as he could go until we were both covered in a thin sheen of sweat, gasping and moaning around kisses.

"Fuck, baby, I'm not going to be able to last if I keep this up," he groaned as he tried to slow down his movements.

"Don't stop. I want to feel you," I whispered against his lips.

I couldn't believe those words came out of my mouth but they were true. I wanted to feel him lose control and get pleasure from my body. I needed to know I could do that to him.

He growled and attacked my mouth with a deep, mind-blowing kiss as his hips slammed into me at an even faster pace. The bed creaked with each thrust. I dug my nails into his back and wrapped both of my legs around his waist to hold on for the ride. His tongue pushed through my mouth just like his hard length pushed into me, and it was so hot I might have had another orgasm if I didn't just think I heard a tiny knock at the bedroom door.

Carter was oblivious so I closed my eyes and hoped our son wasn't outside the door listening and being scarred for life.

Carter pulled his mouth away from my lips and started thrusting erratically. I knew he was close. I really didn't want to stop but I definitely didn't imagine the knock at the door this time.

Shit! Shit! Shit! For the love of God, Gavin, please don't say anything. I want this to be good for Carter and not ruined by a tiny voice saying he had to pee.

I am a horrible mother.

"Oh fuck Claire, oh fuck," Carter groaned.

Oh God, should I shush him? Subtly put my hand over his mouth?

He thrust hard one last time and I felt him pulse inside me with his release.

Oh thank God. I mean, oh darn, is it over already?

"Mommy, I'm thirsty."

Carter laughed in the middle of his release, sliding in and out of me a few more times before he collapsed on top of me. We lay there for a few seconds trying to catch our breaths.

He is never going to want to have sex with me again. Forget about scarring our kid, I just scarred his penis. I just had the best sex ever and I will never get a repeat performance because Carter's penis just died.

Rest in peace, my friend, rest in peace. Here lies Carter's penis: beloved member, hard worker and all around good guy.

"Mommy!" Gavin yelled from out in the hall.

"Just a minute!" I yelled back right next to Carter's ear.

Carter pushed up and looked at me with a smile.

Here it comes, the penis kiss-off.

"Give me thirty minutes and we're doing this again. Next time though, we're duct taping him to his bed."

18.

Baby Daddy

I wasn't gonna lie. Mid-thrust, I swore I heard someone knock on my bedroom door. I couldn't, for the life of me, think of who would be knocking on my bedroom door. Especially at one o'clock in the morning, while my dick was buried in the girl of my dreams. What if it was a serial killer? Frankly, even if one did kick the door down right then, I wasn't stopping. Unless he had a gun. We could quite possibly outrun someone with a knife. A gun, though, we weren't going to get away from that. I might as well die happy and inside of Claire.

Then I wondered briefly if Jim broke in and was going to stand outside the door harassing me by yelling things like, "I hope you know what you're doing with that thing," or "Claire's like a sister to me. If you don't make her orgasm six times, I will gut you like a fish."

Thinking about Jim during a time like this was all sorts of wrong and almost made my dick go soft.

Almost.

Claire did some super power maneuver with her vagina that made it feel like that thing had a fist and squeezed my penis like a stress ball. Holy mother of vaginas!

My head was back in the game at that point—a little too back in the game. She felt so good I never wanted to stop, but her little vagina hand kept squeezing me and I wanted to weep it felt so good. She was warm and tight and fit me so perfectly. I wanted to be a total douche and tell her that her vagina felt like warm apple pie, just

232

like in the movies. But not just any apple pie, McDonald's apple pie. The kind that is so warm and delicious they had to put them on the dollar menu so you could afford to eat eleven of them. I would eat eleventy-billion Claire vaginas. The little sounds she made as I drove into her forced my orgasm up through me faster than I wanted it to. Hearing her tell me she didn't want me to stop and that she wanted to feel me almost made my head explode...both of them.

I kissed Claire in an effort to try and slow down my impending orgasm but that just made it worse. Her mouth was the most delicious thing I ever tasted and her tongue sliding against mine made my dick pulse inside of her. Pushing into her welcoming heat as deeply as I could go, my orgasm burst out of me and I almost had a moment of panic that I was going to come so hard it would burst through the condom.

We all knew I had super powerful sperm. It could happen. Again. Those little fucker's heads were banging against the end of the condom screaming in anarchy, "The man is trying to keep us down! Damn the man!"

After the first throb of my orgasm, a little voice came through the closed bedroom door.

"Mommy, I'm thirsty."

I burst out laughing in the middle of shooting thousands of furious, fist-shaking little sperm into my condom. Claire's legs and arms were wrapped tightly around me and I collapsed right on top of her, careful not to put all of my weight on her. I would like her to still be alive so we could do this again. I'm not much into necrophilia.

We lay there breathing heavily for a few minutes and I started to chuckle again. How could I have forgotten there was a kid in the house? I actually thought an axe murderer might have broken in and was courteously knocking on my door before barging in. For some reason, that seemed more logical than remembering I had a child and he was in the house.

"Mommy!"

"Just a minute!" Claire screamed right by my ear.

I pushed myself up so I could see Claire's face and asked her if we could duct tape him to the bed the next time we did this. I really didn't expect her face to light up as brightly as it did. I was joking about the duct tape. Sort of.

"We'll have to come up with some kind of lie to tell him about what we're doing," she said.

"Do you – fuck, shit-fuck, unnngf!" I sputtered while making the "o" face.

There it was again. That vagina squeeze. What the fuck was that?

"Okay, what the fuck did you just do with your vagina? I think I just came again."

She laughed and the motion pushed my shrinking dick right out of her vagina. I wanted to pout at the loss, but then I realized Gavin was still outside our bedroom door.

Wow, we suck. I hope he isn't bleeding from the head or anything.

Sorry, son, Mommy and Dad were busy playing hide the salami. How's the head wound?

I shifted off of Claire and grabbed some Kleenex from the nightstand to dispose of the condom. I almost smirked at the jizz inside and gave them all the finger. Ha ha little fuckers. Not this time!

"Kegels," Claire said as she quickly grabbed her shirt and threw it over her head and then shimmied into her skirt. It didn't escape my notice that she didn't put her underwear back on.

"Wait, what? Did you say kegels? Why are we talking about cereal?"

At this point Gavin was rattling the door handle so hard I wouldn't be surprised if the thing came off in his hand. I swung my legs off the side of the bed and threw on my boxer briefs, walking over to the door with Claire.

"Not Kellogg's, Jenny, kegels," Claire laughed. "And they are the explanation for my awesome vagina."

I wanted to swat her cute little ass for the Jenny comment but didn't have time. She swung open the door to find Gavin standing there with his head against the doorjamb looking bored.

Claire knelt down and took him in her arms.

"Hey, bud, are you okay? Did you get scared or something?" I asked, ruffling the hair on top of his head.

"What were you guys doing in here?"

Geez, nothing like getting right to the point.

Claire pulled back from him and looked up at me.

"Uh…ummmm," she stammered.

"Were you guys playing a game?" he asked.

I snickered at that, wondering if Claire would punch me if I told him about the rules of hide the salami. *The first rule of hide the salami is to never knock on a locked door during the game unless you are bleeding from the eyes or something is on fire. Like your hair. Anything else can wait until the game is over.*

"Well, we were making a phone call. A very important phone call," Claire explained.

Gavin looked at her like he didn't believe her.

"It was a long-distance phone call," I explained. "And it was really big and important. We couldn't wait one more minute to make the phone call and once we made the call, we couldn't stop or it would have been… painful. So that's why we didn't answer the door when you knocked. Yep, really big phone call. Your mom screamed when she saw how big it was."

Claire reached up and pinched my thigh for that one, but I couldn't help it.

"Your father is over exaggerating how big this phone call really was," she said dryly.

My mouth popped open and Gavin looked at me funny. Claire just knelt there giving me an annoyed look, not even realizing what she just let slip.

A swarm of butterflies started flapping around in my stomach, and I wanted to reach down and scoop both of them up and jump around the room. We hadn't talked yet about telling Gavin who I was. I wanted more than anything for him to call me "Dad," but I didn't want to rush things with Claire. She had done this all on her own for so long; I didn't want to step on her toes. I wanted her to come to this decision on her own, knowing that she trusted me with Gavin.

I could see when the realization hit. Her face got horribly pale and I was a little worried she might barf on my bare feet for a second. She looked back and forth between Gavin and me several times before her eyes landed on mine and she quickly stood up.

"Oh my God. I'm sorry. I have no idea why I just blurted that out," she whispered, glancing back down at Gavin to see if he could hear her. He just stood there looking at both of us like we were idiots.

"Shit. I'm sorry! I'll just tell him I was kidding. I'll tell him I was talking about the phone call or something. Oh my God! I am such a dumbass," she mumbled.

I rubbed my hands up and down her arms to calm her.

"Hey, listen to me. It's fine. Actually, it's more than fine. I wanted to ask you about telling him but I was afraid you would think it was too soon," I explained.

She let out a sigh of relief.

"Are you sure? I don't want you to do something you're not ready for."

"Baby, I was ready for this as soon as I pulled the stupid out of my ass and came to talk to you after that first week."

She leaned up and gave me a quick kiss before turning around to pick Gavin up.

"So, Gavin. Do you know what a daddy is?" she asked him.

He stared at me and thought about it for a few minutes. I started to get worried. What if he didn't want me as his dad? What if he thought I was too strict or too stupid? Shit, I shouldn't have made him clean up the toothpaste on his floor. Cool dads didn't make their kids do shit like that. Cool dads took their kids to strip clubs and let them throw big parties at their houses and smoked pot with them on Sunday afternoons while they picked their fantasy football teams.

"Is Papa your daddy?" he asked.

Claire nodded. "You are very smart, little man! Yes, Papa is my daddy. And Carter is your daddy."

We both stood there in silence while Gavin looked back and forth between us.

He is totally sizing me up right now.

"I'll take you to get a lap dance and smoke pot with you during fantasy draft week," I blurted.

Claire looked at me like I lost my mind.

"Can I call you punk-daddy?" Gavin finally asked nonchalantly, ignoring my outburst.

Gavin asked for a father and saw that he was good.

Yes, I quoted the Bible and compared my son to God. Shut up.

Claire laughed at Gavin's request.

"How about you just call him 'Daddy'?" she asked.

"How about I call him 'Daddy-face'," Gavin countered.

This kid was bartering on what version of "Daddy" he could call me. He was a genius. And I was concerned for no reason at all. I reached over and took Gavin from Claire's arms.

"How about we let Mommy go to sleep and you and I discuss my new name while I put you back to bed?" I asked.

Claire reached up on her toes to kiss Gavin's cheek and then leaned over to do the same to mine. Gavin put his head on my shoulder and wrapped his arms around my neck.

"Okay, baby-daddy."

Claire and I both burst out laughing at that one. As I walked out into the hall, I turned my head and mouthed the words, "thank you" to her before walking Gavin back to his room.

☉ ☉ ☉

I really didn't know why I was so worried about Carter freaking out when I called him Gavin's father. It proved to me yet again just how wonderful he was.

While Carter was putting Gavin back to bed, I reached into my overnight bag and pulled out the tank top and boy shorts I brought for pajamas and changed into them. I brushed my teeth and then got back into bed to curl under the covers and wait for Carter to come back. I just started to doze off when I felt the bed dip and his arms circle around my waist. I smiled and snuggled back into his warm body.

"Everything go okay?" I murmured sleepily.

"Yep, he decided he wasn't thirsty anymore but he made me read him a story. And we compromised on 'Daddy-o' for now," he said with a chuckle.

"You're getting off easy. Two weeks ago he kept referring to me as 'Old Lady'."

I lay there wrapped in Carter's arms and it was the most comfortable I had ever been.

For about five minutes.

This just proved that everything they did in the movies was a load of bullshit. His arm was under my neck on the pillow, which tilted my head at an awkward angle. I could already feel the beginnings of a kink. I was starting to sweat like a whore in church with his other arm heavily draped over my waist and his legs tangled with mine. With my sweaty ass and his itchy leg hair, it felt like I had a hundred mosquito bites on my legs.

It would be wrong to kick him now, right?

I shifted my body just the tiniest bit. I didn't want him to think I didn't want to cuddle, but I was going insane trying to lie perfectly still. Maybe if I waited long enough, he'd fall asleep and I could shove him off me. The Cunninghams had it right when they slept in separate beds on *Happy Days*. That's why all those people back then looked so well rested and blissful. Marion didn't have Howard's hairy legs rubbing all over her.

"Out with it, Claire," Carter mumbled close to my ear.

Shit. Now it was going to get awkward. We *just now* had sex for the first time in years and I was going to tell him to get away from me so I could sleep. I am the most unromantic person in the world.

"Out with what?"

"You've been fidgeting and sighing for the past ten minutes," he replied.

I have Tourette's, restless leg syndrome or a baboon heart that gives me the shakes and makes me sigh every time the furry thing beats.

Crap, wasn't I always teaching Gavin about honesty? And here I was trying to figure out a way to tell Carter I had monkey organs instead of just telling him the truth.

"Soooooo, I've never spent the night with anyone before. Well, except for Liz but we've always been drunk."

Carter made some sort of choking cough sound behind me.

"Can you say that again? Slowly, and with more details," he mumbled.

I laughed and smacked his arm at my waist.

"I'm being serious."

"So am I. You were naked when you did this correct? Tell me you were naked," he replied.

Baboon heart, truth. Baboon heart, truth…

"My neck is killing me and I'm so hot right now my skin could start a blanket fire," I rambled.

Carter was quiet. Too quiet.

Shit, I hurt his feelings.

"Oh, thank fucking God," he said as he pulled both of his arms out from around me. "My arm fell asleep and my legs were getting a cramp."

☉ ☉ ☉

"The bugs got lotion when the dog tickled. Ha ha farmer!"

I had been lying in bed for a few minutes, watching the first light of dawn creep through the curtains. I had to slap my hand over my mouth when Carter started talking in his sleep.

Jesus, talk about "like father, like son." Obviously no one ever clued Carter in on his sleeping habits. Just the thought of some other woman sleeping in the same bed as him made me feel stabby so I pushed those thoughts away for the time being.

He was on his back with one arm flung above his head on the pillow and the other resting on top of his stomach. If I was in a porno, he would be naked under the sheet with his Olympic-sized penis sticking up, and I would be all slutty and pull the sheet down to blow him.

Bow-chica-wow-wow.

I wasn't slutty, and this wasn't a porno. But I had seen enough of them to sort of know what to do. I glanced at the clock on the night-stand and figured I had at least an hour before Gavin would be up. I looked back at Carter's peaceful face and remembered how it felt to have his mouth between my legs last night.

Okay, I could do this. He gave me two mind-blowing orgasms since I met him. Right now, I'm in the lead. Time to even things up a bit so I didn't feel so selfish.

I slowly reached over and tugged the sheet down his body until it pooled around his shins. Leaning up on my elbow, I used the tips of my fingers to gently pull the waistband of his boxer briefs away from his skin so I could peek inside.

Well, hello there, big guy.

Wow, I felt all sorts of slutty now. I wanted to lick his dick.

Heh, heh. That rhymed.

Focus!

I scooted my body closer to his and then eased my way down lower so my face was even with his waist. My elbow slipped a little on the sheet, making my fingers jerk away from his underwear so

I could brace myself and not fall right on top of his sleeping form. The elastic snapped back against his skin and I stopped all movement and held my breath, staring at his face for any sign of waking up.

"Muffins in the basement," Carter mumbled in his sleep.

I glanced back between his legs and noticed that Sir Cums-a-Lot was waking up. Huh, go figure. Dreaming about muffins turned him on. I should make muffins for breakfast. I wonder if Carter had any blueberries. You really couldn't beat fresh blueberry muffins but I guess if I...

Dammit! Why was it so hard for me to focus on the penis? Especially a really nice one like Carter's.

Heh, hard penis!

I closed my eyes and channeled Jenna Jameson but without the nasty lip injections and black eye from Tito. As slowly as I could, I got up on all fours and straddled Carter's legs. Without giving myself any more time to think about muffins or porn stars, I dipped my head and nuzzled my nose against his length on the outside of his boxers.

Wow, he just got harder when I did that. Neat! I wanna see it grow.

Cha-cha-cha-chia!

Shit, no Chia Pet theme songs right before licking a dick.

I rested my elbows on the bed on either side of Carter's hips, my ass sticking up in the air so I wouldn't touch his legs and disturb him. Ever so carefully, I pulled the elastic away from his skin and peeled it down over his erection.

I glanced quickly up at his face, satisfied that he was still asleep. Letting out the breath I had been holding, it skimmed over his penis since my mouth was about an inch away at this point. I watched him get incredibly harder and longer.

Seriously? My breath on him did that? Or is he still dreaming about muffins?

I shrugged to myself. I was not going to question the penis. It was great and powerful, like the Wizard of Oz. And right now, the Wizard wanted me to lick his yellow brick dick. I jutted my chin forward and placed my tongue against the base of him, right above the edge of his underwear that I still held onto. I slid my tongue up the length of him, completely amazed at how smooth and soft the skin was there. My tongue dipped into the little valley right below the head of his penis and I added some pressure with the tip of my tongue like I saw in *Beat the Heat*.

Carter let out a little moan in his sleep and I smiled to myself.

I inched my body up a little further, letting my tongue glide up and over the head of his penis. I swirled it around the tip a few times then brought my lips down around the head and sucked it into my mouth.

Carter whimpered this time and I glanced up to see he still had his eyes closed.

Okay, this wasn't too bad. I could do this. I was a dirty cocksucker! Liz would be so proud.

That reminded me I needed to call Liz later and see if she wanted to help me make three hundred chocolate penises for one of her parties this weekend.

I dipped my head a little lower and took more of Carter into my mouth, letting my tongue continue to swirl around the head. I tasted a bit of wetness that leaked out of him and it was magically delicious, like Lucky Charms. But saltier. And without the leprechaun.

Green clovers, yellow horseshoes, pink penises!

I giggled a little when I thought that. I was giggling with Carter's penis in my mouth. Thank God he was still sleeping. I don't think laughing at a man's penis would make him feel good.

I sucked harder on him and took him as far into my mouth as I could without gagging. Throwing up on his penis wouldn't be a good introduction into the world of blowjobs.

He was big and full in my mouth and I seriously couldn't believe this was happening right now and no one was witnessing it. I, Claire Morgan, had a penis in my mouth. There should be applause or pats on the back. Maybe I should have waited until Carter was awake for this. I bet he'd give me one of those slow golf claps like in the movies. Or at least say "way to go."

I slowly moved up and down his length, letting my wet lips glide over his smooth skin.

Carter's hips jerked forward a little and he moaned again, making me completely giddy with power. Until I made one more pass up his length with my Hoover Mouth (Yes, I was changing its name to that of a vacuum cleaner. Don't judge me.), and I glanced up to see his eyes jerk open and his body completely freeze.

My lips were fastened around the head of his penis when he let out a yell.

"THERE IS NOTHING WRONG WITH MY WIENER! IT HAPPENS TO EVERY GUY!"

His legs jerked out from under me, sending me sprawling backwards to the foot of the bed while I watched him scramble up to the headboard, covering the part of his penis sticking out of his underwear with both of his hands.

"Where's Gavin?" he asked, his eyes frantically searching around the room. "He doesn't have a vagina."

I lay there on my back at the end of the bed, propped up on my elbows, wondering what the fuck just happened.

"Um, I'm assuming he's still sleeping. And I'm guessing you are too," I replied.

"Where's the farmer with the muffins?"

I extended one of my legs and shoved his thigh with my foot.

"CARTER!" I yelled. "Wake up!"

He finally looked at me then, his face scrunched up in confusion. He blinked rapidly and shook his head quickly like he was trying to jar things into place.

"I had another dream that you were giving me a blow job, just like the other morning when Gavin was in the living room watching me sleep. Damn, this one seemed so fucking real," he muttered.

I had no idea what he was talking about right now.

His eyes still glanced worriedly around the room like he expected Gavin to jump out from under the bed or something and shout, "Surprise! I saw Mommy blowing you!"

He looked back at me again. "Why are you laying at the bottom of the bed?"

I sighed and then pushed myself up so I could move back to the top of the bed next to him. When I got up there, I leaned my back against the headboard and glanced down at his lap - where his hands were still crisscrossed over his penis that stuck out of the top of his underwear. He followed my line of sight, moved his hands quickly and yanked his underwear up to cover himself.

What a shame.

"Well, Carter, this time you weren't dreaming. My mouth was on your penis when you decided to start flailing about, yelling about your wiener and our son with a vagina."

The look on his face would have been hilarious if my mouth wasn't depressed from the loss of his penis in there. His penis should be allowed to have the Twizzler slogan, "Makes mouth happy."

"Oh my God. Tell me I didn't interrupt a blowjob wake-up call. Say it isn't so and we can pretend I didn't just kick you off of my dick. I don't think my ego will recover from something like that."

I reached up and patted his cheek.

"Sorry, sweets, my mouth and lips were in fact all over your penis while you slept," I whispered.

He groaned.

"I have to say though, I'm a little surprised I never knew blowjobs included donkey kicks to the sternum."

He groaned again but this time in irritation.

"Shit! It's not my fault. Whenever I'm around you, even if I'm unconscious, my dick gets hard and I have dirty dreams about you. I thought I was having a repeat of the other morning and I freaked out."

He looked at me and pouted his lips.

"Pretty please, do it again?" he begged.

I laughed at how much he sounded like a child right now.

The door to the bedroom suddenly burst open and Gavin flew in the room, scrambled up onto the bed and in between the two of us.

"Morning, Mommy," Gavin said as he snuggled into my side.

Carter sighed, knowing there was no use in begging any more. He smiled though and watched me wrap Gavin in my arms and slide down the headboard to get under the covers.

Once we were situated, Gavin looked over his shoulder at Carter.

"Morning, crabby-daddy," he said, before turning back to face me and play with my hair.

I laughed at that one. Carter did look a little crabby.

He just shook his head and laughed right along with me.

Gavin's hand cupped my cheek and he looked seriously into my eyes.

"Hey, Mom," he said.

I squeezed him tighter and smiled.

"Yeah, baby."

"Lemme see your boobs," he said.

19.

This Patient Needs an Enema, STAT

Her mouth was on my penis.

We were sitting on the couch after lunch and all I could do was stare at Claire's mouth over top of Gavin's head.

This is wrong on so many levels.

But Jesus fuck, those red, plump lips were wrapped around my penis and I kicked her away. Sure, it was unconsciously but still... I punted her like a football off of my dick. That was like rule number one in sex. Never kick a girl away from your dick if she's got her mouth there. If her teeth were clamped down on it and she's whipping it around like a chew toy, that's another story.

I let out a big sigh and turned my attention back to the movie.

"What is this one called again?" I asked.

Gavin was curled up into my side with his feet on Claire's lap.

"*Finding Nemo,*" Gavin mumbled.

We watched the movie in silence for a few minutes and I felt like a kid again as I enjoyed the happenings on the screen. It had been a long while since I watched a cartoon.

"Holy shit, did they just kill off that fish's wife?" I blurted in shock.

"Yep," Gavin replied. "That big, mean fish ated her."

He said it so calmly - like it was no big deal that a sweet, loving cartoon fish just got murdered. What the fuck was wrong with this movie? This couldn't be appropriate for kids. I didn't think it was appropriate for me.

"Are you sure this is a kid's movie?" I asked Claire.

She laughed and just shook her head at me.

An hour later Gavin was asleep with his head on my lap and Claire was leaning in the opposite direction from me, her elbow on the arm of the couch and her head in her hand.

If I had to listen to Nemo calling for "Daddy" one more time, I was going to blubber like a baby. I snatched up the remote and turned the movie off.

Claire lifted her head off of her hand and gave me a questioning look.

"We need to put another movie in. This is too depressing. They killed off the poor fish's wife in the first five minutes and then we have to spend the rest of the movie watching that same, poor sap search for his son who ran away. What kind of sick fucks made this into a kid's movie?" I whispered angrily, trying not to wake Gavin up.

"Welcome to the Disney/Pixar School of Hard Knocks," she said dryly.

I laughed at her comparison.

"Oh come on. There's no way they're all like this. I do not remember being horrified by a children's movie when I was little."

"That's because you were a child. You didn't understand what was happening at the time, just like Gavin doesn't really understand. I think they make these kids movies more for adults anyway," she explained.

I shook my head in disbelief.

"Sorry, but I remember all of the great Disney classics and there is no way you can find anything nightmare-inducing in any of them."

She raised her eyebrow at me in a challenge.

"Okay fine. *Bambi*," I said.

She just laughed.

"Oh please! That's the easiest one. Bambi's dad headed for the hills as soon as the stick turned pink. His mom was a single deer, living in low-rent housing in the crack-whore part of the forest where there are gangs of bunnies. His mom gets killed in a drive-by shooting, leaving Bambi alone and forced to grow up much too soon."

Damn. I forgot about that. It had been a while since I watched *Bambi*.

"Okay, fine. How about the *Little Mermaid*? Beautiful sea creature falls in love with the handsome prince."

Shut up. I had little cousins. And Ariel was hot. Men could spend hours looking at a hot mermaid and wonder just how in the hell he could stick it in her.

But seriously, how do mermaids bang?

Claire nodded her head, "Oh yes. Sweet Ariel who has to give up everything, including her identity, for a man. God forbid Prince Eric grows some gills. Nope, Ariel has to give up her friends, her family, her home and her entire life for him. Eric just takes and takes and never gives."

I racked my brain trying to think of another classic kid's movie and continued to contemplate the process of fucking a mermaid. Maybe you could just bend a mermaid over a chair and your dick magically finds the hold in the one-legged fin thing.

"Fine, then how about *Beauty and the Beast*? The most beautiful girl in all the land falls for the beast's personality instead of his looks. You can't find anything wrong with that. Plus, it teaches a great lesson."

I gave her a smug grin.

Maybe there was a magic button that made a mermaid's legs separate long enough to bang her. Ooooooh, like a magic nipple! Push the nipple and watch her spread.

"Wrong," she replied. "A pretty girl with no money falls for a rich, abusive monster. But she loves him so much that she makes excuses for the abuse. 'Oh that bruise? I tripped down a flight of stairs.'"

She angled her body to face me.

"I could go on all day with these, believe me," she said. "You also can't forget the awesomeness that is the penis drawn on the original

Little Mermaid VHS box cover and the whisper of, "Kids, take off your clothes," in *Aladdin*."

I looked at her in horror.

And I'm not gonna lie, I glanced down to her boobs and wondered what it would be like if she had a magic nipple. That would be some Nobel Peace Prize shit right there.

"From now on, Gavin only watches wholesome movies like *Anchorman* and *The Seed of Chucky*, I told her. "And you're dressing up as Ariel for Halloween this year."

Claire just rolled her eyes at me, reached over to scoop Gavin off of my lap and then disappeared down the hall. A few minutes later, she was back and I watched her walk across the room to me. She straddled my lap and my hands went right to her hips to hold her in place while she slid her hands around my neck and tangled them in my hair.

"He should be out for a little while. Wanna mess around?" she asked with a giggle.

"Can I touch your boobs?" I asked hopefully.

It wasn't like I'd tell her no if she wouldn't let me play with the twins, but it was always good to set the ground rules ahead of time so there weren't any awkward foul plays.

She laughed and kissed the corner of my mouth.

"Yes, there will most definitely be boob touching," she said against my lips. "I'm not wearing a bra."

Easier access to the magic nipple.

"Sweet!" I cheered.

I swallowed her laugh with a kiss, taking my time while I explored every inch of her mouth. I had been in a state of semi-hardness since she walked in the room. Listening to her soft moans while I kissed her was enough to send me right into boner territory. My hands rubbed her ass and pulled her down so she nestled right onto my hard length that strained through my jeans. She slid her hips back and forth over me and I ran my hands up under the back of her shirt so I could feel here bare skin. My fingertips skimmed her spine all the way up and then back down, slowly, until I felt goose bumps break out over her skin.

Our tongues swirled together while I wrapped both of my arms around her body, underneath her shirt, so I could pull her right up against my chest. Her hips continued to move against me, and I felt like a teenager again, dry humping on my parents' couch in the basement.

Except this time, Abby Miller's braces wouldn't get stuck in my hair when she tried unsuccessfully to lick my ear lobe. And by lick, I meant drooled a gallon of spit in there until it sounded like I was swimming under water.

I slid my hands around to Claire's sides and up the front of her body. My palms moved in circles around her breasts, and I felt her nipples harden beneath my hands. She pushed herself down harder on my dick and it made us both let out a gasp. Fuck, I wanted to be inside of her but it wasn't something we could do out here on the couch with a four year old down the hall.

Her hands retracted from the hair on the back of my head and she pushed them up under her shirt until they rested on top of my own. She squeezed my hands and helped me put more pressure on the soft flesh that I would give my left nut to put my mouth on right now.

Okay, maybe not my left nut.

Or the right one for that matter.

Shit, forget the nuts. I just really, really wanted to lick her boobs.

The kiss deepened as we worked together, cupping and stroking her breasts. Her thighs squeezed my hips tightly and she whimpered into my mouth as she ground herself harder against me. Making Claire have an orgasm every single day was my new mission in life. The sounds she made and the way she moved against me were heaven, but I needed to touch her. I needed to feel how much she wanted this.

Just as I had that thought, she pushed my hand off of one breast and down the front of her body until both of our hands slid under the waistband of her yoga pants.

"Fuck, you're not wearing any underwear either," I muttered as she pushed my hand through her soft curls and my fingers easily slid through her wetness. She couldn't do much more than moan softly as I coated my fingers with her. Claire's hand stayed on top of mine and showed me when to increase the pressure or slow down the speed. It was the hottest fucking thing ever to have my fingers sliding through her heat while her small, soft hand guided my way.

With her other arm wrapped tightly around my neck, she flung her head back so her neck was exposed. I easily slid two fingers inside of her and kissed my way down her neck while my thumb moved in quick circles around her most sensitive spot. Her hips bucked against my hand while I started moving my two fingers quickly in and out of her. I held my thumb in place so that the motions of her hips made her slide back and forth over the pad of my thumb and she could set the pace for her release.

I grabbed the back of her head and pulled her down for a searing kiss. As soon as our lips and tongues collided she exploded. Her moans and whimpers were muffled by my mouth, which was a pretty good thing. I had a feeling she would be screaming if our mouths weren't fused together.

She rode my fingers while I kept them inside of her tight heat until every last drop of her orgasm surged through her. She pulled away from my mouth and collapsed against my chest with her face nestled in the crook of my neck.

My fingers stayed deep inside her while she caught her breath, and I felt every single pulse of her. Claire lifted her head and spoke with a dreamy look on her face.

"Give me two seconds to recover and I will suck you like..."

"Ga ga ah-ah-ahhhh, rama llama llama, want your bad bromance."

The sound of Gavin singing at the end of the hall froze us in place. He was headed this way and we both turned to stone.

Claire stared at me with wide eyes and I couldn't move my fingers from her vagina.

Why the fuck couldn't I move my fingers from her vagina?!

I wanted them there twenty-four hours a day under normal circumstances, but I started to see the error of my ways. There are some situations that do not condone having your fingers in a vagina. Like when you're getting an oil change, having your teeth cleaned, or when your four year old is in the room.

"Whatcha doin'?"

The only saving grace was the fact that the couch faced away from the hallway. Right now all he could see was the back of my head and Claire's mortified face.

"Um, Daddy needed a hug," Claire replied.

"Ooooh I wanna give Daddy a hug!"

"NO!" we both screamed.

Claire looked down at her lap and then up to my face with a look of panic.

I just shrugged. I refused to move my fingers now. What if Gavin wanted to shake my hand? I know that's not a very four year old thing to do but Jesus H. Christ! He would need therapy for years after that.

I tipped my head back as far as it would go, so I could see an upside-down Gavin standing there absently kicking his toe into the carpet.

"Hey, buddy, can you do me a favor? In my room on my dresser is a whole bunch of money. Can you carry it into your room and put it into your new piggy bank?" I suggested.

His eyes got big and he started bouncing on his feet.

"Yes! I LOVE money!"

With that, he turned and ran down the hall. We could hear the jingle of change as he scooped it off my dresser and took it to his room.

We finally relaxed when we realized it would keep him busy long enough for us to get our act together, or at least for me to get my fingers out of Claire's vagina.

She slid off my lap and collapsed next to me on the couch while we listened to the clunk of coins being dropped into the ceramic pig and another verse of "Bad Bromance."

"I really need to teach him some better music. Like Zeppelin or The Beatles," I said as I shifted the problem in my pants to a more comfortable position.

"Actually, I was thinking about recording our own Kidz Bop album. Except I'd called it Kidz Bop - The Forbidden Songs," she said with a smile.

"That's a stellar idea. That kid has been loafing off you long enough. It's time he gets a job."

She nodded with a serious face.

"This is true. He's already got "S&M" down pat. Maybe we could throw in a little 'Golddigger' from Kanye."

"I think he might sell more if he did some rap," I said. "'Bitches Ain't Shit' or 'Ninety-Nine Problems.' We just need to teach him a little more attitude."

While we laughed, Gavin ran back to the living room.

"You got eleventy-seven nickels, Daddy-O. Go buy me some beef turkey for lunch, dicky."

I guess we could skip the attitude lessons.

☉ ☉ ☉

As the next couple of days went by, all I could do was thank God for Carter. He helped me with everything he could and took Gavin off my hands every single night when he got home from work. Well, almost every night. He took a night off when Liz offered to keep Gavin overnight so we could finally have some alone time without the fear of another dick kick. I swore Liz to secrecy with that story but I'm pretty sure Carter knew the jig was up when she started asking him random questions like "Hey Carter, have you seen that new movie *Donkey Punch* yet?" or "Claire and I were thinking about taking a kick-boxing class, what do you think Carter?"

I was happy to find out that the sex between us was just as awesome when we were alone and didn't have to fear that a child would walk in on us at any moment. I earned five gold stars that night in "Blow Jobs 101" and did not get kicked out of class...or in the face.

I drastically cut my hours back at the bar, so I had more time to get everything ready for the store opening. Basically, right now, I worked when I could. If I had a few hours of free time, I gave them a call to see if they could use me. Even though it wasn't my dream job and I never planned on being there forever, it was still bittersweet not spending every night there. The Fosters had been good to me, giving me a job, no questions asked, when I showed up five years ago as a pregnant college dropout.

I cried like a baby when I called up there last night and T.J. told me they didn't need me. That bar was my home away from home and held so many memories. My water broke in the storage room when I was grabbing a bottle of vodka. Gavin took his first steps over by the door when my dad brought him by for lunch one afternoon. But most importantly, it was where I found Carter again.

The bar was right down the street from the store, and I knew I'd still spend a lot of time in there; it was just strange not to be there every day. I'd be lying if I said a big part of my sadness wasn't also due to the absence of P.O.R.N in my life. However, T.J. came through with flying colors while I stocked the front cooler of my store with chocolate last night. I heard the door chime behind me and figured it was Carter stopping by with Gavin. As soon as I turned around I was hit right in the face with three ping-pong balls. T.J. screamed something about how I'd never had that many balls smack me in the face while I was sober and then turned and ran out the door.

I spent the rest of the evening drafting up a couple of new rules for P.O.R.N, one of which included a penalty shot if multiple balls were handled without prior approval. A cup would be placed on a table, a ball would be thrown and if it made it into the cup, you were in the clear. However, if the ball failed to land in said cup, the thrower of the ball had to take a direct shot to the face. I called this the "Cupping of the Balls" rule.

Drew stopped by to help lift a few heavy boxes for me and found a copy of the rules by the register. Three hours later he came back with shirts for everyone that said "I Love P.O.R.N." and made himself an honorary team captain.

Before I even had a chance to be worried about how I would pay my bills until the store started making money, Carter sat me down the night after Gavin and I first spent the night and told me he was going to take over paying for everything until I was up and running. It was the night of our first fight. I had been on my own and provided for Gavin and me all this time. There was no way I wanted to take Carter's handout. My stubborn ass refused to see it from his point of view, hence the big fight. He had missed out on so much, and he felt guilty about that every single day, even though it wasn't his fault. Being able to pay my phone bill and buy Gavin new shoes and pay for his doctor's appointments made Carter feel like he was finally a full part of our lives and not just some guy with the title of "Dad." As independent as I was and as much as I hated the idea of someone paying my way, I couldn't deny him this if it was what he really wanted and it would make him happy. I ended my temper tantrum, agreed to what Carter was asking and then we had hot as hell make-up "phone calls" locked in the laundry room while Gavin watched a movie in the living room.

So, with Carter's help and my decreased hours at the bar, I was able to get almost everything done a few days before the opening. The only thing left to do this far ahead of time was fold all of the brochures Jenny made for me. Carter took Gavin for the night so I could have some down time with the girls and they could help me with the folding.

Jim and Drew were going to keep Carter company since I would have their women all evening. I had to put my foot down though with Drew. I told him I would buy a tennis racket and go John McEnroe on his ass if my son came home with any new, colorful words.

Liz, Jenny and I were sitting on the floor of my living room surrounded by thousands of folded and unfolded brochures and four empty bottles of wine.

Wait, make that five. I emptied the fifth bottle into Liz's glass after she jumped up and ran to the bathroom holding her hands between her legs like a toddler because she had to pee so badly.

I got up and walked to the kitchen to grab another bottle of wine. As I passed by the bathroom, I found the door wide open.

"Liz, are you peeing with the door open?"

She looked up at me with crazy, drunk eyes while she swayed back and forth on the toilet and peed.

"Yes. Does it bother you?"

"Only if you fall off the toilet and piss on my floor," I told her as I walked away.

"Fair enough, hairy muff!" she yelled to me.

After I popped the cork on another bottle of wine and refilled everyone's glasses, Liz came back into the living room, shoved the brochures out of the way and lay down on her belly with her chin in her hands.

"Okay, skank whores. Time for a little Truth or Dare," she slurred. "Jenny, what nickname have you given your vagina?"

Jenny blushed and bit her lip, looking down in her lap. After several long minutes of Liz and I goading her, she finally mumbled something that sounded like, "Water."

"Repeat that, please. I don't have dog hearing," I told her.

"You do have a vagina that smells like a dog though," Liz laughed.

"Fuck you, anal warts."

"I call my vagina, Waterford," Jenny said, interrupting the banter between Liz and me.

We turned to her with equal looks of confusion on our faces.

"Explain," Liz said as she took a sip of wine.

Jenny shrugged. "You know, Waterford is like, good dishes and stuff. So, I only let the best eat off my Waterford."

Liz snorted. "Why don't you just call it China then?"

Jenny thought about this for a minute.

"But, I've never been to China," she replied with a puzzled look on her face.

"Okay, next!" I announced. "Liz, same question. Name that beaver!"

Why is this room tilty?

Liz took another big gulp of her wine.

"Vajingo. As in "maybe the vajingo ate your penis," she said in an Australian accent.

The radio that played from the kitchen finally stopped the sequence of commercials and switched to music.

"I love this song. It really envelopes me," Jenny said dreamily.

"Does it put a stamp on you too?" Liz laughed.

"Yeah, a tramp stamp!" I yelled.

Why am I yelling?

"I don't have a tattoo," Jenny argued.

"It's Claire's turn and I'm choosing dare," Liz stated.

"Hey, I'm the one that gets to choose," I protested.

"Shut up, whore! I dare you to send Carter a picture of your tits."

"Wait, what did you say?" Jenny asked. "I can't hear you without my glasses on," she mumbled as she poured more wine into her glass. Liz ignored her and scooted across the floor army-style, grabbed my phone that lay in the middle of us and handed it to me. I only hesitated for a second before I snatched it out of her hand and pressed the button for the camera, chugging the rest of my glass of wine for liquid courage.

I lifted my shirt and bra up to my neck, held my arm out in front of me as far as I could and quickly snapped a picture. My shirt and bra were back down and I was scrolling through the contacts in my phone before anyone said anything.

"Holy shit, dude! I just meant a cleavage picture. I didn't need you to whip out the fun bags right in front of us. I have to say though, I'm kind of proud of you right now," Liz said in awe.

"Claire has pretty boobies," Jenny muttered while she looked down the front of her shirt.

I attached the boob shot to a blank text message and typed the words, "We miss you," then hit send.

That was empowering! I felt all sorts of Joan of Arc-like now, but maybe more *The Legend of Billie Jean* movie version of her. Burning at the stake doesn't sound like fun. But I could totally rock a short haircut and get people to chant, "fair is fair" as they follow me and my outlaw friends across state lines. I turned my phone towards Liz and showed her the text.

"Oh, young grasshopper, it is clear you can be taught," Liz said as she wiped a fake tear out of her eye.

"I don't feel very lurid right now," Jenny slurred as she flopped onto her back and stared at the ceiling.

"Lucid! It's lucid, Jenny. For fuck's sake, someone get this bitch an Encyclopedia Britannica," Liz yelled from her spot on the floor.

"FAIR IS FAIR!" I yelled as I fist pumped.

I started folding some more of the flyers while Liz crawled over to Jenny and tried to lead her in a Hooked on Phonics boot camp. While Liz made her do push-ups and repeat words back to her, I got up and went to the kitchen to cut up some cheese and grab a plate of crackers.

In hindsight, wielding a cheese grater when my blood type was currently Merlot positive wasn't the best idea.

⊙ ⊙ ⊙

"Kick him in the nut sack!"

I sat down on the couch and rolled my eyes as the UFC fight we watched started a new round.

"Okay, seriously. Enough with the nut kicking talk," I scolded.

Drew looked at me and pouted, "Oh come on, your kid isn't even awake."

I looked behind me where Gavin had fallen asleep on the couch. His little body was draped over the arm of the couch, his head and arms dangling down towards the floor, his knees pushed into the cushions. How in the hell does he fall asleep like that?

"I'm just trying to save you from the wrath of Claire. Really, it's for your own safety," I told him as I looked at his shirt that showed a couple walking in the sand with the words, "I enjoy long walks on the beach...after anal."

"I'll put my nuts on all of you," Gavin's muffled voice said from his hanging position off the end.

I looked at Drew pointedly.

"Hey, Carter," Jim said as he walked back in from the kitchen. "Why is Claire sending me a picture of her tits with the words, "Me fish Lou," in it?"

"What?" Drew and I both asked in unison.

Jim held his cell phone out to me as I leaned forward to see it.

"Seriously? Claire's tits are on that phone?" Drew yelled as he jumped up from the couch and tried to grab the phone before I got to it.

I panicked, flew off the recliner in the corner and onto Drew's back, wrapping my arms around his neck.

"What the fuck are you doing? Get off my back you dumbass," Drew yelled as he twisted and turned, trying to throw me off.

"Don't you even think about looking at that picture, dick licker," I threatened as I tried holding on to his neck with one arm and reached for Jim's phone with the other.

The phone suddenly beeped and Jim pulled it towards him, rolling his eyes at what he saw.

Drew stopped moving and we both just stood there. Well, Drew just stood there; I was still hanging from his back like a wet noodle.

"Okay, now Jenny is asking me if I want to eat in China tonight. What the fuck is wrong with your women?"

I dropped off Drew's back and Jim handed me his phone. I scrolled to the text from Claire and my jaw dropped.

Yep, those were her tits. Sweet Jesus. I forwarded the text to my phone, you know, so I could ask her about it later...and stuff.

The phone rang in my hands and caller I.D. said it was Liz.

"Go ahead and answer it. You can ask her why Claire is sending me nudey pictures," Jim said with a laugh.

I hit "send" and put the phone to my ear, quickly pulling it away when I heard muffled screams through the receiver.

"Jesus Christ, who's screaming?" Drew asked with a cringe.

I shook my head and shrugged my shoulders, attempting to put the phone back to my ear.

"I swear to fucking God if you puke in this cab I will punch you in the neck! Stop being a pussy!"

"Hey!" I yelled, trying to be heard over the screams. "HELLO!"

The screams continued and the three of us moved into the kitchen so we wouldn't wake Gavin.

"You're a mother for Christ's sakes! It's just a little blood. Will you stop screaming?"

"LIZ! HELLO!" I yelled again, once we got to the kitchen.

Drew was laughing but I knew those screams. And hearing Liz mention the word "blood" freaked me out a little. Was Claire bleeding?

"Drew, call Jenny," I said quickly.

A few seconds later I heard ringing through my end of the phone call and the sound of Jenny's voice over Claire's screams and Liz's yelling. I hung up since I wasn't getting anywhere and turned to face Drew.

260

"Awww, I love you too, Snuggie!"

I punched Drew in the shoulder and indicated that he should get to the point by giving him the finger.

"Hey, baby, what's going on? Why is Claire screaming?" he asked, pulling the phone back and hitting the speaker button.

The screaming and arguing burst into the room and we all winced.

"Claire's got nice boobies," Jenny said.

I rolled my eyes.

"Baby, focus. What is going on? Where are you?" Drew asked her.

"I'm dying! Oh my God, I'm going to bleed to death in a cab that smells like pee and curry!"

Why the fuck is Claire bleeding in a cab?

"Claire had an assident. Axiscent. She's got a boo boo," Jenny slurred.

"Alright ladies, Butler General Hospital. No, don't pay me; just get the hell out of my cab."

☉ ☉ ☉

Drew and Jim stayed at my house with Gavin and I raced to the hospital.

What if Claire had a freak garbage disposal incident and lost a hand? Or a really heavy meat cleaver fell on her leg and they needed to amputate? My house was not wheelchair accessible. Fuck! Could you buy wheelchair ramps at Walmart?

By the time I made it to the emergency room, I sorely regretted leaving Jim and Drew back at the house. I was stuck in a room with three drunken women - one of whom was sobbing hysterically about orphaning our son while the other two knocked shit over and yelled random things to people who walked by.

"Excuse me sir, do you know where we can get an x-ray of the stapler stuck in her vagina?" Liz asked an orderly that walked by as she pointed her thumb at Claire.

I gave the guy an apologetic look before focusing my attention on Claire.

"Baby, it's fine. It's just a little cut on your finger. Two stitches really aren't that big of a deal," I told her as I held her in my arms and rubbed her back.

I snapped my fingers at Jenny and Liz who were now in the corner of the room trying to get rubber gloves on their heads. They gave me innocent looks, smacked each other and kept giggling.

"Not a big deal? Not a big deal?" she said loudly. "They asked me if I had a living will. I almost DIED tonight!"

I chuckled, but quickly masked it when she shot me a dirty look.

"Claire, that's normal. They ask everyone that," I reassured her.

"I concur, do you concur?" Liz asked.

"Not helping," I growled.

"Not caring," she replied before turning back to the supply cabinet in the room.

"What if I died? My baby would be alone," she sobbed.

"Um, hello? Father, standing right here," I reminded her.

"Fine. But what if something happens to both of us? They could ship him off to my Aunt Gertie the hoarder who talks to her curtains and eats soap," she whined.

I grabbed her face in my hands and wiped away the tears, giving her a soft kiss on the lips.

"Okay, if there's a natural disaster tomorrow and neither one of us is here, I'm sure your dad wouldn't mind stepping in. Why are you so worried about this right now?"

"They asked me if in the event of an emergency, someone could administer Last Rites to me. They thought I was going to die tonight, Carter. This is serious!" she cried. "What if my dad has a heart attack tomorrow or an asteroid lands on him when he's walking to his car after work?"

No more Sci-Fi channel before bed for Claire.

"I swear to you that they ask everyone about Last Rites. But would it make you feel better if we get something in writing so you don't have to worry about this? We can make a list of people that is ten pages long if it will make you feel better."

She nodded happily and threw her arms around my neck.

"Thank you so much, baby. I love you more than a hooker loves free VD testing day at the clinic," she told me drunkenly.

I rubbed her back and shot dirty looks to Liz and Jenny when I saw that they'd taken over the dry-erase board with important hospital phone numbers that hung on the wall. Instead of "Order Meals" it now said "Order Hookers," and instead of "For a Chapel Visit, ask a nurse" it now said "For a Happy Ending, ask a nurse."

The doctor walked in then with Claire's discharge papers and a prescription for an antibiotic. He explained everything to us and turned to leave the room.

"Doctor, wait! This patient needs an enema STAT!" Liz yelled while Jenny waved a rubber tube over her head like a lasso.

I think we could safely say that some people will already be crossed off of the guardian list.

20.

Have You Seen Mike Hunt?

Oh Jesus fucking hell. Where's the monkey that kicked me in the head and shit in my mouth?

"I think I'm dying," I croaked.

Carter's laughter shook the bed and forced a little bit of vomit up into my throat. I clamped my hand over my mouth and started breathing through my nose to make it stop.

"Please don't start the 'I'm dying' thing again. It's too early and I'm not awake enough to say anything comforting," Carter replied as he slowly rubbed circles on my back.

I started to ask him what the hell he was talking about when the pounding in my head turned into flashes of memories from the night before.

"Oh my God, I sent a picture of my boobs to Jim," I moaned as a fresh wave of nausea rolled through me.

"You also threw up in the emergency room parking lot, called Drew and told him you were the Donkey Punch Dick Queen and filled out a Last Will and Testament on a Burger King napkin and then asked the drive-thru worker to notarize it."

I am never drinking again. I am never drinking again.

"Why can't I be one of those people who black out when they drink? It would be really nice right now if I didn't have to remember these things," I muttered.

I felt the bed shift behind me, and a few seconds later Carter's arm came around me and held a napkin in front of my face.

"Sorry, baby, even if you did black out, I still have proof of your stupidity," he said with a laugh. I grabbed the napkin from his hand and squinted at the messy writing that was all over it as he got back under the covers behind me.

"I don't wanna be def. Death. Dead. This Burger Twin nappykin just got served as my will, BEOTCH! The fries here suck, by the way. If I die, don't feed my son your shitty fries. Don't give my son to the creepy child molester king you put in your commercials either. What the fuck is wrong with that guy? He's got a normal body and a plastic face that is always smiley. It's not right, man. It's just not right. My ears feel funny."

I wondered if someone gave me a roofie last night. This was the one time in my life I hoped I got roofied, so I could blame it on something other than me being a horrible drunk.

"Wow, okay, so I've been meaning to bring up the subject of having a will drafted by a lawyer and getting a new birth certificate for Gavin that has your name on it. I probably should have done that before I drank my weight in wine," I explained.

"Well, lucky for you, I'm fluent in Claire's Drunken Ramblings. Even though you barely knew what you were saying last night, I could tell this is important to you. It's important to me too. God forbid anything should ever happen to us, but if something does, it would make me feel better knowing Gavin is going to be okay. I mean, I know we have your dad and even though you haven't met them yet, my parents are absolutely on board with anything that has to do with Gavin, but I agree that we should also have someone younger as a back-up plan just in case. I know you're going to be insanely busy for the next month or so once the shop opens tomorrow, and we'll have no time to really sit down and discuss this, so I thought maybe we could just sort of pop in on our friends in the next few days and see how they do when they're around Gavin. You know, sort of like a secret interview."

I really wanted to throw up right now, but I had to choke it back because Carter deserved my undivided, non-spewing attention.

"I can't believe you actually took me seriously about anything last night."

Carter slid over to my side of the bed, pressing his body up against mine as he wrapped his arms around my waist.

"I take everything you say seriously. Even when you're sexting our friends and screaming into the drive-thru window that whoever is making your burger better not spit in it," Carter said, placing a kiss to my temple.

I lifted my hand up in front of my face and noticed the bandage wrapped around my middle finger for the first time.

"I guess it's fitting I almost sliced off my middle finger. It will be fun to flip everyone off when they ask me what happened," I said with a sigh. "You know what I just remembered? Liz and Jim are babysitting his little cousin for a few hours today. I was planning on going over there so she and Gavin could play while Liz and I filled out the last of our paperwork. You could come with us and we could do our first super secret spy interview."

Carter leaned up on his elbow so he could look down at me.

"Will I get to wear a secret decoder ring and make up a spy code name, like Ichybon Snagglewhip or Bonanza Challywag?"

I turned my head and looked up at him.

"Will I ever have to say those names out loud, in front of people we know?" I asked.

"Only if our cover is blown."

He laid his head back down on the pillow behind me and within seconds, I could feel his hard penis up against my ass.

"Really? Talking about Bonanza Challywag excites you?" I asked with a laugh, trying not to grimace when the action made my stomach churn.

His hand, which rested on my stomach, snuck under my tank top and slid up the front of my body until it came in contact with my bare breast.

"Anything I say, do or think about with you excites me," he said softly as his palm feathered over my nipple. I pushed my hips back and rubbed my ass up against his length while he kneaded my breast and pressed a kiss to the side of my neck. His head jerked away from me abruptly and his hand stopped its exploration of my flesh.

"You're going to throw up, aren't you?" he asked as I squeezed my eyes shut and thought about rainbows and kittens and other things that didn't make me want to puke.

It didn't work. Rainbows made me think of, "Taste the rainbow," which made me think of Skittles and the half-pound bag I ate last night before bed. Kittens made me think of fleas and litter boxes with little poops that looked like tootsie rolls covered in rocks and…

I bolted out of bed and raced to the bathroom, barely making it in time before I emptied the contents of my stomach—which coincidentally looked a bit like a rainbow.

"It's okay, my penis is not offended in the least that it just made you throw up," Carter yelled from the bedroom.

⊙ ⊙ ⊙

Carter got Gavin up, dressed and fed him breakfast while I took a shower and tried to feel human. As much as I hated to do it, puking actually helped. I exorcised the demons.

When I got out of the shower, I realized I didn't have any clothes… well, aside from the tank top I wore to bed and underwear. Where the hell did my clothes go?

I went through Carter's closet and found one of his shirts and threw it on then dug through his underwear drawer for a pair of boxers. Instead, buried way in the back, I found a teeny, tiny pair of red banana-hammock briefs.

The revenge gods were smiling down on me today, my friends.

I shimmied into them and made my way out to the kitchen where Carter was cleaning up breakfast and Gavin was giving him a run for his money.

"Mommy always lets me have candy right after breakfast."

I stood just outside of the doorway so I could see them but they couldn't see me. Gavin was seated at the kitchen table and Carter had his back to him, loading things in the dishwasher.

"Right, candy after breakfast. And I'm Santa Claus," Carter muttered quietly.

"You're Santa Claus?!" Gavin asked excitedly, standing up on his chair.

Carter whipped around to face him with a panicked look on his face.

"What? No. Well, technically...Wait, no. No, no, no. I am not Santa Claus. That was just a figure of speech," he explained.

"What's a finger of peach?"

"Shit!" Carter muttered.

Gavin pointed at him.

"Awwwwww, you said *shit*," he accused, making sure to whisper the bad word.

"So did you," Carter argued. "Don't tell your mother."

"Don't tell me what?" I asked, walking through the doorway with a smile.

Carter sighed. "You heard that didn't you?"

I walked up to Gavin and scooped him off of the chair and into my arms for a hug.

"I have no idea what you're talking about," I told him as I kissed both of Gavin's cheeks.

"How did you sleep last night, little man?"

He squeezed me as hard as he could until I had to pry his arms from around my neck so I could breathe.

"I slept good. But you crawled into my bed wif me last night and told me never to talk to kings with smiley faces," he told me.

Carter laughed while I groaned.

I gave Gavin one last squeeze and then set him down on his feet.

"Run into your room and find your shoes, okay? We're going to see Aunt Liz and Uncle Jim in a little bit."

He let out a cheer of excitement and ran out of the room.

I walked over to Carter and leaned my body into his while he lounged against the kitchen counter.

"You look good wearing my shirt," he said as he wrapped his arms around me.

I kissed his chin and looked up at him.

"I look even better wearing your tighty underoos," I said with a laugh as I reached back and lifted up a corner of his shirt so he could see.

He shook his head and sighed.

"I can't believe you found those. My boxers made me chafe at work so I thought I'd try..."

"Don't worry," I interrupted him. "I'll make sure everyone knows you wear big boy undies now."

I laughed and wrapped my arms around his neck. He bent down and gave me a sweet kiss, sucking my top lip into his mouth and making my toes curl.

"Where are my clothes?" I asked between kisses.

"Your shirt is in the garbage. You threw it there last night when we got here and you saw the blood all over it. You said you couldn't possibly ever wear something again that reminded you of how you almost died in a horrific accident. I took your jeans from you before you did the same to them. They're in the dryer right now."

I shook my head and sighed while Carter tightened his hold on me and placed another kiss on my lips.

"Move in with me," he said suddenly.

His lips stayed against mine and I opened my eyes so I could see him. He stared at me so intently there was no way I misheard him.

"I love you," he continued quickly. "I love Gavin. I love waking up to both of you in this house with me. I don't want to miss seeing him tie his shoes for the first time or write his name. I don't want to wake up in the morning and not see you drooling on the pillow next to me."

I laughed and smacked his arm, the conversation immediately turning lighter.

"Besides, I need a woman here to be barefoot and pregnant in the kitchen making me chicken pot pies every night," he said with a smile.

"Well, then we've obviously never met if you want me to take on that role."

We stood there in the kitchen, wrapped in each other's arms with Carter's junior jockeys creeping up my ass, and I realized I had never been happier.

"Yes," I told him.

His eyebrows went up and his face lit up with a huge smile.

"Yes? Really?" he asked. "I thought for sure I'd have to resort to bribery or extortion."

I nodded my head and laughed. "Yes! We will move in with you so I can monitor the stupid shit you say and punch you in the kidney when you suggest I should be barefoot and pregnant in the kitchen again."

⊙ ⊙ ⊙

A few hours later, Liz and I were just finishing our paperwork at her kitchen table. Jim and Carter were sitting at the table with us carrying on their own conversation while Gavin and Jim's eight year old little cousin Melissa played.

Gavin was currently in the living room watching a movie, but Melissa had been running through the kitchen at warp speed, yelling as loud as she could for the past fifteen minutes. Carter and I passed each other secret looks every so often about the conversation we had in the car on the way over here. We weren't going to discipline Gavin at all the entire time at their house. We would let Liz and Jim take over and see what they did. I had first hand experience on the type of caregivers they were since they were my best friends, so this was mostly for Carter's benefit. I knew for a fact that Liz and Jim were wonderful with kids and Carter would be more than willing to assign them as Gavin's back-up guardians after today.

Surprisingly, we wouldn't need to discipline Gavin anyway. He was being very well behaved. Melissa, on the other hand, reminded me yet again while some animals in the wild eat their young. She was a terror. After her twenty-seventh pass through the kitchen, waving her hands above her head and screaming, Liz finally had enough.

"Melissa! Stop it," she said sternly.

The little terror did indeed stop. For two seconds. Then she started back up and ran out of the room screaming like her ass was on fire. Her ass would be on fire soon if she didn't shut the hell up.

"Is that all you're going to do?" I asked.

"No," Liz replied as she looked up from the paper she was signing. "Next time she runs by I'm going to kick her."

Not conventional by any means, but I was okay with that. I was daydreaming about shoving a Roman candle in her pants and dousing it with lighter fluid.

"So, Melissa seems a little...high strung," Carter said to Jim.

Jim nodded his head in agreement. "She's a cute kid, but I can only stand her in small doses. This one time we took her to dinner with us and she was being a nightmare so Liz made her go sit out in the car while we paid the bill. We got halfway home before we realized she wasn't in the car," he laughed. "Remember that Liz? Hilarious!"

Carter looked at me in horror and I tried not to make eye contact. The whole way here all I did was brag about how good Liz and Jim were with Gavin and how they'd be naturals at parenting. Oops. I forgot about that story. In their defense, Melissa was Satan. I would have driven off without her too.

Melissa made another lap through the kitchen, and true to her word, Liz stuck her foot out. The annoying third-grader went sprawling across the floor.

"NO WIRE HANGERS EVER!" Liz yelled at her.

"You're weird," Melissa stated as she stood up and went running back out of the room.

"Nice work there, Mommie Dearest," I told her.

"So, Liz, when you have kids of your own, how are you going to discipline them?" Carter asked.

I gave him a pointed look. We were supposed to be inconspicuous here. Asking blunt questions like that was sure to send up a red flag.

Liz shrugged. "Eh, I'm not big on discipline. If it's funny and no one is bleeding, you're not in trouble. That's my philosophy."

Gavin walked in then and leaned his head on my arm.

"Melissa told me no one is allowed near her no-no zone. What does that mean? I don't like her. She's loud. I told her my mommy wasn't afraid to punch a kid," he said with a sigh.

We heard Melissa yelling in the other room and some loud banging.

"What the hell is she doing in there?" Liz asked.

"The cat's being bad," Gavin said.

Liz and Jim's cat was known to be a little ball of terror, wreaking havoc on unsuspecting people when they least expected it. One time, when I was on the floor tickling Gavin, she hurtled through the air from God knows where and landed on my back with her teeth and claws inserted two inches deep into my skin. I hated that cat, but I think I hated Melissa more. Hopefully the cat was putting her in her place.

"Did the cat scratch you guys?" I asked, looking over his arms for claw marks.

"No, she won't stay in the suitcase," he explained.

All the adults at the table looked at each other in silence. At the sound of another thump from the living room, we all jumped up and ran out of the kitchen.

⊙ ⊙ ⊙

After making sure Melissa hadn't immediately moved herself into serial killer territory by suffocating a cat, we headed home.

"That really wasn't the best representation of their parenting skills," I tried to explain as Carter pulled out of their driveway.

"Hey, Gavin," Carter said as he glanced in the rearview mirror. "What new word did Aunt Liz teach you today?"

"Ladyboner," Gavin said as he looked out his window.

Carter gave me a pointed look.

"Aunt Liz said you got a ladyboner for Daddy. Did you buy him a present? I want one too," Gavin complained.

After stopping at my house to pick up a few things, we went back to Carter's and put Gavin down for a nap. Carter finally gave up trying to convince me that Liz and Jim were off the list when I said one word.

Drew.

If I was willing to give that giant child a try, he needed to keep an open mind with my friends. At least we agreed to wait until after the store opening tomorrow to tell Gavin that we would be moving. If we told him now, he would bug us every minute from now until we moved asking if it was time yet. I didn't need to fight the urge to lock him out of the house while I was busy with the store. One person can only take so much.

⊙ ⊙ ⊙

After Gavin's nap, Claire's dad stopped by to pick him up for a sleepover. He walked right in the front door without knocking and proceeded to make his way through every room. Once he had seen all there was to see, he told me the house was "good enough." Oddly, that was the nicest thing he had said to me since we met, and I kind of felt like we had a moment.

I leaned in to give him a hug and he stopped me with his hand to my forehead.

"You don't want to do that, son."

I stepped back and gave him a sympathetic look.

"'Nam, huh? Still hard for you to get close to people?" I asked.

"No. I'm still not sure you aren't gay and if you try to play grab-ass, it's gonna get real awkward when I have to snap your fingers in two."

I was going to break that man one of these days, mark my words.

We said our good-byes to Gavin and Claire left soon after to head up to the shop and get a few last minute things made for tomorrow's opening.

I offered to meet her up there after I showered and ran a few errands.

Claire had given me a spare key to the shop, so I let myself in through the front door two hours later. It was dark outside and I left the lights to the store off as I carefully made my way to the kitchen in the back.

I heard music playing and rounded the corner of the kitchen to see Claire licking melted chocolate off of her middle finger. My dick sprang to life as I watched her swirl her finger through her mouth and sway her body to the erotic beats of the song that played.

I rounded the edge of the counter where she worked and stood behind her, placing my arms on either side of her with my hands flat on the counter. I leaned my body close to hers, bringing one hand up to move her hair away from her neck and pushed it behind her shoulder. She continued to work, flipping chocolate molds over and tapped the finished product out onto towels so nothing would break, her body swaying to the music and sliding against me every so often. When I put my mouth on the side of her neck, her motions got choppy.

"Are those chocolate penises and boobs?" I asked.

"Yes," she moaned as I let the tip of my tongue taste her skin. "Party favors...shit...mmmmm."

I smiled against her neck when she moaned and placed another open-mouthed kiss there, this time letting my teeth graze her skin. I watched as goose bumps flushed her skin and listened to her take a shuddering breath. I continued to nip and gently suck on the side of her neck until she finally got fed up with concentrating on the chocolate molds. She dropped them to the counter and smacked her hands down next to mine, dumping over a bowl of melted chocolate in the process. The warm liquid splattered onto her hand and ran off the edge of the counter, pooling on the floor.

"Shit!" Claire laughed as she lifted her hands from the counter and tried to shake off some of the chocolate on them. She bowed her head to look at the puddle on the floor, and I reached up and moved her hair all the way around to the front of her other shoulder so the back of her neck was wide open. I swiped my finger through the mess of melted chocolate on the counter and then trailed it along the back of her neck, leaving a smudge of chocolate behind on her skin.

"Did you just get chocolate in my hair?" she asked distractedly.

My hand snaked around her waist and I pushed it under the hem of her shirt until I touched the smooth, warm skin of her stomach. I moved my mouth towards the back of her neck and slid my hand down into her pants. My fingers slid right inside her underwear and through the soft triangle of curls. I attached my lips to her chocolate-coated skin and gently sucked as two of my fingers slid down and glided through her.

"Oh my God," she moaned softly as I pushed and pulled my fingers through her, coating them with her wetness. "Forget it, you can put chocolate wherever you want."

She felt so good, better than anything else in the world. I could stand here touching her all night and never tire of it.

I nibbled and sucked at the back of her neck, making sure to remove all of the chocolate I'd placed there. I was happy to learn that the spot right below her hairline drove her insane. Every time my teeth grazed that area, she would moan and jerk her hips into my hand. I lifted my free hand from the counter and pushed it under her shirt, lifting the cup of her bra up and over one of her breasts as I went. I cupped the fullness of her in my palm and then took two fingers and circled them all around her nipple. I copied the same motions with my other hand, my fingers circling through the heat between her legs.

The beats of the music and the sound of her soft moans filled the room, and I was about two seconds away from exploding in my pants just by listening to her and feeling her come apart in my hands. I rocked my hips into her ass and it was my turn to moan. She was soft against my hardness, wet against my warm fingers and the skin of her neck tasted salty and sweet, like the chocolate covered pretzels she made. I was about to say something really stupid like tell her she was the yin to my yang. But in all honesty, she was. I wanted more than anything for her to be mine. Forever. That thought should have scared me. If it was any other woman, it probably would. But not Claire. Nothing about her scared me, except the thought of losing her.

Her hips started moving faster and I kissed my way over to her ear.

"I love you so much," I whispered, sliding my hand lower and pushing two fingers into her tight heat. Claire moaned loudly as I moved my fingers in and out of her and my other hand continued to tease her nipple.

My hands were suddenly empty as they were pulled out of her and off of her breast when she abruptly turned to face me. We both looked down at the front of her shirt at the mess of chocolate that was all over it from my hands and from her leaning into the spill on the counter. I laughed until she brought both of her hands to my cheeks and wiped the chocolate on them all over my face.

"I love you more than chocolate," she said with a smile.

Her hands slid down the front of my shirt, leaving a trail of chocolate in their wake, and went to work on my pants. Before I knew it, she had them shoved down to my thighs. I reached for her hips but she batted my hands away.

"No, no, no. It's my turn to play," she said with a wicked smile on her lips.

My dick jumped against my stomach like it was getting ready to do a jig. When she licked her lips and looked down at it, I whimpered. She reached behind her back for a second, fiddling around with something. Before I could tell her that now was not the time to start cleaning up our mess, she kissed my lips and I felt something warm and wet slide around the head of my penis.

She pulled back, slid down my body and my mouth dropped open.

Oh, sweet Jesus, is that...is she going to...

She wrapped her hand around the base of me and her lips around the head and sucked me into her mouth. I didn't even know what kind of incoherent expletives flew from my mouth. I may have said the words "shamwow" and "jiggidy" somewhere in there. I leaned over her and my hands smacked onto the counter sending splatters of chocolate all over the front of my shirt as Claire began licking all around, making sure to get every last drop of melted chocolate she rubbed there with her fingers when she kissed me.

She was licking chocolate off of my dick. I felt like I was in a porno—a really, really good porno with better music and a superb story line. Not like that really creepy one with the guy who put peanut butter on his johnson and let his dog...

Her lips slid around and down my length, taking as much of me in her mouth as she could, and I forgot about the dick licking dog. Thank God. She started a slow rhythm, moving her head up and down, sucking harder every time she got to the tip, before plunging her mouth back down on me. I felt like I should pump my fists in the air or give Claire a round of applause, but that would quickly turn this into bad porno territory.

I could feel my balls tighten and I wrapped my hands around her arms and pulled her up to me. As good as it felt to be in her mouth, I needed inside of her right now. I slid my hands into the waistband of her pants and underwear and slid them down her hips far enough so she could pull one leg out.

Lifting Claire up, I sat her on the counter right at the edge, moving her to the side a little so she wasn't sitting in chocolate. I pushed her knees apart so I could get between them. Her hands fell into the puddle of chocolate on either side of her hips and I held her around her waist as she started to slip through the mess. She smacked a gooey-coated hand onto my shoulder, leaving a chocolate handprint behind and making us both laugh. She brought a chocolate coated finger from her other hand up to her mouth and spread the sugary wetness along her bottom lip.

Oh, sweet Jesus, was that porn music playing in the background? Was I starring in *Cocks and the Chocolate Factory* or *Chocolate Melts in Your Vagina, Not in your Hand?*

I swooped in and kissed her, sucking her lip into my mouth and greedily licking the chocolate off with my tongue. Once I got it all, she pushed her tongue past mine and swirled it through my mouth. She tasted like Claire and chocolate, and I had a moment where I wanted to cry like a baby because my dream for the past five years was right in front of me. I grabbed the back of both of her knees and pulled her legs up around my waist, my hands sliding down her thighs and over her ass. I sucked her tongue into my mouth and pulled her closer to the edge of the counter, my hardness resting against her wet heat.

Her arms wrapped around my shoulders and I pushed my hips forward, sinking into her slowly until my pelvis was flush against hers. My mouth never left hers as I stayed deep inside of her and swiveled my hips, grinding myself against her. She whimpered into my mouth and pushed herself harder against me, creating friction right where she needed it. Her legs tightened around my hips and I squeezed my hands onto her ass, rocking her harder and faster against me. It was killing me not move, not to slide in and out of her heat that squeezed around me, but I knew she liked what I was doing and that's all that mattered.

Our kiss never ended as I felt her start to tighten around me. Her hips moved faster and she clawed at my shoulders as I moved against her and rotated my hips, pushing her into oblivion.

I deepened the kiss and swallowed her cries as she came. Her hands latched onto my hair and I couldn't have cared less that I'd have to wash chocolate out of it tonight. I removed a hand from her ass and rested it on the counter next to her for more leverage as I pulled almost all the way out of her and slammed back inside, stars bursting behind my closed eyes at the sensations that shot up through me.

Claire's moans and muttered curses spurned me on to move faster and harder. Thank God for that because there was no way I could be gentle now. I needed to fuck her on the kitchen counter, plain and simple.

My free hand slid under one of her knees so her leg draped down over the crook of my elbow. I lifted her leg higher and pushed deeper inside of her until we both moaned.

I thrust into her hard and fast, my hips moving at lightening speed. The smell of chocolate filled the air, her hot wetness coated me as I pumped in and out of her and the sounds of our bodies slapping together shot my orgasm through me like a freight train. I only lasted a few more seconds, shouting her name as I came, my thrusts never slowing down. My orgasm ripped through me and I swore it was the best one I ever had. I pushed into her one last time and held still until the last few tingles of my release disappeared.

I dropped my forehead to hers and we stayed where we were, trying to catch our breaths. My arm slid out from under her leg and it fell limply down my side. I felt myself pulse inside of her as I wrapped my arms around her and pulled her body close.

After a few minutes of staying just like that, I finally recovered the ability to speak.

"I'm really going to like this whole chocolate business you own if this is how we get to spend our evenings."

Claire laughed and looked around. "It looks like a chocolate bomb went off in here."

There was chocolate in both of our hair, I could feel dried chocolate on my face and arms and our shirts were completely covered. I looked down and saw chocolate handprints on Claire's thighs and hips and the half of her pants that hung off of her were sopping wet from the chocolate that still dripped off the edge of the counter. We were so busy with our post-coital glow and laughing at the mess we made, that we didn't hear the connecting door to Liz's store open.

"SURPRISE!" several voices yelled as we looked towards the door in shock.

"Oh my fucking God, are you kidding me?" Liz yelled as she cringed and tried not to drop the cake she held in her hands.

"Oh Jesus, my eyes. MY EYES!" Jim screamed as he covered his face with both hands and turned around.

"Are those chocolate boobs?" Drew asked, walking towards us and grabbing a piece off of the counter and popping it into his mouth.

My dick, completely shrunken now, was still in Claire. This was like the damn finger in the vagina day all over again. What the fuck was wrong with my life?

"Sorry I'm late! Claire, were you surprised?" Jenny asked as she pushed her way past Liz and Jim, stopping suddenly when she saw the position we were in. On the counter. With both of our asses showing, covered in chocolate.

"Heh, heh, Claire has boobs and penises stuck to her ass!" Drew laughed.

So that explains the weird bumps I felt on her ass. I was a little worried there for a minute that she might have boils or some creepy skin condition I didn't know about.

"I hope to God you bleach this counter," Liz scolded.

"And my eyes," Jim muttered with his back still to us.

Claire hadn't moved or said a word and I almost wanted to stick my finger under her nose to see if she was still breathing.

"We wanted to surprise you with a "Good Luck with the Store Opening" cake but it looks like you guys started celebrating without us," Jenny laughed. "Drew, why haven't we played with chocolate yet? We need to remedial that."

"Remedy, babe. Remedy," Drew corrected as he grabbed another chocolate boob from the counter a few inches from Claire's ass and ate it.

Why the fuck was everyone still standing in this kitchen?

"I brought you a sample of my new edible lotion. It's funnel cake flavor. I figured you and Carter-boy could spice it up by playing dirty carnie and innocent fair-goer," Liz said as she tossed the bottle of lotion on the counter. "Looks like I should have brought you a drop cloth instead."

"I'm guessing you and Jim already tested out the funnel cake lotion, right? Did you pretend to be the slutty clown car with millions of midgets flocking out of your vagina?" Claire said sarcastically.

"This is the Butler Broadcasting System, coming to you live from the kitchen of the snacks side of Seduction and Snacks, the new business opening tomorrow, right in the heart of Butler."

A woman in a business suit suddenly walked through the door with a microphone in her hand and a man with a camera followed behind her. The giant spotlight on top of the camera blinded us and everyone started yelling, but not before we heard the words, "Coming to you live..."

This is a dream. It has to be a fucking dream.

The perfectly coiffed woman with the bouffant hair stopped in her tracks when she saw my chocolate covered ass. Her shout of, "Holy fuck," was now being broadcast into several thousand Butler living rooms.

Thankfully, the cameraman took in the scene in front of him and reacted faster than she did. He whipped around, smacking his camera into Jim's head before stumbling backwards, slipping through the spilled, melted chocolate and crashing down on the floor on his back.

⊙ ⊙ ⊙

"Son of a bitch that hurt," Jim could be heard shouting off-camera as the view on the television suddenly flew to a shot of the ceiling and a loud "ooomf" came through the speakers, signifying the point in the broadcast when the cameraman landed on his ass.

Liz fell off the couch, landing on her side in a fit of giggles. Jim managed to stay on the couch but bent over at the waist, holding on to his stomach as he laughed right along with her.

All Claire and I could do was stare in shock at the replay of tonight's broadcast that Liz managed to catch on her DVR. After the kitchen debacle and plenty of apologies from the staff of BBS for deciding a surprise interview would be fun, we came back to Liz and Jim's house to clean up and see if by some miracle there was a cable outage in the area.

No such luck.

"Ooooh, here comes my part!" Drew said excitedly as he jumped up from his spot on the floor and reached over to turn up the volume on the television.

Drew's face suddenly came into the shot as he bent over the downed cameraman, the view of the shop's kitchen ceiling behind his head.

"Stop by Seduction and Snacks for the grand opening tomorrow and try some of Claire's boobs. They're delicious!" he said with a smile as he bit off one of the chocolate boobs he held in his hand.

The camera turned to the side where the stunned TV anchor stood with Liz and Jenny, waving frantically into the camera behind her and Jim off to the side rubbing his head and muttering, "Fuck that hurt."

"B-b-back to you in the studio, Sam," she stuttered as she stared wide-eyed into the camera without blinking.

The shot went back to the studio where they immediately began talking about the weather.

"Well, the good news is the cameraman managed to avoid showing Butler that you guys were taste testing the chocolate with your penis and vagina," Liz said from her spot on the floor.

"If that's the good news, what the hell is the bad news?" Claire asked.

"Well, Drew is now the face of Seduction and Snacks," Liz laughed.

We all glanced over at Drew as he picked lint off the front of his shirt that had been the main focus of the camera shot.

I guess there were worse things Seduction and Snacks could be famous for than a t-shirt that read, "Have you seen Mike Hunt?"

21.

Itchy Feet and Fading Smiles

Surprisingly, the airing of our dirty laundry, or should I say dirty kitchen and mouths, didn't deter anyone from stopping by the grand opening of Seduction and Snacks today. But if one more person asks me if Mr. Hunt is available, I'm going to punch them in the kidney.

Carter, Gavin, Liz, Jim and I all arrived at the shop a few hours before we opened to finish last-minute details and set everything up. Thankfully, today's opening didn't require the chocolate boobs and penises. Drew ate all the ones that weren't stuck to my ass last night. Come to think of it, he may have eaten those as well. I remembered him saying something about a "Five Second Ass Rule," not to be confused with the original "Five Second Rule" for when you drop food on the floor. I tuned him out when he told Carter, "Her ass better be so clean you can see your face in it!"

Much to our shock, there was a line of people on the sidewalk waiting for us to open.

Was this really my life right now? How did I get to this point? A few months ago I was a single mother with no social life or romantic prospects anywhere in my future, and I was stuck at a dead-end job at a bar. Now, I was opening a business, doing what I loved every single day, and found the love of my life, who was the best father in the world to our son.

Oh, and my vagina was getting regular workouts on an almost-daily basis. Couldn't forget that tidbit since it was probably the most important. I thought if my vagina had to wait any longer for some action, she would have just got up and walked out of my underwear to find another pair of legs to sit between. I would have turned into a fake woman. If you spread my legs, I'd look like Barbie with her plastic who-ha that had no hole. At least Ken wasn't missing out on sticking it to her. Poor guy just had a pair of tighty whities with no bulge. That's probably why when I was younger I always made them dry hump. There wasn't much else they could do, really.

The store had been open for two hours and it had yet to be empty. Liz and I kept the adjoining door to our places open so people could file back and forth. I was a little leery about how the good people of Butler would take to having a sex toy shop downtown, but I was pleasantly surprised to find out how many dirty people lived here. Liz was going to resurrect the sex lives of everyone in this town, one dildo at a time.

She kept the front of her store to the bare minimum, mostly lingerie, lubes, massage lotions, candles and other things that were PG rated and wouldn't freak anyone out that walked by. She kept catalogs on the counter with pictures of all the other items that were located in the back of the store. You could simply point to what you wanted and she'd go in the back and get it for you, wrapping it in a small black bag so no one would know what you got.

My dad took in Liz's side of the store with as much enthusiasm as I expected him to. He walked through the adjoining doors and stopped dead in his tracks in the middle of a rack of garters and corsets. He took a look around and proclaimed joyously, "Humph," then walked back over to my side.

Gavin was the life of the store, naturally. He walked around handing out samples with the motto, "One for you, six for me." He was so hopped up on sugar by twelve o'clock; I was going to have to scrape him off of the ceiling by the end of the day.

I stood at the cash register ringing up a customer's cookie order when I noticed Carter talking to a guy by the front window. He was holding a small boy in his arms and Carter was laughing at something the guy said. He had his back to me so I had no idea who it was but something about him was familiar. I thanked the customer, gave her a flyer and headed over to Carter.

Carter noticed me walking towards him and smiled.

"There's my girl," he said as he lifted his arm so I could ease into his side.

The guy turned at Carter's words and when we saw each other, I wasn't sure who had the more shocked expression on their face.

"Oh my God, Max?"

"Claire?" he answered, equally surprised.

Carter looked between the two of us, obviously puzzled.

"Wait, you two know each other?" he asked.

"Um, yes. But more importantly, how do *you* know him?" I asked.

This was so awkward right now I kind of wished a meteor would crash out in the street. I needed total chaos right now to distract everyone from this insane situation.

"I met Max at the library when I took Gavin that one afternoon so you could work, remember? He gave me some tips on the joys of fatherhood," Carter laughed.

Max hadn't taken his eyes off me during the exchange and I laughed nervously. I didn't see this ending well. At all.

"So, anyway, how do you two know each other?" Carter asked again.

I looked at him and tried to convey with my eyes that this was about to get really weird really fast. Carter didn't get the hint and just stared at me expectantly.

"Hello, earth to Claire," Carter said with a laugh. "What's wrong with your face?"

I sighed, figuring I might as well get this over with.

"Carter, this is Max," I said, with a raise of my eyebrows, hoping he would get it.

He just laughed and shook his head.

"Yeah. We've already established that. Are you okay?" he asked as he leaned towards me.

"Carter. This. Is. MAX," I said again, punctuating Max's name with a big, fake smile.

Carter looked at me like I was insane for all of three point two more seconds when the light bulb finally went off in his brain. Really, how many fucking Maxes did he know? It wasn't like the guy's name was John or Mike and he might have just assumed it was someone else. His name was Max for fuck's sake. As soon as he met him, shouldn't a red flag have gone off in his head?

It was certainly going off now. Carter's head jerked back and forth between Max and me so quickly it almost looked like he was shaking his head no. Maybe he was. His brain might just be on overload right now and it was screaming, "Noooooooooooo! Does not compute!"

"You're Max?" he asked.

Max just nodded, finally looking away from me and at his son squirming in his arms.

"You're Max," he stated.

I laughed uncomfortably. "I think we've covered that already, hon," I said through a smile and clenched teeth.

Let the insanity commence.

Carter started chuckling.

I closed my eyes, not wanting to witness what surely was going to follow. Why had I ever though it was necessary to share every detail of this story? Why?

"Two pumps!" Carter said excitedly, followed by more laughing.

Max just stood there with a befuddled look on his face.

Then Carter raised his arm and pointed at him, still laughing, I might add.

"You're the chump!"

"Oh Jesus," I muttered.

"What?" Max asked.

Carter was smiling like a nut job.

"Nothing," I told Max. "Don't mind him."

"Where's her underwear?" Carter asked, suddenly serious.

Max's son started kicking his little legs around in an attempt to get down. He hefted him up higher in his arms and gave me a smile.

"Well, I better get going. It was good seeing you again, Claire. Good luck with the store," he said as he moved to the door and used his back to push it open.

"Could you say that TWO more times," Carter laughed.

I smacked his arm as Max lifted his hand in a wave.

Carter waved good-bye to him, shaking his hand in the air frantically like he was a little kid watching a parade.

"Come back again!" Carter shouted as Max got out the door and onto the sidewalk. "Claire likes it when people stay more than TWO seconds."

Max finally disappeared out of sight and Carter turned to face me, a lingering smile still on his face.

"What?" he asked when he saw the look on mine.

"When you're ready to start acting like an adult, let me know," I told him.

"Adults are the little ones, right?" he shouted to me as I walked away.

I shook my head as I made my way to the counter. Just then my dad walked back over from Liz's side with a black bag clutched firmly in his hand.

Oh sweet Jesus, my brain couldn't handle anymore crazy today.

We stopped in front of each other and he tried to hide the bag behind his back.

"Dad, did you just buy something from Liz's store?" I asked bewilderingly.

What in the fuck of fuckery would he need from over there? WHAT? Oh God, where's Jim? I need his eye bleach.

"Well, I've got a date tonight," he stated matter-of-factly.

"So take her some chocolates! Or a box of cookies. I'm pretty sure what's in that store isn't first-date material," I said in a panic.

There could be flavored lube in that bag right now. Or a cock ring. Or a strap on. Oh sweet mother fucking Jesus, what if it's been so long since my dad has been with a woman that he bat for the other team now? Nothing against gay men. I love gay men. I had a gay friend in college that I wish I still kept in contact with. He liked to show me the awesome gaydar he possessed by pointing out every gay man within a two-mile radius. What would he say if he was here right now? "Oh, Claire, that man is gayer than Richard Simmons sweatin' to the oldies on a rainbow."

When I took Gavin to the library last week there was a book called *Daddy's Roommate* in the children's section. Should I go back and get that book? Maybe I should buy a copy for future reference. There was also a book called *I Wish Daddy Didn't Drink So Much* and *It Hurts When I Poop*.

What the fuck has happened to children's literature since I was little?

I knew no matter what, I would love my father. That was a fact. To quote my favorite movie, "I love my dead, gay son!"

Well, I love my dead, gay father. Er, I mean my gay father.

I need a drink.

"Never fear, Mr. Hunt is here!" Drew proclaimed as he walked through the door holding Jenny's hand. My dad raised his eyebrow at Drew's shirt that read, "Jam out with your clam out."

"Hey there, Mr. M, how's it hanging?" he asked as he walked over and shook my dad's hand.

It's hanging a little to the left of Perez Hilton Avenue.

"Oooooh, look at you already sampling the merchandise," Drew said, patting my dad on the back in a congratulatory way as he smiled at the black bag still tightly clutched in his hands.

"Claire, the store looks great!" Jenny told me as she gave me a quick hug.

"Thanks, my dad has a roommate," I blurted.

All three of them looked at me in silence.

"Mommy, can I have another cookie?" Gavin asked, running up to me and slamming into my leg.

"No, no more cookies. You already had a chocolate chip cookie. Obviously it wasn't enough for you and now you want to try a different one. I bet you want to try a peanut butter cookie, which is the exact opposite. Peanut butter cookies are on a different team than chocolate chip cookies. I guess chocolate chip cookies just don't satisfy you anymore do they? One day you just woke up and decided you wanted to eat a completely different cookie from the one you've always liked since you were born. You can't just decide at your age that you want a different cookie. It doesn't work that way. You pick a cookie and you stick with it!"

Gavin looked up at me in confusion. His poor four year old brain was probably going to explode.

"Fine, can I have a chocolate sucker then?" he asked innocently.

I was well aware that no one was moving and they were all standing there looking at me like I was having a nervous breakdown. Maybe I was. I had a gay father; I was allowed to freak out.

"Hey, Mom, guess what? Last night Papa was kissing somebody," Gavin said with a smile.

Oh God, here it comes. Who was it? Bill from the hardware store? Tom from the corner coffee shop? Who would be my new step-father-in-law-uncle-friend?

"Gavin, that was supposed to be a secret," my dad laughed uncomfortably.

Ha, ha, what a funny story. My dad and Gavin had a secret. Isn't that cute? Isn't that fucking cute? I like how my son isn't at all fazed to see two men kissing. It shows great promise for the future of this country. However, I don't like that he isn't at all fazed that he saw his grandpa sucking face with a dude!

"Oh, ha, ha, a secret!" I laughed hysterically. "I guess the cat is out of the bag huh, Dad? Or should I say, out of the closet? Whew, is it hot in here?" I rambled, fanning my face with my hand.

Carter walked over then, leaving his station at the front door greeting customers. He must have seen my crazy eyes from across the store and knew I was seriously freaking out. Worse than that one time I ate a pot cookie in high school and then watched *The Wizard of Oz* while listening to Pink Floyd's "The Wall," when every pot smoker worth his weight in gold knows you're supposed to listen to "The Dark Side of the Moon," and I started crying because Toto was looking at me funny and when he barked it came out as, "Hey you, standing in the aisles with itchy feet and fading smiles, can you hear me?" and I could totally hear him and my feet started to itch. I cried for three hours telling everyone the cookie was evil and would kill me in my sleep.

Don't do drugs.

"Claire, you okay?" Carter asked, picking Gavin up into his arms to stand next to me.

"I'm super! I've never been better! This is the best day of my whole life!" I said with a big smile. "We should all go out back and smoke some pot."

What the hell was I spewing out of my mouth?

"George, you forgot your receipt," Liz said as she walked over from her side with a slip of paper in her hand.

"Sue is going to love that nightgown, I'm telling you. The silk is so soft and that peach color is going to look awesome with her skin tone," Liz said, coming up next to my dad and handing him the receipt.

Wait, what? Sue? There was a guy named Sue in Butler? Shouldn't I know this?

My dad actually blushed and quickly glanced at me.

"Uh, yeah. Thanks, Liz. I'm sure she'll love it."

She! Sue's a she. She's a Sue-she.

"She's a she!" I proclaimed.

Carter's arm that wasn't supporting Gavin wrapped around my waist to hold me up. I was sure he figured any minute now I was going to crack up permanently, probably even fall face-first onto the floor without putting my hands out to stop me like some of those idiots on *Tosh.0*.

I could hear Tosh's voice in my head, *"Okay, let's watch that one again in slow motion. Now watch as she just falls forward, never putting her arms out and then BAM! Face plant! Wow, that's gotta hurt!"*

"I probably should have told you this sooner, Claire. I'm kinda seeing Sue Zammond. You know, that woman who runs the travel agency over on Short Avenue? So, yeah. I'm seeing her," my dad said, shuffling his feet.

"Good for you, George," Carter told him as I gave him a quick hug in congratulations. My dad hadn't dated anyone seriously since my mom left. By the look on his face, I'd say things with Sue just might be heading in that direction and I was happy for him.

Carter, George and Drew walked over to the front counter to help out a few customers while the girls and I stood back and watched.

"I am so in love with Drew," Jenny said with a sigh. "I just can't look at him without thinking about his orgasm face."

"Jesus, Jenny! Over share," Liz complained.

"So you guys are really serious, huh?" I asked her, trying not to dry heave thinking about the words "Drew" and "orgasm face" all in one sentence.

She nodded her head and smiled.

"We are! He's taking me to Chicago next week to meet his parents. I'm so excited! I've never been to the Windy Cindy," she said happily.

Liz opened her mouth and I quickly covered it with my hand.

"Don't. Just…don't," I told her.

Drew came up behind Jenny then and wrapped his arms around her waist, leaning down to kiss her cheek.

"Excuse me, I was wondering if you had someplace I could put my boner?"

Jenny giggled and Liz gagged.

"So Liz, have you and Jim set a wedding date yet?" Drew asked, keeping his arms firmly around Jenny.

"As a matter of fact we did. So you guys all better keep your calendars wide open for the next couple of months. There will be meetings and discussions and appointments and fittings," she said as she ticked the items off on her fingers. "Oh and Claire, we want Gavin to be our ring bearer."

I looked at her like she was insane.

"Have you met my son?" I asked her.

She just laughed at me.

Poor confused Liz. She'll find out soon enough. Like when she's standing at the back of the church on the most important day of her life and my son runs down the aisle at full speed in front of her, chucking the pillow at her grandma's head and calling Jim's uncle a dirty nut sack.

"Liz, how do you feel about facial hair for the wedding?" Drew asked seriously as he ran his fingers down his chin.

"Don't even think about having a soul patch at my wedding, Drew. No douche-tags allowed," she replied.

Liz turned her attention in my direction. "Speaking of the future, what's next for Claire and Carter?"

What's next? What isn't next is the better question. So much was changing. Jesus, so much already HAD changed.

I watched Carter walk towards me with Gavin in his arms, tickling him and making him giggle. I took a few deep breaths and calmed down. Everyone I loved was standing here in this room, in my store, happy and healthy. Carter walked to my side and draped his arm around my waist, reminding me that no matter what came my way, I wouldn't have to face it alone. I had my friends, I had my family and I had Carter.

Next week I was putting my house on the market. It freaked me out just a little. I became a mother in that house. I learned how to love another human being more than my own life in that house. But it was time to say good-bye and move on to bigger and better things. In a few months we would begin our future together and handle whatever life threw our way. I knew we would have hard times. I knew we would have a lot of adjusting to do as we learned how to live with each other, but I also knew we would do whatever it took to make it work.

I met a boy at a frat party, beat him at beer pong and let him take my virginity and give me a baby in return. Not a fair trade, but one I wouldn't change for the world.

I turned towards Carter and wrapped both of my arms around his waist and stood on my tiptoes to kiss Gavin's cheek while our friends chatted behind us with my dad.

"Hey Gavin, guess what? Daddy and I have something to tell you."

Carter looked down at me with a surprised look. We agreed to wait until the time was closer to tell Gavin, but I couldn't hold it in anymore. I didn't care if he drove me insane asking if it was time yet. I was happy and excited and I wanted my little man to feel it too.

I waited for Carter to give me the go-ahead to continue. I mouthed the words "I love you" to him and tried not to cry. This man was everything I had ever dreamed of and more. And he was all mine.

He nodded his head in agreement and his lips formed an "I love you" back to me.

I reached up and smoothed Gavin's hair off of his forehead, letting my fingers trail down his cheeks and over his sweet dimples.

"We're going to sell our house and then you and I are going to live in Daddy's house with him," I explained.

Gavin stared at me for a few minutes and then shifted his focus to Carter.

"Really?" he asked.

Carter nodded his head, "Really, buddy."

Gavin looked back at me and smiled, opening his mouth to hopefully tell us how happy he was.

"HOLY SHIT!"

The End

Futures and Frosting

A SUGARCOATED HAPPILY EVER AFTER

1.

Green Jell-O and Snapping Turtles

I have a dream.

And in this dream I'm under the covers in bed, just a few scant inches away from Carter's body. I stare at his prone form lying next to me, the greenish-blue glow from the alarm clock on the bedside table providing just enough illumination for me to see the shallow rise and fall of his chest. The sheet is draped low over his hips as he sleeps peacefully with one arm flung over his eyes and the other resting on his taut, naked stomach. I slide my body ever so slowly across the bed, careful not to disturb him, until I'm so close I can feel the heat from his skin warming me from head to toe. I pull my arms out from under the sheet and my hands reach out towards him. I connect with his smooth, muscular chest, slide my fingers up his body, and...choke the ever living shit out of him.

Okay, that's not really a dream. It's more of a wish if you will, something I fantasize about when business is slow at the shop, when I'm waiting in line at the grocery store, or pretty much every waking moment of every single day when I find myself yawning and cranky from lack of sleep. But it's not like I would ever follow through with this fantasy. I love Carter. I really do. Sometimes it's just a toss-up on whether or not I love sleep more.

A few months ago, I hadn't even known Carter existed. Okay, I knew he existed; somewhere out there, over the rainbow, in a land far, far away living his own life. I never believed in a million years that he would ever stop and give me, his one-night-stand from college, a second thought. Turns out I was wrong on both counts. A land far, far away had turned out to be a few miles from where I lived and that second thought I figured he had never given? Well, much to my dismay, and using a Harlequin Romance novel cliché, he had spent years pining for me and searching the world for *'the one that got away'*.

That's me by the way, in case you haven't been paying attention.

Here I am, a twenty-four-year-old single mother to Gavin (the wonderful parting gift I received in appreciation of my mad virginity-giving-up skillz, 'yo) when suddenly, the guy I spontaneously gave said virginity to after a rousing game of beer pong at a frat party shows up in my home town to whisk me off my feet and claim the son he never knew he had. This doesn't happen in real life. Something this perfect only happens in books or John Hughes movies.

Alright, so Carter has never stood outside my window holding a radio above his head and he's never run down the street to sweep me up into his arms for a toe-curling kiss and hand me a pair of diamond earrings he gave to some other skank just moments before. Our story isn't necessarily a textbook eighties movie. There have been anxiety attacks, freak-outs, drunken ramblings, inappropriate cursing, misunderstandings, arguments, two-finger eye-threats, and chocolate covered sex in a public place that only by the hair of a gnat's testicle avoided being publicly televised. Through it all though, Carter and I have managed to work through our problems with the speed an accuracy of a thirty-minute sitcom on prime time television. It's no "*Some Kind of Wonderful,*" but it's damn near close. I'm still waiting for my street kiss and diamond earrings, though.

In the middle of all this chaos, I am also busy following my dream of opening my own candy and cookie shop. I know right? Why not add one more thing to worry about to my growing pile. There's a reason why I have a magnet on my fridge that says, "You can sleep when you're dead."

My best friend Liz and I had always talked of one day owning businesses together. While I was busy with the whole single mom gig and put my aspirations on a back burner, Liz was finishing up college and got a head start on her dream. Little did I know, she had also made plans to assure that my hopes didn't die along with my ability to sneeze and not piss myself.

I've always been a pretty independent person, so having someone hand me my dream in a neat little package with a bow on top took some getting used to. Liz had inherited a good chunk of change from her grandfather when he passed away years earlier and putting that money to good use by purchasing a building where we could have adjoining businesses was the only option for her. It had taken me a few days to get my head out of my ass and realize that she didn't do it out of pity. She had done it because she loves me and having her dream come true wouldn't have meant nearly as much to her if mine wasn't becoming a reality right along with her.

So in summary, I am EXHAUSTED. And I guess that brings us back to my choking fantasy. Living with another human being takes a little getting used to. So far there are only minimal amounts of irritating qualities we find in each other, and we've overcome those obstacles and are still growing strong. I love Carter more than I ever thought possible, and he has proven to be the best father a woman could ever want for her son. But I swear to God, Jesus, Mary, Joseph, and Christ's childhood friend, Biff, that if he doesn't stop waking me up at four-fifty-eight in the morning, every fucking morning, with his buzz saw snoring, I am going to go David Carradine on his ass.

Oh yes, young grasshopper, you shall choke in your sleep.

Although the more I think about it, David Carradine choked *himself* in some weird sex thing, didn't he? I don't think I can convince Carter to choke himself out no matter how naked I get.

I've tried everything to make my nights of sleep less irritating. I've gently pushed his arm so he would roll over because according to Google, a simple change of position will put a halt to the snoring.

False. And shut up, everything on Google is true! How else would I know that the world's oldest living goldfish is forty-one and his name is Fred? Or that when you type the word "askew" in Google search the page will tilt slightly clockwise? These are facts, people!

My dad had told me to try buying a box of nasal strips for Carter to fasten across the bridge of his nose every night before bed.

Didn't work. I woke up the next morning with nasal strips stuck in places where nasal strips should *never* be stuck.

It's all fun and games until you need to lock yourself in the bathroom with tweezers, a mirror, and a flashlight.

I've kicked my feet and smacked my hands against the mattress repeatedly in frustration while whisper-screaming about cock-sucking snorers and their lack of respect for people who sleep quietly, and I've jerked the covers off of him, hit him in the face with his own pillow, that I yanked out from under his head, while plugging his nose.

Hey, don't judge me. I'm losing sleep here.

And I had only plugged his nose long enough for him to start choking on his own spit. As soon as he could speak, he told me all about the dream he was having where he thought he was suffocating and how he realized while he was dream-dying that he forgot to tell me he loved me before he went to sleep. Yes, I felt guilty. Yes, I made it up to him by having sex with him at five in the morning, and no I have never told him that it was me who actually tried to off him in his sleep.

Sometimes couples need a few secrets.

Carter thinks my irritation with his snoring is cute. Of course he does. He's not the one with his ears bleeding in the middle of the night, praying for his bed mate to asphyxiate in his sleep. Oh no, he is off in dreamland, wondering why the soundtrack of his really good sex dream suddenly includes the melody of knives being sharpened.

Last night, one of my well placed kicks to his thigh, er, I mean gentle taps, finally got him to shut up and roll over. It was a thing of beauty. The silent, peaceful tranquility that flowed through the bedroom almost made me weep with joy. Sadly, as soon as I fell asleep and began happily frolicking through my own dreamland, Carter was shaking me awake and asking if I said something. Because according to him, he had been sleeping like a rock but could have sworn he heard me ask him if the green Jell-O should go in the trunk with the snapping turtles.

A public service announcement for men: If you see that your significant other is fast asleep and your initial whispered question doesn't get a response, don't be surprised if we start spewing green vomit out of the mouths of our rapidly spinning heads as you shake us awake to ask your stupid question fifty decibels louder than the first time.

So here I am again, wide awake at five in the morning, giving the love of my life the stink eye in the dark and wondering if I will be able to keep a straight face when looking at him if I go ahead and order that chin strap contraption I saw on the Home Shopping Network the previous week. As I stare at the ceiling and wonder why a snoring prevention mechanism has to look so much like a jock strap for the face, I suddenly remember something *else* I read on Google not that long ago that I haven't tried yet (Fred, the forty-one-year-old goldfish – FRED IS REAL, dammit!). The article had stated that a short, loud yell of a random, one-syllable word will break through the snoring person's conscience just enough to get them to stop snoring without fully waking them up.

I roll my head to the side to stare at Carter's profile. Watching him sleep soundly while I currently reside in insomnia-land, as a direct result of his deviated septum, makes me feel stabby. Since I can't take my anger out on his septum without making him bleed, I figure I might as well try one more thing. Especially since buying the chin/jock/anti-snoring strap will require that I address Carter as Dick Face from now on. Something I'm assuming he will frown upon.

I take a deep breath and let out my one-syllable word. "F-U-U-U-U-U-C-K!"

In the blink of an eye Carter jolts awake with a scream, flailing his arms and legs and scrambling across the bed until he falls off the side and lands on the floor with a loud thud.

"Son of a bitch! What the hell was that?" he mutters from the floor.

"I think there's green Jell-O in the trunk with the turtles," I state before rolling over and snuggling under the covers.

2.
My Dog Has the Hungry

"I just don't think it's a good idea, Claire."

I roll my eyes at my dad as I shove a tray of fresh Butter Brickle Bars into the display case under the front counter a little harder than necessary. A few of the bars jump out of their spots on the tray due to my irritation, and as I reach in to fix them, I have to force myself not to eat another one. As much as I love making sweets, I normally don't eat very many. My tastes tend to lean more towards salty snacks. I don't know what is wrong with me lately though. If I keep sampling the goods like this my ass is going to grow another cheek to make room for all the fat.

"I really don't think you've thought this through," my dad continues as he leans his hip against the counter and folds his arms across his chest.

I take that back. I know exactly why I've been pigging out on chocolate and cookies.

I reached into the glass case and grab the Butter Brickle Bar closest to me and shovel the whole thing in my mouth at once. I take a moment to savor the taste of brown sugar, vanilla, and toffee bits, letting the sugary sweetness do its trick of removing some of my stress. Since I can't physically chuck the six-foot-two tension problem I currently have out of the store without giving myself a hernia, this will have to do. I swallow the mouthful of cookie bar and try not to think about it forming little legs and sprinting straight to my ass, leaving pats of butter behind on my hips as it goes. I take a deep, fortifying breath so I can deal with my father.

303

"Dad, Carter and I have been living together for two months. It's a little late for this speech now don't you think?"

My dad has never said one word for or against mine and Carter's living arrangements ever since we first announced it on the day of Seduction and Snacks' grand opening.

He had grunted, glared at Carter, and then walked away. That was approval as far as I had been concerned.

Now that it's been two months and I haven't changed my mind like he probably thought I would, suddenly he has an opinion.

"Everyone says, 'why buy the bar when you can get the beer for free'."

I stop with my arm in midair as I reach for a towel to wipe down the counter.

"Dad, no one says that."

"*Everyone* says that," he replies, pushing himself away from the counter and moving his hands to his hips.

I roll my eyes and began wiping crumbs off of the top of the display case.

"Really? Who?" I challenge as the bell above the door chimes and a customer walks in.

"People," he states firmly.

I sighed and turn away from my dad to smile and greet the woman who is perusing the white chocolate section at the opposite end of the case from where we are standing. After making sure she doesn't have any questions, I glance back at him.

"Dad, it's two-thousand-and-twelve, not the nineteen-fifties. People live together all the time before they make any kind of huge commitment. We just need some time to get used to each other and learn to live together as a family without killing each other. It's not that big of a deal."

My dad huffs and it is his turn to stare at me in irritation.

"Really, Claire, when have I ever given you any kind of indication that I'm old fashioned? I just don't want this yahoo to think he can move you and Gavin into his place and then never have to do anything to make it official. At least if he married you, I wouldn't have to worry about your whiny ass showing up on my doorstep anytime soon wanting your old room back."

I wonder how many Butter Brickle Bars I can fit in my mouth at one time.

"Did you really just call Carter a *yahoo*? How about we take a seat on the davenport so we can discuss that little hooligan and how you aren't old fashioned in the least?" I state sarcastically.

"I should have sold you to that traveling circus when you were four. I could be out on the lake fishing right now instead of having this conversation," he mutters.

My dad had been married twice before he married my mom, and he had his first wife Linda's name tattooed on his arm. When I was younger I tried to change Linda to my mom's name, Rachel, with a sharpie marker when he was sleeping. Unfortunately, he woke up before I could finish. It took him three days to wash Rinda off of his arm. When I told that story to Carter, he started singing like the Chinese men in *"A Christmas Story"*. *Deck da hars with boughs of horry, fa-ra-ra-ra-ra, ra-ra-ra-ra!* He tried joking with my dad once about it saying, "You reary roved Rinda." My dad thought he was impersonating Scooby Doo and didn't find it funny. Could be why he wasn't one hundred percent sold on the whole living together situation. And all of it was a prime example of why I wasn't jumping on board the marriage band wagon just yet. My dad had struck out three times and my mom twice when she had finally decided marriage wasn't for her when I was twelve and packed up to get a condo in the city.

I don't really have shining examples of happily ever after in my life.

Anyway, the point is everyone makes their own decisions about life, some good and some bad. They all teach us something about who we are and blah, blah, blah. No matter what my dad's opinion is, I need to know if Carter's snoring and his inability to put a new roll of toilet paper back on the holder is going to be a deal breaker before we do something legal that we can't back out of.

So far, stupid bad habits aside, we are doing quite well cohabiting. Gavin has adjusted nicely, and I haven't smothered Cater in his sleep. That's total win right there.

My dad can finally tell by the look on my face that I am closing the conversation for further discussion or arguments, and he has given up on the beer/sex/whatever the fuck analogy. He grabs the newspaper he set down on the counter when he first walked in, tucks it under his arm, and walks over to one of the small tables by the front window to drink his coffee. Regardless of the mood he had put me in, seeing the four black, round tables set up in front of the picture window at the front of the store makes me smile. They had just been delivered the prior week and seeing someone sitting in them, even if it is my father, made me giddy. This is *my* store and those are *my* tables and nothing can mar the elated feeling that gave me.

The chime above the door sounds again, and I glanced over to see my friend Jenny storm in with an angry scowl on her face. Never in a million years have I ever picture myself being friends with someone like her. She is runway model beautiful and the things that come out of her mouth rarely make sense, but she's proven to be a good friend in the few months since I've met her and would help anyone with anything they asked without a second thought. Much to everyone's surprise, Jenny had managed to grab onto Carter's best friend, Drew, and wrap him around her little finger. Drew is the biggest man whore you will ever lay eyes on, but for whatever reason, Jenny is able to tame him. Somewhat.

"Hey, what's going on?" I ask Jenny as I round the counter to meet her halfway. I glance down at my watch and see it's only eleven in the morning. "Why aren't you at work?"

Jenny works for the same computer design company she has since her freshman year in college.

She had started off as an intern and quickly made her way up the ranks and was now one of the most talented graphic designers they had on staff. She helped me out in a pinch when I was opening my store and made all of the flyers, brochures, and business cards in her free time and refused to take any payment. It had been one of the main reasons I decided I liked her.

Anyone who doesn't charge me for services rendered is good people in my book.

Jenny laughs manically at my question about work and crossed her arms in front of her. "That's a great question, Claire. And the answer would be, I got fired," she replies before bursting into tears, flinging her arms around me, and burying her face in my shoulder.

Oh Jesus God no.

I awkwardly bend my elbow and pat my hand against her lower back. She still has her arms wrapped around me in a vice grip and that's as high as I can reach. I shove my other hand into the pocket of my jeans and pull out my cell phone, sending a quick "please help me, God" text to Liz next door.

Jenny continues to cry, sniffle and every few minutes wail. After subtly spitting out some of her hair from my mouth as she burrows further into my neck and shoulder, I anxiously glance down at my cell phone wondering how much longer I will need to pretend I enjoy soothing people during breakdowns before Liz gets her ass over here and rescues me. It probably won't be very friend-like of me if I start freaking out that there might now be a pile of someone else's snot pooling on the shoulder of my tee-shirt. My phone buzzes in my hand and I crane my neck over Jenny's shoulder to see the message.

I am busy with customers. You are going to have to MAN UP and comfort her yourself. Start acting like you have a vagina for fuck's sake and hug her.
XOXO – Liz

I grit my teeth at the knowledge I am on my own in the pits of consoling hell.

"There, there," I say, patting her on the back again. I really think I should have been born a guy. I don't know many women who get skeeved out by displays of emotion. If I see a woman crying, I usually run in the other direction. I am not one of those people that throws my arms around her and tells her everything will be okay—because it probably won't. It will most likely suck just as much whether I hug you or not, so it's probably best for everyone involved if I just stand off to the side and let someone else do the touching. I feel much more comfortable wallowing in anger and stewing about something privately until my head explodes. That's natural. Hugging and crying and snotting all over someone isn't.

"Didn't you just get a raise? Why in the hell would they fire you?" I ask as I worm my way out of her arms and try to subtly back away from her.

Don't look at the snot on your shoulder, don't look at the snot on your shoulder. I know you can feel it there, but for God's sakes, DON'T LOOK AT IT!

Jenny finally releases her hold on me and uses the back of her hands to wipe the tear streaks off her face. If only she would have done that with the snot instead of using my shoulder.

"I don't have any idea why they really fired me. They gave me some song and dinner about positive attitude." she pouts.

"You mean dance?" I ask in confusion.

"Claire, focus! I got fired! This is no time for talk about dancing," she yells.

I take a deep, calming breath and put my hands on my hips to keep from strangling her.

"Okay, so they fired you because they didn't like your attitude?" I reiterate.

Jenny looks at me incredulously. "I know, right? I told them I was the most positive person in that dump."

"Verbatim?" I ask her.

"I didn't forbid them anything. What are you talking about? Are you even listening? Have you been drinking?"

The last is stated in a stage whisper as she looks over at the customer who came in earlier. I pinch the bridge of my nose and try not to stomp my foot and throw a temper tantrum like Gavin does when I tell him he is grounded from PlayStation.

"What am I going to do without a job?" she whines as she paces back and forth in front of me. "It's mine and Drew's three month anniversary and I was going to buy him something really special and now I'm not going to be able to afford it."

I grab onto her elbow to stop her pacing and pulled her back behind the counter with me when I saw the customer was finally ready to order.

"I'm sure Drew will understand," I tell her as I start filling a box with the woman's request of a pound of white chocolate covered pretzels.

"No he won't. He's going to be so upset. I already told him what I was buying, and he was really looking forward to the vagina mold," she says dejectedly.

I drop the metal candy scoop on the floor and look over at Jenny as she sighs miserably.

As I pick up the scoop and toss it into the sink before grabbing a clean one, all sorts of thoughts swirl through my mind that shouldn't be when I am waiting on a customer—like who-ha's covered in green fuzz and moldy cheese vaginas dancing around the Tupperware container in the back of my fridge with two-month old spaghetti in it.

Jenny looks over and sees the horror on my face as I try to block out the mental image of moldy cheese vaginas singing, "Mold, mold, baby," in the voice of Vanilla Ice in my head.

"Claire, didn't you see the new product Liz got in last week? It's a mold you can make of your vagina. So your guy can...you know..."

Jenny uses the age old finger gesture of a penis going into a vagina by making a circle with her index finger and thumb and using the index finger of her other hand to move in and out of it.

"Eeeew, what? That's disgusting," I whisper, smacking her hands to get her to stop making that motion with her fingers as I hand the customer her chocolate.

"It's not disgusting," Jenny says. "It's romantic. Drew wants a replica of my..." she glances at the customer and then lowers her voice "...love tunnel so he can be with me whenever we're apart."

I step away from her to ring up the customer, trying not to picture Drew holding on to some little floppy, silicone vagina-looking thing, talking to it in a baby voice like it's Jenny. *"Oooooh, I wuv my wittle fake Jenny-vagina! Yes I do!"*

"Wouldn't it be easier to just get him a blow-up doll and tape your picture over its face?" I ask as I watch the customer leave the store with her purchase and hope she didn't hear enough of this conversation to prevent her from ever stepping foot in here again.

Jenny shakes her head at me in pity. "You have absolutely no sense of romance, Claire."

I huff in indignation as I get busy filling a box with chocolate covered strawberries for an order that's being picked up after lunch. I am plenty romantic.

Just this morning while he slept, I had left Carter a box of his favorite candy next to his pillow–Globs: piles of white chocolate covered, crushed potato chips and pretzels drizzled with caramel. I figured it would soften him up to the note I placed next to the box telling him if he left the toilet seat up one more time and my ass got an involuntary bath at six in the morning, I would put super glue on the head of his penis while he slept. I had even signed the note with a couple of Xs and Os.

Who says romance is dead?

I close up the box of strawberries and finish it off with my signature pink bow and a sticker with the name and address of the store. Setting it aside, I turn to face Jenny and find her inhaling an entire pan of white chocolate covered Nutter Butter cookies that I had been experimenting with that morning.

"Jenny, put the chocolate down and step away from the tray slowly." I speak to her in my best hostage negotiator voice. "I wanted to ask you if you'd be able to help out with a few things for me, but I knew you were busy with work," I explain as I reach around her and take the tray from her hands before she harms herself or others with her unemployment gluttony.

"Work!" Jenny says with a whimper as her lip starts to quiver. She reaches out with both hands and grabs back onto the tray of half-empty chocolates.

"Oh Jesus, will you let me finish?!" I scold as I smack her hands.

She sighs and finally lets go of the tray of chocolates, spitting out a half-eaten Nutter Butter into the middle of the pile before she turns to face me.

"Those are delicious, but I feel kind of pukey right now," she mumbles, putting a hand to her stomach.

I move the tray far out of her reach and my line of sight before I myself become pukey.

"As I was saying, I have a bunch of things you could do for me here. I need a website created and maintained, advertising managed, and everything that goes along with marketing this place that I know nothing about. I got a call just the other day from a magazine wanting to set up an interview, and I have no idea what I'm doing. I know it's not your ideal job, and I probably can't pay you anywhere near as much as you're used to making, but in the interim, until you find something else, would you like to work for me?"

The squeal that erupts from Jenny breaks the sound barrier and makes small dogs throughout the land howl in terror. She throws her arms around me and bounces up and down, making me feel uncomfortable once again at the displays of affection people feel the need to give.

"Thank you so much, Claire! I promise you won't be disappointed. I will do such a good job you'll want to bang the shit out of me!"

I glance up to see my dad standing behind Jenny looking like he'd rather eat the regurgitated chocolate covered Nutter Butter at that moment than inadvertently hear our conversation.

"I just...I'm gonna...my dog has the hungry," he mumbles before turning and walking away.

Jenny lets go of me and watches as he quickly exits the shop. "You're dad has a dog?"

I shook my head and let out a deep sigh. "Nope."

3.

He Went to Jared

"Hey, Carter, when I drunk dialed you last night, did I by any chance mention where I put my keys?" Drew asks as I walk into the living room.

He rummages through the couch cushions, cursing and pulling out loose change, McDonald Happy Meal toys, and other goodies he finds in the cracks and crevices. I grab my baseball cap off of one of the end tables and stick it on my head before turning to watch him.

Drew and I haven't shared a living space in months, yet somehow, even now that Claire and I are living together, I still manage to find him passed out on my couch every once in a while.

"How did you even get home last night if you didn't have your keys? And I hope you know that I use the term "home" loosely. As much as I enjoy your company and watching you stumble drunkenly around my home at four in the morning when Jenny won't answer her door because she thinks you're an axe murderer, this is not where you live. Even though you might think so since I always seem to answer the door and let you in."

A cell phone sails out of the couch as Drew continues to dig to China in search of his keys. I walk over and scoop it up, putting it in my back pocket. Now I remember why I let Drew in the door. He isn't afraid to stick his hand down into the bottom of a couch. I had known exactly where I lost my cell phone; I was just too afraid to go in search of it. There are scary, scary things living in the bottom of those cushions. Something I had quickly found out was a direct result of living with a child.

"I probably took a cab. Or walked. I don't know, the evening got a little fuzzy after I found produce stickers on my penis when I went to take a piss," he replies in all seriousness as he gets up from his knees and turns to face me. The wrinkled and stained shirt he wears that states, "Ask me about my huge penis," has one of the sleeves torn off and proves he had a rough night.

I don't even bother trying to tell him that if he didn't have his keys when he left the club or wherever he ended up last night, it stands to reason they won't be hibernating in my couch. I have other things on my mind at the moment though. I walk away from Drew and into the kitchen, making my way to my coat that's hanging on the back of one of the chairs. I reach into the inside pocket, pull out the small, black velvet box, and open the lid to look inside for the ten thousandth time since I picked it up last week.

The sight of the one and a half carat, platinum, diamond ring nestled in the white satin makes my heart pound with excitement. And I'm not going to lie; it also makes me want to throw up in my mouth. Just a little bit. I stare down at the precious metal that that took me eight days and six trips to the jewelry store to pick out. The main diamond is princess cut and framed by twelve, three-quarter carat round diamonds. The ring is complimented by lines of round diamonds along the band. It's elegant and beautiful.

Yes, I know I sound like a walking advertisement for a jewelry store and men everywhere are humming the tune of "Taps" right now and brain screaming, "MAN DOWN!" but I feel a little fist pump is in order due to the fact that Claire will be able to look over at her friends all smug-like and say, "He went to Jared!"

If she says yes. Which she totally will, ha ha! I'm not nervous at all. I don't feel all itchy and ball-sweaty thinking about popping the question and the possibility that she just might laugh in my face and tell me I'm bat shit crazy. Who gets married after only being together a few months? Who has a one-night-stand in college and finds out five years later it resulted in a child? Who spends all those years turning into a creeper that stalks bath and body shops every time they get a new chocolate-scented lotion line and gets a hard-on at work when some guy, whose wife just had a baby girl, passed out Hershey bars with the cutesy little wrapper that says, "HERESHEIS!"

This guy right here. Don't even ask how I explained away the boner and how I am NOT a child molester and that it's totally natural to get turned on when a co-worker is talking about a baby.

That sentence sounded much better in my head, so let's just pretend I never said it and move on.

The fact is, I spent years wishing I could see my one-night-stand again and find out if she was real, hoping I could one day meet her again and see if she could still make me laugh and turn me on with just a brush of her hand or the smell of her skin.

I had tried to fill the void with a woman whose mouth could hold more balls than a Hungry, Hungry Hippo, but walking in on her playing hide the salami with our neighbor made me realize two things. One, I should have never tried to blot out the memory of my dream girl with someone else. And by "someone else" I meant a whore. And two, our neighbor had Elephantitis of the ball and should seriously get that looked at by a medical professional of some sort. And no, that wasn't a mistake. I really meant *ball*, as in singular. Dude only had one ball and it was the size of a coconut.

Seriously. Google a picture of a coconut. I'll wait. Because you really need to get the full effect of what I saw dangling there for the twenty seconds it took for me to get my head out of my ass and scream insults at both of them.

All of this, while nightmare inducing, had made me realize that when I found Claire, I knew I would do whatever it took to never lose her again.

We may have done everything ass backwards, but I wouldn't change a thing. Claire and Gavin are my whole world and I want to make it official. I want her to know that nothing could tear me away from them and that I am in it for the long haul. Pushing the nerves aside, I smile as I stare at my future and a big chunk of my savings account tucked into the small, velvet box. I close the lid with a *snap* just as Drew walks into the kitchen dangling his keys from the tip of his index finger, holding them out away from his body as far as possible.

"So you're really going to do it, huh? You're going to make an honest woman out of Claire?" he asks as he runs water in the sink, dumps in about a half a bottle of liquid soap, and throws his keys into the growing pile of bubbles. He shuts the water off and turns around to lean against the counter. I give him and the sink a questioning look and he just shrugs his shoulders.

"I found them in the tank of the toilet. Better to be safe than sorry."

Gavin chooses that moment to run into the room and I lift him up into my arms before I can ask Drew why this is the second time in a month he's lost his keys in my toilet.

"Why is Uncle Drew washing dishes?" Gavin asks as he wrapped his arms around my neck.

"I'm not washing dishes. I'm washing my keys," Drew explains with his back to us as he splashes in the water trying to retrieve them. He flings them out of the sink as he turns back around, splattering Gavin and I with suds.

"You don't wash keys. That's dumb," Gavin replies seriously.

"Um, hello? You do too wash keys. Especially if they have *your* poop on them because they were in *your* toilet," Drew replies as he shakes the excess suds off of his key ring.

"I don't poop on keys! YOU poop on keys!" Gavin yells angrily. "I'm going to stick your head in the toilet!"

I probably should have intervened by now, but sometimes this is the highlight of my day. I unwind Gavin's arms from my neck and set him back down.

"Okay, that's enough. Gavin, go in your room and get your baseball hat. It's almost time to pick up mommy and go to the game."

Gavin takes off running but not before giving Drew a dirty look.

"Dude, that kid has anger issues. I hope you sleep with one eye open at night," Drew mutters as he watches Gavin run off. He turns back to face me and crosses his arms in front of him. "So, you took my suggestion and went with the baseball game proposal. Nice. Good work."

"As much as it pains me to say this, it was a really good idea. A guy at work got a bunch of free tickets to the Indian's game today because his daughter works for the concierge desk at Progressive Field. According to this guy, they don't allow you to just pay for a proposal to be put up on the scoreboard anymore. He gave me his daughter's work number and she told me about this whole proposal package they have. So, for three hundred dollars I am now the proud owner of a Cleveland Indian's Proposal Package," I explain proudly.

"Will those three hundred dollars assure that they might actually win a game this year?" Drew asks.

I shake my head. "Probably not. But, it does get us moved to VIP seating in a loge after I propose, a five-by-seven glossy photo of the proposal as it was seen on the scoreboard, a dozen red roses, and a gift certificate to the Terrace Club restaurant right at the park so we can have dinner to celebrate," I say with a smile as I grab my non-toilet-infested car keys off of the counter along with my wallet.

"If she says yes, you mean. Otherwise that's just going to be the most depressing photo you will ever have hanging on your wall and a *really* uncomfortable dinner," Drew supplies with a sad shake of his head.

"Thank you so much for that vote of confidence," I deadpan.

And now the nerves are back. But I won't let them get to me. I've been wracking my brain for weeks trying to come up with a unique and special way to propose to Claire, and when she mentioned casually that she'd never taken Gavin to an Indian's game, I knew it would be the perfect setting. It will be in front of thousands of people and our son will be there to witness it. What could be better than that? And really, what woman wouldn't love it?

◉ ◉ ◉

During the sixth inning is when everything went to shit. Aside from the Drew-induced nervous stomach I suffered from during the first five innings, we are having a great time. Gavin is amazed by the ballpark and the Indians were up by seven. As my knee bounces up and down, and I force myself not to buy another hot dog to give myself something to do because eight ballpark hot dogs is where I draw the line, I try not to think about the fact that I never asked Claire's father for her hand in marriage. That is something people still did nowadays, isn't it? Would George be mad at me that I didn't have a formal sit-down with him to discuss our upcoming nuptials and whether or not he approved? And now that I have said the word, "sit-down," I am having flashes of George wearing a three-piece suit and fedora staring at me across a plate of half-eaten linguini while he steeples his fingers under his chin and then excuses himself to go to the bathroom so he can get the gun he hid behind the toilet and shoot me in the head.

"Leave the gun. Take the cannoli!"

A few people in the row in front of us turn around to look at me quizzically and I just shrug. They won't judge me if they know my future father-in-law is a mobster who wants me dead for not going through the proper channels to marry his one and only daughter.

Claire is too busy arguing with Gavin about how a third bag of cotton candy will not, in fact, give him superpowers no matter what he saw on television so she has no idea about the minor freak-out I had going on. Not that I would talk to her about it anyway. This is supposed to be a surprise—a huge, life-changing surprise that could make or break our future. Or my kneecaps if George decides he really does hate me.

I continue my manic foot tapping as Jose Cabrera goes up to the plate and repeat the words I plan to say to Claire in my head.

I never thought I'd find you again…you are my heart and soul and my reason for living…every moment I spend with you is like-

Claire's laughter breaks my concentration, and I glance over to see her pointing to the outfield and snickering with a few people sitting around her.

"Oh my God, would you look at that!" she exclaims.

I glance out beyond third base to see what has caught her interest. When I see what everyone else is staring at, my stomach plummets all the way to my toes and the eight hotdogs I just consumed threaten to make a reappearance in a totally unflattering way that won't be near as much fun as dancing meat singing the Oscar Mayer wiener song.

There, televised on the jumbotron for all of Progressive Field to see, is a guy down on one knee somewhere by the first base line holding up a ring box to a hysterically sobbing woman with her hands over her mouth in shock. In big, jumbotron-sized, blinking red letters below their picture are the words, "Crystal, will you marry me? Love Rob!"

Claire snorts and shakes her head. "What a tool that guy is. How cheesy can you be? Proposing at a baseball game in front of tens of thousands of strangers and putting it up on the scoreboard? That's got to be the most clichéd thing ever.

"REALLY ORIGINAL THERE, MORON!" she yells as everyone around us claps and cheers when the woman on the screen nods her head up and down emphatically and the pair embrace.

Oh sweet Jesus. Sweet mother fucking fuckery of fucks.

I am going to win the *'Tool of the Year'* award if my proposal shows up on that screen in the next five minutes like it's scheduled to. I don't even know if there *is* a *'Tool of the Year'* award. There must be. It's probably a huge, gold penis trophy with an arrow pointing to it that reads, "This is you! A giant dick! Congratulations." There's probably even a *'Tool of the Year'* book they print every year like that *'Darwin Awards'* book that really has nothing to do with winning an esteemed award and everything to do with the fact that people are pointing and laughing because you died from trying to slow dance with an ostrich that would rather peck out your eyes than learn the Cha Cha.

Claire is going to peck out my eyes if I propose to her right now!

"Carter, are you okay? You look like you're going to throw up. I told you no one should ever eat more than six hotdogs. That's just asking for pig snout disease or whatever the hell they make those things out of," Claire scolds as she looked me over worriedly.

"I ate a pig snout?!" Gavin asks elatedly. "What's a pig snout?

Claire turns to the other side of her to try and explain to Gavin that hotdogs are, in fact, not made out of dogs, and I take that moment to jump up from my seat, mumbling something about throwing up before I race up the stairs to the concierge desk to cancel my Cleveland Indian's Proposal Package before I die a slow, horrible eye-pecking death.

4.

He Loves Me, He Loves Me Not

"I think he's going to break up with me."

Liz's sigh through the phone line is loud and clear. I know she's irritated with me. *I* am irritated with me. It's getting to the point where I can't even stand the sound of my own voice and yet I can't shut up about this.

"He's been acting really weird ever since the Indian's game last week," I explain as I pull my car into the driveway and let the engine idle.

"Carter isn't going to break up with you. Will you shut up about this already? Maybe he's just stressed about work or the fact that his parents are finally coming for a visit. Did you try out that move on him I told you about the other night? The one where you take your fingers and put them in his-"

"LA-LA-LA, I'M NOT LISTENING TO YOU!" I yell over her voice and try to block out the words "prostate" and "gentle massage".

"Fine, but I'm telling you – it will totally relax him," she says matter-of-factly.

I turn off the ignition and rested my head against the steering wheel.

"Have you tried, oh I don't know, *asking* him what's wrong?" Liz continues.

"You're rolling your eyes at me right now, aren't you?" I reply. "No, I haven't asked him. I've done what every other woman in a new relationship does when her boyfriend is acting all twitchy and nervous. I completely ignore the situation and pretend like it isn't happening while making a list of possible responses and comebacks I can lob at him when he finally decides to give me the brush-off. I am NOT going to be one of those people who clam up when he tells me, 'It's not you, it's me,' and then six hours later when I'm sitting alone in the dark with a bottle of vodka scream, 'OH IT'S TOTALLY YOU AND YOUR SMALL PENIS!'. I'm going to have viable retorts ready to go so I don't come up with them later when I'm drunk and alone, and they do no one any good."

I sit back in my seat and stare at the front door of the house I now live in with Carter. The white, three bedroom ranch with black shutters is nestled in a lush cluster of pine trees. I love this house. But more importantly, I love the two men inside of it. My heart literally hurts to think about not being with Carter.

"Carter doesn't have a small penis, by the way," I say, breaking the silence.

"So you've told me. Several times," Liz deadpans.

"I'm sorry I keep bugging you about this."

"Don't apologize. That's what I'm here for. Just talk to him about it. You can thank me for my sage advice by remembering that, as my maid of honor, you are required to keep any and all passé bachelorette party activities as far away from me as possible this weekend," Liz reminds me.

Liz and Jim's wedding date is fast approaching. Being as far removed from a typical bride as possible, Liz had vetoed a traditional bachelorette party and instead decided it would just be one big co-ed night out. Maybe that's what Carter and I need - a night out with friends without any work or parenting responsibilities. I thank Liz again and quickly hang up the phone so I can go in the house and greet my boys.

☉ ☉ ☉

"I'm home!" I yell as I close the front door behind me and set my purse down on the table next to it.

A flash of color darts into the room and barrels into me.

"Mommy's home!" Gavin cheers as I pick him up and start walking further into the house.

"Where's Daddy?" I ask as I rub his back while he clings to me.

"He's gettin' ready for work."

I walk into the bedroom and set him down on top of the bed, bouncing onto the mattress next to him. Gavin stands up and starts jumping up and down and singing.

"Woke up dis mornin', got myself a gun!"

Before I can tell him to stop, Carter walks out of the bathroom, popping his head through the neck of a tee shirt and then pulling the material the rest of the way down over his stomach.

"Hey, baby," he greets me with a smile as he makes his way over to the bed, leans over, and gives me a kiss. He lingers against my mouth and rubs his lips back and forth against mine before pulling away so he can look at me.

"Did you let our son watch *'The Sopranos'* again today? I ask him with a raise of my eyebrows.

Carter laughs nervously and backs away. "No, why would you think that?"

Gavin stops bouncing on the bed and looks at Carter.

"Yes you did, Daddy. Don't you wemember? Big Pussy cried and you called him a pansy-ass," he says earnestly.

I look at Carter pointedly.

"And tell me you didn't take him out in public today with that shirt on."

We both look at Gavin's shirt that boldly states, "They shake me."

"I can neither confirm nor deny those rumors," Carter says as he sits down next to me on the bed so he can put his shoes on. "Let's just say we had lunch with Uncle Drew, and if I didn't put the new shirt on Gavin that he bought him, there would have been a scene."

"I'm pretty sure Gavin would have been fine if you refrained from putting him in that shirt," I tell him.

"I'm not talking about Gavin. Have you *met* Drew?"

Gavin takes a leap off of the bed and runs out of the room. I scoot closer to Carter and rest my head on his shoulder. He lifts one arm and wraps it around my shoulder, pulling me against his side. He seems okay right now, so I figure there is no need to ruin the moment and ask him what his problem has been the past few days and if he still loves me.

"Sometimes I really hate that you work nights," I tell him softly, wrapping my arms around his waist.

He turns and kisses me, easing both of us back onto the bed so we are laying in a tangle of legs and arms.

"You don't have to lie. I know you like the peace and quiet during the week and having control over the remote," he says with a smile as he brushes a piece of hair out of my eyes.

"You're right, I do. But it doesn't mean I don't love you. It just means *'The Real Housewives of Orange County'* can be watched without eye rolls and sarcastic comments. If anyone is going to judge Gretchen and Slade for their poor life choices it will be me," I explain.

"Oh, that reminds me. I've got something for you," he says as he pulled his arms out from around me and rolls onto his back so he can dig into the pocket of his jeans.

"Are you going to tell me that you have a present in your pants for me? Because I've got to tell you, I've been to that pants party a bunch of times. I almost got a concussion last time."

Carter digs deeper into his pocket and huffs at me.

"It is not my fault I was unprepared for road-head. I thought you weren't feeling good and were just going to put your head down in my lap. When a man's penis suddenly makes an appearance in a moving vehicle on a Saturday night, an involuntary hip thrust WILL HAPPEN."

He finally pulls his hand out of his pocket and holds it out to me, palm up.

"This is your present," he says to me.

I look into his hand to see two small, orange, bell-shaped pieces of foam resting inside of a tiny plastic bag. I look at them quizzically trying to decide the correct response one should have when receiving something that looked like dresses for Polly Pocket dolls.

"Um, you shouldn't have?"

Carter laughs at my obvious confusion.

"Oh I should have. Especially if I want to live through another night of sleeping next to you. These, my dear, are the best earplugs ever. They have bins and bins of them at work. If you like them, let me know and I'll bring a bunch more home."

He got me earplugs. He really DOES love me.

I take the bag from his hand and tear open the plastic with my teeth so I can pull the squishy orange plugs out and look them over. I roll one between my finger and thumb to shrink it, and then I push it into my ear.

I repeat the process with the other one and lie perfectly still as the foam slowly expanded until I can't hear a single sound except for the *whoosh* of my breathing.

"THANK YOU SO MUCH, THESE ARE PERFECT!" I tell him.

At least I assume that's what I said. To me it had sounded more like the teacher in a Charlie Brown cartoon.

Carter smiles and I see his mouth move.

"WHAT?"

His mouth moves again.

Does he not understand the concept of earplugs? The word itself is pretty self-explanatory. Ear. Plug. From the Latin root, "I can't hear a fucking thing that is coming out of your mouth."

I stick my finger in my ear and yank one of the plugs out.

"As I was saying, you're welcome. I have to go to work now. Does this ensure that I can go to sleep from now on knowing all of my appendages will still be attached when I wake up?"

He pushes himself up off of the bed, and I pull the other ear plug out and toss them both on my nightstand so I can follow him out of the room.

"I do solemnly swear not to Lorena Bobbet your penis," I tell him as we make our way down the hall and out into the living room.

Carter says a quick good-bye to Gavin who is sitting on the couch watching cartoons and then grabs his work bag off of the floor beside the front door.

"Don't forget Liz and Jim's co-ed pre-wedding party, that we are never to refer to as a bachelor-slash-bachelorette party, is this weekend," I remind Carter as I plant a kiss on his cheek.

"I know. Drew already sent me three texts since lunch trying to get me to admit that I was joking when I told him there wouldn't be strippers. I got a call from his phone after the last text I sent but he never spoke. I think he was just silently weeping in the background."

Carter opens the door and then turns back to me before walking out.

"Oh and don't *you* forget that my parents are coming in this weekend from Columbus. I can't wait for you to finally meet them!"

I close the door behind him and lean my back against it.

"Yay. Meeting the in-laws," I cheer to myself in a completely non-cheery way.

5.

Suck for a Buck

Friday night is finally here and the work week is over. Not that I really have anything to complain about in that regard. I own my own business (someone pinch me!), and every moment I spend in the shop makes me happy. But even when you love what you do, it's still nice to forget about it for a few hours.

The minor freak-outs about Carter are pushed to the back of my mind since everything has been so perfect between us the last couple of days. He doesn't jump when I walk into the room anymore, and he isn't whispering on the phone when I get out of the shower. A normal woman would probably suspect cheating, but not me. I had already followed him a few times and checked his text messages.

Seriously. Don't judge me.

Gavin is spending the night at my dad's house, so as soon as I get home from work, I pack his overnight bag and then got ready for the party. I still haven't stopped thanking Liz after she informed me that she didn't want a traditional bachelorette party where a group of girls get in a limo and go to a strip club.

Thank God.

Don't get me wrong, I'm all for getting liquored up and heading to a female strip club, but a male one? That's just gross. Have you been to an all male strip club before? These oily, long-haired, jacked up on steroid men come prancing out in banana hammocks, thrust their hips in your face, and dry hump your leg. It's disgusting. Have you ever had a sweaty man you don't know rub his penis on your knee? It makes me throw up in my mouth a little just thinking about it. And let's be honest here, the penis – not the prettiest thing in the world to look at. If it's some guy who calls himself the Italian Stallion, wearing a Speedo with the Italian flag on it, dancing to the theme song from *'The Jersey Shore'*, while he has one foot up on your knee and hip thrusts his dangling... Okay, I'm just going to stop myself right there before Carter finds me curled up in the fetal position in the corner mumbling about Italian penis, and he thinks I'm saying "penne" and doesn't understand why pasta is making me cry.

As I was saying, Liz doesn't want any of that. She wants to rent a nice limo bus and go to a few local wineries. I'm pretty sure the evening will still include inappropriate behavior, but at least it won't also include ruining a man's self esteem by pointing and laughing at his junk. Unless of course Drew decides to get naked for some reason. I can't be responsible for my actions at that point and it won't be my fault of he cries.

Once Carter and I are dressed and ready to go, we placed Gavin in the car and head over to my dad's to drop him off.

When we stop at a red light, Carter takes one hand off of the wheel and places it on the inside of my bare thigh.

"You wore that short skirt just to torture me, didn't you?" Carter asks softly so Gavin won't hear him from the backseat.

"I have no idea what you're talking about," I say with a smirk as I cross my legs. The movement forced his warm hand higher up my thigh and his fingers graze just under the hem of the tattered jean skirt material.

I'm not lying when I say I kind of enjoy the fact that Carter and I work opposite shifts. I like the peace and quiet during the week and spending alone time with Gavin. It makes the adjustment from being a single mother to living with the father of my child not so bad. I had spent so many years on my own and having my son all to myself, it was nice we weren't thrust right into something that was a complete one-eighty from what we were used to. Even so, it doesn't stop me from missing Carter during the week.

Or more specifically, missing having sex with Carter during the week.

When you have sex once, get pregnant, and then go years before you ever have it again and when you *do* have it again, it's mind-blowing and delicious and better than finding a pot of gold, a unicorn, and a leprechaun who shits diamonds at the end of a rainbow, having to wait a whole week in between having this wonderful sex is torture. Just having Carter's hand on my leg puts all sorts of dirty thoughts in my head - thoughts that have no business being there when our son was in the backseat.

"I think you and I are going to need to make an *important phone call* tonight," Carter says with a wag of his eyebrows.

I laugh, remembering the first time we had sex again after the night he took my virginity at the frat party.

When Gavin had knocked on the bedroom door right at the tail end of our *reunion* (emphasis on union) and then asked us what we were up to, in a panic I told him we were making phone calls. It had seemed like a good idea at the time.

I place my hand on top of Carter's and slide it just a little bit further under the edge of my skirt.

"You missed a lot of *phone calls* this week while you were at work. I had to take care of them on my own. My *phone* has a dead battery now," I tease him.

"Did you record these *phone calls*? That's something I'd like to listen to," he says with a wink before turning his focus back to the road as the light turns green.

"Sorry, the *answering machine* doesn't have a battery either," I joke.

"Probably because you took the batteries out of every single major appliance in a five-mile-radius and put them in your *phone*," Carter replies with a sneer.

"Don't be jealous because the *phone* gets more time with me during the week than you do," I console him with a pat on his hand.

"I'm not jealous. I just used my *Palm PDA*."

I roll my eyes at him.

"Your *Palm PDA* is no match for my...*Vtech Cordless*," I stammer.

What are we even talking about anymore? Is there a point when innuendos jump the shark?

"I know what you guys are doin' when you make a phone call," Gavin pipes up nonchalantly from the backseat.

You know how when you've told a lie and someone catches you in it your face gets all hot and you get butterflies in your stomach? It's ten times worse when it's your own freaking toddler calling you out and looking at you like, "Are you kidding me with this shit?"

"Heh, heh! What do you mean, buddy?" Carter asks, laughing nervously.

He looks at me and I look at him, and we both look in the backseat at Gavin. Thank God we are stopped at another red light. I don't think Carter can be trusted to keep the car in our lane at this moment. Frankly, I don't think *I* can be trusted not to open up the door and jump out. TUCK AND ROLL!

I'm going to have to tell my son about the birds and the bees in the car on the way to my father's house. I don't even *get* the term, "the birds and the bees". How does that properly teach a kid about sex? You never see a pigeon railing a dove or a honey bee sticking it to a bumble bee. They really need to call it, "the cows and the horses". Just the other day we drove by a farm and one cow was mounted up on another cow and Gavin said, "Awww look, Mommy. That cow is giving the other cow a hug!" I could have explained it easily then. I could have used correct terminology like penis and sperm and fertilization. It was a farm for fuck's sake. That sort of stuff can be seen every two feet between goats and pigs and roosters and chickens. I could have given him plenty of examples. But then I would have to answer the age old question about which came first, the chicken or the egg and that question still boggles MY mind. Now I'm going to have to make up some type of analogy that has to do with phones. "First, you pull the antenna out so it's nice and long, then you push the right buttons so the other phone is in the mood to make a call…"

I can't do this. I'm not ready for this. He's too young to know about long distance phone calls and roaming charges!

"M-o-o-o-o-m! Did you hear me? I said I know what you guys are doin' when you make phone calls," Gavin repeats.

Sure, go ahead and repeat it. Obviously you need to make sure we are sufficiently freaked out. CHILDREN ARE THE DEVIL.

Maybe if I just completely ignore the situation, he'll forget about it. I turned on the radio, frantically searching for a song he knows that he can butcher the lyrics to.

Why is there so much fucking talk radio at five o'clock in the evening?

"Ooooh, this is a good song, Gavin! Do you know this song?" I ask overenthusiastically.

Carter looks at me like I'm insane as Kenny G notes filled the car.

Fucking Kenny G. Couldn't you record ONE song with some lyrics? Michael Bolton taught you nothing. Epic fail, Kenny. Epic fail.

"You guys always lock your door when you make phone calls," Gavin says.

Son of a bitch, Kenny G! You put everyone to sleep but my son. The ONE thing you had going for you and now it's gone to shit.

"You guys kiss in there, don't you?" Gavin asks.

I stop swaying to beat of Kenny G and shut off the BIC Lighter App on my phone, noticing that Carter is still looking at me funny. It's like he's never met me. I'm trying to get Gavin's mind off of fertilization and bees fucking pigeons!

"YES!" Carter shouts. "That's *exactly* what we do. We kiss. That's all we do. Just kiss. Sometimes Mommy and Daddy need to lock the door so we can kiss. And…just kiss. What else would we do in there besides kiss? Ha ha! Mommy and Daddy sittin' in a tree, K-I-S-S-"

I reach over and squeeze his arm to get him to stop talking as we pull into my dad's driveway. Gavin unbuckles his seatbelt and scrambles out of the car to race to my dad, his attention already diverted. My dad scoops him up into his arms and meets us at the car as Carter gets Gavin's overnight bag out of the backseat, and I stand by my open door, breathing a sigh of relief that Sex Ed with our four-year-old is finally over.

"Hey, Papa! Mommy and Daddy lock their door so they can kiss!" Gavin tells him excitedly.

My dad looks a little grossed out and quickly changes the subject.

"I got that movie *'Gnomeo and Juliet'* for us to watch tonight," he tells Gavin.

Sadly, Gavin isn't going to be deterred even for garden gnomes that come to life and ass rape a small community while they sleep. I'm sure that's not what really happens in a children's movie, but in my mind it is. Garden gnomes are creepy. I firmly believe they come to life after you go to bed at night and violate you.

"Mommy and Daddy make a lot of noise when they kiss. Mommy talks to God a lot. I talk to God sometimes too. I asked him for a puppy and a new monster truck but I was nice and didn't yell at him like Mommy does. He still hasn't gotten me the puppy though."

And on that note, we kiss Gavin good-bye, jump into the car, and take off. My dad can deal with the birds and the bees and cows and the chickens and the kissing horses while visions of his daughter screaming for Jesus dance in his head.

We pull up to Liz and Jim's house fifteen minutes later and park in the street behind the biggest limo bus I've ever seen. Liz had told me she rented something small and modest to drive us around so we wouldn't have to worry about ruining someone's night and forcing them to be our designated driver. Obviously her version of small and modest differ greatly from mine. This thing could house an entire football team with room to spare.

"It's about time you two fuckers got here!" Drew yells as he meets us at the end of the driveway, tossing a beer through the air towards Carter.

In honor of the wine tours that evening, Drew dons a shirt with a picture of a corkscrew on the front that reads, "I pull out."

We walk up the bus steps to join everyone else, noticing they are all well on their way toward getting drunk, everyone except Liz. She is all alone at the very back of the bus with her arms folded and a scowl on her face.

I take one look at her and know I had made it there just in time.

How could this have happened? Why wasn't anyone helping my poor friend?

Leaving Carter at the front of the bus with Drew, Jim, and Jenny, I hurry down the aisle and sit down next to Liz.

"Who did this to you?" I ask angrily as I wrap my arm around her shoulder.

She looks at me and I swear I see her lip quiver.

"It's okay. You can tell me. We'll fix it," I reassure her as I rub soothing circles on her back.

I see hope flare in her eyes, and I know she's going to be fine. I will make this better for her if it's the last thing I do.

"My mother! It was her. It was all her!" she wails in anguish.

I quickly glance to the front of the bus, fearing that just *thinking* about Mrs. Gates will suddenly make her appear. Forget bridezilla! Mrs. Gates is mother-of-the-bridezilla. She is the biggest wedding Nazi in the world. Every single wedding tradition, old wives tale, ritual, and custom, Mary Gates believes in it, practices it, and forces everyone around her to participate in it.

Right now, my poor best friend is wearing a rhinestone tiara with a veil attached, a sash across the front of her that reads, "Bride to Be", and underneath that sash, a tee-shirt with individually wrapped suckers strategically attached directly on top of her boobs. In bright pink glitter puff paint are the words, "Suck for a Buck".

"I'm in bachelorette party hell!" Liz screeches.

I reach over and started plucking suckers off of her boobs.

"It's okay; I'm going to get you out of this," I tell her.

"Claire Donna Morgan, I hope you're giving my daughter a dollar for every one of those suckers you are removing from her shirt!"

It's like something out of a movie. The music that pumps out of the limo's speakers screeches to a halt and all of the laughter from our friends immediately dies.

"Run! Save yourself!" Liz whispers loudly as she tries to shove me away from her.

I slowly stand up and put on a brave face, letting my friend know that I will take one for the team. I will stand in between her and sudden bachelorette party death. I turn around just in time to be bum rushed in the aisle.

"Can you believe my baby is getting married?!" Mrs. Gates squeals as she throws a sash over my head that reads, "Maid-of-Honor" before I can blink.

She pulls me into a tight hug, bouncing me up and down like we're long lost sorority sisters, the cloying scent of White Diamonds perfume surrounding me and threatening to make my eyes water.

Where my family is more along the lines of the Connor family from the show Roseanne, Alice's family leans more toward The Brady Bunch.

On crack.

Or maybe acid.

Which is the one that makes you see fuzzy bunnies singing about lollypops and kittens and puppies frolicking on a rainbow?

"Claire, I am entrusting you to make sure my baby has a great time tonight," Mrs. Gates says sternly as she pulls away from me and thrusts a piece of paper in my hand. "This is a treasure hunt for Liz. You have to make sure she does every single thing on the list before the night is out. I've been told this is all the rage with you young people."

Don't look down at the list; don't look down at the list.

"Well, don't just stand there, Claire. Look at the list!" Mrs. Gates demands excitedly.

"Get a stranger to give you his underwear," I mutter, reading the first line.

Mrs. Gates squeals like little girl. "Oh my gosh this is going to be a hoot! Keep reading!"

I take a deep breath, forcing the vomit that had lodged itself in my throat to remain where it is and not splatter all over the piece of paper in my hand.

On second thought…no list equals no scavenger hunt.

"And don't worry, I made enough copies for everyone!" Liz's mom says enthusiastically as she pulls a handful of papers out of her purse and starts passing them out.

I cover my hand over my mouth as I scan the list. No point in puking now. I'll never be able to projectile vomit far enough to reach all the copies.

Find a guy with an accent.

Meet a guy with the same name as the groom and take a picture with him.

Make out with one of the bridesmaids.

I really don't think I should be sober for this right now.

"Mrs. Gates, you are looking positively radiant this evening. Have I mentioned that yet?" Jim states sweetly as he comes up behind his future mother-in-law and puts his arm around her shoulder.

"Now, don't try and distract me, James. I've got something for you too," she says as she unfolds a baseball hat that said "Groom" on it and places it on his head.

"Folks, if this is everyone, I need you all to take your seats so we can leave," the limo driver informs us as he pokes his head in the door of the bus.

"Well, I guess that's my cue to leave," Mrs. Gates says as she stands there, not making *any* attempt at moving.

She glances around at everyone expectantly, waiting for someone to beg her to stay and join us.

No one speaks.

Or moves. There might have even been an uncomfortable cough that I think came from the driver.

"Okay....well...you kids have fun now!" she finally says as she walks to the door of the bus. "Oh my goodness, I almost forgot the most important thing!"

She turns back around and rushes down the aisle towards Liz. Everyone groans quietly.

Mrs. Gates stops in front of her daughter and reaches into the giant suitcase she calls a purse and pulls out a penis. Or should I say, "*penis products.*" Lots and lots of penis products, things I didn't even know they made in the shape of a penis, and now I will have to bleach my eyes at the thought of Liz's mom walking into a store and purchasing these items:

A candy necklace full of sugary penises, a penis-shaped water bottle, a penis-shaped pacifier that she decides needed to be tied around my neck.

Yes, I am absolutely going to stay classy this evening.

But she isn't done yet, oh no. Next out of her bag of tricks: penis-shaped pasta. Seriously? What the fuck do we need with a bag of penis-shaped pasta on a limo bus? We're not going to fill a pan with some water from the tiny bathroom at the back of the bus and stick it on the engine to boil it so we can make maca*weenie* and cheese.

She hands Jenny a box of penis gummies that Drew tells her to open up immediately because he wants to hear her say, "This penis tastes so good." Last but not least, she hands everyone different colored rubber penis pen caps. Because you know, at some point during the night there might be an emergency that calls for someone to write a note using only a pen with a penis pen cap.

I should check the scavenger hunt. It could be on the list.

Mrs. Gates looks like a perverted Mary Poppins pulling penises out of her carpet bag. I'm waiting for her to pull out a penis-shaped lamp or a penis-shaped coat stand. When she finally emptied her bag of all things phallic, she steps off of the bus and we all let out sighs of relief—and then we rip every single sash, hat, veil, and suck for a buck item off of us.

Drew pours everyone a shot of Tequila Rose (in penis shot glasses, of course) and passes them out.

"What is this pussy shit?" Jim asks as he sniffs the thick, pink liquid in his shot glass.

"It smells like strawberry milk," I say with a cringe. I don't know about anyone else, but milk and liquor just does not sound like it should go together.

"It tastes like strawberry milk too. And it's good shit. I thought I'd start us off with something girly tonight so know one hurls in the first hour," Drew explains.

We all nod in understanding. No one wants to be the first one to puke.

The six of us sit at the back of the bus around the semi-circle leather couch. We raise our shot glasses in the air until they all clink together in the middle.

"I'd like to propose a toast," Drew says. "Here's to you, here's to me – fuck you, here's to me!"

We all down the shots as the bus starts up and pulls away from the curb.

6.

Back Door Action

Oh. My. God. What is that noise? WHAT IS THAT NOISE??

It feels like someone is screaming in my ear with a bullhorn. I let out a groan, roll over, and pull the covers up over my head in an effort to stop it from exploding.

Sweet Jesus what did I do last night?

"CLAIRE! For fuck's sake shut your alarm clock off!"

The yelling from Liz on the other side of my door makes me cringe. I pull the covers down just far enough so I can squint at my alarm clock.

Sure enough, the sound that's threatening to make my ears bleed is coming from that little bastard on our dresser across the room.

The repetitive flash of the time, its bright red numbers, and the staccato beeping on that thing makes me think its judging me. I can hear it— tequila, shots, vodka, karaoke, you're an idiot.

"Carter," I mumble.

Jesus, my voice sounds like I swallowed a bucket full of gravel. It feels that way too.

"Carter," I groan again. "Shut off the alarm clock."

With my squinty eye, I turn my head as slowly as possible and see the spot next to me in bed is empty.

"Shit."

I stick my arm out from under my cocoon and grab the first thing my fingers touch on my nightstand—a vibrator with a leash on it. It's a sad, sad day when something like this doesn't faze me. I

338

whip it across the room and watch the giant pink rubber penis and its diamond-studded leash crash into the alarm clock and effectively shut it up.

Small bursts of memories from last night flash through my addled brain and make me wish I can have a lobotomy.

Did I sing "Like a Virgin" at a winery? And why am I not wearing any underwear?

With my eyes squeezed shut so the bright rays of sun shining through the window don't light them on fire, I stumble out of bed and throw on a pair of yoga pants that are crumpled on the floor. I slowly make my way out of the bedroom and into the living room.

"Yo, Claire Bear! You're alive!" Drew shouts from his spot on the couch as I peel my eyes open and gave him the finger for being so cheerful and not hung-over.

How is that possible? He drank way more than me. I think. And why is he in our living room? I'm going to start charging this asshole rent.

I stare at the annoying smile on Drew's face and another memory from last night assaults me as I walk up to the kitchen table and pull out a chair.

"Why do I remember you peeing somewhere in this house?" I ask with my gravelly voice that I hope is just from yelling and singing and not from puking somewhere I can't recall.

"Did you pee on this chair?" I ask angrily as my ass hovers above the seat cushion.

"Yes, he peed in that chair," Liz answers as she emerges from the laundry room off of the kitchen.

"Fuck, it's like we have a puppy," I mutter as I move to take a seat at one of the bar stools by the island instead.

"I didn't pee *that* bad on it," Drew complains as he walks into the kitchen and makes a show of looking really hard at the chair in question.

"There is no GOOD level of pee on a chair, Drew!" I yell as I take the glass of water and aspirin Liz had set down on the counter in front of me. I throw the pills in my mouth and chug the entire glass of water.

I hear the faint sound of music coming from somewhere and realize my purse is singing the theme song from "Golden Girls". Liz and Drew start cracking up behind me as I reach to the end of the island and grab my purse, realizing by their snickers that one of them must have changed my ring tone.

I dig through my purse trying to find the damn phone before that fucking song is stuck in my head all day.

"…..*traveled down the road and back again. Your heart is true; you're a pal and a confidant…*"

My hand finally wraps around the offending cell phone and I quickly hit the send button to stop the song before I even get it out of my purse.

"Hello?" I turn around to glare at Liz and Drew, mouthing the words *"What the fuck?"* to them silently as I answer the phone. That just causes them to laugh even harder.

"Wow, I didn't think you'd be awake yet after last night."

The sound of Carter's voice makes me forget that my so-called friends put some stupid ass song on my phone that I won't be able to stop humming now.

"Did we have sex last night?" I ask, having no shame whatsoever in the fact that I don't remember. Generally, I like to know why I wake up with no pants or underwear on. It's just a little quirk I have.

"Are you referring to before or after we got home?" he asks.

"Uh, both?"

Carter sighs. "I don't think you're awake or sober enough to discuss the sex we had before we got home. After…well, I do believe sex was the general idea until I got your clothes off and you puked on me."

"Ooooh, sorry about that," I apologize sheepishly.

"It's my fault. I should have never introduced you to Drew," he replies jokingly.

"He peed on our chair," I complain, giving Drew the two-finger eye salute.

"You puked on my dick," Carter deadpans.

"Fine, you win," I say with a sigh. "So where are you?"

"DUDE! LET ME TELL HER ABOUT THE BACK DOOR ACTION ON THE BUS!" Drew yells into the phone as he comes up next to me.

I turn to look at Drew with a horrified look on my face.

"What are you talking about?" I ask him. "Carter, what the fuck is he talking about?" I screech into the phone. "Oh Jesus. Did I let you... did we...OH MY GOD WE DID THAT ON A BUS SURROUNDED BY OUR FRIENDS?"

The laughter comes from all around me now. Liz bends over so far in hysterics that she's fallen on the floor; Drew wipes tears out of his eyes as he leans against the counter, and Carter was snorting on the other end of the phone.

"No! No, it's not what you're thinking. Even though you begged me repeatedly saying, 'Come on just stick it in my ass!' I figured that was not a decision you were making with one hundred percent clarity. Tell me you at least remember being in the bathroom with me," Carter begs.

I put my elbows up on the counter and lean my head against one hand, closing my eyes to try and conjure up the bathroom rendez-vous Carter speaks of.

Everyone piles back on the bus after the third winery, a little louder and a lot drunker. Carter slumps onto the leather bench, pulling me down next to him until I am practically sprawled on top of him with my chest resting against his. He holds my face in both of his hands, and as the bus starts moving and our friends start yelling and goofing off in the front of the vehicle, he leans in and kissed me. His tongue slowly pushes past my lips and sweeps through my mouth causing butterflies to erupt in the pit of my stomach and warmth to spread between my legs. After a few minutes he pulls his mouth away from mine, and I let out a groan at the loss.

"You wanna go in the bathroom?" Carter asks with a wag of his eyebrows.

"No. I don't have to pee right now," I tell him as I leaned toward him so I can kiss him again. He tastes so yummy, like wine and sunshine and kittens.

"I'm not talking about going to the bathroom to GO to the bathroom. I'm talking about going to the bathroom so I can stick it to you," he says with a snort and a laugh.

"You're so romantic. Say it again," I tell him as I bat my eyelashes at him. Carter looks over my shoulder and then back down at me.

"Seriously. No one is looking. We could sneak into the bathroom and no one would even know. I'll make it quick."

"No really, keep going. This is totally turning me on," I tell him in a monotone voice.

Carter pulls my face back toward him and our lips crash together. His tongue skates over my bottom lip before plunging back into my mouth. The pain of the week-long exiles while we work opposite shifts have become glaringly obvious as we deepened the kiss, and I practically crawl onto his lap.

Carter's hand slides down the side of my body, brushing over one breast and curving over my hip to clutch my ass and pull me closer to him. He moves his mouth away from my lips and starts planting warm, wet, open-mouthed kisses along my neck and collarbone until I feel like I'll melt into a puddle of goo on the floor of the bus. He gently grazes the side of my neck with his teeth and slides his tongue over the spot. I'm panting like a dog at this point and know I won't make it much longer. If he keeps this up, I'm going to throw him down on the seat and bang him in front of everyone.

"Okay, fine. You win. Bathroom. Now," I mumble through my drunken, lust-induced haze.

We stand up quickly and stumble our way to the tiny bathroom directly across from us. I vaguely hear one of the girls shout, "NO, no, no! I have to pee!" before we slam the door closed and fumble with the sliding lock. The bathroom is about the size of an airplane bathroom so maneuverability is nil. Carter's body is pressed up against my back and he begins kissing and sucking on the back of my neck as I try in vain to get the stupid lock to slide closed.

"I can't get the fucking door to lock!" I complain through moans of pleasure as he brings his hands around my waist and slides them up my body until they cup both of my breasts.

"Fuck it. I think it locks automatically anyway. That slide thing is just for the little sign on the outside that switches to 'occupied' or some shit. Everyone already knows we're in here," Carter says as he starts massaging my breasts.

We turn as one so I can rest my hands on the edge of the sink and Carter can lift my skirt. A quick breaking of the bus makes me jerk forward and slam my shoulder into the wall above the sink.

"Son of a bitch!" I yell. "This is going to be dangerous."

I giggle as Carter slides his hands back down my sides and grazes over a particularly ticklish spot.

"You're not supposed to be laughing. This is supposed to be awesome and hot," he states as his hands slide down my thighs and then immediately back up, pushing my skirt up to my hips as he went.

"Oh believe me, it's totally hot," I say with another giggle as the bus takes off and we fall backwards. Carter falls on top of the toilet, and I landed on his lap with an "oooomph".

"Okay, this might not have been one of our best ideas," I say with a laugh as I try to get up but the bus takes a curve and we both crash our shoulders into the wall on the left right beneath the little bathroom window.

"Dammit! We WILL have sex in this thing if it kills us," Carter states as he pushes me off of his lap and stands back up behind me.

"Carter, I think this IS going to kill us. My dad is going to have to tell his friends that his daughter died in a limo bus bathroom with her skirt up around her hips. That is not okay!"

The bus straightens and maintains a steady, non-deadly speed and a quick glance out of the window shows us that we were on a long stretch of highway.

"Are you sure no one can see us in here?" I ask in a panic as I feel Carter's hands slide up the back of my thighs and then pull my underwear down a few inches.

I hear his zipper open and fabric rustling and before I can think of any other reasons why this isn't such a great idea, one of his hands slide around to the front, between my legs, and his fingers slide through my wetness. I had been aching with need for him since he first put his hand on my bare thigh in the car earlier. Having him touch me like this, for the first time in a week, makes me throw all rationale out the window - where I am pretty certain no one could see us.

"No one can see us," he whispers against my neck, practically reading my mind as two of his fingers plunge inside of me, and he slides his smooth, hardness between the cheeks of my ass. "The window in here is made of special glass. When you shut the door, it hits a trigger so we can see out, but no one can see in. Jim told me about it earlier."

He continues to slide his fingers in and out of me in a slow, tortuous fashion and like he wasn't just talking about the sexual safety features on the bus.

"Holy hell," I moan as he pulls his two fingers up to circle my clit.

I think I hear horns honking and shouts coming from outside but at that point I don't really care if we are stopped in a rest area and people are eating popcorn while staring in the window.

"Fuck, I need you," I tell him as I let go of the sink with one hand and reach back to grab onto his hip and pull him harder against me. "You should TOTALLY give me 'nother baby," I murmur drunkenly.

Carter laughs as he pulls a condom out of the back pocket of his jeans and rips open the foil with his teeth.

"I'm pretty sure you don't really mean that," he says as I feel his hands graze my ass while he sheathes himself.

"Who cares if I mean it? The wine and vodka mean it. And they are ALWAYS serious. Give me your seeeeeeed."

I snort and blink my eyes a few times to get the room to stop spinning.

Carter places both of his hands on my hips and I feel the tip of his penis at my opening. I let out a loud moan and Carter quickly reaches up and puts his hand over my mouth with a laugh.

"Not so loud, baby. Everyone will hear you."

I pull Carter's hand off of my mouth long enough to spout even more nonsense as he slowly pushes himself inside me.

"You should stick it in my ass."

"I am not going to stick it in your ass," Carter says with a muted groan as he moves a little deeper.

"Come on, you know you want to stick it in my ass," I goad him loudly.

His hand comes back up to cover my mouth and my laughter turns into a pleasure-filled whimper as he pushes all the way inside me and holds himself still.

"You should know that as a guy, I am pre-programmed to always want to stick it in your ass. I hope tomorrow you will appreciate my self control," Carter explains as he slowly starts moving inside me.

"If you knock on my backdoor right now, I will totally let you in," I giggle.

Carter stops again and takes a couple of deep calming breaths.

"Careful back there, though, there's a rickety step. Don't fall in my backdoor."

Carter tries not to laugh as he begins thrusting harder, forcing my hips to bump against the edge of the sink. Thoughts of sperm and the porch by my backdoor flow out of my mind.

"Fuck, why did you have to start talking about sticking it in your ass? I'm not going to be able to last long," he complains as he tries to slow down.

"Just shut up and keep going. I'm too drunk to care right now, and you should appreciate that shit!" I yell around his hand that's still held against my mouth.

The faint sounds of horns honking still make their way into my brain as he curses and moves faster against me, his orgasm barreling through him like a freight train.

His hand drops from my mouth and he braces his arms on either side of mine on the edge of the sink as he buries his head in the side of my neck. He comes with a muffled shout and I grip the sink tighter so we won't topple over.

We stood there breathing heavy for a few minutes before he pulls himself out of me and we right our clothes. He gives me a quick kiss and promises me five of my very own orgasms in repayment before we open the door and walk out into the aisle of the bus.

All of our friends are standing there cheering and clapping, and it was then that we noticed the bus was stopped and a police officer was standing behind them with his arms crossed in front of him.

"Oh my God, we got arrested?" I ask Carter.

Why the fuck don't I remember going to jail? Was I somebody's bitch now?

"No," he laughs. "We just got a ticket for indecent exposure. Turns out Jim didn't explain the bathroom door situation clearly. That little lever you were trying to slide over? THAT'S what blacks out the window so no one can see in. Oops."

Drew starts laughing and I noticed that he inches close enough to me so he can put his ear right next to mine and hear Carter's end of the conversation I shove him away when I realize that's what he was doing.

"Ha ha get it, Claire? Back door action? I was talking about the bathroom door. Or was I talking about you shouting for Carter to fuck you in the ass over and over? Hmmm, I'm not sure. They are equally entertaining to think about," Drew says with a laugh.

Oh my God. This day can't get any worse.

"So anyway, I was just calling to make sure you were alive. As you can see, everyone ended up crashing at our place since the bus stopped there first. Jim gave Jenny a ride home this morning to take a shower and left Liz and Drew behind to make sure you didn't choke on your own vomit or anything. I'm on my way to pick Gavin up from your dad's and then we're meeting my parents for brunch. There's been a slight change of plans. Instead of them coming to our house, they rented out the small party room at the Oberlin Inn where they're staying. They wanted to invite your dad, Drew, Jenny, Liz, and Jim and they didn't want to impose on us."

I quickly say good-bye to Carter and kick Liz and Drew out of the house so I can take a shower and start to feel a little more human.

Hopefully, that will be the extent of my embarrassing behavior from last night.

7.

Whore Dizzle

I shower, dress and walk through the lobby of the Oberlin Inn in record time. I no longer reek of stale liquor, but I'm pretty sure I still look like ass. A view of my reflection in a mirror behind the registration desk confirms my suspicions.

"Mommy, you look old today," Gavin says as we walk hand in hand around the corner and down the hall. "Like old lady and eye balls."

"Gee, thanks. I love you too," I mumble.

Carter had got a call to come into work to fill out a form that will add Gavin to his health benefits, so after he picked Gavin up from my dad's and dropped him back off with me, he ran up there and said he would meet us at the inn.

Yeah, that's exactly what I want to do. Walk into the lion's den alone.

I had made a quick call to Drew and Jenny and asked if I could pick them up on the way for moral support. I've spoken to Carter's parents a few times on the phone since we moved in together, but this will be the first time they actually see me and meet Gavin. I am beyond nervous about making a good impression. They are the complete opposite from what I'm used to. They never swear, they only drink on special occasions, and I'm pretty sure they've never puked in anyone's lap after a night out bar hopping. I figured since Mr. and Mrs. Ellis already know Drew and haven't forbid Carter from hanging out with him yet, I should be okay.

"I still can't believe you don't remember screaming at that old lady in the parking lot. It was priceless!" Drew whispers from behind

347

me as we walk into the party room and see Carter and his parents talking to a waiter.

"I'm so glad I downloaded the theme from "Golden Girls" to her phone right after that occurred," Jenny says to Drew.

"It really was a stroke of brilliance," he replies.

I roll my eyes and try not to think about the events from last night that Drew and Jenny regaled me with on the ride over. Some things are best left forgotten—or lost in a drunken haze that no one should ever speak of again.

As we walk through the doorway of the room, Carter turns and we make eye contact. I suddenly don't want to kill the two people behind me. Everything is momentarily forgotten when I look at him.

I can do this. Parents love me.

He excuses himself from the discussion and hurries over to us, scooping Gavin up in his arms and peppering his face with kisses. He reaches out and grabbed my hand to pull me in close and place a soft kiss on my lips.

"Mmmmm. You don't taste like vomit and desperation anymore," he whispers with a smirk as he pulls his face away from mine.

"Remind me to never drunk dial you again for a booty call," I reply with mock irritation.

"Don't worry," he says as he turns and pulls me over to his parents. "If that's your idea of a booty call, I'm never taking another call from you again at two in the morning from the kitchen while you're down the hall in the bedroom. My penis can't handle another rejection like that. Or should I say *projection?*"

Drew and Jenny start giggling behind us.

"Alright, get it all out of your system now you guys. We are never, ever speaking of what happened last night again. We all need to pretend like it never happened," I state firmly as Carter wraps his arm around my waist and hefts Gavin up higher.

"Yeah, about that," Drew says sheepishly, "you might want to check Facebook when you get a free moment."

My mouth dropped open, and I could do nothing but stare at his back as he pushes us out of the way and drags Jenny up to greet Madelyn and Charles and give them a hug. I barely paid attention as Drew introduces Jenny to them. Before I know it, all eyes are on me and Gavin.

"Say hello to your grandparents, Gavin," Carter prompts him.

"Hi, I'm Gavin. When I'm ten I can drink beer and mow the lawn," he states with a smile.

Nothing like a little tension breaker.

"Well, isn't that sweet," Madelyn says in a voice that clearly states it's anything but.

"It's good to finally meet you Clarissa," Charles says distractedly as he stares at Jenny's ass when she bends over to pick up her lip gloss that she had dropped.

"Dad, it's *Claire*," Carter reminds him in a low voice, giving me an apologetic look.

As Gavin and I are pulled in for impolite hugs and air kisses, all I can do is try and think about what I may or may not have put on Facebook. The fact that I am pretty sure Carter's mother hated me on sight and his father is too busy ogling my friend's assets to get my name right doesn't even touch a nerve. If I had put a picture of my boobs on Facebook, I'd throw myself off of a bridge anyway, so their judgments won't matter.

Under normal circumstances, I own who I am. I like to have fun and go crazy, occasionally, and when that happens, it usually involves alcohol. I don't drink and drive and I don't spend my money on hookers and crack. I don't waste my paycheck every week filling up entire shopping carts with bottles of Jack like Nicolas Cage in *Leaving Las Vegas*, and sometimes my shenanigans are broadcast on Facebook either by my own stupidity or by the stupidity of my friends. Typically, this is only slightly embarrassing, and we would all have a good laugh over it for months to come. However, in a moment of insanity a few days ago, I had decided to friend-request Carter's mother and a few other members of his family on Facebook. I really should be supervised any-time I go near social media. There should be an actual human being whose only job is to sit next to me and say things like, "Do NOT post that," and "You should seriously consider removing your tag off of that picture," or "No, dick does not rhyme with delicious, and you are not good at poetry when you're drunk, contrary to what you've been told," and "That comment sounds a lot better in your head than it will under her picture. And that's not how you spell cock sucking whore anyway".

After we conclude a few minutes of small talk, Madelyn and Charles whisk Gavin away and begin spoiling him by letting him order anything he wants on the menu, even if it's five different des-serts. I turn to glare at Drew as Carter moves behind me and wraps his arms around my waist.

"Why the hell do I need to check Facebook?" I practically screech at him. "What did you let me do?"

"Well, the word 'vagina' may have been used in several posts last night," Drew informs me seriously. "As well as a few words even *I've* never heard before."

I can feel Carter's rumble of laughter as his chest presses up against my back.

"Oh this should be good," he says absently as he rests his chin on my head.

I shake my head in denial, completely horrified at the fact that I drunk Facebooked last night.

How can he be so calm? God only knows what I did that his mother might have seen.

"No wonder your mother isn't very impressed by me," I state.

"Nah, don't take that personally. Madelyn Ellis was born with a stick up her ass," Drew reassures me.

"It's true, she was," Carter agreed. "And they love you so stop it."

A few minutes later, Liz, Jim, and my father arrive and after introducing themselves to Carter's parents, they make their way over to our little group.

"So, I'm guessing since you're still alive Carter's mom either hasn't read her Facebook page yet or she has a really good sense of humor," Liz says with a laugh.

Oh my God. That's it! I'm putting an ad out for new friends.

"I should have been nowhere even remotely near Facebook in that condition. What is wrong with you people?!" I yell in a loud whisper so Carter's parents won't hear my hysterical breakdown from their table over by the kitchen where they are currently showing Gavin what each utensil is for and how to place the napkin in his lap.

Oh Jesus. They have manners. They have manners and they're all proper and know which fork to use, and I took a dump on their Facebook page last night.

"You guys let her near the internet when you went out? Jim should especially know better. How many times has she lifted your cell phone and hacked your Facebook page to tell everyone you like to eat baked beans off of hookers?" My dad asks with a chuckle.

"I wouldn't laugh if I were you, George. I remember when she changed your status to say, 'Can anyone tell me what it means when your penis has a blue discharge that smells like egg salad?'" Jim reminds him.

"So who let the dip shit near a phone?" my dad questions.

Can you feel the love? Can you? It feels almost like having my toenails ripped out.

"Well, at first we thought we should take her Blackberry away for her own safety and for that of those around her. But when she posted, "Spitters are quitters" on every one of Carter's cousin's pictures in her photo album, at that point it was just too funny to put a stop to." Drew laughs.

Oh fuck me.

I vaguely remember while Carter was up at the bar buying a bottle of wine at the fourth winery, I told everyone the story about how his cousin Katie gave some guy a blow job in college and gagged on his spunk. The very same story she had just told me a few days ago when she accepted my friend request and swore me to secrecy. Yes, I realize this is very personal information to be sharing with an almost-stranger, but we bonded quickly over Facebook email, what can I say? I may have suggested that if I told anyone her deep, dark secret she could shave my head.

Double fuck.

"I really don't want to hear the story about my cousin that goes along with that, do I?" Carter asks as I crane my neck around to see the grimace on his face.

"Probably not," I mutter as I look back at Liz.

"Give me your phone. Now," I state with my hand out to her.

Of course, today of all days my phone's battery is dead and I've left the fucking thing at home.

Liz pulls her iPhone out of her purse and slaps it into my open palm. I yanked it to me faster than a fat kid with a piece of cake and quickly click on the Facebook icon and log into my account.

"Holy fucking shit," I whisper as the little globe symbol at the top of the screen tells me I have sixty-five new notifications.

Liz moves over next to me and glances over my shoulder.

"Oh don't worry. Most of those were you replying to your own posts using my account. You were really cracking yourself up last night."

This is doing nothing to make me feel better. I go to Katie's page and clicked on one of the two photo albums she had in there. I quickly scan through the pictures and don't find any offending comments. Maybe I had deleted them.

Right, and maybe fairies will start shitting money on my front lawn.

"Wrong photo album," Drew states as he also comes around behind me so he can peer over my other shoulder. "The photo album you want is the one titled, *'Missionary Trip to Jerusalem.'* And yes, I totally just said 'missionary' without laughing."

I am going straight to hell.

At this point, Carter moves his head to the side, right next to mine, so he too can look down at the phone.

I click on the correct album and sure enough, under every single photo from her trip to Jerusalem with people from her CHURCH GROUP, I have posted the words, "Spitters are quitters."

"Oooh, oooh, wait! This is my favorite part!" Drew says excitedly as he snatches the phone out of my hand and navigates to the last picture in the album.

He finds what he was looking for and barks out a laugh before handing the phone back to me. I grab it out of his hand roughly and shoot him a dirty look for his excitement at my epic fail.

Not only does it say "Spitters are quitters" under the last photo in the album, but below that stellar use of the English language I have written, "Jesus is my homeboy."

"Your cousin is never going to forgive me," I said with a sigh.

"Eh, she's a bitch anyway. Someone needed to put her in her place." Carter laughs as he tightens his hold on me.

I reach my arm out to hand the phone back to Liz and notice a funny look on her face.

"What?" I ask with trepidation, my arm just hanging there since she hadn't reached out to take the phone from me.

"Oh fuck, there's more?" I question her as my shoulders drooped.

"You might want to take a gander at the conversation we had on Carter's mom's page," she says, not even bothering to contain the laughter at this point.

I'm sure my eyes are the size of dinner plates as I just stand there staring at her.

"Oh my God! I forgot about that! I read it again this morning and almost pissed myself!" Drew chuckles. "Not on any furniture," he says to me in total seriousness.

I regretfully bring the phone back to me and pull Madelyn Ellis' Facebook page up.

At exactly 12:28 a.m. I had posted the following on Madelyn's page:

"You are a gigantic, stinkotic, vaginastic, clitoral, liptistic whore dizzle."

Three minutes later Liz responds with: *"Dude, was this meant for me? You just posted this on Carter's mom's page. Ha! You dumb ass!"*

I stare at the rest of the conversation, ON CARTER'S MOM'S PAGE, and I want to vomit. His MOM'S page, people! I don't think you understand the level of suck we're at right now.

Claire Morgan: *You are a furry nut sack on the giant dick of my life.*

Elizabeth Gates: *You are the taco to my furry heart.*

Claire Morgan: *Where is your Dumbo-earred vagina? I can hear it flapping from here. Are you trying to fly back to me?*

Elizabeth Gates: *My vagina is way nicer than anything you own you drizzly, weighted down orca of a woman.*

Claire Morgan: *Your vagina is like a burning clown car...this flaming taco with hundreds of screaming people trying get the fuck out of it.*

Elizabeth Gates: *Dumb shit whore.*

Claire Morgan: *Dick weed.*

By the time I got to the bottom of the thread, Carter has stepped away from me and is practically convulsing with laughter.

Carter's parents choose that moment to walk Gavin back over to us, and I am praying to God, Allah, Buddha, and Ryan Seacrest that she had not logged into her Facebook account yet today so I can get in there and delete everything.

Drew and Jim are now huddled together behind me quoting those posts back and forth to each other in loud whispers and laughing like hyenas.

"Claire, you have raised quite the charming young man," Madelyn says with a kind smile. "Gavin is just so precious, and Carter's father and I just want to thank you for taking such good care of our grandson"

Fuck, why does she have to be so nice? She's like a sweet, Disney princess and I'm Girls Gone Wild on crack.

"Right, Charles?"

When he doesn't answer her immediately, she elbows him in the side and he jerks his head back around, no doubt from checking out the waitress.

"Oh, yes. Absolutely, Candy. Wonderful job."

Now it's Candy? Do I look like a fucking stripper?

"Thank you, that means a lot to me," I tell her, pasting on a smile.

"You're looking a little tired today, Claire. Did my son keep you out late last night?" she asks.

Carter tries to cover up a snort from behind me, and my elbow meets his stomach, much in the same way his mother's just had with his father.

I'm pretty sure his mom doesn't want me to tell her my late night involved sex in public, back door begging, sperm demanding, wine drinking debauchery. Although with my luck, those things could be somewhere on Facebook and she'll find out soon enough.

Someone calls Madelyn's name and while she looks away, I pull Liz's phone out from behind my back and furiously pull Facebook back up so I can begin the deletion process. Before I can even get to Madelyn's page, the phone is seized from me.

"Ah-ah-ah! This is a no cell phone zone! And we have a surprise for both of you," Madelyn exclaims with a huge smile as she drops Liz's phone in the front pocket of her dress pants and I try not to whimper. "I'll be right back with your surprise."

She quickly turns and walks away from us, her heels clicking on the wood floor as she exits the party room.

"She's probably going to get her gun. At least she's giving you a head start," my dad whispers.

Carter's father stays with our group and attempts to start up a conversation with my dad while I try to figure out a way to sneak my hand into Madelyn's pants pocket when she comes back without her thinking I'm trying to get to second base.

My dad looks blankly at Charles while he yammers on and on about the stock market and their last vacation to France. The first time he had smacked my dad on the arm trying to be all buddy-buddy with him, I feared for Charles', life. My dad looks down at the spot where Charles' hand connected and then back up at him before walking away without another word. Charles doesn't seem phased by it since Liz bends over the table to set her purse down right then and he has something else to occupy his mind.

Drew and Jim are in a deep discussion about having another bachelor party, this time with strippers, when Liz suddenly latches tightly onto my arm and jerks me towards her.

"Oh my God! Who is that?" she whispers in horror as Carter and I turn to see who she is pointing at.

"That's my grandmother," Carter replied with a huge smile as we watch his mom escort an older version of herself into the room. "This must be our surprise. I had no idea she was going to be in town."

At that moment, Drew turns around and spits out the mouthful of water he was drinking. Something about the woman is a little familiar, but I have never met Carter's grandmother. He talks about her all the time and I know that Carter's mother does whatever she asks. Thank God she doesn't do Facebook, at least I don't have *that* to worry about. She'd tell Madelyn to put a hit out on me.

By now, Drew is bent over at the waist with his hands on his knees choking on the water he managed to swallow, and I'm wondering what the fuck his problem is. Jenny smacks him on the back and is making weird head gestures at me and Carter's grandmother like she has some sort of neck tick.

What the hell is going on with everyone?

I'm clearly looking at her with annoyance and put my hands up in the air in a "what the fuck?" gesture. She opens her mouth but before she can say anything, Liz grabs onto my arm with both hands now and is trying to drag me away from everyone. She's alternating between giggles and repeatedly whispering, "Oh sweet Jesus." I'm starting to wonder if everyone around me has been roofied.

I yank my arm out of her clutches and turn around, coming face-to-face with Carter's grandmother. I put a big smile on my face and began to introduce myself when she cuts me off.

"You," is all she says as she looks me up and down.

The look in her eyes and the tilt of her head as she scrutinizes me suddenly forces a memory from last night to surface from the depths of my subconscious.

"She's going to take our cab. Are you kidding me with this shit?" Drew yells indignantly. "I've been standing here trying to hail a cab for like three years and this skank just waltzes in and takes the one that stopped for us."

"Dude, we came in a limo bus. It's parked over there," Jim tells him.

"I don't care if we came here on a magic carpet. That was OUR cab!" I pipe up indignantly.

I stumble over to the back door of the taxi that is still open while the old woman gets situated and stick my head in.

"You're a dick. Go fuck your face," I yell drunkenly before I'm yanked back out by my friends so my head doesn't get mangled by the shutting of the door.

"Dude, you just say that to a seventy-year-old woman!" Drew yells while patting me on the back.

And here that seventy-year-old woman stands with a cocky smile on her face when she sees that I have made the connection to who she is.

The entire room is silent as they watch the exchange between us. I look horrified and Carter's grandmother looks like she's going to throw her little arthritic fists of fury in the air and beat my ass.

There will never ever be another moment in my entire life that is more embarrassing than this one right here. Mark my words.

Madelyn interrupts the stare-down Grandma is giving me, and I suddenly wish there was a hole in the floor that would swallow me up when I see Liz's cell phone in her hand.

"What does 'gigantic, stinkotic, vaginastic, clitoral, liptistic whore dizzle' mean?"

8.

The Incredible Shrinking Penis

"No, Drew, a trip to the strip club will not make everything better,"
I say for the third time. "Claire is completely mortified after brunch
last weekend and thinks my family hates her. She's also pissed at me
because according to her, my number one rule as her boyfriend is
to stop her from doing anything remotely stupid while she's drunk."

I let out a huge sigh and lift my arms in a "T" so the store owner
could measure the length of my chest. While the girls are over with
Liz getting a last minute fitting for their dresses, I meet the guys
across the street at the mall with Gavin so we can get measured for
our tuxes. This might come as a shock, but I've never been measured
for a tux or a suit before. When I tell you this is the most awkward
moment you will ever have with another person, I'm not lying. It's
right up there with prostate exams.

Some strange man named Steve who barely mutters a greeting
when we walk in, immediately pushes me in front of a set of mirrors
and then gets down on his knees and sticks his hands in the general
vicinity of my balls.

Where exactly are you supposed to look when there is a man
between your legs cupping your nut sack and he isn't a doctor asking
you to bend over and cough? His head? Deep into his eyes when he
glances up at you to yell at you for squirming? I'm sorry but I can't
stand still when there is all this unwelcome ball-handling going on.

I really don't see why it's necessary to take four measurements
that go from where my balls hang to my ankles. My balls haven't

moved; you're going to get the same number each time so just write the fucking number down and move on - preferably to a spot away from my nuggets.

Is a store owner even qualified to do this shit? Doesn't he need some type of degree or something before he can just go off wielding a measuring tape and sticking pins in people?

I glance over at Drew and he is looking up at the ceiling and whistling like it's no big deal, like he always has strange people with their hands all over him while they are eye-level with his junk. Wait, look who I'm talking about! It probably had just happened to him at the gas station a half hour before we got here.

"Claire needs to chill. If your parents don't hate *me* by now, they don't hate her. I've done much worse things to them over the years, believe me," Drew says.

"Yeah. I know. My mom still brings up what you did to her parakeet back in high school."

Drew rolls his eyes.

"That wasn't even my fault."

"Uh, you opened the cage and it flew straight into the glass door and died," I remind him.

"Is it my fault that thing was stupid?" he argues. "I thought it would just fly around the room, maybe shit on the carpet. How was I supposed to know it was suicidal? It's your mom's fault really. She should have known her bird was depressed. And frankly, what I did to her Mynah bird was way worse."

Steve spends a few minutes pinning the legs of my pants and gives me a reprieve from ball cupping.

"That bird is *still* saying 'Where my ho's at, bitch?' whenever my dad whistles. My mom couldn't get the bird to stop so she put a ban on whistling in the house," I tell him.

"I really thought she'd be more pissed about the 'Jesus loves me' one. It was just boring every time your mom said that and it replied, 'This I know.' 'Jesus loves me, *fuck a ho*' is much more entertaining," Drew explains.

The person measuring him tells him to turn around so his back is to me.

"Anyway, back to the subject of strippers," he yells over his shoulder. "You are drastically underestimating the power of naked women dancing on poles. That shit could cure cancer or put an end to war if people would open their eyes. Give pole dancers a chance!" Drew shouts with a fist in the air.

"I think you mean 'Give peace a chance.' And watching strange women gyrate on stage is not going to make Claire *less* angry with me. I'm pretty sure that is the exact definition of something that is guaranteed to piss off your girlfriend," I tell him, flinching when a measuring tape is spread across my ass and then as hands glide up and down my legs.

My penis is shrinking. MY PENIS IS SHRINKING!

"Sylvia, come here and make sure you have everything you need," the owner yells in the general direction of the back storage room as he stands up and wipes his hands on the front of his pants like being in that close proximity to my manhood made him feel dirty. Shouldn't it be the other way around? I feel violated. I'M THE VICTIM HERE. I just want a tux, not go to second base with Steve, the handsy man who sews.

"I think I have what she needs," Drew leans in and whispers conspiratorially. I glanced up to see a blonde Amazon with a measuring tape draped around her neck walking towards us. You're probably thinking, "Okay, he has nothing to complain about now. Some hot chick is going to get on her hands and knees and touch him!"

False.

Sylvia the Seamstress is stalking towards me, and I suddenly realize just how many people are in this store with nothing better to do than stare at me while they wait for their turn. The lights shining down from above are making me hot and now that I know everyone is watching me, I'm getting the ball sweats. I want to pull the dress pants and my boxers away from my junk but I have to just stand here like an idiot with my arms out to the side because Sylvia is already in front of me...on her knees...reaching for my penis.

I know she's not actually reaching for my penis, but my penis doesn't know that. He's a simple creature and all he knows is that there is a hot woman assuming the position and reaching for him.

I know this is going to be hard for you to comprehend, my friend, but this does not mean she wants to have sex with us. I know it's crazy. I know it doesn't make sense but there it is. Stay strong little buddy, stay strong.

Stop judging me. All men talk to their penises.

Wait! Is the plural of penis, penises? Or is it like the word deer and it's just penis? I have five penis. No, that's not right. Maybe it's peni, long "I" like, "There are too many peni in this porno."

"Could you stand still please?" Sylvia says in an irritated voice.

If she had sweaty balls and an almost-boner she wouldn't be so judgmental. Am I right, or am I right?

"Gavin, you almost dressed?" I call into the dressing room, momentarily forgoing my penis grammar lesson to realize my son had gone in there ten minutes ago, claiming he was a big boy and didn't need any help trying on his tux. I begin to wonder about the brilliance of that decision when I don't hear a reply. Part of me secretly hopes he lit something on fire in there so we can finally put an end to this trauma. At least it forces Sylvia to finish the hell up and move on to the next victim so I can stop giving my penis pep talks.

"Gavin, are you okay in there?" I yell as I take a few steps in that direction. Gavin steps out of the room then in a crisp, brand new toddler tuxedo. Lucky little shit doesn't have to worry about Sylvia or touchy-feely Steve. The suit fits him to perfection and I have to say, he is one handsome little boy.

"Wow, Gav. That looks really good on you," I tell him as I squat down in front of him and fix the buttons he fastened wrong.

"I know. I'm a bad ass, man," he replies as he turns away from me and looks at himself in the mirror. He holds onto the lapels of the suit coat like he is James Bond the Toddler Years and twists from right to left to get a better look.

"Gavin, don't talk like that," I scold.

"Nice suit, little dude," Drew says as he walks up behind Gavin and ruffles his hair. "Mine looks better though."

Gavin turns around and looks up at Drew with an angry look on his face.

"I'm going to put corn and hot sauce on your wiener, and then I'll hit you in the face with it. Hit you in the face with your corny wiener."

"Dude, you are an angry little man," Drew tells him as he shakes his head.

"You're a juice bag!" Gavin yells.

"Okay, time-out. Both of you. Gavin, go put your other clothes back on."

Gavin sticks his tongue out at Drew and turns to run back into the dressing room. I stand up to face Drew and fold my arms in front of me.

"What? He threatened my wiener. He's lucky I didn't throw down fisticuffs with him. And just because he said 'juice bag' doesn't mean we don't both know what he was really thinking. That kid is an evil, evil genius, and I never want to be left alone with him. So, strip club, yea or nay?"

⊙ ⊙ ⊙

"It needs to be tomantic...tmotmantic...ramtantic...dude, it needs to be all loving and shit," Jim states as he goes to sit down next to me on the couch, missing the cushions by about six inches and landing on his ass on the floor.

After all of the fittings are over, the girls take Gavin up to the shop so they can help Claire with some last minute orders, and Drew and Jim decide to stick around our place until they are done.

Somehow the topic of my proposal to Claire is brought up and after rehashing the debacle from the Indians game, we all need copious amounts of liquor.

Since Drew's proposal during a ball game idea has gone straight to the shitter, Jim decides it is his turn to try and make this thing work.

"WHY IS THERE A DR. SEUSS CONTACT IN MY CELL PHONE?" Drew yells from his spot sitting Indian-style in the middle of our kitchen table.

"You need candles and you need a violin and you need your shoes shined and a guy in a tux with a white towel thing over his arm and OOHHHH! You need a piano. Chicks dig a guy that can play piano. Can you play the piano, Carter?" Jim asks, finding his way back up to the couch and sprawling across the cushions, kicking me repeatedly in the process.

"Yes! I can play the piano!" I shout.

Why am I shouting?

"I'm not talking about your little Casio keyboard where all you have to do is press the "demo" button and then pretend you're really a piano prodigy," Jim says with a roll of his eyes.

"Whatever, asshole. I can fake-play the SHIT out of "Cherish the Love" by Kool and the Gang. You don't even know. You DON'T. EVEN. KNOW."

I rest my head on the back of the couch and stare up at the ceiling wondering why it's moving.

Ceilings shouldn't move, should they? If ceilings moved, floors would be moving. We'd never be still like broccoli. We'd constantly be moving like in a funhouse. Funhouses are creepy. Funhouses have clowns. Clowns are always moving because they're out to get you and eat your face while you sleep. I wonder if a moving ceiling could kill a clown.

"I DON'T EVEN FUCKING LIKE GREEN EGGS!" Drew shouts from the kitchen, still staring at his phone in anger.

"On my keyboard I used to know how to play "London Bridge is Falling Down" and "Chop Suey".

Heh heh. I said Chop Suey when I meant Chopsticks.

"Chop sueeeeeeeeey, chop sueeeeeeeeey!" I sing.

"London Bridge is a SWEET song! Wait, I know! You should take her to Paris and propose. That's where London Bridge is, right?" Jim asks, grabbing the bottle of tequila off of the coffee table and taking a swig.

"I don't know. Carmela went to Paris and was all depressed and shit. I don't want Claire to be depressed when I propose."

Jim stared at me blankly.

"Who the fuck is this Carmela person? Are you cheating on Claire? I will FUCK YOU UP!" Jim yells.

"Dude, simmer down. Carmela Soprano. Remember? Tony sent her to Paris with her friend Ro so she could 'find herself'. It really was a beautiful gesture on his part since he was banging the Russian chick with one leg," I state.

"Hey, fuck face. You know these people only live in your television, right? THEY. AREN'T. REAL," Jim argues.

"Take it back," I whisper menacingly. "Take it back right now."

"FUCK YOU, SAM I AM!" Drew screams at his phone, holding it up in front of his face.

"And anyway, I think they moved London Bridge. It's in Arizona or some shit like that now," I explain as I took the bottle back from him and rest it on my thigh.

"WHAT THE FUCK ARE YOU SAYING?" Jim yells right in my ear. "London Bridge is in Arizona? When the fuck did this happen? Does London know about this? The queen has got to be pissed."

"It was on 'Real Housewives' so you know it's true," I state.

"Orange County or Atlanta?" Jim asks.

"Orange County, what the fuck is wrong with you? Does anyone even *watch* Atlanta?" I argue.

"YOU AND YOUR STUPID RED AND WHITE STRIPED HAT! FUCKING CATS DON'T WEAR HATS!" Drew screams in frustration before throwing his phone against the wall.

What the hell are we even talking about? I feel like I'm going to puke. And why the fuck is Drew meowing in the kitchen? Do we have a cat? Oh fuck, did I forget to feed a cat? Claire's going to kill me if I murdered her cat.

The last thing I remember before passing out is Jim telling me in a moment of drunken brilliance that Claire would marry me if I fed her lobster and that we should call the queen and ask her if her she would trade us some Grey Poupon for the bridge she doesn't know she lost.

9.

No Nut Shots Before Lunch

The muffled vibrations of my cell phone from its spot under my pillow forces my eyes open. I blink the sleep out of them, pull my ear plugs out of each ear, and slide my hand under my pillow to answer the phone.

"Jesus, Claire. What the hell is that noise? It sounds like a monster. Is there a monster in your house?"

I chuckle at Jenny's question and roll over onto my back and look over at Carter who's fast asleep next to me.

"No, there isn't a monster in my house," I whisper. "That growling snort you hear is Carter snoring."

Once again I thank the good Lord for blessing me with the best earplugs in the world. Not something people typically give thanks for, but I am pretty sure God felt slighted because he is only remembered for the big stuff. I firmly believe there is a special place for me in heaven because I remember to thank him for Southern Butter Pecan coffee creamer and Coochy Cream shaving gel.

"Wow, he really needs to get that checked out," Jenny informs me. "You know, I read something the other day that maybe he should try. It said taking those relaxative things for a few days will make your whole body healthier. Maybe that would fix his sinuses."

"Did you say *relaxative*? Jenny, what the hell is a relaxative?"

I fling the covers off of me and sit up in bed so I can wake up a little more and be able to talk to her with a clear head. I doubt it will help, but here's to hoping.

"You know," she says with a huff, "R-E-L-A-X-A-T-I-V-E."

The fact that she feels the need to enunciate the word like *I* am the one with the problem and my inability to understand is irritating *her* makes me want to shank her.

"I heard the word. I just don't know what the hell you're talking about," I complain as I get out of bed and stretch before making my way out into the hall.

"You know, those pills you take to flush out your system. Relaxatives."

I open Gavin's bedroom door across the hall from our room and peek in on him. He was still out, lying on his back horizontally across his bed with his head hanging off of the edge. There's no way that can be comfortable but I'm not about to move him back up to his pillow and run the risk of waking him up before I've had my coffee. I shut the door quietly and go back to dealing with Jenny while I head to the kitchen.

"I think you mean *laxatives*," I tell her with a sigh. "And they aren't really supposed to be used to flush out your system. Where the hell did you even read that about snoring?"

"Google. So you know it's true. Tell Carter to try it and you can thank me with chocolate when it works," she replies.

I stop in my tracks in the kitchen doorway at the sight before me, unable to even formulate a reply to Jenny about how making Carter shit his brains out most likely would not stop his snoring.

"So anyway, I was calling to ask you if Drew was still at your house. I got a text from him last night as I was leaving your shop that the Cat in the Hat told him he should spend the night. I have no idea what that meant, but as long as I got the whole bed to myself I didn't care."

After the girls had helped me put together the huge chocolate and cookie order last night for a wedding today, we all left to go home. Gavin had fallen asleep in the car so when I got in the house, I bypassed the kitchen and went straight down the hall to his bedroom and then put myself to bed next to a snoring Carter.

I don't know whether I should be happy that I didn't see this sight last night or not. On his back, with his arms and legs flung out to the side, is Drew. Asleep. ON MY KITCHEN TABLE. His ass now rests exactly where I usually put the salt and pepper shakers.

"Yes, he's still here. I need to hang up now so I can beat his ass," I tell her as I walk up to the table, hold the phone between my cheek and shoulder, and then use both of my hands to shove him as hard as I could. His limp body slides easily across the table and crashes to the floor on the other side.

"Don't hurt my pookie-bear!" Jenny yells through the phone.

I walk around the table and stand by Drew's head, looking down at him as he groans.

"Wow, did I sleep on your floor all night?" Drew asks as he opens his eyes and glances up at me from the floor. "You really should consider putting in carpet instead of hardwood. This stuff is really uncomfortable."

Drew rolls over onto all fours with another groan and slowly stands up, twisting and turning as he moves to try and crack his back.

"Get. Out. Of. My. House," I tell him as calmly as I can without screaming and waking up Carter and Gavin.

"Tell him I love him and that my vagina misses him!" Jenny yells excitedly.

"Jenny says to tell you that you need to GET YOUR SORRY ASS OUT OF MY HOUSE!"

"Heeeeey, that's not what I said," Jenny mutters.

"Jenny, I'll call you back."

I hang up the phone and open my mouth to tell Drew to get out of my house again, just in case he hadn't hear me the first two times, when Gavin comes running into the kitchen in his pajamas.

"Hi, Uncle Drew!" he says excitedly as he runs up to Drew. Just as Drew starts to bend over to greet him, Gavin pulls his elbow back and catapults his fist right between Drew's legs.

Drew falls down on his knees with a yelp and I laugh. I know you're not supposed to laugh when your child does something he shouldn't, but I feel this was deserved. I had just found Drew passed out in the middle of the table we eat on. He's lucky I didn't stop Gavin and give him a baseball bat first.

"Gavin, dude, we had a rule!"

At the sound of his voice, I turn to find Carter walking into the room rubbing sleep from one eye. He kisses my cheek as he steps around me and kneels down to Gavin's level.

"Gavin, what was our rule?" Carter asks while Drew clutches his junk, alternating between coughing and making some strange whining noise that reminds me of the sound a balloon makes when you pinch and stretch the opening of it and slowly let the air out.

"No nut shots before lunch," Gavin replies solemnly.

"Right, no nut shots before lunch. And do you know what time it is?" Carter asks.

"I can't tell time," Gavin states.

"Have you had lunch yet?" Carter asks.

"No."

"Then it's before lunch. Tell Uncle Drew you're sorry."

Gavin sighs and turns to face Drew who has finally stopped moaning and is in the process of getting back to his feet.

"I'm sorry I shot you in the nuts before lunch," Gavin mumbles. "Can I have some cereal now?" he asks as he looks at me and away from Drew.

"Sure, baby," I tell him with a smile as I take his hand and walk him toward one of the kitchen chairs. I take one look at the table and veer us in the direction of a bar stool at the island instead. I need to bleach Drew's ass from that table before we ever eat there again.

"My testicles are sitting in my stomach right now. How can you even think about cereal?" Drew asks as he limps over to the counter and grabs his keys.

"Your tentacles are dumb and I'm hungry," Gavin replies around a mouthful of Lucky Charms as I finish pouring the milk in his bowl.

"Whatever, kid. Thanks for letting me crash, guys. I'm gonna make like a fetus and head out."

I let out a big sigh when the door closes behind Drew.

"The next time I find him asleep on any piece of furniture in this house, I'm taking it out on you," I tell Carter.

He comes up behind me and wraps his arms around my waist and places a kiss to the curve of my neck.

"Deal," he replies as he rests his chin on my shoulder.

"You realize you made a rule with your son that states he has permission to punch people in the nuts *after* lunch, correct?"

"Yeah. It sounded good at the time when I made the rule. He had just shown me for the second time the power of his punch, and I was crippled on the ground at the park at the time, so I might not have had full brain function."

I stand there for a few minutes, enjoying the feel of Carter's arms around me as we watch our son scarf down his breakfast.

"I want to have your parents over for dinner," I told him as I turn in his arms and rest my hands against his chest. "I want to cook something really delicious, ply them with alcohol and chocolate, and make them like me. Or at least drunk enough to forget why they don't."

Carter chuckles and tightens his arms around me.

"Babe, they like you. I swear. My grandma even said you had spunk."

"That's old person speak for 'she's bat shit crazy and I'm afraid I'll bust a hip just being in the same room with her when I beat her ass.' I need a chance to make a better first impression," I explain.

"Your FIRST, first impression was just fine. You're forgetting who my best friend is. The first time they met Drew he crashed at our house one night in high school. My mom found him sleepwalking in the middle of the night. She walked into the living room and he was peeing on the couch. Believe me, they've seen it all," Carter reassures me.

"Drew is a moron. He shouldn't be allowed in public without a leash and a handler. I am the mother of their grandson. I shouldn't be talking about a whale's vagina on their Facebook pages. I should be posting pictures of their grandson at a museum studying the works of Michelangelo and posting status messages about my philanthropic work like holding babies in orphanages and hugging homeless people."

Carter stares at me quizzically for a few minutes.

"Will you say something?" I demand.

"Sorry, I'm just trying to figure out if you're serious or not."

"Why the hell wouldn't I be serious? I could totally be that person. I could be that person and you wouldn't even know it," I tell him indignantly as I cross my arms in front of me.

"Oh, I'm pretty sure I would notice if you suddenly turned into a completely different person," he tells me with a laugh.

"Are you saying I'm not a nice person? That I wouldn't cuddle a strange baby or make a homeless guy feel special? Because I would totally do all of that. Maybe I've already been doing it behind your back. Maybe instead of going to the dentist the other day I went to a PETA meeting and threw fake blood on rich people wearing fur. Maybe Gavin has been learning French at night while you're at work."

I crane my neck behind me to look at Gavin.

"Hey, say something in French," I tell him.

"I like french fries," he tells me as he looks up from his cereal bowl with milk dripping down his chin.

"See?" I say as I turn back to face Carter. "He can already use a word in a sentence."

"Okay, stop. Take a deep breath. Of course I think you're a nice person. I think you're an amazing person. But I think we all know that you are not a Stepford Wife and Gavin isn't conjugating French verbs while listening to Mozart."

"MY WIENER EXPLODED!"

Carter drops his arms from my waist, and I jump around in horror at Gavin's scream.

"Never mind. I just spillded milk on it. I have a milk wiener now."

I shake my head and turn back to face Carter.

"I rest my case," he says with a laugh.

I frown and try to act indignant but Carter can see the wheels turning in my head and cuts me off.

"I love both of you exactly the way you are. I love that you have no filter, and I adore that Gavin can make grown men cry. There is not one thing I would change about either one of you, and if anyone doesn't like it, they can kiss my ass. You guys are my life and my family now. Nothing else matters."

Carter bends down and presses a soft kiss to my lips and pulls me tighter against him. His words push aside some of my fears about his family, but it doesn't change the fact that I still want to try again with them. I plan on spending a very long time with this man. I'm still not sold on the whole marriage thing, but I still want him in my life forever, which means I needed to find a way to get on his parents' good side one way or another. If I have to get them drunk, so be it.

"Thank you. But I still want to have your parents over for dinner. I want to at least show them I can act like an adult most of the time."

10.

Ceiling Fan Baseball

"Oh my God! You guys are doing it all wrong. Obviously we need to go over these rules one more time. The dinner roll needs to be thrown *under* hand at the ceiling fan. That's the only way you'll get the arc you need for a good pitch. We're not going for speed, people. We're going for accuracy. Someone pop another batch in the oven so we can start the third inning for fuck's sake!"

After my mother finishes her explanation, she hefts the wooden cutting board up to her shoulder by the handle and readies herself for the pitch.

"Carter, if you bend over like that in front of me again, I might have to grab that sweet little tush of yours and call your mother and thank her."

I'll toast to that.

I raise my wine glass in the air for a toast while Drew does a couple of practice throws.

"I got this one, Mom. Dear Mrs. Ellis, thank you for pushing Carter out of your vagina and having such good genes that he has the most perfect ass I've ever seen," I say with a snort and a wink in Carter's direction.

"Um, thank you?"

My eyes go wide and with my wine glass still held above my head. I turn around slowly and find Carter's parents standing in the dining room doorway looking around at the scene in front of them in shock and awe...but mostly shock.

In hindsight, I should have known better than to listen to anything my mother suggests. Carter's parents had canceled coming to dinner at the last minute because his father was feeling under the weather. How was I supposed to know they would just show up an hour after dinner was over only to find me talking about her vagina, her son naked from the waist up with his shirt tied around his forehead, my dad sitting in the far corner of the room with a bowl of mashed potatoes in his lap, Drew wearing an apron that said, "I didn't wash my hands before I fondled your meat," and Liz and Jenny crawling on all fours around the kitchen table, eating the broken pieces of dinner rolls off of the floor and giggling.

From now on when my mom says, "Beating a dead horse around a bush during a blue moon won't fix anything," I'm going to plug my ears and walk away.

Two hours earlier

"Does it make me a bad person if I feel really bad that your dad doesn't feel well, but feel even worse for myself because I did all this work and now they won't see it?"

Carter laughs and uncorks a bottle of wine.

"I still can't believe you thought their anniversary was the perfect day to have my parents over for dinner."

He pours me a glass of wine as I slide on oven mitts and pull the roast out of the oven.

"Daddy, I wanna help cook the food. What can I make?" Gavin asks as he comes bounding into the kitchen.

"Well, I think Mommy's got everything just about done. How about you take people's coats as they come in the door?"

The doorbell rings and Gavin, happy with the chore he has just been given, scampers off to see who is here.

"I know. It was a crazy idea to do this on their thirtieth anniversary, but I just wanted them to come here, have a nice, family dinner and see that I can be a normal, well-balanced adult. What better day to do that than on a day where everyone has to rejoice in their love, and it would be against the spirit of the marriage in general if anyone said the words whore, vagina, or penis out loud?"

I set the roaster pan on top of the stove and toss the oven mitts onto the counter. The sound of Gavin answering the door puts a halt to our conversation.

"Hi, Uncle Jim. Give me a dollar and I'll cut you."

Carter hands me the glass of Chardonnay and sighs.

"How did he go from, 'Can I take your coats please?' to 'I'm going to murder you for ringing the doorbell.'?"

I shrug and take a sip of the chilled wine.

"Maybe it's a blessing in disguise your parents couldn't come. I think we need a trial run to get this normal thing down pat first," I tell him with a smile.

"I am *not* going to say I told you so," Carter says with a kiss to my cheek.

"Good. Because if you did, I'd have Gavin take your coat and shiv you."

Carter walks out of the room when the doorbell rings again to make sure Gavin doesn't make good on his cutting threats.

With my wine glass in one hand, I start placing serving spoons in all of the side dishes and then pull out the big carving knife so Carter can cut the roast. While I work, I listen to the sounds of a football game coming from the television in the living room and my family and friends talking quietly amongst themselves as they show up. Even if Carter's parents couldn't make it, I know it will still be a good day and a great dinner.

"Claire Bear! Who is this sexy beast you have answering the door for you now?"

I choke on a mouthful of wine and turn to see my mother walk into the room with her arm linked through Carter's. "Have you been working out, Carter?" she asks as she rubs her hand up and down his bicep.

"Mom? What are you doing here? I thought you were going to an art gallery opening?" I ask.

She lets go of Carter's arm and practically skips across the kitchen to me, wrapping me in her arms and squealing in delight.

"Nonsense! When you called the other night and said you were nervous about making a good impression on Carter's stuffy parents, I knew I needed to be here for my best girl," she explains as she pulls back and fiddles with a lock of my hair that has come loose from my pony tail.

"Oh my God, Mom! I never said his parents were stuffy!" I argue as I smacked her hand away from my hair. My mother, while well-meaning, treats me more like a best friend than a daughter and possesses even less of a filter between her brain and her mouth than I do.

I give Carter a look of embarrassment and beg him with my eyes to not listen to a word she said. My mother continues talking like I'm not even there.

"Now, Carter, you look positively yummy and not at all tired. Shouldn't you be exhausted from staying up all night sleeping with my daughter? Claire, why aren't you keeping this man up until the wee hours of the morning having lots of sex?"

"Jesus, Mom! Can you tone it down a bit please?" I beg.

Carter had met my mom the day we moved in when she came to help us unpack and has stopped by for dinner several times since then. He is quite familiar with the way she acts but that doesn't mean I can't try to nip it in the bud before it gets out of hand.

"What? Can't a mother be concerned for her daughter? I just want to make sure your vagina doesn't get full of cobwebs like before. Those things can take a pounding so don't worry about breaking anything. I once pulled a muscle in my vagina. Did I ever tell you that story?"

So much for the no vagina talk today.

I chug the rest of my glass of wine, reach for the bottle on the counter, fill the glass back up, and then took a swig right from the bottle before setting it back down.

"Mom, did I tell you dad brought Sue with him today? You know, the woman he's been seeing? She's really nice. And never, ever talks about pounding vaginas. Ever."

I think maybe making my mom a teensy bit jealous will deter her from all things inappropriate but sadly I'm mistaken. Sometimes I still forget just how cordial my parents divorce was.

"Ooooooh goody!" she squeals, clapping her hands together like a two-year-old. "I've wanted to meet her ever since your father first told me about her. We have so much to talk about. I wonder if he's used his Sean Connery accent on her yet and tried that move where he puts his foot on the headboard and then thrusts-"

"STOP! Jesus Christ, please stop," I plead before taking another big gulp of my wine. "Carter, can you let everyone know dinner is ready and we're doing it buffet style. They can all come in here and fill up their plates before sitting down at the table. If you need me, I'll be in here with my head in the oven."

☉ ☉ ☉

An hour later everyone is still picking at their food after going back for seconds and thirds. My mom sits next to Sue and the two of them have been whispering and giggling like school girls through the entire meal, stopping every once in a while to glance over at my dad before falling into a fit of hysterics all over again.

"Hey, Claire, does this apple pie have nuts in it? I don't like nuts," Drew states.

"I like nuts. Nuts are delicious," Gavin pipes up, taking a big bite of apple pie to prove it.

"Well, *I* don't like nuts," Drew argues.

"Guys, that's enough nut talk," Liz complains as she pours herself another glass of wine from the bottle in the middle of the table.

"I'M GOING TO PUT MY NUTS ON ALL OF YOU!" Gavin yells through a mouthful of food.

Carter clamps his hand over Gavin's mouth and then leans over to quietly tell him it isn't polite to yell at the table.

"So, Claire's mom, do you have any good stories to tell us about your little cupcake when she was growing up? Any slumber parties with naked pillow fights or lesbian experimentation?" Drew asks.

"What's a lez bean? Is that like a lima bean? I don't like lima beans. I am NOT going to eat a lez bean," Gavin declares.

"Oh, you'll change your mind about that someday," Drew tells him with a wink.

"Gavin, how about you go pick out a movie, and I'll put it on in the living room?" Carter suggests. He obviously doesn't want our son learning about the fine art of carpet munching just yet.

Gavin lets his fork clamor to his plate, jumps down off of his chair, and takes off running to the DVD shelf in the living room.

"Sorry, Drew, my childhood was pretty uneventful," I tell him, bringing the conversation back to the original subject. "No one has anything even remotely interesting to tell," I inform him as I hold my glass across the table towards Liz so she can give me a refill.

My mom nods in agreement and gives Drew a sad look.

"Unfortunately she's right. Claire was a very boring child. She liked to read and take naps. We used to invent things to do just to mess with her and try to fuck her up a little bit. She was entirely too well-rounded. It was disturbing. George, remember that time you had your friend Tim call the house when she was eight because she wasn't listening to you? Didn't he pretend he was Santa Clause?"

My dad leans back in his chair and comes an inch away from sticking his hand in the waistband of his pants in post-dinner bliss before he realizes he isn't alone in his own home. He quickly switches directions and moves his arm to the back of Sue's chair.

"Yep, she was being a mouthy little shit so I had Tim call and put the fear of Santa into her," he says with a chuckle.

"Hey, that wasn't funny. He told me I was a very bad little girl and that he'd been watching me. He said he lived in the basement and came up at night to watch me sleep. He's the reason I still take the basement stairs two-at-a-time when I run up them and why I called America's Most Wanted when I was nine because there was some killer on the loose hiding in people's basements," I explain. "I told them the killer was Santa, that he called me the year before, and that he was probably still in our basement."

"I remember that afternoon. The police questioned us for two hours so they could make sure we weren't harboring a criminal," my mother states. "That was such a long, boring day."

"No, don't worry about me. I was totally fine," I deadpan.

"Oh quit your bitchin'. It wasn't that bad. You're still alive, aren't you?" my dad asks. "And don't lie, Rachel. They only questioned us for about thirty seconds. Then you asked them if they wanted a joint and all was forgotten. Cops were way more fun back then," he says to the rest of the table.

I turn towards Carter. "Never, ever ask me again why I am the way I am. NEVER. AGAIN," I whisper.

"I did walk in on her playing with her Barbie's one time, and she had them all undressed, humping each other. It was some weird sex circle, and Ken was sitting in the middle just watching them, fully dressed. I wanted to light some incense and set the mood for her, but then I saw she had one of the horses in the circle of sex and it just got disturbing at that point. I never knew Barbie was into bestiality," my mother states solemnly.

I lean forward and start banging my head softly on the table.

"Nice! Getting freaky with the Barbie dolls. I like it," Drew exclaims.

"I think in honor of this family dinner, we need to remember the best part about our holiday dinners, Rachel," my dad tells her with a gleam in his eye. "Ceiling fan baseball."

My parents start laughing as they remember dinners of the past, and I just continue to bang my head harder.

This was supposed to be a nice, peaceful dinner.

"Oh my God! I remember ceiling fan baseball from high school!" Liz says excitedly. "Except didn't we play it with tater tots a few times?"

"Yes, we've been known to make substitutions," my mother states.

"Okay, what the hell is ceiling fan baseball? It's not what I think it is, right?" Drew asks as he looks back and forth between my parents. They each look at me expectantly. Liz is practically bouncing up and down in her chair in excitement.

Oh what the hell.

I roll my eyes and drain my glass of wine in one gulp, slamming it back to the table with a *thunk*.

"Alright, fine. Carter, grab the wooden cutting board with the handle. Liz, put all the extra rolls on the stove into a basket. Jim, turn the ceiling fan on low and Drew, move the table to the side."

Everyone stares at me with their mouths open for exactly three seconds, and then they all jump into action and start gathering supplies.

"I'll get more booze!" Jenny announces happily.

"I got the mashed potatoes," my dad states casually.

"What do we need mashed potatoes for?" Carter asks as he walks back into the room with the cutting board, a.k.a "baseball bat".

"Claire, this man is hot as balls but he's kind of dumb," my mother says as she pats Carter's cheek affectionately. "The mashed potatoes are the catcher's mitt. Duh."

11.

Mommy!

I think it's safe to say that my parents will never understand the whirlwind that is Claire and her family. I'm okay with that. It's not like I've ever been that close to them anyway. Their parenting style had always been a bit more standoffish than most. I think it's one of the main reasons I knew I needed to do right by Claire and Gavin. I never want my son to feel like there is anything even remotely more important to me than him. Don't get me wrong. My parents are good people. They love me and they have done a good job raising me. They had sent me to the best schools and had high hopes for my future. When I dropped out of college because it bored the shit out of me, they didn't take it very well. They had wanted me to be a doctor or a lawyer and share their country club membership. They like things calm, neat, orderly, and pretentious. They most definitely aren't ceiling fan baseball-playing people, and they never will be. It had taken them a while to stop trying to fit me into a certain mold and realize they need to just let me make my own choices and live my own life. They had been really excited to find out they were grandparents and I know they will be good at it. On the bright side, at least Gavin will have someone in his life who could teach him how to sit on the board of a company, complain about paying taxes, and hide money from the government. Since he already has people showing him how to swear like a truck driver and throw food at ceiling fans during dinner, I do believe this will make him the most well-rounded human being on the planet.

It takes a lot of explaining and even more wine to get Claire on board with my line of thinking. She wants everyone to like her and considers herself a failure because my parents have only seen her at her worst. When I tell her that after twenty-five years *I* have yet to impress my parents and therefore she shouldn't let it get to her, she finally relents and decides against writing an apology note to them in chocolate on their front yard.

After my mother apologizes for showing up unexpectedly, and Drew throws a wild pitch into the fan that results in a dinner roll right to her neck, my parents realize the importance of calling ahead. They do their best to not make faces as they tiptoe around clumps of bread that litter the dining room floor to find an available seat. My father explains he thought he was coming down with a cold but after a short nap, he felt much better so they decided to stop by for dessert. Claire does her best to stick to the original plan of plying them with a bunch of alcohol and sweets to suck up to them, but after thirty minutes of Rachel trying to get my mother to admit she would love to try a threesome some day and goading my father to confess he dropped acid in the sixties, my parents decide it's past their bedtime.

After they leave, everyone helps clean up before they head to their own homes. When the last dish is put away and the final crumb is swept from the floor, we finally have the house all to ourselves and nothing can be heard except the ticking of the clock in the living room.

I walk into the kitchen after putting Gavin to bed to find Claire standing in front of the sink, staring out the window, lost in thought. I don't want her to feel guilty about my parents. I won't let them make her feel like anything less than the amazing woman I know her to be.

I come up behind her and slide my hands around her waist and clasp them together on top of her stomach. I rest my chin on her shoulder, waiting for her to speak.

"So. This was a fun day," she says sarcastically, bringing her hands up to rest on top of mine.

I turn my face and place a kiss on the side of her neck, inhaling the subtle hint of chocolate that always lingers on her skin.

"Actually, it was a very fun day. I had no idea you ever called America's Most Wanted," I tell her with a smile. "And that Barbie likes horse cock. Who knew?"

Her body shakes with laughter.

"Hey, don't judge me. Ken had underwear that wouldn't come off. What's a girl to do in that situation?" she asks as she turns into my embrace, slides her arms around me, and rests her cheek against my chest. "I was an only child with two crazy parents. Unless I wanted to hang out in the basement with my mother and smoke pot, there wasn't much else to do other than have Barbie orgies."

I laugh along with her and rub my hands in slow circles around her back.

"You can still run you know. If you want to make like the Road Runner and bust through the door leaving an imprint of your body behind, I won't blame you."

She looks up at me and smiles but I can tell she is kind of serious.

"Listen to me. Nothing matters but you, me, and Gavin. There is absolutely nothing that either one of our families can do to ruin this."

Ask her to marry you. Do it now!

"Claire…"

"Don't say it," she warns.

What the fuck? Can she read my mind? Claire, nod once if you can hear me.

"Don't tell me it was no big deal and that you don't care what your parent's think."

Oh thank God.

"Fine, I won't say it. I'll just think it."

Will you marry me? Will you marry me? Why the fuck is this so hard to say? There is nothing else more important right now than asking this question!

"I have a great idea. How about you take my mind off of everything by having sex with me on the kitchen counter," she says with a wag of her eyebrows.

Okay, this might trump the proposal.

Before I can stop her...oh who am I kidding? Like I'd really stop her from banging me in the kitchen. She leans up on her tiptoes and presses her mouth to mine. The kiss quickly turns deeper and her tongue sweeping through my mouth instantly makes me hard. I pull away from her mouth long enough to lift her up onto the counter next to the sink. Her legs wrap around my waist and her hands go to work unbuttoning my jeans. Before I can even take another breath, her hand is inside my boxers, wrapping around my length.

"Fuck," I mutter, leaning my forehead against hers as she works her small hand from base to tip, tortuously slow. As my hips rock with the movements of her hand, I slide my palms up the outside of her bare thighs, my fingers inching slowly under the hem of her skirt until I wrap them around the strings of her thong that rest on her hips.

She unwinds her legs from around my waist and lets them dangle off of the edge of the counter so I can slide the black, lacy scrap of material off of her and fling it to the floor.

My eyes travel up her long, smooth legs, and her skirt pushes up to the top of her thighs. I let my hands follow the movement of my eyes, touching every inch of skin I look at. I part her thighs as I go, sliding my hands around her hips to cup her ass and bring her body closer to the edge of the counter.

Her hands move to the waistband of my boxer briefs and I almost whimper at the loss of her warm palm and fingers stroking me into oblivion. She uses both hands to push my boxer briefs down my hips just far enough for my cock to free itself.

I step closer between her thighs until the head of my erection meets her wet center. Gritting my teeth with the need to bury myself inside of her, I slide the tip of my cock up through her heat and circle it around her clit. Her legs slide back up the outside of my thighs, and she locks her feet behind my back, her ankles digging into my ass as she pulls me harder against her, and I slip inside of her one slow inch at a time.

"Jeeeeesus, you feel good," I whisper against her lips as I rock my hips against her.

"This is the best *phone call* we've ever made," she says with a laugh as she wraps her arms around my shoulders.

"I've never made a *phone call* in the kitchen before. It always seemed unsanitary," I state as Claire lifts her hips to meet my thrusts.

"Please don't make me think about the fact that you just sliced a roast on this counter," she says between moans.

"At least we're doing this *after* I cut the meat. Otherwise we would have served our family and friends ass-roast with a side of sex juices."

Claire's fingers slide through the back of my hair and clutches onto it so hard I wince and slow down my movements.

"Seriously? Do you want me to throw up on you while we're doing this? Never, ever use that sentence again."

I chuckle and pull her body tighter against mine, wrapping my arms around her. I try to keep my movements slow but it just feels too fucking good. I kiss a trail down her neck and start to swivel my hips in a circle. Claire's fingernails dig into my shoulder blades, and I feel her entire body shudder.

"Oh my God, keep doing that," she moans.

I should ask her to marry me now. If I do it while she's coming, she probably won't be able to say no. It would be physically impossible. Like performing a sex exorcist. THE POWER OF THE ORGASM COMPELS YOU!

"Oh fuck!" she cries as she pushes herself harder against me and lets her head fall back against the cabinet behind her as her orgasm builds.

Marry me, marry me, marry me.

"Yes! Oh my God yes!"

I wonder if I could pretend that conversation just happened outside of my head and convince her of it. Just start going around telling people she said yes. "Yes, Grandma, we're getting married! What's that you say? How did I do it? Oh, I was fucking her on the kitchen counter, you know, where we prepare food, and it just slipped out! No, not my penis. The question."

I smack a hand down on the counter next to her to hold myself steady as I plunge in and out of her faster and harder, trying to banish all thoughts of talking to my grandmother about slippery penises.

It helps that every time with Claire is like the first time. Just without all the booze, virginity robbing, and not knowing each other's names. I know more than ever that this is the person I want to spend the rest of my life with. I slide my other hand off of her ass and glide my fingers down to where we are connected. Claire lets out a gasp as I touched her with the tips of my fingers and draw her orgasm out of her. She comes quickly and moans my name, her breath hot against my ear. It's the sexiest thing in the world and my own release shoots its way up through my body and explodes out of me. I bury my face into the side of her neck and shout the words I've been worrying about for weeks. Well, I don't shout them so much as muffle them really loudly since my mouth is pushed against her skin.

We clutch onto each other for several minutes, breathing heavy and not uttering a word.

Shit! She's probably mortified I asked her to marry me while I came and thinks it's just post orgasmic bliss or something equally as fucked up. That's why she isn't saying anything.

I pull my head out of the crook of her neck and chance a look at her. She's looking at me funny, almost like she felt a little sick to her stomach just from the sight of me.

Oh that's just super. The thought of marrying me makes her want to hurl.

"Um, Carter?"

"It's okay. You don't have to say anything," I tell her quickly.

I think it's safe to say my humiliation level at this moment is at an all time high. My penis is still inside of her. Does she WANT to make it shrivel up and die by discussing this?

"No, I really think we need to talk about this," she pleads with a worried look on her face.

I laugh uncomfortably. "Nope, no we don't. Let's just pretend it never happened. I've already forgotten."

She pushes on my shoulders and holds me at arm's length.

"Carter!" she scolds.

"I'm sorry, were you saying something?"

She huffs and rolled her eyes, clearly irritated with me that I don't want to have a nice, friendly conversation about how she'd rather yak up a fur ball than become my wife.

"Cut it out! This is serious."

As a heart attack. Or a penis dying in a vagina from a broken heart.

"I'm pretty sure we need to talk about the fact that you screamed 'MOMMY!' when you came," she hisses angrily.

"Whoa that's kinky, Carter! Who knew you had it in ya?"

Claire yelps in surprise and my head jerks around at the sound of Rachel's voice in our kitchen.

"MOM!" Claire yells as she tightens her thighs around me in an effort to get us closer and shield the fact that we are still intimately connected.

"Tsk, tsk. Shouldn't Carter be the one shouting that?" Rachel asks with a laugh. "Sorry to interrupt kitchen sex. Great idea by the way. Did I ever tell you about the time I had sex in the kitchen of a McDonald's?"

Claire growls and narrows her eyes at her mother.

"Another time maybe! Just stopped back to get my purse that I left here," she says as she takes a few steps over to the kitchen table and picks it up off of one of the chairs. "You kids have a nice night. And may I just say you have a very nice ass, Carter. Claire, don't forget to do your kegels."

With that, she turns and breezes out of the kitchen, and we hear the front door open and close.

"What was that you said earlier about neither one of our families being able to ruin anything?" Claire asks sarcastically.

12.
Stinky Wiener Ticks and Twice Baked Potatoes

"Dude, she thought you called out 'Mommy'? Oh sweet Jesus, that is the best thing I've ever heard! Seriously. You just made my week." Drew laughs as he pats my back.

"It's always a pleasure when my humiliation amuses you."

Drew continues laughing and shaking his head as he works on the car panel in front of him. We have three minutes to do our job on the car in progress before the conveyor belt starts moving the car down the line again for the next pair of workers.

"How in the hell did you diffuse the situation? That's what I want to know!" Jim walks up behind me to grab a clipboard off of the table and makes some notes, waiting patiently for my answer.

"Well, having her mother walk in on us helped. Claire was completely focused on her making comments about my ass rather than on the fact that I may or may not have called out something completely inappropriate during sex. Is it wrong that I'd rather she thought I *did* call her 'Mommy' instead of just admitting I really said 'marry me'?" I ask.

"I dated a girl once who liked to call me 'Daddy' in the sack. It was kind of hot until I actually met her dad. He looked like Danny Devito, but shorter and with less hair. He always smelled like farts and swiss cheese and liked to bark at hot chicks when they'd walk by him in public," Drew tells us.

"I take that back. It would have been less painful for her to think I proposed than to hear that story," I say disgustedly.

"So what's the plan now? So far a baseball game and post-coital hasn't worked for ya. Got any other tricks up your sleeve?" Jim jokes.

"I was thinking about doing it over dinner maybe. Someplace really romantic. Isn't that what you said I should do that night after we tried on tuxes?"

Jim looks at me in confusion. "I did? I don't recall. Although I woke up at three in the morning in your bathtub with no pants on that night, so it's possible I had some really good ideas."

"Ooooooh! You should totally propose at our rehearsal dinner next weekend," Jim says excitedly as he slams the clipboard down on the table.

"Really? I don't know. It seems like kind of an intrusion on you and Liz. That's your special day."

"Slow down there, Miss Manners. I'm not asking you to have a double-wedding with us. Just pop the question over dinner. Please, God, give me something else to think about right now other than aisle runners, boutonnières, and swatches," Jim complains.

"Are you wearing a *Swatch Watch* for your wedding?" Drew asks, forming the letter "X" with his arms in front of him and pronouncing the words with flair.

"Funny. Just wait until Jenny gets her hooks in you and you have to deal with her psycho mother. Every time Mary Gates walks in the room and shows me a ribbon sample I want to say, 'Did you see that? The fuck I give. It went that way.' I'm about one tablecloth color away from just telling everyone to bring a side dish and a lawn chair to our backyard and have Drew get ordained on the internet to do the ceremony," Jim complains. "Liz asked me the other day what I thought about twice baked potatoes. How the fuck should I know? Was I supposed to be thinking about twice baked potatoes all this time? Is this where I went wrong? Are grown men *supposed* to have an opinion about twice baked potatoes?"

389

Jim looks like his head is about ready to explode. He stands there with his arms outstretched like he's pleading for understanding or some sort of man hug. Since Drew and I aren't the man-hugging type, Jim finally drops his arms and continues with his rant.

"And my parents, being the good Christian people they are, think one bottle of wine on every table is enough liquor. My mother's exact words were, 'If we run out, we run out. People will just have to make do with water.'"

Drew's mouth drops open as the car we finished moves down the line and a new one follows in its wake.

"Water? At a wedding? I don't understand," he asks in confusion. "Did you invite Jesus? That's the only way that will be acceptable."

"Please, for the love of God, propose to Claire at the rehearsal dinner so my future mother-in-law will squeal in someone else's ear for one night. I beg of you," Jim pleads.

I think about Jim's suggestion while I get to work on the next vehicle. The restaurant where the rehearsal dinner will be held *is* a really beautiful place. And our friends will all be there to witness the event, something I'm sure Claire will love. The more I go over the idea in my head, the more excited I become. The rest of the night at work flies by as Drew and Jim help me come up with the perfect plan to ask Claire to be my wife.

⊙ ⊙ ⊙

The following Friday evening, Claire, Gavin, and I pull into the parking lot of Pier W, a beautiful landmark restaurant in Cleveland that is designed to resemble the hull of a luxury liner. Its location, perched high on a cliff overlooking Lake Erie, gives it a breathtaking view and makes me one hundred percent certain I have chosen the best location for a marriage proposal.

After a short run-through of the ceremony at the church where the wedding will be held the following afternoon, everyone is looking forward to a relaxing evening with good food and drinks. Jim and Drew keep eying me with furtive glances the entire time we are at the church, winking at me and nudging my arm whenever they can. I come close to punching Drew in the stomach directly under a statue of Mary at one point.

"Hey, Carter, can I pop you a question?"

It's the fourth time Drew has made a reference to asking a question, and I've had enough. The groomsmen are standing in a straight line at the side of the altar while the priest speaks quietly to Liz and Jim in the center of the aisle.

"Will you shut the fuck up already? Claire's going to get suspicious you dick-fuck!" I whisper angrily at him.

"Whoa, dude, slow your roll. You just said f-u-c-k in front of the Virgin Mary. Show some respect," Drew scolds.

"What's a virgin?" Gavin asks from his position standing next to me as he swings the ring bearer pillow around his head like a lasso.

"Uh, it's a kind of chicken," I stammer. "Very rare. No one talks about it."

It's impossible not to be nervous as I take Claire's hand and help her out of the car. My palms are sweating, and I hope she doesn't notice as I stand there for a minute staring at her while she helps Gavin out of his car seat.

She's so fucking beautiful I want to cry like a baby.

She closes Gavin's car door and catches me staring at her.

"Are you okay? You seem a little out of it," she says as she looked me over.

Shit, is my forehead sweating? Is she looking at me right now wondering why I look like a chubby man with a heart condition who just ate his weight in chicken wings and Jell-O salad at a buffet? That's not a good look to have when you want the woman you love to look into your eyes and pledge her undying love by saying 'yes' to marrying you.

"Mom, my stinky wiener ticks," Gavin states, interrupting the sweat fest and giving me time to wipe my forehead.

"Um, what does that mean?" Claire asks him.

"It means GET A MOVE ON! I wanna eat some beef turkey!"

The three of us turn and make our way up the sidewalk to the set of stairs that will lead us to the rock face where the restaurant sits.

Once inside the doors, the maître d' escorts us across the room to a long table set up in front of panoramic windows that overlook the lake. We are the last to arrive, as per the plan devised by Drew and Jim. The last three empty seats are strategically placed at the end of the table, the perfect spot for everyone to see what is going to happen.

Our friends are all in the midst of quiet conversations amongst themselves when we walk up but stop long enough to greet us and for Jim to make sure we know not to order any drinks since they are getting champagne. The mention of champagne is over exaggerated with a wink when Claire turns to help Gavin into his seat.

As the conversation moves to talk of the wedding the following day, I try to listen while going over my lines in my head. It doesn't seem appropriate to use the same speech I had prepared for the Indian's game proposal since there were words like "grand slam" and "switch hitter".

Hey, I never had said it was the best speech.

Since that plan had tanked, I needed to start from scratch. On our lunch hours at work every night this week, Drew and Jim helped me write the perfect words to say to Claire. Okay, *Jim* helped me write the perfect words. Drew wanted me to just throw a ping pong ball at her face, reminiscent of her bartending days at Fosters' Bar and Grill where she made up the game P.O.R.N. According to him, I should whip it at her chin and say, "That won't be the only ball bouncing off your chin if you say yes!"

After three rough drafts of the proposal and several uses of thesaurus.com, Jim and I had written the most perfect proposal ever.

This night needs to be flawless. Claire will spend countless hours retelling the story of how I proposed to everyone she knows, and even a few strangers, for the rest of her life. She deserves the most romantic story to tell.

The waitress comes around a few minutes later to take everyone's order.

"So, little man, what can I get you?" she asks as she bends down to Gavin's level.

"I want a virgin," he states.

Claire starts choking on her water and Liz reaches over to pat her on the back.

"I'm sorry, what do want to order?" the waitress asks him in confusion.

"A virgin. I want to order a virgin," he repeats, looking at her like she was a moron.

"Don't we all, son. Don't we all," Jim's father mumbles from a few spots down, receiving a smack on the arm from his wife.

"I think he means chicken," I clarify sheepishly.

"Yes, because *that* makes perfect sense," Claire says under her breath as she picks up her water glass and attempts to take another sip.

With our orders taken, the waitress disappears and conversation resumes.

"Jim, I've been meaning to ask if you were able to finish hot gluing those crystals to all the ribbons for the church programs," Mrs. Gates asks. "And also, don't forget to put Preparation H under your eyes tomorrow morning."

Drew starts laughing and Jenny kicks him under the table.

"I'm totally calling him Hemorrhoid Head all day tomorrow." Drew leans over and whispers to me. "I know he's been stressed about the wedding, but I didn't realize it would cause ass itching under his eyes."

Jim's mom hears Drew and gives him a stern look that instantly wipes the smile off of his face.

"Andrew, it is well documented that this type of cream can reduce puffiness under one's eyes. Very effective when one needs to have their pictures taken," she states primly.

"Also very *funny* when one's eyes now have anal leakage," Drew says under his breath.

"Jim, before you leave tonight remind me to give you the magazine photos of the two different floral arches for you to look at. You'll just need to tell the florist which one you want her to use at the reception tomorrow when she delivers the boutonnières," Liz's mom adds.

Jim is right. This woman is a walking, talking wedding robot.

"Jesus Christ, do it already before she starts talking about wedding favors and I grow a vagina," Jim begs in a low whisper.

I give him a nod to let him know I'm ready. A big grin breaks across his face as he completely ignores Weddingbot 2000 and signals our waitress while Claire is busy discussing the difference between good words and bad words with Gavin.

Jim and I had met with the manager of the restaurant and our waitress the day before to go over the plan for the evening. The waitress will bring over a tray of champagne for everyone at the table as soon as she is given the signal. At the bottom of Claire's glass will be the engagement ring I had dropped off this afternoon when I ran out to pick up Gavin's and my tux.

I couldn't believe it was finally time to do this. I am going to propose to the woman of my dreams who I thought I'd never see again after our one night in college.

The waitress is back and has served almost half the table their glasses of champagne. I figure it's now or never.

I reach down and clasp Claire's hand that rests on my thigh, bringing it up to my lips, trying to calm the frantic beating of my heart.

When she feels my lips on her hand, she turns to look at me.

"I love you so much, Claire," I say softly as I see the waitress move closer and closer to us out of the corner of my eye.

"I love you too, Carter," she replies with a smile.

The waitress only has two more people to serve before she gets to us. I know I need to speed things up a bit if I want to time everything just right.

"Oh my gosh, wait until you hear what Jenny said to me earlier. I can't believe I forgot to tell you," Claire says as she leans in closer to me and glances over my shoulder to make sure Jenny isn't listening.

I look behind me as well and see the waitress rounding the table, heading right for us. I need to be down on my knee when she places Claire's glass in front of her.

Shit!

"Claire, hold that thought. I have something I need to say."

She completely ignores me and turns sideways in her chair so she can face me and get closer.

"Wait, this is really good! You're going to love this," she says excitedly as my foot starts bouncing frantically on the floor when I see the waitress stop right behind Claire to say something to Gavin. "Okay, so Jenny said Drew's been acting funny lately. Talking about weddings and marriage proposals and asking her hypothetical questions like, 'If I were to propose to you, what would you want me to say?' Drew is so damn obvious."

I look back at Claire, barely registering what she is saying and wondering if it's bad manners to tell her to shut the hell up right before I ask her to marry me.

"Huh? What did you say?" I ask her as she continues to talk and I miss the last few sentences.

"I said Jenny thinks Drew is going to propose to her tonight. Can you believe that shit?"

My head slowly turns to face her, my mouth falling open in shock, the waitress with the champagne long forgotten.

"Drew? Propose? Tonight?"

Fuckshitballdamn!

"I know, right? First of all, they haven't been together that long and second – who the hell proposes at someone else's rehearsal dinner? That's in poor taste if you ask me. You're taking the spotlight off of the soon-to-be-married couple and putting it on you. It's like a slap in the face to them. Like, 'Oh hey, look at me! I'm an asshole and want all eyes on me instead of the two people they should be on! Ha ha, I'm such an asshole, who has a camera to document my assholeness for all of eternity?'" Claire says with a laugh and a shake of her head for the imaginary asshole in her mind.

Except *I'm* the asshole! I'm the mother fucking asshole!

An arm slides between our bodies and in the haze of my asshole pity party, I realize there is a champagne glass attached to the end of it. I literally feel my brain shutting down. I hear a computerized voice in there counting backwards from five and feel like I'm in the movie *"The Hurt Locker"* and don't know whether to cut the red or the blue wire.

The red or the blue?? THE RED OR THE MOTHER FUCKING BLUE?!

Claire reaches for her glass of champagne.

You know how people always talk about how during a moment of panic they feel like they're in a dream and everything is in slow motion? I have never experienced that before and always just assume they are full of shit and trying to make their story sound better.

Well, I'm right.

This shit isn't moving in slow motion; it's moving faster than the speed of light, and I'm cutting the wrong wire and exploding into a complete jackass spaz.

My arm, as if completely detached from my body, flies away from its spot resting on the table, knocking over a lit candle, the salt shaker, my own glass of champagne, and two full water glasses until my hand grasps onto Claire's champagne flute right before it touches her lips.

I yank the glass out of her hand, sloshing expensive champagne everywhere in the process. In the back of my mind I could hear some-one yelling, "Nooooooooooo!" and am completely oblivious to the fact that the bat shit crazy screamer in the middle of Pier W is me.

Not even taking one second to think about my actions or the fact that everyone in the place is looking at me in horror, I quickly bring the glass to my lips, tip my head back, and dump everything into my mouth, including the ring.

Drew leans over and whispers in my ear when I slam the empty glass back down on the table. "Dude, are you changing the plan? Because if the new plan is that you're going to try and shit out that ring, I gotta tell ya, that's not very romantic."

13.

Tee Time

I'm going to cry.

I'm going to cry like a God dammed baby and there's nothing I can do to stop it. It's getting hard to swallow because my throat is so tight, and I'm starting to feel like I'm at a rave with a really bad strobe light because of the way I keep blinking my eyes to keep the tears at bay.

Son of a bitch, I'm going to *ugly cry*. Some women can pull off crying without their make-up running or fluids leaking from every hole in their face but not me. I'm in a gorgeous gown, my hair is professionally done, my make-up is flawless and in three seconds I'm going to ruin it all by losing complete control of the muscles in my face. I'm going to try really hard to stay quiet which is going to fuck me over because it's going to force me to make sounds that you only hear in the middle of the night on the Discovery Channel. By the time I'm finished, I'm going to look like I have pink eye after being punched in the face by Mike Tyson.

This is all Liz's fault. Why does she have to look so beautiful?

We're standing in the alcove at the back of the church, just seconds away from walking down the aisle. The other bridesmaids have already left to meet their groomsmen at the front of the alter, the doors leading into the church closing behind them to keep the guests' first view of the bride a secret until the last minute.

Mrs. Gates is busy fluttering around Liz making last minute adjustments to the train of her dress and reminding her to smile, but not too much or the creases at the corners of her eyes will show in the pictures. She's standing up and squatting down over and over as she circles Liz, and I giggle-snort around the tears forming in my eyes since she reminds me of a horse on a merry-go-round. I suddenly want to ask Liz if she has a riding crop I can borrow so I can whip her mother and make her go faster.

"I can't believe you're getting married," I whisper to my best friend as we both ignore her mother reminding Liz to clench her butt cheeks as she walks.

"Me either," she says with a smile through her own tears.

"I love Jim and I know you two will be so happy together," I reassure her. "But as your best friend, it is my duty to tell you that should you need it, my car is right outside, fully gassed with the keys in the ignition and a suitcase with vodka in it in the trunk. I've also been keeping my pimp hand strong, just in case Jim gets out of line and needs a little bitch slap."

She laughs and I lean in to give her a quick hug, careful to avoid tugging on her veil or messing up any part of her. I do not need the wrath of Mary Gates raining down upon me.

"Thanks, BFF. I love you."

The sound of gagging and thumping interrupts our Hallmark card moment and we turned to see Jim's little cousin Melissa in her flower girl dress straddling Gavin on the floor and trying to choke him. Gavin flails and kicks beneath her, trying to dislodge her hands from around his neck.

"Hey!" I whisper-yell. They both cease all movement and turn to stare at me. "What are you doing?!"

Gavin shoves with all of his might and Melissa tumbles off of him. He scrambles up, grabbing his fallen ring bearer pillow and clutching it to his chest.

"She freaking hell took my pillow! Stupid punk!" Gavin says loudly.

"He kicked me in my no-no-zone!" Melissa complains with a stomp of her foot.

"Oh my," Mrs. Gates mutters.

"You should eat dirt!" Gavin turns and yells at Melissa.

"I will NOT eat dirt!" she counterattacks.

"EAT IT WITH YOUR CHICKEN FACE!"

It's complete and utter child anarchy and before I can pick a kid to yell at, the organ music changes and begins playing the song that I needed to walk down the aisle to with Gavin and Melissa right behind me.

I quickly bend down in front of both of them and stare them square in the face with as stern of an expression as I can muster.

"Both of you little monsters, listen up. As soon as you step foot out of those doors, you better have smiles on your faces and your outside voices duct taped inside your bodies. If you speak, push, shove, swear, argue, or even blink at each other I will haul your asses out of that church and lock you in the basement with the scary clowns."

I huff to emphasize my point and stand, tugging up the front of my strapless dress.

"If I see a clown, I'm going to punch him in the nuts."

"Gavin Allen!" I scold.

"What? We didn't step fru dose doors yet," he argues, pointing behind me.

"Kid has a point," Liz whispers.

"Behave," I whisper through clenched teeth as I turn and nodded to the two church attendants so they can open the double doors for my entrance.

"My mom's not afraid to punch a kid," I hear Gavin whisper to Melissa as I take my first step down the aisle.

Thankfully, my threat pays off and both kids make it to the front of the church without killing each other. The ceremony is beautiful and the only interruption came during communion.

Liz is Catholic so she had wanted a full, Roman Catholic service. Carter is a "sort-of" Catholic in that he was baptized, made his First Communion and everything else he was required to do while growing up, but he only goes to church for holidays, weddings, and funerals. Regardless, when it comes time for communion, he gets in line and takes Gavin with him since Gavin is on his side of the church through the ceremony.

I really don't believe in any one religion, but I have been known to sit in on a few services every once in a while just in case someone up there is taking notes. I sit in my seat in the front row with one other bridesmaid who isn't Catholic and we watch the procession and smile at those who walk by. I crane my neck and watch happily as Carter holds Gavin's hand while he stands in front of the priest and receives his little Jesus wafer. In the quiet serenity of the process, with only the beautiful sounds of the organ to fill the silence, Gavin's voice bursts through the tranquility.

"Whatchu got in your mouth?"

I bite my lip and cringe at how easily Gavin's voice carries through the church. Carter bends over and whispers something to Gavin as they turn and start to walk back to their seats in the front row on the opposite side of the church from me.

"GIMMEE WHATCHU GOT IN YOUR MOUTH!"

I cover my eyes with my hand but not before seeing Gavin try to shove his little hand into Carter's mouth. Carter smacks his hand away and as they both sit down, Carter pulls his cell phone out of the pants pocket of his tux and hands it over to Gavin. His face lights up with glee as he snatches the phone out of Carter's hand and sits down quietly next to him. Obviously, Carter is quickly learning that as a parent, nothing works quite as well as bribery. Seconds later the opening notes from Angry Birds blare through the soft din of organ music, and Carter quickly grabs the phone from Gavin to silence the sounds while Gavin yells, "Heeeey! I was playing that!"

The ceremony finally ends and we spend the next couple of hours getting pictures taken. Before I know it, we are finishing up dinner at the reception and the wait staff begin clearing tables. As part of the wedding party, we are all seated at the long head-table at the front of the room. It's always fun to sit facing a group of two hundred strangers so they can watch you eat.

Carter takes his seat next to me after a quick trip to the bathroom, and I noticed he was rubbing his shoulder in pain.

"What happened?"

"I passed Jenny and Drew on the way back from the bathroom. She wanted to know if I loved the *Balsa McChicken* we had for dinner," Carter explains with a raise of one eyebrow.

"I take it you told her it's called *balsamic chicken?*"

"No. I asked her if that was something new McDonald's was serving on their menu with the McRib. Drew punched me."

I glance around the room until I find my father and see him getting up from his table. He offers to head out early and take Gavin home with him as soon as he gets tired. I look at the chair next to me where Gavin is currently asleep on his stomach with his head, arms, and legs dangling down towards the floor.

"No, I didn't club him like a baby seal," I assure my dad as he puts his hands on the table and leans over it to get a look at his grandson.

"Your mother is starting to tell people about Tee Time. I think that's my cue to leave," my dad tells me as I stand with Carter while he scoops Gavin up into his arms and passes him off to my dad.

"What's Tee Time?" Carter asks as we watch Gavin sigh and snuggle his face into my dad's shoulder, muttering something about flashlights and donkey kicks.

My dad smiles evilly at Carter and then looks at me. "I'll leave you two to discuss the Rachel Morgan Tee Time tradition."

We say our good-byes and as the reception hall door closes behind them, my mother's voice comes over the microphone's speaker.

"TEE TIME! IT'S TEE TIME! Everyone meet over by the bar in five minutes!"

I close my eyes and sigh as I hear Jim let out an excited yell and jump up from his seat.

When I open my eyes, Carter is watching as a crowd of about twenty people, led by Jim, walk over to the bar.

"What is going on?"

"Carter! Now that you are part of this family, it's time you learned about the grand old tradition that is Tee Time," my mother exclaims as she pushes her way between us and grabs both of our arms to leads us to the bar. "This is an age old ritual that my family performs at every wedding to ensure the married couple lives a long, happy life together and that all of their ups and downs are in the bedroom."

Jim stands by the bar, bouncing on the balls of his feet in excitement as we made our way up to him.

"Mrs. Morgan! What's our first order of business at this Tee Time gathering?" he asks with a big grin.

"I do believe whiskey is the first on the agenda tonight, my handsome groom," she replies with a smack to his ass as she waves someone over from another table.

"Hold on, wait just a second!" Liz's mom yells as she comes running up to us. "The cake needs to be cut, and you still haven't done the first dance and the photographer still needs-"

My mom steps in front of Mary's path and puts her hand up to stop her from getting any closer to Jim.

"Mary, dear, you look stressed. When was the last time you used the bullet I gave you for your birthday last year and gave yourself a nice, big orgasm?"

My mother, after having dealt with Mary Gates for enough years, knows exactly how to divert her attention onto something else. It's nice to see her focusing on someone else's sex life for once. With Mary sputtering and at a loss for words, the wedding reception checklist is forgotten.

"I have to say, I'm a little bit astounded by the fact that you were still a virgin the night we met. How is it possible your mother never bought you a male hooker for your birthday?" Carter asks.

.

Jim lets out a cheer when he sees his mother-in-law practically running away from the bar and yells to the bartender for twenty shots of whiskey to go around.

"So really, Tee Time is just another excuse to get trashed at a wedding?" Carter asked.

"That would be correct," I reply as I take the shot glass filled with amber liquid that is handed to me. "Calling it Stupid Time would just be too obvious."

"I guess since you're drinking that means this gorgeous stud hasn't impregnated you again," my mother states as she takes her own.

"MOM!" I scold.

"What? Can you blame me for wanting another grandchild? You two make beautiful babies. The man obviously has super sperm. And by the looks of your late-night kitchen trysts, he still knows where to put it."

Mortification, party of one, your table is now ready.

"Did I ever tell you about the boyfriend I had in college who thought blow jobs could cause pregnancy? It's a shame really. I can suck a tennis ball through a crazy straw but he missed out."

Shouldn't there be some sort of law about people knowing these things about one of their parents?

My mother finally shuts up as Jim leads the group in a toast that consists of everyone raising their shot glasses, chanting "Tee Time, Tee Time, Tee Time!" before downing the whiskey.

Carter quickly learns the ins and the outs of Tee Time. Basically, the person in charge (my mother) borrows the microphone from the DJ and announces when it's Tee Time. It starts off as being every twenty minutes. After the first few rounds everyone quickly forgets just how far apart Tee Time is supposed to be. Eventually, it's every ten minutes, then every five minutes, and then there is someone puking in the middle of the dance floor and the bartender is out of a job because Tee Time attendance quickly jumped from twenty people to seventy-eight people and they've taken over the bar so they can pour the shots faster.

Every single wedding I have ever attended since I was three had a Tee Time. And frankly, even some of the funerals adopted the same tradition since honoring the dead can only be accomplished with adults sitting by the casket snort-laughing and loudly discussing how they think they just saw the body move.

Two hours after the first Tee Time, I plant my ass down at one of the tables, slide off my heels, and prop my feet up on a chair so I can watch Carter, Jim, and Drew attempt to break dance to a Celine Dion song. Drew has long since shed his tuxedo coat and white dress shirt, not really caring who sees the tee shirt he wore underneath that says "I'm not the groom, but I'll let you put a ring on it" with a picture of a cock ring below the words. I watch Carter attempt to do the Running Man, unable to stop the huge grin that spreads across my face.

"Good thing I caught you in a good mood," Liz states as she suddenly appears next to my chair and grabs my hand, pulling me up and out of my seat. "Get your ass up. It's bouquet-toss time."

I let go of her hand and sit right back down.

"Nice try," I say with a chuckle.

Liz moves to stand right in front of me with her hands on her hips and glares down at me.

"Don't you give me that look," I threaten. "I am not standing out there in the middle of the dance floor pretending like I give a rat's ass whether or not I catch your stupid bouquet."

All around us, single women are shoving people out of the way to make it up to the dance floor in the hopes *they* will be the chosen one: the woman deemed worthy enough and loved enough to be the next one to walk down the aisle. It doesn't matter if you have a boyfriend or not. If that bouquet filled with all of the good luck from the recently married woman arcs through the air in your direction, you are as good as wed in the eyes of everyone around you.

Even if I don't really believe in that whole thing about how if you catch the bouquet you'll be the next person to get married, I'm still not taking any chances. I had learned early on that I'm probably not a good candidate for marriage. I don't really have shining examples of success in that area. My parents have five marriages between the two of them. I share the same genes as people that stayed married because the healthcare was cheaper. And also because the one time they had made an appointment with a lawyer, eight years ago, my mother got a flat tire on the way there. She still claims it was a sign from a higher power that they shouldn't get divorced. Something about "If you love something you shouldn't set it free or you'll get down to brass tacks in your tire."

I won't admit to anyone that I've been secretly wondering what it would be like to be married to Carter. Frankly, I shouldn't even be thinking it or lightening will strike and ruin everything. Our life is perfect just the way it is. A few stray thoughts here and there about what it would be like to sign the name Mrs. Claire Ellis doesn't mean anything. It just means that every once in a while I can act like a typical girl. It doesn't mean I have any desire to don a white dress and parade myself in front of hundreds of people whose only thought about me at that moment in time is whether or not it's appropriate for me to be wearing white.

And besides, men run for the hills as soon as you get the tiniest inkling you might want to someday be married to them. If you so much as glance in the general direction of a bridal magazine in the store, they start hyperventilating and imagining balls and chains permanently secured to their legs for all of eternity. Really, I'm doing this for Carter. I'm saving him from a coronary or some other life threatening illness that comes from thinking about marriage. I think I read somewhere that just saying the word *marriage* makes a man's balls shrink. It must have been Google.

Before I know what was happening, both Jenny and Liz are dragging me onto the dance floor amid hordes of women who are foaming at the mouth and practically punting away young children who ran from their parents to join in on the game of catch.

Once I'm firmly ensconced by giddy, annoying females on all sides, Liz turns and flees the scene.

"Oh my gosh, oh my gosh, oh my gosh! I hope I catch the flowers! What if I catch the flowers? Could you imagine?! We should move closer to the front. Or maybe go to the back. Can Liz throw really far? I hope they don't get stuck in one of the chandeliers."

I cross my arms in front of me in protest and roll my eyes as Jenny's incessant chatter rings in my ears like an annoying cow bell.

"These parents need to come out here and get their kids. What happens if one of them catches the bouquet? Will someone tell them to give it back? This is like, a really important thing. They're not opposed to be out here."

I sighed and scan the crowd looking for Carter, hoping to get a smile of encouragement from him to brave this storm. He would feel my pain and know how miserable I am in this moment, surrounded by crazies.

As my eyes move through the sea of people standing around watching, Liz is handed the microphone and with her back to the single women, she begins her countdown.

"5, 4, 3, 2, 1!"

Finally, my eyes lock on Carter standing not far from Liz. The corners of my mouth begin curling up when a sudden blur of activity around me causes my focus to wane. Heels are flying, taffeta is swirling, and women are going down like dominoes. I unfold my arms to move away from the chaos when the bouquet Liz throws drops down into my hands like a gift from the heavens.

All movement on the floor around me stops and the pile of wrestling women stare up at me with reverence like I hold the Holy Grail in my palms. I have the strongest urge to spike it to the ground like a football and get as far away from it as possible.

I don't know what scared me more. The fact that the impulse to get rid of the bouquet disappears as quickly as it comes and I find myself cradling the flowers like a baby out of fear that someone will try to take them from me, or the look of sheer horror on Carter's face when my eyes find his again.

14.

Porn and Snozzberries

My best friend has been gone on her honeymoon for a week and I feel lost. I need someone to talk to. I'm sure I could have called her if it was an emergency, but trying to explain to her that I think Carter thinks I want to get married and I think it's got him freaked out while she's lying on a beach in Maui would probably be wrong.

"Hey, Liz! How's the honeymoon? Oh that's wonderful! Speaking of wonderful, I think Carter is afraid I want to get married, so I've been trying to let him know I don't really want to get married when secretly it's all I can think about but it scares the holy fucking hell out of me."

Yeah, that makes perfect sense.

All I've been able to think about for the past few days is the look on Carter's face when I catch the bouquet. He looks like he did the day he met Gavin and got kicked in the nuts. And who knows what the hell *my* problem is. Suddenly I'm crying during an episode of *"A Wedding Story"* on TLC and thinking the bride is totally justified in refinancing her house to pay for a third wedding dress with the Swarovski crystals on *"Bridezillas"*.

I had woke up the other day at four in the morning because I didn't want Carter to know I set the DVR so I could see if the girl from New Jersey on *"My Fair Wedding"* let her fiancé dress up like a Yeti and sing John Denver songs at the rehearsal dinner. Carter came home from work a few minutes early and I jumped up from the couch in shock and turned off the television as fast as I could.

"Hey, what are you doing up?" Carter asked. He set his work bag down on the floor and walked over to the middle of the living room to pick up the blanket I dumped on the floor in my haste to shut off the TV.

"Um...uh...nothing. I wasn't watching anything," I stammered, looking nervously back and forth between the TV and Carter.

He raised an eyebrow at me and looked down at the remote in my hand where my finger was still poised above the power button.

His eyes slowly moved back up to my face that was now covered in a thin sheen of sweat from my nerves going haywire. I could feel my cheeks heating up and knew he must be wondering why they were turning red if I had nothing to hide.

He was going to know I recorded *"Say Yes to the Dress: Atlanta"*. I couldn't just be happy with Kleinfeld's. Oh no, I had to get greedy and see what people bought from Bridals by Lori.

Carter turned to look at the TV again and then back to me, his eyes suddenly going wide.

"Oh my gosh. Claire, were you watching-"

"No!" I interrupted him. "I wasn't watching anything."

I laughed nervously and looked down at the remote in my hand, chucking it onto the couch so fast you would have thought it burned me.

"Holy hell...yes you were," he said as he stared at me in awe.

I had no idea what was going on but if he was this happy that he caught me watching the wedding channel then maybe we didn't have as big a problem as I thought.

"It's okay. You don't have to be embarrassed. It's actually kind of hot."

I looked at Carter like he was insane. And maybe he was. Maybe working all these late nights finally got to him. While I stood there half awake in my yoga pants and tank top, hair all askew, face flushed and embarrassed, he stared me up and down like he wanted to devour me. I had started to ask him what he was talking about and why he was looking at me that way when it had suddenly occurred to me. Four in the morning and I had been sitting in the living room under a blanket all alone looking like I just had a very fulfilling romp in the hay...with myself.

"OH MY GOD! You think I was watching-"

"Honey, really, it's fine! You don't have to be freaked out. Everyone watches a little porn now and then. I just wish you would have waited for me," he said with a leer.

So there's that. My boyfriend thinks I'm a closet porn watcher, that I sit alone in the dark while he's at work every night watching Skinemax and diddling myself. There's something wrong with me if I'd rather he think I had a porn addiction than a deep seeded need to find out if David Tutera could turn a camo, guns, and ATV wedding into a masterpiece.

To try and deter him from my fake inclination toward porn benders, alone in the dark on the couch, and to try and erase the memory in my mind of the sheer look of terror on his face at Liz and Jim's wedding when I had caught the bouquet, I've decided reverse psychology is the best route to go. It works well on kids. And men are pretty much giant babies most of the time anyway, so I figure I've got a fighting chance at getting things back to normal between us. Ever since the wedding he's gone back to being on edge and jittery around me. I think he's afraid he's going to wake up one morning strapped to the bed in a tux with me standing over him in a wedding dress, waving a sledge hammer over my head Kathy Bates-style, threatening to smash in his kneecaps if he doesn't marry me.

He should be more concerned with my father doing that, frankly.

I start off slow by telling him I absolutely don't believe that whole tradition that whoever catches the bride's bouquet is the next to marry. I believe I might have used the words *hogwash* and *twaddle* in that conversation to bring my point home. But Carter thinks I said *twat* and then it turns into an afternoon of him saying, "Twat did you say? I cunt hear you. Let's see if I can finger it out," while I try to show him just how unconcerned with this custom I am by throwing the bouquet away. The beautiful gerbera daisy, orchid, and lily nosegay that looks stunning in my hand.

Shut up. *"The Wedding Planner"* had been on the other night and Jennifer Lopez taught me what a nosegay is. I had also learned that Alex, the hot doctor from *"Grey's Anatomy"*, isn't so hot when he's playing a guy a few fries short a Happy Meal with a shitty Italian accent. And also, the guy from the Magic Bullet infomercial looks a lot like Nigel from *"So You Think You Can Dance"*. Also, late night television should be illegal in all fifty states and maybe I really would be better off watching *"Sweet Home I'll-a-Slam-Ya"* or *"Driving Into Miss Daisy"*.

"Claire, what the hell is your problem? You've been moping around all day," Jenny says as she comes out of the office of the shop with some invoices for me to sign in her hand.

I jump at the sound of her voice and realize I've been dipping the same pretzel in chocolate for the past twenty minutes.

Liz might not be here, but at least I have *someone* to bounce my thoughts off of.

"Carter thinks I have a porn addiction," I blurt out.

"Ooooooh me too!" she replies with glee.

My mouth dropped opens and I stare at her in shock.

"Oh no! I don't mean I think *you* have a porn addiction. Well, not that I know of. I mean Drew thinks *I* have a porn addiction too. We're like twinsies!"

Yeah, I don't think so.

"I have a membership to a porn-of-the-month club. It's kind of like a jelly-of-the-month club except you don't get jelly. And I can't tell my mom about it. The porn, not the jelly. She likes jelly so I could tell her about that. I just got *'Weapons of Ass Destruction'* and *'Forest Hump'*. *Sex is like your box on my cock-o-late,"* she says in her best Forest Gump voice. "We should totally watch that one together!"

Not gonna happen.

"Awww, you miss Liz, don't you? I know what will cheer you up. I'm going to call Drew and have him come up and help you frost all those cookies for the baby shower order tomorrow. He took the night off of work tonight, but we don't have any plans. Did I tell you his mom's been making these amazeball cookies for his sick uncle and the guy just raves about them and keeps asking for more? I'll have Drew bring some up so you can try them. Maybe they'll spark a little creative genius in you. You can put us to work, kick back, relax, and enjoy someone else's cookies for once," Jenny rambles as she pulls out her cell phone and starts dialing. "Don't forget you have that interview with *'The Best of Baking'* magazine so we can go over some things for that while we're at it."

Even though I'm now privy to more of Jenny and Drew's sex life than I ever wanted to be and the sound of her voice droning on is starting to give me a headache, I have to admit that hiring her to help out with all my back office stuff was a stroke of brilliance. She had secured me my own domain name instead of a website that included the words "freesite4everyone" in the address, and once I forbid Drew from sneaking in thumbnail pictures of his penis in the "about me" section, it actually looked very professional. Customers can place orders online and even print out coupons thanks to Jenny. She's organized my schedule so I can work around Gavin's three days of preschool a week and see Carter before he leaves for work every day, and she's managed to get me an in-studio interview with the local news station and three write-ups in local baking magazines; the first of which is scheduled for tomorrow.

In just a few days, my best friend will be home from her honeymoon, and I'll be able to get her advice about Carter. I am so worried about saying or doing something to scare him away that I might have taken it to the extreme. When he had asked me this morning if I wanted more cream for my coffee I replied, "Speaking of cream. Why do women wear cream to their wedding? Weddings are stupid. Married people are stupid. I think I broke my thumb."

No, I don't know why the fuck I told him I thought I broke my thumb. I had panicked. And now I'm pretty sure he thinks my maybe-broken-thumb is due to the late night pornography habit I just can't quit and it's either from A) pressing the rewind and or pause buttons too quickly or B) pressing MY buttons too quickly. Either option is not something I care for him to be wondering about me every time he looks in my general direction.

I spend the rest of the afternoon trying to think of ways to convince Carter I'm not going to pressure him into marriage while at the same time making sure I don't look like I need thirty days in a Betty Ford Triple X Clinic. I've been trying to come up with new ideas for things I can cover in chocolate for the shop. The chocolate covered potato chips and crushed pretzels mixed together had been a huge hit and are one of the main attractions lately. I want something fun and new to talk about in the magazine interview the next morning, so I put all thoughts of doom aside and concentrate on what I do best. For once, I'm not dreading a visit from Drew. With his appetite, I'm sure we could come up with something spectacular.

☉ ☉ ☉

"These snozzberries taste like SNOZZBERRIES!" I yell.

In the far recesses of my mind, I realize I was licking a scratch-n-sniff chocolate-covered strawberry sticker that Jenny had affixed to my shirt, but I don't care.

It smells like it tasty smells. Like snozzberries in a mountain of sticker glue. Why don't more people eat glue? It's delicious. Snozzberries should be our national fruit.

"I should cover these stickers in chocolate and sell them," I mumble as I continue swiping my tongue along the bottom hem of my shirt that I hold up by my mouth.

Drew laughs and I stop the manic sticker-licking to glance up at him. I blink really hard and try to get him to come into focus but it's not working. It's like I'm looking at him through a pair of binoculars backward. He's really small and really, really far away. I can feel my head swaying from side to side and I keep making my eyes open really wide in an effort to see more clearly. It's not working. Take your hand and make a fist then hold it up to one eye. Open your hand just enough to let some light in and that's the view I have right now.

Maybe that's what the problem is. There's someone walking around next to me holding their fists in front of my eyes.

I start flailing my arms all around my head to smack the hidden fists away until I start running into things and knocking shit off of the counters. I'm seventy-four percent positive the noise I make while doing this scares those assholes with their sneaky fists away.

"This chocolate is burning my hand! HOLY FUCK IT'S BURNING! WHY IS IT BURNING?!"

If I squint I can kind of see that Drew is holding his hand out from his body and it was dripping with hot, melted chocolate.

"Your hand looks delicious," I tell him as I absently bring my shirt back up to my mouth and began chewing on it.

"This was the best idea EVER," Jenny states as she helps Drew hold his chocolate hand over the sink so it won't drip on the floor. "Everyone will love chocolate-covered Drew. Make sure you tell them during the interview that this was my idea. I want street cred for it."

I feel my head bobbing up and down in agreement and watch the room go in and out of focus and wonder why the walls are moving closer to me all of a sudden. I look down and my feet aren't moving. I look back up and scream because the wall is right against my nose.

HOW THE FUCK DID THE WALL GET ON MY NOSE?!

"Claire, stop sniffing the wall. It doesn't have any flavor left," Jenny tells me.

Stupid wall. It runs out of flavor too fast.

I step away from the wall and look up at the ceiling. There are marshmallows on my ceiling.

Marshmallows is a funny word.

"M m m m m m a a a a a a a r r r r r s s s s s h h h h h h m m m m a aaalllloooowwwwsssss. Who invented that word? It's a great word. I wonder if they used to be called something else. Like *shmashmoos*. But people couldn't say shmashmoos and babies were crying because they really wanted shmashmoos but couldn't say the word and their mothers kept giving them cookies when all they really wanted were shmashmoos. Babies were crying, parents were crying, the streets were filled with people who just wanted shmashmoos. Total anarchy, dudes. I bet that was the real reason for World War II. It's one big shmashmoo conspiracy the government doesn't want us to know about."

"Claire, you are so smart," Jenny tells me seriously.

"I know, right?"

I should light a fire and make S'mores.

"Quick, someone get me a lighter, STAT!" I yell.

Drew jumps down off of the counter and with one hand, pulled his cell phone out of his pocket and started fiddling with the buttons while he holds his chocolate hand out from his body.

"Are you calling the cops? Oh shit! JENNY RUN! IT'S THE FUZZ!" I yell as I run in circles around the kitchen island.

Somewhere in the distance I hear Jenny crying. At least I think it' Jenny crying. It might have been me.

Am I crying? My face does feel kind of weird and wet. Like a wet fish.

"Give me that fiiiiiish. Give me that Filet-a-Fish fiiiiish, ooooh!"

I wish McDonald's delivered. I want some ketchup.

Drew steps into my path and I slam into him. He shoves his phone in my hand and smiles. "You're welcome. Now get in that kitchen and make me some S'mores, beotch!"

I clutch the phone to my chest and look up to thank him. But he isn't up anymore, he's down. Down, down, down like a tiny little dwarf. I squint and bend down so I can see him better. He's jumping up and down, and I'm pretty sure he's trying to bite my ankles. He's like a little chocolate covered munchkin from the Land of Oz and he's angry.

Why are munchkins so angry all the time? They're in a club called the Lollipop Guild. The mother fucking Lollipop Guild! All lollipops all the time. Munchkins are ungrateful little bastards. Those lollipops died so you could be happy. RESPECT THE LOLLIPOP!

"What in the mother fucking of all fucks happened here?" Carter asks as he steps into the kitchen of the shop.

"Oh shit, the jig is up! HIDE THE COOKIES!" Drew yells as he belly flopped onto the floor and army crawls away as fast as he could.

15.

Just Say No to Necrophilia

When my foreman had told me I could take the night off, I didn't even take a breath or say a word to anyone. My work bag is slung over my shoulder and I'm racing through the plant before the guy even finishes his sentence. Being two people short, with Jim still on his honeymoon and Drew taking a vacation day, it's a rare thing to still have enough people to send someone home. There is no way I'm going to give anyone a chance to change their minds. All I can think about is going to see Claire.

Too many thoughts have been running through my head all week and I just want to put my arms around her and get some reassurance that everything is okay between us. She's been saying some really strange things ever since Liz and Jim's wedding, and I can't stop thinking about them.

Does she really think marriage is stupid? Maybe her idea of happiness isn't settling down with someone for the rest of her life. It's not like her parents have given her any kind of good examples of finding the one you're meant to be with and spending forever loving them. They change spouses more than Drew changes his underwear. But I see her get misty eyed more than once while watching a wedding or a proposal on television when she thinks I'm not looking so I don't think she's completely opposed to the concept.

Shit, maybe it's just *me* she opposed to. Maybe she just doesn't want to marry *me*. The thought makes me sick to my stomach. Everything about her makes me happier than I have ever been in my life. Becoming a father overnight is something I never thought I wanted but now know I can never live without. Ever since the wedding this past weekend, all I can think about is the way Claire looked standing in the middle of the dance floor holding that bouquet of flowers she had just caught.

There had been a sparkle in her eyes and a smile on her face that lit up the room. It made me wish that it was *our* wedding we were at and that it was *our* celebration of love. I actually reached into my pocket to pull out the ring I always carried with me and panicked when I didn't feel it in there. It took me a minute to realize I decided right before we walked out of the house that morning to leave it at home. I had been to enough weddings with Drew to know that there would be break dancing and tuxedo jackets swung around and didn't want to chance losing the ring. After the way she reacted when she only *thought* Drew and Jenny might be getting engaged at the rehearsal dinner, I was glad I'd left the ring at home. Standing there and staring at her with a wedding bouquet in her hand had almost forced me to do something she'd hate, and I'd have no control over if that ring was in my pocket.

Claire seems genuinely happy, aside from the past few days and the weird, off-the-wall comments she makes about marriage. Could it be that seeing her best friends get married has made her realize she'll never have that for herself? She's watching porn in the middle of the night by herself while I'm at work. That's either the sign of the apocalypse or I'm just not doing it for her. Jesus, maybe I need to up my game. She shouldn't be watching porn alone unless I'm not enough for her.

Am I not enough for her? WHY AREN'T I ENOUGH FOR HER? Why can't she be happy with me instead of lusting after some actor on the television? Why, God, why? It's not like those men are real anyway. Everything about them is fake, including their six pack abs and horse cocks. And seriously, who needs that much cock? Maybe she's watching those men wishing I could learn some of those tricks.

But come on, give me a break. No one is that bendy or has that much stamina. That's what film editing is for. She probably thinks it's not cheating since all she's doing is watching them on TV but God dammit, she's cheating with her MIND.

Oh my Jesus. I think I just grew a vagina.

I have to believe that if Claire is really that unhappy with me or my sexual prowess, she'd say something. Chicks like to tell you all the time what you're doing wrong, don't they? Why would Claire be any different? I'm acting like a giant pussy over this. We're fine, she's fine, I love her more than anything in the world, and I WILL make this proposal happen. Enough with the chicken shit stuff.

I try calling Claire on the way out of work to see if she's still at the shop but her phone goes straight to voicemail. When I drive through town I see that her car is still parked out in front of the building, so I pull around back and go in through the back door that brings me into the kitchen.

The sight before me leaves me speechless and confused. I really don't' know where to look first. There is chocolate splattered everywhere and as I take a step into the room, something covered in chocolate dripped down from the ceiling in front of me and lands by my foot with a *plop*.

It's dead silent in the room which is my first clue that something is off; Claire always has music playing in the kitchen when she works.

Actually, my first inclination that something isn't quiet right is seeing Jenny sitting in the sink crying. My eyes pass right over Drew lying on his stomach on the floor lapping up a puddle of chocolate like a dog. That's not something I haven't seen before unfortunately.

Since Jenny is closest to me, I start with her.

"Hey, what's going on? Why are you crying? More importantly, why are you crying in the sink?" I ask her as I reach in and scoop her out of the big, stainless steel commercial sink like a baby. It takes a few minutes to steady her once I get her on her feet. She clutches onto my shoulders and stares up at me.

"I think Drew ate Claire," she whispers. "She was sitting here a minute ago and then Drew said he was hungry and now she's gone. He ate four batches of chocolate chip cookies and one batch of Claire."

Jesus God what the fuck is going on?

I gently push Jenny away from me until her back is leaning up against the counter and I am certain she won't fall. Turning around, I stare at the mess that has transformed this sparkling clean kitchen into a chocolate nightmare.

Are those chocolate covered Twinkies stuck to the wall?

I gingerly step around small puddles of melted chocolate on the floor, careful not to slip and fall, and make my way over to Drew who has given up sucking chocolate off of the floor and is now curled up in the fetal position asleep.

"Hey, ASSHOLE!" I yell. "Wake up!" I shove the toe of my shoe into his stomach and push until he rolls over onto his back and lazily opens his eyes to look at me.

"Duuuuuuuuuude," he says on an exhale of breath.

"Don't *dude* me. What the fuck happened here? Claire sent me a text a few hours ago that you were going to help her frost cookies. Why does it look like a bomb exploded?"

Drew blinks a few times and shakes his head to clear out the cobwebs or whatever the fuck is in his brain right now sucking out all of the functioning parts.

"Help me up so I can think," Drew says as he sticks his arm up towards me.

I shake my head in annoyance, grab onto his hand and yank him up off of the floor.

"You're hands are so soft. Do you moisturize?" Drew questions as he pets the top of my hand like a kitten.

I rip my hand out of his grip and smack him upside the head.

"Cocksucker! Pay attention!"

Drew rubs the back of his head and glares at me.

"Don't get your panties all in a twist. Claire is in her office. She's fine. Her dad is in there with her."

Okay, so it can't be that bad if George is here.

I leave Drew with Jenny so I can go in search of Claire. Jenny isn't going to stop crying until she sees Claire with her own eyes and realizes she hasn't been eaten.

Only in MY life would those words make perfect sense.

Claire and Liz share an office and it is situated right in the middle of their connecting stores. They each have a door that leads into the office. It's really no bigger than a walk-in closet. It houses a computer table and chair, a loveseat, and two metal filing cabinets. I walk over to the closed door and press my ear against it trying to figure out if Claire and her father are in some deep discussion while all hell breaks loose in her kitchen. I'm pretty sure her father still plots fun and exciting ways to kill me so there is no way I'm going to interrupt them if that's the case. I don't hear anything so I turn the knob and slowly open the door.

I had to do a double-take when I see George curled up in a ball on the loveseat. How he had managed to get his six foot frame wedged in between the arms of that thing I will never know. I decide to let sleeping dogs lie for the moment and turn in a full circle, my eyes finally coming to rest on Claire.

She's sitting on the floor behind the door with her knees pulled up to her chest. She has a spatula in one hand held out from her body with chocolate frosting dripping off of it and what looks like Drew's iPhone pressed up against the wall with her other hand. Her eyes are glassy and vacant as she stares off into space, never once blinking as I walk up to her and crouch down in front of her.

I don't know what I'm dealing with here so I speak in a soft, calming voice. "Hey there, Claire. How are you doing sweetie?"

She moans in response, but still doesn't blink.

I look over my shoulder and see George is still fast asleep. Obviously he isn't going to be any help here.

"Can you tell me what happened here tonight?"

Another moan coupled with a bit of a whimper. Still no blinking. *How long can someone go without blinking before they go blind?*

I feel like I walked into a horror movie and found the sole survivor of a serial killer rampage. I'm afraid to say the wrong thing for fear I'll spook her and will never get to the bottom of the truth.

"I ate cookies," she finally mutters.

"Wow, that's great, sweetie," I tell her kindly.

I don't really know if that's great or not but at least she has ingested something that will sop up whatever it is that's turned these guys into chocolate covered zombies.

"I don't want to feel this anymore," she says in a pitiful voice. "Make it stop."

Maybe I should try and get her to throw up. Should I stick my fingers down her throat? I've never done that before. Not even to myself. I've only ever tried to make Drew throw up, and usually all I have to do is talk about his grandmother having sex.

I reach over and take the dripping spatula out of her hand and set it on the floor. I do the same with Drew's cell phone, flipping it over first and noticing it's set to the BIC Lighter app, the fake flame flickering back and forth on the screen.

"Honey, why are you holding Drew's phone against the wall?"

"I wanted to make hot. Stupid fight wouldn't lire. Flight wouldn't flier. Fire wouldn't fire. Fire. Fire, fire, fire, fire, fire-"

Sweet Jesus.

I slide an arm between Claire's back and the wall and bring her forward so she's leaning over her bent knees. Hoping she won't hate me for this or bite me, I push my finger passed her lips and into her mouth. She blinks then and looks up at me, trying to focus on my face. My finger is in her mouth but she won't open her lips, they just stay wrapped around my finger while she squints and tries to see me better.

I wiggle my hand and try to push my finger in further. Her throat has to be in there somewhere. If I can just get back there far enough I'm sure she will puke.

"Come on, Claire. Open up wider. I can't get it in."

I grunt with the effort of holding her up and trying to get the knuckle of my first finger past her teeth.

"Don't bite me. You'll feel much better after this is done, I promise. I've done this a bunch of times, just let me in."

Either she isn't hearing me or she doesn't care. I move my hand around her mouth and try every angle I can but she just won't open her mouth so I could reach her throat. Her tongue presses against the tip of my finger preventing it from moving.

"Claire, don't be difficult," I groan. "I need to do this deeper."

Claire bites down on my finger at the same time I feel a hand slap down on my shoulder.

I yank my finger out of her mouth and whip my head around and up to find George towering over me with his hands on his hips and a glare on his face.

"Carter," George greets.

"Hi, Mr. Morgan," I say as cheerfully as possible, considering he's looking at me like I'm a bug he's getting ready to squash under his shoe.

"Have you seen my shotgun?" he asks.

I gulp loudly and try to remember all of the reasons it would be bad to piss my pants right then. Under normal circumstances, I'm quite used to the death stares and silent threats I receive from Claire's dad, but this seems a little excessive. I'm trying to save his daughter's life. How can he possible be angry with me about that? He had been asleep on the couch two seconds ago. He must have opened his eyes and seen me...

You'll feel much better once this is done. Don't be difficult, I need to do this deeper. Just let me in...

Oh sweet Jesus. He had probably looked across the room and saw just the back of me trying to force something in his daughter's mouth.

Why the hell couldn't Rachel have been the one here tonight? She would have woken up and cheered me on, probably even booing me when she found

424

out I was only trying to make her daughter puke instead of forcing my penis in her mouth.

"I am NOT into Necrophilia," I state firmly to him.

"There is something wrong with you," he mutters.

"I just wanted her to throw up," I complain.

"I really don't want to know about the weird, kinky shit you're into."

"Yo, Mr. Morgan, you're awake!" Drew exclaims as he lounges in the doorway. "And Carter, dude, it's called *Poutiphilia*. You just told Claire's dad you weren't into banging dead people. Which is a good thing, but probably not what you were going for. Poutiphilia is a person who enjoys sexual relations with people who are passed out."

Drew is a walking, talking Urbandictionary dot com.

"I was NOT trying to have sexual relations with this woman!" I shout.

"Slow your roll there, Clinton," Drew says as he came further into the room and squats down next to me.

"HOW ARE YOU DOING, CLAIRE?" Drew yells, talking to her slow and loud like she doesn't understand English. "DO YOU KNOW WHO I AM?"

He snaps his fingers in front of her face a few times. She finally blinks and looks up at me.

"Make it stop," she whines.

I'm not sure if she is referring to Drew or whatever is in her system. I decide to err on the side of caution and punch Drew in the arm.

"What the fuck did you give her?"

"Just some cookies. My mom makes them for my uncle all the time and he loves them," Drew tells me.

"Did you guys get food poisoning or something? Why the hell is this place such a disaster and Claire is almost comatose?"

I briefly wonder if I should try again to make her puke, but I'm a little afraid George really does have a shotgun hidden somewhere in the room.

"Claire wanted some help coming up with some new ideas for things to cover in chocolate. It was a process. A *creative* process. You wouldn't understand. It's an artistic thing," Drew explains. "Chocolate covered carrots were a bust, but we might have something with chocolate covered gummy bears."

This still doesn't make any sense. I'm obviously missing something.

"So you guys ate some cookies and brainstormed. What kind of cookies did you eat? Were they undercooked?"

Maybe Claire has Salmonella poisoning. Is that contagious? Does she need to be vaccinated or have her stomach pumped? I feel like I should know the answer to this since I have a kid. What if Gavin eats some raw chicken and I don't know whether to give him mouth-to-mouth or Pepto Bismol? Is he even allowed to have Pepto? And where the fuck is he getting raw chickens from?!

"Dude, I'm not Betty fucking Crocker or anything. I don't know what was in the cookies. They were mocha coffee nut something or other. Wait, maybe it was the nuts. Is Claire allergic to nuts? She might be going into anal flaccid shock," Drew says nervously.

Oh my God. It's like he shares a brain with Jenny.

"It's Anaphylaxis Shock, dumbass, and no, she's not allergic to nuts," I say with a roll of my eyes.

"My uncle begs my mom for these cookies. Seriously. They actually STOP him from getting sick so this makes absolutely no sense. My mom makes them for him every couple of weeks before he goes in for chemo."

I stare at him blankly and repeat in my head the words that just came out of his mouth just to make sure I'm not hallucinating.

"Jesus fucking Christ! You gave her POT COOKIES???

I whip my head around and stare at George in disbelief.

"YOU ate a pot cookie?" I ask incredulously.

"I was in Nam," he huffs like that's sufficient enough evidence this is perfectly okay. "Where's my grandson?"

I stare at him in wonder for a few minutes, realizing (not for the first time) that Claire's father is the epitome of the saying "The man, the myth, the legend". While everyone else has been one step away from bath-salts-crazy, George has curled up on the couch and slept off his pot cookie high.

"Gavin is with my parents for the night. They're in town for a wedding and are keeping him overnight at their hotel so he can swim in the pool," I explain as I tighten my hold on Claire and help her stand up.

"I'm hungry," Claire announces to no one in particular as she suddenly regains the use of all of her faculties and pushes away from me. Her eyes are bright and clear as she walks out of the office, squeezing her way past Drew, like nothing is wrong.

"Well, it looks like the problem is solved thanks to me. Claire now has a new item to put on her menu and rave about tomorrow during her magazine interview," Drew states proudly.

"She's not putting pot cookies on the menu," I tell him with a shake of my head as we all amble out of the office. "It's illegal."

"You're a real buzz kill, you know that?" Drew complains.

16.

Son of a Face Turd

"I eat my poop."

"Drew, I swear to God if you don't stop playing with that fucking computer, I'm going to shove it up your ass," I threaten as I finished chiseling the last bit of chocolate off of the walls of the shop kitchen.

Drew has recently learned how to turn on text-to-speech in Microsoft Excel. Everything he types into a box on the spreadsheet is repeated back to him in a computerized voice. He had stopped by my shop first thing this morning under the guise of helping me clean but instead has spent the majority of his time making the computer say random, stupid shit.

"I like to touch boobs," the monotone, computerized voice announces.

"Boobs, boobs, boobies, boobs. I like boobies."

Drew sticks his head out of my office a few seconds later and smiles.

"Claire Bear, do you have a pot hangover?"

I growl as I throw the dirty rag into the sink and turn on the tap to wash my hands of the sticky mess they'd become since I started cleaning up the mess we made of the kitchen the previous night.

"After what you did to me last night, you're lucky I'm not shoving a spatula in your eye.

I turn off the water and dry my hands on the towel next to the sink. When I look back over my shoulder to throw another insult at Drew, he isn't there.

"Claire has an angry vagina."

I roll my eyes and take one last look around the kitchen to make sure I haven't missed a spot. In hindsight, I should know better than to eat anything Drew gives me. He always looks guilty and says stupid shit though, so when he hands me the cookie and tells me to "Eat the entire thing or else," I don't think twice. All I had wanted was a nice, quiet evening of brainstorming and keeping my mind off of anything to do with weddings and marrying the man of my dreams.

Be careful what you wish for.

I had woken up this morning with a sinking feeling in the pit of my stomach that I did something stupid. I rolled over and found Carter sitting on the edge of the bed staring at me.

"I was just getting ready to stick a mirror under your nose to make sure you were still breathing," Carter said with a laugh as he stood up from the bed and walked over to the dresser to put on his watch and stick his wallet in his back pocket.

"What the fuck did I do last night?" I groaned with a raspy, morning after voice.

"Which part exactly are you referring to? Eating an entire pot cookie or redecorating the shop by painting the walls with chocolate?"

"Okay, first of all, I didn't KNOW it was a pot cookie until after I took the first bite and second…I don't know. I have no excuse for the rest of it," I trailed off.

"If you knew it was a pot cookie after the first bite, why in the hell would you keep eating it?" Carter asked with a chuckle as I scooted up in bed until I could sit against the headboard.

"Why wouldn't I eat it? The damage was already done. And it was a delicious cookie."

Carter shook his head at me and sighed.

"Claire, you are only supposed to eat a little bit of a pot cookie, never the entire thing at once."

He stared at me like I was an idiot and this was clearly something everyone knew.

"How in the fuck am I supposed to know something like that? Do I look like the type of person who goes around eating pot cookies all the time?" I asked angrily.

"Everyone knows this. I've never eaten a pot cookie, and I still know the rules."

"The rules? Is there a Pot Cookie 101 class I missed or something? It's not like the fucking thing came with an owner's manual. I was handed a cookie, and I ate a cookie. Who in their right mind only takes one bite of a cookie and then puts the rest back for later?" I demanded.

"Someone who eats a pot cookie," Carter deadpanned.

After I had showered and dressed, I left the house with an obvious bug up my ass.

And now my magazine interview is in an hour and the only things surrounding me are bad, hallucinogenic ideas – chocolate covered gummy bears, pickles, moon pies, M&M's, every Little Debbie snack treat imaginable from Twinkies to Swiss Rolls, and a computer printed picture of Drew's hand covered in chocolate. Trays of chocolate covered crap litter the counters, and I berate myself for all of those hours we spent NOT coming up with a good idea. At least Drew manages to frost all two-hundred cookies for the order that's being picked up today. It makes my hatred for him go down just a tiny bit.

"The peanut butter on your cock is delicious."

"DREW!" I yell again in warning.

"Sorry!" he yells back, trying to mask his giggles.

"Cock, the other white meat."

I open my mouth to scream another threat at Drew, this one to his manhood, when an idea strikes.

I glance at the clock and quickly rush around the kitchen, grabbing the ingredients I need. While I wait for the chocolate to melt, I grab a small, white packaging box from under the counter. I prepare it by adding a sheet of pink tissue paper inside to line the box and affix a "Seduction and Snacks" sticker to the outside. I watch the clock out of the corner of my eye as I get down to business, crossing my fingers, toes, and even my legs that this idea would work.

Thirty minutes later I finish placing the last of the new candy inside the box, seal the lid closed, tie a neat, pink and white ribbon around it, and grab my purse from under the counter.

"Drew, I'm leaving. Don't forget to go next door and wait for Liz's delivery so you can sign for it," I yell to him as I head to the front door to make sure the "Closed" sign is in place. I have about twenty minutes now to run home, pick up Gavin, and drive to the meeting spot. The magazine adamantly insists that I bring Gavin with me. This magazine interviewes people due to customer recommendations. Customers write into the magazine and suggest businesses they believe should be spotlighted for one reason or another.

The magazine had done some research, made some calls, and for whatever reason decided "Seduction and Snacks" needed a write up. When the magazine called to set up the interview, they told Jenny that the customers raved not only about the sweets we sold but also about the owner's mouthy little son that ran around the store and made everyone laugh. It had been a toss-up on whether or not I should be horrified by this or happy that Gavin's penchant for swear words and constant talk about his wiener was finally doing something good in the world.

It's still hard to wrap my head around the fact that our businesses had taken off so quickly. Never underestimate the need for sugar and sex in small-town-America. With one last look around the darkened store to make sure everything is in order, I step outside to the faint sound of the computer speaking one last Drew-initiated command.

"Son of a face turd, you whore. Touch my taint and tickle my balls."

⊙ ⊙ ⊙

I walk into Playland McDonalds with butterflies flapping in my stomach and my hand clutched tightly around Gavin's.

I don't know why I'm so nervous. I've done a few phone interviews since we opened and those had been a piece of cake. Maybe it's the fact that I've never done something like this with my son right next to me - my lovely son who likes to talk to random strangers about his poop.

This will be fine. No big deal. Just a couple of questions. Easy peasy.

"Remember, best behavior," I remind Gavin as we make our way through the crowded restaurant to a booth in the back. I can see the interviewer already seated with her laptop open on the table. We make eye contact and she gives me a wave.

"I want to play in the playland," Gavin whines.

"You will, as soon as the interview is over."

"That's dumb," he mutters.

"Too bad. Be good and you can get a Happy Meal."

"Can I have pop too?" he asks.

I pause, contemplating his request. Being a parent is tough, especially when it comes to negotiations. You don't want your kids to think they can have whatever they ask for, but you also don't want them to tell the interviewer of a national magazine that their nuts smell like cheese and it's because she's so ugly. Pick your battles, people.

"Yes, you can have pop. If you're good."

We arrive at the table and introductions are made. I direct Gavin in first so he can sit by the window and then slide in next to him.

"Hi, Gavin, my name is Lisa. I love your shirt," the interviewer from *The Best of Baking* says with a smile.

Gavin looks down at the shirt Drew had bought him a few weeks ago. It's black and in white writing reads, "Parental Advisory: Lock up your daughters."

He just shrugs in response, and I resist the urge to shoot him the evil eye and remind him to be good.

"This is just going to be an informal type of interview," Lisa explains. "I just want to ask some questions and chit chat. Just pretend like I'm one of your girlfriends."

She has a huge smile on her face like I totally understand what she's talking about. She obviously has never met my girlfriends. We don't sit around in dresses, sipping daintily from glasses of champagne while we politely discuss politics. We chug beers, do shots, and call each other thunder cunts.

I slide the white box across the table towards her, figuring I might as well start right off the bat with the bribery.

Lisa's eyes light up when she sees the white box with our signature pink ribbon around it.

"Oh my goddness, you brought me chocolate!" she exclaims.

"It's something new I'm trying out. I crumble up crispy bacon and mix it with white chocolate. The clusters are drizzled with caramel and butterscotch. They're called Bacolate Bunches," I tell her.

She tears into the box and takes a bite out of one of the clusters. She moans and groans and sighs for so long it gets a little uncomfortable. I'm now privy to what Lisa sounds like when she has sex. Awkward. But at least she likes my spur of the moment candy invention.

"So, Gavin, how are you doing today?" Lisa asks after she finishes the chocolate and finally gets down to business.

"I wanna play, this is boring," he complains while staring longingly at the other children who are running and screaming around the play area.

"Gavin, be nice," I warn under my breath with clenched teeth and a smile on my face for Lisa.

"Oh, it's fine!" she tells me cheerfully. "I'd like to play on those toys too," she says to Gavin.

"You're too old to go on the slide. Your butt would get stuck 'cuz you're old."

With the evil eye in full force, I glare at Gavin. "If you don't watch your mouth, you're going home to take a nap," I say quietly.

"Naps can suck it," Gavin whispers as he smacks his elbows on the table and puts his chin in his hands angrily.

Obviously, he's already forgotten the Happy Meal and pop he was promised. *God, if you're listening, just help me not kill him. At least until we're home.*

"So, Claire, how's business been going at the shop?"

I stop glaring at Gavin and hope that by some super mom power he will still be able to feel my wrath floating around him and keep his mouth shut.

"Business has been going very well. I still have to pinch myself every morning when I walk into that place. I am absolutely amazed that people actually want to buy things I make," I tell her with a laugh.

I can't believe someone is interviewing me for a magazine. I'm nobody. How is this happening?

"Are you finding it hard to juggle owning a business and spending time with your family?" Lisa asks as she typed away on her laptop.

"That's the beauty of owning a business. Basically, I can do whatever I want."

Lisa laughs and continued typing.

This sort of IS like talking to one of my girlfriends. Liz never pays attention to anything I say and is always busy doing other shit when I'm pouring my heart out to her.

"Can you elaborate on that just a little bit?" she asks.

"Well, if I want Gavin to spend the day with me, he can. I don't need to find a sitter or send him to daycare when he isn't in preschool. And if I need to close up early to take him to a doctor's appointment or to go to a function at his school, I can easily do it without having to get permission from someone else or have my pay docked for missing time," I explain.

"My doctor gives me cookies and stickers. His mean nurse is a wiener face and gives me shots," Gavin adds.

Lisa chuckles, her eyes never leaving her screen as she types furiously.

Oh my God, please tell me she didn't just type the words "wiener face" in my interview.

"In just three short months of being open, Seduction and Snacks is already turning a profit. That's almost unheard of for a new, small business. What do you think is the key to this success?"

Do I look like Donald Trump?

I don't know anything about anything. I cover things in chocolate and bake cookies. The key to success is pretending like it's not really happening so that you don't freak the fuck out thinking about it.

I answer her question as best I can without looking like a clueless moron. I tell her it's all about luck and how I honestly have no idea how this happened to me.

Lisa finally takes a break from her typing to look up at me.

"It doesn't hurt to have such a famous son either, right?! Everyone I spoke with about Seduction and Snacks told me I absolutely HAD to meet the owner's son."

Oh dear God. Here we go.

"I'm almost afraid to ask what else they said about him. He's lucky he's cute or I would have put him out on the curb with the garbage years ago," I tell her as we shared a laugh.

"You shut your mouth when you're talking to me!" Gavin shouts.

I quickly reach over and cover his mouth with my hand.

I should have packed duct tape and a taser.

"If you can believe it, I've actually been asked by several customers if they could take him home. If only they knew. A marine sergeant stopped in a few days ago on his way to work and joked that he should take Gavin with him to basic training. He figured Gavin could get the men to cry faster than he ever could," I tell her.

She types with a small smile on her face, and I wonder if this will be my first and last magazine interview ever.

"As you know, we do a little research on the people we're going to interview. Being from a small town, it's no secret that you got pregnant and had to drop out of college. It's a huge struggle to be a single mother. What advice do you have for other women who might be going through the same thing?" Lisa asks as she bends her head and goes back to clacking away at her keyboard.

Lovely. I bang a guy at a frat party, get knocked up, and have to work at a bar to make ends meet. The only other option available to me at the time had been pregnant stripping. Is this really something the people of *"The Best of Baking"* want to know? They seem like a conservative group - ones who talk about petit fours and balsamic reductions, not beer pong and vagina pounding.

"Um, yeah. I'm definitely not the best person to come to for advice in that area," I tell her honestly. "I did everything wrong. Luckily, Gavin's father is an amazing man and we were able to find our way back to one another. I honestly don't know what I would do without him. I can't imagine my life without him in it."

Shit! Can I retract that statement?! That sounds entirely too much like saying I want to spend the rest of my life with him. Which I do. But he can't know that. He'll freak out like a guy. Which he is. When he reads this, his mind is immediately going to go to marriage and he'll probably start screaming. *CHANGE THE SUBJECT, CLAIRE!*

"Also, I like to watch a lot of porn."

NO, NO, NO! ABORT MISSION! What the fuck am I supposed to be talking about? Oh, right. Advice.

"Don't look a gift horse in the mouth or he'll bite the hand that feeds you."

Oh sweet Jesus I just became my mother.

Lisa doesn't show any signs of thinking she's talking to a lunatic. She just keeps on typing. It's starting to freak me out.

Is she seriously typing every single thing I say? I suddenly have the urge to scream the words "ANAL WARTS" just to see if she keeps right on clicking away without batting an eye.

I want to ask her if she heard me say I was addicted to porn. Maybe the noise of kids playing around us or Gavin's loud huffing and sighing block out what I said. Obviously, I can't bring it up and *ask* if she heard me because if she hasn't, she'll want me to repeat it. And knowing me, I *will* repeat it to be polite and that will just fuck up this entire freak out I'm currently having.

I am hereby restricting the word "porn" from my vocabulary. It's getting me into too much trouble.

Lisa stops typing and gives me the universal one-finger, hold on a minute sign as she answers her ringing cell phone.

"Son of a bitch," I mutter.

"You said a bad word," Gavin informs me.

"I'm allowed. I'm an adult."

"I wanna be a dolt!" he says excitedly.

A few minutes later, Lisa ends her call and turns her attention to Gavin.

"How about I ask you some questions now? Would that be okay?"

"Sure," he says with a shrug.

"Do you have a nickname? Can I call you Gav?" Lisa asks.

"Can I punch you in the face?" he asks.

"Gavin!" I scold.

"What's your favorite color?" Lisa asks, both of them ignoring me.

"I like green. Green is green. I fart green."

Oh wonderful. This is turning out to be a stellar interview.

"What's your favorite food?"

"Skabetti and meat balls. Balls are delicious!" Gavin exclaims.

Lisa and I both share a snicker over that one.

"If Phineas and Ferb and Spongebob got into a fight, who would win?" Lisa questions.

Gavin thinks about this for a minute before answering.

"Spongebob 'cuz he's a big tough man. Phineas and Ferb are dumber than his wee-wee."

I roll my eyes and shake my head. This interview has officially gone in the shitter.

"What is your favorite holiday?"

"Fart."

"Gavin," I warn.

"What's your favorite animal?"

"Sheep, 'cuz they're stupid," Gavin answers with a laugh.

"What's your favorite smell?"

Oh that's a super question to ask a four-year-old who just said his favorite holiday is passing gas.

"Smelly cat. And feet," Gavin says with a giggle.

"What's your favorite song?" Lisa continues.

Please don't say "99 Problems But the Bitch Ain't One" or I will smother Carter in his sleep for downloading that to his iPod.

"SMELLY CAT, SMELLY CAT, WHAT ARE THEY FEEDING YOU!" Gavin sings as loud as he can.

"How do you even know that song?" I ask him.

Gavin replies with a shrug.

"You like to say big people words a lot. How come?" Lisa asks.

"'Cuz I like it. 'Cuz I'm a man."

"I've heard you like to talk about your wiener a lot. Why do you do that?"

"'Cuz it's stupid. I crapped my pants."

Gavin laughs out loud at himself.

"Excuse me? You know you aren't supposed to say that word," I scold.

"I can't say the s-h-p word either. What the heck am I 'sposed to say?" Gavin asks with a roll of his eyes.

This is what I have to deal with. Am I supposed to correct him when he spells "shit" wrong? Why the fuck hasn't anyone printed a parenting handbook yet?

"What's your favorite thing to do?"

"Fart in everyone's face," Gavin says in between giggles. "FART!"

"You sure like to say 'fart' a lot," Lisa says with a laugh.

"'Cuz I like saying it forever, punk!"

I put my elbow on the table and my head in my hand. There is no point in even trying to put a stop to this train wreck.

"What do you like better, cookies or girls?" Lisa questions.

"My mommy makes yummy cookies. Girls are stupid. Except for Mommy 'cuz she has boobs," Gavin replies earnestly.

"Gee, thanks, sweetie," I mumble as I lift my head and glance at Lisa to see if she looks as horrified as I feel.

"When you grow up, who do you want to marry?"

Obviously, the fact that any chance at a Pulitzer for this interview is long gone doesn't matter one iota to this woman.

Gavin gets up on his knees on the bench seat and places a loud, wet kiss to my cheek.

"I want to marry Mommy. We'll kiss and we'll marry and I'll take her on dates and we'll be best friends forever and make lots of phone calls with each other."

No, no, no, no. Just...no.

"Phone calls? Do you mean you'll call your mommy a lot when you're older?" Lisa questions.

Don't do it. For the love of God, don't do it.

"No, we'll make phone calls like Mommy and Daddy do when they go into their bedroom and lock the door and yell and make weird noises," Gavin replies.

17.

Midget and Donkey Shows

"When asked if he enjoyed preschool, the precocious four-year-old asked me if I was the police. When I told him that no, I was not the police, he informed me that I should go to jail and called me a 'dicky punk'."

Carter laughs as he reads the magazine interview aloud. Lisa had sent me an email copy of the interview right after she finished it so I could look it over, but seeing it in print in one of my absolute favorite magazines that I have read cover to cover for years and only dreamed about one day being in makes me feel a little sick to my stomach.

"How can you laugh about this? This isn't funny."

"Gavin is quite obviously fond of both of his parents. When asked what his favorite thing about his father was he replied, 'He tucks me in at night and tells me that if I eat my green beans my wiener will grow big and strong just like his,'" Carter reads with a laugh.

"I'm buying that kid a Porsche. He just told all of America that I have a big, strong penis."

I shake my head at him and get up to dump the rest of my now cold coffee into the sink and rinse out my cup. My morning coffee, which usually brings me close to orgasm and gives me the strength to make it through the day, leaves me feeling queasy. I've only been able to stomach two sips of it. I'm guessing that the combination of seeing my name in print in my most beloved food magazine and listening to Carter read back to me the embarrassment of that day three weeks ago is the culprit for my upset stomach.

"Claire, this interview is awesome. She raves about how amazing you are by making your dreams come true and how absolutely delicious everything you make is. This is going to drum up so much business for the store. You should be proud," Carter tells me. "Although, I really think we need to sit down and talk about this porn comment. I get that you're uncomfortable about it, but you don't need to be with me. I like porn. I like to watch porn. I would especially like to watch porn with you," he states as he set the magazine down on the kitchen table, stands up, and walks over to me.

He rests his hands on the counter on either side of me, caging me in. He presses his body up against my back and places a kiss to my shoulder. I sigh, memories of the last time we stood like this in the kitchen flooding my mind. Even having my mother walk in on us doesn't diminish the hotness that is kitchen sex.

"What's really going on in that head of yours?" Carter asks as he rests his chin on my shoulder and we stare out of the little window above the sink. I watch Gavin in the front yard, sitting on the walkway right in front of the porch drawing with sidewalk chalk. "I can tell something has been on your mind, so what gives?"

Just tell him. Tell him that all of a sudden after Liz and Jim's wedding, all you can think about is donning a white dress, standing in front of everyone you know, and committing the rest of your life to this man.

"Ever since the wedding you've been on edge. Don't worry, I have no intention of dragging you to the altar if that's what you're worried about," Carter says with a laugh.

I close my eyes and let my head fall forward. I should have never made those little comments all these months about how I'm not sure about the whole idea of marriage. How the hell am I supposed to know I'd change my mind?

"It's nothing, really," I reassure him, turning in his arms and putting on a happy face I don't really feel. I place my hands on his cheeks and pull his face to mine, kissing him with all of the love I feel bubbling in side of me. Carter moans softly and wraps his arms around me, holding me tight.

The front door opens and closes, and we end the kiss that's sure to heat up if we don't stop. No matter what we have going on in our minds, no matter what kind of struggles we are dealing with, nothing can change the spark between us or how much we want and need each other. That is one thing I'm absolutely positive of. Right now, that is the only thing I am sure of.

"I love you," I tell him, staring into his gorgeous blue eyes and trying to push my worries to the back of my mind. "I'm just out of sorts. Liz has been crazy busy since she got back from her honeymoon. We haven't had a lot of time to talk and I miss her. And I just haven't been feeling well."

Carter puts his hand to my forehead as Gavin comes running into the room.

"You do look a little flushed. Are you coming down with something?" he asks, pressing the back of his hand to one of my cheeks.

"I'm sure it's nothing. Just stress," I reassure him.

"Hey, Dad, guess what my favorite word is?" Gavin asks as he stands next to us, bouncing back and forth excitedly from one foot to the other.

"I don't know, what's your favorite word?" Carter asks as we separate from our embrace, and I go back to rinsing out my coffee cup and the other couple of dishes in the sink.

"Nutjob. Nutjob is my favorite word."

"Of course it is," Carter states with a sigh as he lifts Gavin into his arms and starts walking across the kitchen, no doubt to once again explain to him the difference between little people words and big people words. I know it's wrong to staple something to someone's head, but I am two seconds away from writing this rule down on a piece of paper and smacking it to Gavin's head with the black Swingline that's on our computer desk. And just that quickly, I feel like crying for even thinking about doing that to my son. I'm obviously having issues.

"I'll give Jim a call and see if they have any plans tonight. I think you just need a night out to take your mind off of everything," Carter tells me as I watch him walk out of the room giving Gavin a few tickles and blowing a zerbert on his cheek.

He's probably right. I just need a night out with friends, particularly my best friend. Liz and I haven't had any alone time since she's been home. She has told me more than once to just say the word and she'll drop everything so we can sit down and talk, but I feel bad about imposing on her. She's a newlywed with her own business to worry about. I don't want to bring her down with my insecurities. If I don't talk to someone, though, I'm going to explode. I can feel it.

Or maybe throw up. I suddenly have an image in my mind of a person literally being blown to bits with blood and gore and body parts splattering against a wall. With my hand to my mouth I race to the bathroom to throw up the small amount of coffee I consumed.

⊙ ⊙ ⊙

"Seriously, Claire? How is it that we've been friends all these months and I didn't know that you've never been to one?" Jenny asks with a shocked expression on her face.

"What are we discussing here, ladies? Donkey shows? Midget and donkey shows? Ping pong shooting vaginas in Tijuana?" Drew asks as he gets back from the bathroom and takes his seat at the table.

Carter calls everyone earlier in the day and demands they clear their schedules for a night out. It really isn't too hard to convince anyone to do this, but I still appreciate the fact that he's organized it for me and knows how much I need it. We are just finishing up dinner at Lorenzo's, our favorite local pizza place that's famous for not only good food but cheap draft beers. My stomach still isn't feeling one hundred percent better after that morning so while everyone around me enjoys their drafts, I stick to 7 Up in the hopes of settling things down.

"Claire has never been to a sex toy shop," Jenny informs him.

"Wait, I'm confused. Liz owns a sex toy shop, and it's right next door to Claire's," Drew tells her, turning his attention on me. "Dude, you've never walked over to the shop that's connected to yours? That's a little weird."

"Of course I've been to *Liz's* store. I've just never been to any other store. And I don't really think her store counts since it's not like it's full of sex toys right out in front," I explain.

"True. My store is like a mullet. Business in the front, party in the back," Liz states.

"Or like anal," Drew says with a laugh.

Everyone stares at him.

"What? It's totally like anal. Business in the front, party in the back. Hello? Why is that not funny?"

Jenny pats his arm for comfort and we all resume our discussion.

"If you guys will remember, I never even *owned* a vibrator until Liz conned me into doing one of her at-home parties," I remind them.

"Ahhhh yes, the infamous dinner where we talked about your vagina and sex toys all night long," Jim says with a laugh.

That night still goes down in history as one of the most mortifying nights of my life. It had been the night after I saw Carter again for the first time since our one-night-stand. I walked into Liz and Jim's house, talking nonsense about my vagina and how I'd never had an orgasm with another human being when I turned around and saw Carter and Drew sitting on the couch listening to every word. Jim met them earlier in the day and unbeknownst to Liz or I, invited them over for dinner. The rest of the night had been spent discussing how many sex toys I received at the party earlier that evening and the fact I only had sex one and a half times in my life.

"Anyway," I say with a glare to Jim, bringing the conversation back around. "No, I've never been inside a real, live sex toy store."

Drew pushes his chair back and stands up, placing his hands on his hips.

"Grab your keys, folks. We're going to pop Claire's toy store cherry!"

Everyone pays their bills and Liz announces to the guys that the girls need some alone time. The men all pile into Drew's car and Jenny and I get into Liz's car to head to the Adult Mart a few towns over.

"Okay, spill it bitch. What's going on with you?" Liz asks as she pulls out of the parking lot and follows Drew's car.

That's all it takes for the dam to break. I immediately start crying. *God dammit, what the fuck is wrong with me?*

Jenny leans forward from the back seat and hands me a kleenex. I take it and blow my nose, taking deep breaths to calm myself down.

"I don't think Carter wants to marry me," I say between sniffles.

"Whoa, wait a minute. Did he say that to you? I will kick his fucking ass," Liz threatens as she turns on her blinker and gets onto the ramp for the highway.

"No! No, he didn't say those exact words. It's just little things that have happened the past few weeks," I tell her.

"Okay, what little things? And why is this news to me that you even care about getting married? You have always been a staunch supporter of living in sin because of your parents. Why the sudden change of heart?"

This is where I feel stupid. Does it sound dumb that my change of heart came from being jealous of her and Jim? That seeing them so happy and pledging their love to one another has made me realize how much I want that for myself?

"I know that's what I've always said, and I guess part of me really believed that. I mean come on, my parents don't exactly have the best track record. What makes me think I would be any good at that kind of thing?" I ask.

"Sweetie, no one knows if they will be good at that kind of thing. It's not like you're born with a marriage gene. It all just depends on the person you're with. If you can look at that person and know without a doubt that you want to spend the rest of your life kissing them goodnight and waking up next to them, marriage is for you," she tells me.

I start crying again and put my head in my hands.

"When I caught the bouquet at your reception, you should have seen the look of horror on Carter's face. He seriously looked petrified that the old wives' tale would come true," I explain as I wipe the tears from my cheeks and take a deep breath.

Liz stares at me while we sit at a red light.

"What?" I ask.

"You mean that's it? That's where all of this doubt and sadness is coming from? He looked at you a little funny when you caught a bouquet at a wedding? That doesn't exactly scream 'I hate marriage' you know. He could have just been a little surprised. Did he actually *say* he was freaked out that you caught the bouquet?"

I huff and my sadness is immediately replaced with irritation.

"No, he didn't come right out and say it, but I could tell. And I don't know, there's been a bunch of other little things here and there. He was all weird at your rehearsal dinner, smacking the champagne out of my hand and he's made these comments about how he won't be dragging me to the altar and how he's glad he'll never have to worry about asking my dad for permission because my dad still scares the shit out of him," I tell her.

"Um, not to butt in here or anything, but do you think maybe he's saying stuff like that because he knows how *you* feel about the whole subject? Maybe he really does want to marry you but he doesn't want to freak *you* out about the whole thing since you've made it clear your parents left a lasting impression on you in that area," Jenny says from the back seat with a surprising amount of insight.

"Shockingly, I agree with Jenny. Until you sit down and talk to him about this, you're just going to keep jumping to conclusions and making yourself miserable. I love you, Claire, but you're acting like an asshole," Liz says as she pulled into the Adult Mart parking lot. "You know what happens when you assume things."

I let out a sigh. "You make an ass out of you and me."

She maneuvers the car into a spot right next to the guys and shuts off the car but makes no move to get out.

"No, you just make an ass out of *you*. Me, I would never be this assy," she replies. "You love Carter and it is obvious how much he adores you. Stop being a dick, man up, and talk to him. Sit him down and tell him that you don't really have a late night porn addiction but you've been secretly watching wedding shows and sneaking into the magazine aisle at the grocery store in sweats, slippers, sunglasses, and a trench coat to scan the bridal magazines like some deprived housewife needing a Playgirl fix," Liz tells me firmly.

"Ooooh, I love Playgirl!" Jenny said. "I have a prescription to it. I learned how to deep throat while hanging my head off of the end of the bed last month. You know how in the movie *'The 40-Year-Old Virgin'* Steve Carell screams out Kelly Clarkson's name when he's getting waxed? Drew screamed out Willie Nelson's name when he came. It was so hot."

"Oh my God, Jenny. Too much information," I tell her with a grimace as I cover my mouth with my hand and swallow back a little bit of vomit I burped up at the thought of that moment in time in Jenny and Drew's bedroom.

"Hey, are you feeling okay? You look a little green," Liz states as we opened our car doors and step out into the night air.

I take a few deep breaths and will my stomach to calm and not bring up dinner.

"And what the hell was wrong with you tonight drinking pop at Lorenzo's? That's like blasphemy," Liz tells me as she clicks the automatic door lock on her keys and the car horn beeps once. "You're not pregnant are you?!"

She and Jenny start cackling with laughter as they walk ahead of me to meet up with the guys who stand holding the door to the store open for us.

I trail behind them a few steps, the smile dying from my lips as I start doing calculations in my head. I stop in my tracks a few feet from the front door and stare in horror at Carter.

He gives me a heart-stopping smile and in response, I throw my hand over my mouth and run to the bushes on the edge of the sidewalk, depositing two slices of pizza, two glasses of pop, and my dignity onto the front lawn.

18.

Benjamin's Balls

As we walk up and down the aisles of Adult Mart, I keep a close eye on Claire. She looks better after throwing up her dinner, but I'm still worried. I've never seen her sick before, unless you counted hangovers, and it puts me on edge. I hate that she's coming down with the flu and there is nothing I can do to make her feel better.

"This has burnt nut sac written all over it," Drew yells from the end of the aisle, interrupting me from my thoughts as he holds up a candle that doubles as massage oil when it's melted.

I reach for Claire's hand and give it a squeeze as we make our way down one aisle, glancing at things as we walk. I watch her carefully out of the corner of my eye, looking for warning signs on her face in case I need to rush her out of the store to defile more shrubbery.

"I'm fine, stop staring at me," she says without looking at me.

"Sorry, I'm just making sure you aren't going to throw up on the carpet. Out of all the fluids that are stained on this floor, I'm guessing vomit isn't one of them."

"Oh that's disgusting," she says with a laugh.

Seeing her smile puts me at ease a little bit. If she can still laugh, she isn't dying from some horrible, unnamed disease.

Claire suddenly stops and moves in front of me with a serious look on her face.

"You see?" she whispers conspiratorially. "This is why I have never set foot in one of these places," she states, looking over her shoulder and then back to me. "Look at that creepy, old guy over there in front of the 'Buy One, Get One Free' bin. He is about one 'Shaving Ryan's Privates' away from whipping his dick out in the middle of the store and throwing his goo at us like in 'Silence of the Lambs'," she complains.

She gives one last nervous look over her shoulder at him and lets go of my hand to go down a different aisle, clearly needing to distance herself from the guy who now has both of his hands in his baggy pants pockets and is jerking them at an alarming speed. The guy obviously hadn't read the sign hanging above the movies that said, "Please do not jerk off in our store. Thank you!" There is even a smiley face on the sign. It's oddly disturbing, yet comforting all at the same time.

I turn to follow Claire, stopping at a random display and grabbing the first bottle I see and read the back of it to see what it does. I read a few words when the sound of Claire's whispering brings my head up. I see her talking animatedly to Jenny a few feet away, most likely sharing her views about the DVD section and its inhabitants. I stand there for a few minutes just watching her when she suddenly throws her head back and laughs. It's one of those deep, full belly laughs that is impossible to stifle and it gives me goose bumps hearing it. It feels like someone punched me in the stomach and my heart starts pounding faster.

I love her so fucking much.

This isn't a revelation, but all of a sudden in the middle of Adult Mart I feel like nothing else matters but the fact that I love Claire. She is my dream come true, my life, and my everything. Does it really matter if I plan the best proposal in the world and spend weeks trying to come up with just the right words? She isn't the type of girl who cares about that stuff and I know it. I want everything to be outlandish because it's what I think is expected, not because it's what I think will be perfect for her. Asking her to be my wife and to grow old with me – that's what matters, not the amount of money I spend renting a jumbotron, or the meetings I have with the manager of a restaurant, or the stupid three-page speech I memorize. Waking up every morning next to this woman and tucking my son into bed every night is all that I care about. Claire and Gavin are my whole world, and I don't want to wait one more second to ask her to make it official in the eyes of God and everyone we know.

Spur of the moment. Isn't that the way you were supposed to do these fucking things anyway?

I swallow the knot that forms in my throat, suddenly nervous that the moment is here. The one I have been planning for and rehearsing – it's here and it's right fucking now.

I tear my gaze away from Claire for a moment and glance around me. Porn, dildos of all shapes, sizes and colors, and a shelf full of anal lube.

Jesus, does that say cinnamon-flavored anal lube? I don't even want to think about a situation that requires flavored anal lube. I must be insane that I am actually contemplating this right now.

I stand there with my hands sweating, heart pounding, and a bottle of Lickity Stiff Arousing Cream clutched to my chest.

Fuck it.

I take a deep breath, my decision made. With determination, I walk over to where Claire is still chatting with Jenny. She turns to face me just as I reach her and takes the bottle I'm holding out of my hand to read its contents.

"Lickity Stiff Arousing Cream? I'm pretty sure you don't need this," Claire says with a laugh.

She turns around to place it back on a shelf, and I take a deep breath for good measure, reach into my pocket, and wrap my fingers around the velvet box that I still carry around with me just in case. With Claire's back to me, I pull out the box and start to kneel.

"Holy shit!"

The exclamation interrupts my descent to the floor, and I pause with both of my knees slightly bent, looking like I'm getting ready to take off sprinting in a race. Claire turns around just as a hand clamps around my bicep and dragged me backwards.

"Liz, what are you doing?" Claire asks.

"Just need to talk to Carter for a second. Need a guy's opinion about porn, no worries!"

I stumble and shove the ring box back in my pocket as I try to turn around and keep up with Liz. Despite my protests, she continues to hold onto my arm and walk faster.

"Liz! What the fuck?! I was kind of in the middle of something," I complain as we get further away from Claire who stares at us with confusion on her face.

"Oh I know what the fuck you were in the middle of, dumbass!" Liz whispers loudly.

She finally stops when we are on the opposite side of the store from Claire and turns to face me.

"You're proposing to Claire?" she asks with her hands on her hips and a mixture of awe and anger on her face

"Well, I was *trying* to until I was rudely interrupted," I tell her, putting my hands on my hips and staring her down. She is small and feisty, but I have cocks on my side. Hundreds of them I can fling at her and then flee in the other direction when she attacks.

"You're proposing to Claire."

This time it's a statement rather than a question.

"Um, I think we already covered this. Let me guess, you think it's too soon. Or you're afraid I'm going to hurt her. Go ahead, give it to me. Wait, shit! Did she say something to you about not wanting to marry me? Fuck! She's been acting weird since your wedding, and I know she's talked a good game about not wanting to get married, but I figured it was just talk. What girl doesn't want to get married? Oh fuck, *Claire* is the type of girl who doesn't want to get married. Oh my God she doesn't want to marry me," I ramble as I pace back and forth in front of a display of chocolate body paint.

"Oh for fuck's sake, calm down, Nancy. I swear the two of you are the stupidest people I have ever met. You live together and you never talk. How is that fucking possible?" Liz asks in irritation.

"What are you talking about?"

Liz sighs. "YOU. ARE. STUPID," Liz repeats, enunciating each word and making up random hand gestures to go with each one so it looked like she was using sign language. Except I'm pretty sure the sign for "stupid" isn't a middle finger.

"I shouldn't be telling you this because Claire is my best friend and this seriously violates the best friend code of honor between girls, but we have a situation on our hands. I am willing to take a kick to the vagina for you when she finds out about this so you better clean out your ears and listen the fuck up!" she says with a poke to my chest with her finger. "Claire has been freaking out lately that *you* don't want to marry *her* because she has this idea in her head that you're a typical guy and the idea of marriage makes you want to puke, which could explain the purging she did in the landscaping out front. She doesn't have a porn fetish. She just didn't want you to know that ever since my wedding she's done nothing but think about marrying you, and she's scared to death it's going scare you away."

I stare at her with my mouth open, not sure which fact makes me more sad: Claire thinking I wouldn't want to marry her or Claire not really being addicted to porn. That is a problem I'm sure we can overcome together and without the tears or vomiting...unless that was the type of porn she was into, but I'm pretty sure we can get through that together as well. Maybe. But I guess that's a non-issue now.

"Okay, then why the fuck did you stop me? I was seconds away from easing all of her fears," I complain.

"Um, take a minute and look around, Romeo. Do you really want to propose to Claire in front of a display of cock rings?"

I glance around me and really take in my surroundings and think about what I'm doing.

"Years from now when she's retelling this story to your grand kids, do you really want her to say, 'Well kids, your grandfather popped the question right next to the anal beads and ball gags.'?" Liz says in a grandmotherly voice.

"I'm sorry, I don't get what the problem is here," Drew says as he suddenly appears next to Liz, licking a sucker shaped like a pair of tits.

"Go away, this is a secret," Liz tells him.

"Nice try, twat waffle. I heard the majority of what's going on. And I kind of want to take Carter here out back and rub my nuts on his head for not telling me he planned to propose to Claire in the happiest place on earth," Drew states, giving me a dirty look. Well, as dirty a look as he can with sugar boobs on a stick hanging out of his mouth.

"Isn't Disneyland the happiest place on earth?" Liz asks.

"It's like you don't even know me," Drew tells her.

"Look, this was a last minute decision. It's not like I planned to drop down on one knee in the middle of this place."

I look away from them to take another glimpse around me.

Why the fuck did I think this was a good idea? Claire would have killed me, murdered me where I stood. My obituary would read, "He died under a pile of pink and purple rubber cocks and double A batteries."

"I was caught up in the moment and just reacted," I tell them sheepishly.

Drew pats me on the back. "Awww, you got sentimental in a porn shop. Will you marry me instead?" he asked with a laugh.

I shut him up with a punch to his chest.

"Wait, if you didn't plan this, why are you carrying a ring around in your pocket?" Liz asks suspiciously.

"Uh, I, um, kind of carry it everywhere with me," I tell her, feeling beyond uncomfortable that I'm admitting this out loud. "I've had a few proposal plans go belly up the last few weeks. I've been wracking my brain trying to come up with the perfect plan and every time, something has gone wrong. I like to keep the ring in my pocket so I can reach in and touch the box. It gives me reassurance to keep trying."

Liz's bottom lip quivers and Drew stares at me blankly.

"Dude, you've been fingering that box in your pocket all this time? I thought you had crabs or something. I was going to let you borrow my cream," Drew says with a sad shake of his head. "That's pathetic. You have officially lost your man card. If you take it all back right now and tell me there's a hole in your pocket and you were just diddling yourself like the old guy over in aisle twelve, I'll forgive you."

Liz pinches the skin of his underarm, and Drew lets out a howl, rubbing the spot that is now turning red.

"Shut up, ass fuck. That is the most romantic thing I've ever heard," Liz says with a sniffle. "Let me see the ring."

I look behind me and find Claire perusing DVD's now that the guy playing pocket pool is gone. I slide the ring out of my pocket and quickly opened it for Liz to see.

"Holy shit, you went to Jared's," she whispers in awe.

"YES! Ha ha, vindication!" I shout with a fist pump.

Liz and Drew shush me and we all turn around to see if Claire has heard the commotion. I quickly snap the ring box closed and shove it back in my pocket to see that she is oblivious to the noise and is still neck deep in the clearance porn bin.

That is so hot.

Even if my grandmother walked in right now, I don't think I'd be able to get rid of my boner.

Sorry, Nana, my girlfriend is in a sex shop trying to pick out the perfect porno for us to watch later. Carter Junior isn't going anywhere for a while. Please pick girl-on-girl, please pick girl-on-girl.

"Oh for God's sakes, close your mouth, Carter, or you'll catch flies," Liz scolds, bringing my attention back around. "And Drew, quit staring at Jenny's ass. You'll have plenty of time for that later."

"Actually, we've already done it three times today. I'm kind of spent," Drew replies with another lick to the sucker.

"First of all, that's disgusting and I would have slept a whole lot better tonight if you hadn't shared that, and second, when the fuck did you even find time to have sex three times? You were at my shop all day helping me unload inventory. You didn't even see Jenny until we got to the restaurant," Liz questions.

"*First of all,*" Drew replies, mocking Liz. "You said 'load' and we need to acknowledge that. Heh, heh, load! And second, it was more like one point two times if you want to get technical. I had sex with the Jenny mold twice in the bathroom of your store, and I had sex with *Jenny* in the bathroom of the restaurant."

And there goes my boner.

"There are so many things wrong with that statement I think my brain just exploded. You're bleaching my bathroom tomorrow, asshat," Liz says angrily.

"Hey, what are you guys talking about?" Claire asks, coming up to the group.

"We're talking about how many times I spooged in Jenny today," Drew states proudly.

"Sorry I asked," Claire replies, turning right back around and walking away.

"Never, ever use that word again. Ever," Liz tells Drew once Claire is out of earshot. "Okay, Carter, I get where you were going tonight with the whole 'spur of the moment' thing and it's a nice touch. But you need a plan."

"Hey, Christopher proposed to Adriana without any kind of plan. He just walked into her mother's house and handed her the ring. Maybe he had the right idea," I told her indignantly.

"Who the hell are Christopher and Adriana?" she asks.

"Um, duh! From Sopranos," Drew replies.

"Come to think of it, though, it didn't really end all that well. He fucked everything in a skirt, snorted coke, shot up heroin, and had her killed. Plus, the reason he proposed was because he just beat the shit out of her," I reason.

"Gee, it's amazing you were able to come to the conclusion that basing your marriage proposal off of an HBO mob show isn't the best idea," Liz says with a roll of her eyes.

"Hey, as long as Claire doesn't go to the FBI and rat us out it could totally work," Drew states. "That's common sense right there. Bitches are snitches," Drew says, throwing down gang signs to emphasize his point.

"It's obvious I'm going to have to do this for you. Give me a few weeks and I'll have your problem solved," Liz assures me.

I'm not so sure having someone else plan my proposal to Claire is a good idea, but Liz *is* her best friend. Who better to help me out with this? Plus, it will alleviate some of the pressure I feel.

The three of us make our way back to the other side of the store where Claire and Jim are standing, staring slack jawed at Jenny.

"What should I do? He tells me to test them out, so I did. How was I supposed to know how far in to stick them?" she whines as we got to the group.

"What happened? What's going on?" I ask to no one in particular.

I notice Claire is looking a little green again, and I put my arm around her waist and pulled her in to my side.

"I bought some of those Benjamin Wa Balls, and I know you're supposed to try stuff out before you leave the store to make sure it works. Now I can't get them out," she complains.

It's not until that moment I notice she is standing with her legs slightly spread like she was getting ready to take a dump on the floor.

"Did she just say *Benjamin* Wa Balls?" I whisper to Jim standing next to me.

"Seriously? That's what you're concerned with? She stuck a product up her vagina before she left the store. And was planning on putting it back if she didn't like it," Jim whispers back in a horrified voice. "I should never have touched anything in here."

Jenny rocks back and forth from one foot to the other and shakes her hips a little in an effort to shake them loose I'm guessing.

"This Benjamin Wa guy should have come up with a better removal plan," Jenny states.

"Jesus, will you stop calling them that? They're BEN WA BALLS," Liz shouts. "And you're not supposed to test the products out IN the store. That's only for toys that require batteries and the clerk will put some batteries in to make sure the thing actually runs before you leave with it."

"How the hell was I supposed to know any of this? And I thought that was just a nickname for them and they shortened it to fit on the packaging. I was using the formal name," Jenny tells her as she continues to move her hips around in a giant circle like she's trying to hula hoop in slow motion.

We all just stand around staring at her while she does her weird mating ritual to get Benjamin's balls loose. It's like a train wreck we can't turn away from.

"I am never letting anyone use the bathroom in my shop. Ever," Liz says under her breath.

"Ooooh, I think I got one loose!" Jenny exclaims.

"I totally love you right now!" Drew tells her.

"I think I'm going to be sick," Claire states, throwing her hand over her mouth and running for the exit.

19.

Oops, I Did It Again!

After a week of being sick off and on, Carter forces me to go to the doctor. Other than throwing up a few times, I feel fine. I know he's making a big fuss over nothing. But regardless, I haven't been to my doctor for anything other than my yearly pap test since Gavin was born. He's a general practitioner so he is Gavin's doctor as well. With all the time I've spent in that office with my son and his check-ups, colds, shots, fevers, diaper rashes, and everything else under the sun, there is no need for me to go in there if it isn't absolutely necessary. I'm the type of person who doesn't go to the doctor unless I'm bleeding from the eyes or monkeys are flying out of my ass. I figure my heath and well being will be perfectly fine through osmosis just by walking into that place every couple of months with my son.

When I call my doctor and tell him my boyfriend is being mean and making me get a physical, his exact words are, "Claire, you know there's more to you than your vagina. I've scheduled you for tomorrow."

Whatever. What if my vagina *is* the best part? What do you have to say about that, Doctor Dick?

Actually, I really do love our doctor. I have never seen him wearing anything other than jeans and a t-shirt. He's very down-to-earth and Gavin loves him. Plus, if I'm going to let a guy stick his hands up my snatch once a year, he better make me feel comfortable if he isn't buying me dinner first.

I'm currently sitting on the exam table in a lovely ensemble of a paper shirt that opens in the front and a paper blanket the size of a newspaper that is supposed to fit around my ass. The room is a balmy fifty-two degrees, and I have been waiting forty-five minutes so far. Needless to say, I'm in a super mood by the time Dr. Williams finally shows up.

"Claire, how are you doing today?" he asks as he walks into the room with a nurse following close behind.

"Oh, I'm just super. Did you do something new with these gowns? They seem to have much more coverage," I say sarcastically.

"Ah, Claire, you always say the nicest things," he laughs as he takes a seat on his little stool with wheels and looks over my chart.

The nurse comes up next to me and takes my blood pressure and checks my pulse, reporting the numbers to Dr. Williams so he can notate them.

"Well, your BP is good and you don't have a fever. When was your last menstrual cycle?"

I count backward through the weeks in my head and then stop and count again.

"Well, it was…I remember it was a Tuesday because that's the day my supplies are delivered, and I was in the middle of signing for the white chocolate when I felt cramps," I ramble, trying not to panic.

One, two, three, four, carry the seven, multiply by eight…FUCK!

I glance over at the calendar hanging on the wall. This month shows a black and white cat with wide eyes and both of its paws covering its mouth as if to say 'Oops!'.

Fuck you, you stupid cat! I can't count with you staring at me like that. And if cats really could say "Oops" they'd do it when they shit on the SIDE of the litter box instead of in it.

I stare at the squares and the numbers on the calendar until they all start to blur together, either from eye strain or tears, I'm not sure which.

"First, how about we just have you scoot down to the end of the table and we'll check you out. You're due for your yearly exam next month anyway so we might as well get that taken care of," Dr. Williams says as he slides his chair closer to me while the nurse pulls out the extension at the end of the table and adjusts the stirrups for my feet.

I lie back and put my legs up in the air while the nurse slides a table over with the pap test kit already set up on top.

Right now, I wouldn't mind a little Drew humor to take my mind off of things. Something to the effect of, "How's that cunt scrape coming along?"

I squeeze my eyes shut while the doctor goes to work, sticking his hands where only one man has gone before.

"So, have you been watching the new Bachelorette? That chick is a train wreck!" Dr. Williams says with a laugh.

"Um…"

"Did you see when she got all trailer park on that one guy? Wagging her finger and shaking her head? You can take the girl out of the trailer park…" Dr. Williams trails off with another laugh as I hear the metal clink of the speculum.

"My daughter likes to watch that stupid show just to see the pretty dresses she's going to wear," he tells me as he continues working between my legs.

No really, it's perfectly fine to talk about reality television and YOUR KID while your fingers are all up in my business. How does this work when he's at home? Is it the exact opposite when he's sitting around the dinner table? "So did I tell you about this woman today? Her cooch hadn't been shaved in days. What a trainwreck! Can you pass the potatoes? I only treat her because she's got a pretty uterus. How did you do on your spelling test, Cindy Lou?

Dr. Williams finishes digging to China, slides back and slips off his rubber gloves while he stands.

The nurse takes my arm and helps me sit up. I try to situate the paper shirt and skirt thing to cover myself back up but it seems like the fucking thing shrunk. I give up and just keep my legs as tightly together as I can. It doesn't seem appropriate to flash the goods to the doctor now that the exam was over. It would be like walking up to your dentist in the grocery store and showing him your teeth. There is a time and a place for everything.

"So? Is everything okay? What's next?" I ask, hoping since he hasn't said much during the exam, aside from television gossip, that all is good and I'm worrying for nothing.

"Well, we'll order up some blood work, and I'll see you back here in four weeks," he said with a smile as he wrote something else on my chart. "Congratulations, you're pregnant!"

☉ ☉ ☉

Did you know The Dollar Store sells pregnancy tests? It's true. And even though all these stupid dollar stores should change their names to "The Dollar Store – Everything Isn't Really a Dollar, We Just Like to Fuck With You", pregnancy tests are in fact one of the few things there that actually only cost one dollar. Which begs me to ask the question why the hell did I get a dirty look from the cashier when I asked for all thirty-seven tests? Like that's never happened before? They are pregnancy tests for ONE DOLLAR, people. Gavin gets one dollar for doing chores around the house every once in a while. Even HE can afford to buy a pregnancy test. Why a four-and-a-half-year-old would need to buy a pregnancy test is beyond me, but these are the facts.

Arguing with the cashier and telling her I hope she slams her ginormous tits into the drawer of the cash register probably isn't my finest moment, but it keeps my mind off of the fact that I might be pregnant.

Yes, I said *might*. I have just finished peeing on the twenty-third test and Dr. Williams had told me I was pregnant when he fondled my uterus, but he could have been wrong. Doctors get things wrong all the time. They remove a kidney when they mean to remove a gallbladder, and they forget to take clamps and shit out of someone before they sew them up. He could definitely be wrong about my uterus. How many uteri does he stroke on a daily basis? Maybe he's just off his game. Maybe he hadn't even been touching my uterus but had his hand around my spleen. But that would probably mean he was up to his elbows in my vagina. It had been uncomfortable, but not elbows-deep uncomfortable.

I stand at the sink in the bathroom and stare at the pregnancy test in my hand, waiting for the five minutes to be up so I can gouge out my eyes when I see another positive result. When the timer on my cell phone beeps with the new tone ("SWEET MOTHER FUCKING JESUS IT'S TIME!") I downloaded just for this purpose, I glance down and try not to cry.

An hour later, Carter and Gavin come home from the store and find me curled up in the fetal position on the floor of the bathroom, surrounded by used pregnancy tests, instructions, and ripped open boxes.

"Mommy, where did you get all these magic wands?!" Gavin asks excitedly as he runs into the bathroom.

He picks up one of the tests and pretends like he's Harry Potter, aiming the test at random objects around the small bathroom yelling, "I curse you with my magic wand, punk toilet paper!"

I don't even lift my head from the cold tiles; they feel too good on my tear-stained cheeks to move. I watch him with my eyes and wonder briefly if I'm a bad mother for letting him play with something that I peed on. That just starts another crying jag when I realize I will be a bad mother to *two* kids now. I have a vision of the future where both of my children are sitting in a tub of pee while I'm comatose on the floor.

Carter walks to the doorway and takes one look at me and the litter on the floor and jumps into action.

"Hey, Gavin, how about you put down that wand and go get the bubbles we just bought. I'll even let you blow them in your room."

"Sweet! This wand smells funny anyway, and it's making my hand wet," Gavin states as he drops it on the floor and runs from the room.

"You should probably tell him to wash his hands," I mumble from the floor.

"Eh, he's going to be playing with bubbles, which are like soap, so it will all even out," Carter replies as he steps into the room and sits down on the floor next to me.

I sit up, pushing tests and boxes out of my way so I can cross my legs and sit Indian style across from him with our knees touching.

"So, how was your day?" Carter asks gently as he reaches over and brushes my hair out of my eyes.

I sniffle and look around at the mess.

"Oh you know, the usual. I worked, ran some errands, some guy put his hands up my chimichanga, complimented my uterus, and I got into a fight with a clerk at The Dollar Store."

"Was it because practically nothing in that store is a dollar?" he asks.

"Oh my God, right? What the fuck is up with that? I don't go into a store called The Dollar Store to buy a five dollar toy. Someone needs to school these people on proper advertising," I complain.

A few seconds of silence lapse, and I knew Carter was waiting for me to mention the huge "I'm pregnant" elephant in the room. Fuck that elephant! He can just sit there in the corner eating peanuts and shitting on the tile while giving me looks of disgust.

You're the one shitting on the floor, elephant, don't give me that look.

Carter spreads his legs out on either side of me, reaches over and grabs onto both of my ankles, unwinds my legs, and pulls me across the floor to him. He re-hooks my ankles together behind his back and puts his hands on either side of my face, forcing me to look him in the eyes.

"Say it," he whispers. "I missed out on this the first time. I want to hear you say it."

My throat is so tight I'm positive I won't even be able to take another breath, and he wants me to talk?

"Please?" he pleads softly.

He smiles at me and I can see his eyes start to fill with tears. I want to tell him so many things, but I'm too overcome with emotion and frankly, a little bit of puke. Two words are about all I can muster.

"I'm pregnant," I whisper back with a sniffle.

"You're pregnant?" he asks with a huge smile.

Um, duh? What the fuck do you THINK all this is about? Oh my God, what is wrong with me? I'm sorry! I love you!

"Are you not happy about being pregnant?" he asks, showing the first sign of worry since he stepped into the room.

"I figured YOU wouldn't be happy. You're totally screwed now. If you decide you don't like me, I've got you for eighteen years. I'm your baby mama times two. That's triflin', yo."

Carter laughs and wrapped his arms around my waist so he could pull me up against him.

"Stop trying to quote Kanye. You're not a golddigger, and there's no question whose kids they are," he tells me as he cups my cheek with one hand and rubs it softly with his thumb.

"That's what you think. Sperm from the floor of the sex toy shop might have jumped off of the carpet and up into my vagina. No telling who this one belongs to."

He stares at me for a few minutes before kissing the tip of my nose.

"I know you're freaking out. It's okay. Just talk to me. Whatever you're feeling, I want to know. And I am perfectly fine with this. In fact, I am EXTATIC with this. There is absolutely nothing that could ruin my good mood about this news," he affirms.

There cannot be a more perfect man in the world than him. Fact.

"Really? Because I'm pretty sure we conceived this child the night I ate that pot cookie. I'm eighty-four percent positive our child is going to be born a pot head. It's going to come out with dreadlocks and wearing a Bob Marley onesie. Its first word will probably be, 'Whaaaaaazzzzzzzzuuuuuup'. It's never, ever going to sleep through the night because it's always going to have the munchies."

Carter chuckles and tightens his hold on me. I wrapped my arms around his neck and rest my chin on his shoulder.

"If that's the case, we'll just have to make sure we have plenty of Cheetos on hand at all times and some Grateful Dead music to play in the nursery," he states.

I sigh and turn my head so I can rest my cheek on his shoulder and burrow into the side of his neck.

"It's going to be fine. I promise you. I love you and I'm not going anywhere. This is the best news you could have ever given me. Nothing could make me happier right now."

Gavin suddenly comes bursting through the doorway.

"Dad, woke up dis morning, got myself a gun' is on!" he says excitedly. "And my wiener feels funny again. It won't stop being tall."

"Oh my God. I take that back. THIS is the happiest moment of my life. My son just got a boner for Sopranos," Carter whispers.

"Like father like son," I deadpan.

Carter pulls me up from the floor of the bathroom and tells me to leave the mess and that he'd clean it up later. He tells me I'm not allowed to do anything else for the rest of the day but lie on the couch and let him wait on me. He always knows exactly what to say to make me feel better, and he takes such good care of me. I'm an idiot for being disappointed that he doesn't immediately ask me to marry him. He loves me and he's happy we're going to have a baby. I can't help but wonder though why he hadn't asked. He obviously isn't in shock like I am so there has to be another reason. As I curl up on the couch with my head on Carter's lap, I try to ignore the pain in my heart at the thought that maybe he doesn't think I was marriage material.

20.
Did Not Finish

Three months later

"So what you're telling me is you wanted him to drop down on one knee and ask you to marry him in the bathroom?" my mother asks.

I roll my eyes and reached for another balloon to blow up. My mother has offered to help me set everything up for Gavin's fifth birthday party the next day. We are having it at the shop after hours. I let Gavin invite a few of his friends from preschool and think having a party in a candy store will be fun for them. As soon as my mother walks in the door of the shop she can tell I'm not myself. I blame my mood swings and crying jags the last few months on pregnancy hormones, but she knows better. The number of times we've talked on the phone, I gloss over what's wrong. Now that she can see me in person, I can't hide anything from her.

"Don't roll your eyes at me, chickadee. I'm just trying to make sure I understand this correctly," she says as she hangs a "Happy Birthday" banner on the wall. "You thought it would be romantic and beautiful if, once he found out you were pregnant, proposed immediately. So you wanted him to propose out of guilt and obligation for knocking you up instead of out of love."

Well when you say it that way…

"No! I mean…I don't know. I just would have liked for the effort to have been made. Maybe even a comment about us getting married or getting engaged at some point in the future. The fact that he hasn't said one word about it in three months just sucks," I tell her. "Every day I keep waiting for him to bring it up and every day that goes by and he doesn't, I get more upset. What if he doesn't think I would make a good wife? I know he loves me, but maybe he's not IN love with me. The kind of love that makes you want to do everything in your power to ensure you spend the rest of your life with that one special person. Maybe I'm not that special person for him."

Jesus. Talk about depressing. How does anyone even stand to be around me lately? I'm a disgusting, emotional, needy chick. No wonder Carter doesn't want me.

"It makes sense I guess. Look at all the years I spent hating the idea of marriage. I thought it was pointless and could only end in disaster. Karma is biting me in the ass."

My mom walks over to me and pulls me into her arms, my growing stomach acting as a stopper to keep us from getting too close.

"Baby, any fool can see that Carter is IN love with you. Have you ever paid attention to that boy when you walk into a room? His whole face lights up. And he's constantly touching you in some way. A brush of his hand on your cheek, wrapping his arms around your waist, kissing your shoulder...he does whatever he can to be close and connected to you," she says, pulling away so she can look at me. "And don't give me that bullshit story about you hating the idea of marriage."

I give her a pointed look and laughed.

"Are you kidding me? You and Dad were married five times total. FIVE TIMES! When you know your parents crashed and burned so many times, it's kind of obvious that you're going to have the same luck," I tell her.

"Oh, sweetie, you are a jackass. I love you, but you are dumber than a one legged duck in an ass kicking contest when pigs fly," she tells me.

"Am I supposed to know what the fuck that means? You either told me this was impossible or called me a pig."

My mom reaches up and wipes a tear off of my cheek I don't even know is there.

"Marriage was never for me. I knew that early on but I chose to ignore it. I never dreamed of having a family or a house with a white picket fence and being a soccer mom. But then I had you and I knew I needed to try. It just didn't work for me. But your father? He is definitely a marrying man, and he is a wonderful husband. The problem was never him. It was the losers he married," she says with a smile. "You may have always been afraid to try because of how you grew up and what you believed, but that doesn't mean it's who you are. You have more of your father in you than you know. You are already a better mother than I ever was, and I guarantee that when Carter *does* pop the question, you will be an amazing wife."

For the first time in my twenty-five years, my mother actually says something that made sense and gave me pause. And not the "What the fuck is she saying?" pause.

I had put up a wall all my life to protect myself. If I pretended like I didn't really want the American dream of a husband and kids, then eventually I would believe it and no one would be able to hurt me. Until Liz and Jim's wedding, I didn't realize just how much I wanted that wall to crack. Now that it had though, I was right where I never wanted to be - scared, confused and upset. I knew I needed to get my emotions under control and stop acting like a crazy person. I needed to man up and talk to Carter. I could feel the distance between us growing every day that I continued to lie to him and explained away my detachment and rocky emotions by saying they were all just because of the pregnancy. I had acted like a big baby all these months when all of it might have been fixed by one little conversation.

After Gavin's party, I will make sure that we sat down and talked.

"What about Carter's family? Are his parents still trying to recover from ceiling fan baseball?" my mom asks with a laugh, changing the subject to something a little less depressing.

"They've been okay. His mom actually sent me a big box of brand new baby clothes and a few blankets. His grandmother is the one I'm most surprised about. She really should want to kill me but she sent me something too, and I found out she actually has a sense of humor."

"Oh? What was it?" my mom asks.

"A onesie that said 'Too cute to play with your ugly ass kid'."

⊙ ⊙ ⊙

"Why the hell are those bitches over there giving me a dirty look?" Liz asks as she stares down five mothers who have accompanied their sons to Gavin's party.

"I'm guessing it's because the woman who brought her husband just noticed that he's been staring at your boobs that are spilling out of your shirt," I tell her as I finish cutting the cake and placing it on paper plates.

"Oh give me a break. One look at that guy and you can tell he's wound up so tight that if I blew him a kiss he'd probably bust a nut. None of those women look like they ever have sex unless it's to pro-create," she complains.

"They probably only do it in the missionary position with the lights off," I add.

"I bet they think doggy style is a type of line dance," Liz says with a laugh, blowing the husband a kiss.

I smack her hand and give her the evil eye.

"Will you cut it out? I have to be around these mothers all the time at Gavin's school. Play nice," I warn her.

"Look!" she says excitedly. "That poor guy just adjusted his junk. He totally came in his pants."

So far the party has been a success. The kids are yelling and run-ning all over the shop now that they are hopped up on sugar. I had thought having them frost their own cookies would be fun until they forgot about the cookies and started shoveling frosting into their mouths by the handful. Having Drew wrap up a bag of Pixy Stix and a twenty ounce can of Mountain Dew as Gavin's present doesn't help matters either. He tears into the present and has half the candy and all the Mountain Dew gone before I even notice. By the time I get a hold of him, he looks like he's been snorting coke off of hookers. His eyes are bloodshot, his hair is a mess, and he has white powder all around his mouth. When I see Drew whisper in his ear right before Gavin runs up to me and yells, "I have tiger blood running through my veins!" I know it's time to take the kid-crack away from him.

And of course I get nothing but dirty looks from the world's most perfect mothers. They can't just drop their kids off and come back like normal parents who foam at the mouth when they find out they'll get a few hours of peace and quiet and make their kids jump out of the moving vehicle at the curb before peeling off to get a massage or go to the bar. Oh no, they have to stand in the corner in their perfect little clique, judging me with their pastel sweater sets, linen pants, and string of pearls. Drew has already told one of them he has a much better pearl necklace he can give her later that night, hence the huddling in the corner. I think they really thought he was going to whip his dick out at a children's party and jerk off on one of their necks. Actually, this is Drew I'm talking about. There's a distinct possibility he might do it.

They spend the whole day looking put-out that they had to be here. They turn their noses up at my store-bought decorations and one even says, "Oh, so you didn't do centerpieces and table favors? And I heard you say this wasn't catered? That's a shame." Um, correct me if I'm wrong, but this is a party for a FIVE YEAR OLD. Not a fucking Bar Mitzvah. I'm not decoupaging anything, using a glue gun, or whittling an ice sculpture, and I sure as hell am not serving lobster and filet. I feed them pizza and hot dogs and fill goodie bags with Play Doh and bubbles. Where I come from, that's how you celebrate a toddler's birthday. I hold my tongue, though, because

I don't want to be *that woman* who got into a cat fight at her kid's birthday party.

I'm tired, cranky, and on edge as it is because I haven't talked to Carter yet. He had worked last night and we drove separately to the party so he could sleep. If another one of those uppity bitches says anything else to me, I'm not going to be responsible for my actions.

Liz grabs two plates of cake and leaves to take one over to Jim and antagonize the lone father whose wife probably threatened his manhood if he didn't come with her to the party.

She probably told him he wouldn't get missionary birthday sex this year where he could rub on top of her for thirty seconds while she was fully clothed. Poor guy.

"Hey, how are you feeling?" Carter asks as he comes up next to me and helps put forks on all the plates with a slice of cake on them. We've only said a few words to each other in passing since he got here. Both of us have been running around making sure everyone was happy and the party was a success. He had looked a little horrified at first when he got here, having never experienced a little boy's birthday party before, but he quickly jumped right in, grabbed a can of Silly String and began screaming and running around with the kids.

"I'm okay. Just tired," I tell him. I want to throw my arms around him and tell him I'm sorry for being such a bitch lately, but I know it will make me cry and I'm not about to do that in front of all these people. He seems nervous standing here with me and it makes me sad that I've done this to him. Instead of wrapping his arms around me and making a joke like he normally would, he keeps his distance, probably afraid I will snap at him or burst into tears like I've done for three months.

I am the biggest bitch in the entire world.

I turn to face him, knowing I need to say something to clear the air even if it's just to tell him I love him, when one of the she-wolves stalked over and interrupts us.

"Excuse me, but I think you should know that your son just said a bad word," she informs me haughtily with her hands on her hips.

Son of a bitch. This is so not what I need right now.

"I'm sorry. What did he say?" I ask.

I wonder if she's too appalled to say whatever the word is out loud. She's probably going to spell the word for me, and I'm going to have no choice but to point and laugh at her. F-U-C-K, A-S-S, S-H-I-T…what's it gonna be? Hopefully she knows how to spell bad words or this is going to be a whole new level of awesome.

Drew comes up to us and the woman looks at his shirt that says "Have you seen my perfect man ass?" and huffs in irritation.

"What's the dillio, folks?" he asks, taking a bite out of a cookie and spitting crumbs as he talks.

"I was just telling Claire that Gavin said a bad word in front of my son," she explains again.

"We're really sorry," Carter reiterates.

"So what did he say? Cocksucker, thundercunt, fuckholes, balls-actitties? Drew asks in all seriousness.

Under normal circumstances I would have probably smacked him in the arm for this, but the shock on Mother Theresa's face across from me is satisfaction enough. I put my hand over my mouth to cover up my giggle.

She sputters and gasps a few times before she finally replies angrily. "For your information, he said the word c-r-a-p."

The three of us stand there looking at her funny.

"Well? Aren't you going to do something about that?" she asks when no one says or does anything.

"I'm sorry, did you just spell the word *crap*?" Drew asks in confusion.

"Yes, that's the word Gavin said," she tells him.

Drew starts laughing. Loud, gut busting laughs.

"Oh my God! You totally had me going there for a minute," Drew tells her between laughs. "I really thought G-man was going to be in trouble."

The other mothers must have heard the commotion and walk over to join our small group.

"I should have known you wouldn't do anything about it. I mean, it's obvious you don't know the first thing about being a good parent. The parenting skills you have shown are appalling. Letting your child run amok, talking like a veteran trucker or a sailor. Real people do not talk this way to each other. The amount of times I've heard the word v-a-g-i-n-a alone is shocking. If this whole display was a story I was reading, it would be a disappointing 'did not finish' for me."

Oh no she DIDN'T!

I stand there for a few minutes with my mouth hanging open in shock while the other Stepford mothers get on the "you're a shitty parent" bandwagon and nod their agreements. These women are real pieces of work. I mean, I would totally talk about you behind your back, but I'd never be that mean and bitchy to your face or say something to hurt your feelings.

Until now.

You bitches messed with the wrong pregnant woman.

"Oh, I'm sorry. I didn't realize you cornered the market on perfect parenting. Isn't that your son sitting on the floor over there eating his boogers and naming his farts? Real genius you've got on your hands there. And you," I say, turning to one of the other ones. "Your kid told me when he got here that he wasn't allowed to eat processed sugar, white flower, red dye number five, or watch Spongebob because it was too violent. Isn't he the one sitting on the chair by the door rocking back and forth chanting 'I hate humans'? My child may be mouthy, and he may say inappropriate things from time to time, but I am a damn good mother. I just found out today my son scored higher on his kindergarten testing than all of your little fuckwits put together. He may watch Spongebob, he may eat sugar, and he may pick up on phrases the adults around him say, but I can guarantee you that when he's older, you won't find a human head in his freezer like little Johnny over there who's been banging his head against the glass for an hour because he's in shock from having a piece of cake for the first time in his life. And for your information, real people *do* actually talk like this. Really cool people who have awesome friends don't have giant sticks up their asses like you obviously do."

Carter leans close to my ear. "Gavin scored that well on his testing?"

"I know, total shocker for me too. He obviously doesn't get his brains from us," I whisper to him.

I turned back and realized all of the women have dispersed from our fun little pow-pow, grabbed their kids, and scurried out the door without another word.

"Oh and by the way, we should probably look into some new pre-schools," I state.

21.

I Swallowed a Penny!

"What do you mean you aren't going to do it?" Liz screeches. "Carter, we've been planning this for weeks. You HAVE to do it."

Liz and I are in the kitchen of the shop doing dishes while Claire is out front with everyone else taking down decorations.

I know Liz means well, but I just can't do what she wants me to.

"Liz, this just doesn't feel right. It was a great idea before she got pregnant, but I just can't do this now. Claire hasn't been herself since she found out she was pregnant. No matter how many times I try and tell her that everything will be fine, I don't think she believes me. If you hadn't told me what you did about her being afraid I didn't want to marry her, I would have thought she was cheating on me," I say.

"Um, dude. She's got your sperm inside of her. That would be gross. And if you were so worried, why the hell haven't you proposed yet?" Liz questions.

"Because you told me you'd cut off my dick if I did!" I argue.

"Okay, that may have been a little extreme. But I knew she would think you were doing it just because she was pregnant. I figured if you waited a while and I kept telling her she was an idiot, everything would work out and you could propose without her thinking bad things."

I sigh and crossed her arms in front of me. "I can't wait any longer, Liz. I know we planned on me doing this next month on the anniversary of when we first met, but I can't put this off one more day. There is this huge wedge between us right now and I have a feeling it's all because of this. I should have just said something to her months ago. To hell with the surprise."

"Fine. Have it your way. But I swear to God if you just walk up to her and hand her the ring, I won't cut your dick off, I'll just cut one ball off. You'll be forever known as Uniball Carter," she warns.

We stare at each other for a few minutes, her eyes narrowing with each second that passed.

"You don't have a plan, do you?" she finally asks.

I should tell her to move away from the knives.

"Um, not exactly. I mean, I know what I want to say. I just don't have all of the details yet," I admit.

"Well, I'd help you, but I kind of want to punch you in the face. You're on your own with this one," she tells me, throwing the towel she dried the dishes with onto the counter. "Now I'm going to have to tell everyone that the plan is off. It was the one time I was looking forward to wearing a shirt that Drew picked out."

I feel bad that Liz has spent all this time helping me plan something amazing for Claire. At the time, we had both agreed it would be awesome if our friends were there to see the proposal, and Drew of course wanted everyone to wear matching shirts that Claire would see right after I proposed. They *were* pretty great shirts and that is the one thing I will regret not doing, but I know this is the right decision.

"So does that mean no Gavin either?" she asks as she leans her hip against the counter.

"No, no Gavin. As cute as it would be for him to be the one to hand her the ring, I need to do this by myself. It was just the two of us the day I met her, and I want it to be just the two of us when I ask her to spend the rest of her life with me," I explain.

Liz let out a great big sigh and finally concedes.

"Alright, I get it. Your ball is safe from my wrath. But just so you know, I'm going to hold this against you for a long time," she tells me with a pat on my back.

"I wouldn't expect any less. I just need you to do one more little favor for me."

"What now? My first born, a pint of blood, one of my limbs? I've already given so much!" she wails in mock horror.

"Oh quit being such a drama queen. I already told you I appreciated your help so cut the shit out. I just need you to get Claire out of the store for about an hour. Can you do that?" I ask.

"No problem. I have this raging yeast infection from having too much sex in our hot tub. I'll tell Claire she needs to come to the pharmacy with me and help me pick out the right YEAST INFECTION cream," she says, putting the emphasis on the words that make my skin crawl.

"Liz, too much information," I say with a grimace.

"But it's really yeasty. I could make a loaf of bread with this shit."

"OH MY GOD! Cut it out. I'm going to puke," I tell her.

Liz laughs as she walks around the counter to go out front and talk to Claire.

"Payback is a bitch. And YEAST INFECTIONS really itch," she yells back to me with another laugh.

I try to block the last few minutes of conversation from my mind as I get to work planning how this will go down. Claire sticks her head into the kitchen doorway a little while later to tell me she was running to the store with Liz. I can't help but laugh a little when she whispers, "She's got an issue. And she needs my help. It's…an issue. I'll be back soon."

Right after she disappears from sight, Liz pops her head in to give me one more parting shot.

"Say 'bacterial vaginosis is delicious'. SAY IT!"

⊙ ⊙ ⊙

I honestly don't remember a time when I've been this nervous. I would have taken a minute to run to the bathroom and throw up the contents of my stomach, but I just heard the bell over the door of the shop ring and knew Claire was back.

I take my place at one end of the kitchen island and wait.

Claire walks through the doorway seconds later and stops, a look of confusion on her face as she takes in the sight before her.

"Um, why are there red Solo cups all over the counter?" she asks.

"I thought we could take a trip down memory lane and play a little beer pong," I tell her with a grin.

She walks further into the room.

"Nice sentiment and all but I don't I want our child to be born a pot head *and* a drunk."

I laugh and pick up the empty milk jug for her to see.

"Technically, this is milk pong."

She laughs when she gets to the other end of the island and glances into the cup closest to her.

"Ahhh gotcha. If I remember correctly, I kicked your ass the last time we played," she says with a smile.

"Oh I don't think so. I'm pretty sure all of the ass kicking was done by me. You sucked at beer pong."

"Lies! Not only were Liz and I the lap dance champions in our dorm, we were also beer pong champions," she told me with a satisfied smirk.

"Wait, what?"

She laughs again and shakes her head at me. "I know I told you this story."

"No, I'm pretty sure I would remember every part of a story that involved you and lap dancing," I argue.

"Liz and I used to do lap dances on each other for free beers at the college bars. I was a little bendier then so I was usually the one on top," she says nonchalantly.

Claire, bendy, girl lap dances…my penis exploded. That JUST happened.

"Promise me I will get to see this someday very soon," I tell her.

"Yeah, okay. Because pregnant chick lap dances are so hot." She chuckles.

"I don't think you understand how serious I am right now, Claire. This is right up there with meeting God and winning the lottery."

Seeing her happy and smiling confirms my decision to do this right now, this exact way. If only I could get the image of Claire grinding on another woman out of my head.

Damn you, penis, you aren't in charge tonight! Take a break, go back to sleep, nothing to see here.

"As much as it pains me to say this, the lap dance can wait, but you're going to have to prove to me right now that you've still got it in beer pong. The ping pong balls are right in front of you. Put your ball where your mouth is."

She raises her eyebrow at me.

"Hmmm, that didn't come out right. But I kind of like it," I tell her with a shrug.

She picks up one of the balls and lines up her shot. It bounces off the rim of the first cup and lands in one behind it.

"Yeah, that's what I thought," she taunts as I remove the ball from the cup and drink the milk.

I set the empty cup to the side, pick up my own ball and take aim while trying to keep my hand from shaking. I know I need to make as many shots as I can for this to work out the way I want it to. I toss the ball and it sinks right in the cup closest to her. I let out a huge sigh as she removes the ball and picked up the cup.

"Lucky shot," she tells me before downing the milk.

"I love you more than I ever thought was possible," I tell her softly as she sets the cup down. She cocks her head to the side and smiles at me.

I pick up another ball and quickly throw it before she could say anything back to me. It sinks into another cup right in front of her. As she picks up the cup to drink it, I speak again.

"I love you because you make me laugh and you make me want to be a better man."

I already have another ball in my hand and throw it into the air before she even finishes the last cup of milk. She stares at me wide-eyed as the ball plops into the next cup in line and she hesitates before picking it up. I wait until the cup is by her mouth before I continue.

"I love you because every day you amaze me."

A lone tear escapes from her eye as I throw another ball right into a cup. I've never played this well in my life. I guess it's only fitting since this is the only game where I'm playing *for* my life.

She picks that cup up and sniffles before taking a drink.

"I love you because you are the best mother in the entire world."

One more to go. And this was the one that counts. I aim and watch the ball sail in an arc toward the last cup on her side of the counter. I hold my breath until it drops right where it needs to go. I walk around the counter until I'm next to her and wait for her to finish the last cup of milk.

A surprised gasp sounds from her when she tips the cup back and something bumps against her lip. As she pulls the cup away from her mouth and looks into the bottom of it, I get down on one knee.

With shaking hands, she reaches her fingers into the cup and pulls out the diamond ring I have been carrying in my pocket for months. She turns to look at me and gasps again when she sees where I am.

"The first time we did this, every time one of us sunk a shot we would tell each other a fact about ourselves. I remember you told me your favorite color was pink and that you watched the movie 'Girls Just Want to Have Fun' once a year because it made you nostalgic for the time when Sarah Jessica Parker didn't look like a troll."

Claire laughs through the tears that are now falling freely.

"This time, I needed you to know every fact about why I love you. I wanted to marry you the first time I saw you again. I wanted to get down on my knees and beg you to never leave me. And I should have done it. I should never have waited this long. There is no one else in this world I could imagine spending my life with. I want to teach inappropriate things to our children with you forever. Claire Donna

Morgan, will you please, *please* marry me and love me for the rest of your life?"

She leans over and throws her arms around me, holding me tight as she sobs out the one word I have waited forever to hear from her.

"Yes!"

I pull out of her arms long enough to take the ring from her hand and slip it on her finger. Our happy moment is interrupted seconds later by Gavin running into the kitchen.

"Mom, guess what? I swallowed a penny!" he announces.

Claire and I pull away from each other and turn to see all of our friends and Claire's father standing in the doorway wearing the shirts Drew had picked out that say, "I played beer pong and all I got was this lousy t-shirt, knocked up, and a fiancé".

"Sorry, Carter, I couldn't resist the shirts. And really, they're still appropriate considering how you proposed," Liz says with a smile.

"Wait, I'm sorry. But did Gavin just say he swallowed a penny?" Claire asks, wiping the tears off of her cheeks.

"Oh, yeah. Well, we *think* he swallowed a penny. We're not quite sure," Drew explains. "He wanted some candy so Liz dumped out her purse on the floor because she knew she had a bunch of Tic Tacs at the bottom. He started scooping things up and shoving them in his mouth before we saw what he was doing. According to him, he swallowed a penny. But kids are liars."

Gavin stomps his foot. "YOU'RE A LIAR YOU BIG FAT TURKEY!"

"I am not fat. I'm muscular. Get your facts straight," Drew argues.

"Okay, can someone please tell me if my kid really swallowed a penny?" Claire asks loudly, putting a halt to the arguing.

"Well, I Googled 'kids swallowing pennies' and you'd be surprised how many hits I got," Liz says. "Anyway, as long as the penny was made before 1982, he'll be fine."

Claire and I stare at her for a few minutes before Claire explodes.

"What the fuck?!"

"Awwwwww, Mom," Gavin scolds as he pointed at her.

"I'm sorry, what the f-u-c-k does t-h-a-t mean and w-h-a-t do we do n-o-w?"

She has officially turned into one of the Stepford mothers, spelling words she doesn't even need to spell because she is so freaked out. She is not going to be happy about this.

"It's fine, Claire. I used my metal detector on him and the penny wasn't there," George stated.

"You're kidding me, right? You know there's this fancy thing called a hospital you can go to, don't you?" she asks.

"I walked uphill both ways in a snow storm with no shoes just to get to school when I was his age, and I ate metal shavings for fun. A little copper isn't going to hurt him," George argues.

"Unless the penny was made after 1982 because then it's made with enough zinc to melt his esophagus," Drew said matter-of-factly. "I'm pretty sure that would have happened by now though, so he's probably good."

Claire bends down next to Gavin and pulls him into her arms.

"Sweetie, how do you feel? Is your tummy okay?" she asks him.

"My tummy is good. Papa said I need to drop a deuce and check it for money. I can poop money!" he says excitedly.

"I wish I could poop money," Drew complains.

I bend down next to Claire and Gavin, gathering both of them in my arms.

"Just so you know, we're totally eloping," I tell her.

"Oh thank God," she replied.

22.

Hump, Hump, Hump

"So you really like it?" Carter asks for the hundredth time.

We are finally in bed relaxing after the long day, and I can't stop staring at my ring.

"I think I like it more than you."

Carter laughs. "Very funny."

"Oh, I'm totally serious. I've been thinking all this time that you just didn't want to marry me and here you were carrying a ring around in your pocket. I kind of want to whittle my toothbrush into a shiv and stick it in your eye," I tell him seriously.

He rolled over onto his side and rested his hand on my stomach.

"I'm sorry. I should have done it the day I bought the ring. I just wanted it to be perfect and then we found out you were pregnant and I know how your mind works. You would have never believed I was doing it for the right reasons if I did it right when we found out," he says as he gently rubs his palm in a circle on my protruding belly.

"I know, you're right. My mother said the same thing," I tell him, placing my hand on top of his and pushing it down towards the bottom of my stomach where I usually feel the teeny tiny kicking of little feet. To me it feels like bubbles popping, and I'm not sure if he would be able to feel it yet but it doesn't hurt to try.

"Rachel actually said something that made sense?" he asks in surprise.

"Yeah, it shocked me too," I say, turning my head on the pillow so I can see his face. "I should have just talked to you. Obviously I suck at the whole communication thing. I'm much better at suffering in silence."

Carter scoots closer and moves his hand out from under mine, sliding it up the front of my body until it rests on my cheek.

"I think we both have a long ways to go in the communication department. We'll get there though," he assures me.

"Did I tell you that when all this doubt crept into my mind I told Liz about it and she suggested that I give you a prostate massage?"

"Oh my God, stop. Don't say any more. Jim actually told me about the night she did that to him and it was horrifying. Please don't say any more," he warns.

"I don't know, you might like it," I tease.

"Hey, I don't even let anybody wag their finger in my FACE," Carter says in a Brooklyn accent.

"Seriously? A Sopranos quote now?"

"Um, yes. There is a Sopranos quote for every occasion. Hence, the reason for its awesomeness. Respect The Sopranos," Carter tells me seriously.

I roll over onto my side toward him and slide my leg up and over Carter's hip, running my fingers through his hair.

"I think we should celebrate this momentous occasion by me sticking my penis in you," he says with a smile.

"You're lucky you gave me jewelry today or I might have punched you for that."

Carter pulls me closer and brings his lips to mine. Just like always, his kisses make me forget about everything. The softness of his lips and the smooth glide of his tongue against mine remind me of just how long it has been since we've had sex. With our crazy schedules and my attitude problem, it's been a while and I am more than starved for him. His arms wrap around me and his hands slide down to my ass, cupping it and pulling me in against his hardness. I shift my hips against him and let out a groan.

"Wait, hold on. Shit," he mutters, breaking off the kiss.

I pull my head back and shoot him a questioning look.'

"What? What's wrong?"

Is his penis broken? Oh dear God please don't let it be broken. I NEED IT TO LIVE.

"I have to pee. Hold that thought," he says, pulling out of my arms and scrambling off of the bed.

I roll over onto my back and stare up at the ceiling. A few minutes later I still hadn't heard the toilet flush.

"Hey, are you okay in there?" I yell.

"SHHHHHHH! NO TALKING!" he yells back.

What the fuck?

"What do you mean no talking? What the hell is going on?"

I hear a few expletives coming from the bathroom, and I raise myself up on my elbows so I can look at the closed bathroom door.

"I can't pee!" he finally yells back.

"What do you mean you can't pee?"

Holy shit, it really IS broken. I knew I should have used it more these past few months. Son of a bitch! It broke from non-use.

"Seriously, you need to stop talking. You're making it worse."

"What the hell are you talking about? How am I making it worse?" I argue.

The door to the bathroom finally opens and he stands there with his hands on his hips and a tent in the front of his boxers.

"Because, your voice turns me on and I can't get rid of my fucking boner! I would never say this to you under normal circumstances but this is an emergency. So shut the hell up for a minute so I can pee!"

With that he goes back in the bathroom and slams the door closed behind him.

Well, at least it still works.

⊙ ⊙ ⊙

"Oh it was awesome once we got past Carter's freak out," I tell Liz the next day on the phone. "He was convinced the baby could see his penis and would either get jealous or have nightmares for the rest of its life about a penis monster trying to eat its face. Then he wanted to try and find a condom because he though his sperm might drown the baby. I actually had to bring my laptop into bed and show him that his penis would need to be two feet long for it to get anywhere near the baby."

Carter is working the day shift today and I'm spending the late afternoon taking down wallpaper in the room that will eventually be the nursery. I'd been at it for a few hours and was exhausted. I had taken a break to call Liz and report to her about how the rest of our evening went. Since she had constantly berated me the last few months about how often we WEREN'T having sex, I felt she deserved an update. After a few minutes we end the call and I decide to take a trip up to the local corner store to get one of my current pregnancy cravings: a black cherry slush. So far I've had one every single day since the day I found out. They are delicious and refreshing and the only place that sells the black cherry ones is the place right around the corner from our house.

I pack Gavin in the car and head down the street. Once inside the store, I make a beeline for the slush machine in the back, dragging Gavin along with me. I get to the machine and stopped in my tracks, staring at the sign that's taped to the front.

"Out of order? What do you mean, out of order?" I say out loud.

"It means it don't work," Gavin says.

"I know that's what it means. But it's a slush machine. It turns water into ice and you add cherry syrup to it. How hard can it be for a machine to do that?"

I see that the machine is still plugged in so I let go of Gavin's hand, grab onto it, and start jiggling it back and forth.

The power light doesn't come on so I start pressing all of the buttons over and over. When that doesn't work, I start smacking the side of the machine with the palm of my hand.

"Mom, you're gonna break it," Gavin warns.

"Stupid piece of shit machine. All you have to do is make ice you worthless pile of horse shit!" I say to it, completely ignoring Gavin.

Oh my God I need this slush. I need it like I need air to breathe. Why the fuck won't it just work!

At this point I'm pretty sure my brain has left my body. I continue to physically assault the machine, hitting it with my fists and cursing at it like it's a person who can fight back.

"Nothing to say for yourself, asshole? You can't even TRY to work? You lazy piece of shit. Get off your ass and make me a slush!"

People are starting to stare. I can feel their eyes on me as I rape the slush machine with my hands. I pull cords, I stick my finger in holes, and I remove the entire front cover, exposing all of the inner workings.

"Ma'am, I'm going to have to ask you to step away from the slush machine," a man in a corner store uniform tells me.

"Why the hell isn't your machine working? You need to fix the machine," I tell him, standing there with the cover of it in my hands like it's a shield.

"I'm sorry but there's a part that isn't working. We had to order a new machine and it won't be in until next week," he explains, prying the cover out of my hand and setting it aside.

"Next week? NEXT WEEK? What are people supposed to do for slushes if they have to wait a week?" I ask.

"God doesn't want you to have a slush," Gavin tells me.

I look down at him questioningly.

"God is king of the world and he says you don't need a slush. Can I get some ice cream?" he asks.

"God doesn't know. HE DOESN'T KNOW," I complain.

I'm pretty sure I'm having an out-of-body experience. I can see myself acting like a complete douchebag, but there is nothing I can do about it. I'm like a junkie that needs a fix. My hands are shaking, my head hurts, and I'm about two seconds away from selling my kid and my shoes for another hit of black cherry slush.

I take Gavin's hand, walk calmly out of the store, and drive home.

As soon as we get in the house I grab the phone and call Carter. He picks up on the first ring and all I can do is sob hysterically.

"OH MY GOD, CLAIRE?! What's going on? Is everything okay? Is it the baby? Did Gavin get hurt?" he shouts.

"The slush machine was broken!" I wail.

Dead silence on the other end.

"I'm sorry, what?" he asks.

"Did I stutter? The slush machine was broken. I couldn't get my slush. I need a fucking slush!" I cry.

"Wait a minute, this is all because of a slush?" he questions.

Oh my God, it's he doesn't know anything about me. How can I marry someone who doesn't understand me?

"I thought something serious happened," he says irritably.

"Something serious DID happen! Are you even listening to what I'm saying?"

Carter sighs and I try to calm myself by NOT thinking about how much I want a slush. Instead, I think about how I want to stick my fist up Carter's ass and give him a prostate massage with my fist.

"I'm getting off of work in a few minutes. My parents should be there in about an hour."

Oh shit. The future in-laws are in town for a visit. *Thank God I didn't get arrested at the corner store. That would have been awkward.*

"I'll bring you a slush on my way home," he promises.

"Black cherry?"

"Yes, black cherry," he confirms.

"I love you! See you soon!"

☉ ☉ ☉

Carter's parents show up right on time. Thankfully I finish my big gulp slush by then and can carry on a normal, non bat shit crazy conversation. Madelyn walks through the door first and tells us all to come in the living room and close our eyes because she has a surprise for us. A few seconds later, Charles says, "Okay, open them!"

Gavin and Carter let out excited yells and I groan.

"A puppy! A puppy! You got me a puppy! I can hug it and squeeze it and ride it like a bike and give it haircuts!" he shouts excitedly as he gets down on the floor.

The puppy, if you can call it that, is almost the same size as Gavin, and it looks like a polar bear.

"Is it even legal to own one of those?" I question. The more I look at the thing, the more I wonder if they really did just bring us an endangered animal that will grow to be nine-hundred pounds. Do you have any idea how big of a shit a nine-hundred pound animal takes?

"This is a pure bread Great Pyrenees," Madelyn tells me, expecting me to be impressed.

I'm not.

"Wow, this is awesome. Thank you guys so much. You know I've always wanted one of these," Carter tells them.

I look at him in shock. He's always wanted a horse for a pet? This thing is going to be bigger than our car.

"How exciting. We get to house-train a dog AND a new baby. Can they both be taught to shit outside? Or should we put a diaper on the dog? Pick one, because we're not doing both," I whisper to Carter as he pets the dog, and his parents take a seat on the couch.

"Don't worry. It will be fine," Carter whispers back as he stands up and lets Gavin run around the room with the dog playfully following behind him.

"The first time he shits in my shoes I'm going to rub *your* nose in it," I threaten.

"I have all of the American Kennel Club paperwork for you out in the car as well as the authenticity papers from the breeder," Madelyn tells us.

Super. Our dog has more class than we do.

"What's his name?" Carter asks.

"Reginald Phillip III," Charles answers.

"Oh, that's getting changed immediately," I mutter.

"I want to call him Bud," Gavin states as he runs around us in circles with the dog right on his heels.

"That's a good name," Carter tells him.

"I know. I'm naming him after the daddy juice you drink."

"How about we wait a little bit before deciding on a name," Carter tells him.

"Reginald Phillip, get down!" Madelyn scolds.

We turn around to see the dog mounted up on Gavin's back with his paws on his shoulders. Gavin just keeps moving and laughing. It looks like a freaky version of the locomotion dance.

"Ha ha. What's he doing?! This is fun!" Gavin laughs.

"Oh my God, he's humping our kid," I mutter, smacking Carter on the arm so he will do something.

Carter runs over and pulls the dog off of Gavin by its collar.

"Heeeey, why'd you do that? We were having fun," Gavin complains.

"Uh, he was trying to pee on you," Carter tells him.

I look at him like he's insane and he just shrugs. "What? I panicked. I can't tell him what humping means," he says quietly.

Gavin lets out another excited yell and once again, we find the dog hugging onto his shoulders and thrusting his hips behind him.

"Hump, hump, hump. I'm gonna pee on you! Hump, hump, hump!" Gavin chants as the two hop around the room and Carter tries to separate them again.

"Obviously you'll want to have him neutered as soon as possible," Madelyn states with a straight face.

Gee, you think? The dog is trying to breed with my son.

"All aboard the choo-choo train, all aboard the choo-choo train, WOOT WOOT!" Gavin sings with the dog happily enjoying his caboose position.

"Carter, get me the hose."

23.

Scittly Scat-Scat

Five months later.

"Last chance to change your mind. You're sure this is what you want to do," Carter asks as he starts the car and backs out of the driveway.

"I swear to God if you ask me that one more time, I'm going to straight up murder your ass. It's like you *want* me to wreck my vagina," I tell him.

Today is the big day. The one I have been equally dreading and looking forward to: my scheduled c-section. We are on our way to the hospital now so I can get checked in. Carter has been questioning my decision to have a repeat c-section since the day the doctor asked me about it six months ago.

"It's not that. I just want to make sure you don't regret never having the experience of actual childbirth. I've heard that some women who have c-sections get really depressed because they didn't get to know the joy of pushing their child out," Carter explains.

"I'm sorry, who are these women you spoke to? Did you make a trip to a mental hospital recently? What woman in her right mind would regret that her vagina didn't turn into a gaping, bloody wound with bodily fluids pouring out of it and a baby clawing its way out, sometimes ripping and tearing until her vagina and asshole are just one big disgusting abyss?" I ask.

"Forget I said anything. I just want you to be happy," Carter states diplomatically.

"Some women take a dump on the birthing table when they are pushing their kid out. Do you really think that's an experience *you* want to have?" I question. "I've heard the nurses make quick work of cleaning it up before anyone notices, but you'll notice. Believe me. How can you NOT notice the room suddenly smelling of fecal matter?"

"Stop, please stop," Carter begs.

"I am very happy with my decision. And you should be happy that six weeks from now, banging me won't feel like waving a stick in a cave or dipping your pinkie into the Grand Canyon."

"Okay, I get it," Carter says as he pulls into the hospital parking lot.

"Thrusting a pencil into a fireplace...shoving a piece of straw into a barn door," I add.

"Why am I getting turned on right now?" Carter asks as he finds a parking space and we get out of the car.

"Are you into scat play? You're not going to make me poop on you at some point are you? Tell me now so I can give you this ring back."

Carter ignores me as we get into the elevator and make our way up to Labor and Delivery. But I will not be ignored. Oh no, I will not be ignored.

"Scittly scat-scat, do bop dee scat!" I sing as we walk up to the nurse's station and hand them my admitting forms.

The nurse gives me a funny look so I feel it's only right to explain to her my song choice.

"My fiancé wants to me to poop on him," I tell her. "Scat-scat, dee didily bop!"

"Oh Jesus, I'm sorry. I don't know what has gotten into her this morning," he explains, shooting me a dirty look.

"It's perfectly fine." The nurse laughs. "It's just nerves. Believe me, I've heard worse from other women checking in." she told us.

What nerves? I'm not nervous. I've done this before. Piece of cake.

"We'll just get you settled into a room down by the O.R., start an I.V. of fluids, and have you fill out your registration forms. The doctor will come in and talk to you as well as the anesthesiologist. I'll stop by after that to give you a dose of Bicitra to drink. It's a small little cup of liquid that will help if you happen to get nauseous during the procedure. After that, it's go time!" she says excitedly.

What the fuck have I done?! Turn back NOW!

"I changed my mind. Maybe I do want a black hole for a vagina. How bad could it be? I wouldn't need to carry a purse anymore. I could just shove things up my twat. 'Oh, you need a pen? Hold on, let me check in my vagina. What's that you say? Do I have a flashlight? Let me stick my hand up my vag and find out.' Let's go home. We could do a home birth in the bathtub. It might be a tight squeeze but I bet we could both fit in there," I ramble to Carter.

"Can we get some morphine to go?" I ask the nurse.

She just chuckles as she shows us to the room and gets busy typing things into the computer while Carter pushes on my shoulders to get me to sit on the bed.

"Everything is going to be fine. Take a deep breath," Carter tells me.

"They are going to cut open my stomach and pull a human out, Carter," I whine.

"I know, babe. I'm nervous too. But you've done this before, and you know exactly what to expect. You know what it's going to feel like, you know how long it's going to take, and you know what the end result will be...finally being able to see our baby," he says with a smile as he leans down and kisses the top of my head. "At last we can find out if we'll have a Carmela or a Tony."

"Oh I don't think so. We've already had this discussion and we are NOT naming this kid after some ass munchers on the Sopranos. Get that thought out of your head right now," I tell him.

"You are such a killer of dreams, you know that?" he complains.

⊙ ⊙ ⊙

"Just remember, Carter, when the baby is out, we'll have you come down here to the foot of the operating table so you can take pictures and watch your little one get cleaned off, measured, and weighed. But don't forget, whatever you do, don't look at Claire," the doctor warns.

"What the hell is he talking about," Carter whispers, leaning down by my ear.

I'm strapped to the operating table with my arms stretched out in a T on either side of me. A huge, blue drape is attached to two I.V. poles on both sides of the table and placed strategically so I can't see past my boobs. When I had my c-section with Gavin, I wondered what the big deal was of putting this drape up. Maybe I wanted to see what was going on down there and make sure they didn't screw up. Then a few months later, I had watched a c-section on the medical channel and I almost threw up. NOT something you ever want to see being done to yourself, mark my words.

"I'm pretty sure they just don't want you to look over at me with my guts hanging out all over the place and freak out," I tell Carter.

"Okay, Claire, you're going to feel a lot of tugging now as we get the baby out," the doctor tells me.

I definitely remember this part from the first time. Not painful, but really fucking weird. Like someone is grabbing onto your stomach skin with both hands and yanking it all over the place. The fact that I know there's a doctor shoulder-deep inside my stomach right now is what's more painful.

Carter sits on a stool right by my head next to the anesthesiologist and keeps smoothing a few stray pieces of hair out of my eyes that have escaped from my hospital cap. He continues to ask me how I'm doing and kisses my forehead every few seconds, telling me how much he loves me and how proud he is of me. He is so strong, and I am once again reminded of how lucky I am to have this amazing man in my life.

"Okay, Carter, get your camera ready. When I say the word, you can stand up and aim your camera over the top of the sheet to take a picture," the doctor says.

"Try not to get my internal organs in the picture. They don't photograph well," I tell Carter.

He fiddles with the digital camera and gets it ready. I look back at his upside down face and see him smiling from ear to ear. Everything about this past year from the good and the bad to the ugly is all worth it because of this moment right here. Carter had missed out on seeing the birth of Gavin and that fact still makes me sad. But he is here now and I hope that seeing his next child born will ease a little of that ache for him.

"The baby's out! And it's a girl!" the doctor exclaims. "Get your picture, Dad!"

Carter jumps up and holds the camera above his head, quickly snapping a picture before sitting right back down and raining kisses all over my face while I cry.

"A girl? Are you sure? Is she okay?" I ask through my tears.

The next sound we hear is the wail of a healthy set of baby lungs.

Carter laughs through his own tears and continues kissing away mine.

"Oh, baby, you did it! I'm so proud of you. We have a girl!"

The anesthesiologist makes some adjustments to my I.V. now that the baby is out, and I momentarily wonder if would be okay for me to just start chanting "Morphine, morphine, morphine!" really loudly.

"Come on back, Dad, and see your little girl," one of the nurses says.

Carter gives me one more kiss on the cheek before he gets up and begins to walk around the I.V. pole to make his way to the end of the operating table.

"Carter, don't forget, don't look at my "

"OH JESUS CHRIST! IS THAT HER INTESTINES?? WHAT THE FUCK IS THAT? OH MY GOD!"

I hear the sounds of tennis shoes squeaking on the floor as nurses most likely race to Carter's side to get him away from the horror show.

"Oh fuck me, did I just step over a tube of blood that is draining out of her and into a bucket? What the fuck is that for?"

When you have a c-section, there's not much you can do but lie there and listen to the commotion going on around you. It's not like you could be all, "Hey, Doc, can you give me a minute? I need to get up and check on my fiancé and make sure he doesn't puke on our new baby." I had been given a spinal before this thing which meant I was numb from the neck down. I'm not any good to anyone right now.

"They told you not to look!" I shout to Carter.

"That is the number one thing you should never say to anyone! Of course if you tell me not to look, I'm going to look," Carter says as his voice gets closer and closer. Oh my God, Claire, I think I saw your spleen sitting on your chest."

The next thing I know, Carter is right next to me holding a tiny, perfectly wrapped bundle of baby. She looks like a little burrito wrapped tight in her white, blue, and pink hospital blanket and pink baby hat on her head.

Carter brings her right up to me and sets her down on the pillow next to my head so I can kiss her cheek.

"Oh my God, she's perfect," I cry as I stare at her sleeping face.

"Well, kind of perfect. I think she has Elephantitis of the vagina though," Carter tells me quietly.

I laugh and reach an arm over to stroke her soft, pink cheek.

"That's normal. All babies have enlarged genitalia when they're born," one of the nurses says as she walks past us to get something from a drawer against the wall.

"Oh yeah, you should have seen the size of Gavin's balls when he was born. Jesus. He could have fit a small country into those things," I say.

"Hey, maybe that's just the way he was supposed to be born. You know, taking after his father and all," Carter says as he leans down and kisses our little girl's cheek before kissing mine.

"Okay, Dad, if you want to go with your little girl down the hall to the nursery you can help give her her first bath and give the good news to your family members," the doctor says. "We'll have Claire down in recovery in about forty-five minutes. We just need to sew her up."

A nurse comes and scoops up our little girl and places her in the bassinet with a sign on the end that reads "Sophia Elizabeth Ellis, 7lbs, 10oz."

I refuse a Sopranos name, but I concede by letting Carter pick an Italian name.

"I love you so much," Carter tells me, cupping his hand on my cheek and leaning over my head to kiss my lips upside down.

I turn my head to the side and watched the love of my life walk behind the bassinet that holds our new daughter.

When they are gone, I close my eyes and try to enjoy the morphine coursing through my veins and count all of the amazing blessings I have been given. Unfortunately, I keep losing count. As the doctor sews me up, he and the nurses count out loud and it's very distracting. I had asked during Gavin's c-section what the hell they were doing and I was told that they have to count all of the instruments and sponges to make sure none are left behind. At the time, I thought it would be funny to start saying random numbers out loud to see if it would break their concentration. Two, seven, one, fifteen, thirty-five. But then I had realized it wasn't as funny if it was *my* body cavity they were losing these things in. It's hilarious when it's someone else, not so much if I have to go back to the hospital six months later because there's a pair of scissors stuck to my kidney or I'm shitting out sponges.

I block out the incessant drone of counting and think about just how perfect my life is now. I can't wait for Gavin to meet his new little sister, and I am actually excited to show her off to Carter's parents. It's a toss-up though on whether or not I'm so happy because I know the next four days will be spent getting waited on hand and foot with morphine and vicodin to cheer me up should I ever feel like slitting my own wrists.

The man I love more than anything wants to marry me, we have an amazing little boy who keeps us on our toes, a new, healthy baby girl, and the best family and friends. Okay, maybe not the best. Tolerable. Life is good. Nothing can take this feeling away right now unless the anesthesiologist turns off my morphine drip. I'll just take away his manhood if that happens. I'm sure the doctor can find an extra scalpel in my intestines for me.

"Wow, would you take a look at that?" I hear the doctor say.

"Oh my," one of the nurses replies.

"Uh, what's going on?" I ask.

"Can someone get me a camera?"

Okay, that's not something you need to hear when your stomach is cut open and you're strapped to a table.

Someone take this mother fucking sheet down. I don't give a rat's ass if I can see right through my stomach and out my vagina. I'll even help you stuff shit back in.

I can hear some whispering, which makes me a little uncomfortable. I mean, what could they possibly be whispering about? Is there another baby in there no one knew about? Have they found an extra stomach? Maybe I'm supposed to be a twin and I ate her. Have they found my twin sister? Is she looking at them right now like, "What the fuck, people? Get me the hell out of here. I'm twenty-five and I'm the size of a fist. Do I look like I'm comfortable?"

I have always wanted a sister. I can carry her around in my purse like Paris Hilton carries her dog. I can perch her up on my shoulder and she can be like the good angel telling me what decisions I should make.

What if she's mean though? Twenty-five years is a long time to be in someone's stomach. Jesus himself would probably even drop a few F bombs about that nonsense. She might sit on my shoulder and just shout insults at everyone.

"You're tired? Fuck you. I've used a uterus as a pillow for twenty five years."

"I've taken dumps bigger than your penis. And I had to do it in a stomach with a baby looking at me."

"You're so ugly I wouldn't even let you fuck my tiny, fossilized punany."

Mmmmm, this morphine is delicious. Like pot cookies and vodka but without all the weird side effects like hallucinations and crazy talk. I love morphine. It's so pretty.

"Oh, no worries," the doctor finally answers. "Your uterus is just in a weird shape right now. We have a wall of pictures in my office of people's organs and it's kind of like when you look up at the sky and guess what a cloud looks like. Except we do it in my office with pictures of afterbirth and uteruses. I'm just going to take a quick Polaroid and then finish sewing you up."

Nope, that's not at all weird. Doc, can you supersize that morphine for me?

"So, what does it look like?" I asked.

I don't really want to know the answer to this do I? The drugs say yes but the brain says no.

"It actually looks like a face. And it's smiling at us."

OH MY GOD, SISSY! I'm coming for you sissy!

"HOLY SHIT!"

Epilogue

"I think this will be the first bubble bath I've taken alone in three years," I tell Carter as he sets a glass of wine on the edge of the tub and bends down for a kiss.

I wrap a wet hand around the back of his neck and hold his face to mine. He sweeps his tongue through my mouth and I taste the wine he had taken a sip of before he gave the glass to me. Even after all these years I can never get enough of kissing this man. It's our third wedding anniversary and a few months after Sophie's third birthday. For the past three years, we've spent our anniversary the same way – at home with the kids. And I wouldn't have it any other way. We don't need a fancy restaurant or a night out with friends. We have all we need right here.

Our wedding had been just a simple ceremony on the beach with our family and friends. After all the drama about getting engaged, both of us realized we didn't care about anything but becoming husband and wife. It didn't matter where it happened, just as long as it *did* happen. For an early wedding gift that year, Carter had given me all four seasons of "My Fair Wedding" and a box of porn. He still holds out hope my porn addiction would become a reality.

Carter slides his hand down into the water and lets it rest on the inside of my thigh. As the kiss became more intense, his hand inches further and further down. I groan into his kiss as his fingers graze between my legs and make goose bumps break out on my skin.

"Happy anniversary, Mrs. Ellis," Carter whispers.

The wet, smoothness of his fingers slide through my slit and I thrust against his hand as he slowly pushes one finger deep inside me.

A commotion from outside the bathroom door ceases all activity and we pause, my lips brushing against Carter's and his hand resting between my legs.

"What was that?" I whisper.

"It's nothing. The kids are in Gavin's room playing. I gave them a piggy bank full of pennies to count," Carter reassures me as he begins kissing his way down my damp neck and goes back to gliding his finger in and out of me.

"Ohhhhh fuck," I moan, tilting my head back until it rests against the tile wall. "You should probably check on them. The penny thing worked when Gavin was four. I don't think it's going to work now. He's almost nine, knows how to use the internet and is tall enough to reach the matches and lighter fluid in the laundry room."

A crash and a yell sound down the hall and I sit up quickly, splashing water over the side of the tub, forcing Carter to fall back onto the floor on his ass.

"Shit. I'll go check it out," he says with a sigh as he stands up and opens the bathroom door. "We'll continue this after I've duct taped them to the wall."

He closes the door behind him and I lean back into the warm, soapy water with a smile on my face.

The past few years have been hectic, but I wouldn't change them for the world. A year after Sophia was born, we had moved into a new home. The small, ranch house was perfect when it was just the three of us, but once you had a baby, it came with a lot of shit. We had quickly outgrown that house and moved into a two-story colonial a few streets away from Liz and Jim.

Business at Seduction and Snacks is still booming. I've added more items to my menu so people can have breakfast or lunch there, and I've hired five additional people to the staff. Liz and Jim had just gave birth to their second baby girl last month and Jenny and

Drew are planning a weekend wedding in Vegas in a few months. I'm pretty sure that plan includes being married by Elvis and spending time in a lot of strip clubs. Jenny had finally found another job in marketing but still works for me on the side. She refuses to take any money from me though so I pay her in chocolate. Drew still begs me to pay her in sexual favors and is sadly disappointed every time I refuse.

Gavin is now eight and a half years old and getting ready to start third grade and our baby Sophie is growing up entirely too fast. She'll be going to preschool this year and I want to sob every time I think about it. Gavin is an amazing big brother and has spent the past three years teaching his little sister everything he can about tormenting us. The other day, Sophie had come into our bedroom and announced she had a song she wanted to sing us. It had gone a little something like this, "I have a vagina, vagina, vagina. I love my vagina, vagina, vagina." So far I haven't been able to convince her that this song should never be sung at the top of her lungs in the middle of the cereal aisle of the grocery store.

My father had married his long-time girlfriend Sue a few months ago in a small ceremony in his backyard. Gavin, Sophia, and Sue's granddaughter Sarah made up the wedding party. Sarah and Sophia were the same age and Gavin escorted both of them down the aisle. And by escorted, I meant kept the two girls separated since they kept trying to smack each other with their flower girl baskets as they walked until they eventually took Gavin down with them in a big pile of flailing arms, legs, screaming, and crying. Carter and I ran down the aisle and tried to break up the fight but Jesus, those girls were strong. Carter got kicked in the nuts and dropped down to his knees, and I got scratched in the face. Regardless, it was a beautiful ceremony and my mother, in her usual fashion, took control of Tee Time at the small reception. Jenny almost became "that person" who puked on the dance floor, but a cousin of my father's dragged her into the bathroom and showed her a trick where you drink straight from the faucet and then make yourself burp three times. Jenny had wound up making out with her as a thank you, and Drew passed out cold when he witnessed it.

I sink down further into the water and let out a big sigh. We've all come a long way since that frat party nine years ago. Carter and I still play a round or two of beer pong on the anniversary of when he asked me to marry him though. There are some traditions that you just can't put a stop to. Beer pong is how we started and beer pong is how we will end. I have a picture of us on our death beds years from now with a hospital table set up between us as we argue over who sucks more. And then that happy picture is ruined by Drew ambling in with a walker shouting, "Jenny can still suck a golf ball through a garden hose and she gums my cock like a champ since she misplaced her false teeth!"

I can't wait to see what the future will hold for us. We've had our ups and our downs, and we've had our fair share of struggles over the years, but we have proven that we can get through anything. Our beast of a dog, aptly named Gigantor, recently became a big brother himself when Carter's parents dropped off a cat for Sophie. Of course it had come with special hoity-toity cat papers that said it would walk around with a stick up its ass and demand to eat off of our good china. Since I nipped the whole Sopranos thing in the bud when we named our daughter, Carter had adamantly insisted we name the cat Meadow, after Tony Soprano's daughter. Aside from that, Carter has proven a thousand times over what a wonderful father he is. I had been a little nervous at first how he would handle having a little girl, but he was amazing and he was very protective of his daughter. So much so that my father had bought him a shirt that said "Sure you can date my daughter. In a completely unrelated topic, have you seen my shotgun?"

And now my wonderful husband is off taking care of the kids so I can relax in a bubble bath alone without someone coming in to pee, brush their teeth, or ask me why monkeys have nipples. Nothing can ruin this perfect moment or my happy mood thinking about the future.

"Hold still for a second. I need to get it in the right spot," I hear Gavin say softly on the other side of the door.

"What's going on out there? Where's daddy?" I shout out to him.

"He poopin', Mommy!" Sophie yells back.

Thanks for letting me know.

"You guys be good out there, okay? Mommy will be done in a minute," I shout to them as I picked up my wine glass from the edge of the tub and took a healthy sip.

I close my eyes and let the tension ease from my body until a few minutes later, words are loudly whispered by Gavin that you never want to hear on the other side of the door when you're taking a bath.

"Okay, the clothes basket is in the ready position at the edge. All systems go. Sophie, hold on tight. And don't let go of the cat."

The End

Troubles and Treats

A SILLY JOURNEY THROUGH A STICKY SITUATION

1.

You Ruined My Pens!

Candles – check.

Flowers – check.

Deodorant – *shit. Did I remember deodorant?*

Raising my arm above my head and taking a whiff, I find I am all good. Nothing left to do but wait for Jenny to get home from her night out with the girls. Ever since our son Billy was born three months ago, Claire and Liz have to force Jenny to leave the house every few weeks so she can go out and have a few drinks with them. I love my wife to death, but getting her to leave our kids for a few hours every once in a while is like pulling my dick.

Okay, not the best analogy since I've made dick-pulling into an art form. Think of something really hard (HA! That's what she said!) to pull and there you have it.

Taffy? Is taffy hard to pull? *Dat laffy taffy, shake dat laffy taffy… What a good song!*

Jenny had almost canceled tonight's outing too—which I absolutely could not let happen. I have a surprise planned and for it to work, she needs to be far away from the house for a few hours.

It had taken me an hour of me begging and pleading for her to agree to go and enjoy herself, followed by thirty minutes of her locking herself in our room, crying because she thought I was sick of her and just wanted to get rid of her, which made me wonder for the hundredth time: where the fuck did my fun, outrageous, sexaholic wife go?

Gone are the days of pulling over on the way home from dinner to bang in the back seat of the car. Vanished into thin air are the nights of putting anal ease on my junk to see if I could still feel my orgasm. I couldn't, by the way. Jenny also couldn't feel her tongue or her lips for eight hours. Don't try this at home, kids.

In fact, gone are the days of having sex *at all.* I have resorted to jerking off alone in the bathroom after my wife's asleep. It's a sad, lonely existence when you have to take your cell phone into the shitter so you don't wake your wife when you pull up the YouPorn app and crank one out. The worst part is the SpongeBob SquarePants shower curtain in the bathroom. Do you know how difficult it is to keep an erection while SpongeBob is staring at you with his big, googly eyes and you keep hearing the song "Jellyfishin', Jellyfishin', Jellyfishin'" in your head?

Okay, it's not that hard (yeah it is!), but still. It's the principal of the thing. Every night for the past year I've hunched over the toilet bowl with my cell phone in my hand, furiously yanking my wank and hoping I don't drop my phone into the water. Which only happened once, thank God. And you'll be happy to know porn still keeps playing under the water. It's a bit fuzzy and the sounds of "Ooooooh, fuck me harder!" sound more like, "Mwaaaa, mwaaa, mwaaaaagurgle!"

When our daughter Veronica was born three years ago, Jenny's already remarkable libido shot through the roof. It was like a dream come true. We had sex in the morning, for brunch at lunch, at night for a midnight snack, on the baby's changing table, in a Walmart bathroom, in three neighbors' pools and one neighbor's hot tub, and one really strange night that involved the jungle gym at the park, a free range chicken, and sparklers.

Jenny had been insatiable, and I actually wondered if my dick would fall off from overuse.

I'll tell ya, though, what a way to go. "Oh man, did you hear about Drew? His dick fell off. Yeah, just separated from his body and plopped to the floor. He just got done having monkey sex with his wife on the roof of their house though, so it's all good."

I honestly don't know what happened to make everything change. Billy had been a planned pregnancy so it's not like the shock of her getting pregnant again put a bucket of cold water on her vagina. It's like the day the stick turned pink, her lady bits put up a giant "Out of Business" sign.

Do not enter, closed for repairs, zombies will eat your face if you try to touch this vagina.

I've tried everything. I've whispered sweet nothings in her ear like, "My penis misses your vagina," and "I heard a rumor that your love canal misses my jizz." Nothing. I know, I can't believe it either.

I know Billy's pregnancy was a lot harder on her than Veronica's. She'd been sick a lot, and Veronica was in the middle of the Rotten-Horrific-Appalling-Terrifying-Twos. No, I'm not joking. Fuck the Terrible Twos. I half expected our sweet little daughter to cut off our heads while we slept at night and feed our bodies to rabid dogs while overdosing on ring pops and Lucky Charms. One minute she was hugging us and telling us she loved us and the next she was running around in circles screaming about sugar and throwing toys at our heads. Jenny was freaked out by Veronica's behavior and sick all the time from the pregnancy so sex had gone on the back burner. Like, the back burner twenty miles down the road at someone else's house back burner.

But tonight, I am going to fix it all. I am bringing sexy back, bitches!

I can't take one more night of playing pull and tug with SpongeBob. Aside from the fact that I've watched every single YouPorn video ever made—twice—I've also read every story on Erotica dot com, and when I started reading the stories just to see how they ended instead of for the sex scenes, I knew I was in deep shit.

I've spent the last few weeks trying to come up with the perfect plan. Carter had suggested I sit down and talk to Jenny about what's bothering me but that just seems like something a chick would do. I don't need to cry and talk about my feelings. I just need to have sex with my wife.

I'm too nervous to do anything but sit on the couch and stare at the door. At nine o'clock, Jenny's car pulls in and she's unlocking the front door.

"Where are the kids?" she asks as she closes the door behind her and glances around the living room.

"I put them to bed already," I tell her proudly.

Jenny is always nervous about leaving me home alone with the kids at bedtime. I seriously think she expects to come home to our daughter's hair dyed green from lime Kool-Aid and our son sucking on a black Sharpie after painting his face with it. That's only happened once but you'd think I burned the house down or sold them on the black market. And really, the fact that a three month old can draw a perfect Hitler 'stache on his upper lip and a Harry Potter lightning bolt on his forehead without a mirror is just fucking awesome.

I don't miss the smile falter from her face when she realizes the kids are already asleep and she won't get to do it herself. She rarely, if ever, misses a chance to bathe the kids and read a bedtime story to them.

I remember a time when she never missed a blow job. Ahhhhh, memories.

"Did you have a good time with the girls?"

She shrugs as she puts her purse and coat on the table in the foyer.

"It was okay. I wasn't up for drinking so Claire and Liz probably thought I was a board."

"You mean, they thought you were a bore?" I ask.

"I'm too tired to care," she says, flopping down onto the couch next to me and resting her head on the back cushions.

Shit! Claire and Liz had one job and one job only - get my wife drunk. I needed her drunk for this to work! They are so fired the next time I see them. Oh well, looks like we're doing this sober.

"I've got a surprise for you. Go on upstairs to our room and get comfortable," I tell her with a wink.

She looks at me funny for a minute and then pulls herself slowly off of the couch and makes her way up the stairs.

I sit on the couch practically bouncing up and down with excitement. I am like a kid on Christmas. I absolutely cannot wait for her to get upstairs and see what I did. Even sober I know she will appreciate this awesome gift. This is going to fix everything. I can feel it. With one awesome purchase from Liz's sex toy shop, I am going to cure the dry spell in our marriage. I am so fucking awesome I can't even stand it. She's going to take one look into the bedroom and announce that I should be nominated for Husband of the Year. I'll graciously accept the nomination and act like I have no idea just how amazeballs I am.

I'll probably need a speech and a tux, because you know, I'm kind of a big deal. "I'd like to thank the little people. And by little people, I mean the people out there still not having sex, who aren't the shiznit like I am."

I hear Billy let out a cry from his nursery, and I'm not gonna lie, I almost run up the stairs to ask him what the fuck he thinks he's doing. I've given him strict orders that he's not to make a sound after he went to sleep. It's like this kid didn't understand a word I said.

Billy's cries stop after a few seconds, and I say a silent prayer of thanks and give myself a reminder to buy him a new toy tomorrow to apologize for almost going into his room and calling him a cock blocking asshole.

I'm a little concerned that I haven't heard Jenny let out a happy scream yet, but I figure she just doesn't want to scare the kids or anything. Perfectly understandable. She's containing her excitement and waiting for me to come upstairs so she can thank me properly with her mouth on my schwantz. I approve of this message.

After I give Jenny a few more minutes to enjoy the surprise and get situated, I jump up from the couch, and take the stairs two at a time in haste to get to our room.

I run down the hallway with a grin on my face and push open the door to our bedroom with a raging hard-on just thinking about the night to come. I stop dead in my tracks at what I see and am unable to form any words that can describe the horror show happening right this very second.

"Drew, this is the best present ever! I love it!" Jenny whispers. "And the candles?! Oh my gosh, it's the perfect lighting to do this!"

I stand in the doorway of our room staring at the sight before me, and I want to fall down on my knees and weep. Not in the "Oh my God I'm so happy!" way either. In the "Oh my fuck, what is going on???" way.

After three hours of hard labor while Jenny was out, I had managed to install a sex swing in the corner of our bedroom. A sex swing to end all sex swings. This thing is the shit, and I almost had to crank one out in the middle of installing it. I couldn't stop picturing Jenny hanging in it, naked and waiting for me to rail her. I had to go to the hardware store three different times for materials and ended up removing part of the ceiling to reinforce the beams up there. I had to attach two-by-fours and consult five different guys who worked at the hardware store, all who were anxiously awaiting my return so I could give them a play-by-play of the evening.

Now, instead of waltzing back in there like a God to tell them about the hot sex we had suspended from our ceiling, I'm going to have to walk in there with my head down in shame. I'm not going to have an awesome story to tell about the cops being called because of strange jungle noises coming from our room or windows being broken because of swinging too hard. The only story I'm going to have is the one about me falling to my knees and sobbing like a girl.

When I close my eyes to sleep at night, I'm going to have to picture Jenny, fully clothed, holding our three-month-old son in her arms, rocking him back to sleep in our SEX SWING.

"But...that's my swing," I whine loudly and try not to stomp my foot.

"Shhhhhhh, I just got him back to sleep," Jenny whispers while giving me a stern look as she gently sways from side to side and stares lovingly down at Billy – IN MY MOTHER FUCKING SEX SWING!

"Sex...me...the swing...bad....sex...barf."

Nonsense. That's what is coming out of my mouth. Pure nonsense.

The gift that's supposed to rejuvenate our sex life has now become a new baby rocker.

Barf.

"Come over here and sit with me on the swing, Drew. There's plenty of room," Jenny says softly as she stares down at Billy.

Sit next to my wife on a sex swing and NOT have sex? I do not under-stand what is happening right now. Is she speaking English?

"No hablo SEX! Billy bad! Me want!" I complain, stomping my foot for real this time.

"Drew! What the hell is wrong with you tonight?" Jenny whispers loudly.

MY PENIS IS DYING AND MY EYES ARE BLEEDING! That's what's wrong with me, woman!

"You are ruining my present," she complains.

"You ruined my penis!" I complain back.

"I ruined your pens? What does that even mean? I never touched your pens."

Oh believe me, I'm well aware of how much you HAVEN'T touched my PENS. This whispering thing obviously isn't working.

With resignation, I pull my cell phone out of my pocket and head into the bathroom while I scroll through the newest Erotica dot com updates.

"Where are you going?" Jenny asks softly as she watches me take my walk of shame across the floor of our bedroom.

"To a backyard barbeque where Misty and her friend Buffy cornered their high school Science teacher in a bathroom and asked him to explain the theory of threesome-tivity," I mumble sadly.

2.

Negative, Ghost Rider

Jenny and I have been married going on…uh, something like four years. Or is it three? Our daughter Veronica is three and Jenny definitely wasn't knocked up at our wedding. So, three, take away the one, carry the two…eh, three years and some change sounds about right.

Our wedding was the shit! It was the most romantic, perfect day ever. Our friends and a few family members went with us to Vegas, baby! And the best part? You guessed it, we were married by Elvis. Not the real Elvis. Last I heard he was spotted somewhere in Piedmont, North Dakota. This guy was totally a fake, but he was still shitballs good. Jenny surprised me with a shirt to wear during the ceremony. In big, block letters it had the word "Groom" with a giant "X" through it. Underneath it was written: The Bride's Bitch.

I had known the first moment that I met Jenny I would be her bitch, and I am perfectly okay with that. If I wasn't with her, I'm pretty sure I would be in prison and belong to the dude with the most packs of smokes. This is way better. The day we met she had just finished throwing a sex toy party and sampled the merchandise a few minutes beforehand. I didn't know if it was the glow from her recent orgasm or not, but she was the hottest chick I had ever laid eyes on. I had immediately thrown away my man-whore card and stuck to her like glue.

Every day since that moment, I have never regretted one second I've spent with her. That makes it imperative I fix whatever problems we have as soon as possible.

"So how long HAS it been since you and Jenny had sex?" Jim asks.

The guys know all about the sex swing incident. As much as it had pained me to have to relive the horror of that night last weekend, they knew what I was planning and were expecting a full rundown of the events. The guys at the hardware store had a candlelight vigil for me earlier this evening. It really was a touching moment but it just made me all emotional and shit. When I had walked into work tonight and started sobbing uncontrollably, mumbling words like "*rocking*" and "*sleepy penis*" and saying, "*My kid is the spawn of Satan*," they knew the night didn't go as planned.

After telling them about my cock-blocking kid and showing them the Ziploc baggie filled with rice that had my cell phone nestled in it, they know it was a banner evening at the Parritt house.

"And more importantly, why is your phone in a bag of cooked rice?" Carter questions as he reaches across the table and fingers the contents of the bag. I smack his hand away and pull the bag closer to me.

We are on our lunch break at the automotive plant and seated at a corner table in the lunch room. The three of us still work the night shift, and there is nothing unusual about the fact that our "lunch break" occurs at 11:30 at night.

"I dropped my phone in the toilet," I mutter.

"Again?" Jim asks with a laugh.

"Shut up asshole. I was trying to scroll to the next page of the story. Fucking touch screen phones. And I wasn't even jerking off this time. I was sitting on the edge of the tub. It was a really good part of the story too. Buffy just recited the theory of threesometivity, and Misty was going to reward her for being so smart. I wanted to see if Misty was wearing the pink jean skirt and white tank top like in the story about their senior prom. It was a really cute outfit."

Both men stare at me for so long I'm pretty sure their faces might be frozen.

"You seriously need to get laid. Right the fuck now," Carter tells me. "And you're not supposed to use cooked rice, genius. Why the hell is it brown?"

I roll my eyes at him. The rice is obviously not the important part of this story.

"It's Uncle Ben's beef flavored rice. We were out of white," I explain. "Can we please focus here? What the fuck am I supposed to do?"

"Stop diddling your twigs and berries over a body of water," Jim deadpans.

"I don't diddle anything. I stroke lovingly. I like my penis. He's a good guy. And the berries are never involved in the stroking. Wait, do you guys play with yours?" I ask.

Jim shrugs as he takes a bite out of his bologna sandwich. "Sometimes I do. It's nice to incorporate the boys every once in a while so they don't feel left out."

"I agree. A little ball fondling goes a long way. It just depends where you are and if you can get the right angle to get down there and bring them up to the party. I like to give them a good cupping when I'm alone. Claire does this thing with her fingers where she pushes them up so that her mouth—"

Carter stops mid sentence when he hears me whimper.

"Sorry, man," he tells me sheepishly.

This happens a lot lately. Carter and Jim will start to tell some awesome story about the sex they have with their wives and then they stop when they realize I am sitting there staring at them, hanging on every word and dry humping the table leg.

"I don't fucking get it. You and Claire have two kids, you've been married for almost seven years, and you still have amazing sex. What the hell am I doing wrong?" I ask, pushing my lunch aside.

"I don't think you're doing anything wrong. I just think you guys are going through a dry spell. Everyone goes through it at some point," Jim reassures me.

"So you and Liz went through this?" I ask, feeling a little better about my situation.

"Oh, fuck no. We still bang like rabbits. By 'everyone' I meant other people," Jim states around a mouthful of chips. "But seriously, when was the last time you had sex?"

I sit there for a minute pretending like I am doing calculations in my head. There is no need for that shit. I know exactly how long it's been.

"Good sex, or sex-sex?" I ask.

"That's the dumbest question I've ever heard. We're men. All sex is good," Jim states.

"Negative, ghost rider. The pattern is full. If Claire doesn't get off, it's not good for me," Carter says.

"Did you just quote *Top Gun?*" Jim asks him.

"Um, yes. Best mother fucking movie ever. I feel the need, the need, for speed!" Carter shouts with a fist pump.

"Okay, Homo McFaggy. If you think a bunch of shirtless, sweaty men playing beach volleyball is awesome, I'm going to need you to turn in your wings, Cougar. Your straight-man wings," Jim states.

"Fuck you."

"Obviously. I thought I caught you sneaking a peak at my F-14 the other night when we were pissing. Do you and Claire role play in the bedroom? Does she call you Iceman and you call her Maverick?" Jim asks with a laugh.

"HELLO!" I shout. "Man with a problem here. Can we get back to something important please?"

"Sorry, but I do believe discussing Carter's sexual orientation is important," Jim says as Carter reaches over and punches him in the arm.

"Okay, back to the original question. How long has it been?" Carter asks. "And I'm not talking about the 'just the tip' night after Billy was born. I'm talking full contact, all the way home, screaming for your mommy sex."

"If I recall correctly, the screaming for your mommy sex is only had by you, Carter," Jim says with a laugh.

"Fuck off! I did NOT scream for my mommy. I was trying to propose to Claire," he argues.

"Twelve months, thirteen days, nine hours, and thirty-seven minutes," I tell them, glancing across the room at the clock hanging on the wall. "Sorry, thirty-five minutes."

"Jesus Christ," Jim mutters with a look of horror on his face.

"You know that off the top of your head?" Carter asks.

"You two assholes try NOT having sex with your wives and get back to me on whether or not you keep track," I complain.

"Have you tried talking to her about it, like I suggested?" Carter questions with a smug look on his face.

"Yes, I have, so shut the fuck up."

The loud speaker breaks into our conversation and informs us we have five minutes left before the production line will start back up. We all stand and gather up the remnants of our lunches from the table and head across the cafeteria to the doors that lead out to the plant.

"Did you talk to her like you normally talk to her or did you try doing it without being a douche?" Jim asks as he tosses his garbage into the can.

"Shut up. I'm not a douche when it comes to my wife," I argue.

"Really? Because I recall you asking the Elvis impersonator at your Vegas wedding if he could add a line to Jenny's vows that said, 'I promise to always give blow jobs with a smile on my face and love in my heart,'" Jim reminds me.

"What? That's a legitimate wedding vow that should be a part of everyone's wedding ceremony," I argue. "Do you want a wife who gives blow jobs with a frowny face?"

We make our way across the plant to our spot on the production line, and Jim follows us even though he is supposed to be on the other side of the plant at a foreman meeting.

"Okay, you have a few options. One, you can actually sit down with Jenny and straight up ask her why she never wants to have sex with you anymore. And by talk, I mean ask her in a loving, nice way if something is bothering her. Always ask about her well-being first. If you make this all about you and your neglected Johnson, you'll get nowhere. You have to make her feel like you care," Jim explains.

"But I do care. I care about how she's doing and how she's feeling."

"Yeah, okay. But I'm pretty sure at this point, you care more about how she's feeling about your penis," Jim says.

"True story," I agree sadly.

"So, do not use the words: *bang, anal, blow job, just the tip,* or *it makes him smile when you kiss it,*" Jim tells me.

"What the fuck am I supposed to say then? Those are all the good ones," I complain.

"Yes, all the good ones you used when you conned her into having sex with you six weeks after Billy was born. I do believe she took 'just the tip' literally and you told her, 'If your vagina is sore after having Billy chew his way out, I'd be fine with anal,'" Carter adds.

"I still don't see what was wrong with that. I was trying to be nice and make her feel better."

After not having sex her entire pregnancy and then having to wait another six weeks for her floppy bits to fuse back together, I had been desperate. Telling her about all the nightmares I was having of seeing Billy crowning during the delivery probably wasn't my finest hour. But she cornered me in the middle of the night when I woke up screaming from another bad dream. I had been half asleep and could not be held responsible for the things I said. I knew comparing the birth of our son to the movie *Alien* when that little monster tears his way out of that dude's stomach was a bad idea, but I wasn't fully awake yet! Picture the blood, the gore, the slime, and the goo as this little freaky thing rips someone's stomach open to get out. Now picture that happening with your wife's vagina. The vagina you've touched, sucked, licked, and worshiped for years. It took a little time to separate the two.

Jenny had a c-section with Veronica, and I didn't see anything that happened below her neck. I remembered crying tears of joy when they handed Veronica to us and the nurse helped me put on her first onesie that read: Watch your fucking language, There's a goddamn baby in the room. I stared back and forth between Jenny and our little girl and I knew I had never been happier.

With Billy, the doctor gave her the go-ahead to try and have him naturally since her c-section with Veronica was due to a drop in Veronica's heart rate and not because Jenny had any life-threatening complications. And so Jenny decided she wanted to experience real child birth. And it was horrific. It should have been beautiful and amazing, watching the woman I love give birth to our son, but it wasn't. There was screaming and crying and profanities and that was just from me. You didn't even want to know what Jenny screamed when she saw I had wandered down to the foot of the birthing table and put my face right in front of the action. And once I got there, I couldn't move. I was like a deer caught in the headlights. Or a man caught in the slaughter of his wife's vagina. I expected to turn and see her OB with a butcher knife in his hand because of the mess down there. There had been so many things leaking out between her legs I didn't know what the fuck was going on or how one vagina could pour that much gunk out of it and still be alive. Her vagina should have drowned.

Telling all of this to Jenny at three in the morning a few weeks after Billy was born might be one of the reasons why we're having problems. Talking to her again about something so monumental right now doesn't seem like the best idea.

"What else you got," I ask Jim as the line powers up and I pull my hydraulic drill down from its perch on the shelf above my head.

"Well, you could always ask your dad to tail her. Maybe she's hiding something from you," Jim says nonchalantly before he walks off to his meeting.

My dad is a private investigator who specializes in cheating spouses and workman's comp fraud. Since I am fairly certain there is no way Jenny was guilty of *one* of those, it leaves the other a distinct possibility.

Oh my gosh, could this really be the problem? Why didn't I ever think about this before?

I am immediately appalled that my sweet, loving Jenny could do something like this and that she's been lying to me this whole time.

Why hasn't she told me? Why, God, WHY?

The reason my wife doesn't want to have sex with me anymore is because she has a fake injury she never told me about and now she is trying to milk her boss, Claire, out of money to pay for her fake recuperation.

3

Baste in the Glory

"Wait, Drew installed a baby rocker to the ceiling? That doesn't sound right," Claire says as she signs the stack of invoices I've printed out for her.

When I had lost my job seven years ago at the computer design company I worked at since college, my best friend Claire asked me to help out at her chocolate shop that she shared with my other best friend Liz. After a few months of handling all of the marketing and computer design for her, I had found another job but still helped Claire out when I could. After Veronica was born, I knew I didn't want to do the whole nine to five thing anymore. Claire had asked me to work full time and Liz had begged me to help her as well.

It's been three years and I am now the marketing manager of Seduction and Snacks, which has grown by leaps and bounds. A few years ago, Claire and Liz had decided to turn their business venture into a franchise. There are now ten Seduction and Snacks stores located throughout the south.

Or is it west? I can never remember. I'm not good at geology...or genealogy...or that other thing that starts with a "g" and ends in a "y".

Luckily, since Claire and Carter have two kids, Liz and Jim have three, and Drew and I have two, we are all very family-oriental. The kids are all at the shop at some point during the week, and I can work from home whenever I need to, making up my own hours as I go along.

524

"Yes! It was the coolest thing I've ever seen. It was like these straps that almost look like seat belts and they hung down from the ceiling and I could sit right in it and hold Billy. There were these weird hole things made out of the straps that you were supposed to stick your legs in I guess, but I didn't get what the point of those were for so I didn't use them. And it didn't really have a back on it so I just leaned against the wall when I wasn't rocking. You should have seen how quickly I got Billy to fall back to sleep. It was awesome," I explain as I take the signed invoices and start scanning them into the computer.

"Good morning, hookers!" Liz states as she breezes through the connecting door of Seduction and Snacks and takes a seat on the small couch in the office. "Did you get a chance to print out the order that's coming in next week? I need to make sure I got enough strawberry gag reflex gel. I swear to God, I think Mrs. Molnar drinks that shit like water. Either that or she just needs buckets of numbing gel to get Big Balled Bob's one huge nut down her throat."

We all shudder at the though of Mr. Molnar and his penis. He had come into Liz's store a few weeks ago to tell us about his open heart surgery and somehow ended up showing us not only the scar that ran down the middle of his chest but the effect the anesthesia had on his junk. One of his balls swelled to four times its normal size. It had looked like a grapefruit hugging a toothpick with a sad, lonely prune stuck to the side.

"Can we please not talk about Big Balled Bob this early in the morning? I had a good night last night and want to baste in the glory of it," I tell them.

"Bask. It's BASK in the glory," Liz corrects me.

"Oh whatever. You know what I meant."

People are always teasing me because I get words wrong. I'm really not a dumb person. I know what I want to say in my brain, but by the time it travels to my mouth it usually gets mixed up.

"So what happened last night after your lame-ass left us at the bar?" Liz questions. "Wait!! Oh my gosh! I totally know what happened, you little slut! Drew finally gave you his present, didn't he?"

I look at Liz in confusion.

"How did you know about the present Drew got me?" I ask.

"Duh! He bought it from me," Liz says as she gets up from the couch to pick up a piece of paper from the printer and look it over.

"Wait, that was yours? Did you use it with all three girls? I don't remember you mentioning it," I ask as I power down the computer.

"What the fuck are you talking about? What girls?"

"Uh, your *daughters*? What other girls would I be talking about?" *And Liz thinks I'M the dumb one.*

Liz sets the paper down on the desk and puts her hands on her hips.

"Why in the hell would I ever use something like that with my daughters? That's gross," she states.

Gross? Why the hell would it be gross?

"Oh my Jesus," Claire mutters, covering her mouth with her hand and staring at me with wide eyes.

And then she starts laughing uncontrollably. She bends over at the waist and wraps her arms around her stomach.

"Oh God! I can't! Oh Jesus, it hurts!" she says through her snorts and giggles.

"What the hell is so funny?" I demand.

"Yes, enlighten us, Claire," Liz states seriously. "A swing like the one Drew gave Jenny is no laughing matter. That thing is top of the line. He shelled out a lot of cash for that thing."

"Holy hell! This is the best day EVER!" Claire laughs as she finally stands backup and wipes the tears from her eyes.

"Why did you say it was gross? What is gross about a baby rocker? Did someone puke on it or something?" I ask Liz. "You didn't feed the girls naked on it or anything, did you?"

This just throws Claire into more fits of laughter and causes Liz to stare at me with a horrified look on her face.

"Oh dear God. Please tell me you didn't. No...just...no," she says.

What the hell is everyone's problem? This was the sweetest thing Drew did for me in a long time and they're laughing at it.

"I don't even want to tell you now. You're just going to make fun of Drew for being so thoughtful," I complain.

"Oh, no. You have to tell Liz just how *thoughtful* Drew was. Please. Please tell Liz how super your evening was after you left us. Say it slowly and don't leave anything out," Claire begs with a huge smile on her face.

I roll my eyes at how ridiculous the two of them are acting about a baby rocker.

"Fine. But not a word out of either of you."

They both pretend to zip their lips and throw the key away.

"You guys know how tired I was when I left the bar last night. Billy still isn't sleeping through the night and it takes me forever to get him back to sleep. So, when I got home, Drew told me he had a surprise for me upstairs. I thought it would be another one of his lame excuses to try and have sex."

Claire snorts and then plays it off like she's choking when I shoot her a dirty look.

"I get upstairs and of course Billy chose that moment to wake up crying. I got him out of his crib and walked over to our room and saw that Drew lit a bunch of candles. I've been complaining about how the nightlight we have is too dark to see by when I feed Billy in the middle of the night and the candles were just perfect. I walked over to the corner of the room where I have the glider so I could rock him and in its place was a baby rocking swing that hung from the ceiling," I finish, giving both of them a smug look.

Let's see them make fun of Drew now. My husband is a giant man-child, but sometimes he does sweet, unexpected things. It's been awhile since he's done them but this makes up for it.

I stare at Liz expectantly, waiting for her to apologize for being rude.

"Hold on a second. I need a minute," Liz says as she grabs Claire's elbow and turns so that they both face away from me.

I roll my eyes at their backs.

"It's not working. I can see your shoulders shaking. I know you guys are laughing."

The girls compose themselves and turn back around, trying to keep straight faces.

"So, you guys didn't have sex last night?" Liz questions in confusion.

"No! I told you, I was tired and then Billy woke up when I got home. But oh my God, that rocker was THE BEST! He went right back to sleep, and I actually fell asleep in it too. Now I know why you never told me about it when the girls were babies. You were afraid I'd try and steal it from you. No wonder they were such good little sleepers."

Liz nods her head and closes her eyes, holding one hand up in the air as if to say, "STOP!"

"Sorry, I think I need another minute," she says before mimicking Claire's earlier pose and bending over at the waist to guffaw at the ground.

"What the hell?" I yell.

"I think what Liz is trying to say is that you rocked your baby to sleep in a SEX swing," Claire says with a giggle.

I stare at her blankly.

"A. SEX. SWING. From the Latin words, 'you are supposed to fuck in it, not rock your kid to sleep'," Claire states.

"What she said!" Liz laughs as she stands back up and then covers her eyes with her hands. "Oh highway to heaven, I can't even look at you right now!"

Oh. My. God.

"I rocked my son to sleep in something that people bang in?" I whisper in a horrified voice.

"Well, yes. That's why it's called a sex swing," Claire offers.

"Did you actually put your thighs in the stirrups?" Liz laughs.

"Stirrups? Oh my God. I used those to hold the extra bottles," I complain.

"Oh God, here we go again!" Claire says, bending over and laughing so hard she starts dry heaving. "I'M GOING TO PUKE!" she yells in between heave-laughs.

"I hate both of you. You are both jerks."

I feel awful. Not just because my friends are jerks, but because my husband had tried to do something kinky and fun and I ruined it.

What the hell is wrong with me?

I used to be fun and outgoing and kinky as hell. Me, of all people, should know what a sex swing is. I had made a mold of my vagina and gave it to Drew on one of our anniversaries for God's sake. We had even made an amateur sex video and submitted it to YouPorn. Without our faces of course. There are certain things my grandma should never see. Although why my grandmother would be on YouPorn when she's clearly over the age of legally having sex is beyond me. Isn't seventy when they say you have to pass a test to keep having sex? Or maybe that's for your driver's license. No, I'm pretty sure it's for sex. Regardless, a sex swing is something I should have first-hand knowledge of.

Stuff like this has been happening more and more lately, Drew attempting to spark something between us, and me not knowing what to do or having no interest in it. My friends have the most perfect marriages and sex lives, and they were able to raise their kids while doing it. Drew and I had managed to do pretty well after Veronica was born a little over three years ago. Our marriage strengthened and we had sex all the time. As soon as I got pregnant with Billy, though, everything stopped. Suddenly, I had to juggle a toddler in potty training hell with a pregnancy that kept me puking almost the entire time and a full time job.

It's not that I don't want my husband or don't love him, sleep just takes priority. Even though the job is flexible, there's still a lot of work that needs to be done. Not to mention the fact that Drew works the night shift, and I'm stuck doing most things alone in the evening.

I never used to have any trouble getting up at four in the morning when he had come home from work for a quickie. I loved having sex with him while I was half asleep and still warm from being under the covers half the night. The first time he tried it after I found out I was pregnant with Billy, I told him if he brought his penis anywhere near me, I would tell all his friends about how he wore my silk thongs to work because he liked how they slid through the crack of his ass when he bent over. Any time after that when, he would get his penis within five feet of me, I would run to the bathroom and throw up. I was pretty sure he took defense to that. It wasn't my fault the sight of his penis made me sick to my stomach. He has a very pretty penis, actually, and I even drew a picture of it once. There had just been something about how it looked like a jellyfish with one eye that made me queasy. Once Billy was born, I had just been too exhausted to even think about sex.

Our son STILL doesn't sleep through the night. Right now, I just want a full night of sleep more than I want sex. Okay, I'll take that back. I *do* want sex. Just not at appropriate times. Every time I want it, Drew's either sleeping or he's at work. It never happens when we're in the same room together. I can't even masturbate right anymore. The last time I tried, I fell asleep with my vibrator in my hand. While it was still running.

Drew had come home from work and found me sprawled out in bed with my arm flung off the side, clutching a big pink vibrator that was slowly losing juice. Instead of sounding like *wirrrrrrrrrrrrrrrr*, it sounded more like, *wirr-rrr-wirrrr-r......rr*. I couldn't help that the vibrations lulled me to sleep. Now I knew why babies loved their vibrating bouncy seats. Drew got excited when I loaded up on double-A batteries at the grocery store that week, and I made sure my nightstand was fully stocked with them. I was pretty sure I could hear him weeping in the bathroom when he found out I just needed them so I could stick my vibrator under the mattress to help me fall asleep faster. At least I thought he was weeping. He had made some really funny sounds and when I had knocked on the bathroom door, he said he was busy reading.

I need to do something to re-erect our love life.

Re-erect? Is that a word? That's the word I'm looking for, right? Whatever.

First, I need to do something to get myself in shape. Three months post-baby and I still feel big as a house. I lost all the baby weight pretty quickly, but I still feel like my ass is huge. I also need to do something about my vagina. There is no way it feels the same to him when we have sex. Although, we haven't really had sex since Billy was born. I let him get halfway in and then he made some comment about my sloppy vagina and I told him to get off of me. Plenty of women have natural child birth and they don't have floppy vaginas. I've looked it up on the internet. I've tried to look at mine with a mirror and my leg up on the sink of the bathroom. That had been right after I got home from the hospital with Billy though and it was a hot mess. I probably should have waited a few more weeks, but now I can't look at raw ground meat without crossing my legs and wincing.

Basically, I'm afraid to have sex with my husband. He's always loved my vagina. He even has a shirt that says: I love my wife's vagina. What if having sex with me now is like fucking a bowl of Jell-O Jigglers? That is not at all hot, especially if they're green Jell-O Jigglers. I'm not saying my vagina is green, but I'm sure it's jiggly. I shook it a little when I had looked at it in the mirror and it definitely wiggled when it jiggled. Vagina's should never jiggle.

I am going to leave work early and go to a yoga class. Getting my body in shape might help make me feel better and then I can work on getting Drew to help out more around the house so I'm not so tired all of the time. Drew doesn't work tonight so he's home with the kids all day. Maybe a little bending and stretching will get things back to where they're supposed to be, and I won't have to worry about the lips of my vagina hanging low and wobbling to and fro. You should never be able to tie them in a knot OR a bow.

4.

Downwind Lapping Dog

"HE CALLED SHIT, POOP!"

I laugh out loud and put up my hand so my daughter can give me a high five.

I can't help but laugh whenever Veronica quotes her and her brother's namesake movie: Billy Madison. We are curled up on the couch together, watching the best movie of all time, and Billy is asleep in his swing a few feet away.

Jenny walks in the door a few minutes later. Actually, she limps in the door and hobbles across the room until she makes it to the couch and sits down on the other side of Veronica, giving her a kiss on the head.

"Mommy, you gots a boo-boo?" Veronica asks her.

I stare in horror at Jenny as she pulls the footstool closer and props her leg up on top of it, leaning back into the couch and pulling Veronica onto her lap.

Oh my God. This is it. This is the fake injury. How should I play this? Should I call her out immediately and tell her she's a big, fat liar? Wait, never call a woman fat. Especially after pregnancy, even if you're just joking. Lives will be lost. Maybe I should just play along and keep my cool.

"Yes, mommy has a boo-boo," Jenny replies with a sigh.

"HA HA! YOU GOT HURT!" I yell.

Jenny gives me a dirty look and I quickly wipe the smile off of my face.

What the fuck was that? I shouldn't be happy if she's injured, right? Play it cool, man. Play it cool.

"I mean, that sucks that you got hurt. You hurt yourself. That's just sucky. I mean, because you know, you hurt yourself."

533

There. Much better. Be calm, be cool. She'll never know you suspect anything.

Jenny's dirty look never leaves her face and I start to squirm. "You couldn't have picked up a little today? This house is a mess."

I look around at all of the toys on the floor and the dirty dishes on the coffee table.

"We were busy watching movies," I explain.

She turns and looks at the TV, noticing for the first time what we're watching.

"You have seriously got to quit watching this stupid movie. Veronica doesn't stop quoting it as it is," Jenny complains with a sigh.

This worker's comp fraud has already changed her! She used to love this movie. Nooooooooooo!

"So, how did you hurt yourself? You know, when you really hurt yourself," I ask, folding my hands in my lap and acting concerned.

She can't know that you know. What if it's like that TV show, When Animals Attack? She might just come at you, bro.

"Well, I decided to leave work a little early and try a yoga class. It turns out I'm not as flexible as I used to be," she tells me.

Is yoga her code word for something? Is that what she's calling "sticking it to the man" now? I wonder if she has a group of minions working for her, helping her with this elaborate lie. Yoga – yeah right!

"I tried doing that Downwind Lapping Dog thing and I twisted my ankle," she finishes, resting her head on the back of the couch and closing her eyes.

See? I totally caught her in her lie. Downwind Lapping Dog isn't the name of a yoga move. It's a Chinese proverb or something, like, "He who fart in church sit in stinky pew." I think it goes, "He who is downwind of lapping dog make bump-bump in pants."

"So does Claire know? Did you tell Claire? What did Claire say?" I question.

"No, why would Claire know? After class I just wanted to get home and put my foot up. I haven't had a chance to talk to her yet."

Ahhhh, so she's biding her time, formulating a plan. I got ya.

Jenny picks Veronica up from her lap and sets her back down next to her, pushes herself up off of the couch, and starts hobbling towards the kitchen.

"Where are you going?" I ask.

"I need to get some ice for my ankle," she replies as she uses the wall to support her as she goes.

Wow, she's good. She really thought this through. I would have never thought to go get ice. That limp kind of looks real too. She must have been practicing.

I jump up and go to her side in a show of "helping" her with her "injury", when really, I just want to see if I can trip her up.

As I help her walk into the kitchen, I stick my foot out in front of her and she stumbles over it, grabbing onto the table at the last minute before she falls to the ground.

"Drew! What the hell? Did you just trip me?" she yells.

"How's your ankle?" I ask, staring down at the foot suspiciously as she holds it a few inches above the floor.

"What is wrong with you today? You're acting weird," she mutters before using one of the chairs to help her stand and then hops over to the freezer to grab an ice pack.

"I'm onto you, Jenny," I tell her menacingly.

"What the hell are you talking about?" she asks as she sits at the kitchen table, brings her foot up to a chair, and sets the ice pack on top of her ankle with a wince.

Man alive, how is she so good at this? I never knew she was such a good faker. Oh Jesus, what if this isn't the only thing she fakes? Oh my God. This is why she never wants to have sex with me. She's tired of faking it!

"You're faking it when you have sex with Claire and now you want to cheat me out of my money! Sons a bitchin!" I yell, before stomping out of the room.

☉ ☉ ☉

In hindsight, I'm pretty sure I can pinpoint exactly where I went wrong with Jenny. I blame it all on natural childbirth. No man should ever have to see his wife in that position. No man should ever have to look at a live vagina in that position. Although a dead vagina in that position would probably be just as bad because it would be dead. A dead, gooey vagina. It's a sight you can never un-see.

The day had started off fairly well. Jenny was a week overdue so the doctor had her check into the hospital first thing in the morning so she could be induced. We took Veronica with us since the day would mainly consist of us sitting around waiting for something to happen. Carter and Claire agreed to take her home with them for a sleepover once things started progressing. We did everything we were supposed to do so Veronica wouldn't hate her brother at first sight. We included her when we picked out the name, we let her help decorate the nursery, we brought her to the hospital, and we had a present hidden in Jenny's overnight bag that would be given to Veronica, "from her brother", as soon as he was born - everything necessary so she wouldn't step on his nuts and call him a shitbag when she saw him. Considering that was the name she picked for him, calling him that at first sight actually wouldn't have been that weird. It was her new favorite word, and it was a hard sell to get her to pick another name out for him when we were going through the baby name book.

"But I wanna call him Shitbag! Baby is a shitbag!"

It was kind of hard to be mad when she strung together her first swear word sentence. It really was a proud day for me.

Around lunchtime on the day of delivery was when things got serious. And by serious, I mean seriously fucked up. Jenny's contractions went through the roof and the woman I like to refer to as "Crazy-Ass Bitch" made an appearance. And I mean that in the nicest way possible.

"WHERE THE FUCK IS THE GUY WITH THE DRUGS?"

I put my hands over Veronica's ears and stared in horror at my wife. Jenny never yelled or cursed in front of Veronica. Ever. She raised her voice at times, but it was usually just because someone couldn't hear what she was saying. This was a whole new side of her I wasn't used to.

"The nurse just paged him like two minutes ago, baby. He'll be here soon," I reassured her as I removed my hands from Veronica's ears.

"FUCK YOU!"

I glanced at the contraction monitor and saw that the little squiggly lines were so far off of the top of the page that the thing was flashing a red warning light.

"Breathe, baby. Just breathe. Think about something else," I told her.

"I'M THINKING ABOUT SHOVING YOUR BALLS STRAIGHT UP YOUR ASS, YOU SHIT HOLE!"

Out of the corner of my eye, I saw Carter and Claire standing in the doorway with equal looks of horror on their faces.

"Um, so we'll just come back later," Claire said as she quickly darted in the room, scooped up Veronica, and made a mad dash back to Carter whispering, "GO, GO, GO!"

With Veronica out of earshot, I walked over to the side of the bed and tried smoothing hair off of Jenny's forehead and telling her it would be okay, but she bit off my hand.

And that wasn't an exaggeration. She literally leaned over and clamped her teeth around the palm of my hand.

The doctor had showed up a few minutes later, but when he told Jenny he wasn't the one with the drugs, I actually feared for the poor guy's life. Then he had told her he needed to break her water to really get things going.

What has been happening in here for the last hour? A mother fucking tea party?

I really wish I could erase this part of the story because I look like a giant douchebag, and if I could take it back, I would. But I guess it's necessary for you to understand everything.

The doctor had ripped open a package and pulled out what could only be described as a crochet hook. It was a long stick with a hook on the end, and it instantly made me laugh when I looked at it.

The doctor went to the end of the bed and asked Jenny to spread her legs. And before you ask, yes, I laughed at this too.

"Hey, hon, looks like the doctor is going to do some knitting while he's down there between your legs," I joked. "I bet you he could make a blanket for ten people with all that long-ass pube hair you got going on."

Can you hear that? That's the sound of my nuts being clamped in a vice.

After the doctor broke her water, and I apologized profusely for not shaving her ridiculously long pubic hair before she gave birth, it was back to the waiting game. No, not waiting for the baby to be born, waiting for the god dammed drugs.

"I don't think we should name him Billy," Jenny stated in between breaths as she "heeee-ed" and "hoooooo-ed" and "hee-hee hoo-hoo-ed" through the pain.

"What are you talking about?" I asked her in horror as I paced back and forth over by the door. My nuts still hadn't recovered from the pubic hair crack so there was no way I was getting within five feet of her right now.

"Who names their kids after a stupid movie?" she questioned as she took a big sigh of relief when the contraction ended.

"You must be delirious from the pain. That is the only excuse for the nonsense coming out of your mouth right now."

She glared at me and I instantly covered my nuts with my hands. I wouldn't put it past her to pick up the phone, yank it from the wall, and chuck it at my dong.

"Did you just call me an idiot?" she questioned softly.

I really should have just run right then...turned around and darted out of the hospital room and down the hall until I reached the ward with all the comatose patients who wouldn't scream at me.

"If it walks like a duck and talks like an idiot, then yes, yes I did," I told her boldly, putting my hands on my hips.

Mistake number two.

Jenny's cell phone smacked against my junk two seconds later, and I squeaked out a groan and clutched onto the boys.

"Cheese and crackers! That hurt! Dude, *Billy Madison* was the first movie we ever watched together. And it is the greatest movie of all time. There is no way we are naming our son anything other than Billy. We already have a Veronica, named after his hot teacher, Miss Veronica Vaughn. We can't leave our daughter hanging like that. Think of the children," I pleaded. "Do it for the children."

"You don't love me anymore, do you?" she wailed as tears started running down her cheeks and she put her head in her hands.

Sweet Jesus what is happening right now?

I rushed over to her bedside and wrapped my arms around her while she cried.

"Hon, of course I love you. Calm down," I told her.

"YOU FUCKING CALM DOWN! I'M SITTING IN A PUDDLE OF MY OWN UTERUS WATER!" she yelled.

I tried to hold it in, really I did, but I couldn't. I dry heaved. It was just…uterus water. Water from her uterus. She was sitting in it. She was marinating in uterus fluids.

"OH MY GOD! DID YOU JUST GAG?" she yelled.

I started furiously shaking my head "No", but the damage was done.

The anesthesiologist came in then and pushed his cart of drugs in front of him and I almost begged him to give me a hit of whatever he had. I really should be numb from the brain down for the rest of this day before I fucked anything else up.

The doctor let me stay in the room for the epidural and let me tell you, nothing prepares you for seeing a needle as long as your arm, being pushed into your wife's spine. And since she was in the middle of a contraction, all she did was sigh when it went in. Until I opened my mouth.

"Holy fuck that's a huge needle," I mumbled.

Jenny glanced over at me and scowled. Well, as much as she could anyway since she was hunched over her big belly as far as she could go, and a nurse was pushing down on her shoulders.

"What if he moves a fraction of an inch to the left and you're suddenly paralyzed?" I asked in horror.

"Shut...Up," Jenny muttered.

After the epidural was firmly in place, I double checked that we had a waiver on file that states we would own the hospital should my wife become paralyzed. If I was going to feed her mashed peas and wipe her ass until we die, I wanted to be rich.

"You're never going to want to have sex with me again. I'm going to push a human out of the hole where you stick your penis, and you're never going to want to go there again," she sobbed.

Why God, why? WHY did she have to put that image in my head? I never had a problem having sex with her when she was pregnant with Veronica. Never went through that whole "Oh no, what if I hurt the baby or he sees my penis" bullshit. But this? Oh sweet Jesus, this is the end for me.

"Oh, that's just silly. Why would you say something like that?" I asked nervously.

Maybe because it's true. A human is making his way down that canal, and I'm supposed to not freak out about this?

Seven hours later, Billy had come screaming into the world, and I had thrown up in the trashcan next to the bed.

Somehow, now, I need to convince my wife that I do not fear her vagina. Not anymore at least.

5.

Could It Be...Satan?!

I'm going to kill him. I swear to God I'm going to murder my husband.

The week before Billy had been born, he thought it would be a great idea to get a kitten. Something little to take care of to refresh our memories because it had been three years since we last had something that little to take care of. But when he had said *we*, he really meant *me*.

Granted, the kitten, Miss Lippy, named after the weird teacher in *Billy Madison,* is cute and cuddly and likes to rub her little pink nose against mine when we curl up in bed at night, but she also poops more than the average human. I've never seen so much poop come out of something so little and cute. If she'd been an outdoor cat, I might have guessed that she ate a rotten animal or something and got sick, but she never goes outside. She is strictly an indoor cat. I had almost called the vet to ask them if it was normal or if Miss Lippy was dying from some sort of pooping disease. I had the phone in my hand all set to dial when Drew had finally decided to tell me that he pooped in the litter box a few times to see what it was like.

I've SCOOPED MY HUSBAND'S POOP! Do you have any idea how NOT okay that is?

And yet, it's not even the reason why I want to kill him right now, although it should be. So, not only do I have a three-year-old, a four-month-old, a husband, and a kitten, but Drew has come home tonight with a puppy.

A PUPPY!

Because you know, why not add one more thing to my list? Really, on top of all the crap I already do, it should be a piece of pie to clean up after yet another person. I've already had to potty train Veronica and Drew, might as well try a dog this time. Maybe he'll be easier.

Not only did I have to stop Drew from pooping in the kitty litter, shortly after we got married, I had to get him to stop peeing on trees in the front yard. And this was long before we even had kids, let alone had a puppy. He claimed the pee was good for the trees and helped them grow faster. Our neighbors had the most beautiful, tall trees, and Drew always saw their black lab peeing on them, so he assumed their landscaping looked so nice because of the dog. I couldn't count how many times I'd look out one of our windows and saw Drew holding his penis with one hand and waving to passing cars with another as he "helped our trees grow." It got to the point where I had to start keeping an eye on him at all times. When he had started crossing and uncrossing his legs and shifting in his seat, I knew he had to go to the bathroom. I'd have to grab his hand and take him upstairs and stand him in front of the toilet and say, "You pee here! You pee here right now! You are NOT going outside, do you understand me?" It had taken three months before he would head to the stairs instead of the front door to pee.

Now Drew is fast asleep next to me, and I've been tossing and turning for the last two hours, trying to get comfortable in a bed that not only has us in it but now includes Miss Lippy and our Beagle puppy, Rollo the Janitor, too. While the kitten hisses at the puppy and the puppy whines in fear, I lie here silently plotting how to kill Drew and if my friends will help me hide the body.

"Oh my gosh, stop whining," Drew mutters sleepily. "Do you have to go out?"

I lean up on my elbows and try to see Drew in the darkness. I can just make out his form sitting up and feel the bed shift as he flings off the covers and stands up.

"She just went out," I tell him softly, assuming he's referring to Rollo needing to go to the bathroom. I had taken her outside about an hour before, and since she hasn't crawled all over me and licked my face, I'm assuming that means she doesn't need to go out again. But Drew is either half asleep or doesn't care and mumbles something about how it's his turn to take the dog out. I am not about to argue because if he can bring this thing home without talking to me about it first, he can damn well take it out to the bathroom in the middle of the night.

I put my head back down on the pillow and snuggle under the blankets, listening to Drew curse under his breath about how cold it is outside and how the dog better make it quick since we had a huge snow storm earlier in the day and there is currently about a foot and a half of snow on our back deck where we let Rollo out to do his business as he picks up the dog and heads out of the room.

Why do people say that about dogs going to the bathroom? *Do his business.* How is pooping and peeing like doing business? I do business every day and it involves computers and phone calls and meetings. That's nothing at all like going to the bathroom. Every time someone says that, I picture a dog walking into the backyard with a doggy briefcase in its hand, wearing a suit and tie. It's weird.

Another thing that's weird? Animals wearing clothes. Did you know there's a whole website dedicated to just cats wearing sweaters? Do they "do their business" while wearing sweaters?

While I pounder these thoughts, I reach over in bed to scratch Miss Lippy's head before I go to sleep. But it doesn't feel like Miss Lippy's head; it's not as fluffy.

As I feel around the bed for the rest of Miss Lippy, wondering if maybe I'm nowhere near her head, I hear the back door open downstairs so Drew can let Rollo out. As soon as I hear the door slam shut, I hear a whine in the bed next to me and feel a warm, wet puppy tongue on my chin.

"Oh no! Oh SHIT!"

Drew just threw Miss Lippy out into the snow! Poor, little Miss Lippy who has never been outside a day in her life except for the day Drew brought her home!

I throw the covers off of me, scoop up Rollo, jump out of bed, and run as fast as I can down the stairs. When I get to the last step, I hear the screams and wails of agony.

Oh thank God! Drew must have realized what he did and now he feels bad. He's so sweet for getting upset.

I race through the house and skid to a stop in the doorway of the kitchen.

Miss Lippy, sopping wet and covered in snow, is attached to the front of Drew's chest. And when I say attached, I mean it. He hadn't worn a shirt to bed, so all four sets of claws are stuck deep into his skin as Drew screams and tries to pull her off of him.

"MOTHER SON OF FUCKER SHIT! GET THIS GOD DAMMED CAT OFF OF ME!" he shrieks as he tugs on the cat's fur and the cat yowls and hisses up at him angrily.

"Oh my gosh! Drew, you threw Miss Lippy out instead of Rollo!" I tell him as I just stand there cuddling Rollo and watch Drew spin around in circles, slamming into the counter and chair as he wrestles with the cat.

"GEE? REALLY? I HAD NO IDEA, WHAT WITH THE WET, KILLER CAT STUCK TO MY SKIN!" he screams at me as the cat uses his distraction to her advantage by climbing further up his chest until she can sink her teeth into his chin.

Drew screeches at the top of his lungs while he continues to try and pry Miss Lippy off of him. She's growling now and drooling out of the side of her mouth, so I'm guessing she's not going anywhere for a while.

"I SAID I WAS SORRY, MISS LIPPY! COME THE FUCK ON, THAT HURTS! I SWEAR I DID NOT MEAN TO THROW YOU IN THE SNOW!"

Drew and Miss Lippy are carrying on so loudly right now, I'm sure they are going to wake the kids up any minute.

"Drew, keep it down! You're going to wake up Billy and Veronica," I whisper loudly over the crying and hissing.

"I HAVE A KILLER CAT WITH FANGS TRYING TO EAT MY FACE, JENNY! SHE'S TRYING TO EAT OFF MY FACE!"

Rollo sighs and huffs in my arms at the commotion and rests her head on my arm to continue watching.

Drew bends over at the waist and tries to stick his arm up between Miss Lippy's body and his chest to push her away from him since pulling on her fur is obviously just pissing her off. She takes that opportunity to scramble up his face and onto his head, sinking her claws into his skull.

I'm sorry, but at this point, I have to laugh. Drew stands up when the cat gets to his head and is now trying to head-bang to get her to fall off, screaming the whole time because it's just making her dig her claws in even further.

I sort of feel bad for him when I see the claw marks and blood dripping down the front of his chest, arms, neck, and face. It looks like he got into a fighting match with Freddy Kruger. But then I think about the fact that he's brought home not one, but two new animals at the same time we've had an infant in the house, and it kind of makes me happy that this is going on right now.

"IS THIS BECAUSE I TOOK A DUMP IN YOUR LITTER BOX? I TOLD YOU I WAS SORRY FOR THAT TOO. GET THE FUCK OFF OF MY HEAD!"

I walk across the room in an attempt to help Drew get Miss Lippy off of his head, but he's too busy head-banging and hopping around the room for me to get close to him. Instead, I take a seat at the kitchen table, yawn, and get Rollo comfortable in my lap.

"YOU'RE A VINDICTIVE LITTLE BITCH, MISS LIPPY! NEXT TIME YOU YACK UP A HAIR BALL IN MY SHOE, I'M GOING STRAIGHT UP GANSTER AND POPPING A CAP IN YOUR ASS!"

It's almost like Miss Lippy understands what Drew is threatening. As soon as Drew takes a break and rests against the counter,

Miss Lippy rears up on her back legs and starts smacking Drew on either side of his head with her paws. It's like something right out of *Funniest Home Videos* when the little kid is teasing the cat too much and it smacks the poor little kid in the face. That's always funny because it's happening to someone else's kid. It turns out, this is even funnier.

I'm too busy laughing to see how he does it, but Drew finally manages to remove Miss Lippy from his head and tosses her to the kitchen floor. She hisses once more at him and then runs away.

"I can't believe you didn't help me. I could have been killed!" Drew complains.

I roll my eyes at him and stand up. "Oh stop, she wouldn't have killed you."

Holding Rollo to my chest, I turn and walk out of the room.

"You have no idea what that monster is capable of. You didn't see her eyes. It was like looking into the windows of hell. I actually felt a chill. That cat is Satan. I bet she's upstairs right now trying to suck the souls out of our kids. Why aren't you more worried about this?" Drew demands.

"That cat is a sweetheart. You threw her into a pile of snow. What did you expect her to do?" I ask as I make my way up the stairs and Drew trails behind me, shushing me as we go.

"We need to stop talking about her. She's probably listening and plotting our deaths. I bet she knows thirty-five ways to kill us and make it look like an accident. They'll find our bloody corpses, and she'll just be sitting there, looking up at them with those big, cute Puss and Boots eyes but no one will think she's coming to do the Devil's bidding," Drew whispers as we walk into our room.

He turns and looks both ways down the hallway and then quickly runs away from the doorway, over to the closet. I watch as he rifles through the closet until finally pulling out what he's looking for - a baseball bat. He lifts it up on his shoulder and puffs out his chest.

"You do realize Miss Lippy doesn't weigh more than six pounds, and you're ready to fight her with a metal baseball bat, right?" I ask him as I climb into bed and get Rollo situated next to me.

"Cold, dead eyes, Jenny! How many times do I have to tell you? It's like you're not even afraid of Satan! He wants to eat your soul!" he whispers loudly, creeping around the room and glancing nervously behind the nightstands and under the bed.

"She's just a little kitty, Drew." I sigh as he makes his way into the bathroom.

I hear the water running in the sink followed by cursing as he cleans off his scratches. He comes back into the room a few minutes later with the bat clutched tightly to his chest.

"That little kitty tried to gut me like a fish tonight. Do you want me to go downstairs and get you a weapon? I would totally do that for you. I would brave the wrath of the human-slayer to make sure you could sleep safely tonight," he tells me seriously.

"I could probably make it to the first drawer on the left in the kitchen and get you a steak knife if I can bug out early and stay under cover until I make it back to the barracks without risk of another attack," he whispers to himself.

When he starts talking like his father, I know he's lost his mind.

"Drew, cut it out! I don't need a weapon and you're not going to a freaking war. Good grief! You're not really going to sleep with the baseball bat, are you?" I ask him as he climbs under the covers, still hugging the bat.

"Yes. Yes I am. I am not going to just let that thing terrorize our family. I am going to bed armed and ready to protect the people I love at all costs. You didn't see the evil in that thing's face when I realized I'd thrown it out into the snow and quickly opened the door back up to get her. She flew Jenny! She rose up out of the snow and fucking FLEW at me! There was death in her eyes. She was covered in snow and foaming at the mouth. I'm pretty sure her eyes turned red too," Drew mutters.

I can't even think of a reply to the insanity coming out of his mouth right now. As soon as I roll over and decide to just ignore him, he pops up in bed with a gasp.

"Did you hear that?" he whispers so softly I barely hear him.

"Hear what?" I ask.

"SHHHHHHHHHHHHHH! Listen," he scolds.

I sigh in irritation and listen for whatever it was Drew thinks he's heard. I open my mouth to tell him to grow up, and I hear it. I crane my neck and try to figure out what the hell it is. It almost sounds like a garbled female voice. Like maybe we left the TV on downstairs or something.

The sound gets louder, like it's coming closer. It's definitely a female voice and she's talking like one of those Valerie girls. *"Like, you know! Like, oh my God! Like, totally awesome!"*

"Oh my God, is this like a Ghosts of Christmas Past thing? Is this us if we were born in the eighties? But, would that be Christmas Past or Christmas Back to the Future? I don't want to see my back to the future! I'm not ready!" Drew cries softly.

I elbow him in the ribs and shush him.

What the hell is out in our hallway?

We wait in anticipation on the bed, and now I'm a little glad Drew decided to bring a bat to bed with him. I don't think a bat will work on a ghost, but at least Drew didn't lie when he said he would do anything to protect us.

All of a sudden, right in our doorway we see two red, glowing eyes. Drew and I have completely opposite reactions to the creepy glowing eyes staring us down. As soon as I put two and six together, the girly voices and red eyes, I immediately know what it is.

Drew, on the other hand, does the exact opposite of what he had just vowed a few minutes ago.

"OH HOLY MOTHER FUCKING TAINT BUCKET! IT'S MISS LIPPY! SHE WANTS MORE BLOOD!" Drew screams as he throws the bat to the ground, jumps up to his feet on the bed, and scrambles across it, stepping on my legs in his hurry to run away. Before I can even sit up in bed, he's already made it across the room and locked himself in the bathroom.

"Gee whizzer, Drew! So nice of you to do whatever you can to protect us!" I shout to him in the bathroom as I get up out of bed and stomp out into the hallway to pick up Veronica's Furby toy. She always forgets to shut the thing off when she's done with it, and every once in a while it will just get a mind of its own and wander through the house.

"Jenny! STAY STRONG, BABY!" Drew yells from behind the bathroom door.

I shake my head and decide not to tell him that I found out what was in the doorway, and it wasn't a ghost or a killer cat. I think a night sleeping on the cold bathroom floor is good punishment for turning this house into a zoo.

Rollo repositions himself in the bed until he's curled up in the curve of my legs and Miss Lippy, who had been in bed right next to Drew during most of his freak out, and he hadn't even realized it, slinks down next to Rollo and lies down, her chin resting on Rollo's back.

I fall asleep to the sounds of Drew mumbling through the bathroom door about kittens having killer fangs.

6.

Liquid Courage

"Should we call the guys and see how they're doing?" I ask Claire.

"That is the third time you've asked that question in thirty minutes," Liz complains. "If you don't shut up and enjoy the peace and quiet, I'm going to punch you in the neck."

Drew, Carter, and Jim are all at our house with the seven kids, and we're at Liz and Jim's house. I can't help it if I'm nervous. It's the first time they've all been alone with the kids without us there to stop the screaming and the crying. We're the only ones who can calm the men down when they see how much poop comes out of that many kids at one time.

"What if one of them gets hurt?"

Claire rolls her eyes at me. "Don't worry. Gavin knows how to call 9-1-1 if the idiots we married hurt themselves.

"I'm talking about the kids. What if one of *them* gets hurt?"

"I *know* you're talking about one of the kids. I'm trying to make you lighten up. So lighten the fuck up!"

Claire and Liz have started project "Fake it Till You Make it" with me. They are on a mission to restore mine and Drew's sex life. I still don't understand this whole "faking it" thing. I've never faked anything with Drew. They had decided I need to watch the holy grail of faking it movies so we're spending the afternoon watching *When Harry Met Sally*.

"I'm still confused by the fact that you have never, ever faked it with Drew. How is that possible?" Liz asks as she puts the DVD in and hits play.

"Drew is a very giving lover. He always makes sure I come first. And if I don't, he brings out one of my toys. And if that doesn't work, there's always his tongue."

"Okay, stop. You're going to make me puke," Liz complains.

"Well, it's true. He's ambidextrous so his tongue can be used both ways."

"Oh my God, stop the insanity!" Liz complains.

"So what do you do if you're just too tired to have sex but he's bugging you for it?" Claire asks.

"Um, I tell him I'm too tired for sex and roll over and go to sleep."

Both women stare at me.

"What? What's wrong with that? It's the truth. I'm not going to lie to him."

"In this case, you definitely *should* lie to him. He probably thinks you don't want him anymore," Claire says.

In all honesty, part of me doesn't really mind if Drew thinks just for a minute that I don't want him. It serves him right for what he did six weeks after Billy was born.

"EEEEEEEEEEEEEK!"

I had bolted up in bed at the sound of Drew screaming in his sleep next to me. He sat straight up in bed as well, shivering and rubbing the sleep out of his eyes.

"Are you okay?" I had asked him with a yawn and checking the clock. Billy would probably be up in another hour for a feeding unless Drew just woke him up with his scream.

"I had a really bad dream. Oh my God it was awful. It had fangs and it was trying to eat me, and I tried to scream but it bit off my tongue! Oh, the horror!" Drew wailed.

"Where you dreaming about Miss Lippy again?" I ask him, lying back down in bed and pulling the covers up over my shoulder.

He looked down at me nervously and started biting his nails.

"I don't know. I forget. Let's have sex."

Drew immediately dropped his head to the pillow, wrapped his arm around my body, and pulled me against him.

He started kissing my neck, and I swore I could hear him say, "You can do this. Just don't think about the fangs."

"Drew, I don't know. It might still be too soon," I told him.

I knew it wasn't too soon. It had been exactly six weeks to the day since Billy was born. This was the day we could start having sex again. While Drew was busy kissing his way down to my breasts, I looked over his shoulder at the alarm clock on his side of the bed.

If I fell asleep right now, I'd still get about fifty minutes of sleep before Billy woke up.

"I promise I'll be quick," Drew said around kisses as he slipped my tank top down, exposing one breast and starting to kiss and suck all around the full mound.

"Be careful, I might leak," I warned him.

Since I was breast feeding, my boobs tended to leak at inappropriate times. Now would be a really inappropriate time.

Drew immediately stopped, his mouth hovering over my nipple.

"This is a huge dilemma for me. I know I should back away since it's like, our kid's food, but the pervert in me wants to go grab a bag of cookies and do this thing," he admitted.

"Don't even think about it," I told him, clutching onto his hair and pulling his head back up to mine.

"Are you really going to let me stick my penis in you? Don't tease me right now. My heart can't take it," Drew said.

"Yes, go ahead. But seriously, make it quick. Billy will be up soon."

Drew pushed himself off of me quickly and shoved his boxers down to his knees, lying back down between my legs before I even blink.

"I'll be quick, I promise. Time me," Drew said as he pushes my underwear down my hips and to my knees. I wiggled my legs to get them the rest of the way down, kicking them off of my ankle when they reached that far.

"What was your dream about," I asked him as he wraps his hand around his erection and guides it toward me, running the tip through me and placing it at my opening.

"It was awful. Your vagina turned into a monster and it looked just like it did when you were having Billy, except it had teeth and red, glowing eyes, and it wanted to bite off my face, and it was so saggy and floppy and had all this extra skin hanging around. It was so fucking scary," he explained as he pushes just the tip of his penis inside of me and groans.

I put my hand on his shoulders and pushed him up and away from me a little.

"Are you kidding right now or are you serious?"

He paused and a look of pain washed over his face when he realized I'm stopping him from pushing in any further.

Drew had never been able to lie to me, even about little things. I knew that right then he was wondering if he should really tell me the truth.

"Um, yes?"

I pushed on his shoulders as hard as I could.

"Are you serious with this right now? You're having nightmares about my VAGINA?" I yelled at him as he scrambled to get up on his knees, his penis sticking straight out, pointing right at me.

"I'm sorry! I have no control over my dreams. It's not my fault!" he argued.

"It is if you're thinking about my vagina being floppy and saggy!" I yelled back, digging under the sheet for my underwear and sliding them back on.

"No! Please! I need that!" Drew whined as I roll angrily away from him after I pulled my underwear all the way up.

I felt the bed shift and the heat of his stomach against my back. He rested his chin on my shoulder, and I was hoping he was coming up with a really good apology for this crap.

"Can I just stick the tip back in?" he whispered against my ear. "If your vagina is still sore, we could just do anal. That would be awesome, right?"

I had shoved my elbow back and into his stomach as hard as I could. While he was moaning and whimpering like a baby next to me in bed, our REAL baby had started crying over the monitor.

That episode was six weeks ago and Drew hasn't even attempted to try and have sex with me since then. Well, aside from the sex swing I guess. I've forgiven him for his stupidity because, well, he's a guy and guys are stupid. But I'm still not really in the mood for sex, which brings us back to the lesson Liz and Claire are trying to teach me.

"You don't want Drew to think you don't want him. Hence the phrase, 'fake it till you make it.' If you start off faking that you want it, eventually you'll get back into the flow of things and *really* start to want it."

Does Drew really think I don't want him anymore? I don't want him to think that.

"Drew is never going to buy it. He's going to know right away if I fake an orgasm."

Claire and Liz burst out laughing.

"You're kidding right? There is no possible way he would ever know," Liz informs me.

"Oh believe me, Drew would know. He says he can feel it when I come. He says my vagina squeezes him if he's inside me, and it tastes different if he's going down on me," I tell them.

"What the fuck are you ingesting before you have sex that he can taste it, straight gasoline?" Liz asks.

"Why would Drew lie to me about something like that?"

"Why *wouldn't* Drew lie to you about something like that? Every woman has asked her guy if he can tell when she's coming. We don't ask because we want to know if he can feel just how amazing it is and thereby boost his ego because he can get you off. We ask just to make sure he *can't* tell so when we fake it, he won't be the wiser. Even though we all have the same working body parts, every guy's answer is usually different. Proving that they have no idea, aside from the sounds we make," Liz explains.

"Carter told me he can tell when I'm coming because I start breathing faster. I'm usually breathing faster because I'm tired as shit and out of shape and I think my heart is going to give out," Claire says.

"Jim told me he knows because I always smack his ass right before I come. I do that so he'll hurry the fuck up because I want to go to sleep or because Top Chef is coming on," Liz adds.

I stare at both women in shock and cannot believe this has been happening all these years, and I've known nothing about it. I had never known women faked orgasms with their husbands. It makes no sense to me. Why would you marry someone if they couldn't give you an orgasm? Liz and Claire's marriages are solid as a rock though, so they must be on to something.

"Fine, get to the faking part so I can see what this is all about."

"It will be my fake pleasure," Liz says with a smile as she fast forwards the movie.

⊙ ⊙ ⊙

An hour and a half later, we're sitting at a local hole in the wall bar a few blocks from Liz and Claire's shop, and I'm still in shock by that movie.

"I mean, it was so *real*," I tell them in awe.

"I know, right? You would have totally thought Billy Crystal was giving it to Meg Ryan under the table," Liz says as she drinks the last of her beer and signals the waitress for another round.

We decide that since we were without children or husbands we should make the most of it and get some drinks. Plus, the girls are convinced that a little liquid courage will help with the faking I plan on testing out this evening, but they have yet to order me any.

The waitress comes to our table a few minutes later and Claire and Liz each order another beer.

"I'll take whatever size Liquid Courage you have on draft," I tell her with a smile.

"I'm sorry, what?" the waitress asks in confusion.

"I don't know. My friends told me to order it. Do you guys not have it? Maybe it's new."

Liz leans over and covers my mouth with her hand. "Just bring her a drink with the highest proof alcohol you've got."

Claire is laughing and typing something into her cell phone.

"What are you doing? Are you putting that on Facebook? Don't you dare! How was I supposed to know it wasn't a brand of beer?" I complain.

"Actually, that isn't a bad idea. I wonder if I could market my own beer for the shop. Liquid Courage: helping men get laid for centuries." Claire laughs as she slips her cell phone back in her purse.

The waitress comes back with the girls' beers and a shot glass filled with a pinkish colored liquid for me.

"What is this?" I ask her.

"It's Everclear with a splash of cherry juice," she explains before rushing off to another table.

"Ooooh, Everclear. That sounds pretty," I say before downing the shot.

I immediately start coughing and choking, fanning my mouth with my hand.

"IT BURNS! OH MY GOD IT BURNS!" I try to yell with a raspy voice that feels like it's on fire.

"Here, drink this," Claire tells me as she slides her beer across the table towards me.

I drink the entire thing in three big gulps and smack the glass back down to the table.

"Well, I do believe that is plenty of liquid courage for the evening," Liz says with a laugh.

7.

Fake It Till You Make It

"Holy fucking Wheat Thins. What did you feed this kid?" Jim asks as he brings Billy over to me, holding him at arm's length with a look of disgust on his face. "It smells like he ate a dead dog covered in vomit and yogurt and then shit it out."

He puts Billy in my lap and as soon as I get a whiff, I throw up in my mouth a little and have to hold my breath.

"Jenny stopped breast feeding last week and put him on formula and cereal. Maybe that's it."

Carter shakes his head. "That is not what formula and cereal smell like. That smells like ball sweat covered in Swiss cheese."

I place Billy on the floor at my feet and step away from him so I can take a breath.

"Jesus, that is really bad. How is he smiling? Can't he smell himself? If I took a dump that smelled that bad I wouldn't be smiling," I say.

"Well, at least whatever that was isn't inside of him anymore. Imagine the havoc it was wreaking on his stomach. He's probably like, 'Thank fucking God that shit is out of me.' Literally," Jim says as he plugs his nose and takes a few giant steps backwards.

All of a sudden, the sound of five little girls screaming bloody murder comes from the toy room at the back of the house, and ten-year-old Gavin comes running into the living room with a grin on his face.

"What did you do?" Carter asks him as I dig through the diaper bag for a gas mask and latex gloves.

"Nothing," Gavin replies as he flops down on the couch. "Who farted? It stinks in here."

We all point to the baby. There is still screaming and crying coming from the toy room, but at this point we're all more concerned with the fact that the smell coming from my son might start peeling the paint off of the walls.

Veronica comes charging into the living room holding a headless, naked Barbie in her hand. Behind her is Carter's six-year-old Sophia and Jim's three daughters, Charlotte who is also six, Ava who is five, and Molly who is three. All have tear-stained cheeks and a multitude of naked, headless Barbies in their hands.

"GAVIN TOOK THE CLOTHES OFF OF ALL OF OUR DOLLS AND POPPED THEIR HEADS OFF!" Charlotte screeches.

"My dolly has no head!" Ava wails.

"He drew boobies on my Barbie!" Sophia cries as she waves the torso of her inked Barbie in front of our faces.

"Hey, those look pretty good. Nice nipple placement," I tell him.

"Why does this one have a big red dot in the middle of its chest and a shaved head," Jim asks as he grabs the only one with its head still intact that three-year-old Molly is cradling to her.

"She's got a third nipple because she was abducted by aliens and they experimented on her. The other Barbies shunned her and cut off all of her hair when she went to sleep," Gavin explains.

The wails from the five girls grow louder, and we all wince at the sounds they are producing.

"Oh my God, make it stop!" Carter complains.

"GIRLS! Calm down!" Jim yells in an effort to be heard. Living in a house with three girls and a wife, he is quite the expert at the trials and tribulations of females. But even he looks shocked at the amount of noise that is coming out of them.

They begin crying even harder because they think Jim is yelling at them, which in turn produces snot, dry heaves, and honest to God foot stomping.

"No, no, no! Please stop crying!" Carter pleads with them, getting down on his knees so he is eye level with them.

"I WANT MY MOMMY!" Veronica shouts.

And thus begins a half hour chant of "I WANT MY MOMMY" from five little girls.

Instead of calling the wives and admitting to them that we have no idea how to control the situation, Carter calls his own mother. She tells him to bribe them with candy. Exactly six seconds after he hangs up the phone, each girl has a sucker in her hand and a smile on her face as they walk back to the toy room to play "Headless Barbie Princess Parade".

The peace and quiet lasts exactly fifteen minutes.

I manage to get Billy changed with only a little bit of puke coming up my throat but then I actually throw up in the kitchen sink when I look down and realize I have some poop on my finger. Carter takes over at that point and gives Billy a bottle and rocks him to sleep. Gavin is sitting next to Carter on the couch playing his Nintendo DS when all of a sudden, more blood curdling screams start coming from the toy room.

"You have got to be kidding me with this shit!" Jim complains.

We start to get up to see what the problem is now when all five girls shuffle out into the living room in a giant clump. Upon closer inspection, once we are able to get them to finally stop screaming and ask them why they are walking around with their heads all touching in the middle and refusing to separate, we find out that unsupervised suckers with little girls is a no-no.

"Oh sweet Mary. What happened?" Jim asks them.

They all start talking at once, each one with a different version of the story and who is to blame. One says it had something to do with a giraffe and a cell phone, another says it was because there were birds flying around and the princess fell out of her tower, and yet another says the crayons were talking and told her to do it.

I am beginning to wonder if the girls are dropping acid in the toy room instead of playing nicely while enjoying suckers.

I guess the giraffe on the phone talking to the birds who buzz Cinderella's tower while the red crayon stabs people is the reason there are currently five suckers stuck in five long piles of hair which in turn are all stuck together in one big ball of hairy stickiness. They look like a set of sextuplets joined at the head. It's funny for a few minutes until we realize the only way to get the suckers out is to cut their hair. And there is no way you can cut a little girl's hair without their mother noticing.

The three of us stand there staring at the girls in horror, wondering what to do.

"Claire is going to kill me. She's been growing Sophia's hair out since she was born. She only gets trims," Carter says nervously as he walks up behind us with Billy still asleep on his shoulder. "Maybe I should call my mom again."

"NO! We are not calling your mother. We are grown ass men and we can figure out how to fix this shit!" Jim scolds.

"FIX SHIT!" Molly yells.

"FIX SHIT, FIX SHIT, FIX SHIT!" all five girls chant.

"We're out of our depth, man. We'll never make it out of this alive," I yell to Jim over the girls chanting.

"We just need a plan. Where is the closest wig store?" Jim asks.

"That's the stupidest thing I have ever heard!" Carter argues.

I look at Billy in envy as he sleeps soundly on Carter's shoulder through the chaos.

"Do you have a better idea, genius?" Jim asks him.

The three of us stare at each other blankly, not one single idea coming to mind that will ensure our wives don't gouge out our eyes with spoons.

"Get me some scissors, a razor blade, a jar of peanut butter and some safety goggles," Gavin says, coming up next to us. "I got this one."

◉ ◉ ◉

Jenny walks into our bedroom a few hours later to find me sprawled out on top of the bed, staring at the ceiling.

"Why are their Barbie heads hanging from our ceiling?" she asks as she climbs into bed next to me and rolls over onto her back.

"Well, Gavin decided all the other Barbies needed a warning. He figured if they saw what happens to Barbies that disobey, they'd think twice about putting Ken in a frilly pink tutu and purple stilettos during a Barbie parade."

We stare in silence at the twenty little plastic heads affixed to the ceiling by their hair with scotch tape.

"Where are the kids?" Jenny asks.

"They're both in bed. It was a long day."

Before I even finish the sentence, Jenny is on top of me, straddling my hips and ripping off my clothes. It's been so long since she took control like this, I'm momentarily stunned and don't move. She has my pants and boxers off before I can blink and pulls a Hulk Hogan and rips my tee shirt right down the middle.

"Oh my God! That was my favorite shirt!" I yell, sadly glancing down at the torn lettering that used to say: *Bitches ain't shit but hoes and tricks – Ghandi.*

Jenny pulls her mouth away from my chest, leans back, and glares at me.

"Are you seriously complaining about a shirt right now?"

Oh Jesus, what the fuck is wrong with me? Why am I even talking???

"No, no, no, no! Keep going. Please, God, keep going."

Jenny goes back to what she was doing, kissing her way up my chest and grinding her pelvis into my raging hard-on.

My hands clutch onto her hips and help her move faster on top of my dick.

"You still have your clothes on," I mumble through groans as she licks her way up the side of my neck and sucks my earlobe into her mouth. "OH SWEET SUGAR POPS!"

My hips jerk against her as she swirls her tongue around my ear.

She pulls away suddenly and I groan at the loss of her mouth on my ear until I see she's sitting up and pulling her shirt up and over her head. Her glorious tits are spilling out of her black lace bra, and my hands immediately gravitate to them, palming them and rolling them around in my hands. She hasn't let me anywhere near the twins since she started breastfeeding Billy, and I made that crack about cookies and milk. I feel like a crack addict getting a hit after months of being clean. I want to cry like a baby as I hold their fullness in my hands. I feel her nipples harden beneath the lace, and I'm wondering if I'm even going to last long enough to savor this moment.

Jenny leans over me, sucks my earlobe back into her mouth and starts grinding her hips harder against me. She's moaning and breathing heavy in my ear and the warmth of her breath is making me forget all about the fact that she still has her skirt and underwear on and I'm not inside of her yet. I move my hips faster between her legs, and she says the words that have the power of making me come in a split second.

"Felix wants to purr with Buck."

Yes, we named our privates. Sue me.

Jenny starts thrusting her hips faster, my dick rubbing against the cotton of her underwear, and I really want to reach down, move her underwear aside, and push myself inside of her but I can already feel my orgasm creeping up and my hands are clutched too tightly to her hips to move them.

Before I can stop it, I'm jerking, convulsing, and shooting my load against her white cotton underwear and the inside of her skirt.

"Fuck! Holy crab rangoons!" I shout as the orgasm makes me twitch and my toes curl.

"Are you coming already?" Jenny asks.

"I'm sorry! YES! Oh fuck YES!"

She keeps moving against me and all of a sudden begins shouting her own excitement.

"Oh my gosh me too! Oh yes, yes, yes!" she yells, sitting up on top of me and thrashing her head all around. "OHHHHHHHHHH, OOOOOOOOOH!"

I lie perfectly still wondering what the fuck is going on as she starts slapping her hands against my bare chest and continues to flop her head all over the place, her long hair smacking me in the face as she works out the longest orgasm in the history of orgasms.

"YES! YES! YES! YES! OHHHHHHHHHH YES YES YES!"

I'm completely amazed that she's still going strong. My penis has already started to go soft and her vagina isn't even touching it right now. She's just humping air.

"YES! YES! DON'T STOP! OOOOOOOOOH YES!"

Don't stop what exactly? Don't stop lying here wondering how this is happening right now?

She finally ceases all movement and collapses on top of me, breathing heavy and sighing in contentment.

Within seconds she's up and off of me and standing next to the bed. She leans down and kisses my cheek. "That was amazing. I'm going to go check on the kids."

She walks out of the room, and I'm left in bed with a shirt torn in half, naked from the waist down, my wilted cock resting against my thigh, and twenty Barbie heads silently judging me when I hear her shout from across the hall.

"What the hell happened to Veronica's hair?!"

8.

The Great Swami

It's been two weeks since I attempted the "fake it till you make it" with Drew and I think it was a total success. He knows I still want him and that got me off the hook for a little while to try and get my libido back in shape. I had a little bit of doubt that my performance wasn't good enough and that Drew suspected I had been faking that day, but after a little pep talk to myself, I knew I was a golden shower.

I had made Liz play that scene from *When Harry Met Sally* seven times and then Claire made me act out the scene to make sure I got it right.

"Don't keep your eyes open. You're totally giving it away by staring straight ahead looking bored," Claire stated.

I tipped my head back, closed my eyes, and started moaning loudly.

"How's this?"

"You sound like a dying cat. A dying cat that's trying to catch snowflakes. Put your tongue away and close your mouth," Liz scolded.

"Really get into it. Picture someone telling you that tonight, you will sleep twelve hours straight without any interruptions," Claire instructed.

I screamed in ecstasy and shout words I didn't even know how to pronounce.

"Wow, you nailed that one," Liz said in awe.

"Yeah, I guess we found your sweet spot. Just imagine you're asleep when you're banging Drew," Claire said with a laugh.

"Hey, before we had Billy, our sex life was very exciting and I never would have needed to think about sleep. We were even finalists in a porn home movie contest. The contest required us to use four props. Two living things, one gas operated power tool, and jumper cables," I told them.

"You really need to stop sharing things like this with us," Liz complained. "But seriously. Do it exactly how you just did and it will be perfect."

It *had* been perfect, if I do say so myself. I don't get why Drew is still acting weird though. You would think that since he got off he would be in a better mood. I mean, he came without even having sex. That's got to be a good thing. And since he thinks he got me off too, he should be feeling pretty good about himself. But he's been moody and sad and hasn't even made any comments about bending me over the table in days. Something definitely isn't right with him.

Our neighbors call to invite us over for a cook-out this evening, and I take them up on their offer. In the few years we've lived in this house, we've never done anything with our neighbors. They are a very strict, religious couple, and we obviously aren't.

Before I had got pregnant with Billy, Liz hosted a sex toy party on our back deck. The wife had been outside tending to her garden and saw thirty women waving vibrators around and trying to pop blown up condoms by grabbing a partner, putting the condom between them, and hugging each other as tightly as they could to get the condom to explode. The condoms had been full of lotion and everyone was screaming and throwing vibrators at each other.

I'm pretty sure that's why every time I see her out in the yard, she turns and runs back into her house.

Getting an invite from her for a cookout had been a shock but I figure it couldn't hurt. If anything, maybe this couple could help Drew and I learn to communicate better. I mean, they are religious people. They must know how to talk to each other and how to make a marriage work. I bet I can get some really good advice from them.

"The freaks invited us to their house?"

"Will you stop calling them that?" I complain as I put a pink bow clip in Veronica's hair.

"What's a fweak?" Veronica asks.

"The crazy people who live next door," Drew replies as he pulls a onesie out of Billy's drawer that reads: Screw the titties and milk. Give me a beer.

"No. Absolutely not. You are not putting him in that shirt."

I walk over and snatch the onesie out of his hand and put it back in the drawer, searching through Billy's clothes for something appropriate.

"How do we not have one good shirt for our son to wear?"

"What are you talking about? These are ALL good shirts," Drew argues as he pulls out a red onesie that says, "I shit my pants when ugly people hold me."

"These are nice people who invited us over for a nice dinner. He needs to wear something nice," I state as I keep digging through the drawer.

"Boooo. Nice is lame," Drew states.

"Fweaks are lame," Veronica pipes up.

"Yeah they are! High five sister!" Drew exclaims as he puts his hand in the air for Veronica to smack.

At the very bottom of the drawer I find a shirt that says, "Pooping in progress" with a percentage line under it showing forty-five percent.

"This will have to do. Can you get Billy dressed so I can do my hair?" I ask as I lay out the shirt and a pair of tiny little jeans to go with it. "Also, you need to change your shirt. You are not wearing the shirt with a picture of Jesus and a crying Virgin Mary that says: Bitches be trippin'.

"I just want to state that for the record, I do not think this is a good idea," Drew yells as I walk out of the room.

"Doodly noted," I yell back.

⊙ ⊙ ⊙

"Okay, everyone, it's game time!"

Seven seconds after walking across our yard and stepping foot onto the neighbor's back deck I realize I've made a mistake. This isn't just a fun get-together with our neighbors and a way to make new friends and hopefully learn from them about how to make a marriage work. This is the Twilight Zone and we are never going to escape. We are surrounded by women wearing ankle-length jean skirts and their hair in braids down to their asses. They pray before dinner, they pray in the middle of dinner, and they pray after dinner. They pray so much I can almost imagine Jesus himself sitting up there on a white puffy cloud saying, "Oh for the love of my dad, shut the fuck up already. I heard you the first eleven times."

Drew keeps poking me in the side and snorts every time someone says, "Let's bow our heads and give thanks."

"If they ask us to drink the Kool-Aid, grab the kids and run," Drew whispers as everyone pulls their chairs into a circle in the middle of the deck.

"But I like Kool-Aid. Grape is my favorite," I whisper back in confusion.

"We're going to go around the circle and everyone has to tell an embarrassing story!" the hostess announces.

"Oh this cannot end well," Drew says quietly.

I elbow him in the side as one of the jean skirt women starts to tell her story about her husband playing a trick on her. When she had asked him to get her a glass of grape juice, he had handed her a glass of prune juice instead.

"Oh my fu-fart!" Drew states loudly as everyone around us laughs.

It's been a challenge trying to curb our language throughout the night. At least Drew is managing to catch himself before he lets something awful fly out of his mouth.

"That's not embarrassing. That's just sad," Drew whispers. "You realize that every single one of our embarrassing stories ends with one of us naked, right?"

Thankfully, halfway around the circle, people start running out of stories to tell, and I don't have to try and find a way to clean up the story about how we experimented with popsicles and chocolate sauce and had to use a blow dryer to unfreeze the popsicle from the inside of Drew's thigh.

"So, how did you two meet?" one of the men asks as everyone turns their attention to Drew and I.

I look over at Drew in a panic and wonder how I'm going to explain to these God-fearing people that we met after a sex toy party.

"Um, well…we, um have these friends. And they have a store that sells…um, Tupperware," I flounder. "We met after one of their Tupperware parties."

Everyone smiles and nods and Drew starts to giggle.

"Yeah, they have GREAT Tupperware. Every shape and size you can imagine. Jenny likes the great big Tupperware," he says with a snort.

"Ooooh I love Tupperware too!" one of the women states excitedly. "I use it every single day. It really is a life saver."

I just smile and nod, trying to mentally telephone to Drew that he needs to shut up.

"Do you like to use the gigantor Tupperware or the teeny tiny Tupperware?" Drew questions seriously.

"I like to use both at the same time," another woman pipes up.

"Yeah you do!" Drew smiles and nods, giving her a wink.

"My husband takes Tupperware to work and everyone is always asking him if Tupperware is better than GladWare. I tell them that Tupperware can fit in all sorts of places and can be used for your pets," someone else says.

"Wow, that's disturbing. But good for you," Drew says.

"GladWare is the poor man's Tupperware, that's what I always say," one of the men pipes up.

"Amen brother!" Drew shouts.

A chorus of "Amen's" is muttered all around the circle and I have to cover my face with my hands because I don't know whether to laugh or cry.

"Tupperware really has saved our marriage," one of the women says with a laugh. "Before I filled my pantry with Tupperware, Steve was using Zip Lock bags and his stuff was just spilling everywhere. He made such a mess!"

"Ha ha. Oh, Steve! Look at you spilling your stuff everywhere. You're so bad!" Drew tells the guy sitting on the other side of him.

"I went to a Tupperware party once where everyone was passing around the different sizes and then they sold those at the end of the party. It seemed very unsanitary to me. Everyone touching the Tupperware and putting their hands all over it and then you were supposed to just take it home and use it?" another woman states with a look of disgust on her face.

"Oh, they make a special cleaner for that," Drew tells them.

"Hey, I have an idea," Steve, the "stuff spiller" says. "Drew seems like a good sport. I bet he would love to play The Great Swami game."

The circle erupts into laughter and nods of approval. Everyone starts rearranging chairs so there are two in the middle of the circle, facing each other.

"The Great Swami game, you say? I've never heard of it," Drew tells them.

"Oh, it's great fun! You have to try and do everything The Great Swami does. So far, no one has been able to beat him," Steve says excitedly.

One of the other men takes a seat in one of the chairs in the middle of the circle and a few people direct Drew to the chair opposite him.

"Bring on The Great Swami. I will totally kick his assss-ascot!" Drew cheers, catching himself just in time.

"Okay, so Eric is going to be The Great Swami," Steve informs Drew. "All you have to do is follow along and do the exact same things he does."

I have no idea what's going on but it looks like a safe enough game where Drew won't get in trouble with his mouth, and hopefully it will have something to do with having a good marriage. Eric puts both of his arms up in the air, making a 'V', and Drew does the same. Eric then touches his finger to his nose, which Drew copies immediately.

"Man, this is easy. The Great Swami is going down!" Drew exclaims as he copies every single move Eric does with his arms and hands. I'm feeling even more confident that we will at least end this evening on a good note, even if we don't get any good marriage advice from these people.

Since Drew has his back to me, he doesn't see one of the women sneak up behind his chair with something in her hand. I can't see what it is since she's hiding it in front of her, but everyone around the circle starts to giggle when they see her.

The Great Swami Eric does a few more arm movements that Drew repeats and then suddenly he stands up from of his chair. Drew immediately follows the movement, at which point, the woman sticks what I now see is a huge, sopping wet towel onto the seat of Drew's chair.

Eric quickly sits back down onto his own chair, and Drew follows suit, smacking his ass down onto the wet towel and the puddle it makes in his chair. He quickly pops right back up and twists and turns to try and get a look at his ass while everyone around us is rolling with laughter

"SON OF A MOTHER FUCKING JESUS BITCH! WHAT THE FUCK ASS SHIT BITCH JUST FUCKING HAPPENED?!"

I can almost feel Jesus on his puffy cloud shaking his head in shame at us and saying, "You should have known better than to mix with my people. They will fuck you every time."

We quickly gather up the kids and thank everyone for a wonderful time. Drew tells them we need to leave because Billy has explosive diarrhea just as Veronica begins singing at the top of her lungs, "SHIT POOP DIAWEEA. SHIT POOP DIAWEEA!"

The whole walk back to our house Drew complains, "Fucking stupid ass fuck Swami. Next time we're invited over there, I'm going to fuck that Swami up."

I'm not going to hold my breast for another invitation any time soon.

9.

Great Head

"I can't believe you've never played The Great Swami game before. I'm disappointed that you would fall for the oldest trick in the book."

My dad, Andrew Senior, shakes his head at me in pity as we share a beer up at the local pub and watch the Browns game. I had invited my dad up here to get his take on Jenny and see if he would be up to tailing her for a few days. I'm not one hundred percent positive that she's falsifying a workman's comp claim since she stopped limping the day after she hurt her ankle, but I still have my doubts. Something stinks in suburbia and it's not my balls.

"Can we get back to the topic at hand, please? Will you do this for me or not?" I ask as I signal the bartender for another drink.

"Son, I have had your back for twenty-four-"

"Thirty-four," I supply.

"Thirty-four years. I am not about to quit you now, soldier. I will be on her like flies on shit. She doesn't make a move without me knowing about it. I love the smell of deceit in the morning!"

My father's enthusiasm for trying to catch my wife doing something bad doesn't make me feel better.

My dad used to be a drill sergeant in the Marines until word got around just how scary of a mother fucker he was. The Corps had a hard time finding recruits in his area because no one wanted to be the guy crying like a baby while my dad screamed in his face. He had retired early and opened his own private investigation business. Unfortunately, he's never lost that drill sergeant mentality.

"I need to know that you're on board with whatever I have to do to uncover the truth, is that clear?"

"Yes, sir," I mutter.

"Say it like you've got a set of balls, you pansy ass!"

"YES, SIR!" I shout.

My dad smacks me on the back and tells me he'll start his recon this evening when Jenny is *supposedly* going to be running errands after she gets off of work.

We finish watching the Browns game while dad explains to me every few minutes what he'll be doing to try and catch Jenny in a lie. I feel really bad about the fact that I'm going behind her back, but I need to figure out what is wrong before I can figure out how to fix it.

As the game ends and my dad and I part ways, I get in my car, turn on the radio and the song "I Would Walk 500 Miles" comes on, and I'm immediately transported back in time six years ago when Jenny and I went on our first date.

"I may have had too much to drink," I had admitted with a big smile to Jenny as I leaned my chair back on two legs.

She had smiled back at me and the beauty of it forced me to lose my balance and start windmilling my arms as I began to tip backwards.

Jenny immediately reached out, grabbed onto the front of my shirt with her fist, and yanked my chair back on four legs. The act caused the chair to slide closer to her and suddenly for the first time that night, I was close enough to run my nose against her cheek and smell her hair.

"Did you just smell my hair?" she asked.

I pulled back and gave her a sheepish look. "That depends. If I say yes, will you stick your stiletto up my ass?"

She smiled and shook her head "No".

"Then yes, yes I was sniffing your hair. It smells like mangoes."

"That is so hot," she whispered.

We stared into each other's eyes for a few minutes, and I had to mentally smack myself out of the trance she put me in before I threw her down on the table and banged her right there in front of God and everyone.

"So, I realized I'm not even close to sober when a few minutes ago, when I piss a take…I mean took a piss, I screamed when the automatic toilet flushed. I probably won't be able to drive you home," I told her honestly.

"Oh my God, I hate those automatic flushers! Sometimes they flush before I'm even finished and it creeps me out. Like it knows and can see me and just wants to mess with me," she said.

"Holy hell, I always tell people that. I really think there is a camera in the toilet bowl with some pervy little man in another room watching and laughing when he hits the button early."

We stared at each other for a few minutes and once again, there was nothing I'd rather do right then than to lean in and do dirty things with her mouth. But that wasn't something I wanted to do in the middle of a crowded bar. When it finally happened, we needed to be alone. Preferably in a bed. Or on a picnic table in a random park.

"Come on, give me the keys, I'll drive you home," she said as she held her hand out in front of me. I pull the keys out of my pocket and drop them in her hand.

⊙ ⊙ ⊙

Jenny insisted on stopping at Denny's on the way home because she was hungry and always wanted to order Moons Over My Hammy because it was funny to say. I almost asked her to marry me on the spot.

"Funny you mention ham. I have issues with ham when I'm really, really drunk," I told her, shoveling a mouthful of scrambled eggs in my mouth. "The past few times Carter and I have gone out, we always wind up at the grocery store at the end of the night so I can go to the deli counter and order five pounds of ham."

Jenny laughed and wiped her mouth on a napkin. "Why would you order five pounds of ham?" she asked.

"Well, I've only heard this story from Carter so I'm not absolutely sure it's true since I have no recollection of the events. But according to him, I always buy ham and then walk down the sidewalk tossing ham at people, calling myself the Meat Fairy."

Jenny continued to laugh and when my cell phone buzzed on the table in front of me, I ignored it. She picked it up and started scrolling through the apps. Normally, this would make me want to smack a chick in the ovaries, but with Jenny, I didn't mind at all. I leaned over and saw she was clicking on the Facebook app.

"Check and see if my status still says, 'I suck big cocks.' Carter got a hold of my phone the other day and I haven't figured out how to change it."

Jenny leaned slightly away and typed something into the phone with a smile on her face. I let her do her thing as I finished my food.

While we waited to pay the bill, we continued talking about stupid shit we'd done when we were drunk. Jenny's story about sending an email to her grandmother that said "I finger-banged an orangutan. It was a party at the zoo!" because she'll do anything people dare her to do when she's drunk had my Meat Fairy story beat by a long shot.

Jenny started up the car and I leaned over the console and rested my head on her shoulder, turned on the radio, and flipped through the stations. The gay ass song "I Would Walk 500 Miles" came on and I snorted a laugh.

"There are only two things I would walk 500 miles for: beef jerky and you," I admitted.

Jenny immediately flipped the blinker from turning right, toward my house, to left. I didn't say a word as she pulled out of the parking lot and away from the direction I lived. I was praying to the

Meat Fairy that she was taking me back to her place and I wouldn't want to say anything and spook her into turning around.

A few minutes later, we pulled into the driveway of a cute little blue bungalow with a front porch and flower boxes under the windows.

"So, this is my place. I hope it's okay we came here," she said quietly.

"It is absolutely okay. I live with Carter and he's probably at home jerking off with a bottle of chocolate sauce. My eyes can't take that shit anymore."

We get out of the car and I grab her hand as we round the hood and start up the stairs. She let go of my hand to dig into her purse for her keys and unlock the door. As we walk inside, I was suddenly reminded of the fact that I smell like beer and tequila. I needed a shower and I needed it bad. Even if nothing happened between us tonight, I still wanted to do everything in my power to be close to her. I wasn't doing that when Budweiser is leaking from my pores.

She happily obliged my request, showed me to the bathroom, leaving a folded, clean towel on the back of the toilet for me before leaving and closing the door behind her.

I undressed as quickly as possible and hopped into the shower, not wanting to waste too much time away from her. As always when I was in the shower, I started singing.

"Hold me closer, Tony Daaaaanza. Count the head lice on the hiiiiiiiighway."

While singing and washing my hair, I heard a noise behind me and turned to find a wet, naked Jenny standing in the shower with me, a huge grin on her face as she looked me up and down.

"Holy fuck, am I dreaming," I asked, speaking directly to her boobs. "I'm sorry, I'm finding it impossible to look you in the eyes right now."

I continued staring at the world's most perfect boobs as she took a step closer to me and held up a tube of something for me to see. I regrettably pulled my eyes away from booby heaven to read the label on the bottle that bottle said, 'Great Head'.

"I got this the other night at the sex toy party I went to. It's supposed to numb the back of my throat so I don't gag during a blow job. I've never been with a guy whose junk was anywhere near the back of my throat, but I'm pretty sure you have them beat. Wanna give it a try and see if it works?'

I stared at her with an open mouth and, I wasn't going to lie, a few tears in my eyes. Thank God the shower was throwing mist and drops of water all over the place and she wouldn't see my tears of joy.

All I could do was stare and nod my head up and down, my mouth still open in awe. She opened the tube of gel and squirted a generous amount on her index finger before sliding it into her mouth and sucking it clean. Little Drew jerked down below, and I mentally told him to calm his shit down or he was going to spit all over the place before this even started.

Jenny placed her hands on my chest and gently pushed me until my back was flat against the cold tile wall. She quickly got to her knees and wrapped her hand around my dick, running her tongue teasingly over the head as I squealed.

Yep, totally just squealed and I didn't even care.

I slid my hands into her wet hair and held on for dear life. There was no way I would push her down further, but I needed to do something with my hands before I started clapping them in front of me like a gay dude at a Barbara Streisand concert.

With one hand clutching my ass, her other hand slipped down my shaft and cupped my balls before she slid her mouth all the way down to the base.

"MISSISSIPPI MUD FUCK!" I yelled, thunking my head against the shower wall.

My excitement motivated Jenny to give it all she was worth. She sucked me in even deeper until yep, I felt the head of my cock touch the back of her throat. It was official. I was in the best porno movie in the history of the world. I now regretted my decision not to bring my cell phone into the shower with me. This was something that should be recorded for all time. After she adjusted her mouth around my shaft, she slid me almost all the way back out and then began a lightning fast rhythm with the whole in-out, in-out. Her small hand tightened around the base of my cock and began pumping me in sync with the glide of her mouth.

"Holy chips and dip, you're really good at this," I moaned as I looked down and watched her.

She moaned in answer and the sound vibrated all the way down my cock and through my balls. I started panting like a dog in heat. She moved her hand off of my ass and cupped my balls again, rolling them around in the palm of her hand.

"Goat fucking fucker that feels amazing!"

I continued to mutter nonsense as she quickened her pace. Within seconds, months of pent-up sperm erupted from my cock, and I screamed in drunken, mind-numbing pleasure as she swallowed all of my swimmers. "WILLIE NELSON WONDER CATS!"

My body stood completely still, every bone locked into place and my mouth hung open in shock and amazement while Jenny pulled me out of her mouth and kissed the head of my dick like it was a cute little puppy.

The water pouring out of the shower head went cold a while ago and I hadn't even noticed. Jenny stood up from her knees while I rested motionless against the shower wall, hoping my legs wouldn't give out.

"That stuff totally worked! I didn't gag at all! I tested it out earlier with a banana but it was mushy and I think I swallowed some of the skin. It was gross. You weren't gross at all and you kind of tasted like popcorn."

"I hope you know that I plan on marrying you some day. So keep your calendar open," I told her seriously as I turned off the water and we stepped out of the shower to towel ourselves off.

Jenny laughed the cutest little laugh and leaned up on her tip toes to kiss me on the cheek. Now that my excess sperm had vacated the meat whistle, all of the alcohol I consumed this evening started swirling around in my belly and a headache began forming.

"When I start puking tomorrow morning, just let me be. It will most likely start around 9:37. Just let me heave and don't cook any fish or chocolate pudding while it's happening. Also, if you find me spooning your coffee table or bar stool in the middle of the night, don't be afraid. Just wake me up and bring me back to bed. It usually only happens once."

As we had curled up in her bed, I picked my cell phone up from her nightstand and smiled to myself when I saw that she had indeed changed my Facebook status. Now it had said: I'm totally getting a BJ tonight.

10.

Mace, Tasers, and Giant Testicles

"I'm telling you, Liz, someone is following me," I argue as I put on my blinker at the stop light to turn into Target.

"I think you're just paranoid," Liz's voice states, coming through the speakers of the car. "You haven't had a good night's sleep in months and you're not having sex. I've heard that causes hallucinations."

I roll my eyes as the light turns green and I pull into the parking lot. I check my rear-view mirror every few seconds as I drive up and down the aisle looking for a parking space.

"I've been to three places this afternoon and each time there was a black SUV with tinted windows parked a few cars down from me or driving a few cars behind me. Every time I look in the mirror I see that damn car," I tell her as I finally find a spot. "I have a stalker. I just know it. I know I've always said I wish I had a stalker because I thought it would be cool and romantic, but I changed my mind."

I hear Liz laugh through the speakers as I turn around in my seat and search the parking lot for the SUV.

"If you're seriously freaked out, why don't you call Drew?"

"Because, he'll just race over here and make a testicle of himself," I mumble as I continue searching the lot.

"He's already a giant testicle. Don't you mean *spectacle?*"

"No, he doesn't wear glasses. Didn't I tell you what he did when those Jehovah's Witnesses came to the door and he thought they were threatening me? I didn't want to be mean but I couldn't get them off the damn porch. Drew came around the corner and heard me getting frustrated, pushed me out of the way, flung open the door, and started speaking in thongs," I explain.

"Tongues. For fuck's sake. He started speaking in tongues."

I huff in irritation. "Whatever. He started screaming all this nonsense with wild, crazy eyes and banging his head like he was at a rock concert. Those poor old people hobbled off the porch and ran to their car. If I call him right now, he'll start racing around the parking lot, busting old people's hips and scaring children."

"Alright, I'll tell you what. Claire and I are getting ready to close up. We'll meet you at the Starbucks in town for a coffee in like thirty minutes and see if we notice anyone looking suspicious. Will that make you feel better?" she asks.

"Yes, much better. I'll see you in thirty."

I disconnect the call, get out of the car, and run as fast as I can into Target just in case my stalker wants to try and run me down.

☉ ☉ ☉

"Jenny, this is ridiculous. I am not putting this shit on," Liz complains as she throws the Target bag back into my lap.

We had all managed to pull into the Starbucks parking lot at the exact same time. I had parked next to Liz's car and motioned for her and Claire to get into mine so they could change into their outfits before we did this thing.

"Shut up and just put them on. You don't want this lunatic to know we're on to him, do you?" I ask in irritation as I throw the bag back at Liz.

She turns around to look into the backseat just as Claire pulls off her t-shirt and slides on the black, long-sleeved shirt I bought her at Target.

"Oh my God. Are you seriously changing?" Liz asks her with a dumbfounded look on her face.

Claire's movements halt in the middle of unbuttoning her jeans so she can change into the black leggings I had also purchased. "What? Black is slimming. Even if there isn't a stalker, I'll look good drinking my coffee. Plus, Carter's been begging to do some role playing. I can creep into the bedroom window later and pretend I'm a cat burglar that suddenly wants to bang the man she's robbing."

"Didn't Carter get second degree burns on his ass last time you two role played?" I question.

"Yeah. Pretending to be a cooking instructor and telling him to hop up on the stove so I could 'lick his beaters' wasn't a good idea. We both forgot the stove was on. I went to the emergency room wearing just an apron for a shirt. Okay, so maybe I won't sneak in the bedroom window. Someone could get shot."

Liz is still staring in stunned silence as Claire pulls a black skull cap down over the top of her head.

"You're sure you saw the SUV driving behind you after you left Target?" Liz asks for the third time since getting in the car.

"Oh no!" I yell.

"No you didn't see the SUV?" Liz asks in confusion.

"No! I mean yes! I said *oh no* because the SUV is right there, parked across the street," I explain frantically as I point out Liz's window.

Liz and Claire's heads whip around, and they both stare at the black SUV parked on the corner with no one inside.

"Holy shit. Maybe you *are* being followed," Liz mutters.

"Duh!" I yell as I smack her arm.

"Jenny, last year you made me come over in the middle of the night while Drew was at work because you said a colony of spider eggs hatched and your bedroom was so full of spiders you couldn't even see the floor anymore and you were afraid they would eat Veronica. When I got to your house, there was one spider hanging from its web over your bed," Liz states. "Forgive me if I tend not to believe you."

"You can't blame me for that. Veronica woke me up that night, and when I came back in the room he was just hanging there. Spiders DO NOT work alone. And he was hovering over me, watching me sleep. Who knows what other plans he had in store for me. I bet his friends were just lurking in the corners waiting to pounce on me."

For several minutes Liz and I argue back and forth about what I like to refer to as "the night I almost got eaten alive by rabid spiders" when Claire suddenly grabs both of our shoulders from the back seat.

"Guys. I think I just saw some guy staring at the car," she states in a whisper. "Over there behind that bush."

"Why the fuck are you whispering? He can't hear you," Liz scolds.

"Shut the hell up, crotch rot!"

"Oh you did NOT just call me crotch rot, you twat-faced cum dumpster!"

"OH MY GOD! WILL YOU TWO SHUT UP! There is a man hiding behind a bush watching us!" I yell in frustration.

Liz and Claire give up on their insults to stare at the bush in question and sure enough, a head peaks out for a quick second and then goes right back into hiding.

"Oh it's ON now!" Liz says excitedly as she starts digging into her Target bag and scrambling into her black outfit.

"Okay, Jenny, you stay here. Claire and I will sneak out of our side of the car and double back around the building so we can creep up on this douchebag," Liz explains as she pulls her own black skull cap down low on her head. "How are we going to communicate what's going on though?"

I reach into my own Target bag that rests on my lap and pull out two walkie-talkies.

"I got these at the store too."

I hand one to Liz and clutch the other one tightly in my hand while I continue digging through the bag. "I've also got mace and a taser."

I hand the taser to Claire and the mace to Liz.

"Since when do they sell tasers at Target?" Claire asks, leaning forward in between mine and Liz's seats.

"Oh, they don't. I actually brought that from home. Drew likes it when I use it on his balls."

"Fuck, Jenny. Overshare," Liz complains.

I watch as they quietly and slowly open their doors and slink out of the car. They shut their doors without a sound and crouch down, moving across the parking lot toward the building. I immediately feel nervous and double-check the bush to make sure the guy is still hiding behind it and not paying attention to my friends.

I turn on my walkie-talkie and hold down the talk button.

"Hey," I whisper. "It's Jenny."

I let go of the button and within seconds hear Liz's voice. "No shit, Sherlock. We just made it to the back of the building," she says softly, the sounds of her heavy breathing coming through the walkie-talkie. "Don't watch where we're going. Don't act suspicious. Just keep an eye on stalker guy and let us know if he changes position. Over and out Mrs. Pink."

I stare at the device in my hand in confusion.

"Mrs. Pink?" I ask into the speaker.

"Yes, Mrs. Pink. I'm Mrs. Black, Claire is Mrs. Brown, and you're Mrs. Pink," Liz explains.

I hear Claire snatch the walkie-talkie out of Liz's hand seconds later. "I don't want to be Mrs. Brown. I want to be Mrs. Pink."

"Yeah, I don't get why I'm Mrs. Pink. I don't even like the color pink," I complain.

"Ooooh, I like the color pink. I'll be Mrs. Pink and you can be Mrs. Brown," Claire tells me.

"No, brown makes me think of poop. I want to be Mrs. Blue. Blue is pretty."

Suddenly there's a scuffle and some cursing coming through the speaker.

"You guys are such dicks. We're not changing secret names. Claire is Mrs. Brown because of chocolate and you're Mrs. Pink because pink makes me think of victims and now if anyone is on this channel they're going to know what we're doing," Liz explains in irritation.

"So why are you Mrs. Black?" I question.

"Because I'm going to blacken your face if you guys don't shut the fuck up. We are supposed to be commandeering a suspect, not having a coloring contest."

I sigh and rest my hand with the walkie-talkie in my lap, glancing out of the car window to see if my stalker is still behind the bush. I can see the bush rustling and what looks like a pair of black boots peeking out from underneath. Suddenly, I see Liz and Jenny running full speed from the other side of the building, straight at the bush. Without thinking, I throw the walkie-talkie onto the passenger seat and scramble out of the car, rushing across the parking lot towards them.

As I'm running, I see Liz dive behind the bush and tackle someone. I can hear Claire screaming at the top of her lungs, aiming her taser at the tangle of arms and legs I see flying out from the edge of the bush.

I finally get close enough to hear what's going on and see a quick flash of light burst out from the end of the taser followed by a high pitch scream.

"GAAAAAAAAAAAAAAH! YOU FUCK FACE. YOU JUST TASED ME!" Liz screams at Claire while her body spasms and yet, she still manages to straddle the stalker's back. She's got him face-planted into the ground and her elbow wrapped around his neck the whole time the electric voltage from the taser is ripping through her. She's like Rambo on crack.

"OH MY GOD! I'm sorry! I'm sorry! SHIT!" Claire yells as she yanks the taser back toward her to get it off of Liz.

"AAAAAHHHHHH! IT'S STUCK TO MY SKIN, YOU CUNT WHORE! CUT IT THE FUCK OUT!"

"Oh God, oh God, oh God," Claire mumbles as she drops the taser to the ground and rushes over to Liz while she bounces up and down on the guys back and tightens her hold on his neck.

"Oof, GET, oof, OFF, oof, ME!" the guy wheezes with each bounce as Liz lands on him.

"Tell us why you've been following our friend or I am going to mace you, you sick fuck," Liz yells as Claire gets behind her and gently removes the taser hooks from her ass.

The guy has on a baseball cap and dark sunglasses and I can't see his face, but there is something familiar about his voice. I don't know what to do at this point except just stand there helplessly and try to figure out how I know the man's voice. I know I should get in there and help Liz out, but I'm kind of afraid of her right now. She might mistake me for the enemy and break my face.

While I just stand there, Claire reaches into the waistband of Liz's leggings and pulls out the can of mace, holding it out in front of her as she circles the pair on the ground as they continue to struggle and Liz continues to lob insults at him.

"Just say the word, dude, and I will waste this mother fucker!" Claire says excitedly. "I've always wanted to say that!"

"Last chance, buddy. Why were you following our friend?" Liz asks as she arches her back and brings the guy's head up at an awkward angle since her arm is still locked tightly around his neck.

"I'll never talk. You can't make me!" the guy says brokenly as he pants and struggles to get Liz off of him.

I can't just stand there anymore. I need to do something. I walk up behind Claire and tap her on the shoulder. She must not have noticed I joined them because as soon as my fingers touches her arm, her body jolts in fright and she lets out a scream, the action causing her finger to slip and press down on the red button on the can of mace.

Within seconds, streams of liquid fire are hitting everyone in the face, including Claire herself as she screams and panics, her arms flying all over the place. I immediately drop to the ground coughing hysterically, tears running down my face. This burns worse than the time Drew ate hot wings and then went down on me. It feels like my eyes are bleeding and I can't stop coughing.

In the chaos of screams, coughs and crying, I blindly reach into my back pocket and pull out my cell phone, pressing the button on the side of it for the voice command thingy since I can't see to dial.

"CALL DREW! FUCKING HELL, CALL AN AMBULANCE!"

"Did you say, call Claire?"

"NO! CLAIRE IS RIGHT HERE, YOU IDIOT! I SAID CALL DREW! HELP!"

"Did you say browse the web?"

"YOU ARE SUPPOSED TO BE A SMART PHONE, YOU PIECE OF SHIT!"

"Did you say send a message?"

"NO, ASSHOLE! WAIT, YES! YES, YES, YES! SEND A MESSAGE TO DREW! TELL HIM WE'VE BEEN ATTACKED AND WE'RE DYING. TELL HIM WE NEED THE POLICE, A DOCTOR, AND HANDCUFFS!"

"Sending message to, Doctor Madison.

I throw the phone away from me and curl up in the fetal position in the grass, not even caring that I just sent a message to the new marriage counselor I had scheduled an appointment with for Drew and me. She has Drew's phone number in her records so maybe she'll get the text and call him.

I still hear shouts and crying all around me and squint open my eyes as best I can. The tears are pouring down my face and what I see is blurry, but it looks like Liz now has Claire in a headlock and the stalker is on all fours puking in the bush.

"OH MY GOD, MY EYES!!!" the guy shouts.

And just like that, I know exactly who my stalker is. Just a few years ago he had yelled the exact same thing when he walked into our living room and saw Drew doing a handstand against the wall next to the couch while I gave him a blow job.

With squinty eyes, I push myself up onto my hands and knees and crawl over to the figure still heaving in the shrubs.

"Dad? Is that you?" I ask.

"I am an absolute disgrace! What is your major malfunction, numb nuts? You let a bunch of namby-pamby girls take you down. I ought to take a giant shit on you!" he mumbles to himself between coughs and dry heaves.

Yep, that's my father-in-law. Leave it to him to quote *Full Metal Jacket* at a time like this. As soon as I can feel my face again and see out of my eyes, he's going to explain this whole mess to me.

"1-2-3-4 I LOVE THE MARINE CORPS!"

Well, maybe after the mace is gone from his system. I think it's affecting him worse than it is us girls.

"SON OF A BITCH, LIZ! Will you let go of my hair? It was an accident," Claire yells from behind me. "And I can hear you calling me a dumb fuck whore. I may be blind but I can still hear!"

"Then hear this, you dumb fuck whore! Sleep with one eye open. When I can see again, I will straight up shank you with a whittled down stiletto," Liz threatens with her eyes squeezed shut as she crazily swings her arms around trying to reach Claire, who managed to escape from her clutches, drop to the ground, and crawl away.

Alright, so maybe everyone has ingested a bit too much mace.

11.

Womb Hugging and Penis Loving

"YOU DID WHAT?!"

I wince at the sound of Jenny's screech as she throws the cold, wet towel off of her eyes and glares at me.

I can't help it. I laugh. She looks like she has hickies all around her eyes. They are puffy and red and right now it's really hard to look right at her.

"Look at me when I'm talking to you!"

Shit.

I actually do feel really bad that she was maced. She looks like hell and I'm sure it doesn't feel that great.

When I had got a phone call from some person named Doctor Madison telling me she received a text from my wife saying, "I pooped on the police and killed an ambulance. Bring handcuffs," I was a little confused, albeit intrigued. Who was I to judge my wife's kinkiness? I called Jenny right away and could only hear screaming and crying in the background and something about her eyes melting. When I got to the scene, my father was curled up in the fetal position in the parking lot where he crawled as far away from the girls as he could. He made me promise that I would keep Liz at least ten to twenty feet away from him at all times because she threatened to dig out his eyes with her belt buckle and he really thought she'd do it.

After getting my dad, Liz, and Claire home, I admitted to Jenny in the car about hiring my dad to follow her. I had figured it was safer that way. She wouldn't kill me while she was half blind and I was driving. She had ignored me the rest of the way home.

Now we are here, and she is only a few feet away from a kitchen full of sharp objects.

"You're telling me, you thought I was FAKING A WORK INJURY and you had your dad follow me? I thought I had some crazy stalker tailing me all day and he was going to induct me."

Yep, full on laughing right now. There's no hope for me. I've already accepted my fate of sleeping on the couch for the rest of eternity.

"Was this stalker going to *induct* you into the Stupid Crime Stoppers Hall of Fame?"

Jenny grabs the wet towel from the couch and re-covers her eyes, resting her head on the back of the couch.

"I can't even look at you right now I'm so angry. Why in the hell would you think I was faking an injury and trying to cheat Claire out of money? And your father? Really? You actually hired your insane father to follow me around? Did you see what he was wearing? Full on camouflage, a hat with branches glued to the top of it, and leaves painted all over his face. That is not normal, Drew."

Would now be a bad time to point out that all three women were dressed as slutty burglars?

I shrug even though she can't see me. "What can I say, he really gets into his work. And he said to tell you he was sorry."

She doesn't say a word. She just keeps her head on the back of the couch and the towel over her eyes. I feel like I'm in the principal's office, standing in front of her desk waiting for my punishment like that one time in high school when I put a little black skirt over the figure on the boy's bathroom door in an attempt to get some hot chicks to walk in on guys pissing. Instead, the principal had walked in on a Freshman whacking off during fourth period. The principal had ignored me for an hour before she finally gave me my punishment. I don't want to stand here for an hour. The kids are asleep and *Tosh.0* is coming on soon.

"Um, are we done here?" I ask.

"Did you seriously just say that to me?!" Jenny screeches.

How is it possible for women to hit decibels with their voices that even dogs can't hear?

"Yes, we're done here. You can explain your stupidity to Doctor Madison tomorrow when we go for marriage counseling."

I'm sorry, what?

⊙ ⊙ ⊙

"So, Drew, tell me why you think you're here?"

I stare at the woman sitting across from us wearing a long flowing skirt, Birkenstocks, and yellow tinted glasses. The smell of incense is so strong in here I think I'm going to be sick, and the soft sounds of Simon and Garfunkel coming from her radio in the corner makes me want to take a nap.

"I have no idea what the hell I'm doing here aside from having a bad '60s flashback," I mutter.

Jenny smacks my arm and I let out a big sigh.

"Oh it's okay, Jenny. This is a room of honesty. Your husband is free to express whatever is in his heart and mind when he's in this room without fear of judgment. I'll make this a little easier on you since it's your first time here. Jenny has explained to me over the phone that the two of you are having some communication issues. Is that correct?" she asks.

"Um, sure. I guess," I say with a shrug.

I don't know this woman, and I'm sure as hell not going to tell her the only communication problem my wife and I have right now is that her vagina doesn't want to speak to my dick. Hippy chick here will look right at my penis and wonder what's wrong with me. This stranger is going to think I have a third ball or my penis is shaped like a horseshoe.

"My penis is fine!" I shout.

Might as well put that out there before she gets any funny ideas. She doesn't even bat an eye at my outburst, just folds her hand in her lap and smiles at me.

"You have a real connection with your penis, is that correct?"

Is this really happening right now?

"Um, well, it IS connected to my body, so yes. I'm sort of connected to it."

She just smiles at me again and then points to my shirt. "I was referring to your shirt."

I glance down and realize I'm wearing one that says: I puffy heart my penis. Let me show you why.

"I think I can sense what the root of the problem is here. You two just had a baby not that long ago. Sometimes it's difficult for couples to connect again after something this life altering happens. What we need to do is get you two to connect."

Okay, I take it back. This woman might be a genius. If she can get my wife to connect with me at the pelvis, I will buy myself a pair of Birkenstocks and sit under a black light with her, smoking pot.

"Jenny, I'd like you to do something for me. Turn your body on the couch so that you are facing your husband."

Jenny does as she's told, pulling her legs up onto the couch and sitting Indian style.

"Okay, now, Jenny, I want you to look down at your husband's penis and tell it you love it."

Jenny hesitates and looks at Dr. Madison questioningly.

Do not question the good doctor! Do as she says!

"It's alright, Jenny. This will be good for both of you. Talk to the penis."

Jenny slowly turns back to me and stares right down at my lap.

"Um, I love you."

"Very good, Jenny! Now, I want you to apologize to the penis for taking it for granted," Dr. Madison explains kindly.

I wonder if she'll tell Jenny to suck the penis next. And if so, should I ask the good doctor to leave or stay?

"Uh, I'm sorry for taking you for granted," Jenny says while still staring at my lap.

"Excellent! Okay, Drew, now it's your turn," Dr. Madison states.

I don't even hesitate. "I love you penis! You are the best guy ever! No, seriously. You never let me down, you're always up when I need you to be, and I apologize for some of those issues we had back in college that required antibiotics," I say to my penis.

I look up at Dr. Madison, quite proud of myself for being such a team player with this whole therapy nonsense.

"That was very nice, Drew. But what I really wanted you to do was talk to Jenny's vagina," she explains.

Well alrighty then.

Figuring I might as well be comfortable for this, I curl up on the couch and rest my head on Jenny's thigh. "I love you too, vagina. I miss you like a hooker misses her virginity. True story. Why have you done me wrong, Boo? Why is there such a distance between us? Remember when we used to hang out every day? Now I barely see you once a month. You've changed, vagina. I hate to say this, but you have. You're a different person now, and it's like I don't even know you. I thought maybe you were hanging around with a different crowd of people and they influenced you against me. Maybe we're just growing apart. I don't want to lose you, vagina! I need you like I need air to breathe and football on Sundays. I just can't quit you, vagina!"

I realize when I finish that the room is eerily quiet. I lift my head from Jenny's leg and see both women staring at me with their mouth's open. Okay, so I had cried a little. Sue me. This is emotional shit. This doctor is getting to the heart of all of our problems. My penis and Jenny's vagina.

"Um, that was…uh, unexpected," Dr. Madison states.

I sit up fully on the couch and grab a Kleenex from the side table and blow my nose.

"Wow, that felt really good," I say, rolling my shoulders and stretching my neck from side to side. "It feels like a weight has been lifted. My mind is clear and I feel so free. What should we do next?"

Dr. Madison looks down at the notepad in her lap and flips a few pages. "Well, I think you have made some great progress, Drew. We just need to get Jenny where you are. Jenny, when was the last time you hugged your womb?"

"Hugged my room? I don't get it," Jenny says, confused.

"No, your *womb*. The place where you gave life to your two children," Dr. Madison explains.

"Uh, can I do that here? Shouldn't that be done in a real doctor's office with a table and stirrups? I don't think I can reach it otherwise. Unless you have a mirror and maybe a flashlight."

"If I can reach your G-spot in the middle of the woods with a tube of watermelon Bonne Belle Chap Stick while it's raining and there is a homeless guy in a tent four feet away singing the Sesame Street theme song, then you can hug your womb," I tell her encouragingly.

I probably shouldn't have brought that up because now I'm distracted and can only think about the one time we went camping and got lost in the woods.

And now I have a hard on.

"Actually, I don't mean you actually need to...um, reach up and touch your literal womb," Dr. Madison explains.

"Why is she talking about littering? Is she saying my womb is dirty?" Jenny whispers to me.

"What I need you to do, Jenny, is just cradle your arms around your lower stomach area. Hold your womb in your arms and give it comfort. Let it know you care."

Okay, now this chick is talking crazy.

"And while you're at it, try soothing your ovaries and give them some encouragement to open themselves back up and accept the love that is given. I believe the problem here is that your womanhood has closed itself off and no longer recognizes love."

Bat shit crazy. Talking to my penis and Jenny's vagina is normal. This is one step away from taking all of our clothes off and dancing and chanting around a sacrificed pig.

My awesome wife does as she's told though and wraps her arms around her waist. She gently rocks from side to side and begins talking to her "womanhood" like it's Billy.

"Such good little ovaries. Yes you are!"

I want off this crazy train. Right the fuck now!

Watching my wife rock-a-bye her ovaries makes me wonder what she initially thought we would get out of this counseling session. I had thought it would be a bunch of arguing and pointing fingers about whose fault it is that we aren't having sex anymore. Maybe she doesn't think that's the problem. Shit, maybe that *isn't* the problem. Maybe it's just *my* problem. She's not faking a work injury, she's not cheating on me...what the hell else could it be? A few years ago she cut me off from sex for a week because I gave her a Dutch Oven in bed one night. While hilarious, it's never a good idea when your wife is naked and getting ready to mount you.

There had been another time when I gave her a Wet Willy when she started coming. I hadn't meant for that to be hilarious. I read about it in Cosmo. When she had locked me out of the bedroom, I grabbed the magazine and realized two of the pages were stuck together - sex tips and practical jokes. Well played, Cosmo. Well played.

We leave the cuckoo doctor's office with a promise to keep communicating with our reproductive organs. Unfortunately, I still have no fucking clue how that's supposed to help get me laid.

12.

Baby Bullets

Since cuddling our reproductive organs has done nothing to boost our sex life, there's not much else for me to do except think back to a time when we *were* having sex. Man, those were the days. We had A LOT of sex. Like, a lot. Pretty sure it was impossible to even count that high. And fuck, was it good sex. Even when we were trying to get pregnant with Veronica it was good sex. You would think that since we pretty much used to have sex every single day, it would have been easy for us to get pregnant. I had always thought that shoving as much sperm up there as you could guaranteed you a baby.

I mean, it makes sense right? If you've got this little egg, and you just throw a handful of sperm at it, what are the chances that one will get through? But if you pour gallons and gallons of sperm all over it, that's got to up your chances, right?

False! Those little white-tailed squirmy devils have serious attitude. It's like they think they're too good to fertilize an egg. Little bastards. You've got to trick them into submission. A sneak attack when they're least expecting it.

"What, you say he's going to put us through the tunnel while he's on a Tilt-a-Whirl? Impossible!"

"I do declare he just shot us out of his cannon in a golf cart on the highway. Preposterous!"

You see? Listen to those stuck-up fuckers. They even talk like assholes.

After eight months with no success in getting pregnant, instead of letting it get us down, we had just got creative. We had sex in a supply closet on the maternity floor of a hospital because Jenny thought it would bring us luck. It didn't, but we got two bottles of Windex, three pairs of doctor's scrubs, and a box of rubber gloves out of the experience. That was almost better than a baby!

Another time, Jenny had made a list of all of the couples we knew who either were currently pregnant or had already had a baby. We went down the list and had sex in their beds. She figured there must be some kind of magical power in their beds that made it so *they* could have a baby. Having sex in their beds would get some of that magic to rub off on us. Yeah, that didn't work either. And let me tell you, Carter and Claire were not so agreeable with our magic dust plan. I still didn't get what the big deal was. It wasn't like we had sex while they were in the house. We made sure to wait until they left for work. Geeze, give us a little credit. I still had a scar on my forehead from when Claire threw a lamp at my head. It wasn't our fault they decided to come home early. They should have just followed their normal schedules and none of that would have happened.

The next one was totally genius and all my idea. What has more sperm than it knows what to do with? Yep. A sperm bank. I made an appointment and then made my deposit. In my wife – booyah! I figured this place was getting people knocked up every single day, so there had to be some luck in that, right? Jenny was a little nervous at first. She said she was certain that little particles of sperm were floating in the air at that place, and she was nervous that a particle from someone else would get all up in her business, and then she'd give birth to a baby that wasn't mine. Don't worry though, we took precautions. We kept her lady bits completely covered until I was ready for my deposit, ensuring that my particles were the only ones getting inside. The nurse at that place wasn't too happy when we came back out and I told her I had made the deposit in the wrong cup. Jenny also wasn't too happy that I kept referring to her vagina as a cup for the next several months.

I had been a little sad my idea hadn't worked, but it was okay because we came up with something even better.

It's a good thing and a bad thing the next experiment actually worked. I say bad just because some day Veronica is going to ask where she was conceived and were going to have to tell her in the men's room at a Red Lobster. Jenny had read somewhere that lobsters were lackadaisical, which in her mind, meant they would boost our desire, thereby ensuring we got pregnant. I was pretty sure she was trying to say aphrodisiac, but I wasn't about to correct her when it meant I was going to get laid with a belly full of lobster and delicious Cheddar Bay Biscuits. Before the bill came, we excused ourselves from the table and sneaked into the women's room. As soon as I saw the tampon machine on the wall, I turned around and walked right back out. I couldn't concentrate on banging if I was thinking about the red vagina of pain. I grabbed Jenny's hand and marched us over to the men's room. The coast was clear; the urinals were empty and both of the stalls were unoccupied. I dragged her back to the handicap stall and got down to business.

"Fuck, you look so hot in that dress, baby," I said softly as I slid my hands around her hips and grabbed her ass, pulling her against me.

"Do you think it's unclean to do this in a bathroom? What if I get germs in my vagina?" Jenny asked nervously as she looked around the inside of the stall.

"You obviously have no idea how unclean my penis is if you're asking me this," I told her honestly as I slipped my hands under her dress, pushing it up past her hips.

"Jesus, you aren't wearing any underwear," I mumbled against the side of her neck as my hand glides over her bare ass.

"I took them off at the table," she told me, wrapping her arms around my neck as I sucked and licked the skin right under her ear.

"That's so hot. Did you put them in your purse?"

I felt her shake her head "no" as my hand slid around in front, and I pushed my fingers through her soft, wet skin.

"Oh God that feels good! No, not in my purse. I just left them on the floor under the table."

I pushed and twisted my fingers through her heated center, sliding them up and around her clit with each pass.

"Fuck! Take your pants off!" Jenny muttered as she clutched her fingers tightly into my hair.

I pulled my fingers out of her with a groan, quickly unbuttoned and unzipped my pants, and pushed them down to my knees. Jenny lifted one leg up, wrapping it around my hip so I could hold it in place by her knee. With my free hand, I grabbed my dick and positioned it at her entrance.

"We're totally making a baby right now," I told her.

"This is going to be the best bathroom baby ever made!" she said excitedly.

I thrusted into her smooth and fast, squeezing my eyes closed, trying to calm myself down with how good she felt wrapped around my dick. After a few seconds of getting myself under control, I stopped thinking about anything else but fucking my wife and those snot-nosed little sperms who thought they were better than everyone else. I began moving in and out of Jenny at a rapid pace, loving the little sounds of pleasure that came out of her mouth.

"Fuck, I'm getting a cramp in my leg," Jenny said after a few seconds.

I stopped moving, still buried balls-deep in her, giving her a second to put her leg down and try to get more comfortable.

"Here, wrap both legs around me," I told her as I lift her up, pushing her back against the wall of the stall.

Her long, smooth legs locked around my waist, and I got back to the task at hand. Pretty soon, Jenny was clawing at my back and groaning loudly, and I knew she was close to coming. I sped up my movements until the stall was rattling and slamming against the wall of the bathroom.

"OW! Son of a bitch! This is killing my back," Jenny complained suddenly.

I pulled out of her as I let go of her legs and set her back down on the floor.

She stood there for a minute with her hands on her hips, looking at our surroundings.

"I've got it! I'll kneel on top of the toilet and you can rail me from behind," she said with a smile as she moved past me and put her knees on the seat of the toilet and faced the wall.

"Oh my God, I love you so much right now," I told her as I watch her get situated.

I had a clear view of her naked ass, and I was pretty sure if I didn't hurry up and get back inside her, I was going to shoot these baby bullets all over the floor.

She looked back at me over one shoulder and smiled.

"Saddle up, cowboy. Give me your baby juice."

I closed the gap between us, and she leaned forward awkwardly, resting her forehead against the wall behind the toilet, wrapping her hands around the flusher to keep her steady.

Grabbing onto her hips, I slid back home again, letting out a loud groan when I was deep inside her again.

"Ohhhhhhhhhh fuck," I moaned as I got my rhythm back.

I thought I heard a noise in the bathroom but nothing was going to stop me right now. I was in heaven and I wasn't ready to come out yet.

"Jeeeeeeesus!" I exclaimed loudly, thrusting into Jenny with all my might.

At this point we were both grunting and panting and oblivious to everything else around us.

"Fuck this is good. So good. Uuuuuuunnnnggggghhhh," I moaned.

"I'm sorry, but are you okay in there?"

The sound of another man's voice in the next stall forced us to halt our movements immediately. I was clutching onto Jenny's hips, and she whipped her head around to stare at me with wide eyes.

"Um, ha, ha, yes! I'm super, thanks for asking!" I replied back to the guy.

Jenny gave me a "what the fuck" look and I just shrugged. As she turned back around, she shifted on my dick a little and did that awesome thing with her vagina where it squeezes me.

"Oh my goat milk, that's hot!" I cried out.

"Ooooh, yeah. Goat milk has that reaction with me too. I always get the fire shits from goat milk," the guy in the next stall told me.

This guy needed to shut the fuck up already! I didn't need to hear about his burning asshole while I was trying to make a baby! It was like this guy had no class.

I did my best to ignore the rude guy next door so I could finish this thing before Jenny decided it was a bad idea. She turned her head again and looked me in the eye, mouthing the words, "Hurry the fuck up!"

Don't mind if I do!

Without a second thought, I started banging the hell out of her again.

"Fuck yeah. Oh fuck, I'm so close!" I muttered.

"You're doing great, buddy. Keep pushing!" my bathroom friend encouraged me.

"Oh hell yes! I'm pushing, fuck yeah!" I shouted back, bolstered by his enthusiasm.

"Oh my God, I can't believe this is happening," Jenny whispered.

"Oh, it's happening! It's totally happening, baby!" I told her.

I could feel my orgasm and it was right there, just a few more thrusts and I could send those little sperm fuckers to their home!

Mid-thrust, Jenny lost her grip and her hand slipped, causing the toilet handle to push down, making the toilet flush.

"Well that was awkward," I said as I continued what I was doing.

"Nope, not awkward at all," bathroom man yelled back. "A courtesy flush is always a good idea."

Even with this guy talking my ear off, Jenny felt so good that it was impossible to stop my orgasm from rushing up through my balls.

"YES! YES! YES!" I shouted with my head thrown back.

With one last thrust—that I will argue until my dying day wasn't that hard— Jenny lost her balance on the toilet seat while I came, and one of her knees slipped down into the toilet with a loud splash. Water flew out of the bowl and all over the floor.

"Oops," I said sheepishly as I shivered through the final seconds of my orgasm. I had pulled out of Jenny and backed away from her while she struggled and tried to get her knee out of the toilet, forcing more water all over the place.

"It's okay, man, happens to the best of us," the guy next door had admitted.

"Ain't that the truth?!" I answered.

So, yeah. That's the story of Veronica's conception and now Jenny and I have to figure out how to break that news to her when she's older. Maybe we can leave out the part of the spectator in the next stall over. And the part about never finding Mommy's underwear when we had got back to the table. And how Mommy fell in the toilet. You know what? I think we'll just make something up.

Fuck, now I'm horny.

I glance at my watch and realize I've got some time before Billy will be up from his nap and Jenny will be home with Veronica. Normally, I'd go jerk off, but Drew junior is a little under the weather. Remember when you were little and your mom would tell you that if you whacked off too much you'd get hairy palms? That's so not true. Believe me, I've tried to make it come true. I had thought it would be the coolest thing ever to have hands like Teen Wolf. Who needs a dog when you can pet your own hands? Michael J. Fox had no idea how good he had it. Anyway, it turns out, whacking off too much doesn't cause hairy palms. It causes a raw, chafed dick. I'm blaming this all on Head and Shoulders. Stupid blue and white bottle that looks so friendly with its happy little green bubbles on the bottle. I had thought rubbing my love handle in the privacy of the shower with a little squirt of fresh-smelling shampoo the other day would be lovely. I mean, have you felt shampoo lately? It's soft and soapy and smells like heaven. Plus, if it can give you silky, smooth hair. That should naturally mean it will give you a silky, smooth penis.

Folks, never, I repeat, NEVER, yank your wank with shampoo. It may sound like a good idea at the time; it may even FEEL like a good idea at the time. Just give it a few minutes and then your dick will turn into the fiery pits of hell. It will burn like Satan himself is breathing his fire breath on your Willy Wonka. Oh, and it will also feel like someone is chewing on your dick. With razor blades for teeth.

So, while my dick is on the mend, I think I'll spend some quiet time thinking about ways to make my wife have dirty bathroom sex with me again.

13.

Hiney Duck Hiss

Once a month, the six of us try to get together for a game night. We always say that one of these times we should all get babysitters so the evening doesn't include stopping the game every few minutes to break up a fight between the girls and then forty-five minutes of screaming and crying at the end of the night when it's time to leave. For some reason, the weeks in between game nights make us forget about the fact that we were supposed to get a babysitter. It isn't until the first blood curdling scream comes from a bedroom or toy room that we remember.

Tonight we only have Veronica with us. Drew's dad still feels bad about making me think he was a stalker so he's offered babysitting services whenever we need it.

He had told me as we were leaving to make sure I let Liz know how nice he is for offering up his time for us. He also mentioned to stress the fact that he is doing this out of the goodness of his heart. Drew's mom had called me the other day and said that whenever he leaves the house he runs as fast as he can to his car, gets in, and locks the doors.

I'm pretty sure Liz has scarred him for life.

We pull into Carter and Claire's driveway and park behind Liz and Jim's van.

"Honey, have you hugged your vagina today?" Drew asks me with a smirk as he turns off the engine and pockets the keys.

"Will you stop it with that? I already admitted that Dr. Madison was a bad idea. Stop reminding me," I complain as I get out of the car and get Veronica unbuckled from the back seat.

Drew has been teasing me nonstop about our botched marriage therapy session. I don't understand how I could have judged Dr. Madison so wrong.

"Didn't you Google her or anything first? Find out what she was about?"

"Of course I did," I say in exasperation as I grab Veronica's hand and we walk up the driveway. "Her add in the newspaper said she was 'new age' and 'holyistic'. I didn't understand the 'new age' thing. I figured she was just an older woman who wasn't happy with getting older and instead of telling people her age, she just made up something called 'new age'. Sort of like when babies are newly born. Or like, 'How old are you?' 'Oh, I'm new age!'

And being holyistic, you would think that therapy session would have centered more around being holy and close to God. We could use some holyistic in our marriage. We haven't been to church in years."

Drew closes his eyes and shakes his head as he rings the doorbell. I know he totally agrees with me and is just too annoyed about the whole therapy thing to say anything else.

"It's about time you got here!" Carter says as he opens the door. "Charlotte and Sophia have already pulled hair, clawed eyes out, and one of them shoved the other into the bathtub and turned the shower on. Not sure who did it since we found both of them crying and sopping wet."

Carter steps back and holds the door open for us so we can walk inside.

"Hey, man, nice shirt!" Jim states as he comes from around the corner into the living room.

Tonight, in honor of game night, Drew is wearing the shirt I got him for Christmas last year. It's got a picture of a Twister mat and says: How about a game of Twister? Right hand on my penis, left hand on my ass.

"Veronica, why don't you go on back to the playroom and see what the girls are doing?" I tell her as I bend down to help her remove her coat.

605

"Don't tell me what to do, devil woman!"

I stand up and glare at Drew.

"What? Can I help it if she has everything from 'Billy Madison' memorized?"

Veronica takes off running down the hall before I can scold her. Technically it's Drew who needs scolding, but at this point there's no use.

"Come on, everyone's in the dining room," Jim says as he turns and leads the way.

An hour later we're in the middle of a game of Mad Gab. I hate this game. Well, I hate it when it's my turn because I never get any of them right. But it is pretty funny when it's someone else's turn. On one side of the card is a popular phrase, but the words are kind of jumbled together so you can't tell right away what the phrase is. You have to say the words out loud over and over until it starts to sound like the right phrase. For example, the last one that was done, the card said: Abe Odd Hull Luck Oak. The answer, written on the back of the card was: A bottle of Coke.

"Alright, it's Jenny's turn," Claire announces as she pulls a card from the box.

I groan, preparing for the fact that I will lose again.

Claire holds up the card and I read the words, mumbling them to myself.

"No, no, no. You know the rules, Jenny. Say them out loud," Liz scolds.

I huff and start reading the words really slowly. "Hiney…duck… hiss. Hiney…duck…hiss."

Liz is leaning over close to Claire so they can both see what the answer should be and they are laughing hysterically.

"Hiney…duck…hiss. Hiney duck hiss. Hiney duck hiss," I say, trying to say it a little faster in the hopes that it will spark something in my mind.

Nope.

"Oh God, I can't!" Liz laughs, holding on to her stomach and resting her forehead on top of the table. "Hiney duck!"

"Try saying it really, really fast," Drew suggests, laughing as well.

"Hineyduckhiss. Hineyduckhiss. Hineyduckhiss. This is dumb. It makes no sense," I complain. "Just tell me the answer."

Claire continues to laugh as she turns the card around to show everyone the answer.

"I need a kiss? You have got to be kidding me!"

I really hate this game.

"Oh, I told you guys about the charity thing I'm doing at the shop this weekend, right?" Liz asks as she starts packing up Mad Gab to put it away.

"You mentioned something about it but refresh my memory," Drew says as he leans back in his chair and rests his arm on the back of mine.

"Well, you know how last year we did a silent auction and all the proceeds went to The American Cancer Society? I wanted to do something a little more outrageous this year and with more of a theme that matches my store. So, I am having a vibrator race," Liz announces.

"Whoa, really?" Drew asks. "Is that legal?"

"Why wouldn't it be legal? I'm having it in the lot behind the store which is completely fenced in, and there will be security at the door to make sure only eighteen and up are allowed in. There will be bets and different heats and lots to drink. So make sure you all have a fantastic vibrator to bring with you. Or you could always buy a new one at the store when you get there."

Before I can ask any questions about the vibrator race and how exactly it works, Claire shushes all of us.

"Do you guys notice anything?" she asks.

We all pause and listen.

"It's really quiet. Why is it so quiet?" Jim asks.

With five girls in the house and a ten year old boy, there should definitely be a lot of noise coming from down the hall. The fact that we've been able to play a game uninterrupted for an entire hour should have clued us in that something was up.

We all jump up from the table and race down the hall. Drew is the first one to the playroom door and stops dead in his tracks in the doorway, blocking all of our views.

"Oh, holy Mary Tyler Moore," he mutters before turning around and placing his arms on the doorframe so no one can get in. "You do NOT want to go in there."

We all stand in the hallway giving each other equal looks of fear and horror at what could possibly be happening on the other side of Drew.

Is someone dead? Did the cat fights finally get serious and one of the girls is now missing an eye? What if it's Veronica? Oh my God, my baby is going to have to go through life wearing an eye patch like a pirate! On National Pirate Day she'll be expected to dress up and talk in a funny voice the whole day because she's a pirate every day and everyone will just assume she's really good at it. But what if she isn't good at being a pirate? She'll be hated by all for not knowing what "walk the plank" means. I don't even know what the hell it means!

"Drew, what the fuck, man? What did they do?" Carter asks as he pushes me to the side so he can see over Drew's arms.

"Oh my fuck," Carter sighs. "You might as well drop your arms. They're going to have to see it sooner or later. Claire, take a deep breath first."

Drew finally moves out of the way and we can all see just what has happened in the play room.

All five girls are sitting in a circle in the middle of the room, and each one's face is completely covered in black Sharpie marker. And when I say completely covered, I mean completely. Absolutely. Lips, nose, eyelids, ears…covered. We all slowly make our way into the room, our mouths drop open in shock. It's not until we're fully inside the room that we notice the extent of the damage. As I turn around in circles, I'm kind of amazed at the detail of the scenes drawn on the wall. In black Sharpie. They actually drew a castle with a princess in the tower and a moat. It's a pretty good picture.

"Holy hell, is that a dragon? Dude, who did the dragon? That's pretty good," Drew asks.

"I did!" Charlotte pipes up. She immediately wipes the black smile off of her face when she sees the murderous look on Liz's face.

"I just painted these walls," Claire mumbles as she takes on a catatonic look and stares at the ceiling.

"Gavin! Have you been in here this entire time?" Carter shouts.

I didn't even notice Gavin sitting sideways in a chair in the corner with his legs hanging over the arms, flipping through a book.

"Yep," Gavin answers as he continues turning the pages without looking up.

"Um, and you didn't think it was necessary to tell us the girls were painting their faces and the walls with a marker that doesn't wash off?" Carter scolds.

Gavin finally looks away from his book and notices the girls in the middle of the room, all sitting silently and still clutching the permanent markers in their hands.

"Heh, heh. Nice job, cootie faces!"

"Shut up, you piece of crap!" Ava yells.

"AVA!" Liz yells.

"What? I'm not allowed to call him a piece of shit, am I?" she replies as she crosses her arms and pouts.

"She's got a point. She's not allowed to say 'shit'," Jim whispers to Liz.

"I just painted these walls," Claire mutters again.

"This is the best game night ever!" Drew exclaims as he pulls out his cell phone and starts snapping pictures. "Girls, say, 'Once you go black, you never go back!'"

I walk over and smack his arm, snatching the phone out of his hand. "Alright, girls, everybody up, clothes off and into the bathroom."

Liz and I start herding the girls out of the room and across the hall.

"Gavin, go get some soap and water and start scrubbing these walls," Carter says as he makes his way over to Claire and wraps her in his arms.

"Why do I have to clean the walls? I didn't draw on them. This is HORSESHIT!"

"GAVIN ALLEN! I JUST PAINTED THESE WALLS! DID YOU HEAR ME? I...JUST...PAINTED...THESE...WALLS! IJUSTPAINTEDTHESEWALLS! IJUSTPAINTEDTHESEWALLS!" Claire shrieks.

"Is she losing her shit or is she trying to do another Mad Gab?" Drew asks me. "Because if it's a Mad Gab, I'm going with 'A just plain teddy swallows'."

14.

Racers, Take Your Mark

The weekend is finally here and even though it's been an exhausting week with work, getting up at all hours of the night with Billy and giving Veronica eight baths in the last three days to try and get marker off of her face, I'm excited to go to the charity event that Liz is having. And I'm not going to lie. I'm a little nervous. I've never been shy about sex. Ever. But since having Billy, I don't feel sexy. Most likely from the fact that I get maybe three hours of sleep every night. But still, I think today will be good for Drew and I. The marriage counseling was a bust and the dinner with our neighbors didn't provide us with any kind of help, so I'm hoping maybe this will do the trick. Maybe it will give me the spark I need to feel sexy and get back on the sex train. I feel bad for Drew. We used to have sex every single day, sometimes two or three times. I know he's frustrated. I'm frustrated too. I want to want to have sex. I miss sex. I miss sex with him. I'm determined to make today a success even though all I want to do is go back to sleep.

"Okay, you've got your traditional rabbit, which has rotating beads and tantalizing bunny ears. According to my chart, it has a one hundred percent success rate of completion within five point three minutes," Drew states as he looks at a page of the binder in his hand.

We're in our bedroom with all of my vibrators spread out on the floor. Drew is determined that I win this race today so he has spent all week analyzing vibrators, making flow charts, and running diagnosis tests on them.

"Next, we have your standard silver bullet. It's simple, straight-forward, and could be our ace in the hole. Pun intended. No one would think to use the bullet because it's so small. But this baby's got kick, highlighted by my report of a one hundred percent success rate within two point seven minutes. I think we really need to set that one aside as a contender."

I pick up the silver bullet and set it apart from the rest.

"I'm nervous about this race. Do you really think I have a chance to win?"

Drew closes his binder and squats down next to me at my place sitting on the floor. "Baby, you've got this thing in the bag. You could win this thing with your eyes closed and your arms cut off. You just have to believe."

I nod my head and motion for him to proceed with the binder of stats.

Thirty minutes later, we've narrowed down our selection to the top two, which is pretty amazing considering I have no less than thirty-seven vibrators. As we pack up the rainbow of colorful objects and place them back into our suitcase of fun to slide back under our bed, I hear the front door open and close.

"Are you two soldiers ready for action today?" Andrew Senior states from our bedroom doorway.

Once again, he's offered to babysit for us. I can't possibly stay angry with him since it seems like this babysitting offer is going to be on the table for a long time to come.

"Affirmative, sir. We are locked and loaded," Drew states as he pulls me up from the floor and holds up the small, black velvet bag that houses the silver bullet.

"Did you clean your weapon and load it with new batteries? A clean, properly functioning weapon is a happy weapon," my father-in-law informs us.

"The chambers have been cleaned, the batteries have been replaced, and this soldier here is ready for battle," Drew says as he wraps his arm around my shoulder and pulls me into his side.

"Stay smart, keep your head down, and for God's sakes, don't be a pansy ass," Andrew advises me. "The deadliest thing in this world is a soldier and his or her weapon. Respect your weapon and it will respect you, is that clear?"

I nod my head and mumble, "Yes."

"YES WHAT?!"

"YES, SIR!" I shout, putting my hand up to my head and saluting him.

"At ease, soldier."

Surprisingly, his pep talk has motivated me and taken away my nerves. I'm going to go into the race and I'm going to win it all. I'm going to show all of those fools how it's done. I haven't been an adventurous, sexual person all of my adult life for nothing. This race is mine!

Drew has changed into his motivational shirt that he got just for me. It has a picture of a vibrator on it and the words: My wife is #1 at diddling!

We leave Drew's dad with a napping Billy and a hyper Veronica since Drew had let her have toast with sugar on it for breakfast. I'm amazed at the amount of cars parked all around downtown by Liz and Claire's shops. We finally find a parking spot and walk into Liz's side of the store, which is packed with people checking out her selection of vibrators.

"Look at all these losers trying to pick a winning vibrator at the last minute," Drew whispers as we squeeze our way through everyone so we can get to the back door and out into the parking lot where the event is being held. "With my analysis reports, this race is all ours. You can't go into something like this without a toy you're already familiar with. Do these people know nothing? How do they expect to win a race with a toy they've never used before? How do they know they're even going to mesh with that toy? Total amateurs, I'm telling you."

I get more and more excited listening to what Drew is telling me. He's right. I am very familiar with my bullet. We go way back. It's the first toy I ever bought when I was eighteen. We've come a long way since then. This little guy in my pocket has been with me through the good and the bad. He won't let me down today.

"Hey, guys!" Liz greets us as she rushes over to where we are currently standing next to a food vendor tent. She holds a clipboard in her hand and scans a piece of paper attached to it. "Okay, Jenny, you're in heat one of the first round. It's going to take place in the tent next to the beer stand."

I glance over to the direction she's pointing and frown.

"Um, that tent is wide open. I kind of thought it would be a little more private," I tell her, glancing nervously up at Drew.

"It's okay, we can work with that," Drew reassures me.

"Why would it need to be private? It's just a race. And everyone here knows what's going on. They wouldn't be here if they have a problem with it," Liz explains.

She's right. Everyone here had received an invitation with an explanation of what was going on today, so I guess they know what they'll be seeing. I suppose I just hadn't thought about the fact that they'd be seeing *me*. Oh well, I want to get a spark back so I guess this is as good a way as any.

Liz wishes us good luck and runs off to greet more people and let them know what race tent they are in. Drew and I make our way over to the beer tent next to where I will be racing. He gets in line and orders a beer for each of us.

"Chug it. You look like you could use this," he informs me as he hands me a plastic cup overflowing with beer.

I down the beer as fast as I can and hand him the empty cup. He sets it down and moves behind me to rub my shoulders.

"I've been scoping out the competition in our tent. There are a few old people who look scared. That one chick in the purple shirt looks tough, but see how she's tapping her foot? She's nervous. You're calm as a cucumber. That's how you're going to win this thing. Show no fear, baby. Maybe you should stretch," Drew advises.

As he continues to massage my shoulders, I roll my head from side to side and shake out my hands. I grab onto my elbow and pull my arm across the front of my body, repeating the action with my other arm. Liz makes an announcement over the microphone that the first heats will be starting in ten minutes. Drew turns me around to face him and holds my face in his hands.

"Repeat after me. I'm a winner."

"I'm a winner," I tell him.

"I'm more awesome than all these people," he states.

"I'm more awesome than all these people."

"If I win this thing, I will take my husband home and fuck his brains out."

I stare at him for a minute, raising my eyebrow at his statement.

"SAY IT!"

I sigh and roll my eyes. "If I win this thing, I will take my husband home and fuck his brains out."

Drew sniffles. "I think I'm going to cry."

"What's up, assholes?" Jim asks as he walks up to us with Carter and Claire.

"Just giving Jenny a last minute pep talk before the race," Drew informs him.

"There's no need for that," Carter says. "Claire is going to kick everyone's ass."

Drew laughs and shakes his head. "Oh that's hilarious, limp dick! I know for a fact that Jenny will be the victor."

"The Victor? Who's Victor? Is that like some vibrator champion or something? Is the race named after this Victor guy?"

Claire pats my shoulder and just smiles at me. I guess she already knows about Victor. I'm always the last to know everything.

"What toy did she pick?" Carter asks Drew.

"The silver bullet, baby!"

Carter laughs and shakes his head. "Seriously? The bullet is like the grandfather of vibrators. Are you sure it can last long enough without needing to take a nap? There's no way that thing is going to win."

Drew crosses his arms and glares at Carter. "Really? So what amazing vibrator is Claire using?"

Carter smirks and wraps his arms around Claire's waist from behind, resting his chin on top of her head. "The brand new, hot from the factory Butterfly FX 2000."

It's Drew's turn to laugh now and he throws his head back, letting out a loud chuckle. "The Butterfly FX 2000? You've got to be kidding me! That's child's play! Have you even read the reviews on that thing? Did you conduct wind velocity tests and check water submersion quality? You can't go into this thing half cocked, my friend. You guys really should leave this race to the professionals."

"How about we put a little wager on the race?" Jim asks, pulling his wallet out of his back pocket. "I've got ten bucks on Jenny."

Claire gives him a dirty look. "Hey!"

"Sorry," Jim says with a shrug. "Jenny kind of is an expert with these things. You've only been doing this for a little while. She's got years on you."

The men all place their bets and Jim holds on to the money since he doesn't have a wife in the race. Liz makes another announcement over the microphone that everyone should get into their assigned tents because the races are starting. Claire and I are going to be in the same tent for the first heat and that calms my nerves quite a bit. Even though Drew will be close by, having a friend with me makes me even more comfortable.

We all walk together under the tent and greet the other participants. There are six other women and two men. I really don't understand the men being here and being allowed to participate. How exactly does THAT work? It doesn't really seem fair since they could do this race pretty easily without a vibrator but whatever. I don't make up the rules. I'm sure Liz knows what she's doing.

According to the judge in our tent, everyone in the race will go at the same time. I like that idea better than individually since not everyone will be looking at me. He doesn't really give any more explanation though, and I stare at the table in front of us in confusion.

"Am I supposed to just get up on that thing?" I quietly ask Drew.

He glances around at everyone else and no one is making a move to get on the table. They all have their chosen vibrators out and are testing the speeds on them.

"I don't know what the table is for. It's not like you can all fit on it at one time. Maybe it's for support. Like, you can hold onto it if you need to. It would have been better if they provided cots or something, but you gotta work with what you got."

I shrug and pull the velvet bag out of my pocket, sliding the bullet out and fiddling with the speed control.

"I know you usually start that thing off slow and work your way up, but now isn't the time for slow. Crank that puppy up full speed and take these mother fuckers out!" Drew says excitedly.

"Racers, take your mark!" the judge shouts.

Everyone starts clapping, whistling, and cheering. I clutch the bullet in my hand, double checking to make sure it's set to super high speed. I glance over at Claire and she's got her butterfly resting on top of the table. I notice everyone else in the race has done the same thing.

Am I supposed to put the bullet on the table too? Is that like the starting off position?

I decide to do what everyone else is doing and set the silver cylinder on the table top in between a pink rabbit and a yellow dolphin.

"Get set!" the judge yells.

Everyone around the table hunches over their toys. Drew and the guys have stepped back a few feet away from us to give us room. I kind of want to tell him to come back closer to me because this is always easier for me if he's touching me in some way at the same time, but like he had said, I have to work with what I've got.

"GO!" the judge yells, holding a small air horn above his head, pressing the button for a single, loud noise indicating the race has begun.

I quickly pull the bullet off of the table and close my eyes, pushing my hand clutching the bullet down the front of my pants. Drew's suggestion of wearing yoga pants with no underwear is genius. I have easy access without having to get naked in front of all of these people.

I hear screams and shouts of "Go! Go! Go!" from all around me, but I block it all out, hit the power button on the vibrator, and concentrate.

As soon as the bullet touches my clit, I know this isn't going to take long at all. I wasn't lying when I said I missed sex. Not having the time or energy to even masturbate lately has built up my need even more.

There are some gasps from the crowd and I think I hear someone say, "Oh sweet Jesus," but I don't care about what else is going on with the other racers.

I slide the bullet all around me, and I can already feel the little tingles of pleasure shooting down my legs. I squeeze my eyes closed even tighter and think about the one time Drew and I had sex in our basement on a pile of his old stuffed animals from when he was a child. The things that man can do with a Pound Puppy...

I can't stop the moans that escape from my mouth as I hold the bullet still against my clit and let it do all of the work to bring me to completion. I think again about the basement sex and Drew barking and that's all it takes to send me over the edge into oblivion. I shout my release and my free hand smacks down on top of the table to hold me steady as my orgasm washes through me. When the tingling has stopped and my orgasm is over, I quickly pull the bullet out of my pants and smack it down on the table, throwing both of my arms in the air in victory.

I was so focused on my orgasm and flashbacks of basement sex that I didn't even realize how quiet the tent had gotten. I open my eyes and notice people staring at me and all of the vibrators bouncing around on the table.

"Uh, honey. I think we may have got the rules of the race a little mixed up," Drew tells me as he comes up behind me.

Oh my God. Was I the only one masturbating? What the fuck?!

"Uh, I'm not really sure how to pick the winner of this race," the judge says from the other side of the table, clearly looking a little confused.

"Why the fuck didn't you stop me?" I whisper frantically at Drew.

"It all happened so fast. And to be honest, it was hot as fuck," Drew tells me.

"I do believe I clearly won the wager," Jim says from the other side of me where Carter and Claire are laughing hysterically. "Judge, I think Jenny here needs to be the winner of this heat for creativity alone."

The whole tent lets out a roar of approval and there is so much cheering and clapping that people from other tents have wandered over to see what is going on. I'm so mortified I can't even move. All I can do is stare at all of the vibrators bouncing up and down on the table in front of me until Claire's Butterfly FX 2000 inches ahead of the rest and bounces right off of the end of the table where I now see a black and white checkered finish line is painted.

"Son of a bitch!" Claire shouts. "I would have totally won that thing!"

"So, babe, about that pep talk before the race-"

I cut Drew off before he can say anything else. "Don't even think it. You are NOT getting your brains fucked out tonight!"

15.

Dr. Duke of Earl

Contrary to popular belief, standing around at a vibrator race and allowing your wife to masturbate in a tent full of strangers when she's actually supposed to be putting the vibrator down on a table to race it will not get you laid. Even if she promises. I try to get her to change her mind for two hours after we get home. My dad is no help. Once he had found out what happened, I get a forty-five minute lecture on how you're never supposed to leave a man behind. After he leaves, Jenny tells me to sleep on the couch and console my penis on my own.

I try. But every time I get a good yank and pull session going, I hear Billy crying upstairs to be fed. It's all fun and games until your kid starts crying right before you're going to release the demons. Talk about an erection killer.

Today, I have the house all to myself and you would think I'd spend it comforting my penis, but no. I have other plans. Jenny took Billy to Claire's shop with her today while she does some bookkeeping, and Veronica is at preschool for a few hours. I'm using this time wisely. With the help of the little package I had got in the mail yesterday, I am going to fix mine and Jenny's sex life in just ninety minutes. I ordered a self-help CD called: How to Bring the Spark Back into Your Marriage. I've closed the blinds, locked the doors, and put on my favorite motivational shirt: Camel's Tow Service; ask us about our Moose Knuckle discounts.

I grab the package from my work bag, where I hid it yesterday after I got the mail, tear into it, and pull out the plastic CD case.

Popping it into the stereo system in the living room, I crank up the sound and hit play.

"Hello and thank you for purchasing: How to Bring the Spark Back into Your Marriage!"

"You're quite welcome!" I reply to the man's voice coming from the speakers. He's British and British people always sound smart when they talk so this should be good. "'Ello Gov'na!"

See? He's already made me smarter. I'm talking British.

"How 'bout a spot of tea with the Queen?"

"Make yourself comfortable as we begin our first lesson."

"Don't mind if I do," I say as I take a seat on the couch.

"Lesson One: Compliments. Repeat after me, 'You look beautiful today, insert name of wife here.'"

"You look beautiful today, insert name of wife here."

"Have you lost weight?"

"Have you lost weight? Man, this is so easy. I am going to rock this shit."

"Take your clothes off and give me a blow job."

"Take your clothes off and give me a blow job."

"That was a trick. If you repeated that last line, you will never get laid again."

"Heeeeey, no fair! What kind of self-help is this shit!"

"Lesson Two: Helping out around the house. Repeat after me, 'Can I help you with those dishes?'"

"This is never going to work. She'll know something is up if I say that shit."

"Say it or you're never getting laid again!"

"Son of a birthday cake! Can you hear me?" I ask the stereo in confusion.

I let out a sigh and figure I better do what he tells me or he's going to get really angry. I don't need self-help guy angry at me or he'll stop helping me. "Can I help you with those dishes?"

"It's okay, honey, I'll fold the laundry."

"Seriously? You expect me to believe that folding laundry will get me laid? Do you even know what you're talking about?" I ask the stereo.

"I know what I'm doing. Say it."

Stereo guy is starting to get a little angry. I'm kind of afraid of stereo guy right now. I want to turn him off but I'm scared. He knows where I live.

"It's okay, honey, I'll fold the laundry," I say nervously.

"Say it like you mean it, asshole!"

"I'm sorry. I'm sorry! It's okay, honey, I'll fold the laundry! Really, I will! I LOVE folding laundry!"

"Lesson Three: Helping out with the children. Repeat after me, 'I'll get up with, insert name of child here. You go back to sleep."

"I'll get up with, insert name of child here. You go back to sleep," I say quickly so I can stay on stereo guy's good side. I need to pass this shit or my penis is going to be batting solo forever.

"Why don't you go for a day at the spa. I'll take care of the children."

"Actually, that's not a bad idea. Why don't you go for a day at the spa. I'll take care of the children."

Maybe I judged stereo guy too quickly. I mean he's just trying to help me. He wants what's best for me, and what's best for me is Jenny's vagina.

"I'm not changing that diaper. I don't even know if the kid's mine."

"I'm not changing that diaper. I don't even know if the kid's mine."

"You fell for it again, douchebag! It's like you're not even trying. Why am I wasting my time on you?"

"Dammit! Stop giving me trick questions! You want me to fail, don't you? I hate you, stereo guy!"

"Don't get angry at me. My wife still gives it up every day. You're the one with the problem."

"I don't have a problem! YOU have a problem! You live inside a fucking stereo! You're stupid and your voice is stupid!"

"I'm in your house now. I know where you live and I can see you. Don't make me angry."

"Oh no you DIDN'T just say that to me, you piece of shit!"

I get up from the couch and run over to the stereo, pulling it off of the shelf and dropping it to the floor. "Ha! Try helping my self now, asshole!"

"I can still hear you. You can't get rid of me that easily."

"WHAT DO YOU WANT FROM ME?!" I scream as I turn around in circles in the middle of the living room with my arms stretched out from my sides.

I run over to the plastic CD case I threw on the floor earlier and pick it up, checking the back for information about the guy who recorded it. I will not let him terrorize me!

"Oh, ho, ho, *Dr. Earl Michaelson*! What kind of a British name is that? Wait, Duke of Earl, wasn't he British? Is this the Duke of Earl? Is the Duke of Earl threatening me? I know who you are and where YOU live now! You messed with the wrong man, Duke of Earl!"

I'm going to call this guy and I'm going to give him a piece of my mind.

"I wouldn't do that if I were you."

"Big talk from a little Duke, stereo man!"

I pull out my cell phone and look up this guy's information on Google. Oh, Google, how I love thee. A phone number for the whole world to call. Don't mind if I do. I dial the number and wait for someone to answer.

"Is the Duke of Earl there? I don't know, like the song. 'Duke, Duke, Duke, Duke of Earl, Earl, Earl. Shut up! I have a GREAT singing voice!"

I pull the phone away from my ear when I hear the dial tone.

"Stupid Duke of Earl. You need to hire better help to answer your phones," I mutter as I hit redial.

"Yes, is *Doctor Earl* there?" I say, making my voice deeper. "I don't care if he's with a patient, put him on the damn phone! Don't you dare hang up on me! Shit!"

I hit redial again, clearing my throat and preparing a different voice. "Is Dr. Earl there? This is his mother," I say in a high pitched female voice. "Oh, his mother's dead? Probably because he killed her with his awful advice! Put him on the phone!"

Dial tone again. What is wrong with these people?

"We're not done with our lesson yet, dickwad."

"I'm not a dickwad, YOU'RE A DICKWAD!" I yell to the broken stereo on the ground. How the fuck is he still talking to me? This is like the movie 'Chuckie'. That damn doll just wouldn't die. How the hell do you kill a CD that won't die?

I call the number again and try a different tactic. "Yes, this is Punjab from Czechoslovakia. Dr. Earl ordered something from us and I need to speak to him right away. What do you mean Czechoslovakia doesn't exist anymore? When the fuck did that happen? Wow, 1992, seriously? I probably should have learned that in school, huh. No kidding? But it's still there, right? It didn't like, blow up or something? Interesting. No, no message."

I hang up the phone and realize I was fooled again. Like they would really just get rid of some place called Czechoslovakia. What would they do with all the Checkians? I wasn't born yesterday, I know when someone is pulling my leg.

Since calling the Duke and telling him off isn't going to work, I'll just send him an email. I pull up Gmail on my phone and type in his email address that I found on Google.

Dear Dr. Duke of Earl Dick Fuck,

You are going down, buddy. I will make you pay for this…

⊙ ⊙ ⊙

"Yes, officer. I understand. No, I promise there won't be any more trouble. Tell Dr. Michaelson and his family we're very sorry for scaring him. Just send me the bill for his hotel stay."

Jenny closes our front door and turns around to look at me without saying a word.

"Can I just expl-"

"Oh, I think you've done plenty of talking today," she cuts me off. "Really, Drew? Threatening a psychiatrist and his family? He took his wife and kids to a hotel because they feared for their lives."

Jenny walks away from the door and starts picking up pieces of the mangled stereo on the living room floor. I may have got a little too excited in my need to destroy it. There were pieces that flew all the way into the kitchen when I stomped on it repeatedly. According to all horror movies, you have to dismantle the pieces and spread them out away from each other so they can't get back together and form an even scarier monster that will hunt you down and kill you. I was protecting my family!

"Oh please, like fleeing from his house was really necessary," I explain as I help her pick up plastic pieces.

"You told him you were going to sneak into his house and watch him while he slept."

It turns out the CD I bought was a fake. Some disgruntled employee who worked at the online store I had bought it from replaced a bunch of self-help CDs with one he made at home. Dr. Earl wasn't the only one whose CDs had been replaced. There had been about a hundred other self-help people out there that it happened to as well. Oops.

"Why would you even buy a self-help CD in the first place?" she asks as she gets up and takes a pile of pieces into the kitchen to dump them in the garbage.

I stare at her ass as she walks away and try to remember the last time I had my hands on her ass.

"You look very beautiful today. Don't worry about the dishes. I'll take care of them," I tell her as I dump my own pile of pieces into the garbage can after she does.

"What are you talking about? We have a dishwasher," she says with a shake of her head as she leaves the kitchen.

"It's okay, honey! I'll fold the laundry," I yell to her retreating back.

"I folded the laundry yesterday," she shouts back angrily.

"Fuck you, Dr. Earl. And fake Dr. Earl who recorded fake CDs," I grumble to myself as I turn the lights out in the kitchen and follow Jenny upstairs to see if I'll be allowed to sleep in bed tonight. I'm going to go with no, but it doesn't hurt to ask.

I get to the top of the stairs and my pillow and a blanket are already in the hall, next to our closed bedroom door. With a sigh, I pick up my things and head back downstairs.

I curl up on the couch and pull up the porn app on my phone. "At least I still have you, little buddy."

A few seconds later, a message pops up on my screen that says, "The porn app site is temporarily down for service. Please try back later."

Oh my God, even porn doesn't want me to have any satisfaction.

The universe obviously hates me.

16.

Vagina!

"The cops were at our house for two hours questioning Drew. It was so embarrassing. I'm sure all of the neighbors saw the police car in our driveway," I complain to Liz as I add a new blog post to her store's website.

"Right. Like THAT is the most mortifying thing your neighbors have ever seen in your driveway," she replies as she uses a knife to slice through the tape on top of one of the boxes of inventory that was just delivered.

"That Halloween two years ago was an accident. I didn't realize body paint was flammable, and Drew got a little too close to the jack-o-lanterns we carved," I explain as I turn around in the computer chair to help Liz remove some of the items from the box.

"Drew stopped, dropped, and rolled naked in your neighbor's front yard. Didn't he catch their maple tree on fire?"

I pull out three packages of piña colada lube and set them off to the side. "It was a small maple tree. Not a big one. And the fire was out quickly. It wasn't that big of a deal."

Liz pushes the empty box away and pulls up another one and cuts it open.

"I think it's a big deal when you're both standing in your neighbor's front yard with nothing on but glitter body paint," Liz says with a laugh.

"Still, I can't believe he threatened someone. And a psychiatric person at that. Like the guy doesn't have enough problems being crazy? Now he has my husband to worry about. What if Drew sending him that email pushed him over the edge and he goes on a killing spree or something?"

"He is a *psychiatrist,* not a psychiatric person. He's not crazy; he helps crazy *people*. It sounds like Drew should be his patient," Liz deadpans.

"He was listening to a self-help CD. Did I tell you that part? It was called: How to Bring the Spark Back to Your Marriage. We've lost our spark," I sob.

"I love you, but don't cry. I will punch you in the face if you cry. I don't do criers. You have not lost your spark. It's just…temporarily on vacation," she explains as she unpacks the box.

"Why the hell did it go on vacation? I never said it could go on vacation! I need my spark, Liz. You don't understand. I need my spark to live!" I wail.

"It sounded to me like you found quite the spark at the vibrator race," Liz laughs. "You got a standing ovation during the awards ceremony. People have been asking me where they can buy the video."

"Well, we're already under contract with the company we entered the home movie contest with so I'd have to check with them and see. It might be a conflict of incest," I tell her.

"Jenny. For the love of God, think before you speak. Just say what you want to say in your head first before you open your mouth," Liz tells me seriously.

"What? Incest means that you're related, right? Drew and I are related."

Liz stops unpacking the box and stares at me in horror.

"What. The. Fuck?"

I roll my eyes at her and take the package of Jack Rabbits out of her hand. "Um, hello? We're husband and wife. So we're related. And you think I'm dumb."

Liz puts her head in her hands and whimpers to herself. I lean over and pat her on the back in sympathy. "It's okay, things confuse me sometimes too."

"What should I do, Liz? I tried the faking it thing, and I thought that worked, but the next two times I suggested doing it again he said no. He actually turned me down! He says he misses my vagina but I think he's lying. I used to have such an awesome vagina. What if it's not awesome anymore? I need a second opinion. Liz, look at my vagina."

Liz stands up from the box and starts backing away.

"Take it back," she states.

"No, really, I think this is what I need. I need someone who will be honest with me. Look at my vagina," I tell her as I start unbuttoning my jeans.

Liz throws her hands up in the air and bumps into a shelf against the wall, vibrators and lube falling to the ground. "Back away, Jenny. Just back away and no one will get hurt."

I get my pants unzipped and push them down to the middle of my thighs.

Good thing I wore my good underwear today.

"Just one look, that's all I'm asking. Just look at my vagina and tell me if it still looks okay or if it's a hot mess," I plead.

"Oh my God, my eyes, MY EYES!" Liz yells, covering her face with her hands.

"Liz, LOOK AT MY VAGINA!" I shout as I hobble closer to her and my jeans slide down to my knees. "I AM NOT LEAVING HERE UNTIL YOU LOOK AT MY VAGINA!"

I hear a gasp and turn around to see Jim standing in the doorway staring at us. I put my hands on my hips and glare at him. "Move along, Jim. There's nothing to see here."

He shakes his head back and forth, his eyes never blinking as he looks from me to Liz and then back again.

"I've dreamed of this moment," he whispers. "I've prayed, I've wished on stars, I've wished on pennies in wishing wells…my prayers have been answered. God is good."

Liz huffs and walks around behind me, grabbing onto my jeans and yanking them back up over my ass.

"Nooooooo," Jim whimpers. "They're supposed to go the other way."

"Oh for fuck's sake, close your mouth. Turn around, walk out of this room right now, and never speak of this again," Liz warns him as I button and zip my jeans.

"My dreams...shattering right before my eyes," Jim says with a sad sigh as he turns and leaves.

Liz comes around in front of me and grabs my shoulders. "You are fine, your vagina is fine, and you are going to forget all about this shit and come with me and Claire to the Blossom Music Festival this weekend."

I start to shake my head 'No' and she puts her hand over my mouth when I open it to protest. "You are coming with us. End of story. We'll have a girl's night, drink a lot of beer, listen to '80s cover bands and find your spark. I'm sure it will be at the bottom of the third cup of beer. And if you ever ask me to look at your vagina again, I will punch you in the uterus."

⊙ ⊙ ⊙

"Pretty please? Say it again. Just one more time!" Claire tells the woman we just met standing in line for beer.

The woman laughs and says, "Put another shrimp on the Barbie!"

Liz, Claire, and I laugh hysterically and jump up and down with excitement. I'm not really sure if it's the beer that makes this funny or if it really is funny. The woman in front of us is from Australia and we've spent our fifteen minutes in line getting her to say Australian things.

"Okay, okay, I've got one. Say, 'Fosters. Australian for beer,'" Claire says with a snort.

The woman laughs and does as she's asked without complaint.

"Oh my God I love you! You are our new best friend!" Claire tells her.

"Oooh, my turn!" I say excitedly as I finally think of something for her to say. "Say, 'Sucky, sucky, five dolla. Me love you long time!'"

Everyone just looks at me funny. "What?"

"That's not Australian, dumbass. I don't even know what the fuck that is!" Liz says with a laugh.

We order our beers and make our way over to the smoking section just outside of the fence to go back into the concert. We've spent the majority of the concert out here drinking instead of trying to navigate through the crowd to get to our seats inside. Since the music is so loud, we can hear it just fine out here anyway.

"HEY!" I yell to a group of guys walking by our picnic table. "LOOK AT MY VAGINA!"

Claire smacks my hand down from making a 'V' with two of my fingers. "What the hell are you doing?!"

I scope out the crowd for more people who look willing and able.

"VAGINA!" I shout to a couple walking hand-in-hand to the table next to us. They immediately turn and head in another direction.

"Oh sweet Jesus, she's lost her mind," I hear Liz tell Claire. "She thinks something is wrong with her vagina. She tried to get me to look at it the other day."

There's a guy all by himself two tables over. I bet he'd appreciate the vagina. This beer is delicious.

"Wait, is that why Jim called Carter and was screaming about his dreams dying and how he never gets what he wants? Carter could barely understand a word he was saying."

I take a big gulp of my drink and slam the cup down on top of the table.

"HEY! VAGINA!" I yell to the guy by himself at the other table.

He looks at me strangely for a minute and then replies, "Uh, penis?"

"WOOOOOOHOOOOOOO!" I cheer, jumping up out of my seat and attempting to do the running man. It doesn't go so well and I fall flat on my ass.

"Who put the ground so fucking close to my ASS?!" I yell.

"Okay, I think she's cut off," Claire says as she gets up from the table and pulls me up by my arms.

"Claire, will you look at my vagina?" I ask her as I put my head on her shoulder.

"What is the deal with you and vagina? Is this your new favorite word or something?" Claire asks as she helps me back to the table.

"Ass fuck, I told you. She thinks something is wrong with her vagina and that's why she and Drew aren't having sex or some shit like that," Liz explains as I move my head from Claire's shoulder and rest it on top of the table.

"When was the last time you guys had sex?" Claire asks.

"Um, what day is it today?"

"It's Saturday," Claire answers.

"Last year."

Liz grabs the back of my shirt and yanks me up. "The fuck you say?"

I grab my beer and take another drink.

"Well, if we're talking really good, awesome sex then yes. Before the New Year when I was pregnant with Billy."

Liz lets out a sigh of relief. "Okay, you had me scared there. I thought you meant an actual year. So we're just talking a few months then. That's not THAT big of a deal."

I stare at her in horror for a few minutes.

"Are you out of your fucking mind? A few months? That's like ten years in human years," I complain.

"Actually, that's like a few months in human years, moron. It would be ten years in dog years," Liz informs me.

"What the fuck ever! And you were right the first time. It really has been a full year. Since before I got pregnant with Billy. We used to do it like dogs. All dirty and rolling around in the grass and eating out of bowls and using leashes. It was hot," I say with a sigh as I reminisce.

"This beer is coming right back up. I can feel it," Claire complains.

"It only got weird that one time Drew lifted his leg in the living room. But it was still awesome. SO WHO WANTS TO LOOK AT MY VAGINA?!"

A bunch of guys walking by all start cheering. One guy even yells back, "Vagina, long live and prosper!"

Liz pulls my arms down to my sides and shushes me from yelling at the group of guys.

"You're serious, aren't you? It's been a whole fucking year?" she asks in shock.

I just nod my head sadly.

"You know what you and Drew need? You two need a night out alone, just the two of you without any kids. When was the last time you guys went out on a date?" Claire asks.

"What day is it?" I ask her.

"It's still Saturday, asshat."

I nod and start counting in my head. "Saturday? Then…last year."

"Oh my fuck! You guys haven't been out on a date since before Billy was born either? Isn't he like five months old?" Liz asks.

"No! He's a month old. Wait, no. Three months old. Shit, what day is it?"

"SATURDAY!" Claire and Liz yell at the same time. The guy sitting by himself at the next table yells back, "VAGINA!"

"SHUT THE FUCK UP ABOUT MY VAGINA, YOU PERVERT!" I shout back to him.

I turn back around and face the girls. "Okay, so Billy is something like four months old or some shit. It's Wednesday, right?"

I think my beer has something funny in it. I feel funny. Funny is a funny word.

"Oh sweet mother of fucks," Liz says with a sigh. "So you and Drew haven't been on a date in months. You haven't done anything, just the two of you, in months. Is that correct?"

I nod my head and pick up my cup to find my beer gone.

"Who the fuck drank my beer?"

Liz takes the empty cup out of my hand and chucks it into the garbage can next to our table.

"I need a cigarette. WHO'S GOT A CIGARETTE?!" I scream at the top of my lungs.

Don't judge me. Sometimes I get the urge to smoke when I drink. I think I read somewhere that alcohol causes you to want to do things you shouldn't, like rob a bank or kill a hooker. Wait, no. I think that's crack.

"Oh Jesus, do NOT let her smoke," Liz mutters to Claire.

"You can't tell me what to do if you won't even look at my VAGINA!" I complain.

"YAY VAGINA!" some guy yells as he walks by our table.

"WOOOOHOOO VAGINA!" I shout back. "Hey, stud! Give me a cigarette!"

The very nice gentleman stops and runs back to our table and hands me a cigarette, lighting it for me since I probably shouldn't be in charge of anything that can set things on fire at this moment.

I inhale and immediately start coughing and dry heaving.

"Fuck, she's going to puke," Liz complains. "Take her mind off of it."

Claire pats me on the back and takes the cigarette out of my hand, tossing it over into the grass a few feet away.

"Okay, here's the deal, Jenny. Next weekend, you and Drew are going out together alone. Carter and I will take Veronica and Billy so you guys can go to dinner and do whatever. If you guys are in the groove and you don't want to stop to call me, we'll just keep them overnight," Claire tells me as she and Liz help me up from the table.

"I love you, Claire Bear. You're the best ever," I tell her as I wrap my arms around her waist and put my head on her shoulder.

"I love you too, but I'm still not looking at your vagina."

17.

Jackson

"No, Veronica, you are not having candy for lunch," I tell my daughter for the third time as I help her out of the car and then race around to the other side to unstrap Billy from his car seat before he starts screaming his head off.

"Mommy?"

"Yes, sweetie?"

"I WANNA BEAT YOU UP WIGHT NOW!" she yells in the middle of the driveway while stomping her feet.

Canada, take me away...wait, Canada? Is that right? Why would I want Canada to take me away? They really need to rethink that commercial.

I ignore Veronica's temper tantrum over not having candy for lunch while I try to shush Billy who just woke up from the car ride and is not a happy camper. He's screaming in my ear and smacking me with his little fists, Veronica is screaming by my leg, and I'm trying to pretend neither one of them exist as I reach into the backseat of the car and grab my purse, diaper bag, and the four bags of groceries I just picked up on the way home.

Taking two grumpy children to the grocery store should automatically win me mother of the freaking year. Why do people give me such pissy looks as I'm hurrying up and down the aisles while the kids are screaming? Do they think I pinch my kids so they'll cry and ruin everyone else's shopping trips? Maybe I've purposely decided to go to the store when I know my kids will be the worst behaved. I do it just to piss off all of the old, childless people who are stocking up on Metamucil and Depends.

As soon as I get all of the bags in my arms and heft Billy up higher so I don't drop him, the two heaviest bags break open at the bottom and the milk, apple juice, a jar of tomato sauce, and jar of pickles go crashing to the driveway and shatter all over the place. I'm just about ready to cry and sit down in the middle of the mess when I feel a hand on my back and a voice behind me talking to Veronica.

"Hey, little cutie! Look at the pretty flower I just picked. How about you go on inside and help mom put it into a glass of water?"

I turn and see a guy around the age of twenty or so, bent over, handing my daughter a huge, beautiful sunflower. She immediately stops shouting, smiles up at him, and runs towards the front steps.

The guy stands back up and turns to face me, and I notice for the first time that he isn't wearing a shirt.

Holy fucking sweaty six pack abs. I am so grateful for Indian Summers in Ohio. Yesterday it was snowing and today it's in the seventies.

Billy seems to be just as taken with this guy as Veronica had been and has stopped his fit of rage and is now staring straight at the guy. I can't help staring myself. He's gorgeous. He's about six feet tall, has shaggy, sandy blonde hair, and pale blue eyes. He looks like he could be a surfer. But there aren't surfers in Ohio. Or are there? I mean, Lake Erie turns into the ocean like a mile out, doesn't it? That's how we get waves on the shores of the lake. I'm pretty sure I read that somewhere.

"I hope you don't mind about the flower. I have a niece her age and she loves flowers. My name is Jackson, by the way. I just moved in across the street."

I shake myself out of my stupor of staring at his naked chest and grab the hand he has held out for me. I had seen him move in a few weeks ago and we've shared a couple of neighborly waves whenever we're outside at the same time, but I have never seen him up close.

"I'm Jenny. It's nice to meet you. Thank you for doing something to shut her up. I was thinking about just going inside and locking her out until she calmed down," I joke with a nervous laugh.

Shit, I don't know this guy at all. What if he doesn't get my joke and calls the police. Can I get arrested for saying I'm going to lock my three-year-old out of the house?

Luckily he laughs right along with me and gives me a heart-stopping smile. I'm totally not kidding. My heart stutters for a minute before picking back up.

I start to bend down to pick up some of the mess in the driveway when Jackson puts his hand on my arm to stop me.

"Hey, don't worry about this. I'll clean it up. Give me all of the bags and you go on ahead and get the kids inside."

He smiles at me again and I kind of want to melt into a puddle of goo in the driveway with the pickle juice and tomato sauce.

When was the last time Drew smiled at me like that? Like he wanted to lick my face. And when was the last time he ever offered to help me with anything, aside from those weird dishes and laundry comments he made the other night?

I thank Jackson and leave him in the driveway while I usher the kids inside to put them both down for a nap.

Fifteen minutes later, I am still arguing in the living room with Veronica about taking a nap when there is a soft knock at the front door before it's opened a crack.

"Jenny? Is it okay if I bring these bags in?" Jackson asks, peeking his head in the door.

"Oh, yes! Sorry, I forgot to come back out and get them," I tell him as Veronica jumps down off of the couch and runs over to him.

"Are you a shit turd?" she asks him in an innocent voice.

"Oh my God, Veronica! You don't say that!" I scold her, feeling my face get extremely red with embarrassment as the Greece God in front of me just stands there, still shirtless, laughing his ass off.

"I'm sorry," I tell Jackson as I take the grocery bags from his hand.

"It's fine. Sometimes I can be a shit turd so at least she was accurate," he says with a smile. "Oh, I swept up the mess and put it in your garbage can in the garage and then hosed down the driveway. I hope that's okay."

I stand there with the bags in my arms just staring at him.

I know he said he would take care of the mess, but I just figured he would be a typical guy and shove it out of the way with his foot and then go home. I should ask him if he can teach Drew some lessons.

He looks away suddenly and pulls a t-shirt out of the back pocket of his jeans and slips it on over his head, apologizing to me as he does it like he was offending me or something. I want to scream at him and tell him it's more offensive that he put the shirt back *on*, but then I realize I'm standing here holding a bag full of tampons, panty liners, douche, and vinegar, and the bag is see through and he just freaking carried it in for me.

"The vinegar is for French fries. My husband likes vinegar on his fries, and he likes it on cucumbers when I make cucumber salad, and I also put it in my homemade Italian dressing, and it totally doesn't go with the other stuff in the bag because you know, it's already scented flower fresh. I don't like my 'down there' to smell like French fries or dressing, ha ha!"

Oh my God, why am I shitting out of my mouth?

Jackson just laughs and for once it feels like someone is laughing with me and not at me, and I should just get on a bus and go right to hell because I'm ogling someone that isn't my husband.

"I'm sorry. I'm just really tired. I haven't slept since my son was born."

Veronica grabs his hand and starts tugging on it. "Pway wif me. I have Barbies!"

"Veronica, no. Jackson probably needs to get back home."

"I'd love to play Barbies with you, Veronica!" Jackson says at the same time.

He squats down to Veronica's level and tells her to go get her Barbies and bring them out so he can see if she has the same ones his niece has. She's out of the room before he even stands back up.

"You don't have to do this," I tell him.

"It's fine, really. Why don't you curl up on the couch and rest while we play Barbies."

I stare at him again and I'm pretty sure my mouth is wide open in complete shock.

"I'm sorry, am I being too pushy? I'm kind of a stranger and I just asked if I could play with your daughter. Is that creepy?" he asks with a chuckle.

Is it creepy? Am I a horrible mother for wanting to take him up on his offer? I'm so God dammed tired I could fall asleep standing up right now.

Veronica runs back into the room, her arms full of every Barbie she owns, and she proceeds to grab Jackson's hand again and pulls him down to the floor with her.

"Veronica, do you know about strangers?" Jackson asks her as he crosses his legs in front of him and picks up Malibu Barbie and starts making her walk around in circles on the floor.

Veronica nods her head and picks up her Ken doll, copying the same moves Jackson is currently using with his Barbie.

"Never talk to stwangers," she replies.

"Right, never talk to strangers. Never go anywhere with anyone who isn't your mommy or daddy either. We're going to sit right here and play Barbies while mommy rests. You aren't allowed to leave the house at all, okay? If me, or someone else tries to get you to leave, you scream at the very top of your lungs. Can you do that?" Jackson asks her.

Veronica proves she can by letting out a blood curdling scream, and we both wince at the sound.

"Very good!" Jackson tells her. He looks up at me and smiles and it takes everything in me not to hug him and cry because he's being so thoughtful. He had known exactly what I was worrying about and had made sure to calm my fears.

"Um, I'm just going to sit here. Don't let me fall asleep," I tell him as I sit down on the couch, curl my legs up next to me, and rest my elbow on the arm and watch them play.

"You're fine. We'll be right here getting Barbie and Ken ready for their wedding," Jackson says with a smile as Veronica hands him Barbie's wedding dress.

I sit there watching them for a few minutes in complete awe. This guy who has known me for all of five minutes took one look at me and knew what I needed. How in the hell has my husband, who has known me for years, not been able to do that?

⊙ ⊙ ⊙

I'm having the best dream ever. I'm alone on a deserted island, and I'm sleeping. Just sleeping. No crying kids, no husband begging for sex…nothing but the sound of ocean waves and hours of uninterrupted sleep. I stretch my arms over my head, feeling around for the warm sand and instead, and grab onto the arm of the couch.

I sit up quickly and blink a few times, looking around in fear and wondering why I am asleep on my couch and I can't hear Veronica or Billy. The living room has grown dark and there is a lamp on in the corner of the room so I know I must have been out for a few hours at least.

I jump up in a panic and am preparing to scream at the top of my lungs that my children are missing when I hear Veronica's giggle from the kitchen. I run around the couch and across the room, stopping short when I get to the kitchen doorway.

"Hey there, sleepyhead! We decided to move our Barbie party into the kitchen so we didn't disturb you," Jackson says with a smile as he looks up from the kitchen table that's now full of all of the Barbie crap that used to be on the living room floor.

"Mommy! Jackson let me take Barbie swimming!" Veronica shouts excitedly while she points to the sink that's full of water.

"Hope you don't mind. She wanted to fill up the bathtub but I thought the sink was a better idea. Oh and your son is still sleeping. I checked on him a few minutes ago."

Where did this guy come from? Am I still dreaming? He can't possibly be real.

"How long have I been out?" I ask, coming over to the table and kissing Veronica on the top of the head.

"About three hours," Jackson replies, standing up from the table and sticking his hand out towards Veronica. "My lady, it's been a pleasure playing Barbies with you this evening."

Veronica giggles and shakes Jackson's hand.

I walk Jackson to the door and stand there holding it open while he turns and pauses on the front porch, sticking his hands in the pocket of his jeans.

"I don't even know how to thank you. I think I'm the one that was supposed to welcome you to the neighborhood by baking you cookies or something. You weren't supposed to babysit my kids while I snored on the couch," I tell him apologetically.

"Really, it's okay. I didn't mind. I watch my niece a few times a week so it was a piece of cake. Besides, it was too exhausting trying to do yard work in puddles of melted snow so it gave me an excuse to be lazy for once."

He smiles at me again, and I have to force myself to swallow a few times so I don't start to cry.

"See ya later, Jenny! If you ever need more sleep, you know where to find me. And I love cookies, so feel free to thank me with those sometime," he says with a laugh as he jumps off of the porch and whistles his way across the street to his house.

I stand there watching him walk away and wonder if I've lost my fucking mind for even thinking about taking him up on his offer again. I haven't felt this good or well-rested in years.

18.

Vanilla Sex

Date night! Mother fucking date night! I'm so excited I almost pissed myself. Just kidding, I totally really did piss myself. Just a little. It's all good. I've drank a lot of Pepsi this afternoon.

Jenny has been in the best mood ever this week, and I know it's because she's looking forward to this night as much as I am. I've just dropped the kids off with Carter and Claire with strict instructions not to call us unless one of the kids is bleeding from the eyes. And only if it's a lot of blood, like, "Oh my God, so much blood!" If you're just like, "Eh, some drops of blood from the eyes, nothing to get your panties in a bunch about,"' don't call me. I've already hidden Jenny's cell phone in my pants so she has no choice but to give the meat whistle a little rub if she wants to check on the kids.

I've left Jenny at home to finish getting ready and because I know if she goes with me to drop the kids off, it would have taken at least an hour of her kissing them over and over and apologizing for leaving them and then kissing them both ten more times before we could even walk out the door. At least she doesn't make too much of a scene when I leave our house with them. As soon as I see her eyes start to fill with tears, I do the whole, "Oooh look, a butterfly!" and then turn and run. I would have made it to the car too if Veronica wasn't so slow. I need to practice some wind sprints with that kid for situations like this.

I get back home and pull into the driveway, and when I get out of the car, the new guy who moved in across the street is taking his garbage out and lifts his hand in a wave. I wave back and wonder if the dude even owns a shirt. Every time I've seen him outside since he's moved in, he's been half naked. It's a disgrace to the neighborhood. Especially since everyone on this street knows *I'm* the one who looks the best doing yard work without a shirt. Some people just don't know their place.

Walking through the front door, I check myself in the mirror in the front hall.

Damn, I look good. Screw naked guy outside. I've got it going on.

I straighten my hair and smooth the front of my date night shirt that says: I fuck on the first date. Out of the corner of my eye, I see Jenny in the mirror and turn around, my eyes bugging out of my head. She's wearing a short, red strapless dress with her hair piled up on top of her head, and a pair of red, strappy sandals that are so high I'm surprised she can walk in them. She looks so hot I can already feel myself getting a chubby.

"Holy fuck, baby. You look awesome," I tell her as she walks up to me and smiles.

"Thanks. I haven't fit into this since before Veronica was born."

She grabs her purse and we head out the door, my eyes never leaving her ass.

I am so getting lucky tonight.

⊙ ⊙ ⊙

"Oh my gosh, remember that time you went down on me during my cousin's wedding?" Jenny asks as she finishes off her fourth glass of wine and leans closer to me so our shoulders are touching.

After her second glass of wine, she starts getting chatty, just like old times. Whenever we used to go out before we had Billy, we would always wind up talking about our sex life. We had an amazing sex life. I used to think about Jenny and I doing some sort of seminar for loser married couples who only have sex to get pregnant. I had always thought we would be the best people to teach others about how much fun you could have in the bedroom. We could use props and I could make a flow chart. Listening to her talk about our fun times makes me realize how UN-fun our times have been lately. Hopefully not for much longer.

"Oh my gosh, remember that night we played Monopoly and every time someone landed on Park Place one of us had to have an orgasm?" she asks as she puts her hand on the back of my neck and runs her fingers through my hair.

"That was the best game of Monopoly ever. Didn't we have to throw the board away because we got ketchup and hot wax all over it?" I ask her, trying not to pant like a dog as her nails lightly scratch the back of my neck.

"Yep. And we had to use nail polish remover to get the play money off of your ass when we played 'Pin the money on Drew' with the wax. Best night ever," she whispers in my ear.

The hard on I've had since she had walked out of the bedroom in the red dress is now a full blown state of emergency. One more story about our past sexcapades and I'm going to need to shut this restaurant down, and the waiters will need to put on Hazmat suits.

"What about that time when we first moved in together at your old place when the neighbors used to sell honey at a road side stand in their front yard?" she asks softly close to my ear.

I'm going to come in my pants in three seconds.

I clear my throat and shift in my seat, trying to move Big Drew around a little so I'm not so uncomfortable.

"Ha, they formed a neighborhood watch because they thought there was some huge conspiracy where people were stealing honey to sell it on the black market," I remember with a laugh.

"I never understood that. Why would they think only black people want honey?" she asks in confusion.

I don't even think about correcting her because I don't want anything to ruin this good mood she's in.

"I wonder how many bottles of honey we actually stole that month. It had to be close to a hundred."

She smiles and nods, placing a soft kiss on my cheek before pulling back to continue with the memory.

"That last night was a fun night until we spent a little too long on foreplay and the honey started to dry and get sticky. It was like giving you a Brazilian wax to get that stuff off!"

We both laugh and move a little bit away from each other as the waiter comes to our table and steps in between us to place the check on the table.

"I still have that scar on my ass from when you had to help pull me off of the tree. I don't care though. That was the best blow job ever. Well, aside from the shower one on our first date."

We sit there quietly for a few minutes staring into each other's eyes, and I am trying to force all of my thoughts into her head.

You want to bang me, you want to bang me, you want to bang me.

"I want to bang you," she states.

My brain is an awesome and powerful thing.

I throw all of the money in my wallet down on the table without even looking at the bill. I'm pretty sure I just gave our waiter a seventy percent tip, but I don't give a fuck. I grab Jenny's hand and together we run to the exit and out into the parking lot.

In hindsight, trying to have sex in our four-door, compact car in our own driveway probably isn't the best idea. But after Jenny spends the fifteen minute drive from the restaurant back to our house with her hand down my pants, rubbing me one second away from orgasm, I can't even think about opening the car doors and going inside. I turn off the engine, hit the button to move my seat back as far as it will go, grab Jenny around the waist, and haul her over the center console and onto my lap.

With her legs straddling me, I slide my hands up her thighs and push her dress up to her hips, realizing she isn't wearing any underwear.

"You're wearing my favorite clear pair of panties," I tell her as I slide my hands around her hips and onto her bare ass.

"I wore them just for you," she says with a smile as she leans forward and runs her tongue along my top lip.

I reach between us to unbutton my pants, freeing my dick and feeling quite proud of myself that I too chose to go commando this evening.

With one hand still clutching her ass, I pull her down so I can rub the head of my cock against her. She's wet and warm and even though she hasn't shaved down there since before Billy was born, I don't give a fuck. I love her pussy whether it's smooth or has a porn bush fro. As I use my hand to glide myself back and forth through her, she starts to move her hips to create more friction, and we both moan against each other's mouths.

"Fuck, you feel so good, baby. I wanna fuck you like an animal."

She stops the movement of her hips and pulls her face away from mine.

"Don't quote Nine Inch Nails when we're about to have sex. It's creepy. I don't want to think about animals having sex. Remember that time we saw my cousin's dogs having sex? Oh my God, I had nightmares for weeks. I kept dreaming we would have sex and your penis would be stuck inside me until you finish like those stupid dogs," Jenny complains.

"Sorry, no more animals fucking talk. Let's just talk about us fucking. Right now. In the car," I tell her as I move the head of my penis to her opening and push my hips up slightly so I enter her just a little bit.

"Son of Al Sharpton," I moan as she pushes her body down a little more and I go deeper.

Jenny doesn't hesitate to slide the rest of the way down on my cock, and I have to squeeze my eyes shut so I don't blow my load right this second.

She grips onto my hair and yanks me towards her mouth.

"You're such a dirty whore," I mutter against her lips.

She stops and pulls back to look at me again. "Eew, don't say that."

I look at her in confusion for a minute. She's always thought that was hot. In the past, she usually begs me to call her a dirty whore. I want my dirty whore!

"It's just weird. I'm a mom now," she explains.

"You were a mom the last time I called you a dirty whore," I complain with a pout.

I know, I know. My penis is finally home and I'm complaining. But you don't understand! This is our thing! She's my dirty whore and I'm her big, bad slut.

"Just...I don't know, do it normal. Call me Jenny and I'll call you Drew."

Normal? What the fuck is normal?!

"What? But that doesn't even make sense! We're not normal. We're dirty and filthy, and I don't know what is going on right now!"

I think my penis is dying. I'm inside my wife's vagina and I'm starting to go soft. No, no, no! This is NOT happening right now!

"Can't we just have vanilla sex?" she asks as she leans back from me as far as she can while I'm still inside of her.

"Vanilla is white! WE'RE NOT WHITE! We're...fuck! We're Napoleon or whatever the fuck the three colored one is. We're fucking Superman or the chocolate kind with peanut butter in it. I don't even know what vanilla means! WHAT DOES IT MEAN?"

I know I'm yelling while my wife is on top of me, naked from the waist down but this is a complete and utter mind fuck right now.

"You're not hard anymore," she tells me as she looks down where we're still, sort of, joined.

GAAAAAH I'm not listening! I'm not listening! I'm always hard! I'm hard when I'm grocery shopping in the frozen food section. Son of a motherless goat!

"Quick, call me a slut. HURRY!" I yell.

"I'm not calling you a slut. This was a bad idea," she says as she lifts herself off of my wilted willy and crawls over to her side of the car, pulling her dress down as she goes.

NOOOOOOOO bring it back!

Jenny opens her car door and gets out, and I stare down at my limp dick in disgust.

"You are a disgrace to all of penis kind. That's what you are. You couldn't just keep it up for like five more minutes. Oh no, you had to be a quitter. QUITTERS NEVER WIN!"

I angrily shove my dick back in my pants and get out of the car and come face-to-face with Mr. Naked Guy from across the street.

"Hey there, buddy! I saw you guys pull in and I just wanted to make sure everything was okay. My name's Jackson," he says with a smile as he sticks his hand out for me to shake.

The only good thing about this moment right now is the knowledge that the hand I'm touching this douchebag with is the one that was just on my dick.

"Hey, Jackson! How were those Snickerdoodles yesterday?" Jenny asks him as she comes around to my side of the car.

Who the what? Snickerdoodles?

"Oh my God, those were the best cookies I've ever had. Seriously, Jenny. You can bake a mean cookie," Fuckson tells her with a big smile.

I know his name is Jackson. Shut up. Bitch ate my Snickerdoodles. He's Fuckson from now on.

"Well, my girlfriend owns a bakery so I get all the inside tips," she says with a giggle.

A FUCKING GIGGLE.

"Oh, before I forget, tell Veronica my niece left Barbie's giant Malibu house at my place the other day, so I'll bring it over on Wednesday for our play date."

The fuck you say!

"Oh my God, she will absolutely freak out!" Jenny tells him.

Fucky McFuckson says his good-byes and jogs back over to his house, whistling the whole way.

Who the fuck whistles while he walks? The Seven Dwarfs, that's who. Fuckson is a dwarf. He's Fuck Head Dwarf; the sneaky bastard dwarf that tries to steal wives and children and makes them suddenly want vanilla instead of Mint Chocolate Chip.

"I'll call Claire and let her know you'll be over in a little bit to get the kids," Jenny says as she turns and makes her way up the driveway to the house.

I stand there in the driveway long after she's gone inside, staring over at Fuck Face's house.

"As God is my witness, I shall never like vanilla again."

19.

Brazilians and Fupas

I have a headache of mass promotions. Sticking around Veronica's preschool the whole two hours she's here probably isn't the best idea. There's a parent viewing area with a two-way mirror so we can see the kids but they can't see us. Unfortunately, we can still hear all twenty-three kids screaming.

"You look like shit," Liz says as she sits down next to me and hands me a cup of coffee.

Her three-year-old Molly goes to the same preschool as Veronica and usually we alternate who picks up and who takes the kids. Today is Liz's day but I need a break from work and had decided to spend my free time watching Veronica learn and play.

"I *feel* like shit. I have the worst headache and Jackson had to cancel our play date yesterday so I didn't get a nap," I tell her.

Liz knows all about Jackson ever since she stopped by last week to drop off some hand-me-down clothes from her girls for Veronica. She had walked through the front door to find me asleep on the couch, Jackson giving Billy a bottle, and Veronica sitting next to him watching cartoons.

"I still can't believe you have a manny," she says with a laugh as I take a sip of my coffee.

"His name's not Manny. It's Jackson. Remember, I introduced you?"

She laughs and shakes her head. "A manny is a male version of a nanny. And as far as I know, they are young and hot and usually gay. But your manny definitely isn't giving off the gay vibe," she explains.

"He's not a nanny or a manny or whatever. He's just a friend help-ing me out."

"A hot as fuck friend that I would bang seven weeks to Sunday if I wasn't married. Oh, who am I kidding? If Jim was a complete loser of a husband and never helped me out around the house or with the kids, I'd still bang him," she laughs.

I look at her in shock while she laughs and doesn't even realize that she just summed up my life lately with that one statement.

"It's a good thing you and Drew are back to fucking like twisted, demented rabbits, right?" she asks with a smile.

Her smile drops as soon as she sees the look on my face.

"Oh no, what the fuck? You guys just had date night four days ago. That was supposed to cure everything. I assumed you looked like death warmed over from having sex in a bounce house or some shit like that. What the hell happened?"

I can feel the tears stinging my eyes and my lip start to quiver, and I know I'm going to break down any second.

"Shit. Don't cry. Not here. Come on, we're going for a walk."

Liz grabs my arm and pulls me up from my chair and drags me out into the school hallway.

We walk down past a few other classrooms and she stops and turns to face me. "Talk."

I take a deep breath and let it all out in one enormous explosion of truth. Everything I've been feeling and have worried about and stressed over for the last few months. It all comes pouring out of me.

"I'm so tired, Liz. I'm physically tired and brainy tired and Drew is just no help at all, and I don't understand how he can NOT see that I need help or ever even ask me if he can get up with Billy in the middle of the night or change a diaper or fix Veronica lunch or get her ready for school or help me with the other fucking million and one things I've got going on," I complain, as I start pacing in front of Liz. I grab onto a lock of my hair and start twirling it around my finger, something I do when I'm nervous or freaked out. And I'm freaked out right now! I'm also not paying attention to just how fast I'm twirling and before I know it, my finger is stuck in a knot of hair right next to my head.

"My finger's stuck. MY FINGER'S STUCK!" I yell in a panic.

Liz rushes up to me and puts her hand over my mouth so I stop yelling and tries yanking on my arm with her other hand.

"Mmmmmmmmmmmfffffff!" I mumble-scream into her hand.

Liz huffs and shakes her head at me. "I am going to remove my hand from your mouth. Don't you dare scream."

I nod my head at her so she knows I'll be good, and she slowly removes her hand from my mouth. Once she's satisfied I'm not going to freak out every classroom in the hallway, she gets to work trying to free my finger from my hair, and I go right back into my complaining.

"All he wants me for is sex and then when I do try and give it to him, he wants to do it the same way we always have, and I think there's something wrong with me because I just don't want to do it the same way we always have, and I don't know if I want to be a dirty whore any-more even though he still wants a whore, and I just didn't feel right calling him a slut on Saturday but maybe I will next time, but now I don't even know if there ever WILL be a next time, and Jackson is just so nice and pretty and helpful and he knew immediately that I just wanted sleep and some help, and I don't know what to do! What the fuck should I do if I don't want to be a dirty whore anymore, Liz?!"

The sound of someone coughing stops my rant and Liz and I both turn to see one of the teachers from the kindergarten class standing behind us with a line of kids, everyone staring at us with eyes wide and mouths open. Twenty five-year-olds are looking at me like I'm crazy and who knows, I probably am. I think I'm cranking up. I'm going to have to leave my kids and go live in a nut house with my finger still stuck in my hair and I don't even LIKE nuts.

"Mrs. Dellena, what's a dirty whore?" one of the kids asks his teacher.

"Sorry, please excuse us," Liz says with a kind smile to the teacher as she grabs my arm and drags me down the hall where there are no classrooms or children to horrify, forcing my finger to magically get unstuck from my hair.

"Yay, you did it!" I tell her, holding my finger up in front of her face.

She bats my finger out of the way and looks at me in shock. "What the fuck just came out of your mouth?"

"I thought I'd never be able to use this finger again," I tell her in awe.

"Shut the hell up about your finger! What the hell is really going on with you and Drew?" she demands.

"I know. It's a lot."

"You're damn right it's a fucking lot. Why the hell haven't you mentioned all of this before? I thought you guys were just going through a typical dry spell that everyone goes through when they have multiple kids. This is way beyond that. I want to kick Drew's ass way more than usual right now," she says angrily.

"It's not all his fault," I say with a sigh.

"The fuck it isn't! You're his wife. His soul mate. He should be taking care of you and making sure all of your needs are met, not leaving it up to the eye candy living across the street. And Jenny, that kid is total jailbait. You need to stop any and all thoughts you might be harboring about him."

"Hey, don't judge him just because he's done time. He is a very nice person. And how the hell do you even know he was in jail?" I ask angrily.

"Jenny, he's like nineteen! He's thirteen years younger than you, and he lives with his mommy and daddy. Do you really think you can just divorce Drew and this kid is going to take on a thirty-two-year-old with two kids? How the hell is he going to support you with his paper route money?"

"Wait, what? What the hell are you talking about? I don't want to divorce Drew! Sure, Jackson is nice to look at and he's a big help, but I don't want to marry the guy! I love Drew. I just don't know how to fix this," I tell her as the tears I've been trying to keep inside begin falling.

"Oh thank fucking God," Liz says in relief. "This, we can fix. We just need to kick Drew's ass and get his God dammed head in the game. Why the hell haven't you just told him all of this?"

"I don't know! I thought he would just *get it* like he always has in the past. He's always known what I wanted and needed and after a while, I just started getting pissed that he didn't. Now that it's gone on this long, I don't know what the hell to do!" I wail.

"Lucky for you, I'm here. We're going to fix this shit," Liz tells me.

She puts her arm around my shoulder in a very uncharacteristic show of affection for her and we walk back to the classroom to pick up the girls while she plans a strategy.

⊙ ⊙ ⊙

"When you said you were going to fix things, this really isn't what I had in mind," I complain an hour later.

We drop Veronica off with Drew's dad who was already watching Billy for the day, and Liz tells him in no uncertain terms that he needs to watch Molly as well. He calls her ma'am and scoops up both girls in the driveway and runs back into the house before we can even tell him how long we will be gone.

We are currently sitting in the waiting room of the local salon waiting for my turn to get a Brazilian wax.

"Before we can fix your shit, we need to fix *your shit*," Liz says with a wave of her hand in the general direction of my vagina. "No man should have to get his penis caught in a jungle of pubic hair."

I roll my eyes and cross my arms over my chest.

"It's not that bad," I complain.

"The last time you even took a razor to that area was seven months ago. It is THAT bad. The day you wanted me to look at your vagina I could see those things trying to jump ship out of the sides of your underwear. Your twat looked like one of those freaky clowns that's bald down the middle of its white head with ginormous tufts of hair sprouting out by it's ears."

Before I can bitch at her about comparing my vagina to a clown's head, the receptionist calls my name and we both stand up.

"Are you really going back there with me?" I ask.

"Hell yes I am. Your wish is finally coming true. I will see your vagina. Plus, I really want to see the look on that woman's face when she gets a peek at your plethora of pubes. Your copious curls, your abundant bush, the wild mane that if it sees a spark will start a forest fire," she states.

"Are you finished?" I ask irritably.

"I think so. But give me five minutes and I might be able to get one more in."

"You are kind of dicky," I tell her as we follow the receptionist into one of the private waxing rooms.

"Yes, and in just a few minutes, a dick will be able to find your vagina without needing night vision goggles and a weed whacker."

"Okay, Jenny, if you want to just strip down and wrap the towel that's on the table around your waist, the esthetician will be in shortly," the receptionist says with a cheerful smile before leaving the room and closing the door behind her.

"An anesthetician? Geeze, I had no idea they went to such extremes and the same guy who gives you an epidural during child birth does waxing now. Just how bad is this going to hurt?" I ask as I strip off my jeans and underwear.

"Holy fuck, Jenny! How does that shit even fit in your underwear?!" Liz yells as she laughs and points. "And the guy who gives you an epidural is an *Anesthesiologist.* I'm going to need a fucking anesthesiologist to numb my eyes after seeing this!"

I quickly turn away from her and wrap the towel around my waist so she can stop making fun of me. I reach for the hem of my shirt and begin pulling it up my stomach when Liz stops me.

"What the hell are you doing?"

"Uh, I'm *stripping down* like the girl told me to do," I tell her with my hands still on the edge of my shirt and my stomach exposed.

"Do you have hairy tits or something? Why the hell would you need to take your shirt off?"

I huff at her in annoyance that she just expects me to know what hell I'm doing in this situation.

Pulling my shirt back down, I hop up on the table that's covered in doctor's office paper, careful to keep the towel firmly in place so Liz doesn't come up with any more insults.

"Okay, so really, how long does this take? Is she just going to like, slop some wax right on the upper part and then rip it off?" I ask Liz.

"Uh, no. This is a Brazilian. She is going to get all up in your shit from your FUPA to your asshole," Liz informs me with a completely serious look on her face.

"What the hell is a 'FUPA' and what do you mean, 'all up in my shit?'" I ask her nervously.

"FUPA equals fat, upper pussy area. And all in your shit, like, you know, spread you open and get all in there, then flip you over on all fours and clean up your ass."

Why is she so matter-of-fact about this crap?! And I do NOT have a fat, upper pussy area!

"They're going to spread open my folds and wax in there?!"

Liz lets out a sound of disgust and grimaces. "Please, God, never say the word *folds* again."

This is beyond embarrassing. I really did not expect that the waxing of my bits included someone getting this intimate with me.

"What if I'm like, moist, down there? Will the wax even stick?"

Liz makes a gagging sound at this point and gives me a dirty look. "Seriously. *Folds* and now *moist?* Cut that shit out or I'm going to puke all over this floor."

The door opens before I can ask any more questions and a short, cute, bubbly blonde walks in and introduces herself.

"Hi! My name is Stephanie and I'll be taking care of your waxing needs today," she says as she walks over to the waxing station next to the table and stirs the already melted wax in the warming pot and begins setting out all of the waxing strips and the wooden sticks she'll use to torture me to death.

"Have you ever had a Brazilian before?" she asks as she turns around and helps me lay down on the table.

"No, I usually just shave, but it's been a while" I tell her as she rolls the work station on wheels closer to the table so she can reach it better.

"Careful, you might poke an eye out or something when you get a look in there. Prepare yourself," Liz jokes from her chair over against the wall.

"Don't worry, I'm sure it's not as bad as some of the women I've seen come in here," she reassures me with a smile as she parts my towel to get a look at what she's working with.

"Oh my," she says softly and then quickly steps away. "Well, um. Wow. Okay, I think I'm going to need more waxing strips. And maybe more wax," Stephanie says as she moves away from the table to grab extra supplies out of the cabinet against the wall.

Liz is full on laughing and snorting at this point, and I lift up my hand and give her the finger without raising my head from the table.

Stephanie comes back moments later and adds the extra supplies to the table. She dips one of the wooden sticks into the wax and holds her hand under it to catch any excess dripping, then she spreads it out all over my SUPA – *skinny* upper pussy area.

It's warm and soothing when she spreads it around and I kind of like it.

Who knew this would actually be enjoyab-

"AAAAAHHH MY VAGINA!" I scream suddenly at the top of my lungs, my hands flying down to cover myself and press down on the area that burns like it's on fire to try and alleviate some of the pain.

"OH MY GOD DID YOU PULL MY CLIT OFF?!" I yell at Stephanie in horror as she stands there holding the cloth strip that's full of hair and quite possibly my pleasure button.

"Sorry, I should have probably warned you I was going to do that but I find it's best not to warn someone for the first one because they'll just tense up and it will hurt worse," Stephanie explains with a happy smile as she turns and picks up another wax strip and dips the wooden stick into the hot wax.

"The first one is always the worst. Suck it up, bitch," Liz tells me from her chair.

The next half hour doesn't go by quickly at all, and several times I have to stop myself from smacking Stephanie in her face. Liz must have sensed my desire to choke the poor woman and came up to the table to hold my arms down. Luckily, Stephanie redeemed herself by telling us horror stories about other women she's waxed: women getting their monthly visitor right in the middle of waxing or women having orgasms during the event. That right there boogers my mind but then I remember how much Drew liked it when I had to rip the pieces of tree bark off of his ass during "The Great Honey Adventure".

One thing I can say about this whole thing is my ass has never looked better. When she had me up on all fours so she could get down in that area, she got a mirror for me. Let me just say, it's so smooth I kind of want to pet my own asshole. Liz keeps asking me if I want some alone time so I can finger my ass, and I think she's joking so I give Stephanie's mirror back to her before I get carried away.

The only good part about this day is that I don't feel so self-conscious about myself anymore. Maybe this whole time I haven't really been worried about left-over baby fat; I've been worried about my vagina being too furry. I really do feel a whole lot sexier knowing what's going on down there in my underwear right now. Once Stephanie could actually see my vagina, she had told me it was very nice. And since she's seen a lot of vaginas in her line of work, I trust her judgment.

I'm a little more confident now about talking to Drew as well and telling him what I need. Weird how a hairless vagina can do that for you. I'm pretty excited to finally be honest with Drew and take my new vagina out for a spin. I wish it wasn't frowned upon to go without pants in public.

20.

Who's on Goal, What's on Basket?

"So how good looking are we talking here? Like Chace Crawford hot or Penn Badgley hot?" Carter asks me while we're packing up our work bags and getting ready to clock out for the night.

Of course I tell my boys everything about the fucking home wrecker that moved in across the street. They know he's trying to move in on my territory and take over as hottest guy on the block. Oh, hell no! That position has been mine for four years. Plus, I don't like the way he looked at Jenny the other night. And she had made him cookies. COOKIES! She only makes cookies for me. Just like I'm the only one who ever surprises her with little candy treats. Well, I used to do that. I guess I've kind of forgot lately.

"Who the fuck are Chace Penn and Crawford Badgley?" Jim asks as he walks with us towards the exit doors of the automotive plant.

"It's Chace *Crawford* and *Penn* Badgley. The two leading actors on *Gossip Girl*," I tell him. "It's like you've never even picked up an US Weekly. Live a little, Jim."

We head out to the parking lot and make our way to our cars. I can't get the picture of Fuckson out of my head and the way he was so casually friendly with my wife.

"Oh, Jenny! Thank you so much for the cookies. I can't wait to eat your scrumptious cookies and then fuck you in the living room on a pile of cookies while your husband is at work," I say in a high pitched voice.

"Does he really sound like that? Because I gotta say, if he does, you have nothing to worry about," Carter tells me as we wave to a few other guys heading out to their cars.

"Well, it wasn't exactly like that. It was more like, 'Mmmm, me like cookies. Me eat cookies all gone," I say in a deep, voice.

"So easy a caveman can do it," Jim says with a laugh.

"This is no laughing matter, Jim. I know I made a huge mistake when I had my dad trail Jenny because I thought she was hiding something from me a few weeks ago. and I'm still in the doghouse for it, but what if she's decided to get back at me by *actually* hiding something?"

In all honesty, I really don't think the stuff going on with us lately is that serious, even though I went along with the therapy and the disastrous dinner with the neighbors. I kind of just do it to humor Jenny. If she thinks something needs to be fixed, then who am I to tell her it doesn't? I figure she will just eventually bounce back to the Jenny I know and love. The crazy, nympho Jenny who likes to test out Ben Wa balls in a sex toy store and who lets me put a remote control vibrator on her during our wedding ceremony.

"Do you, Jenny, take Drew to be your-"

"OH MY GOD! OH YES, YES, YES! OH JESUS YES!"

"Well, alright then. I think that means I can now pronounce you husband and-"

"KEEP GOING! OH GOD DON'T STOP!"

"Um, wife? Sorry, that's all I've got."

"Suddenly, after becoming buddy-buddy with Shirtless McFucker Face, she wants vanilla sex. She wants to just…do it. No bells and whistles, no live animals, no power strips for electrical safety precautions, and no elbow pads or helmets. I don't understand," I complain to the guys as we get to Jim's car first and we all stop next to it. "She ruined me for vanilla sex. She ruined me and it was the best way to be ruined ever. And now she just expects me to go back to missionary position only with the lights off?"

Jim opens his car door and throws his bag in the backseat.

"Elbow pads and a helmet?" Carter asks.

"Oh man, best day ever. We went to a skateboard park and did it sliding down the ramp," I tell him. "We had to keep stopping, getting up, and going to the top so we could slip back down again so it took a while, but it was still magical."

Man, those were the days.

"Before we make any snap judgments, I think we need to meet this Jackson guy," Jim explains.

"It's Fuckson. Get it right," I tell him sternly.

"Fine, *Fuckson.* I want to meet him and see for myself if he poses a threat."

Jenny volunteered to coach Veronica's peewee soccer team and they have their first game tomorrow afternoon. She must really be bored with work and the kids to sign up for something like that. Maybe that's why she's been so different lately. She's bored and doesn't have enough to do. Too bad she doesn't know a thing about soccer, so I don't think coaching is going to be as life fulfilling as she might think.

Veronica had told me she asked Fuckson if he would come watch her game and he said yes.

Fucking crapbag.

Of course *she* doesn't call him Fuckson. She calls him her best friend ever. Well you know who my best friends are? My two fists. And they're eager to meet Shit on a Stick's face. Booyah!

The guys are already planning on coming to Veronica's game, so I let them know they will get their chance to form an opinion the following afternoon. As we say our good-byes and pull out of the parking lot, I'm actually excited about this. My boys will meet this tool and realize what a loser he is and then we can all warn Jenny together. Like an intervention. A Fuck Face intervention. She'll thank me by getting naked and our lives will go back to the way they should be.

⊙ ⊙ ⊙

"No! Wrong way, Alex! The touchdown is that way!" Jenny screams, pointing to the opposite end of the field where little Alex is currently running with the soccer ball.

"It's a GOAL, Jenny. A GOAL! Touchdown is in football," I tell her quickly as we both start yelling from the sidelines for Alex to turn around.

"Oh my God, this soccer thing is hard. Why are there so many rules for three and four year olds?" Jenny complains as she pulls one of the kids out of the game for a break and gets Veronica ready to take her place.

"Hey, Drew. I need to tell you something," Jenny says as she hands Veronica her water bottle.

Oh shit, she's going to tell me she's leaving me. This can't happen!

"Nope, no talking. This is a serious game. Pay attention."

Jenny rolls her eyes at me and squats down to talk to Veronica.

"Okay, honey, remember, don't take the ball away from your teammates. And if you get the ball, spike it all the way down the track," Jenny explains to a confused Veronica.

"Or, you could *kick it* down the *field*," I confirm for Veronica.

"Soccer sucks," Veronica complains, folding her arms in front of her and refusing to move.

"I know, soccer totally sucks and it will probably make you gay. But there's not much else to pick from when you're three. Suck it up and go make me a goal!" I tell her as I grab her shoulders, turn her around to face the field and give her a little shove.

"Okay, seriously. You and I need to talk. I have something I need-"

The ref blows the whistle right next to Jenny for the kickoff, and she stops in the middle of her sentence to wince. There's a flurry of kids all racing for the ball, hitting and shoving and pulling hair to get to it. They don't care what team they're playing for; the just want the ball. It's soccer anarchy.

"NO, JUSTIN! WE DON'T BITE IN SOCCER!" Jenny yells to one of the kids.

"Get the ball, Veronica! Take that ball away and pitch it past the catcher!"

"You are majorly screwing up your sports talk. Pitch and catcher are for baseball," I explain to her as the crowd erupts in cheers when someone makes a goal. No clue who made it or what team just got the point because all these little bastards look the same.

"But we get two points for a basket, right?" she asks as the kids come in for a water break.

"No, you get one point for a *goal*. Basket is in basketball."

"But you told the kids earlier to dribble the ball down the field. I KNOW dribbling is basketball," she argues.

"Dribbling is basketball *and* soccer."

"Who stops someone from dribbling in basketball?" she asks. "Defense."

"Then who stops them from dribbling a ball in soccer?"

"The defender," I tell her, wondering if this is going to turn into the worst "Who's on First" moment in history.

"Whatever, as long as they don't kill each other, I don't care. Anyway, we really need to talk about something important and-"

"Shhhhhhhhh!" I tell her, putting my finger against her lips. "Game. We play. No talk."

Fuck! I sound like a God dammed Neanderthal but I can't help it. Whatever important thing she needs to tell me is probably going to be that she's decided she wants a younger penis that likes to eat vanilla.

Luckily, something shiny distracts her. Unfortunately, that shiny thing is Fuckson, Mr. Vanilla himself.

Not to be confused with Vanilla Ice, obviously. If Mr. Ice walked over here right now, I would freak the fuck out! Best rapper since Milli Vanilli.

You can't blame it on the rain without first stopping, collaborating, and then listening. Genius.

He saunters (yes, I said saunters, shut it) over to us and hey, look at that. He's wearing a fucking shirt for once.

"Jackson! You made it," she says with a smile as she gives crap hole a quick hug before ushering the team back out on the field.

"OH MY GOSH YAAAAY! I'm so excited you're here!" I squeal in sarcastic delight, clapping my hands together and jumping up and down.

Jenny gives me a dirty look before turning away to face Vaginal Itch Vanilla.

"I wouldn't miss it for the world! You're doing a great job coaching. Drew, you didn't play soccer in school, did you?" shit dick asks.

What the hell is that supposed to mean? I'm not good enough to play soccer? He doesn't think I know how to play sports? Did this shit on a shingle just insult me?

"What, you don't think I would totally kick ass at soccer?" I ask him, trying to rein in my anger before I'm kicked out of a peewee soccer game for bloodying someone's face.

"Oh, no! I didn't mean that at all! I just meant, with your size, I'm betting you played football or rugby. Some full contact sport where you could really kick ass and not just run around the field. You seem like you could play a mean game of football."

He's right. I CAN play a mean game of football.

"I was a total loser in school and didn't play any sports. You must have been like the coolest guy in school. I can tell just by looking at you that everyone liked you. We're you homecoming king or anything?" he asks curiously.

"Actually, yeah. I was homecoming king AND prom king. It was the first time in the history of the school that it happened. You should have seen how loud everyone cheered when they called my name. Dude, it was fucking amazing."

What the fuck am I doing? I just called him 'dude'! And I'm sharing a memory with him. I don't like this guy. I hate this guy. Do NOT be nice to him.

"Oh man, I wish I could have seen that! I bet you won everything," he says. He stares at me for a few minutes, and I'm starting to feel uncomfortable when the next thing pops out of his mouth.

"Wait, Drew Parritt? Holy shit, I knew that name sounded familiar! You were first team, all-state during all four years of high school and got a scholarship but blew your knee out senior year. Oh my God! You're a fucking legend!"

He knows me! He's heard of me! I am a fucking legend!

"Shit, man! That last game of the season sucked major ass. I could have worked harder with the physical therapy and possibly been back on the field sophomore year of college but I was too busy with the ladies at that point," I say with a laugh, quickly cutting it off and dropping my smile when I remember who the hell I'm talking to – Public Enemy Number One!

"Man, do you still have all of your trophies and awards and shit? I would love to see all of them," he gushes.

Noooo, the force is strong! Resist! Resist!

"Yes! I have them all in the basement on a dinky shelf. I really want to build some kind of cabinet for them but I'm not good with that stuff."

Fuck! What the fuck am I doing? Stop talking to him. He's my arch nemesis!

"Hey, I can totally build that for you. I went to school for carpentry actually and my teachers all said I had great natural talent. I build stuff for everyone in the family, and I'm trying to start my own business. I could come over later and you could show me your trophies, and I can get an idea on how big of a cabinet you'll need," he says excitedly.

Awe, shit. I'm a goner.

"That would be fucking awesome! How much do you charge for something like that?"

Why am I asking him this? I will NOT let him make me a trophy cabinet. I WON'T, no matter what the price is.

"Oh, there's no way I'd take your money. Totally on the house, dude. It would be an honor just to be able to see your trophies, let alone build you something to put them in."

Well fuck, I think I'm falling in love with Fuckson. God dammit!!! At least Jim and Carter have already had a chance to talk to him and they can bring me back to reality with what an asshole he is.

The soccer game finally ends and Jackson says good-bye and that he'll stop by later.

Fuck, I can't even bring myself to call him a bad word anymore because he's too fucking likeable! Now I'M the one who needs the intervention.

Jenny is busy talking to the parents, so I sneak away and walk over to Jim and Carter by the bleachers before she corners me and wants to "talk".

"Okay, give it to me. Tell me every mean, awful, and shitty thing you think about him. Go."

Jim and Carter share a look before turning to face me.

"Actually, we kind of like him," Carter says sheepishly.

"Yeah, he's going to come over tomorrow and watch the girls so Liz and I can go out to dinner," Jim adds.

"He's coming over to our house Tuesday because he has a secret wall cleaner he mixed together that will take black permanent marker off of the walls," Carter says.

Nooooooooo! They were supposed to help me! They were supposed to be my wingmen and now they just fucked me in the ass!

"Did you hear him talk about that thing he did in the fifth grade?!" Carter asks Jim.

"Oh my gosh, that was the funniest story ever!" Jim replies with a laugh.

"I really liked his jeans. I asked him where he got them and he said Target. Who knew?" Carter says with a shrug. "I wonder if he would go shopping with me for jeans if I ask him."

I stare in horror at my two friends as they go back and forth gushing over my sworn enemy that I now kind of like.

"We're going shoe shopping next Friday because he knows a great store about an hour from here that is having a huge clearance sale so make sure you don't ask him to go Friday," Jim says.

"Wait, a shoe sale? I need new shoes," I tell Jim.

I am fucked.

21.

Spoop

"I GOT IT!" I scream upstairs to Jenny as the doorbell rings and I race to answer the door.

It's shoe shopping day and Jackson had told me he would come over and get me when he was ready to leave. I'm still not one-hundred-percent on board the Jackson train yet, but any guy that knows where the best shoe sales are gets a free pass for the day in my book.

I fling open the door and Jackson is standing there next to a four-shelf, hand-crafted, oak trophy case.

"I had some free time last night and was able to build your trophy case. I hope you don't mind," Jackson says with a smile.

Well son of a bitch. Now I'm on the Jackson train waving good-bye to my loved ones and heading off into the sunset with my new best friend.

"Dude, this is fucking awesome!" I tell him as I step outside onto the porch to get a good look at my new case. It's the best piece of furniture I've ever seen. This thing will easily hold all of my trophies and medals, and this guy, who could probably tell I didn't like him at first, had made it for me just to be nice.

Or he still wants to steal my wife and this is his way of distracting me. While I'm busy setting up my trophies, he's going to be upstairs having sex with my wife.

"Oh, I almost forgot. I got this for you too," Jackson says as he steps down off of the porch and picks something up that he had left by our bushes.

When he turns around, he's cradling a garden gnome in his arms. But not just any garden gnome. This little guy is wearing an Ohio State football uniform from my alma mater. Instead of a weird garden gnome hat, he's wearing a silver football helmet with a red and white stripe down the center. He's also got on an Ohio State football jersey with my old number painted on it, and he's holding a football in his arm.

Now, normally, I am not an advocate of garden gnomes. They are creepy little bastards that come to life at night and ass rape you while you're sleeping. They hover over your head on your pillow and just wait until you flip over on your stomach so they can take off the covers and have their way with you. This hasn't been proven scientifically yet, but I'm sure it's only a matter of time. It's also the reason why I always wear a belt to bed. I'm not making it easy for them to get my sweet ass!

Jenny has always wanted to get a gnome for our front yard - the one where the little creepy guy is sitting on a dock holding a fishing pole. Every time we are anywhere near a garden store she begs me to let her buy it. And every time, I have to remind her what those things are capable of. Especially one with a fishing pole.

Good God, woman! Do you know what kind of harm could come to my ass with a garden gnome carrying a fishing pole? Unspeakable acts will be conducted. UNSPEAKABLE.

I had never thought I would see the day where I would welcome a garden gnome into my yard. But this one is a winner. I can see it in his eyes that he would never hurt me. He would never use his evil garden gnome way against me.

"Jenny is always talking about how she wants a garden gnome but that you don't like them. I saw this one the other day and thought you might approve of it, so I had the guy at the store paint your old jersey number on it," Jackson says as he hands the little football guy over to me.

"I'm naming him Buckeye and he will be my friend forever," I say softly as I pat Buckeye's head and then set him down on the first step of the porch.

With one last smile in Buckeye's direction, I help Jackson carry the trophy case down into the basement and then he helps me place all of my trophies into it before going back upstairs.

"Hey, Jackson!" Jenny says as she meets us at the top of the stairs with Billy in her arms. "How was your date last night?"

Jackson laughs and I look back and forth between the two of them.

Date? Jackson had a date? With a woman that isn't my wife? This day just keeps getting better and better.

"Oh man, it was so awesome, Jenny! We had such a good time and you will be happy to know it turned into a sleepover," Jackson says with a smile.

Wow, I didn't know the guy had it in him! Banging on the first date is so me. I feel so close to him right now.

"I'm so happy for you! So you guys obviously hit it off. Are you going out again? Jenny asks as she shifts Billy to her other arm.

"Yep, we're going out again tonight. Although, after the wake-up call I got this morning, I'm surprised I can even function or walk right now!"

Jenny and Jackson laugh and I just want to wrap this guy up in a hug and jump up and down in happiness that he's found a chick to bang, and I can stop freaking out.

I reach over and pat Jackson on the back. "That's awesome news, dude. I'm happy for you."

Jackson smiles again and I think I might even see him blush a little.

"Thanks. It's been a while since I've felt this good about someone. Dave is a great guy. I can't wait for you guys to meet him. Is it okay if I use your bathroom?" he asks.

Jenny tells him to go ahead and use the half bath downstairs which is a good thing because my brain is somewhere in outer space right now and I need a minute without him in the room.

"Dave? Tell me that's some weird chick's name," I whisper to Jenny as Jackson walks down the hall to the bathroom.

"Um, no. Jackson is gay. I told you that," she says as she walks into the kitchen to grab a few bottles from the fridge to pack into the diaper bag.

"No, you most certainly did NOT tell me that! I'm pretty sure that is something I would have clearly remembered," I complain as I glance behind me down the hall to where Jackson disappeared.

"What's the big deal? We know plenty of gay people. You're not turning into a homeopathic are you?" she demands angrily.

"No, I'm not turning into someone who uses alternative medicine," I reply with a laugh.

"This isn't funny, Drew. If you have a problem with gay people, we have a serious issue."

"I don't have a problem with gay people! I have a problem with thinking some guy wants to bang my wife when the entire time he wants to bang the Hershey Highway. This would have saved me a lot of headaches, let me tell you," I explain.

"You thought Jackson wanted to have sex with me?" Jenny asks in surprise.

"Um, yes. Why the hell wouldn't I? He's a good-looking guy and you're hot as fuck. Of course I would think Jackson wants to have sex with you," I tell her. "And another thing...he's been in that bathroom too long. If he's spooping in our toilet, we're going to have words."

Jenny pauses with a bottle in her hand and looks at me in confusion.

"If Jackson wants to poop in our toilet, he can poop in our toilet. He's our friend. Jim poops in our toilet all the time," she says.

"Jim poops in our toilet all the time because he has three girls who constantly knock on the door and ask him if he can paint their nails or brush Barbie's hair. His poop gets stage fright at his house. This is completely different. Jackson is depositing spoop in our home!" I complain.

"Will you keep your voice down! He's going to hear you!" Jenny scolds.

"I think he SHOULD hear me! He can take as many dumps as he likes in my toilet. But they can't be spoop dumps!"

Jenny mutters to herself as she puts Billy down in his bouncy seat up on the counter and buckles him in.

"Stop saying spoop! I don't even know what that is. You know I don't like it when you use big words I don't know," she complains as she zips the diaper bag closed.

"It's very simple to understand. Jackson said he had sex this morning. Thereby confirming that he has spooge floating around in his back door regions. It's not just poop at that point anymore, Jenny. It's SPOOP. He's SPOOPING where we brush our teeth! Now every time I go in there, I'm going to see spoop. Spoop in the toilet, spoop on the floor, spoop on the walls. Everywhere I look there will be SPOOP and it's all his fault!"

Jackson is gay. Jackson does NOT want to sleep with my wife. This makes me so happy. Spoop makes me so sad.

"That man made you a trophy case and is taking you shoe shopping today. He can spoop on our living room carpet if he wants!" Jenny argues.

"Oh, now you're just being silly. Why would he spoop on the carpet? He's not a dog," I tell her as I make faces at Billy while he coos and smiles at me.

"If you turn out to be gay, you'd never spoop in Daddy's toilet, would you, Billy? No you wouldn't! You'd keep your spoop to yourself because you love Daddy."

A few minutes later, Jackson walks into the kitchen and stands next to me. All I can do is look at his hands and hope he washed the spoop off of them. It will be embarrassing if I have to remind him.

"RAPE ME! MOMMY! RAPE ME!"

Jenny sighs and shakes her head when she hears Veronica yelling from the bathroom in the upstairs hallway.

"Um, is she asking you to rape her?" Jackson questions with a laugh.

"Yep, she totally is. She's having a hard time saying 'wipe me' right now after she goes to the bathroom by herself," I explain to him.

I wonder when Jackson is in his own home, if he screams, "SPOOP ME! SPOOP ME!"

"It's not funny when she does it in a McDonald's bathroom that is full of people," Jenny says as she leaves the kitchen and heads down the hall to help Veronica.

Jackson and I are left alone together in the kitchen with Billy, and I'm having a hard time looking him in the eye.

"I take it you didn't know I was gay," Jackson finally says.

"No, but it's all good, man. I don't judge."

Unless you spoop in my toilet. Then I will judge the mother fucking spoop out of you.

"Okay, good. Because I really like this guy, and I really like you and Jenny," he tells me.

And you really like to spoop.

"Oh, I almost forgot. I got something else for you," he says as he jogs over to the front door and picks up a bag I hadn't even seen him put there.

He walks back over and hands me the bag. I dig inside and pull out a shirt that says: I like blow jobs, anal, and shopping. Not particularly in that order.

Oh man. Here it comes. I'm going to cry.

I throw the shirt on the kitchen counter, grab Jackson, and give him a hug.

"You're such a good guy. I hope this Dave dude treats you right, and if he doesn't, I'll kick his ass. And I don't care if you want to spoop in my toilet every single day, man. My toilet is your toilet; your spoop is my spoop. I'm on this train, but just so you know, I don't want to be the caboose," I tell him as I release him from the hug.

I have found a new best friend, and I don't care if he *is* the meat in a triple decker man sandwich. He makes me trophy cases and buys me non-ass-raping garden gnomes and t-shirts.

Spoop

As I throw my new shirt on over top of the one I was wearing, Jenny and Veronica emerge from down the hallway.

"Mommy raped my spoop!" Veronica shouts as she runs into the living room.

22.

I Wanna Strawberry Laid!

"Wait a minute, so you *still* haven't talked to Drew?" Claire asks as we walk over to a rack of clearance clothes and pick through them.

While the guys had gone shopping for shoes, we decided to have a girl's day and go to the mall. Liz's two older girls are playing at a friend's house today so she just has Molly with her. After a lot of protesting from him, Claire had brought Gavin and Sophia was with Carter's parents. I have Veronica and Billy with me, so I'm pushing them in the double stroller.

"No, I haven't talked to Drew yet. I tried like a million times during Veronica's soccer game but he kept cutting me off. It's like he knew I wanted to talk about something serious and wasn't going for it," I explain as I pulled a shirt off of the rack and hold it up to me.

"Gavin, get up off of the floor," Claire scolds.

I turn around where she's looking and notice Gavin has removed an entire pile of folded sweaters from one of the tables and is currently using them as a pillow while he sprawls out on his stomach on the floor.

"Uuugghhhh, this is horseshit!" Gavin complains loudly.

"Horseshit!" Veronica and Molly shout at the same time before giggling.

"Gavin!" Claire yells angrily while Gavin lets out another groan and finally pulls himself up from the ground.

"Okay, so he didn't want to talk at the soccer game, what about after?" Liz asks as she reaches in her purse for Molly's sippy cup and hands it to her.

"He invited Jackson over and the two of them were down in the basement looking at all of Drew's old football trophies for like five hours. And then he left for work and you know how that goes."

Seeing as how all of our husbands work for the same automotive plant and were on the night shift together, the girls are well aware of how hard it can be to have any kind of important conversation with them during the week unless you want to do it by phone, which I definitely do not. This is something that needs to be done in person. I finally know what I want and need from him, and I'm pretty sure I have the confidence to actually tell him without screwing it up. But only seeing him for about ten minutes when I get home from work and then he leaves, makes it a little difficult.

"I'm still surprised he warmed up to Jackson so fast and actually went shopping with them today. I thought he would want to kill him when he found out what was going on with you two," Claire states as she points to the pile of sweaters still on the floor without turning or saying a word when Gavin walks over to us.

"Oh my GOSH! This is the worst day EVER!" Gavin complains before stomping dramatically back to the sweaters to pick them up.

"There wasn't anything going on with us! Don't say it like that," I complain as I shake my head, "No," when Liz holds up an orange tank top and gives me a questioning look.

"The guy is coming over to your house practically every day and spending time with you and the kids, helping you out with laundry, the dishes, and rearranging furniture. He's doing all of the things a husband should but without the extra benefits."

I stare at her a minute wondering what benefits she's talking about.

"He only helped me move the loveseat to the other side of the living room that one time. And he has a real job so he already gets

677

health benefits. Why would I give him benefits for helping me out and being a good friend? That's just weird," I tell her as I pull another shirt from the rack and check the size.

"Sex, Jenny! She's talking about sex!" Liz says a little too loudly.

"SEX! I WANT SEX!" Veronica yells from the stroller.

"No, no, no. Don't say that, honey. It's bad," I tell her.

"You really haven't gotten any in a while if you're saying it's bad," Liz laughs from the other side of the clothing rack.

"Oh shut up. We had sex on our date night. Well, kind of. Okay, not really," I say with an embarrassed shrug.

"What do you mean, 'not really?' How do you 'not really, kind of' have sex?" Claire asks in confusion.

"Well, it started off really hot and awesome. We were in the car in the driveway and going at it. But then he started talking all kinky, and I don't know, it felt weird. Like, we're older now and parents of two kids and maybe we shouldn't be doing it like that anymore. I told him to just do it normally and without the crazy stuff and it didn't go over so well."

Liz and Claire stand there staring at me, and I notice Gavin picking up a pair of lacy thongs from one of the tables and putting them on his head like a mask.

"You told Drew to stop being kinky in the middle of sex?" Claire asks in shock.

"Please, don't ask her anymore questions about that. Words like 'dirty whore' and 'slut' will be thrown around and my brain can't take that memory again," Liz says with a dramatic shiver.

"But, I mean…you guys are the epitome of kinky. That's like telling me I shouldn't bake anymore. It's unnatural."

Is that true? I mean, I couldn't imagine Claire never baking again. It's her life and part of who she is. Is kinky sex part of who Drew and I are? If we don't have it, are we not being who we really are?

"Tell me this, did it feel normal to you trying to have plain, old regular sex? Did it make you happy?" Claire asks.

"No, not at all. It made me sad. But it just felt like it was something I should do and ever since then, Drew hasn't even *tried* to have sex with me again. I think I broke his penis," I whisper.

"No one thinks my jokes are funny," Gavin complains, walking over to us with the red, lacy thongs still on his head, the front of the thongs covering his eyes and nose.

"Uhhhhh, why is that on your head?" Claire asks, pulling her cell phone out of her purse and trying to stifle her laugh.

"It's my mask. It's my joke telling mask and no one thinks I'm funny," he complains again.

"Oh, I think you're HILARIOUS!" Liz says, not even bothering to hide her laughter. "Tell me your joke."

Gavin turns to face her. "Knock, knock."

"Who's there?" Liz asks, giggling with each word.

I hear Claire's camera phone click next to me as she takes a picture.

"Y," Gavin states.

"Y who?"

"Y YOU SUCK!" Gavin shouts, laughing at his own joke.

"Yeah, your joke – not funny. But you wearing women's underwear on your head? Priceless. Make sure you send that picture to me. It's going on my fridge," Liz tells Claire.

"You guys are all a bunch of donkey crap bags," Gavin complains as he walks away from our laughter.

"Okay, anyway, back to our discussion. Why would you think you broke Drew's penis? Just because you told him you didn't want to have wild and crazy sex?" Claire asks.

"Well, he was kind of inside me when I said it. And it made him soft. Like, really quickly. It felt like I shoved a balloon inside me and then popped it with a pin. That can't be good."

"This analogy of his penis and your vagina is really not something I need to be picturing in my head right now," Liz complains.

"Eeew, Drew's penis and my vagina do NOT have analogy. That's just gross. I have never had a green, slimy vagina, and do you think I would honestly let Drew's penis anywhere near my cooter if it looked like that?" I complain.

"Oh for the love of God, focus, Jenny!" Claire says as we make our way up to the cashier. "Making a guy go soft doesn't break his penis. You shocked the horny right out of him. Which as far as I know, is a first for Drew. He's probably freaked out and thinks you've changed and doesn't know how to deal with it. That's why he hasn't tried to initiate anything since then."

I sigh as I pile my merchandise onto the counter.

Is Claire right? Does Drew think I've changed and doesn't know how to act around me anymore?

"I feel like we've grown so far apart and I hate it. It's like we don't even know each other. It's the worse feeling in the world."

Claire pats my back as she finishes placing her items on the counter next to mine.

"You guys absolutely still know each other. Even though it doesn't feel like it, he's still your best friend and the one person who knows everything about you. It's a rough patch. Couples have them and if they are strong enough, they work through them. You guys are strong enough. You just have to get on the same page."

Gavin bounces past us with an umbrella in one hand, swinging it through the air and smacking it into hanging racks of clothes, knocking some to the ground. Now he has a blue bra strapped to the top of his head like the guys in the movie '*Weird Science*'.

"Oh my God, I just had the best idea ever!" Liz shouts as she yanks the umbrella out of Gavin's hand and pulls the bra off of his head while Gavin lets out a groan of protest.

"Seriously, dude. I'm saving your life right now. Your mom already has a picture of you with women's underwear on your head. Do you really want to try and get laid in high school when there's a picture of you with a bra on your head too? I just saved your social life. Tell Auntie Liz thank you," she tells him as she tosses the bra onto a table and leans the umbrella against another.

"I know what getting laid means. Dad told me and it's gross. I'm never doing that," Gavin complains.

"Wait, let me get my video camera out," Claire states as she digs in her purse again for her cell phone. "Say that again, slowly."

"Mommy, I wanna laid!" Veronica shouts from the stroller.

"Me too! I wanna laid! I wanna strawberry laid!" Molly screams in delight.

"This is disturbing, and yet funny at the same time," Liz states. "Anyway, back to my *fantastic* idea!"

Claire and I finish paying our bills and attempt to quiet the girls screaming about wanting laid, using bribery of candy as a last resort.

"Okay, what's this great idea," Claire asks as we make our way out of the store.

"Well, you feel like you and Drew have grown apart and don't really know each other anymore, correct?" she asks me.

"Yeah," I say sadly.

"Do you guys remember that old game show 'The Newlywed Game' from like the seventies?"

Claire nods and gets a huge smile on her face. "Oh my gosh, Liz, you are a genius! That is the best idea ever."

I look at them questioningly as we walk towards the food court.

"I don't understand. We're not newlyweds. How is this going to help us? Do we have to get married again or something? I don't know if I'll be able to fit into my wedding outfit again if that's the case."

"Your wedding outfit was a white tube top, a pair of white boy shorts and white thigh-high stockings. I'm pretty sure anyone could fit into your wedding outfit," Liz states as we find a table and try to figure out what the kids want for lunch. "No, there is no remarrying that needs to happen. 'The Newlywed Game' is answering questions about yourself and seeing if your partner gets them right. It's a great way to see how compatible two people are."

This sounds scary. Drew and I always used to know each other well but not lately. What if we completely blow this game and it only makes things worse between us?

"I don't know guys. What if he gets every single question wrong? That's just going to depress me more," I tell them.

"Trust me, this will work. You will see once and for all that you and Drew have not grown apart as much as you think," Liz tells me.

"This is going to be so fun! I'm officially scheduling a game night for two weeks from now," Claire announces.

"Clear your schedules and get sitters. This is an 'adult only' night," Liz adds.

We get lunch for ourselves and the kids and discuss how the game will work while we eat. I don't know whether I'm nervous or excited. I just hope this whole thing doesn't throw up in my face.

23.

Zombie Apocalypse

"I don't know if this is a good idea," Jim states nervously.

"Don't be a pussy. This is the best idea ever. If the girls can do it and live through it, so can we. Do you really want your wife to go around telling people she did this before you? Get your balls out of her purse and man up," I tell Jim.

Liz is at a meeting with her buyer and left Jim in charge of the store for a few hours before we have to be at work. Not a very wise decision on her part considering the last time she left Jim alone at the store, we rearranged her front window display with naked female mannequins having an orgy. So really, whatever happens here this evening is Liz's fault for trusting Jim to behave.

Carter had mentioned the other night how he's never been maced and we found out that none of us had. It's embarrassing that all of our wives have been through something horrific like that and we haven't. So, I devised a plan. An evil, genius plan.

"Alright, there's no one back in the porn room. Who's going to do the honors?" Carter asks as he emerges from the hallway next to the counter.

Two years ago, Liz installed a porno room in her store. The shelves are lined with every porno movie known to man. To avoid people stealing them and to stop any embarrassment of some poor, lonely librarian having to carry the movie box out in front of other people so everyone in the store knows she likes midget donkey sex, the DVD cases are empty and each one is assigned a three-digit number. If anyone wants to buy one, they just have to come up to the front counter and tell the cashier what number they want. Instead of saying, "I'd like to buy 'Dickman and Throbbinhood'," they can just say, "Could I get number four-twenty-three, please?"

Since neither Carter nor Jim want to actually get maced in the face, we decide to spray some mace in the small porno room where it will be easily contained. Then, we can just walk in there and see how we're affected. We never really have to tell anyone *how* we were maced; we can just tell people from now on that we have "experience" with being maced. It's kind of perfect if I do say so myself.

It's sad, really, that I can't find a good macing shirt for the occasion. Instead, I had to settle for my backup for emergency situations: I'm full of awesome.

"Shouldn't we wait until the store closes?" Jim asks, looking nervously at the door.

"Your wife will be back before the store closes. We need to do this shit now," I tell him, grabbing the industrial size can of mace from under the counter. "The girls were out of commission for what, twenty minutes or so? And they were sprayed directly in the eyes. Since we're just going to be standing in a room where it's lingering in the air, we're probably only going to get a small percentage of what they got. We'll be fine. Even if a customer does come in, they'll have no idea what's going on."

Jim taps his fingers on the counter, looks over at the door again, and then down at his watch. "Okay, fine. Let's hurry up and get this over with in case Liz comes back early."

Carter and I let out a victory yell, and I hand him the can to let him do the spraying.

"Go ahead man, just open the door a crack, spray as much as you can, and shut it really quickly," I explain.

Carter takes the can, gives me a salute, and turns and jogs down the hallway.

As soon as he leaves, the bell above the door rings and Jim and I turn around and see three women walk in the door.

"Shit, customers. What the fuck do we do?" Jim whispers frantically.

"Relax. It's contained in the back room. We just wait on them like normal and then go back there. If the mace all faded away, Carter can just spray it again," I tell him.

The three women are off in a far corner giggling over something on one of the shelves so I wander over to where they are and see if they need any assistance.

"Hello there, ladies. What can I help you with this evening?"

They all start giggling again and each one turns bright red when they try and look me in the eyes.

"Um, well, my friend Jamie here has never been to a sex toy store before. So, what would you recommend for her first toy?" one of the women asks.

Normally, I enjoy helping out the customers in Liz's store. I'm kind of a genius when it comes to all of the things in here but as soon as I start to impart my wisdom on them, my nose starts to tickle and I feel a sneeze coming on.

I let out four rapid sneezes right in a row and apologize to the ladies, asking them to follow me to another display so I can show them a few things for beginners.

As I'm holding up a bullet with a cock ring attachment, I feel my eyes start to itch and I'm wondering if I'm suddenly getting allergies or something. The three girls are so embarrassed they are barely even listening to what I'm saying, and I feel like my sex intelligence is wasted on them. I'm holding the bullet and I'm rubbing my eyes furiously now since they won't stop itching.

"Oh my God, my eyes are so itchy," one of the women complain.

From behind me, I hear hacking coughs and I turn to see what's going on with Jim and Carter but my eyes are watering so bad I can barely see them.

Next to me, two of the women start coughing and complaining that their throats itch.

What the fuck is going on?! Is this the fucking zombie apocalypse? Are we all infected with something that's going to make us foam at the mouth and eat people's faces??!

"Fuck! Did you guys eat bath salts tonight? Did you breathe bath salts on me or something?" I ask the women as I too start coughing and tears run down my cheeks.

My eyes are starting to burn and itch at the same time, and I feel like I can't cough hard enough or long enough to stop my throat from itching.

"Drew!" Jim yells between hacking coughs from the counter.

I drop the bullet and cock ring on the floor and tell the women not to move which is pointless because two of them are now sitting on the floor clawing at their eyes while the other one is leaning against a display case sneezing over and over.

I scramble back to the counter as best I can since my eyes are watering so badly that everything is blurry. My coughing gets worse the closer I get to Jim and Carter, and I see they are having the same problems I am. Carter is sitting on the floor behind the counter digging his fists in his eyes while he sneezes and Jim is dry heaving in between coughs.

"What the fuck is going on?!" Jim yells as I stumble behind the counter and sneeze six times in a row.

"It's the fucking zombie virus! Son of a bitch, I told you this day was coming! No one believed me and you all laughed. Well, who the fuck is laughing now?! If I go first, you kill me before I eat ANYONE'S face off, do you hear me?" I scream at Jim.

A hand clamps around my ankle, and I scream like a girl and jump up onto the counter. I look down and see Carter staring up at me with a scared look on his face.

"I don't want to eat people either! Don't let me eat people! They say it tastes like chicken but I don't believe them. PEOPLE TASTE LIKE PEOPLE NOT CHICKEN!"

I nod my head, too busy coughing and wiping the tears out of my eyes to do much else. I glance behind me to check on the three women and see them crawling on all fours to get to the front door.

"NOOOOOOO! YOU CAN'T LEAVE! THE ZOMBIES!" I scream.

They can't go outside. The streets are probably overrun with creepy bloody people chewing on arms and toes.

The women scream at the top of their lungs and are half crawling, half running as they try to get up off of the floor. They are coughing and crying and screaming and shoving displays and each other out of their way to get to the door. They don't listen to my shouts of warning at all, and before I know it, they are out the door and lost to the zombies.

"It's so sad. They were so pretty. Now we won't even be able to recognize them the next time we see them," Jim says sadly as I continue to cough.

"I need to call Jenny and tell her I love her," I say between sneezes as I reach for the phone on the counter.

I dial our home number and she answers on the first ring but she sounds funny.

"Mmmmmm, mmmmfffuh"

Oh my god, has she been turned already?!

"NOOOOO! Jenny! Baby! Did they get to you already? Are you already a zombie? Oh my God!" I scream into the phone.

"What? Jenny's a zombie?" Jim asks from behind me before dissolving into another coughing fit. "Shit! I need to call Liz."

I hear a cough on the other end of the phone and I know that if Jenny isn't a zombie yet, she will be soon.

"Fight the virus, baby, FIGHT IT!" I scream.

"Drew? What the hell are you talking about? I was taking a nap. What time is it?" she asks.

"IT'S ZOMBIE TIME! Lock the doors, baby. Don't let them eat your face!" I tell her.

"MY FACE IS BURNING!" Carter yells from the floor as he scratches his cheeks.

"We need an antidote! What the fuck is an antidote for zombies?" I yell to Jim.

"What the hell does your Aunt Dottie have to do with zombies?" Jenny asks through the phone line. "Did you eat pot cookies again? You know what those do to you."

A flash of blue and red lights catches my attention, and I turn around and look out the front window.

"It's the cops. They've come to save us," I say.

"Or they're really zombie cops and they've come to eat our legs," Jim adds.

⊙ ⊙ ⊙

"Yes, officer. I'll make sure they are never left unsupervised again," Liz tells the cop as he gets in his cruiser and then takes off.

Jim, Carter, and I are all sitting on the curb outside of the store with wet towels pressed to our eyes and bottles of water clutched in our hands.

Even though we can't see right now, we can tell that Liz is looking at each one of us like she wants to murder us.

"What in the fucking hell were you guys thinking?" she asks.

I can hear her shoes tapping on the concrete right in front of us, and I close my legs to protect my nuts, just in case.

"You three morons thought you would spray mace in the porn room because it was a closed room. And yet somehow, during the planning of this stellar idea, you failed to remember this little thing called a VENTILATION SYSTEM. And you know, since it's winter and all, the heat is on, pushing air and MACE from the fucking VENTILATION SYSTEM out into the entire store," Liz explains angrily.

I remove the wet towel from my eyes and chance a look at her.

"Yeah, we didn't really think that part through," I admit.

"Oh gee, you think? Those three women went running down the street screaming about crazy men and flesh eating zombies that had taken over my store. And Jenny called me in a panic, freaking out because someone knocked on her door, and she thought zombies were going to break into the house to eat your kids. She threw a blender, the toaster, and a lamp at the door before I could convince her that it was my mother dropping off a present for Billy," Liz tells me.

"Which lamp? It wasn't my Ohio State one, was it?" I ask in horror.

"That is so not the fucking point, Drew!"

I look over at Carter and Jim and realize they are much smarter than I am. They are both sitting with their heads down, not making eye contact.

"You three are in time-out! No playing together for the rest of the week!" Liz yells before stomping past us and into the store.

"Yes ma'am," we all mumble.

After we hear the door close, we all finally look at each other.

"Next time we're allowed to play together, we are so coming up with a zombie antidote," Jim states.

24.

I Love Your Mom's Clam

"Tell me again why we're spending our Friday night with your parents?" Drew asks for the tenth time tonight.

"I told you, my mom wants to show us some reward she got from a group she's in."

"Reward or *Award*?" Drew asks.

"I'm not sure. Whatever the one is where you get a trophy or something."

I don't know why Drew is making a fuss about going to dinner at my parents' house. They love him. I think maybe more than they do me.

"My mom said she was making something you mentioned liking a while ago. I tried to get her to tell me what it was, but she said it was a surprise," I say with a shrug.

I can practically see Drew's eyes light up with happiness. My mom is a very good cook. If you ask Drew what three things he would want with him if he was stranded on a desert island, he'd say the July 1990 issue of Playboy, me, and my mom's homemade chicken pot pie. He's been grumpy ever since he was grounded from hanging out with the boys. Hopefully this dinner will put him in a good mood.

When we pull into my parents' driveway, Drew is out of the car and running through their front door before I'm even unbuckled. No matter what kind of a mood he's in, there's no way his stomach can deny him my mom's cooking.

I get the kids out of the car and make my way into the house. Of course, as soon as I enter I see my parents pawning all over Drew, hugging him and squeezing his cheeks and asking him a million questions, like they haven't just seen him a week ago.

"Oooooooh, give me that grandson of mine!" my mother squeals, running over to take Billy out of my arms. She presses kisses all over his cheeks while I bend down to help Veronica out of her coat.

"Give Gammy a kiss," my mom says, bending down to Veronica's level.

"You're a stinkin' dumb stupid head," Veronica tells her.

"Awww, isn't she sweet? I could just eat her up!" my mom says with a smile, standing back up and shifting Billy to her other arm.

My mom has a hard time understanding Veronica when she talks. She had thought it was rude to ask Veronica to repeat something or tell her she didn't understand her, so instead she just sort of tunes her out and pretends like she gets what she's saying. It's almost like that dog whistle thingy that only dogs can hear. Except, Veronica is the thingy and my mom is the dog. Wait, no. Would the thingy be the dog? Or would my mom be the whistle?

I've told her she needs to stop doing that. Just last week Veronica had asked her if she could paint on the walls, and Mom just smiled at her and told her she was a good little girl. My parents now have a lovely drawing of a giant pink blob on their living room wall.

"It smells awesome in here, Ma. What did you make for dinner?" Drew asks as my dad walks up next to him with the business section of the newspaper. A year ago, Drew had watched some stockbroker movie and when my parents stopped over that night, he started quoting the movie randomly throughout the night. My dad now thinks he's a Wall Street genius and has Drew give him stock tips each week. I still don't understand why Drew keeps going along with it.

"Well, remember that conversation we had a few weeks ago and you said something about how a bearded clam was your favorite thing to eat?" my mom asks in answer to Drew's question about dinner.

I throw an angry look over at Drew, but he's too busy snort-laughing with his hands over his face.

"I tried to use the Ga-Google thingy on the computer to search for: How to make a bearded clam. All that came up were some really disturbing pictures, so I decided to just wing it and make something else. I hope it tastes as good as the bearded clam," my mom tells him, passing Billy off to my dad as she walks by him to get to the kitchen.

"Daddy, I wanna eat a beardy clam," Veronica says.

"Veronica, don't say that," I tell her softly while Drew snorts even louder.

"I wanna eat a beardy clam, you stinkin' dumb stupid head!" Veronica shouts.

"Oh, that's it! Time out!" I tell her. "Not another word for five minutes."

Veronica stomps her feet angrily into the kitchen with my mother, probably hoping for some sympathy when she tells her I'm mean. Unfortunately for Veronica, my mom will probably think she's said, "I'm so clean!"

"Okay, dinner is served!" my mom yells from the dining room.

My dad turns to head that way, and I whisper angrily at Drew while we follow. "Seriously, Drew? You told my mom you liked to eat bearded clam?"

Drew giggles and covers it up with a cough.

"I assumed she knew what that was and we'd get a good laugh about it. How was I supposed to know she'd go on Google looking for a recipe?" he whispers back. "Oh Jesus, your mom would have been sitting at her computer in her housecoat and slippers with curlers in her hair looking at pictures of furry pussies! This day is full of win!"

I smack him in the arm as we walk into the dining room and take our seats.

As soon as we're seated, my mom takes the cover off of the pan in the middle of the table.

"Drew, I hope stuffed clams are as good as bearded clams!" she says with a smile.

"That's going to be tough because Jenny has the most DELICIOUS bearded clam, but I'm keeping my fingers crossed," Drew says, trying to keep the laugh in with is hand tightly covering his mouth, but it was no use.

"Jenny, I didn't know you made a bearded clam before. "Does it have mustard in it?" my mom asks.

"Only if you're doing it in the parking lot of a baseball game," Drew snickers.

"So, Mom, what's this award you were telling me about?" I ask, changing the subject as far away from my clam as possible as she goes around the table to serve everyone.

"Oh! I was voted Most Caring at the KC Club this year!" she says excitedly as she gets back to her seat.

"Why does Kasey have a club?" Drew asks through a mouthful of food.

"No, not *Kasey,* KC Club," my mom explains.

"I know. But who is this Kasey chick and why does she have her own club?" Drew questions.

"KC, for kindness and caring. Get it? KC Club," my mom tries again.

"Who decided Kasey was kind and caring? I seriously want to know what the deal is with this bitch. I don't get it."

My mom just continues to try and explain it to him while I help Veronica with her food, trying not to roll my eyes or make them stop.

"No, no, no. KC. Capital 'K', capital 'C'," my mom says.

"That's the dumbest spelling of Kasey I've ever heard of," Drew tells her.

This just keeps getting worse.

"Hey, Dad, did you and Mom ever go to marriage counseling?" I blurt out.

Drew flicks my thigh with his finger and looks at me funny.

He's probably not happy I'm bringing this up because he doesn't want anyone to know about the marriage counselor thing. I don't know what the big deal is. When we got home and Drew asked if he could hug my vagina, I told him no and he started sobbing. He can't say marriage counseling didn't work on him. Look at how he wasn't afraid to show his emotions? That's a total breakthrough. I'm just curious to see if my parents ever went through hard times with each other.

"Nonsense! That crap is for sissies and girly-men. If you can't fix your own marriage, how the hell can anyone else? What those quacks charge in an hour could feed a small country for year," he complains.

"Seriously? A whole country? Like, which one? Texas?" Drew asks in astonishment.

"Drew, you silly! Texas isn't a country!" my mom says with a laugh. "It's a consonant."

My dad continues to complain about how young people now-a-days can't even wipe their own ass without help and how the institution of marriage is going down the shitter. Obviously asking this question hadn't been the best idea.

"Here's another question for you. Have you ever fallen asleep during sex?" Drew asks, looking over at me with one eyebrow raised.

I look away from him because I know exactly why he's asked that question. I'm still living by the fake-it-till you make rule, and I had wanted to try and do something for Drew, so when he got home from work the other night, I asked him if I could give him a hand job. I don't mean to brag or anything, but I'm kind of awesome at hand jobs. Just the right amount of pressure mixed with the right amount of lotion and he's done in fifteen point seven seconds. I really hadn't meant to fall asleep in the middle of it the other night, but come on! Drew gets home from work at four in the morning. I've been exhausted. One minute I'm stroking away and Drew is loving it, and the next, he's shaking me awake, yelling because in my sleep, my grip tightened on his penis and it was cutting off his circulation.

"Please don't ask my parents about sex at the dinner table. I'm trying to eat here!" I whisper to Drew.

"I'm still trying to get over the fact that my penis put you to sleep!" Drew argues back in a loud whisper.

Luckily, my dad had got distracted by Billy spitting up in his arms and the question is forgotten. I don't want to have to hear anything that has the words "my parents" and "sex" in the same sentence, but I kind of wish I would have heard my dad's answer. I cannot possibly be the only woman who has fallen asleep during a hand job.

"Ma, what kind of seafood did you stuff this thing with? It's amazing," Drew tells her.

"A little crab and some lobster. I wanted to put salmon in it, but I'm confused by salmon. I mean, what part of the fish is salmon cut from? I asked the guy at the fish market but he didn't know either. I wonder if salmon is a fancy word for stomach or fin. They should just call it stomach or fin. All these different words for things are weird," she explains.

We finish dinner and then move into the living room for coffee.

My dad puts a blanket down on the floor for Billy and is sitting next to him making funny faces.

"Gammy, I feel pukey. Your food sucks," Veronica tells her.

"That's nice, dear!" my mom replies as she pats her on the head.

"Do you really not feel well, sweetie?" I ask as I lift her up onto my lap and feel her forehead.

"I shoulda never, never ate Gammy's clam," Veronica tells me, resting her head on my shoulder.

"There are so many things wrong with that statement," Drew whispers.

We spend a few more minutes chatting with my parents until Veronica starts crying that her tummy hurts. We pack up the kids and head home, but not before Drew tells my dad to buy low, sell high and to watch his bottom line before the market closes or the risk capital will be higher than the profit sharing.

My dad shakes Drew's hand and tells him that without him, he and my mom would be broke.

Dew asks me to drive home because all of a sudden he feels funny. I swear sometimes the sickness in our family works through osmouses. You know, where one person is sick and a mouse walks by and gets the sickness and then passes it on to someone else by sitting on their head? Halfway home Drew starts groaning and clutching his stomach.

"What's wrong? Are you okay?" I ask him.

"Oh Jesus, your mom's clam made me sick," he mutters.

He moans for a few more seconds until he realizes what he just said and laughs through his pain.

"Your mom's clam was delicious, but now, your mom's clam is vicious!" Drew laughs before suddenly bending over and hugging his stomach.

'It's my turn to groan now as I turn onto our street.

"Seriously, stop saying that. It's freaking me out," I complain as I pull into the driveway.

"Your mom's clam was smooth going down, but now I'm regretting swallowing it," he mutters with a laugh.

"Shut up!" I warn him as I pull into the driveway.

"At least it wasn't bearded. I'd be choking on curly hairs right now. Your mom's clam was as clean as a baby's bottom!"

As soon as I shut off the car and open the door, Drew leans out of his side and pukes all over the driveway.

"Oh my God! Your mom's clam was infected!" he yells and laughs in between dry heaves.

I get the kids out of the car and walk into the house without him, happy to just let him puke alone in the driveway.

25.

Drop and Give Me Fifty

"It's time to turn you boys into men," my dad states, standing in front of the fireplace with his arms crossed in front of him. He gives Carter, Jim, and I each a stern look.

"Hey, I'm man enough," Carter complains while Jim nods in agreement.

"Yeah, me too. It's fuck face here who needs work," Jim says, pointing in my direction.

"Fuck you," I complain, punching Jim in the shoulder.

"GET IN THE KITCHEN AND MAKE ME A CHICKEN POT PIE, BITCH!" Jim yells at me.

"Seriously, fuck off!"

"Hey, I'm just getting you prepared for this challenge and getting your wife back," Jim explains with a shrug.

Carter had called me last weekend once we were finally ungrounded and were allowed talk to each other again. Claire spilled the beans to him about how Jenny has been feeling lately and Carter wanted to give me a head's up. Of course, Claire swore him to secrecy and told him she'd never give him another blow job again if he told me, so Carter obviously threatened my life if I said anything to Jenny about it.

I spent all week trying to be a better husband, but I had no idea what the fuck I was doing or how to be better since I thought I was pretty fucking awesome to begin with. I made sure to remember to put the toilet seat down and the cap back on the toothpaste and when Jenny never commented on it, I brought it up to her and asked if it made her happy. She told me I was an idiot and walk out of the room.

That led to me calling my dad and asking him for help.

I had told Jenny I was helping my dad put together a bookcase and we all met at Liz and Jim's house while she was out grocery shopping with the kids. Jim had said she was taking the girls over to have lunch with her parents after, so we should have plenty of time to get this done without anyone knowing about it.

"Alright boys, listen up. There are three rules to live by when you're married. Number one, don't piss off your wife. Number two, don't piss off your wife, and number three..."

He holds out his hands, palms up, indicating for us to finish.

"Never piss off your wife," the three of us say in unison.

"Wonderful, The Three Stooges can be taught," my dad says.

"Heeeeey!" Jim complains.

"QUICK! Tell me what you do when your wife comes home from work with a box of tampons in her hands and starts complaining that the house is a mess," my dad fires at Jim.

"Uh, um...fuck! Uh, tell her she looks pretty?" Jim stammers quickly.

"WRONG! You tell her to go take a nap so you can clean the house!" my dad answers.

"Fuck!" Jim grumbles.

"Stand up, soldiers!" my dad yells.

We all get up from the couch quickly as he comes over and pushes the coffee table out from in front of us.

"DROP AND GIVE ME FIFTY YOU SNOT-NOSED MOTHER FUCKERS!"

We drop to the ground and start our push-ups, each of us grunting and panting.

"I DON'T HEAR YOU COUNTING, ASSHOLES!"

"Son of a bitch! How is this going to help us?" Carter whispers in between counting while he breathes heavily.

"It's going to teach you pussies some respect," my dad says suddenly, squatting down and putting his face right into Carter's.

"Your dad scares the fuck out of me," Carter mutters as quietly as possible as my dad gets up and walks back over to the fireplace.

We finish our push-ups and groan at the pain in our arms and backs as we get up from the floor.

We watch as my dad turns around and bends down to unzip a duffel bag that's on the floor next to the fireplace.

He stands up and turns around to face us, holding three baby dolls in his arms.

"Time for baby duty, fuckers. Let's see what you're made of," he tells us, handing us each one of the dolls.

Jim holds his by the hair, I hold mine by the foot, and Carter cradles his in his arms, swaying gently back and forth.

"Jim, Drew, right now your babies would be DEAD! You are holding a life in your arms and you just killed it. A man and his baby are a powerful force that can devastate small countries," my dad lectures.

"Don't you mean a man and his gun? A baby can't really devastate a small country," Jim tells him.

"Have you ever been in a room with a baby who is projectile vomiting, screaming his fool head off, and diarrhea is exploding out of his ass so much you think he has a fire hose shoved up there spraying shit instead of water? Babies are the Napalm of western civilization!"

My dad pulls a stop watch out of the pocket of his pants holds it in front of him with his thumb hovering over the start button.

"ON YOUR MARK!" he shouts.

"Wait! What the fuck are we doing?" I ask frantically, putting the baby up on my shoulder as I pat its back.

"You are changing diapers, limp dicks! GET SET!"

Carter gets into ready position, crouching low to the ground, his doll shoved into the back of his t-shirt with the head sticking out of the top and its eyes staring right at me.

"Son of a bitch! Where are the diapers?!" Jim shouts, tucking the doll under one arm like a football.

"This is your house, asshole! Shouldn't you know that?" I ask him, sticking the doll's feet down the front of my pants so its limp body falls forward and it's head is facing my crotch.

"Molly doesn't wear diapers anymore! We don't have any fucking diapers!" he shouts back at me.

"This is real life, soldiers! Sometimes you don't know where diapers and wipes are and you have to make do, especially if you're in the middle of the desert and your baby just shit its brains out!

"When the fuck would that ever happen?" I ask in confusion.

GO!" he shouts, clicking the stop watch.

Carter takes off like a bat out of hell and runs to the front door, throwing it open and racing outside. He has the right idea - he's getting the fuck out of dodge.

Jim and I look at each other in confusion and both take off at the same time, slamming into one another, forcing Jim's doll out of his arms. It lands on the floor on its head and we both pause and look over at my dad.

He just stands there shaking his head in disappointment.

Jim scoops up the doll and clutches it to his chest, giving me the finger before taking off up the stairs.

My dad turns the stop watch around so I can see, and I realize I've wasted a shit ton of time while Jim has probably already found a diaper and Carter is most likely already three miles down the road and has chucked his doll into a ditch somewhere.

I turn and run into the kitchen, the doll's head bobbing up and down and smacking into my dick. If this wasn't a serious situation, I would be laughing my ass off right now.

Oh fuck it.

I stop when I reach the kitchen and lift the doll's head up by its hair. "Was that good for you, baby? You need to work on your technique. It's never hot to just smack your face into a guy's junk," I say with a laugh.

I hear a throat clear and turn around to see my dad standing in the kitchen doorway with his hands on his hips, shaking his head at me.

Twenty minutes later, Jim and I are standing in the living room in front of the couch, holding our dolls. Mine has half of its hair singed off (don't ask), a missing arm with a screwdriver shoved into its body for a fake arm (seriously, don't ask), and a place mat tied around its ass for a diaper.

Jim's doll doesn't look any better. He's holding the body in one hand and the head in the other, with one of its legs tucked under his arm. It used to have a pink pair of footy pajamas on, but now it's just wearing a pair of Jim's tighty whities, held in place with a couple of Liz's giant hair clips.

My dad notes our times on a pad of paper sitting on the coffee table and hits the stop button.

"This is just a sad, sad display of skills gentlemen," he complains.

"Wait, where's Carter? You can't stop the time yet, that asshole hasn't even made it back from wherever the hell he went," Jim complains.

"Carter has been back here for ten minutes. He's in the bathroom fixing his baby's hair that got a little windblown outside."

At that moment, we hear the toilet flush and the bathroom door open and Carter walks out into the living room holding his baby on his hip. Her hair is in two French braids, she's wearing a different outfit than the one she came in, and has a diaper perfectly attached to her ass.

"What. The. Fuck?" I ask him as he walks over to stand in between Jim and I, looking at each of our babies in horror.

He quickly covers his doll's ear with one hand and presses her other ear against his chest.

"Drew! Language!" he scolds in a loud whisper.

"Oh you have got to be fucking kidding me. He totally cheated! You called your wife, didn't you? Did Claire meet you outside or something?" I complain.

"Of course not. I am just better equipped to deal with a baby, obviously," he replies, bouncing gently and patting the doll's back.

"Alright, since you two obviously failed that test, you need a remedial course," my dad says to Jim and me. "Carter, I'm going to need your help."

⊙ ⊙ ⊙

"No, no, no. You're doing it all wrong. You need to support his head more. My God, it's like you've never had kids before," Carter scolds as he repositions my hands and angles the bottle up higher.

"This is not the key to fixing my marriage OR my sex life. You guys all realize this, right?"

My dad walks over to check on things and smacks me upside the head.

"Wrong! A happy wife is a happy life. You learn how to do your share around the house and you will get laid regularly. Just ask your mother."

I groan and dry heave, the bottle slipping out and milk squirting all over the front of me. "Dad, gross. Do NOT talk about you and Mom. Ever."

Carter grabs my hands and puts the bottle back where it was.

"You need to rock and bounce a little. It helps them digest the milk easier so they don't have as much gas. And make sure they don't keep sucking after the milk is gone. They'll just be getting air then, and it will cause a tummy ache," Carter says, putting his arm around my shoulder and forcing me to sway slowly with him on the couch.

"Your mother has no complaints in the bedroom OR around the house. I keep her very sexually satisfied, and I always got up with you in the middle of the night," my dad says while I grimace at his words.

"Wait, are you seriously trying to tell me that if I just get up with Billy in the middle of the night, everything will be restored to its rightful order?" I question.

"You stopped swaying, concentrate and keep swaying or the baby will cry. You don't want the baby to cry if you're doing a nighttime feeding or the whole house will wake up," Carter reminds me, pushing against me again to get me to sway.

"I'm saying that if you put yourself in your wife's shoes once in a while, it will be easy to see what she needs. She needs a night of sleep, she needs help around the house, she needs your love and support, and the proof that you WANT to help her with these things. A wife that isn't getting what she needs is never going to want to give you what YOU need," Dad tells me.

"I need kinky sex," I tell him plainly.

"Then rock that baby like you mean it!" he yells at me.

And that's how Liz found us fifteen minutes later when she came home early from her parent's house. Carter and I swaying back and forth on the couch with Jim spread out on my lap, drinking out of the bottle I was feeding him.

26.

The Newlywed Game

Drew and Jackson are up in our bedroom, and I can hear their laughter from the living room where I pace anxiously for everyone to arrive. Jackson had complimented Drew on his shirt for the night: a picture of that Monopoly guy holding a pile of money in his arms that says, "I like big bucks and I cannot lie." Drew had taken him upstairs to show him the rest of his shirt collection.

When I had told Drew about the game night and what we were going to play, he got really excited and immediately called Jackson and asked him to be our "host" for the evening.

I want to be as thrilled as he is for tonight but my stomach is tied in knots. All I can think about is someone asking him a really important question and him getting it wrong. I had thought about canceling tonight a bunch of times, but I don't want to ruin everyone's night. They are all looking forward to this. I should be too, really. The kids are both spending the night with Drew's parents, and everyone else has managed to get sitters as well. We don't have to worry about bedtimes or cranky kids or anything being lit on fire. We are free to do whatever we want, for however long we wanted to.

The doorbell rings just as I hear Drew and Jackson coming back down the stairs. I run to the door and fling it open to see all four of our friends standing there, each with a bottle of liquor in their hands.

"We come baring gifts," Carter says with a laugh as I hold the door open for them.

704

"I just want to let everyone know that Liz and I are so totally going to win this thing. We *have* to win this thing. It's a matter of life and death," Jim says seriously as he sets his bottle of whiskey down on the coffee table in the living room where I've set out some snacks and a bunch of glasses.

"There's no way you're winning this. Claire and I have been quizzing each other since this morning. We've got this in the bag," Carter argues with Jim, setting his bottle of vodka next to the whiskey.

Jim turns and puts his hands on Carter's shoulders and looks him in the eye.

"For the love of God, man, you *have* to let us win this," Jim pleads.

"Why the hell is he being so dramatic," Claire asks Liz softly.

Liz lets out a huge sigh as she hands me her bottle of wine.

"I made the mistake of telling him that if we win, I'll give him anal. I was kind of joking at the time because he doesn't want to play the game, and I was trying to get him in the mood for it. I may have gone a little overboard," she explains as we watch Jim run over to Drew and get down on his knees in front of him.

"Drew, please, listen to reason. I'm begging you, don't let us lose. Oh God, I can't lose!" he wails.

"Hey, asshole, while you're down there…" Drew says with a laugh.

Jim clenches his fist and punches him right in the nuts and Drew goes down on his knees, holding his crotch.

"Alright, ladies and gentlemen, my name is Jackson and I will be your host for this evening," Jackson says with a grin while I grab Drew's arm and help him stand up.

"Um, Jackson, everyone already knows who you are. Remember?" I whisper to him.

"Pay no attention to the woman behind the curtain," Claire says with a laugh as she takes a sip of the wine she's poured for herself.

"I'm not behind a curtain. Is this part of the game?" I ask in confusion.

"Anyway, I'm going to start by taking the ladies into another room and asking them a series of questions. They will write their answers on these pieces of poster board," Jackson explains, holding up a stack of white, heavy duty cardboard and a couple of black markers. "Then I'll do the same with the guys. Everyone will keep their answers in a stack, face down on their laps. We'll do ladies first, so the women will be answering the questions for the first round. Each couple will get five points for each correct answer. The couple with the most points at the end of the game will be crowned The Best Couple in all the Land."

This seems complicated and Jim is so excited he's bouncing up and down in his chair. He wants to win this as bad as I do. I can't even bribe Drew with anal like Liz did. That ship sailed a long time ago.

"Okay, ladies. Grab your glasses and follow me. Boys, start getting liquored up so you have a fighting chance," Jackson says as he turns and heads into the kitchen.

"Hey, sweetie, do you want a nipple for that drink?" Liz asks Jim with a secret smile.

"You were never to speak of that again!" he complains, throwing his hands up in the air.

"What is he talking about?" Claire asks Liz as they make their way to the kitchen.

"If he pisses me off tonight, I'll let you know," she tells Liz, throwing Jim a warning look over his shoulder.

"Fuck, even if we win I'm not getting anal. This sucks," Jim complains, pouring himself a healthy glass of whiskey.

I let go of Drew's arm and start to follow when he suddenly wraps his arm around my waist and pulls me back against his chest. He leans his head over my shoulder from behind, and with his free hand, swipes my hair off of my shoulder.

"Let's kick some ass, baby," he whispers against the side of my neck before pressing his lips to my collarbone. He holds them there for several seconds, letting his tongue snake out to taste my skin before pulling his mouth away from me.

My whole body tingles from head to toe and a smile lights up my face as I pat the top of his hand that's resting on my stomach before he lets go and smacks my ass as I walk away.

Drew has been different this week. He pissed me off a few times making a big deal about putting the toilet seat down after he used it. I mean, give me a break! You don't need a present and a pat on the back for doing crap like that! But he does deserve a present for everything else. Ever since he helped his dad build that bookcase, he's been super helpful with everything. The past four nights, he's got up each time Billy cried and gave him his bottle, telling me to go back to sleep. Last night Billy had slept through the night for the first time. Drew has even used the sex swing that is still in the corner of our room and agrees that it makes a *great* baby swing, especially when I show him where he could store extra bottles.

On Wednesday of this week, he had shocked me again after work. I was late getting home from running a few errands so I could relieve Drew from kid duty and he could head to work, so we barely had time to even say, "Hi" to each other as we passed in the doorway. As soon as I set my bags down inside the door, the first thing I noticed was how absolutely spotless the house was. Not one toy or dirty dish in sight and there was a basket of folded laundry on the couch. Before I could say anything, he grabbed my hand and placed a small, white box in it before kissing the tip of my nose and then racing to his car to make it to work on time.

When we first started dating, we went to the movies one night and he bought me a giant bag of Skittles. I sat there for fifteen minutes before the movie started and picked out all of the red and purples ones, putting them in a napkin in my cup holder before handing him the bag. From that point on, every once in a while for no reason at all he would give me a little white box that was filled with just purple and red Skittles. I couldn't even tell you the last time he did that for me.

I knew exactly what would be in the box and my hands shook and my eyes filled with tears as I closed the front door and opened the lid. Sure enough, the box was filled to the brim with purple and red Skittles. Not only was he stepping up his game around the house before I even had a chance to sit down and talk to him, he was starting to do the little things that I loved the most like giving me my favorite treats.

And tonight, he had given me another favorite treat: kissing my collarbone.

I can't wipe the smile off of my face as I enter the kitchen and find Liz and Claire seated at the table, arguing over who is going to win the game.

"Ladies, ladies! No more arguing. The winner has just entered the room," I tell them with a smile as I sit down at the table with them.

"Well, it's about fucking time you got your confidence back!" Liz tells me. "Bartender, pour us a round of shots!"

Jackson laughs and turns toward the counter, filling up drinking glasses with a few inches of black cherry vodka.

"You know he's not a bartender, right? He's a carpenter," I whisper to Liz.

Jackson comes back over to the table and places a glass in front of each of us.

"Shut up and do your shot!" Liz tells me.

We down our shots, let out a cheer, and Jackson begins our questions.

⊙ ⊙ ⊙

"Alright, for five points, making your score a grand total of forty-five, Drew – what would Jenny say is her favorite place to make love?" Jackson asks.

"VAGINA! IN HER VAGINA!" Drew screams excitedly.

Jackson looks over at me and nods, and I flip over my card for everyone to see my answer.

Jim and Liz groan from their spots on the floor, and Carter and Claire start to laugh while Drew bounces up and down and gives me a high five when he sees the word "vagina" written really big on my card.

"WOOOHOOO! We are kicking ALL of your asses!" Drew shouts as I throw my card down to the discard pile on the floor.

I don't know why I was so worried about this game. No matter what, Drew and I know each other very well. It doesn't matter if we aren't on the same page or even reading the same book. Which we never are anyway because I like romances and Drew only reads the funny pages, and it just occurred to me that that statement is kind of dumb. Who reads the same book at the same time? I takes me months to read a book and other people might read fast. That's just weird.

Anyway, we were really kicking everyone's ass and unfortunately, poor Jim wasn't going to be plowing the back field tonight since he and Liz are currently in last place with only ten points.

"Jim, who did Liz say is better at handling money?" Jackson asks him.

Jim chuckles and finishes off his drink, setting the glass on the coffee table next to him.

"Man, this is an easy one. Me!"

Liz flips her card over and then smacks Jim in the chest with it.

"Are you kidding me? You went to the store two weeks ago and bought seventy-two bottles of Windex. Who the fuck even USES seventy-two bottles of Windex in their entire life?" Liz complains, throwing her card down on the floor.

"IT WAS ON SALE!" Jim yells at her. "I saved money in the long run!"

"We will DIE before even half of that is used. You WASTED money!" Liz yells back.

"Alrighty then, moving on. Carter, for five points, bringing your score up to thirty-five, if you told Claire that tomorrow you would do one item from her 'Honey-Do List', what would she pick?" Jackson asks.

Carter leans over and kisses Claire on the cheek and answers confidently, "Install the new sink in the guest bathroom."

Claire leans away from him and gives him a dirty look before flipping her card over.

"I installed the sink myself three weeks ago. What did I tell you JUST THIS MORNING that you needed to fix before I smothered you in your sleep and set fire to your Sopranos DVD collection?"

Carter leans forward and looks at her card.

"Ohhhhhh, right. Move the heavy bag I hung in the middle of the garage because now you can't park in there. My bad," Carter says apologetically.

"Okay, final question and for the win. - Drew, you've run out to the corner store late at night to pick up milk. You decide while you're there to get a treat for Jenny. What did she say you would buy her?" Jackson asks.

I look over at Drew and he looks over at me and we both smile.

"Skittles, Funyons and a Chinese finger trap!" Drew says without looking away from me.

I flip my card over and everyone voices their complaints when they see *Skittles, Funyons, and a Chinese finger trap* written on my card.

"With fifty points, the winners are Drew and Jenny!" Jackson shouts.

Drew and I both jump up from the couch and start hugging and jumping up and down. Before I know it, his lips are on mine and his hands are pressed against my lower back, pulling my body up against his. I don't even think twice before sliding my tongue past his lips and swirl it around his. He tastes like whiskey and a hint of the peppermint toothpaste he used earlier, and I want to swallow him whole. I clutch the front of his shirt in my fists and pull him even closer, sucking on his tongue just the way he likes. Drew groans into my mouth, his hands sliding down toward my ass. I bend my knees slightly and prepare to jump up and wrap my legs around his waist when the sound of throats clearing and Jim yelling, "GET A ROOM!" breaks through our haze of lust.

We pull apart, righting our clothes and fixing our hair.

"Now that I'm thoroughly disgusted, tell me what the deal with the Chinese finger trap is," Carter says as he starts collecting all of the answer cards into one big pile.

"Oh, it's just this thing we do every once in a while," Drew explains as he leans down to grab his drink from the table and take a sip. "I put it on my penis and Jenny tries to take it off without using her hands. It gets a little dicey there every once in a while and I've gotten some killer paper cuts on my taint, but she gets it off every single time."

Carter starts howling with laughter and pointing at Drew. "Dude, do you have a teeny tiny weenie?! Those things aren't any bigger than my pinkie finger!"

Everyone joins in on the laughter, and I pat Drew's back in sympathy.

"FUCK YOU! THEY COME IN DIFFERENT SIZES!" Drew yells at them.

"Yeah, needle dick and pinky peen!" Jim says with a laugh.

"Jenny, baby, tell them I don't have a small penis," Drew wails.

"Oh, he totally doesn't. I get cock jaw when I give him blow jobs," I tell them.

"Don't you mean *lock* jaw?" Liz asks.

"No, *cock* jaw. When you're giving a blow job and you have to open your mouth so wide your jaw cocks," I explain to them.

"You cock a gun, you don't cock your jaw," Claire laughs.

"You don't *lock* your jaw either! Who the hell has a lock on their cheek? That's just stupid. Drew has a big penis. That is a fact."

Jim shakes his head and smacks Carter in the arm. "You had to ask the story behind the Chinese finger trap. Now my wife is going to have nightmares tonight about those things and jaws with pad locks stuck through them."

"And my giant penis. Don't forget my giant penis," Drew says, looking over at me and beaming proudly.

27.

Irish Car Bombs

"Am I dreaming? Somebody pinch me!" Drew exclaims as we walk through the doors of the local strip club, *Bare Naked Ladies*. "It's been, one week since you cooked for me. Rocked your head to the side and said I'm hungry."

Drew's off-key singing makes everyone groan and tell him to shut up. He's been singing that song the whole way to the strip club.

"For the love of all that is holy, stop singing that fucking song! Especially if you don't know the words," Jim tells him as we all stand in the doorway.

I don't remember exactly whose idea it was to go to a strip club. After the game, we all had started doing shots and everything got really funny. When someone suggested a strip club, we thought it sounded hilarious. So we had called for a taxi, piled in, and had it take us into town.

"Oh my God, why is the floor sticky?" Liz asks with a disgusted look on her face as she gently picks her foot up and looks at the bottom of her shoe.

"Do you really want me to answer that?" Jim asks her as he throws his arm over her shoulder and they lead the way into the club.

Drew and I have been to plenty of strip club's before so this is old news to us. It's been a really long time since we've been to one though. Just seeing the flashing, colorful lights and hearing the loud music brings back so many good memories, and it makes me sad that things between us have been so strainered lately.

As soon as I have that thought though, I feel Drew's hand slide into my own and we lace our fingers together, following behind Jim and Liz as they find a table close to the stage and we all take seats.

We won the game! We really do know each other, and I'm starting to forget all of the reasons why I haven't been in the mood for dirty sex lately. Even though he can act like a big child most of the time, he loves me and he takes good care of me.

"Drew, Jenny! Oh my gosh! I haven't seen you guys in ages!"

We turn and see Candy, the server whose section we always used to sit in when we would come here.

"Candy! We were hoping you'd be here tonight," Drew tells her as she gives me a quick hug. "I wore your favorite shirt just in case."

Drew turns and holds his shirt out for her so she's a picture of a woman upside down on a stripper pole with the words: I support single moms.

He had made the taxi driver run by our house on the way to the club just so he could change.

Drew makes introductions and when everyone else orders beers, Drew and I look at each other and then at them.

"Oh no. You aren't drinking just beer at a strip club. Shots only, folks!" Drew tells them before giving Candy an order for six Little Beers.

"It's okay, you guys can look at the chick dancing on the stage. You won't go blind or anything," I tell Liz and Claire with a laugh.

Ever since we sat down they have looked everywhere but at the topless woman gyrating on the pole four feet in front of them.

It feels good to finally know more about something than my friends.

Claire is the first to turn and look and Carter rubs his hand in soothing circles on her back.

"I really should be a lot drunker for this right now," she mutters.

As soon as she says that, Candy is back with the shots we ordered, along with another round of shots and six dark beers that she sets in front of each of us.

"You two look like you could use a little more alcohol to get through this night," she says to Liz and Claire with a smile. "The Little Beers are the ones on the left and to your right is everything you need for an Irish Car Bomb. Drop that shot glass with the amber liquid into the beer and immediately start chugging. Enjoy!"

Candy walks away and we all pick up our Little Beers.

"What the hell are in these?" Jim asks.

"It's called Liquor 43 with a splash of cream on top to make it look like foam," Drew tells them.

"It looks like jizz," Carter says, bringing the shot to his nose and sniffing it.

"Don't worry. It doesn't taste like jizz. It's sweeter," I tell him. "Well, except for that one time we went to a bulk candy store and Drew ate two pounds of gummy worms. It tasted like cherry-lime then."

Drew grabs the seat of my chair and pulls it closer to his so he can put his arm on the back of my chair.

"Remember we played that fishing game with the gummy worms? We used my old fishing line from when I was little that we found in the basement, and I tied the worm to the end and shoved it-"

"No! Please God, no," Claire says as she puts her hand up to stop Drew from going any further. "Hurry up and make a fucking toast before I puke on this table."

We all raise our arms in the air and Drew clears his throat.

"To naked chicks on poles and putting our poles into naked chicks!"

Claire and Liz let out disgusted sounds before we all do our shots.

We immediately follow them up with the Irish Car bombs and then order two more rounds of car bombs right after since everyone loves them.

Fifteen minutes later we are all beyond buzzed and Claire and Liz are finally enjoying their environment.

"Oooooh, she's pretty. I wonder if her boobs are real," Claire says, pointing to a blonde that just got off of the stage. "Excuse me, can I touch your boobs?"

Carter clutches on to the front of Drew's t-shirt and stares as Claire calls the blonde stripper over, and she immediately agrees to let Claire touch her boobs.

"If this is a dream, never, ever wake me up," Carter mumbles as he watches wide eyed while Claire cups the girl's boobs.

"Welcome to the dark side, my friend," Drew says, clapping him on the back.

Liz suddenly gets up from her chair, walks around the table, and straddles my lap, resting her elbows on my shoulders and pushing her boobs into my face.

"I'm really drunk," Liz tells me.

"I know, honey," I reply with a laugh as I wrap my arms around her and pat her back.

"I think I should give you a lap dance," she says as if she's discussing painting her nails.

"Yes, yes you should. What a super idea!" Jim says, pulling his chair around the table and sitting right next to us.

"Okay. I'm gonna do it. Don't ask me to have sex with you though, Jenny. Even though this is gonna be awesome, I like penis," Liz informs me.

"I will try to remain myself," I tell her as she gets up from my lap, pushes my knees apart, and turns around.

"It's *refry*. You will try to *refry* yourself from sexing me," Liz says over her shoulder.

I smack her ass as hard as I can. "Shut your mouth and dance for me, bitch!"

Liz immediately starts moving her hips and lowers her ass to my lap, moving with the music. Even though I'm drunk, she's REALLY drunk and unsteady on her feet. When she starts moving faster, she begins to tip over to one side. I quickly reach up and grab onto her hips to steady her and bring her back down to my lap so she doesn't fall on her face.

"This is the best day ever," Jim says dreamily from his chair as he watches us with his chin in his hands and his elbows on the table.

Liz puts her legs on either side of mine and bends completely forward until her head is almost touching the floor and continues to move her hips.

It's a bit strange since her legs are slightly bent and she kind of looks like a female dog backing into a male dog to mate. Her ass keeps bumping into my stomach, and it's really hard not to laugh.

"This is starting to get awkward and not hot," Jim says as Liz sits back up and starts Voguing to the music, her arms flying in every direction, forcing Drew to jerk backwards in his chair so he doesn't get smacked in the face.

The Vogue turns into the Y.M.C.A. and at this point, Liz has forgotten about the lower half of her body and is just sitting on my lap leaning against my chest, continuing to form the letters with her arms.

"Lap dancing is exhausting," Liz says with a sigh.

"It's also no longer a turn on," Jim mutters.

"Wow, that girl was so nice!" Claire says as she turns back around to face our table. "Her name is Aubrey and she just graduated from college with a major in journalism. She bought her first house all by herself last week and her boobs are totally real and she gave me a recipe for her grandmother's famous sugar cookies."

Carter shakes his head and sighs. "You have just ruined the magic of strip clubs."

"What are you talking about? I totally touched her boobs!" Claire argues.

"Let me explain how this works here, Claire," Drew explains. "That girl right there who you just fondled, we already imagined that her name was Star and she was just working here part time to save enough money to go to another country to learn how to be a bendy contortionist. At night, she goes home to her one bedroom apartment that she shares with two other equally hot girls, and before they go to bed each night, they have naked pillow fights. Now, that illusion is ruined. She's not hot anymore. She's a smart chick who knows how to read and write. Where's the fun in that?"

Liz is still on my lap, and I tap her shoulder to get her to move because my legs are starting to fall asleep.

"Hey, Liz. Get up, I need to pee," I tell her.

"Um, I think she's asleep," Carter says.

Right then, her head falls back onto my shoulder, and I can hear her lightly snoring.

"Well, I guess that's it for us," Jim says, scooping Liz up in his arms. "You guys coming? I'm going to go outside and call a cab."

Carter grabs Claire's hand and helps her up from the table and they all turn and look at me and Drew.

"Yeah, we're right behind you," Drew tells them as he starts to get up.

I know for a fact he doesn't want to leave right now. We've never left the strip club this early. He's only doing it for me because he assumes I'm going to want to leave and go home to bed, which I would have absolutely done a week ago. But now? He has reminded me this week about all of the reasons I fell in love with him. I don't know how he finally figured out what I needed from him, but he did. And he doesn't hesitate to do all of those things. There is no way I can just NOT do something for him that I know he needs.

I grab his hand and pull him back down to his seat next to me.

"That's okay, guys. We're going to stick around here. We'll just call our own cab."

Everyone leaves and Drew and I are alone at the table, our hands still clutched together, resting on top of Drew's thigh.

"You really want to stay? Are you sure?" he asks.

I lean forward and run my tongue along his top lip, letting go of his hand and sliding my hand up his thigh until I reach the bulge in his jeans. He immediately grabs the back of my head and deepens the kiss. Our tongues swirl around each other, and I can feel him growing hard beneath my hand.

I've missed this so much. I've missed wanting him like this. I've missed kissing him and thinking only about kissing him instead of folding clothes, orders at work, and whether or not I paid the cable bill. What the hell was I thinking when I told him I wanted normal sex? I suddenly really want to try out that thing we talked about last year with a bowl of mashed potatoes and a ride-on lawn mower.

Drew breaks off the kiss and pulls back to look into my eyes.

"I love you, baby. I know I haven't said that in a while and I'm sorry. I'm going to do better," he tells me.

"Oh, Drew! You don't need to do any better. I love you too. I've just been so tired, and I should have said something sooner. I'm so sorry things got so crazy," I tell him.

"No, I'm the one who is sorry. You have nothing to apologize for. I should have realized sooner that you needed more help, but you know I'm an idiot when it comes to stuff like that. If you don't write it down and staple it to my dick, I'm going to be clueless," he explains.

"I would never staple anything to your dick. I love it too much!" I tell him with a smile.

"Speaking of my dick-"

"Yes! We are totally having lots of sex tonight," I interrupt him excitedly.

"No, that's not what I was getting at, but it's good to know," he says with a smile. "What I mean is, if you just want vanilla sex, then vanilla sex is what I will give you. I don't care if we never use those bungee cords or the box of saltine crackers again. I don't care if we never see Officer O'Connor again because he won't be knocking on our door to tell us there's been a noise complaint. I don't even care if the diamond studded dog collar and French maid outfit that fits me like a glove has to go back to the store. I don't care about anything but being with you, whatever way I can, anyway that you'll have me."

With the biggest smile I've had in a long time, I stand up and pull Drew with me.

"Let's go home. I have a surprise for you."

28.

Peeping Ghost

I mean every word I say when I tell my girl I will have plain old vanilla sex for the rest of my life as long as I can do it with her. After the last few months, I realize I don't care about anything but being with her. She is my best friend and my life, and I will do whatever she wants me to do as long as she's happy. I had been stupid when I got mad about never having crazy, dirty sex ever again. While it's true that wild and sometimes bordering on illegal sex is what brought us together, it's not what has kept us together.

The taxi just drops us off from the strip club and Jenny is leading me by the hand into the house and up the stairs. She had mentioned a surprise at the club and I've been hard ever since, knowing that the surprise will more than likely include her getting naked. And if we're just going to get on the bed and have missionary sex with the lights off, I'm okay with that.

She leads me into our bedroom and stops in front of the bed, turning around to face me.

"Okay, I lied. I actually have two surprises for you," she tells me with a smile. "Close your eyes."

I do as she asks and feel her place one of my hands on top of her belly, sliding it down into the waistband of her pants. In just a few seconds, my fingers slide over perfectly smooth, hairless skin. My eyes fly open and I stare down into her face that has a huge smile on it while she holds my hand in place.

"Did you get waxed?" I ask her in awe.

She nods her head, her mouth opening to reply but letting out a small gasp instead when my fingers graze the top of her clit.

"This is the best present ever!" I tell her softly as my fingers dip even lower and glide through her wetness.

Jenny lets go of the grip she has on my hand and clutches onto both of my shoulders as I use two of my fingers to pull some of her wetness up and circle her clit.

"Oh Jesus….wait, stop!" Jenny exclaims suddenly, putting a hand back on top of my wrist to stop me.

As much as I want to curl up in the fetal position, cry, and suck my thumb like a baby right now, I won't. If she doesn't want to do this, I will be a big boy and not have a temper tantrum. I will respect my wife's wishes.

I will not cry, I will not cry, I will not cry.

"Okay, we can stop. You want to just cuddle?" I ask her, trying not to let my voice quiver.

She looks at me funny for a minute and then lets out a small laugh.

"Oh hell no! There will be no cuddling tonight. I just need to give you your second present," she tells me.

"OH HOLY MOTHER OF PEARL, THANK GOD!" I yell, leaning down and resting my forehead against hers.

"Close your eyes again," she tells me softly.

Once again, I do exactly as she says. I can hear clothing rustling, and I start doing a little Cabbage Patch dance action with my arms knowing that Jenny is taking her clothes off. I hear some other noise that almost sounds like creaking but whatever. My wife is getting naked, and I don't give a rat's ass about anything else.

Unless that creaking means there's a ghost in the house. I've heard some strange noises every once in a while late at night and always wondered if the house is haunted. I bet it is. I bet that freaky little fucker wants to watch us have sex. Fine with me, buddy, enjoy the show. Just don't touch my ass at all during the event or I will call the Winchester brothers from Supernatural.

Dean and Sam will fuck you up! I had a strange hand touch my ass one time in college during a threesome, and that's just something you don't get over. Random ass touching scares me more than spiders.

"Okay, you can open them," Jenny says.

I slowly open my eyes and really, she should have prepared me a little for the sight I am currently seeing. I don't know whether to drop to my knees and pray or have a heart attack.

"Oh, Willie Nelson. Are you...are we...this is...I...biscuits."

I can't even form a coherent sentence right now. My awesome wife is currently naked, lounging in the baby swing, er, I mean sex swing. Our sex swing is really a sex swing! Our sex swing is going to be used for sex and swinging and swinging sex!

Wait, no. Not swinging sex. We're not swingers. No one else can enter this bedroom while we're naked. Okay, scratch that. If a couple of naked chicks suddenly walk in, I certainly wouldn't kick them out.

"Come over here, hot stuff, and bang me in the sex swing," Jenny says as she curls her finger, beckoning me over.

I'm pretty sure I've never moved so fast in my life. My shirt is flung across the room, I shove my jeans and boxers down to my ankles, and start to run over. Unfortunately, it's really fucking hard to run with pants around your ankles and I face plant into the carpet.

"Oh my gosh! Drew, are you okay?" Jenny asks me with concern.

"Fine! Totally fine! Don't move!" I tell her as I quickly crawl on all fours over to the corner of the room.

I grab onto the swing on either side of Jenny's thighs and use it to pull me up so I can stand between her legs.

"You're a dirty, slutty man," Jenny tells me in a sultry voice.

Oh my God! Oh my God!

I giggle, yes giggle, and start bouncing excitedly on my toes.

"I think you should push me on the swing with your ginormous cock, slutty man," she tells me as she leans forward, grabs onto my hips, and pulls me closer to her on the swing until my "ginormous cock" is pushing against her entrance.

Porno Jenny! Porno Jenny is back! Hallelujah, praise Paula Abdul, Porno Jenny is back!

She wraps her legs around my hips and uses her thigh muscles to pull me closer, my cock sliding deeper. We both groan and I stop halfway in when I hear creaking.

I whip my head around and shoot a dirty look over my shoulder to the whole room in general.

Stop moving around, ghost! You're breaking my concentration. If you're going to watch, do it quietly. AND DON'T TOUCH MY ASS!

I turn my head back around and concentrate on the task at hand. Swinging my dick into my hot wife.

Ha ha! Did I totally just make up an awesome pun or what?!

"Do me hard, you dirty slut," Jenny whispers.

Oh hell yeah! It's fucking ON!

I push the rest of the way inside of her heat, and I want to stop and savor the feeling of being back inside my wife but the swing is swaying and causing me to rock my hips against her.

"This swing is fucking awesome!" I tell her as I grab onto her thighs, pull my dick almost all the way out of her, and then slam back home.

Jenny lets out a gasp and throws her arms above her head to grab onto the straps of the swing. I start moving faster and harder, the force of my thrusts causing the swing to really begin swaying from front to back. It's a little awkward and I have to concentrate on not falling. When the swing moves forward, I have to quickly shuffle my feet and follow it so my dick doesn't fall out of Jenny. Then, when it swings back, I have to quickly shuffle my feet forwards, or else it's going to clothesline my thighs, and I'm going to land on my ass on the floor.

I really should have taken my pants all the way off. This shit is hard! Ooooh, another pun right there, motherfuckers!

I'm basically waddling back and forth with the motion of the swing while at the same time, thrusting my hips in and out of Jenny.

It's like trying to pat your head and rub your stomach at the same time.

"Oh yes! Faster, faster!" Jenny screams.

Oh my God, the pressure! If I go any faster this swing is going to take me out at the knees! I need to make this swing my bitch and show it who's boss.

I plant my feet as wide apart as I can with my jeans still wrapped around my ankles, let go of Jenny's thighs, and wrap my hands around the straps that hang from the ceiling to stop the swing from swaying so much. It takes a minute to get it to stop, and I have to arch my back as far as I can, raise one of my knees, and push it against Jenny's ass under the swing to finally get it to stop moving.

"Yes! Keep doing that! Rub my ass with your knee, you whore!" Jenny shouts.

I am nothing if not attentive to my wife's needs right now, so I do as she asks. I hold onto the swing straps with both hands, lean back, keep my leg up, and rub my knee back and forth against her ass under the swing and keep moving my hips, thrusting in and out of her.

Jenny is moving her hips and pushing against me as I bang the hell out of her while trying to keep the swing in place. Around her moans of pleasure I hear another loud creak and I roll my eyes.

Seriously, ghost. Cut that shit out. I know you're there; you don't need to advertise it. Keep it down while you ghostly masturbate over there!

"I'm sorry I ever said anything about your vagina being floppy. It's totally not like fucking a sloppy joe at all! You feel so good baby!" I tell her as I continue to pound into her, sweat breaking out on my forehead with all the things I have to remember to do to keep the swing in place.

"Call me a tramp!" Jenny shouts as she lets go of the grip she has on one of the swing straps, slides her hand down the front of her body, and starts moving her fingers against her clit.

Fuck, best day ever! Even with the pervy ghost in the corner and my arm and leg muscles threatening to give out.

"WHO'S MY TRAMP?! WHO'S MY DIRTY HOOKER TRAMP?!" I shout as I pick up the pace and slam into her harder while her fingers move furiously over her clit.

"ME! ME! I'M YOUR DIRTY HOOKER TRAMP! PAY ME, BIG DADDY, PAY ME!" she shouts.

"I'M GOING TO GIVE YOU A SEVENTY-FIVE PERCENT TIP, YOU DIRTY WHORE!"

"YES! YES! GIVE ME THE TIP! GIVE ME THE TIP!" Jenny screams.

I know she's only a second away from coming which is a damn good thing because I can't hold off any longer. My balls are about to explode like a fucking geyser.

"I'M GOING TO GIVE YOU A TIP AND LEAVE YOU SOME MINTS! YOU WANT SOME FUCKING MINTS, YOU LITTLE SLUT?!" I yell in excitement as she tightens her thighs around my waist, and I feel her orgasm rush through her and squeeze my cock like a vise.

"OH MY GOD! GIVE ME THE MINTS! OH FUCK, I'M COMING! MINTS, MINTS, MINTS! YES, YES!"

She's thrashing her head and bucking her hips against me, and there's nothing I can do to stop the swing from swaying, so I just hold on tight to the straps and thrust into her with all I've got, feeling my own orgasm tingle through my balls. I hear another creak, this one louder than all the others.

"YOU LIKE THAT, GHOST? HUH?! YOU LIKE BEING A PERVY CREEPER, JERKIN' YOUR GHOSTLY GHERKIN?" I shout into the corner of the room.

Just as my orgasm barrels up through me and I start coming, I feel a hand on my ass and scream as loud as I can in fear while still plunging in and out of Jenny.

"EEEEEEEK! I'M COMING! HOLY SWEET AND SOUR CHICKEN, I'M COMING AND THERE'S A GHOST TOUCHING MY ASS!"

Mid orgasm, I reach back to swat the ghost's hand off my ass and hear another creak, followed by a loud ripping sound and this orgasm feels so fucking good right now that I'm not really concerned with the fact that the pervert poltergeist is making so much noise.

While smacking my hand on my ass to keep the ghost away from it, I thrust as hard as I can one last time and the orgasm finishes so good it almost feels like I'm falling.

"OW! SON OF A BITCH!" Jenny screams.

I open my eyes and quickly realize that feeling of falling really was a feeling of falling. I'm sprawled on top of Jenny on the floor with my penis still buried in her and bits and pieces of our ceiling littered in chunks all around us. I reach up and wipe a bunch of white dust off of Jenny's face and hair, and she ruffles her hand through my hair, dust and debris falling down onto her chest.

I crane my neck and look up at the giant hole in our ceiling.

"Wow, guess I should have secured that a little better, huh?"

Jenny just laughs and wraps her arms around my shoulders, pulling me down to her lips.

"Let's do it again. Go get the Skittles in the kitchen, a wooden spoon, and two containers of purple Play-Doh."

29.

Vagina Skittles

"Um, Whitney Houston, we have a problem."

Jenny sits up on her elbows and stares down at me lying on my stomach between her legs with my face resting on her hipbone.

"Problem? What problem? I was almost there, keep going," she complains, letting her head fall back to the pillows.

"Yeah, and that would be the problem. I can't keep going, they're stuck."

Her head flies back up off of the pillow, and she slides her body up the bed until she's resting her back against the headboard, my head slipping off of her hip as she goes.

"Stuck?! What the hell do you mean stuck?!" she screeches.

I push myself up onto my knees and point between her legs.

"Stuck, as in, probably not coming out anytime soon because it was too slippery and they just sort of, shot off, deep into the heart of Texas," I explain with a shrug.

"I'm confused. Are you comparing my vagina to Texas? Is that a good thing or a bad thing?" she asks, momentarily forgetting the problem at hand.

"Well, you don't mess with Texas and everything is bigger in Texas, just like you don't mess with your vagina and…"

She raises her eyebrow and glares at me.

"Your vagina is NOT big. Or large or in charge. Okay, it's totally in charge but it's not large. We will not be renaming your vagina Large Marge so don't even give me that look. Your vagina is tiny and perfect and warm and cuddly, just like it should be," I explain.

We had stared at each other for a few minutes and I wasn't not gonna lie, I sort of forgot about the problem for a minute while I stared at her. I had started crawling up the bed toward her when she reminded me.

"Wait, stop! What are we going to do about the Skittles stuck in Texas?"

Two months after the night of the sex swing crash and the "Taste the Rainbow" incident, Jenny and I are doing better than ever. It had taken a trip to the emergency room that night and a vacuum cleaner nozzle to remove the Skittles from the great state of vagina.

Okay, it hadn't really been a vacuum cleaner nozzle but it may as well have. I could have saved us a hundred dollar deductible and our dignity by just using the Hoover at home. Surprisingly, the nurse told us that wasn't even the strangest thing she'd seen stuck up in someone in the emergency room. While we waited, she told us all about the sorts of things people had jammed up in them and how they had to waddle through the emergency room doors to get it removed.

McDonald's Happy Meal Toys, grapefruit, cell phones, wine bottles, a dozen ping pong balls, and a whisk.

But the whisk was totally not my fault, and I was doing something else that had absolutely nothing to do with sex and it just slipped. I had been grateful that the nurse who helped us was new and wasn't aware of mine and Jenny's frequent flyer miles at that particular emergency room.

Through it all, Jenny and I have learned some very important lessons. Never hire your dad as a private investigator, and Carter cheats when he's in a diaper changing race.

We've also learned to never keep things to ourselves if something is bothering us, and I've learned to just assume my wife always needs help around the house and she shouldn't have to ask for it. Our sex life is better and more adventurous than ever, especially trying to navigate around two children's schedules, but we're making it work and being very creative. Jenny finally admitted to me that she never really wanted vanilla sex, she just though that now that we were older and parents, it's what we should do. I honestly would have agreed to boring sex for the rest of my life, but thank the holy jeans I don't have to worry about that anymore.

My hot, slutty wife is back, and I couldn't be happier.

."Are you nervous?" I ask Jenny as we stand at the front of the room and wait for everyone else to get here.

"You know, I'm not. Is that weird?" she asks with a smile as she pulls things out of her bag and sets them up on the table.

"Nah, I'm not nervous either. I mean, we're kind of experts about this shit so why should we be nervous?"

She nods in agreement and sets the bag on top of the table, walking over to me as I organize my notes. She pulls the pad of paper out of my hands and places it on the table, taking my hands and resting them right on top of her tits.

"This is going to be so much fun," she tells me with a big smile as she stands on her tip toes and runs her tongue along my top lip, giving me the shivers, just like always.

I remove a hand from one of her boobs and place it under her ass, lifting her up so she can wrap her legs around my waist. I turn us and push her back against the wall, sliding my hand down the front of her body and then pushing it back up under her t-shirt, grazing soft, warm skin as I go.

Jenny pulls her lips away from mine and tilts her head to the side so I can kiss my way down her neck to her collarbone. I suck and nibble on the skin while my hand under her shirt pulls the cup of her bra down underneath her breast so I can palm the soft mound and run my thumb over her nipple.

"This is so naughty and dirty. I love it," Jenny says as I push my hips forward and grind my jean-clad erection between her legs.

She locks her ankles together right above my ass and uses the muscles of her thighs to pull me harder against her.

I pull my lips away from her neck and my hand stops its movement on her breast.

"I totally forgot. I have something for you," I tell her as I let go of her ass and bend backwards for my bag on the table without breaking our connection or moving my hand from her bare tit.

I reach the bag and dig inside for the white box, pulling it out and leaning my body back against hers. I hold the box between our bodies and when she sees it, her eyes light up.

"Ohhhhh, Drew!" she says excitedly as she takes the box from me. I put my hand back on her ass and go back to massaging her boob under her shirt with my other hand while she opens the lid.

She looks inside and there's confusion on her face for a moment and I explain.

"Well, I figured you wouldn't be in the mood for Skittles for a while after the 'Rainbow of Fruit Flavor'" evening, so I decided to switch things up."

Jenny reaches her hand inside the box and pulls out a handful of grape and cherry Dum-Dum suckers.

"I stuck with the purple and red theme, but this time they have handles on them for easier removal," I tell her with a wink and a wag of my eyebrows.

"I love you so much, Drew Parritt!" Jenny tells me as she tosses the box to the ground and wraps her arms around my shoulders, her hand still clutching the suckers.

"I love you too, Jenny Parritt, my sweet, fuck-hot wife!"

I hear the rustle of a wrapper behind my head, and Jenny moves one arm in front of me, offering me a lick of a cherry sucker. I wrap my lips around the candy and suck while Jenny twirls the stick, making the candy swirl around my mouth.

I reach up and wrap my hand around hers, pulling the sucker out of my mouth with a *pop* and together, we move the candy to her lips. She runs her tongue all around the outside of the candy just like she does with my dick, and I groan as I watch her tongue and lips enjoy the sucker.

Ten minutes later, we have a slight problem and it involves my pubic hair and a grape sucker.

"Let me just rip it off, like a Band-Aid," Jenny pleads, looking frantically toward the door of the room. "They're going to be here any minute, and I don't think it would be good if you spent the entire hour with your hand down your pants."

I glance at the clock and then back at her. "Well, they would never forget their first class, that's for sure."

After our trip to the emergency room two months ago, we had been approached by one of the doctors and he asked if we would consider doing a sex seminar for married couples once a month at the local community college. We could talk about whatever we wanted, use whatever visual aids we needed. We just needed to teach couples how to have more active sex lives and put a spark back in their marriage.

"I am not ripping this thing off, do you have any idea how much that would fucking hurt?" I ask her.

She glares at me and puts her hands on her hips.

"Oh, yeah, sorry. Forgot about the whole Brazilian thing. Have I mentioned how much I love it, by the way?" I tell her, trying to suck up as best I can. "Maybe you should just suck it off," I plead with her.

"We're in a classroom! I'm not getting down on my knees and putting my face in your crotch five minutes before twenty couples are going to show up," she complains.

"You just put your hand down my pants with a wet sucker in a classroom five minutes before twenty couples are going to show up! What the hell is the difference?!"

Jenny stomps her foot and looks back at the clock in frustration.

"Oh my God, we have no time! At least take your fucking hand out of your pants!" she yells at me.

"I'm afraid! If I let go, who knows what will happen down there. At least right now I'm keeping it contained."

Jenny wrings her hands in front of her and whips her head around when we hear a voice.

"Excuse me, are we in the right place? Is this the 'How to Put the Spark Back in Your Marriage' course?" a man asks from the doorway, his hand holding onto a woman standing right next to him.

Yes, I am well aware of the irony in this situation. Not that long ago I had practically stalked a doctor because of his shitty self-help CD with the same title. I play nice though and sent him and his wife an invitation to our first class. Unfortunately, due to the restraining order, they are unable to attend.

Jenny turns around and flattens her body against mine, blocking me from the couple's view.

"YES! Yes, welcome! Go ahead and take your seats. We're just discussing some last minute lesson changes," Jenny tells them before turning back around to face me.

"Pull that fucking thing off, right now!' she whispers angrily.

"NO! It's going to take a layer of skin with it! You have no idea how tangled it is right now!" I whisper back.

I look over Jenny's shoulder and see two more couples entering the classroom and taking seats, talking amongst themselves.

While I'm busy looking, and before I realize what she's doing, Jenny sticks her own hand down my pants, wraps it around mine, and yanks as hard as she can.

"MOTHER OF JUSTIN TIMBERLAKE DICK IN A BOX!" I scream at the top of my lungs.

Jenny and I stand there staring at one another wide-eyed, the grape pubic-hair covered sucker held in both of our hands between us. My lips are quivering and I can feel tears forming in my eyes.

The pain! Oh my God the pain! It's like no other I've felt before!

Jenny quickly turns back around to face the class, which is now full and all eyes are staring at us questioningly.

I chuck the furry sucker into the garbage can under the table and swallow back my tears, hobbling forward so I'm standing shoulder to shoulder with Jenny.

"Welcome to class, folks! That was just a sample of what we'll be talking about first this evening. Ways to scream out your pleasure without being boring! Who wants to go first?!" Jenny asks.

It takes a few minutes, but pretty soon the class is really getting into the question and having fun shouting out their suggestions. Jenny and I turn to face each other while the class is laughing and yelling.

Some of my dick skin is stuck to a sucker under the table, the people in the emergency room call us by our first names, we've been banned from all major appliance stores and local farms, and yet, I wouldn't change the way our life has turned out for all the hookers and coke in the world.

"You have GOT to be kidding me?!"

We break our eye contact and turn to face the door of the classroom, our looks of surprise and confusion mirroring those of the two couples who are hovering in the doorway.

"Dude, you guys are the teachers?!" Carter asks with a smile as he pulls Claire into the room. "This is going to be fun!"

The rest of the class has quieted down and is watching our exchange with interest.

"This is going to be a horror show, that's what this is going to be," Liz says as she and Jim follow Carter and Claire down the aisle and find their seats. "Tell me you aren't going to be using yourselves as visual aids."

Jenny reaches down to the table and lifts up a pair of tongs and a bottle of honey.

"Nope, we've got plenty of visual aids," she tells her with a smile.

"Drew, get the laser pointer off of my boobs," Claire says in irritation.

Jenny turns her head and sees me standing next to her playing with the pen laser light I picked up at the gas station on the way here.

"Well, Claire, technically this is part of tonight's lesson. Erroneous Zones and how they can make sex hotter," Jenny explains as she takes the pointer out of my hand and sets it back on the table.

"Is anyone else weirded out by the fact that Drew and Jenny are teachers?" we hear Jim ask the rest of our friends.

"If they were teaching children, yes. But let's be honest here. This is the absolute best subject for them to teach," Liz answers with a smile in our direction.

"Just tell me we aren't going to be watching any of your home movies," Claire begs.

"I don't know. I'd kind of like to see those," Carter says with a shrug.

"Oh, we've already seen their home movie. It's a finalist over at Youporn's 'Home Movie of the Year Awards'," one of the guys on the opposite side of the room says. "We Googled you when we signed up for the class. Using the pumpkin and the ice cream scoop was genius, by the way."

My smile is bigger than ever after hearing those words.

"Honey, you can Google us!" I tell Jenny, leaning in to kiss the top of her head.

"Alright, fine. We Googled you too," Liz admits.

"Yeah, so did we," Claire adds.

"And aside from having to see Drew's hairy ass, it was pretty hot," Jim states.

"It was disturbing-hot and I felt a little dirty after watching it, and I'm not sure I can ever look you guys in the eye ever again, but yeah, pretty hot," Carter admits.

"Alright, let's bring this class to order!" Jenny shouts excitedly. "First, we're going to discuss items that should never be placed in a vagina unless you are wearing safety goggles and have a pair of needle nose pliers on hand."

I wrap my arm around Jenny's shoulders as she begins the first part of the lesson, holding up items one at a time from the table and giving explanations on where they can be safely inserted without the use of medical assistance or antibiotics.

While she talks, I glance over at our friends that had decided to sign up for our class even though they didn't know we were teaching it. No matter how perfect you think someone else's marriage is, this just goes to show you we can all use a little spark and a little fun in the bedroom to make life more interesting. I couldn't be happier that our best friends are here with us tonight. It just makes me realize how great my life really is.

Veronica and Billy are happy and healthy, and our best friends are the greatest people ever. I'm beyond glad we've remained friends and raised families with each other. Oh, and I can't forget our new best friend, Jackson, that we brought into the circle of trust. My fears of him trying to steal my wife are long gone ever since the day he brought his significant other over to our house for dinner. Dave is two years older than him and lives one street over from us. My only worry now is that Jackson and Dave might want me to have a threesome. I'd be honored and shit because, come on, I'm fucking hot as balls and of course they'd want me, but any more than one penis in a bed is too many, and I would have to sadly decline. Luckily, they haven't asked yet, so I don't have to worry about the awkwardness.

I had never thought that night seven years ago when Carter and I went to our new friend Jim's house for dinner I would meet my soul mate over a plate of lasagna and a discussion on vibrators. Jenny and I…well, I never had a doubt we were meant to be together. She's my best friend and the best mother and wife there is. No marriage is perfect, but ours is damn near close. And even though we've had some troubles, fixing them has been sweeter than any candy I've ever eaten.

Well, except for Vagina Skittles. Vagina Skittles are delicious.

Epilogue

Six months later.

"This is Matt with Channel 3 News, coming to you live from the store that started it all, Seduction and Snacks. Seduction and Snacks has grown far beyond the little corner business that two best friends decided to open together almost eight years ago. With the combination of delicious chocolates, cookies, and sex toys, Seduction and Snacks is the perfect store to satisfy your sweet tooth or your bedroom cravings. We're here today to speak to the women who came up with this idea, as well as their friends and family who have supported them along the way. Welcome, everyone!"

Seated in a straight line are all three couples: Carter and Claire, Liz and Jim, and Drew and Jenny. Sitting on the floor by their feet are each of the couple's respective children: Gavin and Sophia, Charlotte, Molly, and Ava, and Veronica and Billy.

"Claire, did you ever think that the store you had always dreamed about owning would one day turn into a household name and that you would have locations all over the United States?"

Claire laughs and shakes her head in disbelief while Carter reaches over and covers the hand resting on her thigh with his own.

"This is far beyond my hopes and dreams. Opening just *this* store by itself was something I never thought would happen. And then to have it take off like it did and to be able to franchise it? I still can't even wrap my head around it," Claire states.

"I know you've done several interviews about how you and your husband met, and every time I hear that story, it still makes me smile. How are the two of you handling the success along with raising a family?"

Carter lifts Claire's hand to his lips and places a soft kiss on her fingers. Claire stares happily into his eyes before finally turning back to the camera.

"We're handling it together, one day at a time. Having the support of such amazing friends and family makes things a lot easier," Claire states.

"And we really are pretty amazing," their friend Drew chimes in from down the row. "Well, except for that punk sitting down there surrounded by little girls."

Drew laughs and points at ten-year-old Gavin, who gives him a dirty look.

"Shut up or I will cut your mother," Gavin tells him.

"You don't talk about Eileen Parrit! Eileen Parrit is a saint!" Drew argues.

"So, Liz, did you ever think there would be such a high demand for a store that sells sex toys?"

Jim leans over and places a kiss on Liz's cheek, and she smiles at the camera.

"As long as there are people having sex, there will always be a need for sex toys," Liz tells us.

"What's 'having sex'?" Liz and Jim's five-year-old, Ava, asks.

"It's gross. And people yell like they are in pain. I think it has something to do with killing each other," Gavin tells her.

"Ooooh, that's scary. I'm never having the sex," Ava replies as she goes back to playing with one of the toys her parents brought for her.

"Why do they only pay attention when we're talking about something they shouldn't hear?" Jim whispers to Liz.

"Because children are assholes," Drew whispers back.

"I heard that," Gavin replies without even turning around.

"Good, because you're the biggest asshole!" Drew whispers loudly.

"Will you stop calling my son an asshole?!" Claire scolds Drew.

Drew immediately bows his head in remorse when Claire gives him a dirty look.

"Oooooh, you just got schooled by my mommy," Gavin taunts with a laugh.

Carter quickly leans forward and clamps a hand over Gavin's mouth while Drew sticks his tongue out at him and gets a smack in the arm from his wife.

"Jenny, you're credited with putting Seduction and Snacks on the map with all of your amazing marketing and promotion skills. Can you tell us a little bit about that?"

Drew leans back in his chair and throws his arm around the back of Jenny's and plays with a strand of her hair.

"Um, well, I don't think *I* was the one who put Seduction and Snacks on the map. I'm pretty sure it had something to do with the state of Ohio and where they built the building. I could be wrong though. I did send a flyer to our mayor so maybe that made him add it to the map. Not sure," she says with a shrug.

"You guys have stuck together as friends and been through quite a lot together in the last few years. Where do you see yourselves ten years from now?"

The couples all look at one another, and there are a few smiles and some laughs exchanged.

"In ten years, we'll still be friends. We'll still be talking about sex all the time and doing inappropriate things in public," Jim tells us with a chuckle.

"In ten years, I hope I'm living next door to my best friend so I can just walk over there if I need her. Even if Seduction and Snacks is no longer around, at least I'll still have her. And sex toys," Liz says with a smile.

"Awwww, you're going to make me cry!" Claire tells Liz.

"And you're going to make me puke. Cut it out!" Drew yells at them.

"In ten years, I hope I'm still waking up every morning next to my soul mate," Carter admits with a smile in Claire's direction.

"What is this, *Lifestyles of the Gay and Sappy*? Come on!" Drew complains.

"In ten years, I hope they have a Skittles remover and I can still put my feet behind my head in a hammock," Jenny tells everyone.

"In ten years I hope I've forgotten every part of that sentence," Jim states.

"In ten years, I'll still be banging my hot wife. Hopefully by then they will have invented honey that isn't so sticky and corn stalks that don't chafe so much when you tie them to your penis," Drew states.

"In ten years, I hope Drew stops talking about his penis and the weird things he does with it," Claire says with a roll of her eyes. "But we'll definitely still be friends. We'll all have teenagers then and will need as much support as we can get," she laughs.

"In ten years I'll be twenty. I'll be able to carry a gun and pistol whip Drew," Gavin says.

"You can't carry a gun at twenty! And anyway, I will still be bigger than you in ten years, kid," Drew argues.

"Yeah, but you'll be old. And you'll probably need a walker and someone to change your poopy diaper," Gavin argues back.

"How the hell do you even know what pistol whip means?" Claire asks in shock.

"PlayStation. Duh," Gavin replies back.

"I'm not going to have poopy diapers, YOU'RE going to have poopy diapers," Drew tells Gavin.

"You can't even spell poopy," Gavin replies in a bored voice as his sister Sophia climbs onto his lap and gets comfortable.

"I can spell poopy!" Sophia announces.

"It's called SPOOPY!" Drew and Jenny's daughter Veronica announces proudly.

"SPOOP!" Billy shouts from his place on the floor in between Jim's daughters.

Everyone stares down at Billy in shock.

"Did he just say spoop?" Liz whispers.

"What the hell is spoop?" Carter asks.

"Oh my God, our son's first word is spoop?!" Jenny screeches as she smacks Drew's arm.

"This is NOT my fault. It's Jackson's fault!" Drew argues.

"Do I really have to put that in his baby book? I CANNOT write the word 'spoop'," Jenny says.

"I can. I know how to spell spoop," Gavin tells her.

"So do any of you have plans for more children?"

All three couples chime in at once and without any hesitation.

"OH HELL NO!"

"As we close our interview with the women who started Seduction and Snacks and their loving families, I think it's clear to everyone that this group will remain friends for a very long time. They will continue to follow their dreams and watch their business grow into something none of them ever saw coming. They will also share in the joys of watching their children grow up together and form their own close-knit friendships and who knows, maybe one of *them* will have a story of their own to tell us down the road. I have a feeling we haven't heard the last from the gang at Seduction and Snacks!"

The End

Hearts and Llamas

A SHORT STORY

Claire

As I'm trying to plan the featured dessert items this week at the shop, the ringing of the phone interrupts my concentration. It's the week of Valentine's Day and that means we're going to be slammed with walk-ins—people that have waited until the last minute to get something delicious for their loved ones.

"Hello?" Carter answers.

I listen to his one-sided conversation as I try to remember if the caramel chocolate chunk cookies were featured on last week's menu or the week before and if covering them in red icing would make them "Valentiney" enough.

"No, Gavin isn't home right now. He's at his grandpa's house. Sure, I can let him know you called, Brooklyn. Does he have your number? Okay, got it. Bye."

I stare at Carter with my mouth open as he hangs up the phone nonchalantly and goes about his business of filling his travel coffee mug for work, humming to himself.

"Um, who the hell was that?" I ask, squeezing the pen so hard in my hand I can feel the plastic starting to crack.

"Brooklyn. Some girl in Gavin's class at school," Carter replies, finally turning around and noticing the look on my face. "What's wrong?"

My jaw drops and I stare at him angrily, wondering if he even knows me.

"Brooklyn? Some girl? Who the hell is this slut and why is she calling our son?" I demand.

"Claire, she's ten. I'm pretty sure she hasn't reached slut status yet." With a laugh, he walks over to the table and sits down next to me.

"She's calling our house. What ten-year-old girl needs to call a boy's house? A slutty ten-year-old girl, that's who. She's got her sights on our son, and before we know it, she's going to be giving him blow jobs on the back of the bus and forcing him to watch porn with her. This is our BABY, Carter!"

"Blow jobs and porn? When did fourth grade turn into a brothel?" Carter asks, raising an eyebrow questioningly.

"Oh, just you wait. It starts out innocently enough. She calls the house acting all sweet and harmless and then BAM! Gavin gets the shit kicked out of him by her pimp because he's poaching on the guy's territory!"

I can't stop the word vomit no matter how hard I try. This is Valentine's Day week— one of the most romantic weeks of the year and our busiest at the shop. I should be concentrating on how much I love Carter and the oodles of money I'm going to make selling sweets, but instead I'm worried about my son being led astray by a harlot. A harlot named Brooklyn. Her parents probably named her that because skank was too obvious even though they knew what her future career would be.

"Let's give a great big Bearded Clam welcome to BROOKLYN as she takes the stage! Brooklyn's parents knew she'd be working the pole some day and thank God for that! She's quite bendy and she's dancing for us tonight because, well, she's a great big ho!"

Carter gently reaches over and pries the pen from my hand, pulling me out of my pole-dancing thoughts, and sets the pen down next to my list. Glancing around the table, he thinks better about leaving the butter knife from my bagel earlier within my reach and slides it closer to himself.

"She's just a little girl who likes our little boy. No big deal. I'm going to work now, and you are going to get back to your list and NOT think up ways you can cut this girl's hair off without getting arrested," Carter tells me as he stands up from his chair and places a kiss on the top of my head before walking out the back door.

"Please. Like I would really spend my time thinking of ways to cut her hair off," I mutter to myself as I reach for the pen, tear off the top sheet of paper from my pad and start a new list: Ways of Putting the Fear of God in Ten-Year-Old Girls.

Carter

"So, what are you getting the old ball and chain for V-Day?" Drew asks me as we head to the lunchroom on break.

"I don't know. I haven't decided. I could always send flowers to the shop."

Drew shakes his head at me as we grab a table in the corner.

"Nope, too boring. Try again," he states.

"Um, jewelry?" I suggest, opening up my insulated lunch bag and removing my ham sandwich.

"Nice, but too over the top. Ooooh, what about chocolate?" he asks me excitedly around a mouthful of chips.

"Seriously? Did you just suggest I get Claire chocolate for Valentine's Day?" I ask in astonishment.

"What? She doesn't like chocolate or something? That's like, totally un-American."

Before I can tell him what a jackass he is, Jim walks over and plops down on the chair across from me.

"What are we talking about, dick bags?"

"We're talking about the stupidest holiday in the world and what we're getting our wives," Drew tells him.

"Ahhh, so Valentine's Day," Jim states.

"Hey, did you know Claire doesn't like chocolate? She must be allergic to it or something," Drew informs Jim.

Jim pauses in the process of opening up a bag of Doritos and stares at Drew a few seconds before shaking his head and sighing, then turns his attention back to me.

"What are you getting Liz this year? Any fun plans?" I ask him.

"Hold on, I have a list," he tells me, reaching into the back pocket of his jeans and pulling out a folded piece of paper.

"A list? What the hell do you need a list for? What all are you buying her?" Drew asks in shock. "Awwww, man. You're totally going to make us look like dill weeds, aren't you?"

Jim unfolds the paper and flattens it on the table with the heel of his hand.

"No, the list isn't because I'm buying her a ton of shit and can't remember all of it. The list is from Liz. She told me exactly what I'm supposed to get her," he explains.

"Um, what? That doesn't sound very romantic to me," I tell him in confusion.

"Liz, sweetheart that she is, has come to realize that I suck when it comes to Valentine's Day. Every year she has this idea in her mind of what she wants me to do, and every year I completely fuck it up. I ruin her day and she cuts me off from sex for a week. After an incident that happened four years ago with a pet llama for a day and floor seats to a Cavs game, I handed the reins over to her. A week before Valentine's Day she writes down exactly what I should do, and ever since she started doing that, I have had a stress-free holiday and lots of good sex," Jim explains.

"Dude, a pet llama? How in the fuck could *anyone* hate that? That is just full of awesome right there," Drew tells him.

"Right? I thought so too," Jim complains. "I mean, Liz loves animals. And every time we're at the zoo she always goes to the petting part and spends the entire time with the llamas."

"So what was the problem then?" I ask.

"It was fine at first. I mean, the handler showed up with the llama and explained to me what we needed to do for the four hours we had it. The llama and I bonded before Liz got home from work and I really thought she understood me. Boy was I wrong."

"Jim, I'm home! What time are we – SON OF A BITCH! Why the fuck is there a giant rat with fur in our living room?!" Liz screeched.

I ran into the room from the kitchen and came to a sudden stop when I saw Liz pinned against the door with the llama right in her face sniffing her.

"It's not a rat!" I whispered loudly as I crept over to where they were. "Don't say that so loud. You'll offend her."

Liz looked around the llama's head and gave me a dirty look.

"I'll offend HER? What the hell is it doing here?"

I got next to them and reached over to pet the llama to put everyone at ease.

"Her name is Princess Sugar-Britches, and she is your Valentine's Day present!"

Liz didn't share in the excitement that I obviously did. She inched her way out from under Princess Sugar-Britches stare and punched me in the arm.

"You brought a llama into the HOUSE?"

I shrugged as PSB turned around and looked me as if to say "What's this chick's problem?"

"It's totally fine," I explained to Liz as she paced back and forth behind the couch. "She's totally housebroken. She'll go to the door and spit on it when she needs to go out."

That was probably the wrong thing to tell Liz, but it was too late to take it back. Before she could react to the spitting statement, she let out another horrified scream and darted to the corner of the room.

"Is there SHIT in my brand new Coach purse? OH MY GOD! There is a steaming pile of llama shit in my purse! MY COACH PURSE!"

I glanced over in that direction as Liz held up the purse with the tip of one finger through the strap, as far away from her body as possible.

"Oops."

She stalked over to PSB and held the purse right in front of her.

"Did you take a dump in my purse? Do you have any idea how much this thing cost me, you furry little rat?"

I told her not to call PSB a rat, really, I did.

The next thing I know, PSB pulls her head back and spits right in Liz's face. Great big globs of llama spit dripped down the front of Liz's nose.

"You did NOT just spit in my face!" Liz yelled at her.

And since PSB obviously thought Liz didn't get the memo the first time, she reared back and did it again, while at the same time spreading her legs and pissing all over the carpet by the entryway.

Liz was too busy screaming at the top of her lungs and wiping llama gobs off of her face that she didn't notice PSB turning around, pawing at the ground, and flaring her nostrils angrily.

"Um, Liz, you might want to come over here close to me, very slowly," I told her gently.

Of course Liz didn't listen. She stood right where she was, stomped her foot, and pointed angrily at PSB. And then, all hell broke loose.

PSB's back leg shot out and kicked a hole right through our front door, and then she charged.

"RUN! JESUS H CHRIST, LIZ, RUN!" I screamed as I turn and ran towards the kitchen.

Liz took off hurtling the couch and screaming right along with me.

We flew out into the backyard, and I slammed the door right in PSB's face.

"That doesn't sound so bad. A little shit, a little spit, running and screaming into the night. That kind of sounds like having a kid," Drew says with a laugh.

"When I called the handler to come back and get her, he wasn't surprised. He said no one lasts more than an hour. That asshat should have told me that when he dropped her off. It would have saved me the trouble of buying a new front door, a new coffee table, a new couch, two new windows, new carpeting, and replacing a $400 Coach purse," Jim complains. "But man, Princess Sugar-Britches sure was a sweetie for a few minutes there."

Lunch ends and we throw out our garbage and make our way back out into the plant. We get to our work stations, and as the line powers up, I wonder if Liz and Jim are on to something. Why should I have to be so stressed about what to get Claire? It's just like Jim said. Every year I spend a ton of time trying to come up with the perfect gift, and every year, just when I think I've found it and I can't be more excited, Claire seems less than thrilled even though she tries to hide it by overacting and gushing about it so much that even *I* start to hate what I got her.

This year, I'm going to be smart about it. She is so going to love me for this, and she'll never have to worry about anything pooping in her purses.

Claire

"He what?"

"He said, and I quote, 'How about this year you just tell me what to get you.' Can you believe that? Of all the unromantic things I have ever heard," I complain to Jenny as I put the last batch of Devil's Food cupcakes in the oven.

"If Drew said that to me, I'd cancel *Anal Fridays*, I'll tell you that," she says as she hops up onto the counter next to me and starts swinging her feet.

"Jenny, how many times do I have to tell you that there are just some things you do not need to share with me?" I ask her with a grimace.

"I'm so lucky with Drew. He has never bought me something for Valentine's Day that I didn't like. Last year, he got me a membership to a Jelly of the Month Club," she tells me with a huge smile on her face.

"I'm sorry, but how is that something you would *ever* like?" I question as I start piling dirty mixing bowls in the sink.

"Do you have any idea what you can do with that much jelly, the extra attachment from the vacuum cleaner, and the newest DVD of *Foot Fetish Fantasies, Volume 57*?"

"Jesus God no. And I never, ever want to, so stop talking right now," I beg her as I fill the sink with hot water and soap.

"You know, that's what Liz does for Jim. She told me that a few weeks ago when we were getting many pettings," Jenny informs me.

"Did you just say *many pettings*? Do I even want to know what you're talking about?"

Jenny sighs and rolls her eyes.

"Duh. We had our nails and toes done at the salon. How have you never gotten a many pettings before? It's like you live in a cave or something, Claire," she complains as she shakes her head at me. "Anyway, Liz was telling me that she got so tired of Jim never having a clue what to get her, she started making a list for him. This year, he's supposed to take her to the Cheesecake Factory for dinner and then to see a chick flick after. That way he won't show up with an alpaca or whatever the hell that was that shit in all her Coach purses a few years ago."

Just then, Liz walks through the door carrying a huge box and drops it on the floor in front of Jenny.

"Jenny, can you open this box and make sure everything I ordered is in there?"

She hops off of the counter and begins tearing the tape off of the box and opening the flaps excitedly.

"Ooooooh, we used these at the movie theater and used the extra butter—"

Liz holds up her hand and closes her eyes, stopping Jenny mid-sentence.

"Without a running commentary of the places you've stuck them and the condiments you used to get them there."

Jenny looks up at Liz with a perplexed look on her face.

"We don't use condoms, Liz, you know that. It's like you never listen to anything I say."

Jenny huffs and continues pawing through the box.

"So, I heard you guys discussing shitting farm animals when I walked in. Reliving the Valentine Coach Massacre of 2009, are we?" Liz asks as she leans against the counter while I wash the dishes.

"Jenny told me about how you give Jim a list every year for Valentine's Day. It sounded a little unromantic to me, but I forgot about that whole Queen Shitty Britches or whatever her name was."

Liz nods her head in understanding.

"I agree, it's a little unconventional, but it's necessary so I don't smother my husband in his sleep. It really does make for a much happier holiday all around. Plus, Jim doesn't have to sleep out in the garage for a week, and I don't have to soak my face in bleach to get llama germs off," she explains with a shrug.

"You know, you could have gotten Key Lime Disease from something like that, Liz. Llamas have these little bugs called sticks that carry Key Lime. I saw it on Animal Planet," Jenny states.

"Did you maybe see it on the Food Network instead? With Paula Dean?" I ask with a laugh.

"I think Key Lime Disease is cured with whip cream," Liz adds with a snort.

"You guys are weird. That makes absolutely no sense."

Jenny rolls her eyes and goes back to her sex toy sorting while Liz reminisces fondly about the time she almost got a delicious citrus illness, and I have to pause with the dirty dishes because she starts sobbing uncontrollably about her favorite Coach purse she buried in the back yard that year while she made Jim hum *Taps*.

Maybe Liz is on to something with this idea. Her expectations won't be through the roof because she'll know exactly what she was getting, and it will be what she's wanted because she had spelled it out for Jim. But the more I think it's a good idea, the more I go back to square one and think, where's the romance in that? Carter is amazing and I love him more than I ever thought possible. Even though it's hit or miss sometimes because come on, he's a guy and they really aren't the most perceptive when it comes to knowing what to buy us girls, I still love being surprised and hopeful when it comes to the most romantic holiday of the year. Is it too much to ask that he just put on his thinking cap and really concentrate on something that he knows will make me happy?

☉ ☉ ☉

755

"Hello mothers! Thank you so much for volunteering to help out with your child's Valentine's Day class party this year," the principal of Gavin's school announces to the twenty or so mothers gathered in the lobby of the elementary school a few days later.

As I stand in the corner with my arms crossed in front of me so none of the other mothers will try and talk to me, I glance around and wonder when the hell cupid puked all over these people. Every single mother is wearing red from head to toe. Red shirts, red sweaters, red jeans, red skirts, red and pink striped knee-high socks (no, I'm not joking). Half of them have God-awful headbands on their heads with red springy hearts or glittery pink flowers. A few of them even light up. I look down at my jeans and black t-shirt and shrug to myself. I may not be over the top like these freaks of nature, but at least I've worn *something* in honor of the day. The black shirt had been a gift from Drew when he found out I got roped into being the room mother for Gavin's Valentine's Day party. It has a picture of a voodoo doll on the front with pins and needles sticking out of it all over the place. Under the doll it says: Be mine. Or else.

"When your child's class party is finished, please make sure to sign your child out before you take him or her home. Have a *Heart-stopping* good time ladies!" the principal finishes.

I groan as I bend down and pick up the Walmart bag filled with enough juice boxes for the twenty-four kids in Gavin's class and a cookie sheet full of red and pink frosted cupcakes. I had stopped feeling inadequate years ago when I came to these things and saw all of the Longaberger baskets decked out in pretty little Valentine's Day liners and filled with beautiful little bags of candy tied with perfect little bows or flawlessly made alligators on card stock with cutesy little sayings on them like "I'd snap at the chance to be your Valentine!" I have a full time job and a full time family to take care of. I don't have time to spend forty hours creating Valentines for a bunch of ten-year-olds who will just throw them in the garbage when they get home.

Claire

I follow the other moms down the hallway until I come to Gavin's classroom and step inside to complete and total anarchy. The kids had a day filled with Valentine activities and they are obviously already hopped on enough sugar to take down an elephant.

"Hi! Thanks for coming!" Gavin's teacher shouts over the noise. "Sorry about this. They just exchanged valentines and they're a little excited."

I feel myself breaking out in a cold sweat as I scan the room. I want to get down on my knees and weep at his teacher's feet. Instead, I stand up on a chair and shout at the top of my lungs.

"HEEEEEEEEY! Sit down and be quiet or no one gets a cupcake!"

The kids stare at me for a minute, then everyone scrambles to their seats, everyone except for one little girl who stands directly across from me on the other side of the room. I step down off of the chair and stare at her. She is a tiny little thing with the most amazing head of hair I've ever seen on a ten-year old. It's full of natural curls and it hangs down to the middle of her back. She's impeccably dressed in a Valentine-themed outfit: a red long-sleeved shirt with pink and white hearts on it, a matching skirt, and red glittery shoes. The whole outfit is finished off with a cute little red bow in her hair.

"Hey, Mom!" Gavin greets me as he runs up to my side while the rest of his class, sans miss fashion plate over there, settles in their seats.

"Hey there! Who's the chick over there by the window staring at us?" I ask him as I pull the juice boxes out of the bag and take the foil off of the tray of cupcakes.

"Oh, that's Brooklyn," he says before running back to his desk.

I stop with my hand in midair over the top of the cupcakes, turn my head back over to the corner of the room, and then stand up straighter. We glare at each other for a few minutes, and I swear to God the room suddenly gets deathly quiet and I can hear that weird whistling song that always plays in those old westerns when two cowboys are getting ready for a gun fight at the O.K. Corral.

It's going down, and it's going down right the fuck now. I don't care if there is a room full of witnesses. This slut is getting a piece of my mind.

I square my body towards her and wiggle the fingers of my hands as they hang down at my sides, wishing I wore worn my gun belt. Wishing I *had* a gun belt.

Little Skankasaurus Rex over there tilts her head from side to side, cracking her neck, as we stared each other down. No one in the classroom moves and all eyes are on the two of us. I'm pretty sure I see tumbleweed roll by, but it might have just been a wad of paper one of the kids had thrown. Whatever.

"Mom! What are you doing?" Gavin whispers loudly as he runs back up to me. "You're supposed to be passing out the cupcakes."

"Hey, remember when I used to ask you all the time when you were little who you wanted to marry when you grew up and you would always say, 'I just want to marry my mommy'?" I ask him without taking my eyes off of Fourth Grade Floozy.

"Um, sure. Whatever. Can we have the cupcakes now?" he asks, growing impatient with me.

"You still want to marry Mommy, right?" The desperation is clear in my voice.

"Mom, you know that's illegal, right? Seriously, we're hungry. Give us the sugar and no one gets hurt," Gavin threatens.

"You should go back to your seat, Son. Go back to your seat and cover your eyes. As a matter of fact, cover your ears too," I inform him distractedly.

I take a step in *Brooklyn's* direction. Just thinking her name makes me cringe. Her parents had named her after a city known for housing the Russian mafia and call girls. Not to mention dirty. Dirty, little Brooklyn. It's a nice place to visit, but no one wants to live there. I bet you it says that under her name on her birth certificate.

She takes a step in my direction as well, and before I know it, she's skipping across the room towards me at lightning-fast speed, barreling into the front of me and wrapping her arms around my waist, squeezing on for dear life. I stand there with a look of horror on my face as I stare at the top of her head, unable to move.

Finally, she pulls away from me and beams at me with a huge smile on her face.

"Hi there, Mrs. Ellis! I'm so excited to finally meet you! You're so pretty! And I love your shirt! Wow, you're really young! You don't have any wrinkles on your face like my mom does! I love your hair! When I grow up, I want to look just like you!"

Is this some new form of warfare? Kill the enemy with kindness? Her skills are no match for mine. NO MATCH! And she speaks in nothing but exclamations. I don't know whether to challenge her to a cage fighting match or braid her hair.

"Your son is really nice. And really cute! But you probably know that already," Brooklyn continued.

"Eeeew, gross," Gavin mutters next to me.

I reach out blindly for him and fling my arm around his shoulder, pulling him into my side in a crushing one-armed hug.

"He is cute, isn't he?" I tell Brooklyn. "And he's such a good boy. So nice and polite and did you know he told me he's going to marry me when he grows up?"

Gavin lets out a gasp and whines in a loud whisper.

"Mooooooooom! Cut it out!"

Brooklyn claps her hands together in glee. "Oh my gosh! That is the sweetest thing EVER! You are the best mom in the world. He talks about you all the time," she explains.

I'm totally going to cry. Right here in the middle of this fourth grade class. I am going to curl up in the fetal position sucking my thumb and sobbing like a baby.

I takes me about ten minutes to compose myself, but I manage to do it as well as pass out the cupcakes and juice. Oh, and I tell Brooklyn she can call the house anytime she likes.

☉ ☉ ☉

"Alright, I hope this makes up for the fact that I tried to act like Liz and Jim this Valentine's Day. Open your eyes," Carter tells me later that evening after the dishes from dinner have been cleared.

I slowly open my eyes and on the table in front of me is a vase full of a dozen long-stemmed pink roses, my favorite, and a thin box wrapped with a red bow on top. I quickly tear into the box, lift the lid, and my breath catches in my throat as I look at what's inside.

"Where did you find this?" I whisper, trying to hold back the tears I can feel pooling in my eyes.

"I found it at your dad's. I told him what was going on with girls suddenly calling the house, and he pulled out a box of things from when you and Gavin used to live with him," Carter explains as he scoots his chair closer to mine and rests his chin on my shoulder so we can both look at the eight-by-ten frame in my hands.

Back when Gavin was around four, right before I found Carter again, he and I used to have weddings at night after his bath. It was a huge production. He would come into the living room, tell me it was time for our wedding, and then we'd stand up in the middle of the room, exchange gifts (which usually consisted of two stuffed animals that we traded), and say our vows.

"Mommy, do you wanna marry me?"

"I do!"

"And I wanna marry you, so yay! We're married! Let's go on a honeymoon to the kitchen and have pop and cookies!"

I had no idea my dad took a picture of one of our *weddings*. In the frame, Carter blew up a profile picture of Gavin, in a pair of Spider Man pajamas, and me, in a t-shirt and yoga pants, standing in my dad's living room facing each other, holding hands. How had I ever thought for one minute that Carter didn't know me or that he wouldn't pick out the most amazing Valentine's Day gift ever?

"Carter, this is amazing!" I tell him as I take my eyes off of the picture from what seems like so many years ago to look at the man I love.

He takes my face in his hands and places a gentle kiss on my lips.

"Happy Valentine's Day, baby. No matter what, Gavin will always be your little boy. The first woman he ever asked to marry him. Even when he's in fifth grade and those little bitches pull out the big guns and start getting boob jobs and vaginal rejuvenation surgeries."

The End

Made in the USA
Charleston, SC
17 July 2013